Handbook of
Child
Psycho-
analysis

RESEARCH, THEORY, AND PRACTICE

Handbook of Child Psycho- analysis

RESEARCH, THEORY, AND PRACTICE

EDITED BY

Benjamin B. Wolman, Ph.D.

In collaboration with

Rudolf Dreikurs, M.D.
Michael Fordham, M.R.C.P.
Maurice R. Friend, M.D.
Max Goldblatt, M.D.
Maurice R. Green, M.D.

Paul Kay, M.D.
Humberto Nagera, M.D.
Peter B. Neubauer, M.D.
Gerald T. Niles, M.D.
Sally Provence, M.D.
Estelle Rauch, M.S.W.

Nathaniel Ross, M.D.
Hanna Segal, M.D., Ch.B.
Saul Scheidlinger, Ph.D.
Jerome S. Silverman, M.D.
John J. Sullivan, Ph.D.

Foreword by
Peter Blos, Ph.D.

Susan Knapp
Editorial Assistant

 VAN NOSTRAND REINHOLD COMPANY
New York Cincinnati Toronto London Melbourne

Van Nostrand Reinhold Company Regional Offices:
New York   Cincinnati   Chicago   Millbrae   Dallas

Van Nostrand Reinhold Company International Offices:
London   Toronto   Melbourne

Published by Van Nostrand Reinhold Company
450 West 33rd Street, New York, N. Y. 10001

Published simultaneously in Canada by Van Nostrand Reinhold Ltd.

15   14   13   12   11   10   9   8   7   6   5   4   3   2   1

CONTRIBUTORS

Peter Blos, Ph.D., President, Association for Child Psychoanalysis; Faculty, New York Psychoanalytic Institute.

Rudolf Dreikurs, M.D., Emeritus Professor, The Chicago Medical School; Director Emeritus, Alfred Adler Institute.

Michael Fordham, M.D., M.R.C.P., F.R.C.Psych., Director of Training in Child Analysis, Society of Analytical Psychology, London.

Maurice R, Friend, M.D., Clinical Professor of Psychiatry and Director, Division of Psychoanalytic Education, Department of Psychiatry, State University of New York, Downscate Medical Center, Brooklyn, New York.

Max Goldblatt, M.D., Training Psychoanalyst, the Hampstead Child-Therapy Clinic, London.

Maurice R. Green, M.D., Attending Psychiatrist, Roosevelt Hospital, New York; Assistant Clinical Professor of Psychiatry, New York University Medical Center; Assistant Attending Psychiatrist, Bellevue Hospital, New York; Supervising and Training Analyst, William Alanson White Institute, New York.

Paul Kay, M.D., Clinical Associate Professor of Psychiatry, and Instructor, Division of Psychoanalytic Education, State University of New York, Downstate Medical Center, Brooklyn, New York.

Humberto Nagera, M.D., Professor of Psychiatry, University of Michigan; Director, Child Psychoanalytic Study Program, Department of Psychiatry, University of Michigan.

Peter B. Neubauer, M.D., Director, Child Development Center, New York; Faculty, State University of New York, Downstate Medical Center, Brooklyn, New York.

Gerald T. Niles, M.D., Physician in Charge, Children and Adolescent Service, Karen Horney Clinic, New York.

Sally Provence, M.D., Professor of Pediatrics, Yale Child Study Center, New Haven.

Estelle Rauch, M.S.W., Community Service Society, New York.

Nathaniel Ross, M.D., Clinical Professor of Psychiatry, State University of New York, Downstate Medical Center, Brooklyn, New York.

Hanna Segal, M.D., Ch.B., Member of the British Psychoanalytic Society.

Saul Scheidlinger, Ph.D., Community Service Society, New York; Associate Clinical Professor, Albert Einstein College of Medicine, New York.

Jerome S. Silverman, M.D., Assistant Professor of Clinical Psychiatry, State University of New York, Downstate Medical Center, Brooklyn, New York.

John J. Sullivan, Ph.D., Professor of Educational Psychology, New York University.

Benjamin B. Wolman, Ph.D., Professor, Doctoral Program of Clinical Psychology, Long Island University, New York.

FOREWORD

The history of child psychoanalysis has now extended over half a century. It has lent proof to Freud's discovery, made in the analysis of adults, that a childhood disturbance constitutes both the origin and the model of the adult neurosis. Working directly with disturbed children, however, has called for the adaptation of established technique and has led to the revision of previous theory, in accordance with a more precise knowledge of the various stages of the developing child.

As a result, the study of psychic structure formation by way of child analysis has produced not only a widened application of the analytic therapy of children, but also a deeper understanding of the varied emotional disturbances of adults. The ascendancy of ego psychology and of longitudinal studies has also added the developmental dimension to the conflictual one, thereby leading to an important re-evaluation of the influence of the experiential, in relation to that of endowment or *Anlage*.

The science of child psychoanalysis has reached such a level of complexity over the years that only the specialist could now hope to keep up with its rapid expansion and refinement. As a consequence, there still remain many misconceptions about child analysis in the minds of those who are interested in the origins and treatment of the emotional disturbances of infancy, childhood, and adolescence. It is the merit of *Handbook of Child Psychoanalysis* that it has brought together outstanding child analysts, to present their specialty at an up-to-date level. The relevancy of their presentations is convincingly buttressed by the historical account of theory and the reports on research. This joint effort will greatly assist in delineating the place of child psychoanalysis within the field of child therapy and child development, by offering the reader authoritative expositions on all the significant aspects of the broadening orbit of child psychoanalysis.

Peter Blos, Ph.D.

PREFACE

The psychoanalytic technique is an unusual blend of art and science. Its rationale is derived from clinical, observational and experimental studies conducted by Freud and his disciples, followers, and critics. These studies have led to a formulation of theoretical hypotheses, concepts, and models which serve as a basis for psychoanalytic work. Yet, every practicing psychoanalyst must find his own way of treating his own particular patient. No two analysts are identical, nor are there two identical patients; thus every case of psychoanalytic treatment is an unrepeatable process, a true idiophenomenon. The main tool an analyst uses is his own personality, his intellectual and emotional resources, and his skill and knowledge. Guidelines are supplied by the empirical research and theoretical systems, but the application of these guidelines must remain individual, based on the personality makeup of the psychoanalyst, his patient, and the particular type of interaction that evolves between the two of them.

The complexity of psychoanalytic research, theory and practice is multiplied by the peculiarities and vicissitudes of child development. Statistical averages and growth norms provide little help. The practicing child psychoanalysts face an exasperating variety of developmental patterns, and the individual differences between their little patients turn every new case into a new challenge to the psychoanalyst.

In the present volume a group of prominent psychoanalysts who belong to various schools of psychoanalytic thought have tried to present a coherent but by no means uniform picture of the present status of research, theory and practice in child psychoanalysis. The differences in point of view, experience and personal preferences bear witness to the complexity of the task we have faced. I have restrained my editorial efforts, keeping in mind the fact that we do not agree with one another, and I have planned this volume not as one on technique but as a true representation of the diverse ideas and techniques.

In planning this volume I consulted Drs. Gerhard Adler, Kurt Adler, Grete Bibring, Anna Freud, Elisabeth Geleerd, Heinz Hartmann, Harold Kelman, and the indefatigable and always reliable

Nathaniel Ross. All of them put me in debt by their friendly and wise suggestions, and whatever are the shortcomings of this book, they are certainly a product of my own inadequacies.

In preparation of the manuscript I have received invaluable help from Susan Knapp, Sharonah Koolyk, Shou Fung Yu, and Marcia L. Rosser. The friendly cooperation of Mike Hamilton, the Editor at Van Nostrand Reinhold, deserves special appreciation.

Benjamin B. Wolman

CONTENTS

PART I

FOUNDATIONS

1
FOUNDATIONS

1

BENJAMIN B. WOLMAN*

Psychoanalytic Theory of Infantile Development

HISTORICAL INTRODUCTION

Prior to Freud, child psychology was, as it were a marginal topic. The early scientific studies in psychology were concerned mainly with perceptual and cognitive processes. Sensation, attention, memory, and intelligence were the focal points of psychological research in the second part of the nineteenth century and the beginning of the twentieth. The studies of Wundt, Ebbinghaus, Külpe, Brentano, Ach, Titchener, and Binet, to mention a few, were devoted mostly to intellectual processes of adults.

* With the assistance of Bernard Mimno.

The early studies of child psychology are associated with the observational and biographical method applied by Taine (1877), Darwin (1877), Preyer (1881), Hall (1891), Sully (1895), and others. Preyer's systematic observations of his son's behavior from birth through the third year have established a model for several biographical studies of infant behavior followed by Shinn (1900), Dearborn (1910), Stern (1914), and others.

In 1891 Hall started the publication of *Pedagogical Seminary*, and in 1893 Sully began publishing the series, *Studies in Childhood*. Toward the end of the nineteenth century, child psychologists had accumulated a good deal of empirical data concerning overt behavior. In review of Freud's contribution to the understanding of infantile development, one must not overlook the synchronicity of Freud's discoveries with the early observational studies.

THE FREUDIAN REVOLUTION

Most students of the history of psychology know that Freud's discovery of infantile sexuality scandalized the public's opinion of psychologists and psychiatrists (Jones, 1955, vol. 2), but not all of them are aware of the fact that Freud revolutionized the entire field of child psychology. Freud was an iconoclast, and his new ideas broke the artificial barriers between childhood and adulthood. Freud discovered the roots of adult behavior in early childhood impulses and unraveled the driving forces of mankind in their infantile beginnings. The unholy union of ignorance and hypocrisy put a veil on the driving forces of sexuality and aggressiveness and denied the child the right to be human. It took Freud's genius and courage to destroy the myth of the child's alleged "innocence" and present the growing human being in a sharp light of psychoanalytic investigation. The nonrelated behavioral data and the unintelligible pile of correct though irrelevant facts were replaced by Freud's economic, topographic, and structural theories that presented the infant as a cogent entity driven by unconscious and hitherto unrecognized forces.

At the time when Freud wrote the *Studies on Hysteria* (Breuer and Freud, 1895), his ideas on childhood development were in their beginnings. Freud believed in a traumatic origin of psychosexual conflicts in infancy, caused by attempted or performed seduction. Later on, Freud realized that his patients often confused recollections of actual sexual experiences with vague recollections of wishes for such an experience (1887–1902, pp. 215 ff.). In a letter of January 3, 1897 (pp. 182 ff.), Freud called the mouth an "oral sexual organ"; a few weeks earlier, Freud had formulated the idea of erotogenic zones. The Oedipus Complex was described by Freud in *The Interpretation of Dreams* (1900). In a letter dated November 14, 1897, Freud mentioned the mechanism of repression and the abandonment of infantile sexual zones. In the same letter, he wrote:

> Only one idea of general value has occurred to me. I have found love of the mother and jealousy of the father in my own case, too, and now believe it to be a general phenomenon of early childhood. . . . If that is the case, the gripping power of *Oedipus Rex* . . . becomes intelligible. (Freud, 1887–1920, p. 223)

In *Three Essays on the Theory of Sexuality* (1905a), Freud elaborated the theory of psychosexual developmental stages based on Haeckel's biogenetic principle. This principle, widely accepted at the beginning of this century, has been strongly supported by recent studies (Yazmajian, 1967). The main part of the *Three Essays* is devoted to explorations of infantile sexuality.

The idea of distinct stages of unconscious psychosexual development was reformulated in the "Formulations on the Two Principles of Mental Functioning" (Freud, 1911), and the theory of instincts was revised in the essay "On Narcissism: An introduction" (1914).

The economic theory of libidinal drives, the topographic theory of mental strata, and the theory of psychosexual development seemed to be complete and final, but in 1920 and in 1923 Freud introduced far-reaching changes in his conceptual system and revamped his psychological findings. In *Beyond the Pleasure Principle* (1920) he explained the phenomena of repetition compulsion and the death instinct, and *The Ego and the Id* (1923), Freud's structural theory, completed his theory of child development.[1]

SOME RESEARCH PROBLEMS

Sigmund Freud did not intend to create a fully developed psychological system, nor did he. His initial concern was the understanding and healing of mental ills. "Psychoanalysis," wrote Freud, "has

[1] Piaget, of all contemporary psychologists, is the only one who has introduced a full-fledged, elaborate psychological theory of developmental stages.

never claimed to provide a complete theory of human mentality as a whole but only expected that what it offered should be applied to supplement and correct the knowledge acquired by other means" (1914b, p. 50). Moreover, Freud arrived at his main discoveries in childhood psychology unintentionally, as it were. The theory of repression was a product of psychoanalytic work with patients.

> Another product of this sort was the hypothesis of infantile sexuality. This, however, was made at a much later date. In the early days of tentative investigation by analysis no such thing was thought of. At first it was merely observed that the effects of present-day experiences had to be traced back to something in the past. But enquirers often find more than they bargain for. One was drawn further and further back into the past; one hoped at last to be able to stop at puberty, the period in which the sexual impulses are traditionally supposed to awake. But in vain; the tracks led still further back into its earlier years. (Ibid., p. 17)

Most psychologists rebuffed Wundt's and Titchener's introspectionistic methods and tried to confine psychological research to observation of and experimentation with overt and observable behavior in the belief that that was the only possible research method. Freud went in the opposite direction. He abandoned introspection, but did not embrace extraneous observation of overt actions. Instead he entered a hitherto neglected area, of unconscious motivation and hidden impulses.

Freud's method of study was both idiographic and retrospective. The idiographic method of study of individual cases was widely though not generally accepted in two such different areas as historical and medical science. Windelband (1921) and Rickert (1899) viewed the study of individual cases as the proper method for ascertaining the factual data in humanities and historical studies. Dilthey (1924) and afterward Spranger (1928), Allport (1937), and others advocated the uniqueness of psychological phenomena.

Freud never committed himself to an idiographic philosophy. Starting with the individual case, Freud proceeded toward cautious generalizations in the best spirit of the British empiricists. True, Freud never performed rigorously controlled experimental studies, but neither Pavlov nor Piaget, the greatest psychologist discoverers, conducted controlled studies.

The case study method does not exclude generalizations. Actually, *all* sciences deal with individual phenomena, yet scientists group individual cases in classes and categories. One common denominator suffices for putting a series of individual phenomena into a class or category (Wolman, 1960, Chapter 14). The apparent strength of the case study method lies in its detailed and thorough observation of single cases, and its weakness is no less apparent; case studies cannot compete with rigorously controlled experimentations and meticulously executed surveys.

Moreover, Freud's study of child psychology was an ex post facto study, resembling historical reconstruction. However, historians use more tangible sources than psychoanalysts, and they do not have to rely on memories of past events.

THEORY OF INSTINCTS

The Sexual Instincts

All living organisms act in accordance with two purposes, self-preservation and the preservation of the species. Accordingly, Freud distinguished self-preservation or ego instincts and sexual instincts. These two instinctual forces are often in conflict with each other. The sexual instincts are more flexible than the self-preservation instincts; they can be held in suspense (aim-inhibited), sublimated, diverted into new channels, distorted, and perverted; their gratification can be denied or substituted for, and their objects can be easily changed. Freud said:

> The popular view distinguishes between hunger and love, seeing them as representatives of the instincts that aim at self-preservation and reproduction of the species respectively. In associating ourselves with this very evident distinction we postulate in psychoanalysis a similar one between the self-preservative or ego-instincts on the one hand and the sexual instincts on the other; the force by which the sexual instinct is represented in the mind we call 'libido'—sexual longing—and regard it as analogous to the force of hunger, or the will to power, and other such trends among the ego-tendencies.

He added:

> We have defined the concept of libido as a quantitatively variable force which could serve as a measure of processes and transformations occurring in the field of sexual excitation. We distinguish this libido in respect of its special origin from the energy which must be

supposed to underlie mental processes in general, and we thus also attribute a qualitative character to it. (1905a, pp. 130–245)

Freud did not postulate a single urge leading to fertilization and preservation of the species. He believed that there are a great number of relatively independent instincts that stem from various somatic sourcs. All of them strive toward gratification in their respective somatic zone; that is, all of them strive toward *organ pleasure*. In the process of ontogenetic development some of them merge with the sexual instinct proper that originates in the genital organs; some of these instincts will be eventually repressed, some partially incorporated in the final organization of the adult sexual functions.

Freud distinguished between source, object, and aim in sexuality. The *source* is a stimulation arising in some part or zone of the organism. The parts of the body that are capable of reacting to sexual stimuli are called *erotogenic zones*. The main erotogenic zone is the genitals, but many other parts of the body, such as mouth or anus, may in certain cases serve as erotogenic zones in the pregenital phases of a child's development. The usual *object* of sexual urge is a person of the opposite sex, but often, as in homosexuality, a person of the same sex, or, as in masturbation, the individual himself is the sexual object.

Freud broadened the concept of sexuality to include perversions and infantile sexuality, which do not lead to the usual aim of sex—fertilization and reproduction. In fact, perversions were never excluded from the realm of sexuality. A perverse sexual relation usually ends with orgasm and ejaculation analogous to the normal sexual intercourse, which may lead, in addition to orgasm, to fertilization and reproduction. Sexual activities of persons considered to be normal include several elements which, if performed exclusively and in place of normal intercourse, would be considered perverse. Kissing, for example, is an indispensable part of the sexual foreplay in normal individuals, but actually, kissing gives a pleasurable arousal by a contact of two oral zones. Undoubtedly the mouth is an erotogenic zone, i.e., an area capable of producing sexual excitation. Some individuals achieve orgasm by kissing or some modification of it, such as "deep kissing" (introducing the tongue into the partner's mouth), or by oral-genital contacts. Whenever kissing is a part of the sexual foreplay which leads to the union of the genital organs, it is considered normal. Only when kissing takes the place of intercourse and excludes the union of genital organs does it become a perversion. Obviously, normal and perverse sexuality have much in common. Freud believed that normal sexuality grew out of something very similar to perversions and developed through modification of some elements, discontinuation of other elements, and incorporation of others.

The same applies to any sexual deviations. Onlooking, gazing, touching of erotogenetic zones, etc., are generally accepted and widely practiced parts of the sexual foreplay. If these practices take the place of intercourse and exclude the union of genitalia, the foreplay becomes a perverse voyeurism. Fixation of erotic interest on an object of clothing, for example, instead of on the genital organs, is fetishism.

Perverse sexuality points to the fact that sexuality is not limited to reproduction or to the function of genital organs, nor is it necessarily heterosexual. There are several possibilities regarding source, aim, and object in sex. The genital organs may be replaced by the other organs for the purpose of gratification, as in the normal kiss, or by perverse practices, or by conversion symptoms of hysteria.

Once Freud had assumed that both normal and abnormal sexuality stem from the same source, he had to conclude that sexual deviations are some sort of retardation or thwarting of the sexual development. This was a very far-reaching hypothesis. Comparative studies in biology and embryology led him to believe that Haeckel's biogenetic theory could be readily applied to the development of sex. "Ontogenesis is a repetition of phylogenesis," Haeckel said, and Freud, in his essays about sex, accepted this theory and assumed that the child's sexual development is a recapitulation of the main phases in the evolution of sex in organic nature.

The study of sexual perversions in adults and the biogenetic principles led to the study of infantile sexuality. "The child is psychologically father of the man," Freud said. Infantile sexuality contains all the potentialities for future development, which may lead in any direction—either into a normal or into an abnormal sexuality. Normal development takes place when the source, the object, and the aim of sex are combined in a consistent effort of unification of genital organs of two persons of opposite sex. The normal sexual source is the genitals; the object, an adult person of the opposite sex; the aim, heterosexual intercourse. The normal individual passes through development stages and if, for some reason, he retains the characteristics of one of them (remains "fixated"), he is considered abnormal. What is normal in infancy is abnormal in adulthood. A sexually abnormal individual is a sexually retarded individual. The infant is "a polymorphous pervert" who may or may not eventually become a well-adjusted adult.

The Self-Preservation Instincts

The entire activity of man is, according to Freud, "bent upon *procuring pleasure and avoiding pain.*" This activity is controlled by the *pleasure principle.* "We may venture to say that pleasure is *in some way* connected with lessening, lowering, or extinguishing the amount of stimulation present in the mental apparatus; and that pain involves a heightening of the latter. Consideration of the most intense pleasure of which man is capable, the pleasure in the performance of the sexual act, leaves little doubt upon this point" (1953, p. 311).

Sexual instincts always follow the pleasure principle. Self-preservation instincts, sometimes called ego instincts, do the same as a rule. However, the task of avoiding pain forces them to postpone, or sometimes even to renounce, pleasure. This ability to compromise with reality and to consider what could be done and what price has to be paid for pleasure is the *reality principle.* The reality principle is a modified pleasure principle; it approves of pleasure, but not at any price or at any time. The reality principle is striving for pleasure combined with avoidance of pain; it is the ability to sacrifice one kind of pleasure for another.

The consideration of circumstances apparently makes a great difference between the two groups of instincts. Through ego instincts we learn to comply with reality. Sex instincts are less concerned with reality. The reality principle usually gets an early hold on ego instincts; sexual instincts are not so easily controlled, and it takes years before they become at least partially subordinated to the reality principle.

The other difference between sex and self-preservation instincts relates to their flexibility. The self-preservation instincts have a limited flexibility. One cannot change the zones or indefinitely postpone the gratification of hunger or thirst, nor is there any way to substantially change the objects that satisfy hunger or thirst; all the objects that satisfy the basic needs for air, food, and fluids must contain respectively oxygen, nutritional elements, and water. The sexual instincts can be modified in regard to zone, aim, and object, and they are open to a great number of deviations, perversions, substitutions, and conflicts. This latitude does not apply to the self-preservation instincts.

Narcissism

In 1914 Freud revised his theory of instincts. Originally he felt that the libido or love instincts have to be distinguished from the ego or self-preservation instincts. After several years of clinical experience he discovered that libido may be directed to oneself and not necessarily to external objects only. Love for oneself precedes love for others; the newborn is not capable of loving other people.

Infants learn to divert part of the love primarily cathected (invested) in themselves and to cathect it in their mothers. This self-love was called by Freud *narcissism* after the Greek legendary hero Narcissus, who fell in love with himself.

Narcissism or self-love is a never-terminated phenomenon. It starts probably in prenatal life and accompanies us till the last day of life. At the earliest stage of life it is the only channel of libido cathexis; all the energies at the disposal of the love instincts are invested in oneself in a stage called by Freud *primary narcissism.* Later in life, in cases when the object love is being thwarted, the libido may turn back to one's own person and *secondary,* morbid narcissism may develop.

The discovery of the phenomenon of narcissism destroyed the barriers separating the libido from the ego instincts. The ego instincts had to be considered from now on as a special case of libido cathexis, namely, as an investment of libido in one's own person. Now Freud had arrived at a monistic interpretation of instinctual life: there is but one instinctual force, the force of love, the libido.

The conflict that often takes place between the sex and self-preservation instincts could now be interpreted in a different way. It is narcissism versus object love. In well-adjusted individuals there is a balance of cathexis in oneself and in others which permits the individual to protect himself and to take care of those whom he loves. In some individuals this balance is disturbed. Some develop secondary and morbid narcissism after they have been seriously thwarted in the development of object cathexis. Some are unable to take care of themselves, owing to insufficient narcissism or abundant object cathexis.

Freud united under the name "Eros" all the forces that serve pleasure and enhance the vital functions of the individual. Eros encompassed all sexual and egoistic drives, and libido became from then on the name for all the energies that are at the disposal of the Eros.

Thanatos

In 1920 Freud again revised his theory of instincts. He wrote about this revision as follows:

> After long doubts and vacillations we have decided to assume the existence of only two basic instincts, *Eros* and the *destructive* instinct. . . . The aim of the first of these instincts is to establish ever greater unities and to preserve them, thus—in short, to bind together; the aim of the second, on the contrary, is to undo connections and so to destroy things. We may suppose that the final aim of the destructive instinct is to reduce living things to an inorganic state. For this reason we also call it the death instinct. (1953, p. 20)

This new hypothesis of separate aggressive and destructive instincts was derived mainly from the study of sadism and masochism. The sexual gratification of a sadist depends upon pain and suffering inflicted by him on his love object, and that of a masochist depends on pain inflicted on him by his love object. It was exceedingly difficult to interpret sadism in terms of libido theory, and the existence of a masochistic wish to suffer formed a most serious challenge to the libido theory.

Freud had to look for additional factors, factors that make people wish to inflict or to receive pain. These factors could not be related to libido and Eros. The only possible solution was to assume another driving force or another instinctual power that leads men to cause pain to others in an object-directed situation or to inflict pain on themselves in a self-directed situation. Such an instinctual force could be held responsible for the desire to hurt, to humiliate, and to destroy. The existence of this force was sufficiently proved by daily experience and by the testimony of human history. Humans are born lovers and haters; as much as there is energy (libido) at the disposal of the love instinct, there is no less energy (called *mortido* by Federn) at the disposal of the aggressive instinct. The final aim of the love instinct is to create life, and the final aim of the aggressive instinct is to destroy life and to go back to inorganic nature.

When aggressiveness against the outer world is thwarted and

cannot find satisfaction, it may, in certain circumstances, turn inward. It may, said Freud, increase the amount of self-destructiveness. An impeded aggression entails most serious dangers; it seems that we have to destroy things and people in order not to destroy ourselves. In order to protect ourselves from the tendency toward self-destruction we must find some external channels for aggressiveness.

All instincts, as stated before, turn out to be directed toward the reinstatement of an earlier state of things. As soon as a given state of things is upset, an instinct arises to re-create it. This tendency was called by Freud *repetition-compulsion*. It may become even stronger than the pleasure principle, and often overcomes it. Repetition-compulsion explains the tendency to reproduce in dreams unpleasant and often traumatic experiences.

Life developed from inorganic matter. Once life started, an instinct was born that aimed at reinstatement of the inorganic state and destruction of life. This is, according to Freud, the origin of the destructive instinct, whose final aim is death or the reestablishment of inanimate nature. Life and death are interwoven; construction and destruction are inseparable. No vital process can be free from the death instinct. The erotic instincts try "to collect living substance together into ever larger unities," and the death instincts act against this "and try to bring living matter back into inorganic condition. The cooperation and opposition of these two forces produce the phenomena of life to which death puts an end" (1953, pp. 146–147).

This idea of interrelationship between life and death is not a new one. Freud mentioned in this context the influence of the philosopher Arthur Schopenhauer and the Indian concept of Nirvana. Another philosopher and scientist, Herbert Spencer, elaborated on the idea and postulated a continum of consecutive development and decline, evolution and dissolution, accumulation and dissipation.

In the life of an individual, Eros and Thanatos may combine their resources, but they often fight each other. Eating is a process of destruction with the purpose of incorporation, and the sexual act is aggression that aims at the "most intimate union." Most of the impulses of sexual life are rarely purely erotic, usually sexual impulses are a combination of erotic and destructive instinctual demands.

In extreme cases, when the destructive instincts become the stronger part in the fusion of the two kinds of instincts, sadism or masochism results. In sadism aggressive impulses thrust the sexual aims away and substitute the aim of hurting the love object. Sexual gratification becomes possible only if pain is inflicted upon the sexual object. In masochism the aggression is self-directed, and sexual gratification depends upon pain and humiliation being inflicted by the love object.

When an individual is overwhelmed by the forces of Thanatos directed to the outer world, he becomes hateful and destructive, spreading pain and death around. When these forces are directed to himself, suicidal attempts may take place.

The Id

The major part of Freud's theory belongs, as it were, in the realm of child psychology. Although Freud wrote about adult personality and its aberrations, his psychological studies are largely studies of infantile sexuality, child-parent relationships, and personality development in the first five or six years.

As mentioned before, Freud in 1923 introduced his "structural" theory. This new personality model incorporated the "economic" forces of libidinal and destructive impulses, the "topographic" layers of conscious, preconscious, and finally the three parts of the "mental apparatus," the id, ego, and superego.

According to Freud, "the determining causes of all varying forms of human mental life are to be found in the interplay between inherited dispositions and accidental experiences" (1938a, p. 84). The id is the link between the organic and non-organic processes. It is "somewhere in direct contact with somatic processes, and takes over from instinctual needs and gives them mental expression, but we cannot way in what substratum this contact is made" (1915–1917, p. 104).

The id acts impulsively, irrespective of whether or not its actions protect the organism from danger. The id knows no fear and takes no precautions to insure survival. An immediate and unconditional gratification of instinctual demands is pursued by the id. An id-inspired behavior may lead to clashes with the external world and to the death of the organism.

The entire mental energy, both libidinal and aggressive, is stored in the id. This energy is mainly put at the disposal of the two primal forces, Eros and Thanatos. The energy stored in the id is free, unbound, operating on the homeostatis Nirvana principle and the pleasure principle.

The id, as the seat of all vehement desires and seething impulses, tends to an immediate discharge of energies. The discharge of energies that restores the inner balance was called by Freud the *Lustprinzip*, that is, the principle of lust (usually translated as "pleasure principle"). Undoubtedly, an immediate discharge of libidinal or destructive energy brings relief, thus it is experienced as pleasure. The *Lustprinzip* emphasizes the urgent need to obtain an immediate gratification, come what may. The unbound, uncontrolled energies of the id lead to impulsive discharges of energies according to the pleasure principle. Thus the pleasure principle sometimes indicates the general striving for pleasure and avoidance of pain, while in another context it points to the urgency of obtaining such a pleasure through an immediate discharge of energy.

The id stays entirely unconscious forever; but, under the pressure of the outer world, some of the unconscious material of the id develops into preconscious material, and the ego emerges.

> Under the influence of the external world which surrounds us, one portion of the id has undergone a special development. From what was originally a cortical layer, provided with organs for receiving stimuli and with apparatus for protection against excessive stimulation, a special organization has arisen which henceforward acts as an intermediary between the id and the external world. This region of our mental life has been given the name of ego. (Freud, 1938a, p. 15)

The mental processes in the id, called *primary processes*, defy the laws of logic. Self-directed perceptions and coenesthetic feelings disclose the economy of inner tensions and the balance of the mental apparatus. Whenever the economy or the equilibrium of the mental apparatus is disturbed, the instinctual forces react in the striving for immediate discharge of energy. Indeed, the id blindly obeys the pleasure principle. Id knows no values, no right or wrong, no moral standards, no consideration for other people. It is a "cauldron of seething excitement," Freud said. "Instinctual cathexes seeking discharge"—that is all that the id contains. Infants know of no moral standards.

According to Freud, conative impulses which have never gotten beyond the id and impressions which have been repressed into the id are preserved for the whole life. The repressed material is hardly affected by the passage of time. Long-forgotten infantile memories come back in dreams, and early childhood experiences plays a decisive role in the symptomatology of mental disorders. The two other "agencies of the mind," the ego and superego, develop out of the id and become independent.

This is the essence of the structural theory. The core of the personality is the id. The id itself has no direct relations with the external world and is accessible to our own knowledge only through the ego. All organic instincts operate within the id. The instinctual life is comprised of two primal forces (Eros and destructiveness) in proportions varying for various individuals. The sole aim of all instinctual drives is immediate satisfaction. The id is, as it were, blind, unable to take precautions to insure survival. The id cannot experience, nor is it capable of producing, the sensory elements of anxiety. "The processes which are possible in and between the assumed mental elements in the id (the *primary process*) differ largely from those which are familiar to us by conscious perception in our intellectual and emotional life; nor are they subject to the critical restrictions of logic, which repudiates some of these processes as invalid and seeks to undo them" (Freud, 1938a, pp. 108–109).

The Ego

Fenichel described the origins of the ego as follows. One may say that the newborn infant has virtually no ego. The human infant is born more helpless than other mammals, and is unable to remain alive unless he is cared for. The human neonate cannot move voluntarily, nor is he able to differentiate between oncoming stimuli. Most probably the id has an undifferentiated sensitivity to pain and pleasure and to increasing and decreasing tensions. The contact with the external world (perception), the control of the motor apparatus (motility), and the ability to bind tension by counter-cathexis are functions of the ego.

According to Fenichel, the origins of the ego are not too clear. It starts, probably, with or before birth. At birth the organism emerges out of a relatively quiet environment and faces an overwhelming mass of stimulation with very little protection from the flood of stimuli. This overwhelming state of excitation without an adequate defense apparatus is the prototype of all later anxiety.

> The origin of the ego and the origin of the sense of reality are but two aspects of one developmental step. . . . The concept of reality also

creates the concept of ego. We are individuals inasmuch as we feel ourselves separate and distinct from others. (Fenichel, 1945, pp. 34–35)

The early perceptions of the infant border on primary processes with a good deal of condensation and distortion. The infant perceives the world in a diffuse manner.

The id has its own world of perception. It detects with extraordinary clarity certain changes in its interior, especially oscillations in the tension of its instinctual needs, oscillations which become conscious as feelings in the pleasure-unpleasure series. (Freud, 1938a, p. 109)

The task of the ego is to distinguish between the inner, id-originated stimuli, and the stimuli from without, perceived by sensory apparatus. The archaic ego and the failing ego of psychotics may not be able to distinguish between inner and outer stimuli and may fall prey to delusions and hallucinations.

Perception of the external world starts with the ego's primary, archaic *identification* with perceived objects. Several functions are included in this archaic identification. The infant puts the perceived things into his mouth, in fact and in effect introjecting his first love objects. This *oral introjection* shows that several distinct functions such as perception, motility, and emotionality have not separated from one another. Identification is an effort to master stimuli that are too intense by adjusting one's body to them and imitating them.

The dim picture of the outer world is accompanied by the infant's feeling of his own omnipotence: when his perception of the outer world becomes more precise, the infant begins to realize that satisfaction of his needs depends on external factors.

The "surface" part of the ego is the perceptual-conscious or Pcpt-Cs system. This system "is directed on to the external world, it mediates perceptions of it, and in it is generated while it is functioning, the phenomenon of consciousness. It is the sense organ of the whole apparatus, receptive not only of excitations from without but also of such as proceed from the interior of the mind" (Freud, 1932, p. 106). The mature ego controls the cognitive functions and can perform reality-testing.

Verbalization is of crucial importance in the development of several functions of the ego. The use of words facilitates a more precise communication with other people, more adequate reality-testing, and better control of impulses. In very early childhood and in cases of severe mental deterioration an *autistic* language develops, understandable to the speaker only.

The Superego

In 1914 Freud introduced the term *ego-ideal,* defined as a "critical faculty" within the ego. This ego-ideal was described in 1921 as the heir to the original narcissism, a sort of self-serving legislative organ. The ego-ideal is formed under the influences of the environment and represents the demands which that environment makes on the ego and which the ego cannot always rise to. It is the individual's conscience, the critical self-attitude of a part of the ego. It exercises the power of censorship in dreams, and it serves as the main force in repressing instinctual wishes (Freud, 1921).

The ego grows and develops from a state of merely perceiving instincts toward actually controlling them; from yielding to instincts toward inhibiting them. In this development a large share is taken by the ego-ideal, which is partly a reaction formation against the instinctual processes of the id.

The superego develops as a result of the weakness of the infantile ego. At the anal stage (see following section) the child undergoes toilet training. The fear of punishment and the need for affection and protection force the child to accept the parental demands and to "internalize" them, that is, to consider them as his own.

The actual development of the superego takes place toward the end of the phallic period. The fear of punishing parents comes to its peak at that point in the Oedipus complex when the little boy, shocked by castration fear, is forced to give up his mother as a love object, and the little girl, under the threat of losing her mother's love, is forced to abandon the father as her love object. The frustrated child of either sex regresses from object relationship to identification by introjection. The introjected parental figures are idealized and seem to be more powerful and more glorious than they may be in reality. In most cases the father's image (which usually encompasses the images of both parents) plays the greater role in the child's superego. Originally a new element added to and introjected into the ego, forming a part of it, the superego gradually becomes a separate mental agency, often opposed to the ego.

The id is the sole source of instinctual energies; all the energy that the ego uses for its inhibiting and anti-instinctual functions is drawn from the id; the anti-instinctual forces of the superego are, furthermore, derivatives of the instinctual forces of the id. Since the child's rebellion and resentment against parental prohibition can hardly find satisfactory discharge, the superego becomes cathected with some of the destructive energy, originally directed against the parents, but later internalized and directed against the individual's own ego.

DEVELOPMENTAL STAGES

Mythology has been described as the memory of nations because it tends to convey the irrationality of human nature, the everlasting impulses, and their eternal vicissitudes. Sophocles, for example, immortalized the ancient Greek story of a man who murdered his father and married his mother. In this story, Oedipus acted unaware of the true nature of his deeds and was, therefore, innocent: he did not know that Laios, whom he had killed, was his father, nor that Jocasta, whom he married, was his mother. The Greeks, of course, were not alone in portraying the mythological family drama. The Judean King David had an experience similar to that of the Greek King Laios. He was obliged to flee from Jerusalem, and from his rebellious son Absalom, who had slept with his father's wives.

Freud applied the principle of constancy to personality development. Life starts with conception, and intra-uterine life goes through prehuman evolutionary stages in a sheltered environment. To be born must be a traumatic experience, since it rather dramatically disrupts this sheltered life. The birth trauma, therefore, may be the prototype of all anxiety feelings in later life (Freud, 1926). Since the trauma of birth exposes the infant to stimuli that are far beyond his handling capacity, the natural tendency is to restore mental economy through withdrawal from contact with the outer world. The often immediate gratification of the infant's narcissistic needs gives rise to his feeling omnipotent whenever his wishes are gratified. Failure of need satisfaction creates a feeling of hopelessness and despair. The newborn infant seems to experience an objectless longing and craving for the outer world which Freud (1927) called the "oceanic feeling." It seems that the infant desires to restore the previous state, to return to the uterus, or even to nonexistence.

According to Freud, the normal child passes through a series of dynamically differentiated stages during the first five years of life, following which, for a period of five or six years (the so-called *latency period*), the dynamics become more or less stabilized. At adolescence, the dynamics erupt again and then gradually settle down as the adolescent moves into adulthood. Freud felt, however, that the first few years of life are decisive for the formation of personality.

As mentioned above, each stage of development during the first five years is defined in terms of the modes of reaction of the particular zone of the body that the infant finds pleasurable. During the first year of life, the mouth is the principal region of dynamic activity. This *oral stage* is followed by the development of cathexes and anticathexes around the eliminative functions. This *anal stage* lasts during the second year of life and is succeeded by the *phallic stage*, in which the sex organs become the leading erogenous zones. These three stages, the oral, anal, and phallic, are called the pregenital stages, and they are the ones that will be of concern in this chapter. After these stages, Freud believed that the normal child goes into a prolonged latency period, during which the impulses tend to be held in a state of repression. The pregenital impulses are reactivated by the dynamic resurgence of adolescence, and if these are by then successfully displaced and sublimated by the ego, it is possible for the person to pass into the final stage of maturity, the *genital stage*.

The Oral Stage

The first pleasure-producing objects are the nipples of the mother's breasts or the bottle, and the first part of the body that experiences the pleasure of sucking is the mouth. The *oral stage*, then, is the first erotogenic, or pleasure-producing, stage of development.

Freud borrowed the idea of pleasure from Fechner, whom he quoted as follows:

> Insofar as conscious impulses always have some relation to pleasure or unpleasure, pleasure and unpleasure too can be regarded as having a psycho-physical relation to conditions of stability and instability. This provides a basis for a hypothesis . . . [that] every psychophysical movement crossing the threshold of consciousness is attended by pleasure in proportion as, beyond a certain limit, it approximates to complete stability, and is attended by unpleasure in proportion as, beyond a certain limit, it deviates from complete stability; while between the two limits, which may be described as

qualitative thresholds of pleasure and unpleasure, there is a certain margin of aesthetic indifference. (Freud, 1950, pp. 3–4)

The greatest pleasure is related to sexuality, and non-genital infantile sexuality, when various wishes and desires exist independently, is the forefunner of adult sexuality. Several bodily zones may strive for their own pleasure in childhood, while in adulthood the genital zone dominates.

According to Freud, every human being goes through developmental stages reflecting the level of libidinal organization and the respective erotogenic zone. The first libidinal excitations of the infant are connected with the feeding process. When the infant falls asleep at the breast completely satisfied, it bears a look of perfect contentment which will come back again later in life after the experiences of sexual orgasm. Most infants continue to suck after the intake of food, sometimes in hunger, but often for the pure pleasure of sucking. Sucking was defined by Freud as the prototype of every later sexual satisfaction. For him, the desire to suck included within it the desire for the mother's breast, which is therefore the first libidinal object. Also at this stage, love is intertwined with hunger, and sucking brings gratification both of hunger and of love. At first the infant is unable to distinguish the mother's breast from his own body, but gradually the breast is given up as a love object and is replaced by the infant's own body, and he may suck his own thumb or tongue. It matters little whether the child was breast-fed or bottle-fed, weaned early or late in life; every child still longs for the mother's breast and for the mother as a whole. The mother's image stays in his memory as his first love object and the prototype for all future love.

The attitude toward the outer world is ambivalent at the oral phase and contains elements of both love and hate. The infant swallows what he loves and loves what he swallows, but his love is destructive and cannibalistic. Freud said that cannibals have "a devouring affection" for their enemies, and devour people of whom they are fond. Oral love is destructive and self-terminating. The infant certainly does not care any longer for the milk he drank, and as soon as the tension stimulated by hunger is removed, the infant falls asleep. Oral love, then, is a primitive love. It is a love for a while, that terminates by itself immediately after gratification. There are some adults who have not outgrown the oral stage and who retain these destructive elements in their adult love life. They love their love objects inasmuch as they can exploit them, and love them only as long as they can exploit them.

The wish to be like another person, or *primary identification*, is one of the earliest emotional attitudes toward others. Identification is the wish to possess the other person, but it is not necessarily love. "It can turn into an expression of tenderness as easily as into a wish for someone's removal" (Freud, 1921, p. 121). For Freud, the oral introjection leads to the primary identification. An infant at the oral stage takes things into his mouth and thus incorporates whatever he loves. When he incorporates an object, he may believe that he himself is like the incorporated object, just as savages believe that they become as brave as the lions they eat.

Freud and Abraham suggested a division of the oral phase into *oral-passive* and *oral-aggressive* (Abraham, 1911). The oral-passive phase extends over several months of the first year of life. Near the end of the first year and in the second year of life, the oral-aggressive phase of libido develops. The oral-passive or oral-dependent stage is usually characterized by pleasure derived from sucking. The oral-passive infant probably cannot distinguish himself from the external world, and so he may experience sucking as a self-gratifying phenomenon. The oral-aggressive phase usually coincides with teething. At about this time, the infant becomes aware of the fact that the mother's breast is not a part of himself and that it is not always available. The infant does not take the breast for granted, and, whenever frustrated, he grabs, bites, and seeks oral gratification by acts of aggression.

These two modes or oral activity, passive incorporation of food and biting, are the prototypes for many later character traits that develop. The pleasure derived from oral incorporation may be displaced onto other modes of incorporation, such as the pleasure gained from acquiring knowledge or possessions. For example, a gullible person can be described as one who is fixated on the oral incorporative level of personality; he swallows almost anything he is told. Sarcasm and argumentativeness can be described as displacements from biting or oral aggression. Through the use of displacements and sublimations of various kinds, as well as by defenses against the primitive oral impulses, these prototypic modes of oral functioning may provide the basis for the development of a vast network of interests, attitudes, and character traits.

It should also be mentioned in concluding the discussion of this first stage of development that since this stage occurs at a time when the infant is almost completely dependent upon his mother for sustenance, when he is cradled and nursed by her and protected from discomfort, feelings of dependency arise during this period. These dependency feelings often persist throughout life, in spite of later ego developments, and are apt to come to the fore whenever the person feels anxious and insecure. Freud originally believed that the most extreme symptom of dependency is the desire to return to the womb.

The Anal Stage

Usually in the second and often in the third year of life, infants can derive considerable pleasure from excretion, and they learn to increase this pleasure by a delay in emptying the bowels, with concomitant stimulation of the mucous membranes of the rectum. Freud states:

> Infants experience pleasure in the evacuation of urine and the content of bowels, and they very soon endeavor to contrive these actions so that the accompanying excitation of the membranes in these erotogenic zones may secure them the maximum possible gratification . . . The outer world steps in as a hindrance at this point, as a hostile force opposed to the child's desire for pleasure. . . . He is not to pass his excretions whenever he likes but at times appointed by other people. . . . In this way he is first required to exchange pleasure for value in the eyes of others. (Freud, 1915–1917, p. 276)

According to Freud, the infant sees in his feces part of his own body and is unwilling to part with them. He usually offers resistance to the maternal demands, and he may try to exercise sole control over his movements. Many infants act aggressively in elimination, thus combining libido and hate in anal eroticism by the sadistic holding and expelling of feces. Resistance against bowel training is an expression of rebellion against adults.

The anal stage appears to be ridden with another ambivalence besides expulsion-retention. Masculinity and femininity should be distinguished at this stage by activity and passivity respectively. Masculine impulses, such as scoptophilia (gazing), onlooking, curiosity, and desire to manipulate and to master may develop into cruelty and sadism. Feminine impulses, on the other hand, usually represent a passive desire connected with the anal and the feminine erotogenic zones. The rectum can be easily stimulated by accepting a foreign body that enters it. This anal ambivalence of masculine-active expulsion and feminine-passive reception of a foreign body may lead to a confusion of sexual roles in adulthood.

Abraham (1911; 1924) has suggested a subdivision of the anal stage into the anal-expulsive and the anal-retentive stages. In the earlier, expulsive phase, the infant enjoys the sadistic pleasure of expulsion. Folklore and slang bear witness to these anal-aggressive tendencies, as preserved in the scatological language used by adolescents and some adults. At the later, anal-retentive stage, the infant may develop affection for feces. Feces, after all, are the first possession that the infant may give away to his beloved mother, and as such they are the prototype of a gift and later of gold and money. In dreams feces may symbolize babies, since children often believe that childbirth is a process similar to elimination. Also, children often consider the penis as being analogous to the column of feces that fills the mucous tube of the bowel.

The anal-retentive phase is usually considered to be the source of tenderness, defined as the wish to preserve and to take care of. Freud accepted Abraham's suggestions on this point and elaborated on the concept of tenderness as distinguished from the anal type of love. Even though tenderness seems to originate from the wish to keep and to preserve feces, gradually the care spreads to all pleasurable objects and grows into a consideration for the mother, whom the infant wishes to keep and preserve as a source for a future and continuous flow of gratification. Abraham maintained that the "retention pleasure" outweighed the "elimination pleasure." As tenderness spreads, the child begins to care for his property and pets, handling them carefully and with tenderness.

The particular method of toilet training used by the mother and her feelings concerning defecation may have far-reaching effects upon the formation of specific traits and values in the child. If the mother is very strict and repressive in her methods, for example, the child may hold back his feces and become constipated. If this mode of reacting generalizes to other ways of behaving, the child may develop what is known as a *retentive* character, becoming obstinate and stingy. On the other hand, presented with the same repressive measures, another child may vent his rage by expelling his feces at the most inappropriate times. This is usually considered to be the prototype for all kinds of expulsive traits, such as cruelty, wanton destructiveness, temper tantrums, and messy disorderliness. If, on the other hand, the mother is the type of person who pleads with her child to have a bowel movement and who praises him extravagantly when he does, the child usually acquires the notion that the whole activity of producing feces is extremely important. This idea is felt to be the basis for creativity and productivity. There are numerous other traits of character that are said to have their roots laid down in the anal stage.

The Urethral Phase

The urethral phase is usually not considered to be a stage of development unto itself, but instead is described as transitional to the phallic phase. The urinary tracts are closely related to the genital tracts in both sexes, and childrens' sexual fantasies and dreams often confuse urine with semen and sexuality with urination. Urethral eroticism is basically autoerotic, as one's own body is the love object, but it may be turned toward other objects with fantasies about urinating on them or being urinated on by them.

In girls, urethral eroticism usually leads to holding on and retention, but with the aim of the expulsion of urine which gives the pleasurable sensations. Urination itself can be as active and aggressive as urination on someone. Urethral eroticism in boys usually develops over time into normal and active genital eroticism, but in girls urethrality can lead to a conflict concerning their sexual role, and later may become associated with penis envy (see below). The somewhat passive nature of urination, experienced as "let it go" or loss of bladder control in boys, is related to confusion about their sexual role. In many cases, men who were bedwetters in their childhood exhibit passive and feminine traits as adults.

Training in bladder control can lead to severe conflicts with parents. A child may be punished for his lack of self-control and for his delays in developing full control. These conflicts often hurt the child's self-esteem and may elicit feelings of shame. Children who are bedwetters often become overambitious, as if struggling against the feeling of shame and trying to re-establish their self-esteem.

The Phallic Stage

The term "phallic" is derived from *phallos*, which means erected penis. During the phalic stage of development (ages 4–6), the boy discovers, as it were, the genital organs and learns to derive pleasurable sensations by manual stimulation. During this period the genital organs become powerfully cathected, even though it is some time before all sexual excitement becomes concentrated in the genitals and is dischargd by their interaction in sexual intercourse.

THE OEDIPUS COMPLEX   In the boy, the most important conflict at the phallic stage is the Oedipus complex. The Oedipus complex is named for the king of Thebes who killed his father and married his mother. The tragedy of Oedipus was not a result of malevolence on his part, but a product of inevitable fate. When he realized what he had done, he punished himself by putting out his eyes. Freud saw in this myth a symbolic description of the prehistoric development of human society and, in accordance with the biogenetic principle, a necessary stage in the lives of individuals. Freud discovered that every four-to-five-year-old boy desires to possess his mother physically in the ways which he has derived from his observations and intuitive surmises of sexual life, and tries to seduce her by showing her the male organ of which he is the proud owner. The boy wants to take over his father's place, for, although he loves and admires his father, at the same time he views his father as a competitor and wishes to get rid of him.

To explain the boy's ambivalent feelings toward his father, and as we shall see below, the girl's ambivalent feelings toward her mother, Freud assumed that every person is inherently bisexual. Each sex is attracted to members of the same sex as well as to members of the opposite sex. Freud felt this to be the constitutional basis for homosexuality, although in most people the homosexual impulses remain latent (see below). Bisexuality complicates the Oedipus complex by inducing sexual cathexes for the same-sex parent, so that the boy's feelings for his father and the girl's feelings for her mother are said to be ambivalent rather than univalent in character. This assumption of bisexuality has recently been supported by investigations on the endocrine glands which show rather conclusively that both male and female sex hormones are present in each sex.

Returning to the description of the phallic phase, at this time the penis becomes the main source of pleasurable sensations in the boy. In contradistinction to the more passive, urethral desire to be fondled, a definite need emerges for active pursuit and thrust with the penis. However, the little boy is aware of his inferiority in comparison to his father, whose penis is larger. The boy is afraid that his father will punish him for masturbation and for desiring mother. If the boy has previously noticed the difference between male and female organs, the threat of castration becomes something very realistic and shocking. The boy believes that originally all people have a penis but that it is sometimes cut off by an omnipotent father. This fear of castration is much stronger than the oral fear of being eaten or the anal fear of losing the body content.

Castration fear forces the boy to abandon his incestuous desire for his mother. In fact, some boys give up masturbation altogether and develop a passive attitude similar to that of the mother. This passive attitude usually conceals an increased fear of and hatred for the father, and the resentment toward the father often develops into a defiant attitude against all men in authority. Affection for the mother can turn into a dependence relationship and into a passive need to be loved. Overattachment to the mother, with its feminine components and partial identification with the mother, may lead, in turn, to a submissive attitude toward women in the future. In still other cases, when the mother is strong and aggressive and the father is weak, the boy may repress his phallic strivings toward his mother. Rather than trying to possess her, he identifies with her and forms a passive affection for his father. This so-called *negative Oedipus complex* may lead to homosexuality.

THE ELECTRA COMPLEX　The Oedipus complex in boys creates castration fears that lead to its resolution, but in girls there are no castration fears. When the little girl first realizes the organ differences between the sexes, she develops *penis envy,* which accentuates her love for the father. This is the feminine version of the Oedipus complex and is called the *Electra complex.*

Originally, of course, the girl believes that everyone's body is like hers, but as soon as she discovers that men have penises, she wishes she had one too. Usually girls fantasize that they had a penis but lost it. Freud wrote (1938a, p. 97) that the little girl "begins by making vain attempts to do the same as boys, and later, with greater success, makes efforts to compensate herself for the defect—efforts which may lead in the end to a normal feminine attitude." Girls may masturbate, using the clitoris as a penis substitute. If the girl clings to her wish to have a penis, she may develop masculine tendencies and become domineering and aggressive. If she goes so far as to develop a negative Electra complex, she will become homosexual.

Most girls become hostile toward their mothers, blaming them for not giving them a penis or for taking it away. In addition, jealousy of the mother for possession of the father is always present. The girl wishes to annihilate her mother and possess her father's penis. The feminine Oedipus complex differs significantly from the masculine one, based as it is on jealousy and penis envy. The girl's love for her mother turns to hate. The mother is no longer a love object, and the girl reacts to the loss of the love object by identifying with it. The girl ends up by wanting to take the mother's role and, instead of wanting to have a penis, she desires to be given a baby, which becomes a penis substitute. Her role now becomes passive and receptive, paving the road for normal feminine sexuality.

During the Oedipal period, the girl's sexual pleasure is focused in the clitoris. The clitoral masturbation typical for this age is sometimes accompanied by masculine fantasies in which the clitoris plays the role of a penis. Penis envy may lead to an inner conflict related to clitoral masturbation. For example, a girl with a negative Electra complex may dream about taking the role of the father, inserting her clitoris into the mother's vagina, and having a baby with the mother. Normally, resentment toward the mother and love for the father (the positive Electra complex) lead to giving up the wish for the penis, identification with the mother, acceptance of the feminine-receptive role, and the wish to have (to "incorporate") a baby.

HARTMANN'S CONTRIBUTIONS:
EGO DEVELOPMENT

The publication in 1939 of Heinz Hartmann's *Ich-Psychologie und Anspassungs-Problem (Ego Psychology and the Problem of Adaptation)* is often thought of as a landmark in the development of psychoanalysis. For psychoanalysis it might have meant only the rise of another rebel group, but Freud was no longer present to challenge the new movement, and Hartmann, along with those who contributed to its launching (Hartmann et al., 1946; Kris, 1939; 1941; 1950) did not care to assume a rebel role. Rather, this group sought in Freud's own somewhat ambiguous theorizing a justifying base for their radical proposals. Without surrendering the psychoanalytic concern with depth forces which "scientific" psychologists regarded with distrust, Hartmann was able to propose a revision of the concept of the ego. This revision had the effect of freeing the ego at least partly from its dependence on the id, and so opened up the possibility of a new approach to questions of motivation, learning, thought, perception, and other activities in a form more akin to those which are the concern of the academic psychologist.

Of course, such a revision necessitated some additions to the psychoanalytic view of infantile development, and these additions were in the area of early ego development. Hartmann maintained that the newborn infant is not wholly a creature of drives. In addition to the drives, he has inborn apparatuses (perceptual and protective mechanisms) which appropriately perform a part of those functions which, after the differentiation of ego and id, are attributed to the ego. For Hartmann, then, a state of "adapted-ness" exists before the intentional processes of adaptation begin. He felt that even defenses exist on the level of instincts, and he defined ego development as a differentiation, in which these primitive regulating factors are increasingly replaced or supplemented by more effective ego regulations. According to Hartmann (1958), this differentiation progresses not only by the creation of new apparatuses to master new demands and new tasks, but also and mainly by new apparatuses taking over, on a higher level, functions which were originally performed by more primitive means.

Strictly speaking, then, Hartmann believes that the normal newborn human and his "average expectable environment" are adapted to each other from the very first moment. The newborn seems to be in close touch with his environment not only by his need for its continuous care but also by his reactions to its stimuli (even though at first these reactions are often not specifically adapted). The first signs of intentionality appear near the third month of life, and for Hartmann they mark a crucial phase of development. However, true object comprehension makes a definite appearance only around the fifth or sixth month and is not complete even at the age of one year (Bühler, 1928). Further, the child's needs play a significant role in influencing and directing the development of intention phenomena.

Hartmann is quick to point out that the structural development of the individual also serves his adaptation. This is quite true for the differentiation of the ego and the id, and it is also true for the identifications which build the superego. Here, the relationship between what is achievement and what is disturbance in adaptation is particularly clear. The superego appears to be not only in antithesis to the ego and the id, it is also "to some extent an ideal prototype of that state toward which all the ego's endeavours are tending, a reconciliation of its manifold allegiances" (Freud, 1924, p. 253).

The various processes of adaptation to which Hartmann refers include intelligence, perception, memory, and motility. As they mature, these apparatuses not only enable the child to cope with this environment but also provide some intrinsic pleasure of a "conflict-free" nature. In time, these activities may come to be used in the service of the id. For example, language can be adapted to ego defense by the direction of sharp wit or ironic criticism against those who arouse hostility; what is seen or heard can also be warped by id drives or the defenses against them; walking or dancing can be assimilated to the id system, etc. Any habit once acquired as an ego defense, on the other hand, may develop what Hartmann calls a "secondary autonomy" which insures its persistence even when the need for the defense no longer exists. For example, meticulous orderliness may long outlive the anxiety which originally accounted for its development. Freud had earlier (1905a) recognized the possibility of the separation of a process developed in the service of a drive from that drive, and its subsequent functioning as an end in itself. Therefore, Hartmann's argument that any particular response may be "triggered by the drive," may serve other needs, or may have become an end in itself was a less radical innovation than it might at first appear.

Surveying the functions of the ego according to Hartmann's concept of its development shows the ego to be extremely diverse and complex. Among its many functions, the ego tests reality; controls and directs the discharge of motor energy; inhibits instinctive drives through its defenses; and, in response to danger signals, it safeguards the organism through internalized trial responses and "detour activities" which result in growing independence from the immediate impact of present stimuli. In addition to these functions of adaptation and inhibition, Hartmann also describes integrating and coordinating tendencies, which he called the ego's "synthetic function." For Hartmann, the synthetic function seeks to maintain equilibrium with the adapting and inhibiting activities, and as such it seems to represent the person as something transcending the apparatuses and functions which comprise the ego.

In summary, then, according to Hartmann's psychoanalytic ego theory, the same behavior may be at various times: (1) a simple adaptive response made to the environmental situation; (2) a conflict-free response made purely for the pleasure it gives to the performer; (3) an action which becomes tied up more or less with the id; or (4) at least as an after-effect of this complication remains as a habit carried on with the neutralized energy of the aggressive or sexual drive it once served. Keeping the first two points in mind, it can be seen that thought activities once treated as "rationalizations" can be accepted as reality-oriented means of dealing with the external environment. The same is true of memory or fantasy. The memory of past reality can and will contribute to the solution of immediate problems, and still freer imagination is not infrequently the source of brilliant invention and creativity.

ERIKSON'S DEVELOPMENTAL STAGES

Erik Erikson has remained entrenched in Freudian psychology while at the same time recognizing the effect social factors will have upon the individual's development at each of the psychogenetic stages. A great deal of this thinking has been influenced by field studies of the Sioux and Yurok Indians which he carried on with the cooperation of the anthropologists H. Scudder Mekeel and Alfred Kroeber (Erikson et al., 1950). Erikson is not concerned only with the broad cultural differences which first come to mind when we think of different ethnic groups, however. He is concerned also with "changing historical reality" within an apparently continuous culture. Although the evolution of automation in our own society may have appeared to be very gradual to those who lived through it day to day, its effect on ego development should not be underestimated. Given Hartmann's view that the infant is born with a readiness to adjust to an "average expectable environment," for Erikson (1959, p. 151) it followed that "only a perpetual social metabolism and a constant (if ever so imperceptible) restructuring of tradition can safeguard for each new generation of infants anything approaching an 'average expectability' of environment." Erikson states that the ultimate basis for a healthy personality is security of personal identity. The prototypes or models for identification around which this personal identity is built are likely to be less available in a push-button society or in a society with amorphous goals and ideologies than in a society with organized values and social institutions. In the latter society, the older generation must constantly "rejuvenate" and interpret these values and institutions for the young as they move through the crisis of early child development toward maturity. Therefore, healthy mental adjustment depends upon a healthy mutuality between the child and the parent, since the latter functions in the role of the agent of society.

Erikson, then, utilizes his own terminology, but retains the familiar psychosexual stages of Freud as his framework. He then describes the essential contribution of each phase to the gradual evolution of the individual's ego identity. According to Erikson, the development of positive "psychosocial" effects at each stage will depend on how successful the parents are in handling the inevitable frustrations that represent the crises of each period.

Erikson's first stage of development is the *incorporative phase.* Here, a crisis arises as the infant finds himself abandoned at moments of discomfort with no way of knowing whether relief is near at hand. At this time, the infant requires a feeling of comfort and minimal experience of fear and uncertainty. This stage initially centers around feeding activity, and the quality of the child's physical and psychological comfort during nursing determines his feeling about his early social life. Continuous, dependable, loving attention at this time will cause *trust,* as opposed to *mistrust.* This trust will express itself in the "infant's first social achievement . . . his willingness to let his mother out of his sight without undue anxiety or rage" (Erikson, 1950, p. 219). The second oral stage begins as the first teeth develop and the child learns he can keep what he is given (i.e., the *grasping mode).* Also in this stage, the infant develops his earliest "sense of badness," when the loved source of comfort is abruptly withdrawn as he bites hard to ease his own discomfort.

The next stage, identified by a conflict between self-assertion and denial of the right and capacity for self-assertion, coincides with the Freudian anal period (eighteen months to four years). As interest is transferred to the anal zone, "holding on" and "letting go" become the focal modes on which the *social modalities* will depend. Cultural demands focus attention on sphincter control during this period, and toilet training allows a testing of self-regulation as opposed to regulation by others. As this behavior becomes emotionally charged, the meaning and feelings are transferred into other areas of living. Play assumes an important role in the development of self-control, as self-control is possible in play without a loss of the self-esteem necessary for the development of autonomy. During this period, much depends on the parents' ability to grant independence within relatively "safe" areas. Parental firmness, wisely used, will also help the child to develop a generalized *autonomy* rather than leaving him subject to *shame* and *doubt.*

During the phallic stage, the child's behavior is characteristically "intrusive" for boys and "receptive" for girls, not only in relation to the genital zone but in the handling of objects, walking about and getting underfoot, chattering and asking questions, etc. The primary emphasis in all this is the child's attempt to increase the expansion of his abilities and social awareness. Conscience assumes increasing control of behavior during this period, and ego processes develop toward a sense of identity and purposeful existence. There is also a stress on relationshisp with others and the formation of identity based on the same-sex parent. Testing the limits of inquisitiveness and aggression also become important. How this period affects the individual's later personality depends to a large extent on how skillfully the parents manage to develop a sense of participation, responsibility, and *initiative* out of the child's propensities and interests, rather than impressing him with a sense of *guilt*. A cruel and rigid superego developed at this stage may have disastrous effects all through life.

For Erikson, the latency period is latent only in terms of the sexual drives. Normally, by this time the "organ modes" have been mastered and the child begins to develop the knowledge and skills which will from then on make an important contribution to the confirmation of his identity. Experimentation with basic skills is required by the culture at this time, and the major theme of the period is to master whatever is being done. In the family group and among his peers, the child's status is determined largely by the number and kinds of things he can do. As a result, his activities become less random and more aimful. If the child fails with the tools of his *industry*, his sense of *inferiority* may turn him back upon thoughts of his failure in the Oedipal rivalry and leave him with a lasting belief in his own inadequacy.

Erikson describes four further stages (adolescence, early maturity, later maturity, and culmination) which do not concern us in this chapter. Erikson's important contribution remains his addition to the Freudian psychosexual view, the psychosocial factors that must play a major role in the development of any child.

CONTRIBUTIONS OF ANNA FREUD

In her book, *The Ego and the Mechanisms of Defense* (1946), Anna Freud attempted to clarify the status of the ego in current phychoanalytic theory and to sketch a plan for further study of the concept of ego. In clarifying the concept, she pointed out that early psychoanalytic *theory* would have promptly rejected as apostasy any disposition to dethrone the id and to set up the ego as its independent partner. She pointed out further, however, that psychoanalytic *therapy* had always concerned itself with the unconscious only for the purpose of treating abnormalities and restoring "the ego to its integrity." In fact, the notion that psychoanalytic research should be restricted to depth psychology was explored by Freud's own writing (e.g., Freud, 1920; 1921). Further, Freud (1938b) had explicitly expresed the conviction of an ego "endowed from the beginning with its own peculiar dispositions and tendencies." Hartmann's (1939) later work could really be described as undertaking the task of exploring the ego's "contents, its boundaries and its functions and [tracing] the influences in the outside world, the id, and the superego by which it has been shaped." This is the direction which psychoanalytic theory should take as later prescribed by Anna Freud. In fact, the prestige of her endorsement has without doubt done much to lend strength not only to Hartmann's contributions but also to the work of Ernst Kris, David Rapaport, Erik Erikson, and others identified with the advancement of the concept of the autonomy of the ego.

In addition to recognizing and studying the ego devices which often play a predominant part in the defense mechanism of neurotics, Anna Freud's own contributions to psychoanalytic ego theory have been incorporated into her active professional work with children at the Hampstead Child Clinic in England, her international lectures, and her regular articles in *The Psychoanalytic Study of the Child.* (She has been a co-manager and co-editor of this publication since its establishment in 1945.) Needless to say, her contributions in the area of child development have emphasized ego development rather than psychosexual stages. She accepts the stages originally laid down by her father, but her emphasis on ego processes has resulted in her viewing development as a more continuous process and her de-emphasis of the stages of development.

In a *Panel on Infantile Neurosis* chaired by Ernst Kris, Anna Freud summarized her views concerning developmental stages:

> We have, of course, long left behind that earliest stage when masturbation was regarded as a pathogenic factor, something between a breeding ground and a forerunner of later neurotic symptom formation. We have discarded also a conception held in earlier years, that all other autoerotic activities (thumb sucking excepted) are masturbation substitutes. They merely assumed that aspect for us when we reconstructed events backwards from the study of the phal-

lic phase. When working upwards from the beginning of life, we see them fall into place as distinct expressions in their own right, reaching their respective peaks at the maturation-peak of the libidinal phase by which they are determined. Thumb sucking in the first year of life, anal play and interest in excrement in the second and third, phallic masturbation and exhibitionism between the ages of three and five, have assumed today the settled status of normal and legitimate pregenital activities. (A. Freud, 1954, p. 26)

The years of research in the Hampstead Child Therapy Clinic (Anna Freud, 1967) have produced additional data concerning child development and have enriched the understanding of infantile development. In 1965 Anna Freud stated that there is one basic developmental line which has received attention from analysts from the beginning and which can serve as the prototype for all others. This is the sequence which leads from the newborn's utter dependence on maternal care to the young adult's emotional and material self-reliance. Anna Freud feels that the successive stages of libido development (i.e., oral, anal, phallic) merely form the inborn, maturational base for this sequence. She also feels that the steps in this sequence are well-documented from the analyses of adults and children, as well as from direct analytic infant observations. Although we are interested, in this chapter, only in the first six years of life, all eight steps in this sequence are discussed below for the sake of continuity.

1. The sequence begins with the biological unity between the mother-infant couple, with the mother's narcissism extending to the child, and the child including the mother in his internal "narcissistic milieu" (Hoffer, 1952). Anna Freud follows Margaret Mahler (1952) in further subdividing the period into autistic, symbiotic, and separation-individuation phases, and she points out that there are significant danger points for developmental disturbances lodged in each individual phase.

2. Anna Freud follows Melanie Klein in postulating the next step in the sequence. This is the part object, or need-fulfilling anaclitic relationship, which is based on the urgency of the child's body needs and drive derivatives. She describes this relationship as being intermittent and fluctuating, since object cathexis is sent out under the impact of imperative desires and withdrawn again when satisfaction has been reached.

3. The third step in the sequence is the stage of object con-

stancy, which enables a positive inner image of the object to be maintained, irrespective of either satisfactions or dissatisfactions.

4. The next step is described as "the ambivalent relationship of the preoedipal, anal-sadistic stage, characterized by the ego attitudes of clinging, torturing, dominating, and controlling the love objects" (A. Freud, 1965, p. 65).

5. The fifth step is the completely object-centered, phallic-Oedipal phase. For A. Freud it is characterized by possessiveness of the parent of the opposite sex (or vice versa), jealousy of and rivalry with the parent of the same sex, protectiveness, curiosity, bids for admiration, and exhibitionistic attitudes. In girls a phallic-Oedipal (masculine) relationship to the mother precedes the Oedipal relationship to the father.

6. Following the Oedipal period is the latency period. Here, there is a postoedipal lessening of drive urgency and a transfer of libido from the parental figures to contemporaries, community groups, teachers, leaders, impersonal ideals, and aim-inhibited, sublimated interests. There is also a significant element of fantasy manifestations giving evidence of disillusionment with and denigration of the parents (e.g.,, "family romance," twin fantasies, etc.).

7. The next step is the preadolescent prelude to the "adolescent revolt." During this period there is a return to early attitudes and behavior, particularly of the part-object, need-fulfilling, and ambivalent type.

8. The final step is the adolescent struggle around denying, reversing, loosening, and shedding the tie to the infantile objects. This period is further characterized by a defending against pregenitality, and finally establishing genital supremacy with libidinal cathexis transferred to objects of the opposite sex outside the family.

Anna Freud discusses other developmental lines for which the above serves as the basis (e.g., those toward body independence, from egocentricity to companionship, from the body to the toy, from play to work, etc.). Unfortunately, space does not permit their discussion here. In all of her discussions of developmental lines, however, A. Freud emphasizes their practical value. For example, she maintains that a mere glance at the above developmental line will explain why a child's separation from mother, parents, or home results in such varied reactions. Infringements of the biological mother-infant tie (phase 1) will give rise to separation anxiety (Bowlby, 1960); failure of the mother to play her part as a reliable need-fulfilling and comfort-giving agency (phase 2) will cause breakdowns in individuation (Mahler, 1952) or anaclitic depression (Spitz, 1946), or other manifestations of deprivation (Alpert, 1959), or precocious ego development (James, 1960), or what has been called a "false self" (Winnicott, 1966). Further, any unsatisfactory libidinal relations to unstable or otherwise unsuitable love objects during anal sadism (phase 4) can disturb the balanced fusion between libido and aggression and give rise to uncontrollable aggressivity and destructiveness (A. Freud, 1949). Only after object constancy (phase 3) has been reached can the external absence of the object be substituted for in part by the presence of an internal image which remains stable.

Anna Freud (1965) outlines other practical lessons which can be learned from the same developmental sequence. As these are considered by this author to be one of her major contributions to the psychoanalytic theory of development, they are summarized as follows:

1. The clinging attitudes of the toddler stage (phase 4) are the result of pre-Oedipal ambivalence, not of maternal spoiling.
2. It is unrealistic for parents to expect the pre-Oedipal child (up to the end of phase 4) to show the mutuality in object relations that belongs to the next level (phase 5) only.
3. No child can be completely integrated in group life before libido has been transferred from the parents to the community (phase 6). In other words, if the Oedipal complex remains unresolved, the child cannot be expected to adapt well to school life.
4. Reactions to adoption should be most severe in the later part of the latency period, when all children feel as if adopted and their feelings about the reality of adoption merge with the occurrence of the "family romance."
5. Sublimations are characteristically lost during preadolescence (phase 7), not through any developmental or educational failure, but because of phase-adequate regression to early levels (phase 2, 3, and 4).

It is an unrealistic on the part of parents to oppose the loosening of the tie to the family or the young person's battle against pregenital impulses in adolescence (phase 8) as it is to break the biological tie in phase 1, or oppose pregenital autoerotism in the phases 1, 2, 3, 4, and 7. (A. Freud, 1965, p. 68)

In 1970 Anna Freud published a major paper on "Symptoma-tology." Although the study of psychopathology does not belong here, her remarks concerning symptom formation are also rele-vant for the psychology of normal development. Anna Freud be-lieves that the symptomatic structures can be "ego-dystonic" and create mental pain and discomfort or "ego-syntonic" and become incorporated in the individual's personality structure. It depends largely on the ego's readiness to accept distortions and to accom-modate the pathological manifestation within its structure.

Moreover, such pathological formations depend on the relation-ship between the id and the ego, the unconscious and the con-scious. Neurotic symptom formation does not start until the ego has broken off from the id, but it is not necessarily postponed until the superego has become independent from the ego. The id-ego conflicts, and the first neurotic symptoms representing attempts of conflict solutions develop within the ego under pressure from the environment. The initial conflicts are created "by dangers arising from the object world such as loss of love, rejection, punishment" (A. Freud, 1970, p. 25).

Thus the earliest stages of ego development are connected with the so-called *archaic fears* of the early infancy. The archaic ego has no resources of its own to cope either with the flood of external stimuli or with the disturbing inner tensions.

> When a child's ego is unusually sensitive or when a child's mother is unusually unable to provide the comfort and reassurance to which the infant is entitled at this stage. Where ego development is slow, the archaic fears last beyond infancy. Their undue persistence and prominence can be taken as diagnostic indicators for retardation or arrest in the area of ego functioning. (A. Freud, 1970, pp. 30–31)

Again, Anna Freud stresses the interaction of biologically deter-mined developmental tendencies and interactional patterns.

RECENT DEVELOPMENTS

Mittelmann

In the last ten or fifteen years there have been numerous contri-butions to the psychoanalytic theory of infantile development. Some of these, of course, are not new contributions at all, but are merely clarifications of the orthodox position; others are not worthy of our attention; while still others may turn out to be significant contributions to the theory. Some of those that appear to belong to the latter group are discussed below.

One example of an interesting and valuable contribution is the work of Mittelmann on intrauterine and infantile motility (Mittelmann, 1954; 1955; 1958; 1960; Mittelmann et al., 1959). He states that "there is a period in infantile development in which motility predominates both as an urge and source of pleasure and as a form of reality testing and integration. This period is ushered in by the development of locomotion; the psychological characteristics and pathological implications of this phase are closely connected with various aspects of motility as the dominant function" (Mittelmann, 1960, p. 104).

Mittelmann states that dynamically it is possible to differentiate between motility (1) as an urge, a factor in object relations, and a source of pleasure (id aspects); (2) as a form of reality testing, mastery, communication, and integration (ego aspects); and (3) as relating to the ultimate formation of conscience and ideals (superego aspects). In addition, from the point of view of maturation and relation to the environment, it is possible to differentiate between movement and action. For Mittelmann, the former predominates in the intrauterine or pregravitational period as well as in the first six months of the postnatal or gravitational period. Lastly, studies of motility have suggested that later motor and related psychological phenomena have successive precursors in intrauterine and early motility. The time of the appearance and the quality of the pattern can vary with environmental circumstances, and pathology can arise, immediately or later, because of trauma to motility proper (e.g., being hurt while crawling) or through motility being involved in other traumatic situations (e.g., affect starvation).

Based on this information, Mittelmann has postulated different stages or different kinds of motility through which each infant passes in the course of normal development. These kinds of motility are briefly described below:

1. *Passive motility* has its origin in intrauterine posture and being moved rhythmically. It is reinforced by similar postnatal experiences and by being cared for, and accordingly, it stands for unlimited care and protection. It accounts for the later association of horizontality with helplessness and death.

2. *Active motility* at first involves nonadaptive varieties of motility. One example is "reflex grasping," which is the antece-

dent of later voluntary grasping, of clinging, of grasping for manipulation, and therefore of later adaptation and reality testing. Reflex grasping is also the antecedent to the manifestations of dependent longings, anxious dependency, affection, and adult love-making, particularly when it is dependent love-making. *Random movements,* which have their antecedents in "quickening" *in utero,* are defined as the first manifestations of the motor urge, and are presumably the precursors of regressive diffuse discharge via motility. Affectomotor patterns in this area are said to be antecedents of interpersonal communication and the adaptive handling of objects. Together with *autoerotic rhythmic patterns,* they are also said to be the precursors of adult intercourse movements, of excess discharge through hypermotility, and, via kinesthetic sensation, of foot fetishism.

3. *Adaptive motility* is divided into three basic kinds: manipulative, postural, and locomotor. It is described as one of the main avenues of the development of mastery, reality-testing, motor urge, and object relations. Later, it is also important in the development of aggression, self-esteem (with possible later self-deprecation), and the concepts of self and not-self. The fear of falling and fear of the failure of motor function appear during this stage, and restriction arouses anxiety and rage, which, in excessive amounts, raises the possibility of later neurosis or psychosis.

4. *Sensory motility* (primarily visual), combined with tactile motor exploration of the body, contributes to reality-testing, mastery, differentiation of part-self, self, and not-self, and displacement from the genitals to the extremities. Generalized inactivation while looking at faces, plus later inactivation and staring during anxiety while being looked at, is presumably the precursor of voyeurism, exhibitionism, a "paralyzing" fear (as in Freud's, 1918, Wolf Man nightmare), or hysterical paralysis.

5. *Oral motility* is described as hand-to-mouth movement and support of mouth activity by posture and locomotion. According to Mittelmann (1960), it is an element in self-differentiation, reality-testing, passive or active aggressive devouring fantasies, and the use of the mouth as a manipulative and aggressive organ.

6. *Excretory motility,* when combined with "freezing" in anxiety

and restrained aggression, supposedly contributes to the general muscle tension in obsessive-compulsive states.

7. *Genital motility,* when defined as manual handling or grasping, usually results in incorporation of the male genitals in the body image and in the subsequent relief from anxiety. Rhythmic pelvic thrusts, on the other hand, are the precursor of adult intercourse, and the ease of occurrence of erection, often combined with general motor responses, is the precursor of the symbolic use of the body as a phallus.

Mittelmann adds that although not a particular stage in itself, the early motor crying pattern, reinforced later by slamming of the thighs and head-banging, is the antecedent of aggression directed outward and toward the self, and therefore is the antecedent also of masochism and conscience. Later, when it is combined with the general motor-rage response to restriction, it becomes the prototype of diffuse outbursts of hostility.

Mittelmann himself admits (1960) that while all that he presents is based on observations, some of it is reasonable assumption while some is supported by an impressive array of data; and that therefore its convincing value varies. For example, it is much more reasonable to assume that the infant's gazing at his hands held aloft at three months of age is connected with the development of self-image, then it is to assume that the fetus' being rhythmically moved by the mother's movements contributes to the infant's rocking at six or seven months of age. Still, much of Mittelmann's work is very interesting and could be quite valuable if substantiated by further research.

Escalona

Still another valuable contribution has been made by Sibylle Escalona (1953; 1962; 1963) concerning patterns of infantile experience. She presents an approach to the investigation of early developmental processes which focuses on patterned aspects of the infant's *experience* as the matrix of growth, rather than on innate and instinctual factors. The key word for her is "experience," defined not as the outer stimuli as such, nor as the simple summation of these, but experience as the manner in which these factors alter what the baby feels with his senses, what he does with his body, and the content and quality of successive events in his life. Escalona (1963, p. 240) states, "What I call experience is a series of events ordered on a time-space continuum, unified by virtue of the fact that they occur in a single organism that remains the same."

The data from Escalona's work has suggested that the same developmental transitions may be accomplished by different routes, depending upon the infant's established reaction propensities, and the mother's mode of dealing with the child. The data also suggests that differences in organismic characteristics, such as activity level or perceptual sensitivity, may determine the impact of external stimulation upon the child's experience. In six-month-old infants who are markedly responsive, for example, strong stimulation from the mother is arousing, but it certainly does not usually lead the infant to engage in the most mature behavior integrations of which he is capable. It may in fact lead him to activate simpler, already well-established schemata. In markedly inactive babies of this age, however, the same kind of external stimulation is a necessary condition for the emergence of the relatively most mature behaviors. Therefore, both of these children respond to maternal stimulation and in both the resulting behavior activations have a bearing on the establishment of some early ego functions, but the immediate effect is in an almost opposite direction, as a function of activity level. This is what Escalona means by postulating the infant's experience as the crucial intervening variable.

The central theme, then, in all of Escalona's presentation is to make plausible the notion that very different actions on the part of mothers (or other environmental variations) can have very similar consequences in terms of their impact upon the child's experience (i.e., as reflected in behavior). The converse is equally true, that similar or even identical external stimulation may have varying and opposite consequences in terms of the direction in which they alter behavior. Two categories of variables, then, environmental and organismic, converge and interact reciprocally in shaping the minute-by-minute and year-by-year experience of the growing child. Of course, for example, all healthy children come to recognize an environment that exists independently of their action; they all learn to regulate motor actions in a purposive manner; all develop a selective tie to the mother, etc. But these and other universalities are the necessary consequence of closely similar biological equipment, and a high order of regularity in the encounters with animate and inanimate objects in the human habitat (what Hartmann [1939] calls the "average expectable environment").

Superego Development

Still another major contribution to the psychoanalytic theory of infantile development has been in the area of conscience and superego development. Certainly mere observation indicates that children often experience "guilt" before the age of five or six, and various theories have been put forth to explain this. Although the present psychoanalytic view cannot be attributed to any one investigator, Malmquist (1968) has done a good job of summarizing the work in this area.

Theorists in the fields of learning and developmental psychology have presented various ideas about the development of "moral standards." Controls are most often viewed as a form of learned social behavior which emerges as a result of reward and punishment as well as of secondary and vicarious reinforcement. The development of conscience has most often been ascribed to such factors as the desire for parental approval and praise, and, conversely, anxiety in response to parental rejection and criticism. A great deal of elaborate empirical and laboratory data has been amassed by utilizing social learning theory in an effort to describe the acquisition and maintenance of self-control as well as transgressions (Bandura and Walters, 1963). Of course, any thorough discussion of this work is beyond the scope of this chapter. Let it suffice to say that various measures are used in attempts to delineate conscience growth, such as resistance to temptation, guilt, sex-typing, adult role formation, and prosocial aggression, which are believed to be reflections of identification processes.

One of the difficulties in using the concept of identification, as pointed out by Malmquist (1968), is inherent in the different referents to which this term is applied. It has been used to describe a situation in which the child thinks, feels, and behaves as though the characteristics of another person or group of people belong to him (Bronfenbrenner, 1960). Also, identification has been described as merely behaving like another person, or as having motivational implications such as the need to be like another person. Still further, the concept has been confined to the belief of a child that the attributes of a model belong to the child himself (Kogan, 1958).

The situation seems clearer when identification is confined to "identification with the aggressor." As a defensive maneuver, such identification usually begins during the second year and is generally believed among analysts to be of great significance for the crystallization of a superego. Presumably, it builds on the attachment the child has previously made to a parent, and is almost always described in the oedipal context of the boy fearing castration from his father as a retaliation for his sexual wishes toward his mother. The wish to eliminate the rival is then repressed and gives rise to guilt. Since the child also loves his father, it is possible for him to identify with the threatening parent as well as with the mother, who is loved by both child and father. However, the establishment of this defense within the ego is necessary but not sufficient for the actual development of internalized controls (Spitz, 1958). The process originates in the infant's helplessness and is a primitive attempt to master a situation by becoming the protective or frustrating adult. The change from passivity to activity allows aggression to be discharged against external objects, but it also results in aggression being discharged against the self. The defense which was initially directed against a feared object is now available to the child's own psychological self as a restrictive mechanism (Malmquist, 1968). To conceptualize this economically, energy is withdrawn or "decathected" from the external objects by a process of desexualization and deaggressivization. The same energy is then available to the superego for its own internalized primitive aggressive and loving activities (Hammerman, 1965). Guilt cannot be experienced until this level of development is reached, when the ego can direct against itself some of its functions. It is only now that a separate group of functions are developed under the control of the superego (e.g., self-observation, self-evaluation, self-punishment, a need to expiate for transgression of standards, the bestowing of self-esteem for virtuous thoughts, acts, and wishes, and withholding it for their contraries, etc.). Intrasystemic conflicts are now superseded by intersystemic ones (Beres, 1966).

Malmquist (1968) believes that other attempts to look at conscience formations from the external aspects of socialization and conformity may have delayed a conjoint consideration of the complex psychological processes that are involved in the emergence of the controls. The classic study of Hartshorne and May (1928), for example, viewed "moral character" in terms of overt conformity, such as adherence to rules and not cheating on school tests (i.e., in terms of resistance to temptation). Certainly clinicians working with children during this period are interested in such behavior, but they are more curious to understand the meaning of such outward conformity. It is clear to most clinicians that such external rule-following can be present in children, as well as in adults, and yet be accompanied by severe conscience deficits. In fact, it seems clear that conformity to moral rules has little correlation with the strength of verbalized beliefs in rules or with the intensity of guilt feelings following transgressions. Apparently, judgments and verbalizations about what a moral act is are of little value in predicting whether the individual child or adult will actually act in such a manner. Knowledge of morality is, instead, indicative only of the child's cognitive and cultural background and of his desire to make a good impression (Kohlberg, 1964).

Another issue in this area concerns the extent to which cognition and intellect are involved in the development and function of conscience. Certainly some degree of conceptual capacity is needed before an operational conscience can be present, but many of the functions indicating some type of control system are precursors of the actual conscience. Certain ego functions (e.g., reality-testing, memory, judgment, etc.) are necessary for the elaboration of conscience, but to say that these are equivalent to conscience gives a totally different perspective on a mental agency that functions in the realm of personal values, ideals and social controls. Nor is it an agency concerned merely with conformity as judged by externals, such as cheating on school tests. Conscience refers rather to part of an intrapsychic system that develops in contact with the social environment and with the inner world of wishes and strivings. Further, and perhaps most importantly, at a certain point in a person's development, this structure survives in its own right, independent of the specific social and environmental pressures (Malmquist, 1968). What accounts for this independent functioning is the introduction of true feelings of guilt.

As previously mentioned, in the young child, diverse manifestations of controls exist prior to a functioning superego. Even during the infantile period, some inhibition of direct impulse expression can be observed in children. Originally this inhibition is based on imitation and fear, but later it expands to the stage of an inner danger. However, since warning functions are attributable to the ego, impulse-controlled behavior or conformity does not by itself signify superego activity or anticipation of superego restriction. Ego development is a precursor of superego development, and outward social conformity may thus be a protective device of the ego and not be influenced by the superego. In a similar way, defenses do not imply a superego, since these too are ego functions. Malmquist (1968, p. 325) states:

What does seem to occur in the course of development is that the superego lends a more skilled and specific direction to these ego activities. The presence of a superego can be detected by a different kind of warning signal experienced by the ego—the affect of guilt—in contrast to many other affects which are experienced by the ego.

Malmquist (1968) goes on to point out that defenses are not always initiated by or in the service of the superego. They can be employed by the ego when the ego is in conflict with the environment. Reaction formation, for example, can result in a strict cleanliness to counter the expression of anal impulses when these are prohibited by a strict environment, and need not be the response of a harsh superego. In some cases, therefore, it can be quite difficult to determine whether a certain observed behavior is due to the influence of the superego or is a defensive ego function. To make this determination, it is necessary to know whether other superego functions pertaining to ideals or controls are present (e.g., self-evaluation, prohibitions and injunctions, social feelings, *and the necessary sense of guilt*). Only these factors can give a clue as to the developmental level that has been attained.

Experimental Studies

Direct observation and experimentation can confirm or refute empirical data, but it can hardly prove or disprove theoretical constructs and models. Unfortunately, many experimental studies have operated with the ill-defined concepts, and the early research was rather inconclusive.

A review of experimental research in psychoanalysis concluded as follows: "The triviality of obtained differences in this field makes a most discouraging picture, and the coarseness of the experimental methods so far available for tapping the sensitive dynamics of repression does not augur well for the future" (Sears, 1943, p. 120). A more optimistic report was published by Farrell (1954), who analyzed the observational, nonexperimental studies of Isaacs (1933), Halverson (1940), Levy (1928), and others.

"In the case of the early stages of life," Spitz wrote, "where the usual psychoanalytic methods of free association and verbal communication are not applicable, the experimental-psychological approach used with the framework of the psychoanalytic investigation can offer valuable contributions to the psychoanalytic theory and to the psychoanalytic clinic. It can never replace the exact psychoanalytic investigation of the given individual child with its

whole background, it can only complement it" (Spitz, 1950, p. 73).
Freud's theory of infantile developmental stages has found support in the Blacky-Picture Studies conducted by Blum (1949), in
Cohen's (1957) studies in cognitive responses, and in other studies.

Several experimental studies offered support to Freud's theory
of infantile repression, especially those by Belmont and Birch
(1954), Dollard and Miller (1950), Weiner (1968), Zeller (1950),
and others.

Several authors criticized the design and findings of the experimental studies. Sarnoff (1965) maintains that so far most experimental tests were "an extension of the theory and not merely
a literal testing of formally stated predictions" (p. 278). This criticism is not new; Hilgard (1952), Hook (1959), and Nagel (1959;
1961), and many others, pointed to the difficulty inherent in proving or disproving the psychoanalytic propositions concerning infantile development. However, the main difficulty lies not with
psychoanalysis but with the experimental method (Wolman, 1960;
1964). Psychoanalytic theory, like any other scientific theory, is
a system of hypotheses, logical constructs, and models *explaining*
human behavior. A theory cannot be proven or disproven by empirical test; a theory should be open for deductions open to
empirical test.

Experimental procedures cannot operate with personality models
such as, for instance, Freud's structural theory; experimental research must be preceded by observational studies which will develop testable hypotheses. Anna Freud's Hampstead Clinic and
Marianne Kris' Yale Studies have embarked upon such a long
and arduous road of longitudinal empirical studies. A powerful
experimental support for Freud's theories of unconscious has come
from an unexpected source, namely the Soviet research in interoceptive, unconscious conditioning (Ayrapetyantz, 1952).

REFERENCES

[Note: *The standard edition* refers to *The standard edition of the complete psychological works of Sigmund Freud* (London: Hogarth Press
and the Institute of Psycho-Analysis).]

Abraham, K.   Notes on the psychoanalytical investigation and treatment
of manic-depressive insanity and allied conditions (1911). In K.
Abraham, *Selected papers on psycho-analysis.* London: Hogarth
Press, 1949, Pp. 137–156.

Abraham, K.   A short study of the development of the libido viewed in light of the mental disorders (1924). In K. Abraham, *Selected papers on psycho-analysis*. London: Hogarth Press, 1949. Pp. 418–501.

Allport, G. W.   *Personality: A psychological interpretation*. New York: Holt, 1937.

Alpert, A.   Reversibility of pathological fixations associated with maternal deprivations in infancy. *The Psychoanalytic Study of the Child*, 1959, 14, 169–185.

Ayrapetyantz, E.   *Higher nervous function and the receptors of internal organs*. Moscow: U.S.S.R. Academy of Sciences, 1952.

Bandura, A. and Walters, R. H.   *Social learning and personality development*. New York: Holt, Rinehart and Winston, 1963.

Belmont, L. and Birch, H. G.   Re-individualizing the repression hypothesis. *Journal of Abnormal and Social Psychology*, 1954, 46, 226–235.

Beres, D.   The functions of the superego. In R. E. Litman (Ed.), *Psychoanalysis in the Americas*. New York: International Universities Press, 1966. Pp. 275–288.

Blum, G.   A study of the psychoanalytic theory of psychosexual development. *Genetic Psychology Monographs*, 1949, 39, 3–99.

Bowlby, J.   Separation anxiety. *International Journal of Psycho-Analysis*, 1960, 41, 89–113.

Breuer, J. and Freud, S.   Studies on hysteria (1895). *The Standard Edition of the complete psychological works of Sigmund Freud*. London: Hogarth Press, Vol. 2.

Bronfenbrenner, U.   Freudian theories of identification and their derivatives. *Child Development*, 1960, 31, 15–40.

Bühler, C.   *Kindheit und Jugend*. Leipzig: Hezzel, 1928.

Cohen, H.   The effect of oral need on cognitive responses of children. *Boston University Graduate Journal*, 1957, 6, 47–49.

Darwin, C.   A biographical sketch of an infant. *Mind*, 1877, 2, 285–294.

Dearborn, G. V. N.   *Motor-sensory development*. Baltimore: Warwick & & York, 1910.

Dilthey, W.   *Gesammelte Schriften*. Leipzig: Teubner, 1924.

Dollard, J. and Miller, N. E.   *Personality and psychotherapy*. New York: McGraw-Hill, 1950.

Erikson, E. H.   *Childhood and society*. (2nd ed.) New York: Norton, 1950.

Erikson, E. H.   The problem of ego-identity. In G. S. Klein (Ed.), *Psylogical issues: Selected papers by Erik H. Erikson*. New York: International Universities Press, 1959. Pp. 101–171.

Escalona, S. K. The study of individual differences and the problem of state. *Journal of the American Academy of Child Psychiatry*, 1962, I.

Escalona, S. K.   Patterns of infantile experience. *The Psychoanalytic Study of the Child*, 1963, 18, 197–244.

Escalona, S. K. and Leitch, M. et al.   Early phases of personality development: A non-normative study of infant behavior. *Monographs of* the Society for Research in Child Development, Vol. 17, No. 54, Evanston, Ill.: Child Development Publications, 1953.

Farrell, B. A. Scientific testing of psychoanalytic findings and theory. In H. Brand (Ed.), *The study of personality.* New York: Wiley, 1954.

Fenichel, O. *The psychoanalytic theory of neurosis.* New York: Norton, 1945.

Freud, A. *The ego and the mechanisms of defense.* New York: International Universities Press, 1946.

Freud, A. Aggression in relation to emotional development. *The Psychoanalytic Study of the Child,* 1949, 3/4, 37–42.

Freud, A. et al. Problems of infantile neurosis: A discussion. *The Psychoanalytic Study of the Child,* 1954, 9, 16–71.

Freud, A. *Normality and pathology in childhood.* New York: International Universities Press, 1965.

Freud, A. *Research at the Hampstead Child-therapy Clinic and other papers, 1956–1965.* New York: International Universities Press, 1967.

Freud, A. The symptomatology of childhood: A preliminary attempt at classification. *The Psychoanalytic Study of the Child,* 1970, 25, 19–44.

Freud, S. *The origins of psychoanalysis: Letters to Wilhelm Fliess, drafts and notes (1887–1902).* New York: Basic Books, 1954.

Freud, S. The neuropsychoses of defense (1894). In *The standard edition.* 1962. Vol. 3, Pp. 45–61.

Freud, S. Further remarks on the psychoneuroses of defense (1896). In *The standard edition.* 1962. Vol. 3. Pp. 162–185.

Freud, S. The interpretation of dreams (1900). In *The standard edition.* 1962. Vols. 4 and 5.

Freud, S. Three essays on the theory of sexuality (1905a). In *The standard edition.* 1962. Vol. 7. Pp. 130–245.

Freud, S. Jokes and their relation to the unconscious (1905b). In *The standard edition.* 1962. Vol. 8. Pp. 9–238.

Freud, S. Formulations on the two principles of mental functioning (1911). In *The standard edition.* 1962. Vol. 12. Pp. 218–226.

Freud, S. On narcissism: An introduction (1914a). In *The standard edition.* 1962. Vol. 14. Pp. 73–102.

Freud, S. On the history of the psychoanalytic movement (1914b). In *The standard edition.* 1962. Vol. 14. Pp. 7–66.

Freud, S. *A general introduction to psychoanalysis* (1915–1917). New York: Garden City, 1943.

Freud, S. From the history of an infantile neurosis (1918). In *The standard edition.* 1955. Vol. 17. Pp. 7–257.

Freud, S. Beyond the pleasure principle (1920). In *The standard edition.* 1955. Vol. 18. Pp. 7–64.

Freud, S. Group psychology and the analysis of the ego (1921). In *The The standard edition.* 1922. Vol. 18.

Freud, S.   The ego and the id (1923). In *The standard edition*. Vol. 19. Pp. 12–66.

Freud, S.   Neurosis and psychosis (1924). In *The standard edition*. Vol. 19. Pp. 149–156.

Freud, S.   Inhibitions, symptoms, and anxiety (1926). In *The standard edition*. Vol. 20. Pp. 77–175.

Freud, S.   *The future of an illusion* (1927). In *The standard edition*. Vol. 21. Pp. 5–56.

Freud, S.   *An outline of psychoanalysis* (1938a). New York: Norton, 1949.

Freud, S.   Analysis, terminable and interminable. *International Journal of Psycho-Analysis*, 1938b, **18**, 373–405.

Hall, G. S.   The contents of children's minds on entering school. *Pedagogical Seminary*, 1891, **1**, 139–173.

Hall, G. S.   *Aspects of child life and education*. Boston: Ginn, 1907.

Halverson, H. M.   Infant sucking and tensional behavior. *Journal of Genetic Psychology*, 1940, **53**, 365–430.

Hammerman, S.   Conceptions of superego development. *Journal of the American Psychoanalytic Association*, 1965, **13**, 320–355.

Hartmann, H.   *Ego psychology and the problem of adaptation* (1939). Trans. D. Rapaport. New York: International Universities Press, 1958.

Hartmann, H., Kris, E. and Loewenstein, R.   Comments on the formation of psychic structure. *The Psychoanalytic Study of the Child*, 1946, **2**, 11–38.

Hartmann, H. et al.   Problems of infantile neurosis: A discussion. *The Psychoanalytic Study of the Child*, 1954, **9**, 16–71.

Hartshorne, J. and May, M. A.   *Studies in the nature of character*. New York: Macmillan, 1928–1930. 3 vols.

Hilgard, E. R.   *Psychoanalysis as a science*. New York: Basic Books, 1952.

Hilgard, E. R.   The scientific status of psychoanalysis. In I. Sarason (Ed.), *Science and theory in psychoanalysis*. New York: Van Nostrand Reinhold Co., 1965. Pp. 184–205.

Hoffer, W.   The mutual influences in the development of ego and id: Earliest stages. *The Psychoanalytic Study of the Child*, 1952, **7**, 31–41.

Hook, S. (Ed.),   *Psychoanalysis, scientific method and philosophy*. New York: New York University Press, 1959.

Isaacs, S.   *Social development in young children*. London: Routledge, 1933.

Jacobson, E.   *The self and the object world*. New York: International Universities Press, 1964.

James, M.   Premature ego development: Some observation upon disturbances in the first three years of life. *International Journal of Psycho-Analysis*, 1960, **41**, 288–294.

Jones, E.   *The life and work of Sigmund Freud*. New York: Basic Books, 1953–1957. 3 vols.

Kagan, J. The conception of identification. *Psychological Review,* 1958, **15**, 296–305.

Kohlberg, L. Development of moral character and moral ideology. Vol. 1. *Review of child development.* New York: Russell Sage Foundation, 1964.

Kris, E. On inspiration. *International Journal of Psycho-Analysis,* 1939, **20**, 377–389.

Kris, E. Probleme der Ästhetik. *Int. Z. Psychoanal, und Imago,* 1941, **26**, 142–178.

Kris, E. On preconscious mental processes. *Psychoanalytic Quarterly,* 1950, **19**, 540–560.

Levy, D. M. Finger sucking and accessory movement in early infancy. *American Journal of Psychiatry,* 1928, **7**, 881–918.

Mahler, M. S. On child psychosis and schizophrenia: Autistic and symbiotic infantile psychoses. *The Psychoanalytic Study of the Child,* 1952, **7**, 286–305.

Malmquist, C. P. Conscience development. *The Psychoanalytic Study of of the Child,* 1968, **23**, 301–331.

Mittelmann, B. Motility in infants, children, and adults: Patterning and and psychodynamics. *The Psychoanalytic Study of the Child,* 1954, **9**, 142–177.

Mittelmann, B. Motor patterns and genital behavior: Fetishism. *The Psychoanalytic Study of the Child,* 1955, **10**, 241–263.

Mittelmann, B. Psychodynamics of motility. *International Journal of Psycho-Analysis,* 1958, **39**.

Mittelmann, B. Intrauterine and infantile motility. *The Psychoanalytic Study of the Child,* 1960, **15**, 104–127.

Mittelmann, B., Malkenson, L. and Munroe, R. L. Mannerisms in blindness and childhood schizophrenia: A preliminary report. *American Journal of Orthopsychiatry,* 1959.

Nagel, E. Methodological issues in psychoanalytic theory. In S. Hook (Ed.), *Psychoanalysis, scientific method and philosophy.* New York: New York University, 1959.

Nagel, E. *The structure of science.* New York: Harcourt, Brace, 1961.

Piaget, J. *The origins of intelligence in children.* New York: International Universities Press, 1952.

Preyer, W. *The mind of the child* (1881). New York: Appleton-Century-Crofts, 1888.

Rickert, H. *Kulturwissenschaft und Naturwissenschaft.* Tubingen, 1899.

Sarnoff, I. The experimental evaluation of psychoanalytic hypotheses. *Transactions of the New York Academy of Science,* 1965, **28**, 272–290.

Sears, R. R. *Survey of objective studies of psychoanalytic concepts.* New York: Social Science Research Council, 1943.

Shinn, M. W. *The biography of a baby.* Boston: Houghton Mifflin, 1900.

Spitz, R. A. Anaclitic depression. *The Psychoanalytic Study of the Child,* 1946, **2**, 313–342.

Spitz, R. A. On the genesis of superego components. *The Psychoanalytic Study of the Child,* 1958, **13**, 375–406.

Spranger, E. *Types of man.* Halle: Niemyer, 1928.

Stern, W. *Psychology of early childhood* (1914). New York: Holt, 1930.

Sully, J. *Studies of childhood.* New York: Appleton, 1895.

Taine, M. On the acquisition of language of children. *Mind.* 1877, **2**, 252–259.

Weiner, N. Motivated forgetting and the study of repression. *Journal of Personality,* 1968, **36**, 213–234.

Whiting, J. W. and Child, I. L. *Child training and personality.* New Haven: Yale University Press, 1953.

Windelband, W. *An introduction to philosophy.* London: Allen & Unwin, 1921.

Winnicott, D. W. Metapsychological and clinical aspects of regression within the psycho-analytical set-up. *International Journal of Psycho-Analysis,* 1966, **36**, 16–26.

Wolman, B. B. *Contemporary theories and systems in psychology.* New York: Harper & Row, 1960.

Wolman, B. B. Evidence in psychoanalytic research. *Journal of the American Psychoanalytic Association,* 1964, **12**, 717–733.

Wright, H. F. Observational child study. In P. H. Mussen (Ed.), *Handbook of research methods in child development.* New York: Wiley, 1960. Pp. 71–139.

Yazmajian, R. Biological aspects of infantile sexuality and the latency period. *Psychoanalytic Quarterly,* 1967, **36**, 203–229.

Zeller, A. F. An experimental analogue of repression. *Psychological Bulletin,* 1950, **47**, 39–51.

2

PAUL KAY

Psychoanalytic Theory of Development in Childhood and Preadolescence

BASIC CONCEPTS

As early as 1905, with the publication of "Three Essays on the Theory of Sexuality," Freud had made it clear that psychoanalysis embraced the study of normal development and functioning in childhood, adolescence and adulthood. His concept of normal development at this time was based almost entirely on reconstructions from the analyses of adult patients. Its major features included the unique interaction of biology and environment as embodied in the mother-child relationship, the Oedipus complex, and the sequential maturation of the libido from birth through adulthood, paralleled by and interacting with the development of what we would today call superego and superego functions. He had already taken note of phasic overlapping, phasic irregularity, and the influence of earlier on later phases.

Near the end of his life, Freud stated that "a normal ego . . . is, like normality in general, an ideal fiction. . . . Every normal person . . . is only normal on the average" (1937, p. 235). The normal ego approximated that of the psychotic and was almost indistinguishable from that of the neurotic except for "quantitative disharmonies" (1940, p. 183). "The determining cause of all the forms taken by human mental life," he wrote, "is, indeed, to be sought in the reciprocal action between innate dispositions and accidental experiences."

No human being is spared the traumatic experiences originating in the "instinctual demands from within, no less than excitations from the external world . . . during childhood" (Ibid, p. 185). The parents, representing civilization, and then internalized as the superego restrict "the ego's activity by prohibitions and punishments, and encourages or compels the setting-up of repressions. We must therefore not forget to include the influences of civilization among the determinants of neurosis" (Ibid).

The "greatest trauma" in a boy's life is the "combined effect of a threat of castration and the sight of the absence of a penis in females. . . ." (Ibid, p. 155). For the girl, the discovery that she lacks a penis may also be for her a great, if not the greatest traumatic experience in her life. Freud's concept of trauma was based on the idea of a "sliding 'complemental series'" of two factors: the quantitative aspect of the traumatizing event and the particular constitution which is more or less vulnerable to the traumatic experience (1939, p. 73).

Trauma, frustrations and conflicts "belong to the normal course of mental life . . . " (1931, p. 220). Development, therefore, for these reasons, rarely achieves completion. Referring to the libidinal development in adolescence, Freud stated that "as a rule the processes necessary for bringing about a normal outcome are not completely present or absent, but partially present, so that the final result remains dependent on . . . quantitative relations" (1940, pp. 155–156).

Freud's (1931) concept of libidinal types vividly illustrates his concepts of health and illness. These types, on the one hand, do not "coincide with clinical pictures" and, on the other hand, they include "all the variations which . . . fall within the limits of the normal." He calls them erotic, the narcissistic and the obsessional. A type representing all three, "erotic-obsessional-narcissistic" "would be the absolute norm, the ideal harmony." None of these types need be neurotic, but if they fall ill, then those of the first type would develop hysteria, those of the second, obsessional neurosis and those of the third type, psychosis or criminality.

The study of the normal has remained a "distressed" area in psychoanalysis[1] (Kris, 1951). More than fifty years after the publication of the "Three Essays," Anna Freud (1958) referred to the study of adolescence as the "stepchild" or psychoanalysis. Sixty-five years after the same publication, Buxbaum (1970) referred to latency as the "stepchild" of psychoanalytic literature.

Psychoanalysts have generally tended to loosely equate health and normality, and to define both in terms of the absence of conflict and symptom-formation. Flapan and Neubauer (1970) caution against equating normality and health. Normality, they point out, indicates "average" and adaptation to the values of a particular society. Noting that the "forces that operate to maintain health have been studied less than those" interfering with it, they stress the difficulty in arriving at a concept of health. They define health as the "maintenance of developmental progression. . . ."

The foregoing concept which is probably congruent with the views of many analysts today has been anticipated by earlier concepts formulated by Hartmann and Anna Freud. Hartmann's (1939) "evolutionary" concept of health referred to the "degree of development actually attained"; to adaptation to reality; and to the differentiation, synthesis and hierarchical organization of psychic structure. This concept seems to have foreshadowed those of Anna Freud's (1945, pp. 24, 25) concepts of normal[2] development manifested by more or less continuous drive and ego development and that of "developmental lines" (1965).

Hartmann, Anna Freud and other writers on this subject have stressed the complexity and richness of normal development.[3] Ac-

---

[1] The psychoanalyst has been trained to deal with psychopathology and the suffering to which it gives rise. A psychoanalyst, however, who works with adolescents and children must be as familiar with normal development as he is with neurotic and psychotic manifestations. He is continuously faced, in both his diagnostic and therapeutic work, with the task of evaluating the developmental process.

[2] Anna Freud uses the terms "normal" and "health" interchangeably throughout her writings.

[3] I will be using the word "normal" throughout the rest of this chapter for the word "health" only because it appears to be the most commonly used

cording to Hartmann (1950), "the complex interdependence of a great variety of developmental factors and a branching out of many alternatives on every subsequent developmental stage" constitutes normal development. Anna Freud (1965, p. 87) has referred to the "many variations of normality" resulting from the inevitable "disharmonies, imbalances, intricacies of development . . ." (Ibid., p. 107).

Three basic but highly variable factors are reciprocally involved in normal development: the individual, the environment and the interaction between the two. In regard to the forces operating within the individual, Hartmann (1950) has discussed "partly independent variables," such as aggression and the conflict-free sphere in addition to psychosexual development. In connection with the concept of phasic sequences, he has discussed phase "vulnerability" and phase specificity. Phase "vulnerability" refers to the potential for normal as well as pathological development, experience in previous phases, and the "vulnerability" specific to the particular phase. His concept of phase specificity refers to the "optimal phases for every step in adjustment, integration, and overcoming conflicts. . . ." Phase specificity results from "the average interactions of the child's growth and development, of the psychological characteristics of the relevant figures of his environment, and of the cultural equipment they use in dealing with the child's needs. . . ." All these factors are "variable."

Anna Freud (1965, pp. 86, 87, 105) has pointed to the complex impact on normal development of the different rates of progression and regression of the drives and ego function unique to each individual which inevitably lead to developmental imbalances and variations. These difficulties in development attain their most dramatic and complex form through the interaction between the individual and the environment. The unique development of the individual is due to "accidental environmental influences" (p. 86). She refers to "tendencies, inclinations, predilections (including the tendency to depression, masochistic attitudes, etc.) . . . which are present in all human beings [and which] can be eroticized and stimulated toward growth through forming emotional links between the child and his first object" (p. 87). The child develops those aspects of himself which evoke his mother's love and approval and

---

term denoting healthy development. Actually, Flapan and Neubauer's term "health" as distinguished from "normality" is preferable because it is more precise.

neglects those which provoke her disapproval. Such imbalances and disharmonies are not "pathological as such" (Ibid.).

It is by now an axiom that "psychic life springs from an interaction between biological givens, including instinctual endowment, and the infringement of the outer world" (Blos, 1962, p. 199). Selective internalization of the environment, the mother, in particular, other significant figures, values and ideals occurs, followed by growing independence, an independence which is sustained by continued, reciprocal interaction with the external world.

When the environment is unable to provide what is needed for normal development and functioning, damage to the individual results. Hartmann's (1958 [1939], p. 46) concept of the "average expectable environment" is one in which "on the average the whole ensemble of instinctual drives, ego functions, ego apparatuses, and the principles of regulation . . . have survival value." If, instead of "average expectable stimulations (environmental releasers)," there are "environmental influences of a different sort," then development will be deflected one way or another (p. 35). Winnicott's (1965) concept of the "facilitating environment" is similar to Hartmann's concept of the "average expectable environment" except that it stresses the particular contribution which the environment makes to a specific developmental phase.

What is the average expectable environment? How favorable or unfavorable for development is it? Olden (1952) has described in detail how many American parents in recent decades have distorted psychoanalytic knowledge by assuming that psychoanalysis urged unlimited drive gratification as the precondition for normal development.[4] The application of this distorted view to the rearing of children may lead to disaster. These parents had, it seemed, carefully disregarded what psychoanalysis had to say about other basic aspects of development, such as identification, sublimation, defenses, and the superego. This distortion by the public of psychoanalytic knowledge has not yet disappeared. The implications of this view in terms of the latent attitudes of these parents towards themselves and their children's development is hardly reassuring.

Anna Freud (1965, p. 7) has offered a balanced account of the impact of psychoanalysis on rearing practices and child development. It has led to greater honesty about sexuality between parent and child. It has eliminated or reduced problems associated with achieving bowel control and disturbances in eating and sleeping.

---

[4] This distortion has been created partly by some psychoanalysts, psychiatrists, and mental health professionals.

In helping to eliminate masturbatory conflicts, it has been beneficial in some respects but has had "unwanted side effects on character formation by eliminating struggles which . . . served . . . as a moral training ground." Also, as a result of parents trying to reduce their children's fear of them, the children's guilt feelings increased (Ibid, p. 8). Finally, when superego severity was reduced, children experience the "deepest of all anxieties," the fear of their drives (Ibid).

Olden's (1952) study of rearing practices in America and of parental attitudes towards their children have led her to conclude that the child in this country has generally been viewed as the man to be, the "future citizen, money maker, and future politician" rather as a child.

Deutsch (1967, p. 91) has stressed that today's adolescents have been reared in a "matriarchy." Many parents, especially mothers, have not only abdicated their authority but have also collaborated "in the rebelliousness of their children." These parents have not been successful in their own adolescent revolution and "hope to achieve a kind of delayed victory through identification with their children" (p. 104). Many mothers have encouraged their daughters to act out sexually because of their own real or fantasied sexual deprivations. Some mothers, fearing homosexuality in their sons, have pushed them into a "precocious heterosexuality" (p. 105).

Erikson (1964, p. 33) has not minced words about the "average expectable environment." He has stated that the "general provocation and exploitation of the child's immature emotions by parent and grandparent for the sake of their own petty emotional relief, of suppressed vengefulness, of sensual self-indulgence, and of sly righteousness must be recognized . . . as a universal potentiality often practiced and hypocritically rationalized," and "under the guise of being trained" the child is "being ruefully exploited, only to become in adulthood nature's most systematic and sadistic exploiter" (p. 34). Olden (1953) has referred to children as the "targets par excellence, for adults' aggressive drives . . . perhaps. This is another reason why empathy with children is more rare than empathy with adults."

Beyond the parent, there is the community, and stretching far beyond that the society of the nation and of nations. Society at large, according to Blos, is a mixed blessing, at best, in regard to its impact on development. Our modern democratic, capitalistic society allows for a "high degree of personality differentiation and individuation [but] . . . the discontinuities in social patterning and the burden of self-determination facilitate deviant and pathological development . . ." This society does not "offer youth any status confirmation . . . initiation rites . . . consecration . . ." (Blos, 1962, p. 204). Further, in our society "rational and adaptive behavior . . . may represent instinctual gratifications, condoned or encouraged by society in the form of . . . competition, acquisitiveness and vindictiveness. . . ."

Seen through the prism of the universal traumatization of children by parents and other figures within the environment, how does one evaluate normal development? Flapan and Neubauer (1970) have raised some sharp questions bearing on this issue. They ask, for example, how the health of a child is to be evaluated "in terms of his adaptation to an 'abnormal' environment by means of 'symptoms of deviant behavior.'" They ask about the "significance of a minor deviation in what seems to be a 'growth-supportive environment.'" They ask about the "developmental significance of conformity to or rejection of a family or community." Finally, they ask whether "peer acceptance or rejection mean health or illness."

Emphasis on the environment, however traumatic, tends to obscure the fact that development normally includes traumatic experiences (just as it includes gratifications and achievements) even in a benign setting. I have already referred to Freud's emphasis on the extreme traumatic impact on both the boy and the girl of their discovery that there are human beings without a penis.

Many analysts have come to believe that object loss and the dread of abandonment, especially, early in life may constitute the child's most severe trauma. Rochlin (1961) has beautifully elucidated the significance of the rearing figure to the child. Without the relationship to a nurturing person, the release of tension, the development of the ego and of the drives, the principles of constancy and homeostasis, and the maintenance of sufficient self-esteem to support development cannot be achieved. Personality disorganization and suffering resulting from the loss of the nurturing person is usually catastrophic. Even the threat of loss of such a person may injure the child's development severely since the meaning of the loss remains the same. While the actual loss of a parent through divorce or death in childhood and adolescence is hardly universal, it is by no means infrequent. What is universal in childhood is separation from the nurturing person and the fear of losing their love. What is universal in adolescence is the necessity of permanently relinquishing the original tie to this precious human source of psychic life and development.

Arriving at a concept of normal development is bound up with the problem of acquiring the necessary data and knowledge. Reconstructions from the analysis of adults, children and adolescents have been the main sources of the knowledge on which the psychoanalytic theory of normal development has been based. Despite the many limitations of this method, it has been remarkably fruitful. In the last three decades, direct observation ("spot" and "longitudinal") has gradually become an important and, in certain respects, a unique source of data for the study of normal development.

These two methods, reconstruction from psychoanalysis and direct observation have their advantages and disadvantages. Direct observation has been most helpful in studying the undifferentiated, preverbal stage, the conflict-free sphere of the ego, the early mother-child relationship, separation anxiety, and the effect of different settings, such as hospitalization, on development (A. Freud, 1965, p. 24). Direct observation, however, provides few, if any, clues to psychic structure and function, especially, their unconscious aspects. Hartmann (1950), therefore, has urged the "meaningful interpenetration" of data from both sources, because observational data alone is rarely fruitful without the use of psychoanalytic theory.

The limitations of psychoanalysis are well-known. Many adults, for example, are not suitable for psychoanalysis. A disturbing number of the papers devoted to normal development, especially, in regard to female psychosexuality, are not based on psychoanalytic work at all but rather on psychotherapy and consultations with borderline and psychotic patients. Reconstructions of childhood and adolescence even from the analysis of suitable adult patients are apt to have limited validity. The feelings of adolescence are rarely accessible to the adult analysand, although the facts are remembered, while the opposite tends to hold true for latency (A. Freud, 1958). Further, the direct psychoanalysis of the preadolescent and adolescent is usually very difficult. Detailed reports of such analyses are rare. The preadolescent finds it very difficult to recognize and talk about his thoughts and feelings while the adolescent is either in "mourning" or in "love"[5] (A. Freud, 1958).

The psychoanalyst is often bound by certain professional, cultural and personal limitations. Because his therapeutic aims are primary, he is hardly in the best position to study developmental processes which are usually silent. Pathology speaks with a loud

[5] Or both.

voice. The psychoanalyst may, therefore, according to Sandler (1960; 1962) see the superego as a source of torment and despair, rather than of love and encouragement. Also, the preferred interest of most psychoanalysts is the unconscious. Their reservations about the data of consciousness and behavior make them prejudiced observers.

Erikson (1964) has criticized psychoanalysts for minimizing or ignoring social reality and for securing "clinical evidence" with the "help of inferences based on Freud's theories" which is then "slanted and used" to verify the very theory which had been used to acquire the "clinical evidence."

The psychoanalyst's sexual identity may also affect what he is able to learn from his analysands. Freud (1931) had noticed that women psychoanalysts have greater access to the girl's pre-Oedipal mother attachment since they are more suitable figures for a mother transference. Jacobson (1950) has asserted that male psychoanalysts have neglected the study of the wish for children in men because of a defensive attitude towards their own unconscious wishes for children.

There are other factors besides sexual identity which affect the psychoanalyst's ability to perceive and understand his patient. Atkins (1970) has discussed filicidal impulses in the psychoanalyst due to unresolved adolescent conflicts over aggression. These filicidal impulses may impair the psychoanalyst's ability to analyze the adolescent phase of his patients.

The continuous build-up of the data on which the psychoanalytic theory of normal development is based along with its limitations lead naturally to evolution, ambiguity, and contradictions in the opinion of those working in the field. How can it be otherwise when the subject being studied, normal psychological development, is awesome in depth and scope regardless of approach?

I hope, therefore, that the reader will use the format I have chosen merely as a convenient guide, as I have done, and from which I have often meandered whenever I felt that more justice would be done to the developmental processes under discussion. They cannot be straitjacketed into neat compartments. Also, repetition has been unavoidable but, hopefully, I have repeated productively rather than photographically, as when referring to the same process or function in different developmental contexts. Finally, wherever possible, I have used illustrative clinical data (which is usually scantier than one would prefer) to help make the theory come alive.

LATENCY

Freud

Freud, for the first time in Letter #75 in 1897, clearly speaks about the "extinction of the sexual zones" as a "developmental inhibition" due to "piety, shame, and such things. . . ."[6] (p. 270). In 1905, he used the term "latency"[7] explicitly to refere to a developmental inhibition which was total or partial, "organically determined and fixed by heredity. . . ." (p. 177). It was also due to "education" which (Freud implies) set up mental forces such as "disgust, feelings of shame, and the claims of aesthetic and moral ideals" (p. 177). These mental forces also arose from the individual's unpleasant awareness that his "sexual impulses" were contrary to the "direction" of his "development" (p. 178).

The sexual instinct itself loses its object and becomes autoerotic. But "the activity of those (sexual) impulses do not cease even during this period . . . though their energy is diverted, wholly or in great part from their sexual use and directed to other ends." He refers mainly to sublimation (p. 178). Finally, "some sexual activity may persist through the whole duration of the latency period until the sexual instinct emerges with greater intensity at puberty" (p. 179).

Freud's 1905 formulation of latency is clearly ambiguous and contradictory about two separate but intimately related issues: sexual inhibition and the forces which bring it about. Sexuality is totally inhibited, partially inhibited or uninhibited. In 1917 (p. 320), for example, he noted that the "latency period may . . . be absent" altogether, while in 1940a (p. 153), his last reference to this phase, he stressed the "lull" (and, even "retrogression") in psycho-sexual development. Further, he considered this sexual inhibition as "organically determined" and also due to the effects of education and mental forces. In subsequent writings, Freud stressed one or both of these views.

Sarnoff (1971) has recently traced Freud's thinking on latency in an intriguing piece of detective work. He quoted from Freud's 1909, 1923, 1939, and 1940 papers to demonstrate his biological approach to latency. Then he quoted from a letter (1897) to Fliess

---

[6] In a previous letter, he had referred to the ebb and flow of the instinctual life in childhood.
[7] In this and subsequent writings on latency, Freud placed this period between the end of the Oedipal phase and adolescence.

and from the 1905, 1911, 1914, 1921, and 1922 papers demonstrating Freud's psychological, i.e., defense concept of latency. Finally, Sarnoff showed how Freud, in his 1925 paper, resolved the dilemma by viewing the ego as ultimately rooted in physiology (phylogeny), but very responsive to cultural demands. When the latter demanded sexual latency, the ego complied.

Some of Sarnoff's evaluations of Freud's papers may be questioned. The 1905 paper, for example, according to Sarnoff, demonstrated Freud's concept of latency as a defense, but actually, closer reading of Freud's ideas in this paper demonstrates that he had espoused both the biological and psychological views, as quoted above. Also, in the 1940 paper, according to Sarnoff, Freud had advanced the biological approach, but in this paper, Freud had clearly stated that "repression is prominent" in latency.

The astonishing thing about Freud's 1905 concept is how much it anticipates the thinking of subsequent contributors as well as his own. The resolution of the conceptual dilemma in the 1926 paper, for example, is foreshadowed by two observations. One is that education follows "the lines which have already been laid down organically" and impresses "them somewhat more clearly and deeply" (1905, p. 178). The second is that the "unpleasurable feelings" caused by the individual's opposition to infantile sexuality because it runs counter to the "direction" of his "development" evoke the "mental forces (reacting impulses)" which are sexually inhibiting. The collaborative and complementary operation of biological and psychological forces in this formulation is plain.

Sarnoff (1971), Buxbaum (1970) and others have stressed the absence of drive diminution in latency as if it were a departure from Freud's concept, but even the 1905 paper which represents his first explicit discussion of latency clearly shows that he was aware of this feature as factually and theoretically significant.

Divergencies and contradictions would seem to be inevitable in building up the clinical and theoretical foundations and structure of any science or discipline dealing with human development and functioning, especially psychoanalysis. The real issues consist of the data which is available and the thinking which is brought to bear on it. At this time, the available data does not decisively support latency as defense or latency as a biologically determined drive inhibition. It does clearly support latency as a period in which there is great drive modification by the ego. The true issues seem to be drive modifiability and the modifying elements rather than drive diminution or persistence.

What, to me, is more striking than the ambiguities which Sarnoff points out in Freud's concept of latency[8] is Freud's apparently puzzling attitude towards the latency period itself. In 1940a (p. 153), for example, he considered latency as a "lull" in which "progress is at a standstill . . . much is unlearnt and there is much recession." Much earlier (1926, p. 114), he had characterized this "lull" in which "much is unlearnt" as the "dissolution of the Oedipus complex, the creation or consolidation of the super-ego and the erection of ethical and aesthetic barriers in the ego." The counterpart of this civilizing of a child is the evolution of civilization in general. In a previous paper, he had written that "an extremely serious part of human intellectual activity, the part which has created the great institutions of religion, law, ethics, and all forms of civic life, has as its fundamental aim the enabling of the individual to master his Oedipus complex and to divert his libido from its infantile attachments into the social ones that are ultimately desired" (1925, p. 208). Is this "progress . . . at a standstill" and "recession"?

The implications are clear that the study of the instinctual life and the complexes associated with it has apparently been more compelling to Freud than the study of ego and superego development. That he as well as other psychoanalysts have retained the term "latency" for a period marked by the awesome evolutionary achievements in psychic structure which Freud and subsequent contributors have themselves elucidated suggests that Freud's ambivalent attitude is not unique.[9]

Freud's productive dedication to the study of the ego and superego, or, rather to his uniquely balanced study of the psychic apparatus throughout his life, proves that his apparent ambivalence was not strong. His verbal devaluation of the ego and superego in latency in relation to the drives suggests some residual fascination with the instinctual or biological aspect of human psychology.

Freud's blurring of the concept of latency extended itself to the defenses of this phase. In 1905, he stressed reaction formation;

[8] and in Anna Freud's concept in regard to the drive-defense or biological-psychological nature of latency.

[9] Anna Freud's account of the intellectual development in latency compared to that of the Oedipal phase and adolescence which I shall report on later bears the imprint of a similar attitude.

The significance for a psychoanalytic theory of normal development of these and other attitudes arising out of the natural interests and dispositions of the investigator in regard to the acquisition of data and the development of theory based on that data has already been discussed in the introductory section of this chapter.

in 1911, fantasy; in 1926, regression and, in 1940, repression. This description is somewhat misleading since Freud often referred to more than one defense in the same paper. In general, he seemed to stress regression and repression in initiating latency and re-action formation, fantasy and sublimation in maintaining it.

Freud elaborated directly on the content of the latency phase in terms of superego formation. Indirectly, he elaborated it in terms of psychosexual development, especially that of the girl. In both in-stances, he made it clear that the processes he was describing began prior to latency and reached into adulthood. I shall briefly sketch his description of these processes except where he explicitly refers to another developmental phase and then I will report it in that section. Aside from convenience and clarity, this meandering demonstrates the continuity and variegated impact of develop-mental processes on different levels of structure formation and functioning over the long run, an essential feature which is apt to be crippled or destroyed by thinking only in terms of phases.

FEMALE PSYCHOSEXUAL DEVELOPMENT   The summary of female psychosexual development which follows is based on Freud's papers published in 1923, 1925, 1931, 1933, and 1940. In these papers, he compared the psychosexual development of boys and girls. The castration complex in the boy, for example, brings about the (total) repression or destruction of his Oedipus complex but it leads the girl into hers. Also, the girl, in contrast to the boy, re-solves her Oedipal complex far more slowly and less completely than the boy with profound implications for ego and superego de-velopment. "The number of women who remain till a late age tenderly dependent on a paternal object, or indeed on their real father, is very great" (1933a, p. 119). But this prolonged de-pendency is an advantage, according to Freud, because a few years later he observed that "It does little harm to a woman if she re-mains in her feminine Oedipus attitude. . . . She will . . . choose her husband for his paternal characteristics and be ready to recog-nize his authority"[10] (1940c, p. 194).

The girl's psychosexual development is more complicated than the boy's not only because she is more fearful than the boy of losing her parents' love but, mainly, because of two other separated

[10] Freud's opinion obviously indicates a personal and cultural bias. More data than is available on the dissolution of the Oedipus complex in girls and boys is necessary in order to achieve a more accurate picture of this process in both sexes.

but related factors: her castration complex and the two great developmental shifts which she must accomplish in her progress towards femininity. One shift pertains to the transfer of her love from mother to father and the other is the transfer of sexual excitation from one erotogenic zone to another, clitoris to vagina. The boy, of course, does not have to master such shifts.

The castration complex consists of the girl's reactions to the discovery that she lacks a penis. She may, as a result, give up sexuality (clitoral masturbation) for a while. She may deny the lack of a penis and devote herself to becoming as masculine as possible for longer or shorter periods of time. Or, she may begin her feminine development by substituting the wish for a baby (penis) from her father for the wish for a penis.[11] Before turning to father, she gives up the tie to mother after devaluing and hating her. She devalues her mother for not having a penis. She hates her for several reasons: infantile ambivalence; the failure to give her a penis; and the inevitable deprivations and frustrations of childhood brought about by her mother. In giving mother up, she identifies with her and tries to take her place. She then competes with mother for father, becomes very jealous of her and hates her anew. Following her Oedipal disappointment, the girl gives up her father as a love object, identifies with him and returns to her masculine position, at least until adolescence.

Freud stressed again and again the profound significance of the girl's reactions to the awareness that she lacks a penis. Her "whole development may be said to take place under the colours of envy for the penis" (1940c, p. 193). Penis envy, the girl's outstanding reaction to the lack of a penis, leads to feelings of inferiority and self-contempt (which may be more or less shared by the boy till middle or late adolescence) and then to compensatory narcissistic intensification. The girl also becomes generally more envious and jealous than the boy. Finally, penis envy enhances the girl's bisexuality so that it is greater than that of the boy. A little later, I shall report Freud's observations on the effect of penis envy on superego development.

The outcome of penis envy is ultimately decided by the degree of constitutional activity (which may and does coexist with Oedipal wishes towards father) or passivity. While Freud made no explicit statement to this effect, he clearly implied the primary importance of the girl's pre-Oedipal mother attachment in regard to the fate

---

[11] All these reactions take place to a greater or lesser extent in every girl.

of her penis envy. Freud drew attention repeatedly to the momentous effect of the girl's pre-Oedipal mother attachment on her relationships to her father and subsequent male figures. It is this pre-Oedipal mother attachment which is transferred to the father and which, therefore, constitutes the basis and model for this new tie.

The pre-Oedipal mother is the first seducer. In contrast to the paternal seduction, the maternal one is real rather than fantasied and consists of gratification as well as stimulation. These experiences are inherent in the mother's care and fondling of her child's body. The girl develops active and passive wishes towards the mother in all libidinal phases. If she is to complete her psychosexual development, the girl must give up this tie to her mother.

The boy's pre-Oedipal mother attachment is similar to the girl's. Throughout latency, therefore, boys and girls learn to feel for the people who have been helpful to them "in their helplessness and satisfy their needs for a love which is on the model of, and a continuation of, their relation as sucklings to their nursing mother" (1905, pp. 222–223).

So far as the subject of aggression in latency is concerned, Freud now and then referred to it in the form of allusions to pregenital regression but made no explicit statements about it.

In certain respects, superego formation and functioning is the same in both sexes. The superego is the "heir" of the Oedipus complex and represents the incorporation of the Oedipal objects into the ego giving the "new structure its characteristic qualities" (1925, p. 257). The difference in superego formation and functioning between the boy and the girl arises, as previously implied, in their reactions to the castration and Oedipus complexes. Castration anxiety tends to destroy, (or, repress more completely) the Oedipus complex in the boy resulting in the formation of a comparatively strong superego. The girl, however, develops a superego which is not so "inexorable, so impersonal, so independent of its emotional origins" as the boy's because she lacks castration anxiety and, therefore, the incentive to resolve her Oedipus conflict to the same degree as the boy does (p. 257). Internalization of parental ideals and demands is thereby weakened. Her capacity for social interests, for justice and for sublimation is, as a result, less well developed than in the boy.

The superego represents "every moral restriction" and "strivings towards perfection" (1933b, p. 67). It functions as a self-observer, as a conscience, and as the "vehicle of the ego ideal by which the ego measures itself" (p. 65). The superego represents the values and attitudes of the parents and everything that had influenced them: "the taste and standards of the social class in which they live and the characteristics and traditions of the race from which they sprung" (1939, pp. 122–123).

Freud regarded the ego ideal as a vital part of the superego. The ego ideal is the "target of . . . self-love" and a source of "narcissistic satisfaction" (1914, p. 101). It has a "social side" in its references to "family," "class," and "nation." If the ego ideal is not fulfilled, "a sense of guilt" (social anxiety) ultimately derived from a fear of parental punishment (loss of love) is experienced. Later he also referred to the ego ideal as "the precipitation of the old picture of the parents" (1933b, p. 65).

After Freud

In recent decades, two clear trends have become manifest in the work of other contributors on latency. One trend is in the direction of conceptual dissolution, similar to the recent fate of some other psychoanalytic concepts, such as the superego (Sandler, 1960). The other trend is in the direction of building up a detailed clinical and metapsychological picture of development in terms of psychic structure and psychosocial reality.

The conceptual dissolution of latency is more apparent than real, since it is the result of attempts to be more precise about the occurrence and contents of this phase. Latency, for example, no longer extends from the Oedipal phase to adolescence as it did for Freud, but to preadolescence.[12] Also, Anna Freud (1945, p. 18) has observed that latency is "usually in existence for one or two years before the first tendencies of the infantile period fade into the background." Bornstein (1951; 1953) has divided latency into two distinct phases. The first begins at the age of five and ends at eight-and-a-half, while the second (latency proper) begins at eight and ends at ten. Heightened instinctual pressure and superego-id conflict characterize the first phase, while reduction of instinctual conflict and pressure characterize the second. "Limited orgastic gratification is apparently a normal phenomenon in the latency period, more so among boys than among girls" (Ibid, 1953).

---

[12] I have been using "adolescence" and "preadolescence" instead of puberty and prepuberty, except in quotations, for reasons which I shall explain in the section on Preadolescence.

Other writers such as Deutsch (1944, p. 4) and Williams (Kay, 1969) have tended to stress the merging of late latency and preadolescence. Williams (Ibid), in fact, has subdivided latency into three subphases, the result of which is that both its beginning and end are blurred. She suggests an early phase from five to seven years of age containing residuals of the Oedipal phase; a middle phase of latency proper, from seven to nine years, in which ego development and drive abatement occur; and a late phase from nine to eleven years of age in which preadolescent intrusions take place. These Oedipal and preadolescent intrusions may represent the operation of developmental, defensive or cultural factors, singly or in combination.

To what extent the foregoing conceptions of latency with their emphasis on the drives represent increases in clinical and theoretical knowledge about latency, and to what extent they may represent a particular interest of the investigator in the biological, or, rather, instinctual aspects of this phase is an important issue since it involves the freedom of the investigator to acquire the kind of data needed to form the useful hypotheses.

The second trend I have referred to consists not only of elaborations and refinements of the various elements in Freud's thinking, but also of fresh clinical and theoretical contributions. Sarnoff (1971), for example, has unequivocally expressed the idea that there is no drive diminution at all in this phase. Latency, instead, represents a defense against Oedipal strivings. Sarnoff (Ibid) traces his own position, in part, to a panel discussion on this subject stressing, in particular, Bornstein's opinion (Friend, 1957).

An authentic ambiguity[13] about the nature of latency lies in the definition of words like "inhibition" or "persistence" of sexual impulses. I have already quoted Freud to the effect that they persist but are more or less sublimated. Blos (1962, p. 54) has made a similar statement and then quotes Fenichel who, in 1945, stated that, "During the latency period, the instinctual demands themselves have not changed much; but the ego has." Are sexual impulses which are sublimated still sexual impulses and experienced as such? The most recent concept of sublimation which I shall discuss in a subsequent section does not simplify the issue since it stresses the nearness of instinctual life and conflict to the sublimatory process. What seems to be the central issue here is the degree of unneutralized drive energy present in the sublimatory

[13] He illustrates clearly Anna Freud's ambiguity on this point with suitable quotations.

process, its variation in different individuals as well as within the same individual, and the proportion of aggression involved. Clinical data bearing on this issue would be most helpful.

So far, what is clear is that the clinical data increasingly points to the presence and direct experience of sexual impulses in children who seem to be most Oedipal and who come for analysis or psychotherapy. Are these children, however, latency children psychologically? To what extent do undisguised and unmodified sexual impulses occur in children between the Oedipal phase and pre-adolescence who do not come for treatment? How does one acquire such data? It would be a gargantuan task since it would involve knowing about the accompanying masturbatory fantasies which latency children can barely share with themselves.

Freud's thinking on latency has been further developed by the ideas of individuation and of structural autonomy. This approach has been slowly gaining ground among those studying latency but has yet to achieve the explicitness with which Blos had discussed it in regard to adolescence. These two approaches, dealing with related processes, regard psychosexuality as but one, although very likely the most important one, of several developmental variables. Aggression is another. The first and only elucidation of aggression in latency, by Anna Freud (1949), will be discussed in the next section. The formation of the self and the sense of identity is another aspect of the new approach. Erikson's contribution to the concept of the sense of identity, its association with work and with psychosocial reality in latency (as well as in adolescence) come to mind. Sarnoff has offered a concept of ego structure specific for latency, based upon the type and organization of the defenses.

Most of the work on latency, however, has consisted of amplification, refinement, and modification of the various elements in Freud's concept. One example is the ego-id struggle as elaborated by Anna Freud, Bornstein, Jacobson, and others. An outstanding contribution in this connection is Anna Freud's discovery that masturbation fantasies under certain circumstances may be acted or lived out unbeknowst to the individual.

Another example of outstanding work on latency, resulting in an expansion of Freud's thinking, is Jacobson's integration of the clinical and metapsychological aspects of superego development and functioning, especially in regard to sublimation, drive mastery, adaptation, and the evolution of various ego functions, such as reality-testing, feeling, and thinking. Jacobson's contribution is especially valuable in that it always treats latency sequentially instead of in isolation.

The group experience, the education, the games, and the psycho-motor aspects of the latency child's life are other examples of the creative elaboration of Freud's observations on latency by Anna Freud, Buxbaum, Blos, Jacobson, Peller, Fraiberg, Kaplan and other writers.

Some, like Greenacre and Harley, have questioned Freud's ideas about the absence of vaginal sensitivity before adolescence and the nature of the shift from clitoral to vaginal sexuality. Blos (1962, p. 54), based upon a prior observation by Anna Freud, has pointed to the "shift in cathexis from an outer to an inner object," i.e., the replacement of object relationships by identifications as the "essential criterion" of latency. Lampl-de Groot (1950) has used a superego function to signify the onset of latency, i.e., the fusion of previous parental restrictions against instinctual gratification into a prohibition against masturbation.

Kestenbergy has offered an elegant, comprehensive, psychobiological, or, better still, psychohormonal concept of latency chiefly, I gather, for heuristic purposes.

> A gradual increase in all hormones seems to reflect the struggle of beginning latency when progressive and regressive forces vie with each other as they do at the ages of two-and-a-half or three and later in prepuberty. Based as it is on previous integration and differentiation of psychic structure, the development in early latency is smoother and does not produce disturbances equivalent to the disequilibrium of the two-and-a-half year old and the diffusion in prepuberty. Latency consolidation of psychological gains reinforces the integration of psychic functions that, I believe, develops between the ages of three and four. It anticipates the phase of integration in prepuberty and seems to be a model for the final consolidation of psychic structure in transition from puberty to adulthood. (1967, pp. 458–459)

She states in the paper from which the foregoing quotation was taken that the "earliest beginning of an adult-like steroid metabolism" occurs along with a "significant rise in hormone excretion" at about the ages of nine or ten. The onset of sexual differentiation coincides with these hormonal events. The "hormonal constellation in latency may prove to be a miniature antecedent of the preadult consolidation during which the adult form of hormone production, initiated in puberty, becomes stabilized."

I like her formulation because its correlative, anticipatory, and recapitulatory aspects offer an evocative framework. That her concept of anatomical, hormonal, and psychological correlations need much confirmation only highlights the strong and prior need for analytic and observational data to confirm the other more conventional psychoanalytic concept of latency.

Anna Freud's (1965, p. 66) recent statement on latency is very useful because it is so comprehensive and yet succinct. In latency, there is "post-oedipal lessening of drive urgency and the transfer of libido from the parental figures to contemporaries, community groups, leaders, impersonal ideals, and aim-inhibited sublimated interests, with fantasy manifestations giving evidence of disillusionment with and denigration of the parents ('family romance,' twin fantasies, etc.)." Her concept falters only in its omission of the classical picture of the latency child as reasonable, obedient, industrious, and good natured. I am sure such latency children have existed and still do. I have even seen some of them but how common are they?

The most pithy yet complete statement on latency which I have found is Bernstein's (Becker, 1965). For him, latency consists in accomplishing three tasks: repression of the Oedipus conflict, identification with the ideals of the peer group, and the development of a stable superego.

The following subsections, I hope, will amplify the foregoing preparatory statements.

The Drives

The outstanding feature of the latency drive organization is the regression to pregenitality, "one of the most important occurrences in childhood development" (Reich, 1951). It represents a defensive regression against genitality, which, at least in early latency (Bornstein, 1951), is more typical for the boy than for the girl (Blos, 1962, p. 53). According to Anna Freud (1949b, p, 91), one pregenital fantasy or image, "the embodiment and secret representative" of infantile sexuality and aggression, is expressed in phallic masturbation which commonly occurs in the form of sudden breakthroughs after the defenses have been overwhelmed. Voluntary or involuntary masturbation accompanied by conscious or unconscious fantasies takes place, leading to relief which is then followed by guilt, self-punishments, and depression (A. Freud, 1945).

Discharge of both libidinal and aggressive drives from all pregenital levels in both active and passive modes occurs in masturbation fantasies (Lampl-de Groot, 1950). Wermer and Levin (1967) have stressed the presence of sadomasochistic fantasies and the denial of passive feminine tendencies in the masturbation of latency boys.[14] Bisexuality is actually greater in girls than in boys because of the preservation of the phallic component (Blos, 1962, p. 52).

One of the most important determinants of the degree of masturbatory activity is the mother's attitude (Lampl-de Groot, 1950). The sex of the child also determines the degree of masturbatory activity. Girls tend to masturbate much less or not at all, presumably because of the narcissistic injury related to their perception of genital deficiency compared to boys. Another important determinant is the degree of erotic stimulation to which the child is exposed. A third determinant is the degree to which the ego is prepared to supersede masturbation as "transient regulator of tension" by means of defenses, adaptation, and sublimations (Blos, 1962, p. 54). The superego, of course, exerts the greatest, single influence on the degree and form of masturbation in latency.

While pregenitality is the ego's regressive response to the genitality of latency, it is the aggressive component of pregenitality which is apt to dominate the child's instinctual life at this time. Anna Freud (1949) has observed that aggression originating in actual conflict with members of the family or in fantasy may be normally displaced onto people and animals in the environment. One of the fantasies acted out in the community, for example, is that of sadistic intercourse. In these instances of displaced aggression, the parents do not offer sufficient support to the child in helping him to curb his impulses (Ibid).

Hartmann, Kris, and Loewenstein (1949, pp. 33–34) have stressed drive integration in latency. "It is only the development of the object relation during latency and prepuberty and the maturation of the new modes of discharge provided by the genital organization that allow for what might be considered as optimal integration of the discharge of both drives. . . ."

The Ego

GENERAL CONSIDERATIONS   What is new in the latency child is the fact that a "central agency" has detached itself from the instincts, and "attempts to direct and control them." The child ex-

---

[14] Exaggerated demands for passive gratification in latency (and prepuberty) in boys may occur as a result of intensified primary narcissism due to traumatic restriction of movement in early childhood. These demands may be associated with Isakower phenomena (Brody, 1964).

periences this agency (the ego) as his "self" (A. Freud, 1947). The latency ego has the "leisure to devote itself to other tasks (and to) . . . acquire fresh contents, knowledge, and capacities" because the diminution of drive pressure lessens the need for defenses (Ibid, 936, p. 144). The latency child is as much an ego child as the younger child was an instinctual one (Ibid). He is, in fact, a child who works, compared to the younger child who plays. The ego may now begin to replace sexuality as a tension regulator (Blos, 1962, p. 53), to establish the reality principle, and to adapt to the outside world (A. Freud, 1945). Symptoms and behavioral difficulties subside or disappear. A "spontaneous cure" takes place (A. Freud, 1936, p. 144).

The ego achieves dominance over the drives for the first time in latency following the reduction in drive pressure (A. Freud, 1946, p. 31). Buxbaum (1970) has taken issue with this position, asserting that actual ego strengthening occurs in latency, partially due to identification with the parents and partially due to the stimulating effect of conflict. Actually, Anna Freud has repeatedly illustrated and stressed the actual development of the ego in latency, indicating that its new strength is not merely relative to that of a weakened id. The reduction in drive pressure may help initiate ego development but does not account for it. Jacobson (1964, p. 139) has observed that ego development in latency may be the result of the projection (of ego functions) onto individuals in the outside world with whom the child has formed an attachment and identified.

An increasing number of psychoanalysts have begun to stress the importance of the parents in regard to ego development during latency. In a recent workshop on this subject (Kay, 1969), the participants underlined the significance of the parent as the representative of reality to the child. Some parents hinder the development of their child's reality-testing through being too protective. Other participants were concerned about parents who encouraged pseudo-progressive (often, pseudo-sexual) behavior in their children because of their own anxieties. Buxbaum (1970, p. 95) has stressed the importance of demands and routine in stimulating ego development because they facilitate drive control, especially that of aggression.

According to Bornstein (1951; 1953), ego development in the first phase is marked by the itensification of defenses and the beginning of secondary process functioning in spite of the turmoil at this time. Drive control is achieved in the second phase. Drive control, however, is only one of the major developmental attainments of the latency ego. Reality-testing, control over motility, intellectual and affective development make remarkable progress. Integration, organization, and consolidation of the ego occur towards the close of latency (Jacobson, 1964, p. 139). These latter attainments are essential because of the large and continuously increasing number of contradictory identifications made by the latency child.

The limited ego autonomy achieved during this phase is the precondition for successful mastery of preadolescent and adolescent tasks.

THE STRUGGLE   Normally, the "ceaseless battle" against masturbation gradually subsides with the lessening of drive pressure (Bornstein, 1951; 1953). Between outbursts of sexual feelings and activity, the battle against masturbation is apt to be successful. The fantasy, for example, disappears from consciousness (A. Freud, 1949). The opposition to the act itself may lead to inhibitions, obsessions, and compulsions in the use of the hands. If the struggle is directed against the penis or clitoris, another part of the body may be substituted, resulting in masturbatory equivalents such as ear pulling, nose picking or nail biting (Ibid).

If masturbation is totally inhibited, the drives in the fantasy are "displaced with full force from the realm of sex life into the realm of ego activities. Masturbation fantasies are then acted out in dealing with the external world, which become . . . sexualized, distorted, and maladjusted." This acting out is the "substitute and representative" of phallic masturbation. Adults and children join in the acting out. Its "compulsive and periodic" character reflects the corresponding need to masturbate (Ibid, p. 93).

Regression and repression are normally used to deal with libidinal and aggressive Oedipal wishes, while reaction formation, displacement, and sublimation are used to deal with pregenital impulses. Combinations of defenses are generally used, rather than single ones. Buxbaum (1970, p. 228), for example, has stressed the use of repression reinforced by reaction formation and sublimation. She has also noted that obsessive-compulsive mechanisms and projection occur normally. Repression, reaction formation, sublimation, and obsessive-compulsive mechanism are important for ego development (Ibid).

Sarnoff (1971) has pointed to the importance of fantasy in latency, noting that it allows the child to deal with Oedipal and pre-

Oedipal conflicts without disturbing his actual relationships. A diminution in drive pressure results so that maturation and sublimation can proceed. Towards the end of latency, fantasy formation declines as reality-testing improves.

Sarnoff (Ibid) has offered a useful scheme of latency defenses. Regression, "reality cathexis" and repression defend against Oedipality and genitality. Sublimation, obsessive-compulsive defenses (doing and undoing), reaction formation, and repression deal with regression to anal-sadistic drives. Once latency has been established, then repression, fragmentation, displacement, symbol formation, synthesis, secondary elaboration, and fantasy formation ward off breakthrough of anal, genital, and Oedipal conflicts. He has designated the latter group of defenses as the "ego structure of latency" (Ibid).

Anna Freud (1936, pp. 116, 119, 120) has suggested a complicated defense not restricted to latency which, at the same time, represents an "intermediate stage" in superego development. The child identifies with the aggressor and internalizes the latter's criticism but externalizes the offense. Projection of guilt parallels or follows the identification. Both defenses intensify the child's internal and external conflicts.

Ego and superego identifications are used extensively for defensive and adaptive purposes in latency as well as in preadolescence and adolescence. They are of major, if not crucial, importance in the development of a "coherent, consistent defense organization" (Jacobson, 1964, p. 135). They are also important in the development of realistic goals (Ibid, p. 136). I shall refer to their significance in sublimation in that section.

Like indentifications and externalizations, proxies are not specific to latency but are important in facilitating development (when not used pathologically). A proxy, however, according to Wangh (1962), is a "person other than oneself who is used to experience feelings, exercize functions, and execute actions in one's own stead." The use of a proxy helps the child to strengthen his ability to control himself, maintain reality-testing, achieve internal object constancy, and ward off the anxieties resulting from the loss of narcissistically cathected objects. Friends, siblings, and even groups are commonly used as proxies. Proxies also resemble transitional objects.

That the ego should make extensive use of other people in its defensive and adaptive tasks should not occasion surprise. It must, as a new agency, deal with Oedipal and pre-Oedipal wishes, superego anxiety and with persisting, often difficult environmental demands by parents and others. But not it must do its vastly increased work with continuously decreasing parental support.

TIES, OLD AND NEW   Oedipal frustration and castration anxiety, combined with the need for affection and support, force the latency child to seek new attachments, generally outside the family. Girls, because of their need to hold onto their parental ties, seem less pressured than boys to seek new ones.

Harley (1965, p. 156) has offered a useful picture of latency child society as a "miniature culture within which he finds his place among fellow citizens, and develops his intellectual powers, his self critical faculties, and his own internal controls, thus adding dimensions to his awareness of his separate and independent identity." The latency child, in his new role, "selects and absorbs" the "values" of his friends, contemporaries, and adults.

Object relationships in latency tend to be narcissistic, identificatory, and homosexual, as they are in preadolescence and in early adolescence (A. Freud, 1965, p. 196). The child's failure to free himself sufficiently from the parental ties may lead to defensive, "precocious" attachments or sexuality (Bernstein in Kay, 1969) and to difficulty in joining groups or entering community life. Redl (1942), who was one of the first to study group life in latency and adolescence, had noted that while many children have difficulty in adjusting to the group, adjustment for many other children is only possible through the group.

An increasing number of psychoanalysts in recent decades have stressed the importance of the group as a transitional experience for the child, between the family and the outside world. Bernstein (1965, p. 586), for example, has referred to the group in this regard as a "collective proxy." The group, observed Buxbaum (1945), whose contribution to this aspect of childhood and adolescence is, to me, a classical one, provides highly "welcome shelter" to the latency child, offering him unique help at this "crucial point in his development" when he is "breaking away from home" physically and emotionally, even though the group reaches its greatest usefulness for development in adolescence (Ibid). According to Buxbaum, there are peaks in the formation of groups, between the age of five and seven, during preadolescence, and during adolescence (Ibid). In general, the latency group supports the child's strivings for physical independence from his mother, while the adolescent group helps its members to achieve moral independence from the family (Ibid). Redl (1942) has observed that the latency child prefers the matriarchal or patriarchal type of group in contrast to the preadolescent who prefers the gang type.

The group is the child's new family, a special one in which extraordinary events may occur which uniquely serve the child's development. The transference of allegiance from parents and siblings to the leader and other members of the group and the ensuing identification with them offer the child major assistance in overcoming separation anxiety, castration anxiety, and guilt over Oedipal wishes. The protection and new strength offered by the group permit the child to be assertive towards his parents and other people, to diminish his anxiety in connection with passive as well as active strivings, and to master the trauma involved in feeling or being rejected by the family. He can now, for example, do the rejecting. By permitting the child to take the leader's place as well as to identify with him, the group enhances the child's ability to resolve his Oedipal conflict.

Blos (1962, p. 210) has stressed the importance of the group in the development of the child's "social consciousness." This achievement would seem to be linked up with the development of special ego attainments such as empathy, compassion, and altruism. The significance which these achievements have for the formation of the self, the awareness of one's self, and the modification of the rigid, harsh superego of childhood in the direction of flexibility and ingenuity is obvious.

Jacobson (1964, pp. 137–138) has asserted that the group helps its members to accept themselves and others despite differences. The acceptance of group standards enriches and modifies self and object representations. Groups help boys to sharpen their sense of masculinity. Their anti-girl attitude, on the other hand, also tends to reinforce the girl's sense of femininity. The girl, however, in a group of girls, prefers to be a boy. She tries to "conquer" boys by "seduction." These experiences further the development of the self and the sense of identity. Finally, the group enhances the child's ability to test inner and outer reality, to evaluate the present and past, and to anticipate the future.

While new attachments to groups and individuals make possible the latency child's psychological detachment from his parents and siblings, still other ego achievements and attitudes are necessary to support these great changes. A realistic evaluation of the parents and other adults, for example, is of basic importance in this regard. One intriguing aspect of the way in which the latency child becomes more realistic about his parents is through the family romance fantasies.[15]

The family romance fantasy is a conscious daydream in which a child is deserted by his rich, noble, powerful parents and reared by humble, ordinary ones from whom he is one day to be rescued and reunited with his true parents. The fantasy represents simultaneously the idealization of the parents, the wish for separation from them, and the child's "regressive longing" for his early childhood relationships with them (A. Freud, 1949a, pp. 101–103). The fantasy also anticipates the "ruthless" devaluation of the parents in preadolescence (Ibid).

The effectiveness of the family romance fantasy in assisting the child's ability to give up his old ties and form new ones depends upon and, at the same time, stimulates (or permits) the development of other ego functions, in particular, the advance in thinking. This advance combined with the opportunity to evaluate and compare his parents (and siblings) with the other people in his new life, allows the child to gradually give up his infantile image of them as perfect and magical. Inevitably, devaluation of the parents and the giving up of his previous ties to them means aloneness and loneliness even with new attachments. The ability to tolerate aloneness, therefore, is one of the more important ego achievements making independence possible (Blos in Kay, 1969). Still another basic achievement which advances the latency child's individuation is his increasing ability to regulate his self-esteem both as a result of real achievements and growing superego autonomy.

These achievements and experiences gradually permit the latency child to begin to see his parents as they are, rather than as awesome, and to see himself as separate, different, and quite self-reliant. In this exciting evolution, sublimation plays a unique part.

SUBLIMATION[16]   While the group experience directly fosters the child's resolution of his infantile ties, it also does so indirectly by way of various interests and activities such as play, games, and

[15] Freud first mentioned this series of fantasies in his letters to Fleiss in 1897 and 1898. The paper, "Family Romances" appeared in 1909. Later, Freud (1914) linked another series of fantasies involving the themes of rescuing and being rescued to those of the family romances. (Rescue fantasies are especially prominent in adolescence.)

[16] In their definition of sublimation, Moore and Fine (1968) include "all conflict-free activities that promote the synthesis of the total personality" rather than only the traditionally creative, intellectual, or artistic pursuits.

hobbies. These sublimatory activities and trends, on the other hand, not only facilitate the child's entry into the group but also his successful adjustment in it.

The central function of play, according to Peller (1954), is the "assimilation of anxiety" regardless of source. Play also offers the child gratification, catharsis, and an opportunity for synthesis. Latency play, which generally takes the form of games, is more realistic than the play in previous developmental phases. It is often associated with various interests, hobbies, and group experiences, including "secret societies" (Ibid). Games, in contrast to Oedipal play, stress organization, tradition, ritual, equality, team loyalty, and the observation of rules. The feelings and spontaneity of the individual which are of primary importance in Oedipal play are relatively unimportant in games. Also, in the latter, there is an underlying fantasy usually belonging to the family romance series which is tacitly shared by the group. (Perhaps the reason why games which are apt to involve groups and, therefore, tend to loosen Oedipal ties are more popular with boys than with girls is that girls are more apt to retain Oedipal ties.) Games also assist the child in strengthening his superego and resolving homosexual strivings by means of the mutual identification and attachments provided by group membership and rules. Further, games help the child to translate his daydreams, of which he is apt to be ashamed, into an acceptable, conventional form shared by his peers. Finally, games also help the child prepare to cooperate with leaders and peers in later life.

The psychomotor aspect of latency development has received little attention.[17] Kaplan (Becker, 1965) has elucidated the rhythmic, changing games of early latency and Kolansky (1967) has discussed typical latency motor behavior in the form of climbing, swinging, sliding, jumping and other activities. Both authors agree that these psychomotor activities are important to the latency child

---

Some phychoanalysts, whose opinions I shall report later on in regard to sublimation in adolescence, indicate that conflict may coexist with sublimation. Modern definitions similar to the foregoing and based largely on the work of Hartmann (1950) and Hartmann, Kris and Loewenstein (1946), have stressed the presence of unneutralized aggressive and libidinal energy, the predominance of neutralized drive energy, the intense and lasting pleasure involved, the discharge value, the communicability, and the object-libidinal core in sublimation.

[17] Anna Freud (1954, p. 352) has referred to the "sadly neglected problem of the child's motility," stressing Mittelmann's important contributions to this subject. Mittelmann (1954, 1955, 1957, 1960) has discussed motility as a drive, as an important aid in ego development, and its significance in fetishism.

in warding off incestuous masturbation fantasies, promoting object relationships, acquiring various skills, and consolidating the body image.

The latency child achieves a great deal of libidinal and aggressive gratification through the motor system. Kestenberg (Becker, 1965) has stressed that "normal motility and motor interests are a prerequisite for the establishment of the genital, psychic organization." She also observed that when repression is gradual and balanced, motility is apt to be "free-flowing." When repression is not smooth, motility is affected accordingly.

Play and games involve humor. Wolfenstein (1953) has written a delightful article on jokes in children and adolescents. The joking riddle is the preferred form of a joke. Jokes offer a relatively disguised, pleasant way of attempting to solve emotional difficulties and express unacceptable impulses. Early in life, the child is apt to regard jokes as being stupid because they do not make sense. He is learning to be realistic and logical. It takes some time for the child to realize that it is the nonsense in the joke which makes the joke. The nonsense is, of course, primary process thinking. Joke comprehension is determined by various factors, especially intelligence and motivation. By adolescence, most intelligent children are able to appreciate jokes. (Some of these observations are surprising. I have found jokes and riddles appreciated by latency children.)

Without thinking and learning, there can be no games and jokes. The first systematic elucidation of intellectual development in children and adolescents began in 1936 (p. 164) with Anna Freud. At that time, she contrasted the "brilliant intellectual achievements" of the Oedipal phase and adolescence with the "decline in intelligence" in early latency. The intellectual flowering of the two former phases was due to phase-specific instinctual dangers while the intellectual "decline" in latency was due to the internal prohibition of sexuality. Latency children "dare not indulge in abstract thoughts" because they might lead to prohibited feelings or ideas (Ibid, p. 164).

I have previously remarked on the tendency in Freud and, perhaps, in others to devalue at least verbally the ego and superego accomplishments of latency. Anna Freud's comparison of the intellectual development in latency and the phases immediately preceding and following it is another striking example of this tendency. It is clear that she does not mean that a true intellectual decline has taken place but, in fact, the opposite.

The latency child, for example, does not indulge in abstract thought, not only for the reason just stated but also because he does not need to defensively intellectualize his instinctual processes. His ego is quite strong. His drive pressure has abated. Therefore, the thinking of the latency child, in contrast to the thinking in childhood and adolescence, is relatively realistic, concrete, productive, and associated with action (Ibid, p. 165). The latency child can even learn about things not directly useful to him, although his ability to do so is limited (A. Freud, 1947). His knowledge of the outside world increases rapidly while his self-knowledge decreases. The insight of Oedipal children and adolescents, by way of contrast, is apt to be outstanding.

Anna Freud offers a possible clue to her apparent deflation of the intellectual development in latency by noting the difference between the insight of the Oedipal child and the adolescent and the lack of it in the latency child. He becomes, in a sense, analytically stupid and sterile. Perhaps this is why latency has been the "stepchild" of analytic literature (Buxbaum, 1970, p. 206). The brilliance brought about by the intellectualization of the drives makes or seems to make for productive and satisfying analytic work. This cannot but be of great importance to the analyst even when he is not pioneering in the field.

Erikson[18] (Evans, 1967, p. 27) has laid special stress on the importance of learning, especially in latency. He has referred to the "crisis" of learning at this time owing to the significant association between learning, education, work, identity, and character

[18] Erikson, like many other psychoanalysts interested in intellectual development has been much impressed by Piaget's findings on cognitive maturation in children. I shall refer to Piaget's work because it seems to provide the maturational aspect of cognition without which a complete psychoanalytic theory of intellectual development would be impossible. (I am using the term "maturational" in Hartmann's sense of primary autonomy, a biological "given.") Piaget (1967, pp. 61–64) has found that prelogical thought is characteristic for the child up to the age of seven, after which it is replaced by logical thinking. Prelogical thought appears in three forms: the egocentric type, the animistic type, and intuition. Egocentric thinking is purely subjective. The child discovers and constructs for himself "new realities." He makes his wishes come true. Egocentric thought is expressed in symbolic play. Animistic thinking is characterized by the subjective perception of reality and the use of words. Nothing is fortuitous. Of the prelogical modes of thinking, intuition which is dominated by perception is most closely adapted to reality. It is the "logic of early childhood." Logical thinking develops with the acquisition of the concepts of conservation, causality, time, rate and space. "Schemata of thought" replace "schemata of action or intuition." More of Piaget's findings on cognitive maturation will be presented in subsequent sections.

formation. These processes, in turn, have immediate and long-range effects on the child's social development. Success and failure, with corresponding effects on self-esteem and the ability to identify with growth-promoting figures in the environment are inevitable. Erikson has viewed learning as not just "suppressed or displaced sexual curiousity," but something with "an energy of its own" and as "a fundamental lifelong striving" (Ibid, p. 27).

In all cultures, according to Erikson (1963, p. 259), the latency child receives some "systematic instruction" in the technology of his society. The latency child develops "a sense of industry" and "adjusts himself to the inorganic laws of the tool world" (Ibid). Failure to produce may lead to a "sense of inadequacy and inferiority" impairing the child's ability to identify with teachers and other important persons in his world (Ibid, p. 260). The child may even retreat to the previous stage of family and home away from the "tool world." Failure, therefore, can seriously impair the evolution of the self and the sense of identity.

Learning and working in latency may be decisive for the child's social development because they involve doing things beside and with others as well as the ability to understand and accept the division of labor. Overemphasizing industry and "what works" as the only criterion of "worthwhileness," however, may lead to the danger of becoming a "thoughtless slave of . . . technology and of those who are in a position to exploit it . . ." (Ibid, p. 261). Anna Freud (1957) has described the evolution of the change from the "indiscriminate and immediate wish fulfillment" of play to "indirect and sublimated wish fulflllment . . ." (Ibid, p. 480). Hobbies, which are very common in latency, are not immediately pleasurable but serve a pleasurable purpose in the end. They, therefore, represent a transition from play to work (A. Freud, 1965, p. 214). Hobbies may originate in the child's attempt to free himself from family ties. Children often react to separation from their parents by becoming interested in a particular possession or activity at that time, as if they were transferring their attachment from the parent onto the possession or activity (Anna Freud, 1965, p. 178).

The success of the child's educational experiences depends upon his ability to work and this, in turn, is based on his ability to sublimate. Identifications, which act as general developmental catalysts, are crucial in this regard. Peller (1956) has stressed the overwhelming effect of the child's identification with his teacher on his ability to learn in school. Some of the most important qualities in the teacher which facilitate this identification are his ability to maintain a certain amount of distance from the child in order to help the latter repress his Oedipal conflicts; to represent reality, make demands, be inspiring and, above all, to be warm and accepting. The child's ability to sublimate is determined by his natural endowment, his experience with being loved and well cared for, his exposure to intellectual and artistic stimulation and "unexpected" narcissistic gratifications or injuries.

The child's ability to sublimate is impaired if he has to spend a great deal of time with children of his own age and is, therefore, exposed to the destructive effects of competition and comparison; if he is deprived of opportunities for normal regression; if he has no opportunity to plan and anticipate so that he is deprived of the chance to struggle with challenges; if he is placed in large classes; if his teachers are changed rapidly; and, finally, if he has to depend on mechanical teaching aids. Peller (Ibid.) is pessimistic about the ability of the family or school to foster sublimation in the child because he sees so few adults who enjoy their work in our highly industrialized society.

Within the past two decades, a small but increasing number of papers have appeared in the psychoanalytic literature dealing with specific aspects of education. Emma and Robert Plank (1954), for example, have discussed the acquisition of mathematical and reading skills, especially the former. Arithmetic, they have asserted, is more difficult to learn than reading because, unlike the latter, it does not offer the inducement of being a "key to the secret world of adults." They stress the importance of the pre-Oedipal period in regard to the individual's ability to learn both reading and arithmetic. Based on thin, scanty but fascinating autobiographical and other data, they have concluded that a strong pre-Oedipal tie to the mother associated with the inability to express aggression impairs the ability to learn arithmetic.

Peller (1959) and Fraiberg (1954) have written two intriguing articles on the psychoanalytic aspects of stories and reading in general. Peller has suggested that the child's eagerness for stories is due to his intense desire to see what adults do. Stories enhance the child's ability to remember, because of the characters, the incidents, and, chiefly, the gratification which they offer. Peller has described three main groups of stories: the heroic type, the twin or companion type, and those in which the child acquires an unattainable, "coveted" environment. Each type, of course, has numerous variations.

By means of the heroic type of tale, the latency child is able to realize his Oedipal wishes in symbolic form. In the second type, the reader symbolically gratifies his wish to overcome his loneliness and master disappointments through the devotion of a partner or companion. The companion also helps the child reader to cope with sibling competition and serves as a defense against Oedipal seduction by parents who tend to be too intimate. The companion may be an animal or a contemporary and, in addition, may represent the boy's wish for a child and the girl's wish for a penis. Finally, the idea of a twin or companion may be associated with the idea of "doubling," multiplication and invincibility. In the third type, the child reader may achieve symbolic identification with the father and Oedipal victory.

Stories embody universal fantasies and daydreams, such as the discovery of buried or secret treasure. Fraiberg (1954) has offered a fascinating elucidation of the many meanings to be found in this type of story, which forms the nucleus of myths and legends common to cultures throughout the world.[19] Most of the insights in the paper were gathered from the analyses of two boys in early latency. The outstanding meaning of treasure is that it represents the mother. Treasure also represents the woman's buried penis, baby, and the father's penis. The secret refers to the father's secrets of intercourse and impregnation. In the story, a boy wants to steal the secret. Between him and the treasure stands a formidable adult. The secret also refers to the secrets of masturbation through which the secret of father's sexual activity with mother may be discovered. Finally, the secret represents a displacement from anatomy to "topography." Tales of buried treasure represent, in effect, highly sublimated versions of solutions to the Oedipal conflict.

Conventional education is based on the ability to think and speak in words as well as on reading. There is almost nothing in the literature on language in latency. Geleerd (Becker, 1965) has observed that "thinking in words and thoughts comes in adolescence and is alien to the latency child." According to Blos (1962, p. 55), verbal language begins to replace body language at this time. He refers to Sharpe's findings on the use of the conjunction "because," metaphor and other figures of speech in latency.

[19] Many more papers of this type along with observational data of children who are not in analysis are needed to advance the psychoanalytic understanding of the child's normal educational development.

THE SELF AND THE SENSE OF IDENTITY[20]   The connection between the new interests and achievements of latency, the formation of the self and of the sense of identity, has been clearly stated by Jacobson. The striking physical, intellectual, and moral achievements of latency "enhance the experience of the consistent self which maintains its continuity despite changes" (Jacobson, 1964, p. 54). I found her metapsychological translation of the former statement most helpful: "with the development of aim-inhibited pursuits, the narcissistic cathexes, withdrawn from the erogenous body zones, spread out to representations of the entire body and mental self. These continuous cathectic redistributions and displacements to representations of all the executive organs and functions of the ego, and the correspondingly increasing multitude and variety of coordinated activities immensely fortify the child's experience of his self as a composite and coherent identity" (1964, pp. 136–137).

[20] I shall use the phrase "sense of identity" instead of "sense of self" because it enjoys such widespread usage.

Moore and Fine (1968) define the self as "the total person of an individual in reality, including his body and psychic organization . . . [it] . . . is a common-sense concept; its clinical and metapsychological aspects are treated under self image, self representation, etc."

Jacobson's concept of the self is "one that mirrors correctly the state and the characteristics, the potentialities and abilities, the assets and the limits of our bodily and mental ego: on the one hand, of our appearance, our anatomy and our physiology; on the other hand, of our conscious and preconscious feelings and thoughts, wishes, impulses and attitudes, of our physical and mental activities" (1964, p. 87).

Moore and Fine (1968) offer the following definition related to the concept of the self: Self image is that which "an individual has of himself at a particular time in a specific situation. It consists of his body image and the representation of his inner state at the time. The ego constructs the self image from the direct experiences of sensations, motions, and thoughts, and from indirect perceptions of the bodily and mental self as an object. A self image may be conscious or unconscious, realistic or unrealistic."

Self representation is "A more enduring schema than the self image constructed by the ego out of the multitude of realistic and distorted self images which the individual has had at different times. It represents the person as he consciously and unconsciously perceives himself. It includes enduring representations of all the experienced body states, and all the experienced drives and effects which the individual has consciously or unconsciously perceived in himself and to the outer world. Together with the object representations, it provides the material for all the ego's adaptive and defensive functions."

The sense of identity is the "experience of the self as a unique, coherent entity which is continuous and remains the same despite inner psychic and outside environmental changes. . . . An integrated self representation (self image) is created out of the multiple former identifications contributing to character traits. . . . The sense of identity is the self image as perceived by

Beginning with the child's primitive distinction between himself and his mother or mother surrogate, resulting from pleasure-pain experiences, the child's continuous physical and psychological experiences and achievements steadily and, often enough, painfully promote an awareness of himself as a separate person. Mahler (1963) places the onset of the sense of identity within the first two years of life. The core of the individuation process is the separation of the child's image of his body from that of his mother (with great implications for the development of ego functions, especially those of perception and reality-testing).

By the end of the Oedipal phase, the child's awareness of his feelings, thoughts, attitudes, and actions has grown very considerably. Significant amounts of libidinal and aggressive cathexis have been withdrawn from object representations and deflected onto the self representation (Jacobson, 1964). Now, for the first time, the child regards himself as an "entity" (Ibid). I have already referred to Anna Freud's view of this process in my introductory remarks about ego development in latency.[21]

I will not repeat the many experiences and achievements of the latency child to which I have already referred and which build up the self and the sense of identity. I shall now, instead, refer to additional experiences and achievements in latency with respect to the foregoing developmental processes. Blos (1962, p. 57), for example, has referred to the "novel, keenly-felt differentiation between fantasy and rational thinking" which takes place in this developmental phase along with an increased distinction between public and private worlds. These achievements parallel and are interdependent with the child's increasing ability to tolerate aloneness and aggression. An intensification of the ego-synthetic activity accompanies these processes.

Probably, the latency child's psychosexual development along with his ego and superego identifications are the most profound sources of his self and sense of identity. Sexual differentiation[22]

---

one's self and entails awareness of some, although not all, physical sensations, emotional feelings, and character traits."

[21] The literature on the "self" and the "sense of identity" is often confusing because of the tendency of many writers to equate the "ego" with the "self," and these two terms with the sense of identity, the self-image and the self-representation. An example of this ambiguity is in the quotation by Anna Freud previously cited. A similar and related confusion involves the concept of character.

[22] Most contributors to the subject of development in all phases have been and are women. Perhaps this is one reason why the girl's psychosexual development has received greater attention than the boy's.

continues throughout latency and is apt to be prominent in the latter half when physical changes may often stimulate rivalry among peers. Greenacre (1950), Lampl-de Groot (1950), Harley (1965), Kestenberg (1961) and others have asserted that vaginal sensations and the girl's awareness of her vagina exist long before puberty in contrast to Freud's opinion. Greenacre (1950) has also suggested that there is vaginal-clitorial bipolarity in latency which affects the girl's reality-testing, thinking, and her sense of identity. Kestenberg (1961) has stressed the girl's need to deny the existence of her vagina. (This need, of course, does not preclude the development and awareness of vaginal sensitivity.) The latency girl concentrates on defending herself against phallic-Oedipal strivings. Her femininity generally takes second place. I have already referred to her pseudo-feminine, conquering, seductive attitude towards boys. She is also apt to reject boys as "wild and dirty" (Bernstein, in Becker, 1965, p. 585). This attitude may represent the girl's attempt to repudiate both her envy of the "anally degraded penis" and her aggression (Ibid.). The intensified narcissistic investment of her body due to penis envy may ultimately stimulate the development of her femininity.

Another important aspect of the girl's psychosexual development which bears on the formation of her self and sense of identity is her relationship with her mother. She is angry at her mother for not having satisfied her "diffuse needs."[23] She defends herself against her anger by means of reaction formations (Kestenberg, 1961, p. 34). The mother can teach her latency daughter to be precise and organized. Otherwise, the latter may regress and experience learning difficulties.

Kestenberg (1967, p. 442) has also observed that sex play is sporadic and occurs less frequently among girls than boys. It is masked by other activities and interests such as wrestling and jokes.

Bornstein (1953) has referred to the latency child's perception of his orgastic experience as "craziness" and his feeling that the world is coming to an end when orgasm is avoided.

Common illnesses, including surgical procedures, are apt to be part of a child's "average expectable environment" and may well

---

[23] Originating in her body image and sensations which are apt to be more diffuse than that of the boy because of the greater complexity of her internal and external genitalia, her hormonal organization, and her greater ambivalence towards her body and parents due to penis envy. More details are available on this and related subjects in the section on Preadolescence.

affect not only the child's psychosexual development but his body image and character as well. Illnesses, of course, are not unique to latency, but given the unique tasks of this phase in terms of drive mastery, the building up of psychic structure and the adaptation to external reality, they may well have a particular significance at this time.

Anna Freud (1952) has stressed, for example, the general tendency towards regression and passivity which illness induces in the child. It tends to stimulate or reinforce the child's masochistic attitude towards the physician, the mother, and other caring persons. Further, by increasing the child's dependence on his mother, illness intensifies the notion held by both child and mother that his body belongs to her. Illness may inhibit or accelerate the functioning of affected bodily parts. Erotic and aggressive reactions may result from the nursing care and from restrictions related to movement and eating. Anna Freud has underlined, in particular, the boy's reaction to surgical interventions: "the feminine castration wish in the male child . . . is most frequently responsible for serious postoperative breakdowns or permanent postoperative character changes."

The erotic and aggressive aspects of illness, along with the inevitable injunctions and prohibitions, lead to the uniquely powerful position held by superego and ego identifications in the development of the self-image and self-representation. Conflict, for example, is inevitable as a result of the latency child's many and varied new identifications with people, symbols, and characters in his daily life and in TV programs, cartoons or books. Some of these new identifications, in fact, lead to pseudo-identities rather than conflict. Because children, for example, wish to be older than they are, they are apt to be especially vulnerable to the unsuitable models for identification thrust at them by the mass media (Williams in Kay, 1969). Some mass media models like Charlie Brown, for example, may further development (Ibid.).

Conflicts arising out of contradictory superego and ego identifications are complicated by the fact that the child's ego interests and goals, which are chiefly determined by his identification with the corresponding interests and goals of his parents, may well be different from the morality demanded by his superego, which also originated in identifications with his parents. Added to this maze are the child's unique endowment and tendencies plus the expectations of the environment outside the family (Jacobson, 1964, pp. 150–151).

Severe identity conflicts and isolation can develop if the child cannot integrate and stabilize his numerous and varied identifications. Normally, integration and stabilization do take place with the result that the child becomes less dependent on personal relationships and, therefore, less ambivalent (Blos, 1962, p. 34).

Aside from new and old superego identifications (which include new perceptions of and, therefore, new identifications with old figures), superego functioning promotes the development of the self and the sense of identity through other routes. The superego, a brand new achievement of latency, not only transcends parental and cultural morality but provides a brand new set of feelings and experiences related to guilt, shame, and self-esteem. More than that, the child for the first time has the capacity for "enduring feelings and feeling states" and for the "subtle differentiation [of emotional qualities]" (Jacobson, 1964, p. 89). Finally, the superego promotes the relative constancy of self and object representations, partially by way of its control over the cathexis of the self representation and, partially, through its sublimation of ego development (p. 54).

CHARACTER   Character, according to Moore and Fine (1968) is that "aspect of personality . . . which reflects the individual's habitual modes of bringing into harmony his own inner needs and the demands of the external world." It affects the "drives, discharge, defenses, affects, specific object relationships, and adaptive functioning in general. . . . The integrating, synthesizing, and organizing functions of the ego are significantly involved in determining character."

Permanent character traits are derived from modified, or sublimated drives or reaction formations. No character trait is completely independent of instinctual conflict. Healthy character traits depend upon the "ego's capacity to achieve a degree of flexibility, mobility, and even reversibility within a framework of constancy, which will lead to optimum mental functioning." Erikson, (Evans, 1967, p. 26) stressed the importance of character formation in latency, noting that it had been neglected. For Erikson, the latency child becomes a "very different person."

Anna Freud has viewed character formation in several ways, all interrelated. Character formation represents the achievement of "moral independence," "the outcome of a dynamic struggle" (1965, p. 170). It represents the "firmly established relation" of the ego to the id and superego in which the ego is "unyielding" (1936, p.

147), and the "whole set of attitudes habitually adopted by an individual ego for the solution" of conflicts between id, superego, and ego (1949b, p. 491). Character originates in the "development and fate" of the drives, the identifications with parents and parent substitutes, and the defenses (1947, p. 459).

Blos has offered some interesting, helpful ways of conceiving character. It represents the result, for example, of "the internalization of a stable, protective environment" (1962, p. 261). (Unstable and unprotective environments are also, unfortunately, internalized). He has also stressed the elements of trauma and conflict in his latest formulations (1968). In childhood, however, character is "mainly a pattern of ego attitudes, stabilized by indentifications which . . . can undergo a most radical revision during adolescence" (p. 248).

Anna Freud (1947, p. 459) and Bornstein (1951) have stressed the significance of the battle against masturbation as a source of character formation in latency. Most writers have emphasized the significance of reaction formations as a major source of character formation in latency. According to Bornstein (1951), the emergence of superego functioning in about the middle of latency coincides with the major step in character development. Other important sources of character formation in latency are the lessening of superego rigidity, the decrease in drive pressure, sexual deprivation, masochistic tendencies, the contempt which boys have for girls in order to reject their own femininity and ward off incestuous strivings and, finally, the girl's attempt to reject her phallic wishes (Ibid.).

Spiegel (1958) has referred to the importance of salesmanship in our society, an attainment which is inevitably linked to exploiting oneself and others. The sadistic and masochistic elements implicit in our cultural institutions and values are obvious. What is almost as obvious, it seems to me, but ignored in the impassioned criticism of modern society, is that narcissistic control, subjugation, and exploitation have generally been the outstanding features of all ruling classes in the past, whether secular or religious.

Superego

The development of identity and the sense of identity and character are inseparable from superego formation which arises in reaction to the child's forbidden sexual and destructive impulses. The "wishes, requirements, and ideals" of parents (and later, from teachers and other individuals) are introjected, with the result that the fear of the object is replaced by fear of the superego experienced as a sense of guilt (A. Freud, 1947).

The following list is an elaboration of the foregoing statements and also represents the major features of the development and functions of the superego in latency as I have encountered them in the literature and in my experience: (1) initiation of superego development by castration anxiety (I am uncertain about its analogue in the girl; presumably, it is the fear of loss of love); (2) its dependence upon identifications (which involve the individual and society) and ego development, especially the ability to neutralize aggression, test reality, and think, for its evolution; (3) its powerful stimulation of ego development; (4) its introduction of many profound affective experiences, the most important of which is the sense of guilt; (5) and lastly, its gradual evolution from magical ideals, injunctions, and prohibitions to the beginning of a more realistic and reasonable set of aspirations and standards. Some of the details of this list deserve further examination.

Castration anxiety "propels the development of the ego, of affectionate object relations, of self and object constancy, and of general drive neutralization to the point where the specific type of identification processes can set in which constitute an effective functional superego system" (Jacobson, 1964, p. 126).

Aggression is also very important in superego formation and functioning. The superego, for example, works with aggression neutralized by the ego (Hartmann, Kris, Loewenstein, 1949). Aggression enhances the child's ability to identify with his parents while reinforcing his wish to be big and independent (A. Freud, 1965, p. 180). Aggression lends "moral strength and severity" to the superego (Ibid.).

Hartmann, Kris, and Loewenstein (1946, p. 31) have stressed that "a certain stage of development of intellectual life forms an essential precondition" for the growth of conscience. I found Jacobson's elaboration of this point most helpful. She has pointed to both the "conceptual and emotional understanding" required for superego formation (1964, p. 126). This understanding allows the child to observe in his parents "their mental characteristics, their superego standards, their ideas and opinions, their attitudes and wishes, their expectations and demands, as well as their prohibitions, and of the consistency of the moral codes which they imply." Depending upon the degree to which this understanding develops, "the imagistic components in which the superego originates will mature, change with regard to their content, and assume abstract qualities. Only at this stage can selected ideal, directive, prohibitive, disapproving, and approving parental traits and attitudes and parental teaching become constructively correlated and gradually blended into a consistent, organized set of notions." This developmental process which starts in latency "extends to the end of adolescence and even further" (Ibid.).

Normal superego development is inseparable from ego ideal formation. Because the ego ideal arises from "infantile, magic, wishful self and object images" at a time when self and object representations are still incomplete, the mature ego ideal harbors in its "deep unconscious core . . . the gradiose wishes of the pre-Oedipal child as well as his belief in the parental omnipotence" (Jacobson, 1964, p. 95). This magical core of the ego ideal with its "narcissistic, ambitious strivings" makes possible the internalization of the burdensome parental demands and prohibitions (p. 96). Because of its origin in the ideal self as well as in the idealized object, the ego ideal gratifies the infantile longing "to be one with the love object," a desire which is never fully relinquished (Ibid.). The internalization of the magic, idealized image of his parents is of enormous help to the child in mastering his "dangerous sexual and aggressive tendencies" towards them (p. 109).

The building up of an ego ideal from "idealized parental and self-images and of realistic ego goals as well as realistic self and object representations, appears to reflect the child's simultaneous acceptance of the reality principle and his resistance to it" (p. 111). Ego development allows the child to distinguish between the real parents and his idealized image of them, enabling him to transform the latter into an abstract ego ideal (Ibid.). In this way, the child achieves a "compromise between irrational desires and the demands of reality" (Ibid.).

Ego ideal formation is also "interwoven" with identifications which are based upon "acoustic pathways" (p. 112). These identifications "internalize the daily parental demands and prohibitions" and comprise the "self-critical functions and the 'enforcing' qualities of the moral demands of the superego" (Ibid.).

Erikson (1968, p. 210) has observed that the ego ideal represents the ontogeny of the individual, i.e., the "ideals of the particular historical era as absorbed in childhood" to which it is "more flexibly and consciously bound," in contrast to the superego which represents the highly internalized, "blind morality" of phylogeny.

Only at the end of the Oedipal phase does the ego ideal begin to evolve from highly cathected imagery to the level of an abstraction paralleled by "the development of consistently demanding, directive, prohibitive, and self-critical superego functions" (p. 119). At this time, "the superego comes into existence as a new specific functional system" replacing castration fear with fear of the superego: guilt (Ibid.).

Williams (Becker, 1965), Jacobson (1964), and others have commented, at length, on Freud's concept of incomplete superego development in the girl compared to its development in the boy. Williams has pointed out that the latency girl builds up a "premature ego ideal" because of her great need to be loved. This need is due, in part, to her devaluation of herself and her mother. The superego, which develops on the basis of this ideal, is supported by a weak ego structure in which primary process thinking and primitive modes of expression are interwoven. The boy's ego ideal is, in contrast, constructed much later.

Jacobson (1964, pp. 113–114) has asserted that the femal ego ideal absorbs and replaces the fantasy of the illusory penis. Clinically, this statement means that the girl's narcissistic pride in her inner values, her moral integrity, and ideals have come to represent her unconscious "inner penis." The female ego ideal is a maternal one, emphasizing physical attractiveness, the renunciation of aggressive and sexual wishes, cleanliness, and neatness.

Is it true that the girl's superego is incomplete or, in any other way inferior to the boy's? I see no factual evidence pointing to a clear answer. If anything, one might point to the greater potential for moral and ethical achievements in the girl's developing maternal tendencies than in the boy's introjection of the moral system of his parents and other adults. The latter is apt to be too close to the narcissitic impulses of pregenitality on which to base a superego evolution directed towards humaneness. (Little is known about the boy's fathering tendencies at this time. Presumably, they too might be the potential source of an ethical attitude. Compared to the girl's maternal tendencies, however, they are apt to be invisible and to remain so until well into adulthood.)

Whatever the actual differences are in superego development between boys and girls, feelings of shame and inferiority are hardly restricted to girls. These feelings may well attain special significance in adolescence but they are common and important throughout childhood (and other developmental phases). Shame originates in reaction to the exposure of failure and deficiencies. Inferiority feelings originate in narcissistic defeats (Jacobson, 1964, p. 145).

Feelings of shame and inferiority are often associated with guilt but have a broader, more primitive basis and significance than the latter. While guilt arises in connection with affectionate or hostile impulses towards others, shame and inferiority feelings are generally associated with elementary, narcissistic concerns about the self, such as its power, intactness, and appearance. Shame is especially significant in that it is accompanied by the "strange feelings of helplessness," because the physical deficiencies which evoke it cannot be remedied while moral failure (presumably) can (p. 147). Shame and inferiority feelings, according to Jacobson, involve conflicts which influence "self-esteem in terms of pride and superiority rather than moral behavior in relation to others" (p. 146).

The superego of both sexes, notes Jacobson, plays "an eminent part in the entire psychic economy" (p. 129). Its "contribution . . . to the organization and structuralization of emotional and ideational processes can hardly be over-estimated" (p. 131). By having introduced the new affective experience of guilt, the superego becomes the "motive force of manifold new defensive devices" against "specific, unacceptable instinctual strivings" (p. 129). Through its effect on the ego, the superego promotes the organization and stabilization of the defense system (p. 126). Both superego and ego identifications are important in developing a "coherent, consistent defense organization" (p. 135).

Because the superego can "morally condemn or praise the total self, it can lower or raise the self-esteem[24] and, in this way, control mood vacillations. These, in turn, affect all ego functions and, therefore, the individual's entire emotional state (p. 133). As a result of the superego's control over self and object-directed discharge and, therefore, over the stability of libidinal and aggressive cathexes of the self-representation, it can maintain a "high average level of self-esteem" (p. 132), thus making it a "safety device of the highest order" (p. 133). The superego, therefore, can protect the self from "dangerous external stimuli, and hence from narcissistic harm" (Ibid.).

The superego also makes possible a "wide range of experiences," such as a "general sense of responsibility," "strong feelings of moral conviction," "subtle pangs of conscience," and "moral self satisfac-

[24] Self-esteem expresses the harmony or discrepancy between the self-representation and the wishful concept of the self. It is not identical with the ego ideal (Jacobson, 1964, p. 131).

tion" (pp. 126–127). It provides the ego and id with "complex and valuable" functions far beyond those of "signal fears and simple self-criticism," (p. 129), such as the self-rewarding function, guidance, inspiration, "stop signals," and "positive directions" (Ibid.).

Jacobson has further illuminated the complex and important relationships between the superego, the self, and the ego. The superego, for example, can "deal with the self as with an object," (the reverse is also true) thus making it possible for the individual to deal affectively with conflicts of conscience (pp. 128–129). Finally, in regard to its relationship with the ego, "An effective surveillance of the ego by the superego and a smooth interplay and collaboration between superego standards and the goals and achievement standards of the ego will enable the child to combine the solution of his incestuous conflicts and the development of social behavior with the building up of ego functions, ego interests, and sublimations" (pp. 150–151).

Ego and superego must deal with the inevitable collisions between pragmatic ego goals and interests, such as success, power, wealth, prestige, and other kinds of perfection ultimately derived from pregenital strivings, and the moral and ethical code transmitted by parents and educators (p. 151). The complexity of these collisions and of the difficulty in mastering them may be better appreciated if one thinks of the changing as well as contradictory ego goals and moral convictions of all the people with whom the child identifies, as well as the changes and contradictions within the child himself due to the normal developmental struggle between progressive and regressive tendencies.

The double morality (which is to be distinguished from the issue of idealism versus reasonable standards) of the child is well-known. He displays one set of attitudes and behavior toward adults and another set toward contemporaries and younger children. This double morality involves the magical and manipulative use of words and the denial of behavior. More might be profitably learned, not only about the genesis of this double morality, but its impact upon the integration of the ego and the self. The social and political significance of such knowledge is obvious since it has to do with the explosive issue of vulnerability to deception by the self as well as those who wield any sort of power.

Whatever the complexities of superego development, its basic evolution in latency seems reasonably clear. In early latency, the superego-id conflict results in heightened ambivalence manifested in obedience alternating with rebellion and followed by self-reproaches (Bornstein, 1951). As a result of "new identifications, intellectual growth, educational and religious indoctrination, and the decrease in drive pressure," the "over-rigid" superego in early latency undergoes gradual modification in the direction of benevolence (Hartmann, Kris, and Loewenstein, 1949). Bornstein (1953) regards "light twinges of guilt" over masturbation as normal in latency.

The latency child's superego achieves a relative independence. Having detached himself somewhat from his parents, the child externalizes his superego. (I have already described the mechanism of identification with the aggressor as an intermediate step in superego development.) Because of his continued dependence upon other people for superego functioning, the latency child cannot depend completely upon his superego for adaptation to the adult world (A. Freud, 1965, p. 181). Further development is required to achieve that goal. What follows anticipates the discussion of superego development and associated issues in subsequent phases.

Where the adolescent, for example, is ideological, according to Erikson (1970a, p. 753), the child is moralistic. Because of the child's limited understanding, his superego may preserve throughout life "a primitive sadomasochism inherent in man's inborn moralistic proclivities. . . ." This primitive internalized moralism may then become "isolated from further experience" (Ibid.). Erikson (1963, p. 279) has looked for the dissolution of this primitive superego through "cultural identity" which integrates childhood identifications, "neutralizes the autocracy of the infantile superego . . . [and prevents] the superego's permanent alliance with the unreconstructed remnants of latent infantile rage." How helpful it would be to have clinical material either in the form of analytic reconstruction or direct observation (which would include literary and other products of childhood interests and activities) to confirm Erikson's propositions. Are cultural identities free of "infantile" superego elements and rages? I doubt it.

It is necessary to distinguish the child's perception of the ideals of his culture in their official, inspirational, or exalted form from his perception of the daily translation of those same ideals by his parents and other adults into actual feelings, attitudes, and actions. These translated ideals may turn out to be institutionalized residues of narcissistic pregenital strivings which could hardly offer the young superego the kind of beneficient influence which would tame its "infantile rage." The reverse, in fact, might well happen as a casual reading of the average daily newspaper clearly indicates.

PREADOLESCENCE

Blos (1962, p. 57) has enumerated the preconditions for the successful advance from latency into prepuberty:

> Intelligence must have developed through a sharp delineation between primary and secondary process thinking, and through the employment of judgment, generalization, and logic; social understanding, empathy, and altruistic feelings must have acquired considerable stability; physical stature must allow independence and mastery of the environment; ego functions must have acquired even greater resistivity to regression and to disintegration under the impact of minor, that is, everyday, critical situations; the synthesizing capacity of the ego must have become effective and complex; and finally, the ego must be sufficiently able to defend its integrity with progressively less assistance from the outside world.

Omitted from this formidable list of achievements are superego formation and functioning, which are indispensable for drive control, the maintenance of self-esteem and adaptation to the outside world.

If latency and adolescence have been called the stepchildren of psychoanalytic literature, what can one call preadolescence? In 1936 (p. 145), Anna Freud referred to it as the "so-called prepubertal period" and as "merely preparatory to physical sexual maturity," in what is the first explicit comprehensive account of this phase in the literature. Almost two decades later, Greenacre (1954) regarded it as "one of the most silent areas of analytic investigation." Greenacre's statement appeared a considerable time after a second elucidation of this phase by Deutsch (1944). The panel held by the American Psychoanalytic Association (Galenson, 1964) unanimously agreed that preadolescence existed, that very little was known about it, and that it was a most difficult period to study. Rexford (Ibid.) discussed the analyst's difficulty in studying normal development since his patients' development was not typical, and Maenchen posed the problem of distinguishing between the results of analysis and normal development. She also noted that little could be learned about preadolescence from analytic reconstruction because the patient was as heavily guarded about this period as he was about his adolescence.

Ambiguities, contradictions, and differences as well as increasingly broad areas of general agreement, reward a search through the literature on this phase. Deutsch (1944, p. 4) has regarded preadolescence, for example, as "the last stage of latency" and as the period of the "greatest freedom from infantile sexuality," limiting it to the interval between ten and twelve years of age (or the biological advent of adolescence). Anna Freud (1936; 1947; 1949; 1965) and other analysts have defined this period in terms of a biologically determined augmentation of (pregenital and genital) drives. Maenchen (Galenson, 1964) has stressed the defensive aspect of preadolescent regression to pregenitality. Blos (1962; 1970), Kestenberg (1967) and others have stressed both the biological and defensive aspects of this intensified pregenitality.

Most writers on preadolescence have regarded it as a transitional period between latency and adolescence. Actually, while Deutsch clearly stated that preadolescence (which she calls "prepuberty") is part of latency, she has described it, in effect, as preparatory and transitional to adolescence (which she calls puberty). Blos has written about preadolescence both as a transitional phase and as part of adolescence.

Differences of opinion and ambiguities exist about the occurrence and severity of preadolescent regression. Anna Freud as Blos and Kestenberg have stressed its severity (at least, in boys) Maenchen (Ibid.) has emphasized its lack of severity because no ego regression corresponding to that of the drives takes place, and the pregenitality, therefore, appears in "token quantities." Also, Deutsch (1944), Kestenberg (1967) and others have all noted or described considerable regression in girls as well as boys, but Blos has stressed its predominance in boys and its peripheral presence in girls.

Actually, Deutsch (1944, p. 5) has stated that in regard to the "thrust of activity," which she considers the "principal characteristic" of this phase, boys and girls are alike except for the "form and content of their activities." Unfortunately, she did not elaborate upon this statement.

A very puzzling discrepancy appears in Anna Freud's latest reference to preadolescence (1965, p. 163). In all her writings on preadolescence up to 1965, she has referred to the quantitative increase in all drives which occurs at this time. In 1965 (p. 163), however, she referred to both qualitative and quantitative changes in the drives in this phase. She offered no explanation for this surprising and drastic modification.

Discrepancies and ambiguities in the literature about the physical maturation in preadolescence and its relationship to psychological processes are common. Kestenberg (1967; 1968), various participants at the 1964 panel, such as Benjamin, Prugh and Bell, and others have reported a wide variety of anatomical and physiological changes in preadolescence, including menstruation, ejaculation and secondary sexual characteristics. I have already noted Anna Freud's statement about prepuberty being "merely preparatory" to the "physical sexual maturity." Blos (1962, p. 3) has noted that prepuberty (by definition) precedes the "development of primary and secondary sex characters."

Blos (1962, pp. 7, 8) has provided a useful review of this borderland area. Not only may there be enormous variations in physical maturation from one individual to another and from one sex to another but even within the same individual at different times. Complicating these variations is the normal occurrence of changes seemingly inappropriate to the individual's sex. Feminine body contours due to temporary "adiposity of the lower torso" (Ibid., p. 8) and breast development occur in the boy just as a masculine type body build occurs in the girl. (It is almost as if nature were reflecting somatically the dynamic balancing of heterosexual and homosexual currents prior to the eventual and normal domination of one current over the other.)

One source of confusion lies in the use of terms. Some authors, for example, have used "prepuberty" and "puberty" to refer only to physical maturation. Others have used the same terms to include psychological changes, while still others have used these terms to indicate both physical and psychological changes. Some, like Blos, have tried to distinguish between terminological and phasic differences in terms of explicit physical and psychological events specific for each phase, rather than a mixture of these events.

Blos (1962, pp. 3–8) has defined adolescence as the individual's psychological reactions to puberty, the time when "the physical manifestations of sexual maturation" appear. The nature and extent of the biological changes in prepuberty remain unclear. Preadolescence, in fact "remains independent in its course . . . [it] can continue overly long, unaffected by . . . physical maturation." Deutsch (1944, p. 4) has stated that prepubertal "manifestations may continue far into puberty, and, exactly as is the case with puberty itself, may even persist until the age of the climacterium." Many years before, Jones (1922) made a similar observation and introduced additional dimensions: "The prepuberty period is, I think, longer in man than with any other animal, constituting some 20 per cent of the total duration of life. The strongest attempts are made on the part of society to extend it until it covers as well the most active years of sexual life. . . ." (Note the remarkable prolongation of adolescence in the past two decades. Has it also been happening to preadolescence?)

At a recent symposium (Lilleskov, 1970, p. 32), child analysts discussed several issues related to adolescence. One issue involved the distinction between preadolescence and adolescence. The participants "differed in their characterization of the chronology, biology, behavior and psychology of early adolescence." Some thought that early adolescence followed latency and "was accompanied by prepubertal biological changes." Most agreed with Harley, Blos, Kestenberg and others that preadolescence followed latency and that early adolescence followed the onset of puberty and constituted the beginning of "adolescence proper."

Most of the participants agreed that an "upsurge in drive intensity, loosening of the latency ego structures, and defensive regression to preoedipal conflicts" (Ibid., p. 33) characterized preadolescence and that the "total organization of the personality" rather than the presence of pre-Oedipal conflicts determined whether the individual was a preadolescent or an adolescent. Most participants also seemed to agree that the early adolescent, in contrast to the preadolescent was "much more capable of verbalization and correspondingly less dependent upon actions and objects," more aware of "internal feelings and sensations" and externalized less (Ibid., p. 34). These differentiating achievements are significant in that they reflect changes in the total psychic organization (Ibid.).

General agreement was also reached on the definition of puberty as the period starting with the menarche in girls and ejaculation in boys (Ibid., p. 33). Kestenberg suggested that puberty began with the ability to reproduce (which might not occur for as long as one year after the menarche and varying lengths of time after the first ejaculation).

Freud

Freud made his first and only explicit statement about preadolescence in 1910 (pp. 170–171): "somewhere about the years of prepuberty," the boy begins to learn about the sexual life of his parents, perceives his mother as a prostitute, longs for her, and comes "under the dominance of the Oedipus Complex."

Freud also described, in this context, a series of rescue fantasies created by the boy in prepuberty and puberty. In these fantasies, the boy disguises himself as his mother's idealized lover, rescues his father, gives his mother a child like himself and, in effect, makes himself into his own father. The boy also has himself rescued. Freud linked these fantasies with those of the family romance group.

The foregoing concept of prepuberty stresses several features: its continuity with the next phase; its fantasied gratification of active and passive instinctual impulses aimed at both parents; the defenses against these strivings; the gratification of sexual curiosity about the parents; and, the omission of the girl's pre-adolescent experience. There is no hint of pregenitality in the picture Freud has sketched. Aggression is indicated in the debase-ment, of the mother and the replacement of the father.

The gratification of the boy's sexual curiosity about his parents indicates both the sublimation of erotic (and aggressive?) wishes aimed at the parents as well as the wish to learn about reality.

These fantasies, in general, indicate the main thrust of the boy's new perception of himself as an active person. He does the rescuing instead of being the one who is rescued in the family romance fantasies of the latency phase. This activity may well represent, in part, a defense against the passivity implicit in his wishes to be a child and to be rescued.

The boy not only acts out the identification with his father but, at the same time, seems to reverse positions. Rescuing his father and giving his mother a child like himself suggests that he has made himself into his father, and his father into the child he was. The rescuing indicates parental love and care as well as impregna-tion. The boy's wish to be rescued points to his underlying passive wishes towards his father. From this point of view, the boy's Oedi-pal wishes towards his mother may be translated as a defense against homoerotic impulses as well as the direct representation of developmental processes.

These fantasies may also be understood as the boy's wish for a rebirth and, perhaps, a better rearing than the one he has gotten. They also offer him a chance to deny his past as a child and to emerge directly as the powerful Oedipal father. Finally, they offer him an opportunity to rehearse, in fantasy, his future roles as husband and parent.

After Freud

The following formulations of preadolescence are offered as guides to the detailed expositions of preadolescence which comprise the remainder of this section.

Anna Freud (1936, p. 145; 1947; 1949a; 1965, p. 163) has

stressed the biologically determined drive intensification and the "severe loss" of latency achievements in regard to "social adaptation," sublimation and "personality gains" in this phase. Her descriptions and formulations tend to focus on the boy.

Deutsch's (1944, pp. 5–13) concept of preadolescence is that it is "that last stage of the latency period in which certain harbingers of future sexual drives may be discerned, but which in the main is the period of greatest freedom from infantile sexuality." Its chief characteristics are: the "thrust of activity" ("an intensive process of adaptation to reality and of mastery of the environment"); the "renunciation of infantile fantasy life"; the "turn toward reality"; the abandonment of "earlier identifications," and the devaluation of the parents, especially the mother; the replacement of the mother by a figure outside the family who is loved and idealized as the mother had been; play-acting or "acting out" of transitory identifications; "secrecy"; and friendships. Ego development is most "intense" at this time.

Deutsch has stressed the similarity between preadolescence and the pre-Oedipal phase in regard to the child's struggle for independence from his mother and the negligible influence of the father (1944, pp. 19–20). Liberation from the mother is the "central point" of the preadolescent girl's "psychologic life."

In contrast to Anna Freud, Deutsch has tended to focus on the girl instead of the boy. So far as the "thrust of activity" is concerned, however, boys and girls are alike except in regard to "the form and content of the activity" (1944, p. 5).

Brody (1961) has stressed the "biologically determined" physical activity in preadolescence as its "primary phase-specific mode of expressive discharge" just as play is to the prelatency child and speech is to the adult. The preadolescent is more independent of his parents, more objective about them, and better able to regard "distant objects" as heroes or villains than the latency child. He prefers more abstract forms of verbal communication and has begun to replace identifications with object relationships in contrast to the latency child.

In Blos's (1970, p. 26) last definition of preadolescence, he stressed its phase-specific characteristics such as: increase in drive energy which makes itself felt before any physical signs become evident; the upsetting of the previous balance between ego and id; and the alternation between a "regressive movement" and a "defensive holding position."

The preadolescent girl's task is to resist the "regressive pull toward the preoedipal mother." She does this through a "forceful turn" towards a (defensive, phallic) heterosexuality (Blos, 1962, p. 66). In sharp contrast to the boy, she represses her pregenitality except for that part which she has restricted to the company of girls.

The preadolescent boy's task is the same as the girl's, but he attempts to accomplish it through a defensive homosexuality. He turns to a group of boys. Castration anxiety in relation to the pre-Oedipal mother, the "universal experience" of the preadolescent boy and the "central theme" of male preadolescence, drives him away from the female and toward other males (Blos, 1962, pp. 63–65). The preadolescent boy's "typical conflict" is due to his fear and envy of the female. He must now "renounce again, and now definitively, his wish for a baby (breast, passivity) and, more or less, complete the task of the oedipal period" (1962, p. 63).

According to Kestenberg (1967, p. 578), preadolescence begins with the "activation of the inner genital organs and the appearance of secondary sex characteristics." It is "initiated by a diffusion of psychic functions that is resolved in a phase of reintegration in preparation for puberty genitality." This diffusion "coincides with the rapid increase in sex-specific hormones, and the subsequent reintegration parallels the regularization of sex-specific hormonal patterns." The "influx of diffuse inner genital sensations" during this phase increases the need for externalization and initiates the "reorganization of psychological and hormonal constellations. . . ." She has compared preadolescence to the transitional phase between anality and phallicity.

What is unusual and most helpful in the formulations and data offered by Kestenberg and Blos are their attempts to provide on clinical and theoretical levels lucid, precise, and comprehensive pictures of both the preadolescent boy and girl.

The Drives[25]

The preadolescent boy is apt to be very different from what he was in latency. He is "greedy . . . , voracious . . . , unkempt . . . ,

---

[25] Deutsch (1944, p. 5) has referred to the preadolescent's "thrust of activity" as an "inherent drive of the ego towards growth and independence." She seems to be using the term "drive" in some broad organismic sense rather than in the usual context of a specific libidinal or aggressive impulse.

Her distinction between this tendency and the "turn towards reality" is not clear. The "thrust of activity," as defined, is aimed at the mastery of inner and outer reality.

disorderly . . . , unruly . . . , impolite . . . , conspicuous, brutal to younger children and animals . . . , hostile towards parents (and siblings of the opposite sex) . . . , unsocial . . . , moody . . . , [and] withdrawn. . . ." (A. Freud, 1947). He performs "destructive acts, thefts. . . ." (A. Freud, 1949). "Masturbation and other auto-erotic habits are frequent; so are sexual activities with other children" which include "perverse and homosexual pursuits" (A. Freud, 1947). He seduces and lets himself be seduced (A. Freud, 1949a). "His mind is busy with the exclusion of other interest with sexual imaginings, aggressive thoughts, death wishes" (A. Freud, 1947).

The literature, in general, stresses the intensified pregenitality of the preadolescent boy. Blos (1970, p. 27), for example, has referred to it as "massive, action-oriented and concretistic" compared to that of the girl. Maenchen (Galensin, 1964, pp. 601–607; 1970), however, has referred to this regression in boys as "temporary," "partial," and "symbolic" rather than "real."

Blos (1962, p. 66; 1970, p. 27) has minimized the pregenital regression in girls, referring to it as peripheral, secret, and confined to the company of girls. Deutsch (1944) and Maenchen (Galenson, 1964, pp. 601, 607) have denied its existence in girls. Yet, Deutsch (1944, p. 19) has described the preadolescent girl as disobedient, defiant, aggressive, gluttonous, filled with "hatred and rage" at her mother because she wants to be simultaneously independent and dependent in relation to her. She has also referred to the girl's lack of bodily cleanliness, her sadomasochism (Ibid., p. 21) and the tendency to act out ("gangsterism, prostitution, or criminality," p. 17).

Anna Freud (1936, 1947, 1949) has, in her descriptions, stressed the pregenitality in boys, but her 1965 (p. 163) statement (increased pregenital trends and "severe loss of social adaptation, of sublimation, . . . and personality gains") would seem to apply to both sexes. Kestenberg (1967) has also described pregenital regression in both sexes.

I have already referred to the differences in the literature concerning the origins of this developmental phase. Actually, the literature, except for Maenchen's statements, tends to be ambiguous about this issue. Anna Freud (1936; 1947; 1949; 1956), for example, has over the years repeatedly stressed the biological aspects of the preadolescent pregenitality, but in 1949, she referred to the return from repression of Oedipal as well as pre-Oedipal wishes. The preadolescent boy's "manifest dreams . . . frequently contain intimate sexual scenes with the parents, barely disguised or distorted. . . . "to which he reacts with dread. His "fears subside much later when [he] has succeeded in attaching his mature genital strivings to an object outside the family" (Ibid.). These and other observations of a similar nature indicate that the idea of a defensive pregenitality is implicit in Anna Freud's elucidation. If my inference is correct, it does not, of course, exclude a biological intensification of the pregenital drives. It is likely that the apparent contradiction in Anna Freud's 1965 (p. 163) reference to "qualitative" changes in the drives in this phase can be understood to be a reference to emerging genital impulses.[26]

Blos (1967, 1970) (especially in his latest statement) and Kestenberg (1967) have stressed both the biological and psychological elements which bring about preadolescence. Kestenberg (1967, p. 586), for example, has emphasized the child's reaction to bodily changes with regression to pregenitality even long before such specific major events as the menarche. No data exists which conclusively proves the direct biological or psychological origin of preadolescent pregenitality or disproves the coexistence of both factors. To the extent, however, that one regards the pregenital regression of this phase as a defensive and adaptive reaction to the emerging genitality which is to some degree biological in origin, then one can view this regression as both biological and psychological in origin.

Blos has noted that no new instinctual aim or love object appeared in the phase, emphasizing the continuation of latency pregenitality (1962, p. 57). He made fleeting references to genitality, especially in regard to the girl. Discussing the relationship of genitality to the preadolescent drive organization, he referred to "infantile residues in the emphatic turn to a genital orientation and to its concomitant imagery, thought and behavior" in the preadolescent girl. "Infantile—and this includes preverbal—memories attach themselves to genital modalities. . . ." This genital "elevation" of recathected infantile wishes and effects has both defensive and adaptive aspects (1970, pp. 25, 26).

Earlier, Maenchen (Galenson, 1964, p. 601) remarked on the greater strength of genital impulses in preadolescence compared to pregenital ones, after the initial increase in the latter. Kestenberg (1967, p. 597) has described the genital excitement itself in the girl. She discovers that internal and external stimuli of various parts of her body, especially those related to the reproductive sys-

---

[26] In 1936 (p. 147), she had referred to the "qualitative" change in the drives with the advent of "puberty proper" because of the intensified genitality.

tem, may stimulate genital excitement (Ibid.). "Fantasies triggered by inner genital tensions veer from ambitious plans to breed multitudes of animals to dressing up for dates, going to a wedding, becoming engaged and raising children" like her mother (p. 598). Genital excitement may spread to all parts of her body awakening interest in it as a whole as well as in various parts. Sexualization of her intellect may occur, affecting her schoolwork. She may get anxious, irritable, and depressed. Conflict with the important people in her life may result. The excitement may reach such a pitch that it leads to destructiveness. The preadolescent girl may veer from "feminine slavery to masculine rape," and from masochism to sadism in her sexual orientation. (Ibid.)

It is not genitality, however, according to the main drift of the literature, which colors preadolescence, but pregenitality from which most of the normal homosexual, sadomasochistic, aggressive, and other infantile impulses and behavior of this phase originate. Nonsexual experiences of various kinds can lead to excitement, erection, and emission in the boy (Blos, 1962, p. 64).

Preadolescent masturbation reflects this pregenital diffuseness in that it is not aimed at the symbolic expression of genital sexuality related to a heterosexual object as in adolescence, but functions, instead, as the main regulator of tension. Its "concomitant global affect of excitation and satiation serves as a primitive regulator of tension, and reflects the somatic regulation and maintenance of emotional homeostasis with only dim and tenuous object involvement" (Blos, 1970, p. 59). The phallus, instead of a love object, is the focus of interest in the fantasy (Blos, 1962). The fantasies accompanying preadolescent masturbation consist, as in latency, of pregenital impulses (Blos, 1970, p. 60), and aggression is apt to be prominent in these fantasies, as it was in latency. The boy's masturbation is "undeniable, . . . focused, . . . conscious. . . ." (Ibid., p. 58). The girl may not masturbate at all or rarely. If she does, she may be so indirect as to remain oblivous of the act (Ibid.). By means of thigh pressure, thoughts, and fantasies instead of her hands she may "elicit genital excitation." At these times, she may enjoy "prolonged if slight elevations of excitation, without reaching a climax" (Ibid.).

The literature offers a blurred picture of the sexual behavior and gratification of this phase. Homosexual and heterosexual episodes existing "side by side" occur more or less regularly at this time, according to A. Freud (1965, p. 189). Exactly what this statement means is not clear. Deutsch (1944, p. 15) has stated that the preadolescent girl's only sexual gratification comes from sexual investigations. Kestenberg (1967, p. 589) has referred to "sex play" between girls which may shift to an interest in boys, doll play, or animals. These statements, too, are not clarified.

While the girl's (transitory, usually latent) homosexuality is "harmless," her defensive or acted out heterosexuality may be dangerous (Deutsch, 1944). (I shall elaborate upon this statement later.) I have already referred to Blos' (1970, p. 27) concept of the girl's defensive heterosexuality. It is aggressive, narcissistic, and possessive. It is masculine (in a pregenital sense) rather than feminine. This is the girl's "puppy love" (Ibid., p. 114) stage. The girl, according to Blos (Ibid.), defends herself with pseudoheterosexuality against the pre-Oedipal homosexual attachment to mother. This tie reappears in her friendship with another girl or in her "crushes" on an older woman. It may also reappear in her relationship with a boy.

Several features about the preadolescent girl's heterosexuality stand out. One is its large pregenital component. The other is its normal genital aspect. Blos has, for example, referred to the girl's "exaggerated heterosexual desires" (1962, p. 66).

While Anna Freud (1965, p. 199) has derived preadolescent homosexuality from the "sexually indiscriminate object ties" of pregenitality, Blos (1962, p. 65; or 1970, p. 27), has stressed its origin in the boy's defensive identification with the pre-Oedipal mother as a result of fearing castration by her. (Does a defensive identification with the Oedipal mother also contribute to the boy's homosexuality?) Bell (Galenson, 1964, p. 602) has suggested that as a result of being ignored by girls and noticing their growth in height and breast development, the boy feels inferior and envious. He perceives his rapidly growing testes as if they were breasts and reacts with "consternation." These reactions lead to pregenital wishes for breasts and babies which then confront him with the issues of femininity and castration anxiety.

While the boy may well react defensively to his oncoming genitality with homosexual regression, the reverse also happens. He may perceive sensations originating within his body (resulting from maturational changes) as signs of femininity, react with hypochondriacal anxiety and defensively reinforce a "phallic-aggressive" masculinity (Kestenberg, 1967, p. 603).

Aggression is prominent in both sexes but more directly expressed in the boy. Although aggression may originate in the boy's desperate, often frustrated attempts to control his rapidly changing, awkward body (Kestenberg, 1967, p. 603), it appears to be derived mainly from pregenitality. I have previously referred to Anna Freud's description of the boy's aggression which may take delinquent, quasi-delinquent, and sexual forms. He may also express his aggression in athletics and fantasy. Boys tend to aim their aggression toward their mother's body (Blos, 1962, p. 62). Recently, Blos (1970, p. 200) has stressed two points about the aggression of the preadolescent boy: its large component of phallic sadism and its importance in combating the phase-specific regression, making entry into adolescence possible.

Girls tend to express their aggression indirectly, usually in their seductive, provocative behavior toward boys (Ibid., p. 27). Their "delinquency" is sexual. Kestenberg (1967b, p. 589) has noted the girl's use of aggression (or flight) to defend herself from anxieties originating in sexual wishes aimed at both parents, especially masochistic impulses directed toward their father.

The overall impression which the literature has left me with, and which agrees with my own observations, is best summed up by Kestenberg's (1967, p. 602) observation that the "regressively exaggerated bisexuality of preadolescence is transitional . . . to the heterosexual orientation of puberty genitality." The drive organization is dominated by defensive and adaptive aims. What remains to be elucidated, it seems to me, is the strength and relationship of pregenitality and genitality in preadolescence.

The Ego

Throughout her writings on preadolescence, Anna Freud (1936; 1945; 1947; 1949; and 1965) has emphasized the ego's loss of superiority over the drives gained in latency. "The preadolescent's ego is not equipped to deal with these increased demands from within . . . fails to maintain the previously established equilibrium . . . [leading to] outbreaks of anxiety with increased efforts at ego defense which lead to neurotic behavior . . . symptom formation . . . or . . . breakthroughs . . . in the form of . . . perverse sexual manifestations of dissocial actions" (A. Freud, 1949, p. 98).

For Deutsch (1944, p. 4), preadolescence is a period in which the "sexual instincts are . . . weakest . . ." and ego development is most intense." Blos (1962, 1970), too, has stressed ego development in preadolescence. The "hallmark" of preadolescent regression is the ego's "resiliency" (Blos, 1970, p. 72). I have already referred to Maenchen's earlier views on regression in this phase to the effect that there is little ego (or drive) regression (Galenson, 1964, p. 607). Her (1970) latest expanded and more precise observations on this are illuminating: "the ego is both stronger and weaker. With the genital drives increasing at a time when the auxiliary ego is weakening, the integrity of the self can be maintained by defensive regression of the drives. [There is] . . . an imbalance in the ego . . . ego controls suffer, but, more importantly, the increase of the drives demands more defensive activities . . . [there is] . . . regression of some ego functions but . . . [it] . . . does not correspond" to the drive regression. "The increased defensive activity protects the self. . . ."

The apparent discrepancy between these views and Anna Freud's begins to fade as soon as one appreciates the ego's functioning from the point of view of balance, flexibility, fluctuation, the selective progression and regression of specific ego functions which go on more or less simultaneously, and the elements stressed by a particular writer. Anna Freud has, in various elaborations on preadolescence, indicated that ego development continues in spite of transient fluctuations in its ability to deal with the drives and that this development is essential for a successful adolescence. She has stressed the strength of the drives while other writers have stressed the adaptive and defensive effectiveness of the ego so that contradictory pictures of the same developmental phase emerge.

The main current of thought throughout the literature in regard to the preadolescent ego seems to be in harmony with Rexford's (Galenson, 1964) observation that its accomplishments (like those of the latency ego) are not only important as preparation for adolescence but are valuable in themselves because of the resulting degree of mastery attained over the self (especially in regard to the bodily changes) and the outside world.

Struggle and Mastery

Because of the great changes in psychic structure achieved in latency, the preadolescent boy reacts to his new drive pressures and to his perception of bodily changes with conflict and great suffering (A. Freud, 1947). He is now "horrified" by erotic and hostile impulses towards his parents, in contrast to his innocent excitement of early childhood. He is "laden with guilt and anxieties of the worst kind" about masturbation, which had brought relief in the dim past (Ibid). He "simultaneously indulges in and rejects his instinctual life. . . ." (Ibid.).

Blos (1962; 1970) and Deutsch (1944) have described in detail many of the experiences and states of mind of the preadolescent girl. She experiences conflict and suffering far less than the boy, if at all. "Indeed, the phallic quality of her sexuality is prominent at this stage and affords her for a brief period an unusual sense of adequacy and completeness" (Blos, 1962, p. 67). The gratifying and reassuring masculinity of the preadolescent girl expresses itself in her classical "tomboy" identity and in her teasing, provocative femininity. Her playfulness, her play-acting, and her activities, which constitute a significant proportion of her day and, in some instances, may pervade it, evoke and reflect pleasant, eager states of mind and zestful anticipations.

Kestenberg (1967), on the other hand, has in this and other papers repeatedly referred to the girl's disturbed equilibrium and painful diffuseness because of bodily and emotional changes. The "nagging, unfocused genital excitement" makes her want to "get rid of what is inside and to find a focus in the external world." This "gnawing pressure" (Ibid., p. 591) from the inside (due to hormonal and anatomical changes) may lead to "violent handling of the external genitals, . . . abrasions and pain." Her "intense desire to get rid of the unexplored monster" inside brings about fears that everything will fall out of the abdomen (Ibid.). Also, because of her greater need than the boy's to be good, she suffers more from her pregenitality. She has to lie about her overeating and other pregenital gratifications since she fears the loss of her parents' approval and its damaging effect on her self-esteem (Ibid., p. 587).

How does the child react to his new pressures and the anxieties to which they lead? The preadolescent ego, according to Anna Freud (1936, p. 147), tries to "preserve the character developed during the latency period, to reestablish the former relation between its own forces and those of the id, and to reply to the greater urgency of the instinctual demands with redoubled efforts to defend itself" (A. Freud, 1936, p. 147). The defensive mechanisms and operations of preadolescence are directed against anxieties in reaction to genital and pregenital impulses and to sensations stemfrom internal and external bodily changes, especially those involving the internal and external genitalia. Interwoven with or parallel to the defensive activities of the ego are numerous attempts at adaptations. In general, the literature emphasizes, as I have already stressed, the defensive regression to pregenitality and the repression of genitality in the boy. The girl, in contrast, represses her pregenitality and tends to express her genitality. (I have already indicated the limited validity of such broad views. They can serve, however, as a guide or starting point until something better takes their place.) Both the preadolescent boy and girl deal with their enhanced underlying passivity related to the mother by means of action and acting out. Sublimation and the use of certain other psychological functions for defense and mastery, such as identification or the drives, will be discussed in detail in other sections.

Every available defense is pressed into service. The preadolescent characteristically tries to stay away from his parents (the living source of his distress), although not necessarily from all his siblings. He involves himself in the outside world. By means of hostility toward his or her parents (and siblings of the opposite sex) and with the help of a friend or group of contemporaries of the same sex, the preadolescent (particularly, the boy) tries to ward off incestuous fantasies (A. Freud, 1947).

The preadolescent's drive toward independence may also be viewed as a defense against the return of the repressed strivings of the past (Ibid.). This "independence" generally involves relationships with transitory, underlying or overt homosexual trends of a narcissistic nature. Blos (1962, p. 65), for example, speaks of the "homosexual" or "gang" stage of the preadolescent boy. His homosexuality is used defensively against castration anxiety related to the pre-Oedipal mother (Blos, 1962, 1970). He reinforces this homosexual defense by means of contempt for his mother and girls. Homosexual episodes, however, are of great importance to the boy in helping him to externalize genital sensations (especially in the group), to explore himself by means of another boy, and to repudiate his femininity by means of the phallic cult (Kestenberg, 1967, p. 605).

I have already referred to Blos' concept of the preadolescent girl's defensive heterosexuality, which functions to resist the regressive pull to the pre-Oedipal mother and the "surrender to primal passivity" (Blos, 1962, p. 153). Blos (1962, p. 70) has interpreted Deutsch's "thrust of activity" in the preadolescent girl as the result of her identification with the pre-Oedipal mother in order to experience actively what she had experienced passively in early childhood. In addition to these attempts to give up the pre-Oedipal mother, the girl may use an interest in horses and horseback riding ("horse-craze") (Blos, 1962, p. 70). She may also boast about her parents, especially her mother, or glorify them through lying as a defense against the wish to degrade them. This

preadolescent version of the family romance in the girl also represents another important defense aimed at her longing for the
mother of her early childhood.

Just as the boy may resort to femininity in reaction to castration
anxiety, the girl's tomboyishness may serve as a protection against
feminine masochism. Her indifference to boys, on the other hand,
may be viewed as a defense against feelings of inferiority in relation to them (Deutsch, 1944, p. 18).

Anxieties about bodily changes, especially those related to the
reproductive system, are generally enmeshed in the struggle against
masturbation. In contrast to the boy, the girl defends herself, as I
have previously indicated, against the impulse to masturbate to a
far greater degree. Feelings of being injured, babyish, passive,
dirty, and inferior to the boy in reaction to sensations stemming
from her external and internal genitalia (in addition to guilt and
insufficient relief or pleasure) initiate and sustain (or even successfully terminate) her intense struggle against masturbation
(Kestenberg, 1967, p. 586). The girl may condemn her vagina
and other parts of her genitals and focus, instead, on her breasts
(Ibid.). She may externalize sensations from her inner genitalia
and isolate inner and outer genitals (p. 580). A flight into activity
associated with intensified masculinity and competition with boys
may be another defensive reaction against the wish to masturbate
(Ibid.). The girl may also substitute an interest in her hair for
"pubic masturbatory activity" (p. 586).

As in latency, masturbatory equivalents (the replacements of
"volitional manipulation of the erotic zone for . . . pleasure . . .
[by] . . . compulsions, traits, attitudes, rituals, impulsions [acting
out] . . ." which also result in the reduction of tension) may occur
when masturbation is blocked (Blos, 1970, p. 60).

Kestenberg (1967) and Blos (1962; 1970) are particularly
helpful in showing the profound adaptive value of masturbation
in regard to inner and outer reality, the development of psychic
structure, and the formation of the self. Masturbation, for example, helps the girl to "unify" sensations from all parts of her
genitalia and to ". . . centralize them on the now accepted introitus" (Kestenberg, 1967, p. 429). In indirect masturbation,
"sustained genital excitement" occurs, counteracting the girl's fear
that her "insides have fallen out." As a result, masturbation promotes the development of "organ constancy." This achievement, in
turn, facilitates the integration of the internal genitalia into the
body image (Ibid.). In the boy "externalization of inner tensions

and of extensions of the image of the phallus" and the beginning of an acceptance of his internal genitalia "reshape" his body image and prepare him for the "new identity" to be elaborated on in the next phase (p. 609).

The regulation of tension by masturbation is gradually replaced by the ego as it achieves mastery over the drives and the environment (Blos, 1970, p. 59). Mastery is based upon internalization which then "gives rise to new forms of stimulation and gratification" (Ibid.). This achievement is possible if the ego develops the ability to tolerate tension. This ability, in turn, is based upon the "confident expectation . . . that relief of tension is timed well by the caretaking environment" (Ibid.). The impact of these achievements on psychic structure is obvious.

Ego development is also, enormously enhanced by defensive and adaptive measures which evolve into sublimations or, at least, proceed in that direction. Brody (1961) has suggested that the preadolescent may use his motor activity as a defense against the fear of "surrender" to the archaic mother and psychic dissolution. Kestenberg (1961) has stressed the significance of the boy's gross motor activity as a means of mastering anxieties associated with his genitals. Brody (Ibid.) and Kestenberg (Ibid.) have also pointed to the preadolescent's interest in mechanical devices as attempts to master symbolically those anxieties associated with understanding, controlling, and integrating bodily changes and sensations.

Because of the possibility of evoking sexual excitement, the preadolescent boy may even find his imagination dangerous. He may, therefore, stress reality in his drawing, concentrating on designs and maps (Brody, 1961). In his writing, he may also concentrate on form instead of content for the same reason (Ibid.). Beisner (Galenson, 1964, p. 609) has noted that the preadolescent achieves the ability to draw in formal perspective. Perhaps, in part, this achievement also originates in the wish to avoid sexual excitement.

The revival of denial, projection, regression, magical thinking, reaction formation, and displacement in preadolescence results in a transitory but florid symptomatology but fails, not infrequently, to prevent instinctual breakthroughs. Blos (1970, p. 71) points out that "obsessions and rituals are characteristic of preadolescence." Compulsive behavior is common (Blos, 1962, p. 59). Phobias, various types of hysterical and pregenital conversions, psychosomatic symptoms, "nervous habits" such as nail biting, hair pulling, and "fiddling with things," and psychotic-like manifestations occur

(Blos, 1962, p. 60). Inferiority feelings (often due to guilt) and anxiety states are most frequent in this phase, according to Deutsch (1944). Deutsch (Ibid.) has also noted that the neurotic manifestations of this phase may also be a continuation of previous ones. Traumatic experiences, such as the loss of a friend, seductions, or the birth of a sibling, may also lead to serious symptoms (Ibid.).

Old and New Ties

Because of the sharpness of his struggles and suffering and because of his greatly strengthened wish to grow up and to be on his own, the preadolescent has to give up his parents far more urgently than the latency child. It would seem that the urgency is greater in the boy than in the girl, because she remains longer and feels more comfortable in the Oedipal position. Also, the girl may well feel confident and pleased in her temporarily intensified masculinity, while the boy is horrified by his Oedipal longings, dreads castration, and is ashamed of his femininity.

Anna Freud, throughout her writings on preadolescence, has stressed the child's struggle to sever the tie with both parents, while Deutsch, Blos, Kestenberg, and others, as I have already indicated, have stressed the importance to both sexes of giving up the pre-Oedipal tie to the mother.[27] Father, in fact, may well become the preadolescent boy's much needed ally and model.

Giving up his parents and past pleasures in order to avoid suffering and to become independent is itself an additional source of suffering (A. Freud, 1947; 1949a). These renunciations also include the child's ". . . auxiliary ego and part of the superego" (Maenchen in Galenson, 1964).

The suffering caused by guilt and castration anxiety, the loneliness, the continued, urgent need for affection and for the reinforcement of his ability to function as a person, and the driving ambition to realize himself all propel the preadolescent away from his mother and toward new attachments. The literature, in general, indicates that relationships with individuals constitute the major source of strength for the girl breaking away from her mother. For the boy, group relationships and sublimatory achievements seem to be the crucial sources of his strength in accom-

---

[27] I shall stress the latter formulation because it is the dominant trend in the literature and because I think it is clinically true. There are instances in which the breaking away clearly involves both parents. This is another one of many examples where more clinical data from direct observation, from analysis, and from varied population groups is needed.

plishing this basic task. How much gratification and strength the preadolescent can derive from his new ties is uncertain. Anna Freud (1949a) has stressed the painful dilemma of the preadolescent who, while shedding his old ties, has difficulty replacing them with satisfactory new ones because he is ". . . characteristically weak and wavering in his allegiances, lonely, narcissistic, self-centered. . . ." Deutsch (1944), on the other hand, has stressed the great developmental value of friendships in this phase. Buxbaum (1945, 1970) and Blos (1962, 1970) have stressed a similar value in group experiences, especially for the boy.

The preadolescent's "ruthless disillusionment" with his parents (anticipated by the family romance fantasy in latency and accompanied by the preadolescent version of that fantasy) leads to the "reversal of generations" (A. Freud, 1949a). The preadolescent believes his parents must be "little and despicable" if he is to be big (Ibid.). "To grow in strength, to mature, to become clever is automatically translated . . . into the decline and fall of the parents" (Ibid.). At the same time, the preadolescent may well find it necessary, knowingly or unknowingly, to hold on to some acceptable, idealized version of his mother (or her substitute) as another major, if not crucial, source of strength by means of which he can separate from her emotionally.

I have already referred to the defensive significance of the girl's glorification of her mother (Deutsch, 1944, p. 20). This idealization, however, is also partly genuine. The boy may well idealize his father much more than his mother because of castration anxiety in relation to mother (Blos, 1970, p. 27). Yet, he may also be hostile and vindictive towards his father for having disappointed him (in being less perfect) (A. Freud, 1949a). The preadolescent oscillates between debasing and idealizing his parents as he will continue to do much of the time during adolescence. Paralleling this oscillation are his wishes to be grown-up and childish.

The idealization of the parent and the retention of early identification with one or both idealized parents are of tremendous importance to the preadolescent in maintaining sufficient self-esteem to facilitate individuation. In this way, the original object is not entirely lost, but used instead to promote development.

Giving up or resolving the homosexual tie to her mother allows the girl to progress gradually to the positive Oedipal position in mid-adolescence (Deutsch, 1944, p. 19; Blos, 1962, p. 58; 1970, p. 25). The boy, on the other hand, progresses from the pre-

Oedipal attachment to his mother to the homosexual Oedipal position with his father in early adolescence (Blos, 1962, 1970). By mid-adolescence, he has progressed toward the Oedipal position with his mother after resolving the erotic tie to his father in early adolescence (Ibid.).

The literature is unanimous in indicating that the loosening of the ties with mother may well not be completed by the end of preadolescence, especially in the girl, although explicit statements on these (as well as other developmental) processes often tend to suggest a finality and completion which is misleading. Success is more a matter of progression outweighing regression or inhibition.

The preadolescent replaces the attachment to his parents, especially mother, with new ones which are identificatory, narcissistic, and transitory (A. Freud, 1947; 1965, p. 95). The "part-object, need-fulfilling, and ambivalent" relationships of early childhood reappear (Ibid., 1965, p. 67). The new attachment may be with a contemporary or an older person of the same or opposite sex. The contemporary may well be a sibling. Attachments to older people, in contrast to those with contemporaries, are apt to be partially or wholly in fantasy. The tie with mother may also be replaced by an interest in animals and sublimatory or potentially sublimatory pursuits.

While both girls and boys join groups and have friends, it seems that the girl, as I have already indicated, prefers individual relationships even within a group (Deutsch, 1944, p. 257). Friendships are so important that girls may even try to make themselves more attractive to their girl friends by premature dating and petting with boys (Kestenberg, 1967, p. 585). Friendships may last a lifetime as a result of the sublimation of their erotic elements (Deutsch, 1944, p. 51). They tend, however, to dissolve frequently and to be replaced by new ones (Ibid.).

Mutual identification and acceptance; warmth; the sharing of experiences, burdens and, especially, guilt; seductiveness; complementarity in regard to activity and passivity; sadomasochistic trends; secrecy; play-acting; and, faithfulness all characterize the friendship of preadolescent girls (Deutsch, 1944, p. 27; Blos, 1962, p. 62). On the other hand, preadolescent girls are not necessarily tender towards one another. Neither do they practice mutual masturbation or overtly seduce each other as boys do. Their sexual investigations carried out in secrecy are, as I have previously indicated, their only (direct) sexual gratifications (Deutsch, 1944, p. 15).

Friendships are, therefore, a source of gratification, excitement, learning, and strength. They are essential for normal development. The mutual identification, sharing of guilt, and other features of these relationships serve progression in several important respects. They offer the preadolescent girl the strength and freedom to observe, think, and anticipate the experience of sexuality, courting, marriage, and family (Deutsch, 1944, p. 5). They offer her a special opportunity to express her pregenital interests, one of the main reasons for the secrecy and giggling of these friendships. The secrecy is often associated with sexual curiosity and lying. [Lying often represents a retaliation against the mother for withholding secrets, especially of a sexual nature (Ibid., p. 20).] The connection between secrecy and diaries will be taken up in the section on sublimation.

There are other important aspects to these friendships. They may help, for example, to prevent identity diffusion (Kestenberg, 1967). Also, the girl may use her friend's body as a "mirror" in order to learn about her own body and feelings (Kestenberg, 1967, pp. 584; 588–589). Friendships, then, for all the foregoing reasons serve as a transitory, homosexual bridge between the preadolescent girl's tie to mother and the world of womanhood.

To the extent that the girl attempts to replace her mother with boys, the latter may also represent an important bridge between mother, the outside world, and femininity. The girl, in this way, again preserves the mother tie with adaptational rewards. Contact with boys is actually focussed on gratifying sexual curiosity. The boy, for his part, because of castration anxiety (and envy) belittles and teases girls and shows off in front of them (Blos, 1962, p. 60).

No account of friendships between boys similar to the one between girls reported by Deutsch exists in the literature. My general impression based on the literature and on my own experience is that friendships between boys are basically the same as those between girls. There are differences, some of which I have already mentioned. More direct sexual activity, more stress on athletics and other interests, especially scientific and mechanical ones, and comparatively little interest in emotional and interpersonal aspects of their relationship usually differentiate the friendships of boys from those of girls.

Both the "tomboy" with her unresolved penis envy and the seemingly more feminine girl who is narcissistically preoccupied with her body may attempt to resolve the pre-Oedipal tie with their mothers by becoming more realistic about them and by means of triangular relationships. The latter may consist of two girls and an older woman, such as a teacher or another girl (Benjamin in Galenson, 1964, p. 606). Such triangles may be seen both as an adaptive and defensive recapitulation of the pre-Oedipal triangle of childhood (in which father was the outsider) and an adaptive anticipation of the Oedipal conflict to be painfully revived later on in adolescence.

The older woman with whom the preadolescent girl may choose to replace her mother may be ideal like the idealized mother, someone who is realistically progressive in her development, or someone who is "sexually disreputable" (Deutsch, 1944, p. 21). "Crushes" on older women may also frighten the girl (Kestenberg, 1967b, p. 588). Kestenberg (Ibid.) has interpreted the preadolescent girl's adulation of unapproachable male idols as an attempt to protect herself from physical contact with adults (of both sexes) and, at the same time, to give herself an opportunity to express pent-up feelings.

So far as group ties are concerned, the accounts given in the sections on latency are applicable to those formed in preadolescence. I have already referred to Blos's emphasis on their adaptive importance as a temporary homosexual solution to castration anxiety and envy of the female. Blos (1962, p. 59) has also stressed the importance of the preadolescent group for "direct instinct gratification." By means of the "socialization of guilt," the "disapproving superego" may be set aside (Ibid.). He calls this a "novel solution." (Has not this solution already been discovered and used in latency groups?) Kestenberg (1967) has stressed the preadolescent group experience as a setting in which the boy or girl may externalize disturbing bodily and emotional experiences.

Old and new ties may well be associated with dangers in preadolescence. Deutsch (1944, p. 20) has stressed the developmental impairment resulting from the girl's inability to give up her pre-Oedipal mother tie. She may develop, according to Deutsch, a condition which she has called "psychic infantilism" (Ibid., p. 8). The boy, too, is faced with great danger if he cannot give up the tie to his mother. It may well magnify his tendency towards homosexuality. Other important dangers to normal development in the preadolescent girl are the "excessive solicitude" of the people around her and her own excessive guilt and fear (Ibid., p. 8).

Severe traumatic experiences are apt to occur in connection with new ties. Because of their identificatory nature and because preadolescent identifications tend to be enacted as well as acted out, the new relationships may lead to the dangers alluded to in previous sections (premature sexuality, pregnancy, prostitution, and criminality) depending upon the personality of the individual with whom the girl is involved (Deutsch, 1944, p. 20). The counterpart to these dangers in boys are homosexual episodes in which they are the seducer and the seduced and anti-social behavior. These experiences are potentially destructive in terms of long-lasting, serious symptom-formation; general distortion of development, especially in regard to character; and conflict with the community.

Deutsch (1944, p. 28) has pointed out that the loss of a friend is the "typical trauma of prepuberty and the period immediately following." Severe, and, at times, psychotic reactions may result. Greenacre (1952, pp. 222–223), in fact, has found that prepuberty is ". . . especially favorable for the provocation of traumata . . ." in girls because of their ". . . heightened curiosity," their "thrust of activity" (physiologically determined by growth processes which precede sexual maturation), their normally intensified sadomasochism and their masculine identification. She has concluded that these "fateful traumata" of preadolescence with their profound and more or less lasting sequelae are ". . . provoked by the victim" and represent the ". . . compulsive repetition of pre-Oedipal conflicts. . . ." The victim always chooses an adult to perpetrate the trauma.

No further examples of "prepubertal trauma" of either sex have been reported in the literature since Greenacre's paper. It would be important to find out the frequency of such traumata in both sexes and their effect on development.

Sublimation, Cognition, and More Mastery

While sublimations were important in enhancing the latency child's beginning gropings towards acceptable gratifications, mastery, and independence, they are apt to be far more so in preadolescence. The drive intensification of this phase, the temporary loss of control and ego disorganization, the guilt and suffering which the parents generally magnify thru their retaliatory responses (whether in the form of withdrawal or attack), and the frightening or at least disconcerting challenges posed by new bodily changes catapult the preadolescent, especially the boy, into a desperate situation. He has lost (or, rather rejected) much of the ego and superego support of his parents. The diffusion in body image, thinking, and feeling have, in addition, impaired his ability to make use of powerful psychological equipment in dealing with his new threats. New ties, pregenital gratifications, and masturbation hardly offer unalloyed satisfaction and guaranteed solutions. They are, in fact, apt to lead to conflict with parents or other adults and exaggerate pre-existing anxiety, guilt, and disorganization.

The situation is by no means hopeless. The capacity for sublimation generally offers speedy and considerable assistance as I have already described. I have previously alluded to the transformation of aggression into athletic achievements in both latency and preadolescence, an attainment which reaches its greatest height in adolescence (Blos, 1962, p. 70; 1970).

While athletics tend to be more popular with boys than with girls (a distinction fast appearing), horseback riding or "horse-craziness" is especially common in preadolescent (and adolescent) girls. Blos (1962, pp. 70, 71) has stressed the horse's significance to the girl as penis and father. He has also pointed out that the girl's love for her horse is narcissistic, while her feelings for her dog are maternal and companionable. Kestenberg (1967, p. 590) has emphasized, however, that the girl's "love" in looking after, feeding, and grooming horses represents a desexualized, maternal interest. Earlier, Anna Freud (1965, p. 20) had suggested that the horse represented the mother, masturbation, penis envy, and "phallic sublimation" to the girl.

Kestenberg's (Ibid.) elucidation of the significance of horses and horseback riding to the preadolescent girl bears a more detailed exposition. Through the experience of caring for a large animal, the girl overcomes "one of her greatest fears": that her insides are too small to hold a penis or a baby. Horses also represent "untamed, genital impulses," and, therefore, offer the girl an important opportunity to control them through controlling the horse as well as through the symbolic, masturbatory pleasure of the riding itself (Ibid., pp. 589, 590). The girl also develops tolerance for pain and strong feelings and the ability to recover her equilibrium after a fall through horseback riding (Ibid.). These achievements allow her to prepare herself for menstruation, pregnancy, childbirth, and other great feminine prerogatives associated with pain.

Sublimation also helps the girl to deal with her anxieties about her body, especially her reproductive system. She may, for example, substitute an interest in her hair for pubic masturbation (Ibid., 1967, p. 587). She may transform anxieties about her internal or external genitalia through externalization into an interest in her breasts and then on to brassieres, sweaters, feminine clothing in general, and sketching of the female body (Ibid.).

In a previous section, I referred to the significance which interest in or working with mechanical devices may have for the preadolescent boy. Interest in magic tricks and puppetry (traditionally male), for example, offers the boy an avenue for externalization and activity in order to master anxieties related to his difficulty in controlling erections and testicular movements (Kestenberg, 1967b, p. 606). Working with tools, sports equipment, and machinery offers similar symbolic means of understanding and controlling the different parts of his genitalia. The anxieties which the boy masters in this way are related not only to fantasies about the genitourinary system but also to the resulting intensification of frightening, passive wishes aroused by phenomena over which he has little or no control.

Cognition in preadolescence as in latency not only facilitates sublimation but may also lead directly to important sublimatory achievements of an intellectual nature. Cognition is crucial in assisting the child in mastering all the tasks of his internal and external worlds. It is mainly by means of cognition that the preadolescent, especially the girl, can most effectively carry out the constant evaluations of herself and others which promote mastery over bodily and psychological changes, interpersonal relationships, and integration of all her experiences into a richer and better organized self-representation.

All the writers on this developmental phase have pointed to the preadolescent's intense curiosity about all aspects of sexuality, especially, those of "function and process" (Blos, 1962). They cannot, however, fully grasp penetration and impregnation (Scott in Galenson, 1964, p. 608). Intercourse is considered as a brutal attack by the father on the mother (Deutsch, 1944).

Diaries, which may enhance intellectual and literary creativity, are apt to be about sexuality and kept secret. They are more common among girls than boys. They are ". . . the expression of that part of a girl's inner life which she shares only with her best friend or with a selected group of friends." (Deutsch, 1944, p. 14, 15). Their significance for the enhancement of self-awareness and for socialization is obvious. Cognitive advances enhance the adaptational effectiveness of diaries.

Galenson (1964) has pointed to the maturational advance in abstract thinking which occurs at about the age of ten.[28] Blos (1970, p. 199) has stressed the "proliferation of preological thinking and magic beliefs" in preadolescence after their "spectacular decline" in latency. This primitive thinking coexists with a new, "highly developed rationality and power of observation . . ." appearing at this time. These two contradictory types of thinking possess ". . . potentially equal motivational valences" resulting in contradictory behavior (Ibid.).

Like the girl, the preadolescent boy may find his thinking impaired because of sexual preoccupation. Generally, the diffuseness and disorganization of the girl's thinking is greater than that of the boy. She must deal with a greater influx of sensations stemming from bodily changes more complex and widespread than those the boy experiences. These disturb her body image and ego functions to a greater degree than they do those of the boy (Kestenberg, 1967). Stechler (Galenson, 1964, p. 602) had asserted earlier, however, that there is no essential difference in the cognitive development of both sexes in this phase. Kestenberg's (1967, p. 600) final point about preadolescent girl's thinking is that its evolution towards clarity and organization is very dependent on the attitude and thinking of the parents, especially the mother.

The Self and The Sense of Identity

The preadolescent faces the continuous and increasingly complex tasks of resolving the anxieties caused by intensified drive pressures and bodily changes, and of fitting changing perceptions of himself and others into a workable whole. Sublimation and cognition are two of several major devices available to him for dealing with these tasks.

Sexual experiences (such as masturbation, bodily explorations, homosexual encounters, and the girl's first, defensive heterosexual excursions), externalization, and identification seem to play an even more powerful role in the evolution of the preadolescent's body image and self-representation. This evolution proceeds from diffusion in body image (partially due to actual bodily changes),

---

[28] At twelve, according to Piaget (1967, p. 40), a decisive change in thinking occurs consisting of the transition from concrete to "formal" or "hypothetico-deductive" thinking. Formal thought permits reasoning from "pure hypotheses rather than only from actual observations." This change in thinking leads to ". . . free reflection no longer directly attached to external reality."

thinking, feeling, and speaking and bisexual self-representation to the beginning of clarity, organization, and sexual polarization in body image and self-representation. Preadolescents, according to Kestenberg (1967b, p. 597), face the specific tasks of acknowledging and accepting the existence of their inner genitals and their continuity with their outer genitals (instead of denying them as they did during the prephallic phase); of giving up the illusion of a female phallus, and of accepting sexual differences in preparation for genitality and parenthood (p. 595).

Externalization, "the organizing influences of clear-cut physical[29] and intellectual maturation and . . . identification (p. 580) with the parents result in reintegration towards the close of preadolescence (p. 585). This reintegration permits the preadolescent to "prefer certain masturbatory practices and fantasies" and to look forward to a "progressive increase in sex-specific characteristics" (Kestenberg, 1968, p. 109). It also means, according to Kestenberg (1967, p. 597), the unification and libidinization of the various parts of the genitals in the girl (and, by inference in the boy, too). Vaginal supremacy in the girl and phallic supremacy in the boy over the rest of the genital apparatus is approached as puberty draws near. During this time, both sexes may temporarily exaggerate their sexual differences and condemn this or that part of their genitalia (Ibid.).

Masturbation helps the girl to "unify" sensations from all parts of her genitalia and to "centralize them on the now accepted introitus" (Kestenberg, 1967a, p. 429). In indirect masturbation (tensing of thighs and contraction of pelvic musculature and sphincters), "sustained genital excitement" occurs and affects the girl in a way reminiscent of the boy's awareness of his phallus. It counteracts her fear that her "insides have fallen out," promoting the development of "organ constancy." This achievement facilitates the integration of the internal genitalia into the body image (Ibid.).

In the boy, masturbatory and other experiences previously mentioned promote "externalization of inner tensions, . . . extensions of the image of the phallus," and the beginning of an acceptance of his internal genitalia. These achievements "reshape" his body image and prepare him for the "new identity" to be elaborated on in the next phase (Kestenberg, 1967b, p. 609).

Sharpening and widening of the awareness in both sexes of their

---

[29] As previously defined, menstruation and ejaculation mark the beginning of adolescence and so are not discussed at this time. Their effects on the self and the sense of identity are complex and crucial.

sexual feelings and genitalia are more or less continuous. The girl realizes that her "genital excitement can be stimulated by various parts of her body . . . and may be related to internal changes as well" (Ibid., p. 597). She becomes increasingly aware of the clitoris as a "trigger and romance organ of the vagina . . ." (Ibid.). She becomes aware of her hymen, vaguely perceived earlier in childhood.

Analogous processes occur in the boy. In contrast to the girl, the boy may take a proud interest in his growing genitals since he has been familiar with them for a long time. With both sexes, their attitude towards their genitalia and their sexual experiences is complex and ambivalent, at best.

While struggling to accept her genitalia and genital wishes, the preadolescent girl may well be a "tomboy." This does not prevent her from welcoming and even cultivating feminine interests and charms. The passive, narcissistic preadolescent girl who seems feminine may well reject her fragile, beckoning femininity. So far as enhancing development is concerned, Deutsch (1944, pp. 17–18) stresses the great value of the tomboy's activity.

While the girl may be proud of her masculinity and even flaunt it, the boy may be ashamed of his femininity and conceal it wherever possible except on certain ritualistic occasions such as Halloween (Bettelheim, 1962). Then he may don his femininity exuberantly and publicly in preparation for soon shedding it. His bisexuality, which is based largely upon identification with the reproductive mother, will only slowly yield to a firm heterosexuality in late or post adolescence.

The boy is proud of his masculinity (while many preadolescent and early adolescent girls are shamed and frightened by signs of their femininity). To protect and reinforce it, he avoids girls or treats them with contempt (Deutsch, 1944, p. 17). From friends and the members of his group, he eagerly seeks affirmation of his manliness. Similarly, the girl, "estranged from grown-ups, half-child, half-woman" finds a "double in her girl friend and seeks a new identity through a peer group" (Kestenberg, 1967, p. 599).

Although, in general, most writers on preadolescence have explicitly or by way of description and elucidation confined preadolescent pregenitality largely to the boy, Deutsch (1944, p. 19) has stressed, as I have previously indicated, the girl's defiant and rebellious regression in all the major spheres of her life. This regression expresses her sensing of mother's "attack on her adulthood," her protest against everything in the past embodied in her mother, and "an even more intense longing . . . for her own childishness (Ibid.).

A related aspect of self-definition in the preadolescent is suffering and aloneness. The boy, according to Anna Freud (1947) feels like an "outcast," (to what extent this is true for the girl is not stated in the literature).

While Kestenberg (1967, p. 595) and Deutsch (1944) have stressed the girl's frequent evaluation of her body and bodily functions in the larger terms of childhood, adulthood, and parenthood (as a result of her menstrual experiences), I think that, to some extent, this also occurs prior to menstruation. The literature does not refer to similar evaluations in the boy, but I have come across them in the boy, too, and prior to ejaculation. So far as the girl is concerned, Deutsch (1944) has stressed her adaptation to reality, in general, and with it a heightened self-confidence and a growing perception of weakness. Imitation, identification, evaluation, and devaluation take up a large part of her life. I have encountered analogous processes in boys.

A basic part of this evaluative and self-defining process is the relationships between the preadolescent, his body, and his mother. The literature is not explicit about this but indicates a growing perception by the preadolescent that his body is his, not his mother's, and that he wants full control over it. He may, to repudiate his mother's investment in his body, treat it badly in defiance of previous maternal care and protection. It is as if this were his most effective way of asserting his new ownership of his body. This ownership, which also takes a constructive form, is based upon a certain minimum of skills and understanding.

Identity formation and the sense of identity seem to be ultimately determined by the development of the body image, self-image, and the self-representation. These structures, in turn are, ultimately, due either to identifications or to their influence on those ego achievements which contribute to self-definition.

In preadolescence, identifications are characteristically transitory, superficial, imitative, and playful (Deutsch, 1944, p. 17). Kestenberg (1967, p. 586) has explained these shallow identifications by the preadolescent's powerful tendency toward easy fusion with others because of his diffuse body image. They dominate personal relationships, at least for a while. Their enactment in play (which may become real and, possibly, dangerous) allows the girl, often in the company of her friend, to try out who and what she would like to be. She can, in this way, prepare herself for certain critical life experiences in which feelings are powerful or overwhelming. All kinds of emotional experiences are sought, even those of suffering and persecution (Deutsch, 1944, p. 21). Identifications may be based upon an admired and loved person in real life or a fantasy figure. They are associated with wishes for independence, success, power, and fame as well, as specific aspirations in regard to dating, "falling in love," a career, marriage, and motherhood.

Neither Deutsch nor any other writer has described similar rehearsals for living through identifications in the preadolescent boy in response to present and hoped for pleasures and responsibilities. The preadolescent boys whom I have seen had active fantasy lives in which they performed heroic feats. Their ideal is apt to be a man who is daring and powerful in some sense, usually physical.

In regard to the "choice" (unconscious) of parental identifications, Deutsch (1944, p. 7) has stressed the importance of appreciating the child's numerous mothers and fathers who have their origins in real and perceived qualities. What does not happen is that the girl simply identifies with her mother and, as a result, becomes feminine. The child's past and current ambivalence and his guilt are the major determinants of the specific characteristics in both parents chosen for identification.

Anna Freud (1965, pp. 195–197) has enumerated the various factors responsible for bisexuality throughout all developmental phases: The developmental tendency towards masculinity or femininity, castration anxiety, and reaction formation to anal erotic strivings, facilitate heterosexuality. "Innate bisexuality," primary and secondary narcissism, the need for an anaclitic attachment (especially in girls), anal erotism (particularly in boys), penis envy, overestimation of the penis in boys, and a negative Oedipus Complex in boys facilitate homosexuality.

The bisexuality of preadolescence and, in particular, the intensified penis envy in the girl have been universally accepted in the literature both as its hallmark and as the obstacle to be surmounted if psychosexual development (and all the developmental processes contingent upon it) is to progress. Erikson (1968, pp. 261–294) has sharply disagreed with the penis envy concept of femininity and has offered as a replacement the concept of the "inner space." His critique of penis envy is of interest on several counts. It is enriched, for example, by a refreshing and clear second look at the conceptual, methodological, and emotional origins of the traditional psychoanalytic view of femininity. It is based, apparently, to an important degree upon an experimental study, unique in the literature, of several hundred normal preadolescent youngsters of both sexes. The study, done in the early fifties, sought to understand the way in which the youngsters perceived their bodies, especially their genitalia. Further, the data illuminated some basic personality and cultural implications which these perceptions might have.

With few exceptions, the penis envy concept has dominated the psychoanalytic theory of femininity since Freud devised it early in the century. Erikson has offered several reasons for this situation. First, this concept has grown out of work with "acutely suffering individuals . . . women necessarily at odds with their womanhood." Second, the psychoanalyst has traditionally directed himself toward understanding and alleviating this suffering. Third, psychoanalytic thinking has been (and is?) "atomistic" and "fragmentary," (a reflection of conventional, medical and scientific thinking, in general?). Fourth, this thinking has been continuously reinforced by the "earliest experiences of (sexual) differentiation, largely reconstructed" from such women patients. Also, psychoanalytic thinking "infers . . . meaning . . . from origins" and deals with observable "reality"—what is and what is not there. Finally, the psychoanalytic setting and procedure encouraged the "venting . . . of hidden resentments and repressed traumata." The psychoanalytic theory of normal feminine development, therefore, came to be based on the "so-called genital trauma" (1968, p. 274). The boy had a penis. The girl did not. Instead, she had a "woundlike aperture" which she had discovered early in life and which had "blighted" her development (Ibid.).

Using the "genital trauma" concept as a starting point, certain assumptions followed naturally, such as the prevalence of penis envy in women; the "future baby representing the penis"; the girl turning from mother to father because she finds that the mother had not only cheated her out of a penis but had been cheated herself; and, finally, the woman's disposition to abandon (male) aggressiveness for the sake of a "passive-masochistic orientation. . . ."

The "partial truths" unearthed by psychoanalysis are important but, in terms of development, according to Erikson, they leave out too much. The "complexes and conflicts unearthed by psychoanalysis . . . do threaten to dominate the developmental and accidental crises of life. But the freshness and wholeness of experience and the opportunities arising with a resolved crisis can, in an on-going life, transcend trauma and defense" (p. 276). Erikson has hoped that "future formulation of sex differences must at least include post-Freudian insights in order not to succumb to the repressions

and denials of pre-Freudian days" (p. 268). What were the repressions which led to these "partial truths"? They are man's ancient fears of menstruation, pregnancy, and birth.

This study was based upon contacts over a two-year period with
each of one hundred and fifty boys and one hundred and fifty girls.
Their play constructions demonstrated how differently each sex
used space. The girls had emphasized "inner space" and the boys
"outer space" (1968, p. 270). The girls emphasized peaceful interiors or enclosures containing people and animals who were
usually static. Doorways were elaborate. There were intruders such
as a man or animal. The intrusion usually evoked humor and excitement. Houses with conical protrusions, high towers, people and
animals in motion, automobile accidents, a policeman who channeled or arrested traffic, and the collapse of high structures dominated the scenes created by boys. Ruins appeared only in the boys'
scenes. Exteriors were typical.

It is intriguing to note that Erikson's initial and nuclear position
about feminine development, his "post-Freudian insight" is based
on something which is not there—a Freudian viewpoint which he
has severely questioned for many pages. His unrepressed "post-
Freudian" concept is also about a space, woman's "inner space."

Erikson has proposed that the analyst emphasize the "early
dominance of the productive interior" (p. 235) of the woman instead of her "woundlike aperture." Rather than the "loss of an
external organ . . . a sense of vital inner potential . . ." (Ibid.). He
has suggested viewing the woman's "inner space" as a potential
source of production and danger and the "richly convex parts of
the female anatomy . . . [in terms of] . . . fullness, warmth, and
generosity" (p. 267). Instead of "passive renunciation of male activity" the woman turns to "the purposeful and competent pursuit
of activities" in harmony with her anatomy and physiology (Ibid.).
Instead of masochistic pleasure in pain, the woman has learned
to "stand (and to understand) pain as a meaningful aspect of
human experience in general and of the feminine role in particular"
(Ibid.). The "cumulative experience of becoming a man or woman
cannot . . . be entirely dependent upon fearful analogies (vagina
as devouring mouth, etc.) and fantasies (Ibid.)." "A productive
inner bodily space safely set in the center of the female form and
carriage has . . . greater actuality . . . [than a] missing external
organ" (Ibid.). Woman, then, is to be regarded in terms of her
unique biology and potential for development in every aspect of
her being rather than as a penisless man with a bleeding wound.

A woman is not more or less of a man or a human being with a "body," but a "somebody," an "indivisible personality and a defined member of a group" (Ibid.). For a particular woman, the issue is "how much she varies within womanhood and what she makes of it within the leeway of her stage of life and her historical and economic opportunities" rather than her reactions to being penisless (Ibid.). At the same time, "real women harbor a legitimate as well as a compensatory masculinity . . ." (p. 286).

Women have historically stood for the "realism of householding, responsibility of upbringing, resourcefulness in peace keeping, and devotion to healing" (pp. 201–202). But what man has offered woman and what she has seemingly fought to gain and to accept triumphantly is an opportunity to be and live like man (p. 262). Emancipation for the woman has represented an opportunity to emulate man's "self-made image as a model to be equaled . . ." (Ibid.). But, Erikson has argued, "true equality can only mean the right to be uniquely creative" (p. 291).

I think that I have accurately presented the essence of Erikson's views about femininity in his own words. They are presumably based on the experimental study to which I have alluded earlier and, by implication, on a variety of other sources which are not mentioned. The connections between the findings produced by the study and Erikson's formulations are worth examining. First, a closer look at the study itself is in order. The subjects, preadolescent boys and girls, were presumably normal. This aspect was implied rather than discussed. If they were normal, what criteria were used? Also, while the children were called "preadolescent" and their ages (10–12) given, the criteria used to determine their developmental stage were not mentioned.

The developmental stage, which may vary enormously from child to child and which may have little to do with age, would dictate what the child permitted himself to perceive about his body and to project or externalize onto the scene which he had been asked to create. Defensive and adaptive considerations could profoundly influence the child's body image and his externalization of it. Children normally repudiate part or all of their reproductive system prior to adolescence in the course of accepting and integrating it into their self-representation. They may, in fact, consciously or unconsciously desire the anatomy of the opposite sex. (One-third of the children, in fact, constructed scenes which were like the majority of those constructed by children of the opposite sex, a finding which Erikson [1968, p. 94] has failed to discuss.) It would be helpful in reporting and assessing the results of such a study to have access to the fantasy and behavioral lives of these preadolescents so that the meaning of their constructions is as accurate and as rich as possible.

The children had been asked to imagine that the "table was a moving picture studio; the toys, actors and props; and they, themselves, moving picture directors" (1968, p. 268). They were to arrange "an exciting scene from an imaginary moving picture and then tell the plot" (Ibid.). The children's remarks were recorded and the scenes photographed. The children were complimented.

It would seem that more direction and seductiveness might have entered into the experimental design than one might prefer. Is a setting in which excitement and narcissistic gratification were stressed in gaining access to the child's inner world more scientifically productive than the analytic setting which, according to Erikson, encourages expressions of fear and pain? And do not the specific verbal and nonverbal demands made on the children represent the kind of "atomistic" thinking which Erikson has, I think, correctly discerned and criticized in Freudian thinking? His experimental design could well favor the acquisition of the "partial truths" of Freudian analysis which he has criticized at some length.

The essence of his elucidation of the significance of woman's "inner space," the underlying principle, so to say of this space, is that: "Anatomy is destiny . . . insofar as it determines not only the range and configuration of physiological functioning and its limitations but also, to an extent, personality configurations. The basic modalities of woman's commitment and involvement naturally also reflect the ground plan of her body" (p. 285). It is a very long leap from the findings of the study presented in this chapter to the foregoing assertions, and from those to the concept of femininity which Erikson has delineated. His assertions about the "inner space" and "penis envy" may very well be correct, but a detailed clinical documentation would be most enlightening. Otherwise, his statements take on a teleological, rhapsodic, and exhortative coloration. His view of woman is a noble one. One wants very much to believe it. But such reactions cannot substitute for step-by-step documentation.

Everyday observation and clinical data demonstrate that women with "productive interiors" and warm, generous convexities are, too often, mean, niggardly, and destructive to child, husband, and other people. Erikson's answer to this and to woman's penis envy is that the male society has made her this way, has crippled her basic capacities for loving and nurturing, and made her want to be a man.

Why is this so? No one questions the overwhelming and permanent influence of the mother on her child. How, then, does she produce sons who abuse women and who try to make them into inferior men (or even worse, into beasts of burden)?

In discussing the concept of penis envy and how it arose, Erikson has drawn our attention to something which is just as important as the concept: the method and spirit of the investigation from which the concept had been derived. Process and product are a tapestry from which one element cannot be removed without changing or, rather, spoiling the whole.

Few analysts have discussed, in detail or at all, the derivation of their concepts of normal development from specific clinical sources, as Freud did, for example, in his classical studies of certain patients. The sources themselves are mentioned infrequently, and then, too often, only in a general way. But, however they are mentioned, they are apt to be of great interest. Deutsch (1944, p. 3), for example, preceded her classic account of preadolescence with the statement that the "information about these [preadolescent] processes . . . does not always have the full authority of direct personal observation." Her sources are women whom she has analyzed and "whose behavior can be understood only as a direct contamination of prepuberty and, second, many young girls . . . who have consulted "her about adapting to college life. She made considerable use of "case and life histories recorded by other observers—physicians and social workers—not prejudiced in favor of any psychologic theory" and "creative literature," (Ibid., p. xi). (This is an interesting statement if only because the observers' lack of prejudice in regard to psychologic theory would have nothing to do with the operation of psychological blinders. These could well distort or inhibit their perceptions as much or far more then adherence to a particular theory.)

Blos, in his various writings on preadolescence and adolescence, especially in his last book (1970), has made increasingly successful attempts to present abundant clinical material and sufficient evidence of his own thinking to allow the reader a fascinating and rewarding opportunity to evaluate his theoretical position. Even in this book, however, there are some limitations. The data was acquired through psychotherapy conducted by psychiatric social workers whose work he had supervised (Ibid., p. xvii).

Greenacre's (1952) paper on trauma in preadolescence offers

step-by-step integration with theory. The limitations of the data in this instance consisted of its derivation from the analyses of four adult women, consultative experiences, and the "direct knowledge" of trauma in only one preadolescent girl who remained accessible for study during her adolescence. The papers by Kestenberg (1967; 1968), on the one hand, offer as clinical data a few isolated clinical observations and considerable use of material from creative literature. Yet, she presents remarkably explicit images of the experiences and processes of children in the developmental phase she is elucidating. Almost everything she says seems not only correct but real. Her theoretical formulations and illustrations seem marvellously illuminating until one wonders about the adequacy and sources of her data.

Even so, the point is not that every assertion be accompanied by extensive psychoanalytic reconstructions or mountains of observational data. Rather, all possible sources of data should be used including intuition and imagination. The author should not only identify his sources but, just as important, he should report the reasoning by which he has arrived at his position in the greatest possible detail.

Erikson has failed to convince me of the validity of his "inner space" concept and of the incorrect or "partial truth" of the genital trauma concept, although I feel he is correct. At the very least, he is refreshing and evocative even in his own "partial truths" and omissions. In his explanation of the Freudian view of femininity, for example, he referred to man's old and universal fear of women's reproductive functioning (which includes her sexuality). Why did he leave out man's envy of the reproductive woman? I think that this is just as important a factor as his fear of her. Jacobson (1959) has discussed the possible role of this envy of the female in the work of male analysts.

A much more profound omission in his critique of Freudian procedure and thinking is that the pathologically disturbed individuals with which Freud worked had not prevented him from creating a scheme of libidinal development and of the psychic apparatus which remains astonishingly useful. Moreover, this scheme led to an understanding of developmental differences in male and female and of the meticulous interaction between the environment and the individual in its widest possible sense through the mechanism of identification. Freud's work made possible Hartmann's (1938) concepts of the "average expectable environment" adaptation and the "conflict-free sphere" which, in conjunction with

Freud's theories, could easily cradle Erikson's views. Deutsch (1944) and Benedek (1950), in fact, working within the Freudian tradition did, indeed, precede Erikson's view of femininity with ones which were not dominated by penis-envy and which saw woman on her terms. They did not, however, write about "mom."

The Superego

Identity formation originates largely in identifications, as well as in certain ego achievements which are apt to have been very much dependent on identifications. Who one is, what one stands for, and what one wants to do or can do is, therefore, automatically connected to superego development. The battle between the super-ego and the id in preadolescence, as in latency, is an important source of character traits, more or less transitory.

Anna Freud (1947) and Blos (1962, p. 59) have referred to two features of the preadolescent superego. I have previously referred to the new "inner criticism" and the "novel" solution of dealing with guilt by means of the group. These observations are difficult to understand since the latency child has achieved an "inner criticism" and externalizes his superego within the group.

What is clear to me about the superego in preadolescence from the literature and from my own experience is that its latency achievements undergo continuous enrichment. Both externalization and internalization are intensified. What may be new, perhaps, is that the preadolescent attempts to reason about his reactions and impulses, rather than only reacting reflexly in terms of his notion of his parents' system of what is "good" and "bad." This attempt to replace conscience by reason seems to be beyond most latency children.

Kestenberg (1961, p. 583) has made three observations worth noting about the superego in preadolescence. Parental ideals are rejected and replaced by those of other adults. (The preadolescent idealizes performers, especially, athletes, actors, magicians, etc.) Archaic superego demands are revived and lead to compulsive rituals reminiscent of those at the age of three. Finally, the pre-adolescent makes "secret deals" with himself. He bribes his conscience with "good deeds" in order to perform forbidden ones. These deals serve as "advance punishment" and masochistic submission."

The one paper dealing directly with the preadolescent superego is by Hendricks (1964). He has noted that the preadolescent feels lost without the person onto whom he has externalized his ego ideal, since this psychic structure represents, ultimately, the symbiotic tie with the mother.

The ego ideal also represents the narcissistic homosexual tie with the parent of the same sex, a tie which will be resolved by and absorbed into its formation during the next phase of development (Blos, 1970, pp. 219, 226–227). This achievement, like other developmental achievements is very gradual.

Postscript

Well over thirty years after the publication of the first detailed account of preadolescence by Anna Freud, in which she had plainly shown some reluctance to regard it as a developmental phase (the "so-called prepubertal" period), Maenchen (1970) has recently spoken of it as "the least understood phase." Earlier, Prugh (Galenson, 1964, p. 607) reflected the general uncertainty about this phase in asking how much of "typical prepuberty behavior . . . is innate" and how much is due to "social and parental expectations long before this period is actually reached."

Variations in latency and early adolescent development seem to me to be so frequent and wide-ranging that preadolescence remains for me difficult to conceive and discern.

CONCLUSION

Long before Prugh asked about the ultimate origin of preadolescence, Spiegel (1958) questioned "whether there are cultural forces in our country which tend to interfere with the adolescent process: with the establishment of genital primacy, object love, and a firm sense of self." He answered his own question: "If law-abiding society does not offer the adolescent adequate ego ideals in the form of heroic figures, his hunger for them will tend to drive him to the gang. For the gang represents a social organization that takes care of the functional, instinctual, and value disturbances of adolescents in conveniently institutionalized ways."

The increasing pathological involvement of the preadolescent with drugs and their associated criminality within the last decade, the obvious suffering and regressiveness in so many adolescents (and post adolescents) and the ever increasing prolongation of adolescence in our society (a serious concern since the twenties of Bernfeld, Anna Freud, Deutsch, Spiegel, Erikson, Blos and many others) have introduced a special note of urgency into the psychoanalytic effort to understand normal development in latency and preadolescence. Everything unearthed by psychoanalytic investigation has pointed to the absolute dependence of a successful adolescence on the success of latency and preadolescent development. Prevention of emotional illness as well as enhancement of therapeutic capabilities and learning practices would be facilitated by more knowledge of these phases. Of even greater importance than these benefits might well be the stimulating effect of such knowledge on society's ability to survive and prosper because it could enrich the parental rearing of children through new and sensitive institutions.

I have tried throughout this chapter to point out some ambiguities, discrepancies, and gaps in the literature, hoping that this will stimulate the work necessary to replace them with clarity and new knowledge. With this aim in mind, a more elaborate statement about the incomplete areas and omissions would be useful.

Much more, for example, could be understood about mothering in general and about the vulnerability and invulnerability of mothers to distinctive societal pressures in regard to their mothering. Benedek (1959) has written on parenthood as a developmental phase, in particular, from the standpoint of their identification and superego evolution. Recently, she has published the only account of fathering and fatherhood in the pschoanalytic literature.[30] For the mother, much might be gained from a study of the parenting tendencies of children. According to my impressions, somewhere about the end of latency or the start of adolescence, the child may begin, more or less impulsively, to instruct, advise, admonish, approve and exhort his parents. This tendency which may well evolve by postadolescence into a deliberate and substantial part of the individual's relationship to his parents is, I suggest, a kind of parenting. Some parents crave it, some demand it, some indulge it and some condemn it. This tendency may well start in early childhood as a reflexive, imitative gesture. That this parenting tendency has within it elements other than love and understanding is axiomatic. But I have been impressed by its presence and the possibility that it exerts an important influence on the development of both child and parent.

Kris (1950) has pointed to the necessity of learning to predict

[30] Recently, a psychiatric discussion of fathering has appeared in *Modern Perspectives in International Child Psychiatry*, John G. Howells, Ed., New York: Brunner-Mazel Inc. 1971.

the extent to which the transformations of latency, preadolescence, and adolescence modify predispositions to psychopathology. He has also urged that much more might be learned from the mother's behavior about her latent attitude toward her child, in order to appreciate the full impact of her personality on the child's development. Of equal importance is further illumination of the child's vulnerability to object loss, to the fear of loss of love, as well as to the actual loss of love. The child's ability to accept parent substitutes also merits more understanding.

Anna Freud (1965, p. 106) has pointed to the need for more knowledge about the criteria for the reversibility of regression in childhood, preadolescence, and adolescence. Flapan and Neubauer (1970) have urged the study of affective development in children, the variations in development, the formulation of different developmental models, and individual variability in the developmental process.

Spiegel (1958) and Erikson (1970a) have stressed the need for a better conception of the self and the sense of self. Sandler (1960) has pointed to the need for greater knowledge about superego formation and functioning and the introjection of parental authority in particular. Finally, much more might be profitably learned about filicidal impulses in parents (Atkins, 1970).

The construction of a theory of normal development in latency, preadolescence, and adolescence as a result of the integration of data from analysis and direct observation is a gigantic task. Might not our current sources of knowledge of normal development be enriched if analysts (and their appropriately trained representatives) had access to more data of obervation and introspection than is presently available on children and preadolescents. Arrangements, for example, might be made throughout the country with all these institutions involved in the daily lives of children and adolescents in order to obtain this data. I am referring especially to schools. The data would consist of intellectual, scientific, literary, and artistic productions, illustrating interests, concerns, jokes, and fashions. The arrangement, of course, would be voluntary and the identity of the contributors anonymous. In this way, a child could be followed throughout all developmental stages, including adulthood. This study might provide important supplementary data to that acquired by the ongoing formal longitudinal studies started within recent decades, and traditional reconstructions from psychoanalysis.

REFERENCES

[Note: *The standard edition* refers to *The standard edition of the complete psychological Works of Sigmund Freud.* (London: Hogarth Press and the Institute of Psycho-Analysis).]

Anthony, E. J. and Benedek, T.   *Parenthood.* Boston: Little, Brown, 1970.

Atkins, N. B.   The oedipus myth, adolescence and the succession of generations. *Journal of the American Psychoanalytic Association,* 1970, **18**, 860–875.

Becker, R. E.   Panel report: Latency. *Journal of the American Psychoanalytic Association,* 1965 **13**, 584–590.

Benedek, T.   Parenthood as a developmental phase. *Journal of the American Psychoanalytic Association,* 1959, **7**, 389–417.

Bettelheim, B.   *Symbolic wounds.* New York: Collier, 1962.

Blos, P.   *On adolescence.* New York. The Free Press, 1962.

Blos, P.   Character formation in adolescence. *Psychoanalytic Study of the Child,* 1968, **23**, 245–263.

Blos, P.   *The young adolescent.* New York: The Free Press, 1970.

Bornstein, B.   On latency. *Psychoanalytic Study of the Child,* 1951, **6**, 279–285.

Bornstein, B.   Masturbation in the latency period. *Psychoanalytic Study of the Child,* 1953, 8, 65–78.

Brody, S.   Some aspects of transference resistance in prepuberty. *Psychoanalytic Study of the Child,* 1961, **16**, 251–274.

Brody, S.   *Passivity.* New York: International Universities Press, 1964.

Buxbaum, E.   Transference and group formation in children and adolescents. *Psychoanalytic Study of the Child,* 1945, **1**, 351–365.

Buxbaum, E.   *Troubled children in a troubled world.* New York: International Universities Press, 1970.

Deutsch, H. *Psychology of women.* Vol. I. New York: Grune and Stratton, 1944.

Deutsch, H.   *Selected problems of adolescence,* New York: International Universities Press, 1967.

Erikson, E. H.   *Childhood and society.* (2d ed.) New York: W. W. Norton and Company, 1963.

Erikson, E. H.   *Insight and responsibility.* New York: W. W. Norton and Company, 1964.

Erikson, E. H.   *Identity youth and crisis.* New York: W. W. Norton and Company, 1968.

Erikson, E. H.   Autobiographic notes on identity crisis. *Daedalus,* 1970a, 99, 4, 730–759.

Evans, R. I.   *Dialogue with Erik Erikson.* New York: Harper and Row, 1967.

Fenichel, O. *The psychoanalytic theory of neurosis.* New York: W. W. Norton and Company, 1945.

Flapan, D., and Neubauer, P. B. Issues in assessing development. *Journal of the Academy of Child Psychiatry,* 1970, 9, 669–688.

Fraiberg, S. Tales of the discovery of the secret treasure. *Psychoanalytic Study of the Child,* 1954, 9, 218–241.

Freud, A. *Writings of Anna Freud.* (Rev. ed.) Vol. II. New York: International Universities Press, 1936.

Freud, A. Indications for child analysis. *The Writings of Anna Freud.* Vol. IV. New York: International Universities Press, 1945.

Freud, A. *The psychoanalytic treatment of children.* London: Imago Publishing Company, 1946.

Freud, A. Emotional and instinctual development. *The Writings of Anna Freud.* Vol. IV. New York: International Universities Press, 1947.

Freud, A. On certain difficulties in the preadolescent's relation to his parents. *The Writings of Anna Freud.* Vol. IV. New York: International Universities Press, 1949a.

Freud, A. On certain types and stages of social maladjustment. *The Writings of Anna Freud.* Vol. IV. New York: International Universities Press, 1949b.

Freud, A. Aggression in relation to emotional development: normal and pathological. *The Writings of Anna Freud.* Vol. IV. New York: International Universities Press, 1949d.

Freud, A. Indications for child analysis. *The Writings of Anna Freud.* Vol. IV. New York: International Universities Press, 1945.

Freud, A. Problems of infantile neurosis: contribution to the discussion. *The Writings of Anna Freud.* New York: International Universities Press, 1954.

Freud, A. The role of bodily illness in the mental life of children. *Psychoanalytic Study of the Child,* 1952, 7, 69–81.

Freud, A. Child observation and prediction of development. *Psychoanalytic Study of the Child,* 1958, 13, 92–116.

Freud, A. *Normality and pathology in childhood.* New York: International Universities Press, 1965.

Freud, S. Extracts from the Fleiss papers (1897). *The standard edition.* Vol. I.

Freud, S. Three essays on the theory of sexuality (1905). *The standard edition.* Vol. VII.

Freud, S. Analysis of a phobia in a five year old boy (1909). *The standard edition.* Vol. X.

Freud, S. Family romances (1909b). *The standard edition.* Vol. IX.

Freud, S. A special type of choice of object made by men (1910). *The standard edition.* Vol. XI.

Freud, S. Formulations on the two principles of mental functioning (1911). *The standard edition.* Vol. XII.

Freud, S.   On narcissism: an introduction (1914). *The standard edition*. Vol. XIV.

Freud, S.   Development of the libido and the sexual organizations (1917). *The standard edition*. Vol. XVI.

Freud, S.   Group psychology and the analysis of the ego (1921), *The standard edition*. Vol. XVIII.

Freud, S.   Two encyclopaedia articles (1922). *The standard edition*. Vol. XVIII.

Freud, S.   The infantile genital organization (1923a). *The standard edition*. Vol. XIX.

Freud, S.   Some psychical consequences of the anatomical distinction between the sexes (1925). *The standard edition*. Vol. XIX.

Freud, S.   Inhibitions, symptoms and anxiety (1926). *The standard edition*. Vol. XX.

Freud, S.   Female sexuality (1931a). *The standard edition*. Vol. XXI.

Freud, S.   Libidinal types (1931b). *The standard edition*. Vol. XXI.

Freud, S.   Femininity (1933a). *The standard edition*. Vol. XXII.

Freud, S.   Dissection of the psychical personality (1933b). *The standard edition*. Vol. XXIII.

Freud, S.   Analysis terminable and interminable (1937). *The standard edition*. Vol. XXIII.

Freud, S.   Moses and monotheism: three essays (1939). *The standard edition*. Vol. XXIII.

Freud, S.   An outline of psychoanalysis (1940). *The standard edition*. Vol. XXIII.

Friend, M. R.   Panel report on latency. *American Psychoanalytic Association*, 1957.

Galenson, E.   In panel report: prepuberty and child analysis. *Journal of the American Psychoanalytic Association*, 1964, 12, 600–609.

Greenacre, P.   Special problems of early female sexual development. *Psychoanalytic Study of the Child*, 1950, 5, 122–138.

Greenacre, P.   *Trauma, growth and personality.* New York: W. W. Norton Company, 1952.

Harley, M.   *Masturbation conflicts, adolescents: psychoanalytic approach and therapy.* New York: Harper and Brothers, 1965, 51–78.

Hartmann, H., Kris, E., and Loewenstein, R. M.   Comments on the formation of psychic structure. *Psychoanalytic Study of the Child*, 1946, 2, 11–39.

Hartmann, H., Kris, E., and Loewenstein, R. M.   Notes on the theory of aggression. *Psychoanalytic Study of the Child*, 1949, 3, 4, 9–36.

Hartmann, H.   Psychoanalysis and developmental psychology. *Psychoanalytic Study of the Child*, 1950, 5, 7–17.

Hartmann, H.   *1939 Ego psychology and the problem of adaptation.* New York: International Universities Press, 1958.

Hendricks, I.   Narcissism and the prepuberty ego ideal. *Journal of the American Psychoanalytic Association*, 1964, 12, 522–528.

Jacobson, E. The development of the wish for a child in boys. *Psychoanalytic Study of the Child*, 1950, **5**, 139–152.

Jacobson, E. *The self and the object world.* New York: International Universities Press, 1964.

Jones, E. Joint meeting of the General, Medical, and Education Section of the British Psychological Society, *British Journal of Psychology*, 1922, **8**, 198.

Kay, P. Report of a workshop on latency. *American Association for Child Psychoanalysis*, 1969.

Kestenberg, J. S. *Menarche; adolescents: psychoanalytic approach to problems and therapy.* New York: Paul B. Haeber, Inc., 1961.

Kestenberg, J. S. Phases of adolescence. Part I. *Journal of the American Academy of Child Psychiatry*, 1967, **6**, 426–463.

Kestenberg, J. S. Phases of adolescence. Part II. *Journal of the American Academy of Child Psychiatry*, 1967b, **6**, 577–612.

Kestenberg, J. S. Phases of adolescence. Part III. *Journal of the American Academy of Child Psychiatry*, 1968, **7**, 108–151.

Kolansky, H. Some psychoanalytic considerations on speech in normal development and psychopathology. *Psychoanalytic Study of the Child*, 1967, **22**, 274–295.

Kris, E. Notes on the development and on some current problems of psychoanalytic child psychology. *Psychoanalytic Study of the Child*, 1950, **5**, 24–46.

Kris, E. Opening remarks on psychoanalytic child psychology. *Psychoanalytic Study of the Child*, 1951, **6**, 9–18.

Lampl-de Groot, J. On masturbation and its influence on general development. *Psychoanalytic Study of the Child*, 1950, **5**, 153–174.

Lilleskov, R. K. Workshop report on early adolescence. *Proceedings of the Fifth Annual Scientific Meeting on the problems of technique in the analysis of adolescents*, 1970, 32–35.

Maenchen, A. On the technique of child analysis in relation to stages of development. *Psychoanalytic Study of the Child*, 1970, **25**, 179–209.

Mahler, M. On human symbiosis and the vicissitudes of individuation. *Journal of the American Psychoanalytic Association*, 1967, **15**, 740–760.

Mittelmann, B. Motility in infants, children and adults: patterning and psychodynamics. *Psychoanalytic Study of Child*, 1954, **9**, 142–177.

Mittelmann, B. Motor patterns and genital behavior: fetishism. *Psychoanalytic Study of Child*, 1955, **10**, 241–263.

Mittelmann, B. Motility in the therapy of children and adults. *Psychoanalytic Study of Child*, 1957, **12**, 284–319.

Mittelmann, B. Intrauterine and early infantile motility. *Psychoanalytic Study of Child*, 1960, **15**, 104–127.

Moore, B. E., and Fine, B. D. *Glossary of psychoanalytic terms and concepts.* (2d ed.) New York: The American Psychoanalytic Association, 1968.

Olden, C. Notes on child rearing in America. *Psychoanalytic Study of the Child,* 1952, 7, 387–392.

Olden, C. On adult empathy with children. *Psychoanalytic Study of the Child,* 1953, 8, 111–126.

Peller, L. E. Libidinal phases, ego development and play. *Psychoanalytic Study of the Child,* 1954, 9, 178–198.

Peller, L. E. The school's role in promoting sublimation. *Psychoanalytic Study of the Child,* 1956, 11, 437–449.

Peller, L. E. Daydreams and children's favorite books. *Psychoanalytic Study of the Child,* 1959, 14, 414–433.

Piaget, J. *Six psychological studies.* New York: Random House, 1967.

Plank, E. N., and Plank, R. Emotional components in arithmetical learning as seen through autobiographies. *Psychoanalytic Study of the Child,* 1954, 9, 274–293.

Redl, F. Group emotion and leadership. *Psychiatry,* 1942, 5, 573–596.

Reich, A. The discussion of 1912 on masturbation and our present-day views. *Psychoanalytic Study of the Child,* 1951, 6, 80–94.

Rochlin, G. The dread of abandonment. *Psychoanalytic Study of the Child,* 1961, 16, 451–470.

Sandler, J. On the concept of superego. *Psychoanalytic Study of the Child,* 1960, 15, 128–162.

Sandler, J. The concept of the representational world. *Psychoanalytic Study of the Child,* 1962, 17, 128–145.

Sarnoff, C. A. Ego structure in latency. *Psychoanalytic Quarterly,* 1971, 15, 387–415.

Spiegel, L. A. Comments on the psychoanalytic psychology of adolescence. *Psychoanalytic Study of the Child,* 1958, 13, 296–308.

Wangh, M. The evocation of a proxy. *Psychoanalytic Study of the Child,* 1962, 17, 451–469.

Wermer, H., and Levin, S. Masturbation fantasies: their changes with growth and development. *Psychoanalytic Study of the Child,* 1967, 22, 315–328.

Winnicott, D. W. *The maturational processes and the facilitating environment.* New York: International Universities Press, 1965.

Wolfenstein, M. Children's understanding of jokes. *Psychoanalytic Study of the Child,* 1953, 8, 162–173.

3

JEROME S. SILVERMAN AND NATHANIEL ROSS

Mental Disorders in Childhood and Adolescence: Psychoanalytic Perspectives

A new diagnostic nomenclature (DSM–II) became official for American psychiatrists in July, 1968. It was the first revision of the American Psychiatric Association's 1952 Diagnostic and Statistical Manual, Mental Disorders (DSM–I). Similarly, the eighth revision of the International Classification of Diseases (ICD–8), approved by the World Health Organization in 1966, became effective in 1968. The sixth edition of ICD, which was still appearing in 1968, had been incompatible with DSM–I (1952). Aware of this, the United States Public Health Service sent American representatives to work with the international committee for the revision and publication of ICD–8. The American

Psychiatric Association (APA) in 1965, in conjunction with these committees, assigned its committee on nomenclature and statistics the task of preparing DSM–II, which was to be compatible with the ICD–8 nomenclature on mental disorders.

Alas, not only have these noble goals of international cooperation, communication and compatibility provided little help for the development of a satisfactory nomenclature and classification of the emotional and mental disorders of children and adolescents, the revision of DSM–I to DSM–II is also less than satisfactory. It does contain one slight improvement; namely, the new category: Behavioral Disorders of Childhood and Adolescence. This consists of a new set of diagnoses, designed to describe those disorders "occurring in childhood and adolescence that are more stable, internalized and resistant to treatment than transient situational disturbances, but less so than psychoses, neuroses, and personality disorders. This intermediate stability is attributed to the greater fluidity of all behavior at this age." According to DSM–II, these diagnoses include: hyperkinetic reaction, withdrawing reaction, over-anxious reaction, runaway reaction [sic], unsocialized aggressive reaction, and group delinquent [sic] reaction.

One feels that the sacrifice that has been made by American psychiatrists, with the adoption of DSM–II, for the use of diagnostic categories that are part of an international classification of diseases is a regressive step—at least as far as the classification of emotional disorders of children and adolescents is concerned. As described by E. M. Gruenberg, Chairman of the APA Committee on Nomenclature and Statistics, which prepared DSM–II in collaboration with the World Health Organization and others, there are to be found in both DSM–II and ICD–8 many of the deficiencies that are so often attributed to the approaches of collaborating committees (in this case an international committee). What this committee did was to *negotiate* (in the Revision Conference) the list of diagnoses and their names, a painful bit of surgery for all concerned.

Gruenberg (1969) says:

> To me, a standard set of diagnostic terms functions mainly to improve communication between clinicians, to make the results of research more readily understood, and to classify issues in psychiatry. Improving the usefulness of service statistics is a secondary and doubtful goal. The diagnostic terms and definitions should be as clear as possible and should not introduce or imply judgments about

the nature of the disorders, unless these judgments have been well-established and are generally accepted by competent psychiatrists. (p. 370)

He also reminds us that:

First, a classification of disorders should be a classification of disorders, not a scheme for classfying patients for statistical purposes. Second, an official set of definitions for the list of disorders should specify why psychiatry needs each label, and this means specifying in what way each disorder differs from the other listed disorder. (p. 372)

Aside from the confusing step of dropping the term "reaction," the other added diagnoses notwithstanding, in the absence of a specifically stated etiological basis for a diagnostic classification, there appears to be no basic theoretical change from DSM–I to DSM–II. One is left with a diffuse classification, based primarily on symptom pictures and syndromes, and on some dynamic-genetic-social viewpoints, but dealing mainly with surface phenomena. While these may be superficially similar, they may have quite different underlying psychogeneses and etiologies. A nosology that incorporates recent advances in ego psychology, such as we are attempting here, offers solutions to many of these problems.

According to the Group for the Advancement of Psychiatry (GAP, 1966), "The ideal scheme of classification would . . . permit a synthesis of the clinical picture, the psychodynamic and psychosocial factors, 'genetic' considerations regarding the level of origin, the major etiological forces, a concise prognosis, and the appropriate method of treatment. . . . Such a clinical-dynamic-genetic-etiological scheme of classification is presently premature." (p. 208)

N. Ross (1960) has described how our psychoanalytic nosology has taken the form of a linear series of benign-to-malignant states, with the implication of a decreasing order of accessibility to psychoanalytic therapy. As regards symptom-picture classification—conversions, phobias, etc.—it has become clear that many individual symptoms have deeper etiological roots than had been previously thought. Clearly, a nosology that is based solely on psychosexual stage differentiation requires constant amendment. "Many, if not all syndromes," according to Rangell (1960), "extend across various lines of traditional classification—that is, anxiety states, conversion, phobia, fetishism."

The ontogenetic recapitulation of the development of child

psychiatry is nowhere more evident than in the current confused state of nomenclature and classification of emotional or mental disorders in childhood and adolescence. More than with classification in adult psychiatry, the problem of classifying emotional disorders in children and adolescents compels awareness that the ideal basis for a systematic classification, namely, specific etiology, is as yet unavailable. However, despite the fact that it is not yet reflected in attempts to suggest a rational nosology, considerable progress has been made in that direction.

The list of advances is an impressive one: findings from direct child observation as well as from child and adolescence analysis; recent advances in ego psychology; Hartmann's concept of adaptation; the progressive understanding of the special significance of growth and development and of gradual progression in the child and adolescent; concepts of developmental phases, developmental sequence, continuity, developmental crises, timing in development, development upon maturation, along with concepts of critical phases in development and of optimal triggering stimuli for the optimal development of various ego functions; concepts of developmental variations, asynchrony, precocity, deviations, regression, and fixation points; the significance of object relationships; the concept of the significance, for ego functioning and development, of physical, sensory, and cultural stimulation (and deprivation); concepts of arrests and lags in development; the recently increased appreciation of mutuality in the developing parent-child relationship, as it occurs in a particular family against a particular socioeconomic and cultural background; the general contributions of psychoanalytic psychology, including reconstruction from adult analyses; and the evolving dynamic concepts of constitution, trauma, stress, and anxiety. All of this now enables us to synthesize the most comprehensive organization currently available. That is what we are attempting to do in this paper.

What these recent advances have enabled us to do, above all, is to *go beyond the traditional classifications*, which were based mainly upon the descriptive, behavioristic, phenomenological approach. J. Cramer (1959), in reviewing the common neuroses of childhood, pointed out that there is *no mention of children* in Kraepelin's classic 1904 treatise. It awaited the early work of S. Freud who, at first with Breuer (Breuer and Freud, 1895), clarified the relationship between adult psychoneurotic symptoms and early childhood emotional development, as well as experiences within the earliest social unit, mother and child. It must be noted, however, that we still need a more rational basis for our classification, and that the above scientific advances— particularly those in ego psychology—have not yet been applied *systematically* to the disorders of the child and adolescent.

Stengel (1959) tellingly reminded us that the "fundamental difficulty of classification of mental disease is lack of agreement by psychiatrists on concepts upon which it should be based. . . . Diagnoses cannot be verified objectively, [and] in essence a confusion or babel of names and nomenclatures greets us since we don't speak the same language." He then suggested, as an attempt at the resolution of this difficulty, what he calls "operational" definitions so as "to overcome the lack of knowledge of pathology and etiology and basic principles for international definition." Yet, one need not, on behalf of some assumed convenience, dilute advances that have been made in conceptualization, simply because of continuing differences in theoretical viewpoints.

As Stengel pointed out, it is Kraepelin's basic schemata that have been attacked, not the clinical foundations of his system, namely, his clinical nosology, as based upon methods of descriptive psychology, including long-term observation and follow-up. It is chiefly his view of disease entities that has been criticized, and not so much his descriptive, institutional psychiatric concepts. This is because it is clumsy and confusing to attempt to classify the infinite variety of disturbed forms of behavior mainly on a descriptive, phenomenological basis.

Stengel attributed the confusion to the lack of precision characteristic of psychiatric diagnosis. Along with others, he regarded mental disorders as reactions of the personality to known or unknown pathological factors. This followed from the concepts of psychoanalysis, which in this country were introduced early, or at least implied, in Meyer's "Psychobiological Concepts" (1906). The latter incorporated the etiological significance of stress and the uniqueness of the individual in terms of his past. Diametrically opposed to Kraepelin's system of classification are such recent formulations as the "unitary concept" of Karl Menninger (1959). As Stengel rightly assumed, the strength of Kraepelin's system lay, above all, in his "empirical dualism," which combined cerebral pathology with psychopathology on the basis of clinical observation, and took into account the absence of a precise and differentiated knowledge of etiology.

Among the significant differences between the adult and the child in the clinical picture, which make impossible the utilization of an adult-oriented classification with the child or adolescent, are those based on the developmental thrust and process, and the lack of a complete formulation of the physical, emotional, and structural-psychic development in the child. This implies a special dependence of the child on his immediate society—his family, and particularly on his mother—during the first years of life.

The second edition (1968) of the *Diagnostic and Statistical Manual of Mental Disorders* of the American Psychiatric Association, according to its introduction, sought to reflect "the growth of a concept that the people of all nations live in one world." Although that edition was the result of collaboration with the World Health Organization, in its attempt to develop a more uniform international classification of diseases (ICD–8), that effort appears to have been the occasion for what may be an unnecessary dilution of advances in conceptualization. Even past efforts at classification had followed rather closely the international classification of diseases; as the foreword to DSM–II states: "No list of diagnostic terms could be completely adequate for use in all those situations and in every country and for all time. Nor can it incorporate all of the accumulated new knowledge of psychiatry at any one point in time."

One can readily agree with this statement, insofar as a nomenclature for the emotional disorders of children and adolescents is being sought. To be sure, in the latter manual as with the ICD–8, attempts were made to incorporate diagnostic entities relating to childhood and adolescence. But the manual is less than adequate for use with children and adolescents. The nomenclature that is pertinent to childhood and adolescence is almost entirely and inadequately subsumed under: special symptoms; transient situational disturbances (adjustment reactions of infancy, childhood, adolescence); and behavior disorders of childhood and adolescents. Thus, except for that unsatisfactorily organized group that has been incorporated in DSM–II, along with "mental retardation and schizophrenia, childhood-type," there is no standard nomenclature or classification dealing specifically with the disorders of childhood and adolescence.

The next effort toward developing a standard classification was that of the Group for the Advancement of Psychiatry (GAP), whose Committees on Child Psychiatry formulated and published, in

June 1966, "Psychopathological Disorders in Childhood: Theoretical Considerations and Proposed Classification."

PSYCHOANALYTIC CONTRIBUTIONS TOWARD A CHILD/ADOLESCENT CLASSIFICATION

It is thus apparent that a nosology that is based solely on a symptomatic picture, or mainly on fixation points or even on the sequential ordering of instinctual phases, is incomplete. There is no rigid hierarchy in the ordering of phases; one may desire to obtain a total picture, but one does not look at an individual merely in a unitary manner. From a psychoanalytic point of view, we are always interested in those aspects of the drives and of ego and superego functions that have led etiologically to the conflict that has arisen in a particular situation, social or personal. It is only in that sense that both sequential phasic elements and the external environment are taken into account.

Freud did, of course, develop, in a rather loose manner, a psychoanalytic classification and nosology. This is nowhere better elaborated upon, in the classical psychoanalytic sense, than in Otto Fenichel's *The Psychoanalytic Theory of Neuroses* (1945). Other psychoanalytic contributions to the nosology of childhood psychic disorders, and to the problem of classification generally, have been summarized by N. Ross (1960), P. Neubauer (1963), C. Settlage (1964), and many others.

One of the most valuable efforts in recent times toward the development of a child-adolescent nosology was that made by the Committee on Child Psychiatry of the Group for the Advancement of Psychiatry, referred to above. That organization recognized the pressing need for a useful classification of mental and emotional disorders in children and adolescents and responded to it with a monograph (GAP, 1966). They were sensitive to the "marked discrepancies between current nosological approaches to childhood disorders and the disparities among nomenclature terms" (which, they felt, "underlines the need for a classification based upon explicit and clearly defined categories that can be employed by clinicians from varying conceptual backgrounds . . . for the purposes of ready communications, . . . the collection of comparable data, the study of the natural history of disease pictures, the assessment of treatment outcome and prognostic outlook and the investigation of the epidemiologic factors"); and they set out to draw up a classification.

Such an endeavor, they emphasized, was important in "leading to the induction of testable hypotheses and to ultimate prediction and modification of existing phenomena"—all of which they saw as subsumed under the general rubric of the scientific method. In their classification, the main concepts that had been derived from nineteenth-century basic assumptions were retained, including the "concept of polarity, the need for basic assumptions, and the use of deductive and inductive techniques." Their excellent report then goes on to stress, however, that "20th-Century scientific thinking in a number of fields strives to be multidimensional, relativistic, and dynamic in character, relying on probabilities rather than certainties" (GAP, 1966).

It is apparent that a merely phenomenological approach, based on the traditional nineteenth-century medical model, is inadequate. Freud's metapsychological approach, which, to a large extent remedied this situation, is obviously to be retained in the development of a classification that is pertinent to children and adolescents, since it implies, at the very least, the transcendent importance of early development. We are left, then, with the task of going beyond phenomenologic, behavioristic psychiatry, as well as the limitations implied in the traditional (i.e., somatic) models, toward a synthesis that will include descriptive, clinical, genetic, dynamic, structural, economic, adaptional and psychoanalytic dimensions, and will also incorporate the all-important developmental aspect that is the essence of the nature of childhood.

The child/adolescent is in a continuous process of development, which must be viewed not only in its epigenetic, longitudinal aspects, but also in its cross-sectional appearance at particular chronological and crisis phases of development. This conceptual approach incorporates the later work of Hartmann, and includes more than recognition of stages of instinctual development, or of interactions that have been delineated by Glover between various ego mechanisms. It also includes the dimension of development and further, from an adaptational point of view, all of it within the family and social schema of an individual with a specific constitutional endowment. A classification, in order to be useful, has to aim toward a synthesis of various schemata: phenomenological, behavioristic, etiologic, somatic, and developmental, within the evolving child-parent family relationships as these occur in the total socioeconomic structure (GAP, 1966). For the psychoanalyst, this implies concepts of treatability.

We go along generally with the conceptual views set forth in the GAP report: the role of hereditary, familial, and environmental influences; the significance of developmental vulnerabilities; and the plasticity of the young child's characteristics. We are also in accord with such basic propositions as the psychosomatic concept, which implies physiological, psychological, and social levels of organization. The concepts of stress, structure, conflict, and anxiety also contribute to a picture of mental illness.

The second basic idea, propounded by many since Freud, is that of the *developmental dimension.* This includes the concepts of: maturation and development; developmental variations and deviations, and asynchrony; problems of continuity and consistency; sequential developmental phases, with phase-appropriate tasks; crises, and the idea of a gradual developmental progression that, even under "normal" circumstances, includes lags, arrests, fixations, regressions, distortion and precocity. We would also concur with GAP in their division of developmental stages: infancy (0–2 years); preschool (2–6 years); school and prepuberty (6–12 years); adolescence (13, 14–20+ years).

Developmental patterns include, quite importantly, the development of object relations, as well as of other ego functions, such as those that imply increasing differentiation of reaction to stimuli; the development of thresholds and structures; the functions of identity and identification; and those functions that have to do with the balance of progressive and regressive forces, especially in terms of cognitive development. We incorporate in our conceptual framework the idea of a developmental profile (A. Freud), along with the concept of defensive adaptive maneuvers based on inherent constitution, developmental level, and relations with parents and society. Involved in this is a concept of the balance of internal and external forces.

The third basic proposition, as delineated in the GAP publication, includes psychosocial considerations of the parent/child relationship, to which Erikson has so significantly added (e.g., his concepts of psycho-social phases and of tasks in development). It is particularly apropos in terms of the child/parent relationship and of other family and societal interactions. Starting with these concepts, they describe a classification that also encompases what they termed "Healthy Responses." Other categories included in their classification are: reactive disorders, developmental deviations, psychoneurotic disorders, personality disorders, psychotic disorders, brain syndromes, mental retardation, and other disorders, outlined below.

  I Healthy responses
     A. Developmental crisis
     B. Situational crisis
     C. Other responses

  II Reactive disorders

  III Developmental deviations
     A. Deviations in maturational patterns
     B. Deviations in specific dimensions of development
       1. motor
       2. sensory
       3. speech
       4. cognitive
       5. social development
       6. psychosexual
       7. affective
       8. integrative
     C. Other developmental deviations

  IV Psychoneurotic disorders
     A. Anxiety type
     B. Phobic type
     C. Conversion type
     D. Dissociative type
     E. Obsessive-compulsive type
     F. Depressive type
     G. Other psychoneurotic disorder

  V Personality disorders
     A. Compulsive personality
     B. Hysterical
     C. Anxious
     D. Overly dependent
     E. Oppositional
     F. Overly inhibited
     G. Overly independent

H. Isolated

I. Mistrustful

J. Tension-discharge disorders
1. impulse-ridden personality
2. neurotic personality disorder

K. Sociosyntonic personality disorder

L. Sexual deviation

M. Other personality disorder

VI Psychotic disorders
A. Psychoses of infancy and early childhood
1. early infantile autism
2. interactional psychotic disorder
3. other psychosis of infancy and early childhood
B. Psychoses of later childhood
1. schizophreniform psychotic disorder
2. other psychosis of later childhood
C. Psychoses of adolescence
1. acute confusional state
2. schizophrenic disorder, adult type
3. other psychosis of adolescence

VII Psychophysiologic disorders
A. Skin
B. Musculoskeletal
C. Respiratory
D. Cardiovascular
E. Hemic and lymphatic
F. Gastrointestinal
G. Genito-urinary
H. Endocrine
I. Of nervous system
J. Of organs of special sense
K. Other psychophysiologic disorders

VIII Brain syndromes
A. Acute
B. Chronic

IX Mental retardation

X Other disorders

A "symptom list" ("symptom" in the broadest sense) was included, in accordance with an outline of various disturbances, as they are related to bodily functions; cognitive functions; disturbances in affective behavior; disturbances related to development; disturbances in social behavior; difficulties in integrative behavior; and other disturbances not listed elsewhere.

GAP, stressing the dynamic-genetic approach that is necessary for deepening a clinical-descriptive classification, suggests (and we are in accord) that it would be desirable to incorporate a Developmental Profile (A. Freud, 1962), and/or (as in the standard nomenclature of the American Psychiatric Association) an *estimate* of:

1. external precipitating stress;
2. premorbid (including both contributory and perpetuating factors) personality predisposition;
3. degree of psychiatric impairment.

This may be broadened to include modifying statements, as in DSM-II, pertaining to acuteness or chronicity and degree of severity, and referring to the broad chronological stages and developmental periods (infancy, early childhood, later childhood, or adolescence), as well as, perhaps, an individual statement of prognosis and a treatment plan. This would also be based on the degree of psychiatric or social impairment and the adaptive features that are present. Mentioned too should be the nature of the specific sociocultural setting out of which have emerged not only the child's personality characteristics but those of his parents and siblings as well. Further, their relationships within the marital matrix should be discussed, perhaps utilizing GAP's "Dynamic-Genetic Formulation."

Currently, we have advanced beyond a classification that is based mainly on phases of development of libido and/or aggression to one that takes the structural concept, including the development of ego functions, into full account. We have advanced beyond Glover's complaint, stated in 1953:

> It is still the task of psychoanalysis to produce not only a detailed account of the mental development of children but a satisfactory classification of childhood disorders. Here it encounters the difficulty that the clinical measures adopted in the case of adults are particularly unsuitable for the purposes of child psychiatry. Not only so, the measures of normality are much more elastic than those applicable in the case of adolescents and adults.

He then proposed a classification of disorders, feeling it convenient for that purpose to distinguish "two main groups: (1) disturbances of function [his functional and psychosomatic group] and development; (2) symptom-formations." Disturbances of function were further subdivided according to whether they were of the nature of inhibitions or of exaggerations (perversion). Disturbances in development were divided into regressions, fixations, and precocious advances. Glover classified symptom formations as "psychoneurotic, prepsychotic and psychotic." Preceding his nosology was Fenichel's standard psychoanalytic classification, to which we have already alluded.

In Ross's synthesis of the 1960 American Psychoanalytic Association Panel, "An Examination of Nosology according to Psychoanalytic Concepts," he reported as being generally held the view that "a classificatory scheme, based phenomenologically on symptom clusters and dynamically on levels of psychosexual development, is not adequate." As he said in his own paper on "Nosologic Considerations from the Standpoint of Phobias": "Attempts at revision of classification according to psychoanalytic principles must remain tentative and approximate, but should be sharpened . . . [to] take into account such principles as those of differential regression, ego autonomy, and in general the interplay of levels of ego and instinctual functioning." He affirmed the importance of including the concepts of instinctual fixation and constitutional factors, and according clear recognition to the influence of probability theory. The central importance of development in relation to unfolding ego functions was stressed, and especially the functions of object relationships and defenses, particularly those against aggression.

At the same panel, Leo Stone emphasized Freud's "nosological contribution of genius . . . his differentiation between the narcissistic and transference neuroses, referring to the capacity for transference, thus for object relations, and the actual and potential relation to reality." Rangell remarked that, although we still remain burdened with a classification that we have inherited from the Kraepelinian and post-Kraepelinian eras, a new phase was at hand, marked by the advent of the structural view of the psychic apparatus, the second theory of anxiety, the dual instinct theory, and the steady advance of ego psychology. He credited Otto Fenichel with being the "psychoanalytic Kraepelin who in 1940 organized the accumulated data into a scheme of classification which is probably the one used today in everyday analytic practice."

Everyone on the panel agreed with Rangell's criticism of current nosology as containing no unifying system of etiological principles, and being instead merely a system that leaped from one frame of reference to another. This logical confusion is apparent when one nosological scheme can contain as "equivalents" such varying categories as *end products,* the symptoms themselves (i.e., obsessions and compulsions), *processes* of symptom formation (i.e., conversion), a *quantitative excess of the affect* as the mode for defense (i.e., anxiety state), the vicissitudes of the *relation to reality* (i.e., psychosis), and the state of a *structural aspect,* that of the instinctual drives in the id (i.e., impulse disorders). Everyone further agreed that the concept of specificity, which is indispensable for the construction of a rational nosology and of a firmly established basic etiology, remains unsettled. We urge that the definition of etiology be spelled out more clearly as one avenue for these clarifications that might lead to a rational nosology.

Rangell mentioned various frames of reference as possibilities for a rational nosology, based on such fundamental principles as internal consistency and parsimony: symptoms (end products); processes of symptom formation; defenses against specific affects; and an integrated inventory of ego as well as instinctual functions, including superego and constitutional factors. Incorporated within such a frame of reference could be Waelder's concept of "multiple ego functions," Erikson's "epigenetic ego stages," Hartmann's "ego autonomy" and the 'conflict–free ego sphere," Rapaport's "hierarchical series," Fenichel's distinction between primitive and "tamed" affects, and Stone's inventory of personality resources.

Zetzel (1963) recalled Freud's statements concerning: "(1) the differentiation between traumatic and signal anxiety and (2) the expansion of the developmental hypothesis, in his remarks on the correspondence between each developmental level and its characteristic danger situation." This can be expanded to comprise the metapsychological assumptions proposed by Rapaport and Gill (1959): dynamic, economic, structural, genetic and adaptive. The latter enable us to differentiate: "1. the crucial tasks of the early months of life, which are concerned with: (a) the differentiation between what is internal and what is external, and between self and object, (b) the capacity to develop signaling anxiety, (c) the potential capacity to externalize and maintain good objects; 2. the adaptive goals which may be optimally anticipated at each level."

Erikson's epigenetic schemata (1950) showed many correlations with Glover's (1953). Erikson's concepts, which did not amplify instinct theory, have nevertheless furnished a basis for the establishment of diseases of development and the neuroses.

It was not until 1963 that P. Neubauer reported on the next similar panel discussion, "Psychoanalytical Contributions to the Nosology of Childhood and Psychic Disorders." In that panel the "specific characteristic of childhood—the process of development —became the pivotal point of orientation around which a system of classification was to be built." Correlated with this was the child's capacity to develop progressively—a significant factor in the determination of its future.

Anna Freud's (1962) table assessing health and pathology and drive and ego development, along with her "lines of development," were noted as making a longitudinal perspective possible. Her three categories of development included maturation of drives and ego in the direction of the adaptation to environment; development of object relations; and the organization of psychic structure. These lines were integrated in terms of four general characteristics: (1) level of frustration tolerance; (2) acceptance of substitutes, such as satisfaction; (3) the child's behavioral attitude toward fear and anxiety; (4) progression and regression rate. On this basis Anna Freud (1962) proposed the following nosology of childhood psychic disturbances: (1) variations of normality; (2) transitory symptoms, the by-products of developmental strain; (3) permanent regressions, analogous to the fixation point, and structural (ego, superego) damage: character structure—neurotic, psychotic, delinquent; or symptoms—neurotic, psychotic, delinquent; (4) primary deficiencies: retarded, defective and nontypical personalities; organic nature; distortions of development and structuralization; (5) organic, toxic, and psychic or unknown destructive processes that have affected or are at the point of affecting disruption of mental growth.

Neubauer (1963), pointing to the need for formulating conceptual schemata that can describe the process at work in the constant changes occurring in childhood, utilizes four approaches: (1) development as a measure of health and pathology; (2) developmental disorders; (3) disorders in the continuum between normal conflict and pathology; (4) primary disturbances and their effects on development. Regarding the last, he noted that "Here belong organic conditions that influence development and produce an emotional disorder." He also indicated a primary ego deficiency stemming from unknown factors, yet affecting developmental progression. Neubauer reminded us that, from the standpoint of ego adaptation, Hartmann proposed four "equilibria" in which he formulated psychic functions in terms of a balance of forces. The concept of developmental crisis, said Neubauer, may have overshadowed the study of the regulatory mechanism of the ego, and deemphasized the study of the synthetic function of the ego.

During the panel discussion (Neubauer, 1963), M. Friend expressed his deep concern about the dichotomy between clinical data and metapsychological formulations about the clinical picture and its relevance to sociological factors. He felt that the steps taken to develop the Hampstead Index represented a useful model toward formulating a scientific nosology.

Neubauer described the impressive contribution made by a variety of psychoanalysts, particularly in the diagnosis of childhood disorders proper, e.g., Spitz's "anaclitic depression"; Beata Rank's "atypical child"; Mahler's classic formulation of the autistic-symbiotic disorder; Geleerd's contributions to schizophrenia; Weil's deviational disorders; Alpert's disorders based on maternal deprivation, etc.

The idea of "rate of development" implies acceleration, arrest, delay, regression and unevenness, as well as some form of relationship between development and maturation. One often tries to differentiate clinical pictures that are reactive in nature from those that reveal internalized conflict. With the conception of developmental unevenness, as Neubauer noted—which leads, for example, to disharmony between speech, motility, and the sensory mode— we find a variety of disorders, some of which may be based on congenital activity patterns (Fries), variations in drive endowment, or an imbalance between drive and ego maturation.

At a panel discussion on "Psychoanalytic Theory in Relation to the Nosology of Childhood Psychic Disorders" (1964), C. Settlage stated that the major variables implicit in a nosology are directly or indirectly discernible in the ego and its functions. The advantages of this viewpoint are: "(1) It can utilize observational data, both direct and historical; and (2) it reflects the state of the id-ego-superego equilibrium on the one hand, and adaptive capacity on the other." Furthermore, observed Settlage, the ego is therefore the avenue through which all variables gain expression. It can provide a basis for a nosological system, utilizing the following basic concepts: (1) the timing of traumatic experience, in relation to a particular stage of early psychic development, will determine whether the disorder will be of the order of psychosis or neurosis; (2) neurotic types of disorder are derived from neurotic types of psychopathology, and psychotic character disorders from psychotic types of psychopathology; (3) it is possible further to define subtypes of the major categories in terms of specific defenses and symptoms, as well as the stage of ego and psychosexual development from which they are derived.

Settlage further asserted that traumatic experiences, before or during the process of differentiating the self from the object world and before the attainment of object constancy, tend to predispose the individual to a psychophysiological or psychotic order of mental illnesses; by contrast, traumatic experiences following the establishment of relatively stable images of self and object tend to produce a predisposition of a neurotic order. This conclusion is in accord with recent studies of the autistic, symbiotic, and separation-individuation phases of early ego development.

Settlage proposed the following categories of psychic disorder, in order of increasing severity: developmental disorders; situational disorders; neuroses; neurotic character disorders; psychotic disorders; psychoses; and psychic disorders in association with organic disorder.

In his panel paper, "Juvenile Delinquency: Its Place in the Nosology of Childhood Mental Illness, Irving Kaufman (Neubauer, 1963), divided delinquency into: (1) antisocial character formation (following Kate Friedlander's classification), as an *impulse-ridden character disorder*, belonging neither to the neurotic nor to the psychotic class; (2) organic disturbances; (3) psychotic ego disturbances.

He classified syndromes into: (1) psychoneuroses; (2) psychosomatic disorders; (3) impulse-ridden character disorders in delinquency; (4) psychoses. An interesting conceptual scheme for characteristics applicable to any syndrome, including delinquency, contains the following areas: structure; symptom pattern and unconscious motivation; the developmental level achieved by the organism; instinctual phenomena; anxiety and affective patterns; object relations and family interactions; ego structure and defense; and superego phenomena.

At the same panel (1963), Reginald Lourie, in his paper "The Diagnostic Assessment of Children for Psychoanalysis," observed that currently, "a diagnostic profile seems to be the best we can produce in the diagnostic scheme, to replace the descriptive non-dynamic categories we now have."

As Settlage (1964) noted, "a psychoanalytic nosological system . . . should be based upon those differences in psychogenesis and psychodynamics which underline and explain differing clinical illnesses. Its inherently explanatory nature can convey more meaningful and more consistent implications regarding prognosis and treatment expectations" (p. 776). These are advantages over the existing descriptive-behavioristic-phenomenologic types of noso-logical system. He referred to Anna Freud's paper "Assessment of Childhood Disturbances" (1962), in which the problems involved in diagnosing mental disturbances in children are contrasted with the problems of diagnosing adults. She notes particularly that the child is *still developing.* Thus, the ordinary criteria of "efficiency" or "failure in sex and work" have no comparable counterpart in the child, as she pointed out.

The use of psychoanalytic ego psychology as an approach to the establishment of a psychoanalytic nosological system, such as Settlage attempts, seems most practical. The child's adaptive capacity, a vital variable for a nosological system, can also be observed through the functioning of ego. It is important to take into account the "timing of traumatic experiences," concepts of neurotic and psychotic character disorders, object relationships, and the role of reality in deriving a rational nosology. To elaborate, Settlage attempts to base various types or classifications of disorder upon the study of the patient's specific major defenses and symptoms (A. Freud, 1946). Similarly, the timing of the traumatic experience significantly influences object relationships and ego development, defenses and symptom choice. Along with the concept of fixation, Settlage points out, defenses and symptoms are either derived primarily from the maturational and developmental events that were taking place in the child at the time of the traumatic experience, or from a concept of regression to the phases of earlier development.

From the structural viewpoint, he noted, "once the essentials of psychic development have been laid down, the symptoms and defenses become more genuinely psychological, in the sense of mental mechanisms." Following this, more elaborate defense structures, such as those underlying phobias or obsessive-compulsive neuroses, become possible. Settlage employs the terms "developmental disorder" and "situational disorder" for a disturbance of lesser degree, and "neurosis" as a category of disorder that is applicable when the conflict has not yet been fully internalized. He conceptualizes both these categories as due to a conflict between the child and his environment, going on within the child, although the conflict is not yet fully internalized. Developmental disorders are related to conflicts that are characteristically associated with stages of ego and instinctual development, while situational disorders occur *in reaction* to the environmental pathology.

He also includes a category of "psychic disorders, in association with organic disorder," to describe conditions in which organic factors may play important roles in the etiology of the psychic disorder, or in which "the two conditions have a minimal cause-and-effect relationship to each other."

In his classification of psychoses in children, he distinguishes two general types: psychoses of early childhood (in which the impact of traumatic experience caused defective ego development, with failure to achieve adaptation: the autistic and symbiotic childhood psychoses), and the psychoses of later childhood and adolescence (in which there is a breakdown of functioning of a personality that has already attained sufficient development or achieved a kind of adaptation). The latter states are essentially analogous to a psychosis in adults. Settlage's system of broad categories, in order of increasing severity of psychic disorder, is as follows: 1) developmental disorders; 2) situational disorders; 3) neuroses; 4) character disorders; 5) psychotic disorders; 6) psychoses; 7) psychic disorder in association with organic disorder. He also stresses the importance of constitutional endowment, drawing on those recent childhood observational studies that have indicated the significance of such factors as the constitutional strength of drives and the "biologically provided, substrate ego apparatus," as these enter significantly into the determination of the outcome of potentially traumatic experiences.

In summary, according to Settlage: "Psychogenesis is presented in terms of the timing of traumatic experience and the resulting fixation points in relation to the development of object relationship, the phases of early ego development, and the stages of psychosexual development. The attainment of object constancy seems to be a critical factor in determining whether traumatic experience will eventuate in a neurotic or a psychotic type of disorder."

It is of interest, too, to peruse the practical schemata utilized by the treatment centers and clinics of various psychoanalytic centers or institutes. The New York Psychoanalytic Institute Treatment Center uses a general diagnostic index (preliminary plan) consisting of some thirteen major subdivisions. They are:

1. *Neuroses and related disorders:* hysteria, conversion, anxiety; compulsion and obsessional neuroses; phobias; anxiety neurosis; hypochrondriasis; neurasthenia; manifest sexual dysfunction; neurotic disorders of mood; mixed neuroses;

traumatic neuroses; tics; impulse neuroses (without important social or legal implications: bulimia, nail biting, etc.); neurotic disorders of speech, isolated regressive disorders (enuresis, etc.); circumscribed occupational inhibitions; and dysfunction or disabilities.

2. *Character disorders:* hysterical, narcissistic, masochistic, sadistic, obsessive-compulsive, depressive, oral, anal, infantile, passive feminine [or masculine in a female]; neurotic [neurotic failure] impulsive; epileptic; psychosis-linked personalities; miscellaneous.

3. *Major nonpsychotic behavior disorders:* criminal, psychopathic personality, delinquency, antisocial impulse neuroses and compulsion, malingering.

4. *Addictions.*

5. *Sexual perversions.*

6. *Psychoses.*

7. *Borderline conditions.*

8. *Psychosomatic conditions.*

9. *Mental deficiency.*

10. *Situational and reactive disorders:* war neuroses, postpartum reactions, etc.

In the *International Journal of Psychiatry,* (Vol. 7, No. 6, June 1969) there appeared "A Guide to the American Psychiatric Association's New Diagnostic Nomenclature," by Robert L. Spitzer and Paul T. Wilson, with critical evaluations by a number of others, including E. Gruenberg, Karl Menninger, Francis Braceland et al. Spitzer and Wilson felt that the first revision of DSM-I represented a significant advance toward the use of a standard international classificatory system. That it represents a similar advance in other areas, however, appears to us to be open to question. These authors felt that the elimination of the term "reaction" from diagnostic labels was a striking difference, but they were also aware that many, such as Karl Menninger, would interpret this as a "return to a Kraepelinian way of thinking, which views mental disorders as fixed entities." So far as the utility of this revision is concerned for those who are interested in childhood disorders, the only changes were minimal.

Fish (1969) also felt that the new nomenclature was inadequate for the reporting of children's disorders, although perhaps better than that in DSM-1. She reflected the commonly held notion that the original APA nomenclature made "no provision for the vast majority of children's disorders which lie between transient adjustment reactions on the one hand and the more crystallized personality disorders and neurotic reactions on the other." The new nomenclature, with its category of "behavior disorders of childhood and adolescence," provides, in her opinion, "only an inadequate range of disorders, and includes some inappropriate and confusing items." She echoed the disappointment of many over the omission of the diagnosis of developmental deviations, among other things, and suggested the incorporation of many of the GAP categories.

Stuart Finch (1969) in his paper, "Nomenclature for Children's Mental Disorders Need Improvement" (p. 414) felt that the section on mental retardation was a distinct improvement, but that the section on psychiatric disorders in children "can only be termed unscientific and bordering on the ridiculous." According to Karl Menninger (1969) (in his paper, "Sheer Verbal Mickey Mouse" [p. 415]), the "American Psychiatric Association took a great step backward. . . . In the interest of uniformity, in the interest of having some kind of international code of definitions . . . in the interest of statistics and computers, the American medical scientists were asked to repudiate some of the advances they had made in conceptualization and designations of mental illness." Quoting Spitzer and Wilson's view that one of the most significant changes was the addition of eight specific alcoholic brain syndromes he asked, "is this progress in scientific conception or medical practice? Or is it sheer verbal Mickey Mouse?"

In their reply to criticisms, Spitzer and Wilson first pointed out that DSM-II was intentionally designed to be three kinds of documents or systems: a classification system, indicating what categories of mental disorders exist and how they should be grouped; a nomenclature, indicating what terms to assign to each category; and a glossary, indicating how all categories are to be defined. ICD-8 was only a classification system.

Basil Jackson's (1969) "Reflections on DSM-II" (pp. 385–392) was quite clear: "I must confess to a very definite disappointment over the absence of a completely separate section on child psychiatry, in view of the fluidity of conditions of that period of development." He did agree that the term "childhood psychosis" is a much more desirable term than "childhood schizophrenia," since "There is no definite evidence either that a psychosis in childhood will necessarily eventuate in an adult schizophrenia or, for that matter, that it resembles adult schizophrenia phenomenologically."

At this point we would like to select the problem of psychosomatic disorders to illustrate the enormous complexity of the problems confronting us in the establishment of a sound nosology and the woeful inadequacies of the traditional schemes of classification. Paul Schilder (1951) saw the interweaving of psyche and soma (if, indeed, they constitute a true dichotomy, as seems entirely unlikely) in a truly profound way. One must forgive the vagaries of the verbiage in order to appreciate truly the seminal thinking of this extraordinary man. We quote at length:

> When an organic case feels so, there are always complexes and those wild dissatisfied wishes of childhood; and when there is a tendency to conversion, the conversion will be directed into those parts of the body where he feels this organic strain. Or we would say that conversion goes to that point where there is a feeling of strain, a feeling of uneasiness. This is what Freud calls . . . the somatic preparedness [compliance]; or something in the organic sphere is prepared to meet the psychoneurotic tendencies. (p. 65)
> The beginning or slight trouble finds its magnified expression by psychic influence, but . . . the psychic influence may repress the organic symptoms . . . the psychic influence acts again on the same apparatus but this time not in the direction of the disease but against the direction of the disease. Then we get a picture in which the patient seemingly is normal and still he has an organic trouble, only this organic trouble is compensated by the psychic strength of the individual. . . . The psychogenic influence acts on the same apparatus, but the psychogenic influences is not strong enough to counteract the continual influence of the change in the apparatus which is going on from the organic disease as such . . . the problems about which we speak are not only problems of the quality of the influence but also the problems of the quantity of the influence. It is often true that such a compensatory tendency concerning the organic disease, such as compensatory "health" cannot be maintained for a long time . . . there exists not only a psychogenic disease but also a psychogenic health, so to speak. That plays an important part in some cerebellar cases . . . in some encephalitis cases. . . . The psychogenic health may, if the tendency to compensation persists, and the organic trouble does not increase, become by and by also an organic health. . . . What we see as psychogenic health, as I mentioned, is only one instance of the compensatory functions of the individual.

Compensatory functions are not only in the psyche and in the brain but in the whole organism. . . . I am very much in doubt whether it is possible to influence this deep layer of the organic conflict of the individual by the layer in which the psychic conscious and instinctive unconscious processes are going on.

When we come to the general problem, what is the psychic influence, and what has the psychic influence to do with organic change, I may quote some excellent ideas of Bleuler . . . about abreaction and *occasional* apparatus (*Gelegenheits-apparat*). He means by this term a psychophysical apparatus which is built up for a special occasion. . . . Whenever energy in the psyche in the body is produced and is near to be used or exploded, this energy will always go more to the wrong paths because of this *occasional apparatus*, which makes a wrong shifting over. We have to destroy . . . the occasional apparatus, and we do that by psychoanalysis, finding out what has produced this apparatus. [We suggest the term "improvisations" for this "occasional apparatus."] Such an occasional apparatus is indeed on the borderline between functional and organic. . . . [These building] processes are very near to the organic processes of building up an organ. . . . The occasional apparatus indeed will be in connection with some vasovegetative phenomena and will be in connection with the knowledge of some parts of the body. We can also say the organic structures are built by apparatuses which very likely once were occasional apparatuses. That is our general conception. Whether it is possible to influence an organic apparatus by a newly built occasional apparatus, that is a matter of experience in an individual case. The forces of the occasional apparatus and the forces of the organic apparatus are in some way of the same order but not all on the same level. . . . This is an instance of what we would call a psychophysiological integration. (pp. 67–70)

Clearly to those interested specifically in treatment, in prognosis, a nosology has certain specific and limited value; a profile has considerably more significance. Inasmuch as the current status of scientific advancement precludes a complete etiologic statement, we would suggest the use of a multifaceted profile (see GAP 1966, pp. 293–296)—a coordinated nosological (classificatory) profile organized along these five basic themes leading to a therapeutic statement:

COORDINATED DIAGNOSTIC PROFILE

1. Traditional clinical descriptive phenomenological formulation.

    2. Psychodynamic and metapsychological statement of personality and psychopathology (including chronological age and developmental stages, predisposing, precipitating and perpetuating factors).

    3. Assessment of degree of consonance of lines of development.

    4. Assessment of family, marital integration and interpersonal relations.

    5. Psychosocial, sociocultural assessment.

    6. Therapeutic recommendation and prognostication.

At least the first part of this Profile can be used to adhere to the usual classificatory and nosological requirements.

One may alternately adapt the GAP (1966) Dynamic-Genetic Formulation (which in essence we follow), as indicated in abbreviated form below. Our basic supplementations, as noted above, are italicized.

Although it may appear unduly lengthy and would be sharply abbreviated in practical use, the formulation is presented in condensed form to demonstrate the multifaceted considerations which must be understood in order to assay not only the diagnostic differentiations, but the therapeutic possibilities for effectively treating one small human being. Clearly, it demonstrates the woeful inadequacy of traditional classifications.

DYNAMIC-GENETIC FORMULATION

(from GAP 1966, abbreviated; modifications in italics.)

I Individual personality character of child
    A. Intellectual capacity
    B. Central conflictual areas
    C. Characteristics of ego functioning
        1. predominant defenses and adaptive capacities
        2. reality-testing functions
        3. object-relations
        4. self-concepts
        5. current developmental level (psychosexual, psychosocial, developmental deviations)
        6. integrative functions
        7. nature of superego operation, ego-ideal
        8. impairments in capacity for development

II   *Summary of degree of consonance of developmental lines*
III Individual personality characteristics of parents and other family members
IV   Inter-personal situations
    A.   Nature of marital relationships
    B.   Nature of parent-child relationships
    C.   Nature of other relationships (siblings, children)
    D.   Nature of intrafamilial transactions
    E.   Nature of sociocultural setting
V   *Traditional clinical descriptive phenomenologic statement*
VI   Summary of developmental-etiologic considerations (precipitating, predisposing, contributory, perpetuating factors)
VII Treatment plan and prognostic statement

The following case illustration will demonstrate the principles hitherto discussed.

CASE ILLUSTRATION

Eric was a chubby, robust, attractive, and initially engaging, alert, bright, 5½-year-old preschool boy, one of whose key features was a pressing need for mastery over the environment. This he obtained by means of an active, dramatic, and highly verbal caricature of a precocious oedipality, with a pseudomature poise. Emotionally labile, his active aggressive motor behavior, particularly toward his peers, was obviously causing havoc with his developing object relationships.

His mother was a bright, compulsively organized, severely controlled and controlling, somewhat prim housewife, who took only slightly disguised pride in her son's aggressiveness.

Eric's father, an intelligent professional, was dismayed to find himself in these circumstances; he felt overwhelmed and threatened not only by his wife, but by his son as well. As a result, he would "come on hard" in his losing struggle to stand above these constantly shifting powerful surrounding forces, as he fought a losing battle to maintain his marriage.

Through the history obtained from the verbal, somewhat obsessional parents, a story emerged of a heightened regressive behavioral and symptomatic change, during two to four months, in an anxious, insecure, phallic-Oedipal phase 5½-year-old boy. There were complaints from his nursery school of a tendency toward explosive behavior, aggression against his peers, and general exaggerated activity, alternating with quiet, shy behavior (in a "creative" child with "potential"). He showed stubborn, defiant behavior and verbalization at home, along with the sudden development of a slight speech problem (described by his parents as a stammer or stutter). All of this, superimposed upon a certain environmental background, led to Eric's being brought to psychiatric consultation.

Eric had endured a series of difficult separations, the most recent of which had taken place three months before the consultation, when he was left with a grandmother, who then became ill. Investigation of his behavior at that time revealed transient regressive changes, including occasional bed-wetting, angry verbalization and behavior, and aggressive fantasies directed toward his parents.

At about the same time, a favorite maid, who had been with the family for years and had been mainly responsible for Eric's care, left them. The new maid complained of his genital touching, rubbing, and activity. Questioning by the adults about this exposed overstimulating closeness and behavior kept Eric in a constant state of excitement and frustration, and evoked feelings of being overwhelmed. This was partially expressed in occasional open masturbatory play, disturbing and provocative to his parents, by urethral dribbling, and by occasional nocturnal enuresis. His loud braggadocio was at least superficially oedipal in content. He was in open oedipal rivalry with his father and aggressively seductive toward his mother. The conflict was sometimes regressively expressed in urethral, toilet, exhibitionistic, and voyeuristic ways.

Eric's obvious intelligence and verbal precocity enabled him to attempt to maintain control of his disorganizing anxiety and overwhelming stimulation with an exaggerated fantasy life, embellished with "tall stories" about his prowess, occasional lies, and generally aggressive fantasies, which in turn added to his fear of being hurt or damaged. He experienced nocturnal fears and doubts relating to his sense of self. He also displayed the undoing of adaptive behavioral changes in regressive directions, and showed increased silliness, immature behavior, and regressive interference in social relations with peers and with some authorities.

His defenses were generally obsessional in direction, but not altogether stage-appropriate. They were becoming regressively exaggerated by his heightened separation anxiety, and by the occasional breakthrough of impulsivity, resulting from poorly developed control over states of tension and excitment. Conflict was increasingly interfering with his psychosexual and psychosocial development. He manifested a regressive tendency in problem-solving with his handling of mounting tensions by action and activity. Occasionally he was sad and self-deprecating. All this took place against the background of a failing marriage.

The *Clinical Diagnostic Impression* could be designated variously depending upon the system of terminology used: "conduct disorder in a phallic-oedipal child" would be a satisfactory clinical-descriptive picture. However, in conformity with the preceding discussions of nomenclature, the impression was that of a *tension-discharge disorder—neurotic personality type*. Similarly, the following statements are necessary to complete the diagnostic nosologic-genetic statement.

The *external precipitating stresses* included the increasing tendency by both parents to save their marriage by using Eric as a spearhead for externalizing their own problems. This occurred at a time of poorly established phallic-stage organization in Eric. Their arguments had become overwhelming to him, and the immediate separations were drawing upon the trauma of earlier ones in an increasingly pathological direction. The result was an increasingly regressive perception and conceptualization, on Eric's part, of the total situation. At this time of extreme stress, preparations were made to start Eric in grammar school.

The *premorbid predispositions* have been implied above. There was a parent-child relationship in which the child, representing the externalized focus of the problems in the marital relationship, was used as the scapegoat for these difficulties. The family patterns were ones of externalizing rejected urges and wishes, of denial and projection, of sadomasochistic interpersonal relations, and of obsessive pressure for achievement, status, and power. This was a marital situation with the partners at odds, and it all predisposed to the child's illness.

Along with these went certain hereditary handicaps, such as small size. Chronic minor physical illnesses, capped by relatively minor but emotionally traumatic surgery, enhanced fixations on more infantile libidinal and aggressive (motor) levels. This was complicated by some immaturity in integrative capacities. Development of the latter had been interrupted by real-life events, including repeated traumatic separations from an early age on, leading to early specific personality patterning problems in handling large amounts of tension, anxiety, and perceptual stimuli.

In the same way, *contributory factors* emerged, such as a minor physical finding of *equino-valgus* (flat feet). The use of special shoes served to make some irrational distorted elements of the child's self-image more real. These stimulated reactions in his parents, who already had various problems concerning their own physical health and body images. Varying amounts of depression in both parents contributed further toward illness in the child.

Probably the most important *perpetuating factor* was the parents' use of the patient as a vicarious object. To his controlling mother, he was a sign of fulfillment of certain childhood ambitions, so that a defect in him was seen as a defect in herself. Her domineering possessive aggressiveness was gratified through *his* aggression; in various ways, he was serving as her tool. Similarly, his father attempted to work through his own problems, of having been overwhelmed and rejected by his parents in a similar way. He too strongly identified with the child, not so much in the fused quality of the mother's identifications as in his son's struggle not to surrender, not to submit passively to his wife—a later reflection of his earlier conflicts.

Evaluation

In order for this elaboration to be used as a clinical contribution with a therapeutic aim, *a dynamic-genetic formulation* is in order. We thus focus upon Eric's *individual personality characteristics*.

We have here a *tension-discharge disorder, neurotic personality type*, in a bright, 5½-year-old boy whose central conflicting areas, becoming increasingly internalized, are fixated primarily on an early phallic level. Within this developing personality, the external environmental stresses, of acute and chronic traumatic nature, include an insecure home life with immature, conflicting parents in a stormy marital situation. Certain repetitious past experiences, at this early school stage in his development, helped to precipitate his illness. Along with the constantly shifting structural development and organization of this developmental stage went unresolved repressed conflicted impulses and the traumatizing parental situation.

The *characteristics of his ego functioning* are of determining nature, not only regarding the clinical features, but also with respect to therapeutic prognostication. The defenses of specific note —the most archaic ones in this case—included a tendency toward projection and denial, a little stronger than is age-appropriate.

Eric's *adaptive capacities,* very good in potential, by dint of inherent endowment and through the stimulation of those ego functions that were acceptable to his parents, were conspicuous by their failure in actuality. His bright, alert, imaginative age-appropriate thought processes and his reality-testing functions balked and regressed in the face of overwhelming external and internal stress. There was realistic opposition by his current environment to his attempts to gain mastery. His difficulty in controlling stimuli and states of tension, coupled with low frustration tolerance, inhibited his flexibility and his ability to master anxiety. These reality factors combined to enhance his sense of helplessness and dependency, promoting the instinctualization and hampering the neutralization of various developing ego and superego functions. Diminished satisfaction resulted in strivings for active mastery, for integration, for the balancing necessary for gratification, and for the use of age-appropriate functions, as in play and fantasy. The balance of forces was being tilted in a regressive direction.

Eric's reality-testing was not altogether age-adequate. Children his age may show, at times, what appears to the adult to be an almost delusional belief in their ability to be an adult. For example, the child becomes "the sheriff" by wearing a badge in play, or the father, by speaking loudly or "boldly." This stage-appropriate behavior was exceeded too easily in Eric, particularly in his regressive storms and in his states of near panic.

In his identification with the aggressor, he became too easily the television set or the magical, strong, omnipotent figure within it. His heightened restless motor activity did not give him mastery over his sense of inferiority, nor over his helpless symbiotic needs. Such measures did not adequately reverse the trauma of illness, or of surgery, nor did they promote his independence, because his ego functions were momentarily overwhelmed and secondarily regressed.

These disorders in behavior—i.e., immaturity in various ego functions—presented problems in technique from the first. Direct confronting symbolic interpretation, and at times physical restraint, were occasionally necessary in the beginning. Illustrations of such technical measures were: "Now *you are* superman jumping from the chair. . . . You *like to feel* strong and big like father, and not small."

The interrelatedness of Eric's developing psychopathology with the environmental situation was manifest in his phobic tendencies. A certain degree of phobic reaction can, of course, be construed as age-appropriate or age-adequate in an early-school-age child who is coping with problems of separation control, in the development of a social identity outside the home, and in an early sense of industry. Eric had some fearfulness of the dark, of sleeping, and of noises. But he was overwhelmed with reality information from his parents, by veritable Niagaras of explanations from them about, for example, the origins of noise, the reality of events in daily life, accident, danger, and damage. In these ways, his floating anxiety was made real and crystallized.

In the process of making an assessment, we clarify and differentiate the psychopathological from the age-adequate, adaptive, psychophysiological; the constitutional and environmental and the rest from those temporary phenomena of transitional phases, the circumstances of which, particularly in children and adolescents, determine whether or not the clinical features are age- and stage-appropriate. We may thus appraise the seemingly pathological bedtime ceremonials at the end of the anal stage, or the phobias of the preschool or early-school child, as transitional and phasic, rather than as early signs of permanent pathology. Of course they could be the latter; this depends upon the intensity of past fixations, as well as on past, current, and future traumata. Today, developmental considerations enable us to regard such transient signs as representing phase-vulnerability. Naturally, we attempt to account for what has served to continue the otherwise transitory, relatively phase-specific symptomatology.

To what extent, then, did Eric's heightened motility, repressive aggression, his low frustration tolerance, and his problems in object relations and speech reflect an early and subtle organizational developmental disorder? Were these phenomena, secondarily and in an increasingly comprehensive manner, affecting later motor, cognitive, and affective development, with only the most subtle clinical clues as to their origin?

On the other hand, to what extent were these clinical features indicative of a phase-specific vulnerability, precipitated by environmental traumata? Was his increased motor activity, for example, a primary defect with ever-broadening consequences? Were the disorders in play secondary to organizational deficits that had led to developmental, cognitive arrests? Or to what extent did these clinical elements indicate secondary regression, various regressive discharge phenomena? Were his actions and hyperactivity defenses based upon a developmental ego deficit, or were they defensive out of internal conflict? To what were we to attribute alterations in neurophysiological development, maturation, and environmental trauma? Are these clinical phenomena traceable to internalization of conflict?—bearing in mind the child's neurophysiological development, the sequential phasic pressure of instinctual and ego development and growth, with its phase-specific vulnerabilities, and his experience and environment.

The specific diagnostic and therapeutic utility of Anna Freud's mode of assessment according to *Developmental Lines* suggested itself to us as we considered Eric's hyperactivity and motility. In this approach, we have found it feasible to avoid the inevitable inadequacies and frustrations that result from considering solely the child's chronological age and intelligence in searches for diagnostic solutions. Instead, we have taken into account the maturation along vital structural lines in his progressive, developmental thrust.

Considering in *this* light the complaints bearing upon Eric's immature object relations, his aggression to peers and others, we found that he occasionally treated his friends as objects, to be pushed aside when they interfered, only rarely as partners, and only occasionally as helpers in collaboration toward a common goal. He had not consolidated his appropriate position in the developmental line toward companionship, friendship, and satisfactory social relations. His variability of performance—in which he occasionally fluctuated between just the degree of socialization that was minimally required for kindergarten, to experiencing, however briefly, the more mature partnership considerations required of the early school child—revealed not only regression, but also flexibility of the regression.

To what extent, then, do we assess this variability as age-adequate, and to what extent is it out of sequence with other lines of development? (The latter refers to such elements as constructive play, bodily independence, or emotional maturity.) To what extent is it a result of lack of correspondence in level, or of irregularity in degree of maturation of these developmental lines? Again, we ask ourselves what is the cause of any developmental lag?

It is clear that Eric was immature in his development toward body independence. Occasional episodes of wetting had occurred, and dribbling still occurred. Fixation points were clearly accounted for in the history; namely, as the consequence of parental over-stimulation through exhibitionism and seductive behavior. Early separations undermined his "sense of trust" (Erikson, 1950), and the overwhelming stimulation by the parents, which alternated with frustration, further interfered with incorporation of controls and the establishment of autonomy. All this intensified his sense of shame and doubt. Bodily management was further disturbed by surgical procedures that took place during later anal and early phallic periods of development. Occurring in the phallic phase, the surgical trauma itself resulted in enhancing passive trends and bodily fears, which became focused as castration anxiety. His mother's lack of interest in his bodily "unruliness," adventurousness, and aggression further discouraged him. He was "too physical"; he became more awkward and clumsy, not less so, as he failed to obtain signs of her pleasure in his bodily movement.

We were finally able to develop a picture that indicated a mainly psychoneurotic and not a primary basis for his variations in motility, action, and his subsequent use of activity and play. His restlessness and hyperactivity were manifestations of anxiety—defenses against affects, including anxiety. Hyperactivity and more structured forms of it in play were, to some extent, defensive manifestations of erotic and aggressive discharge phenomena; but they were more particularly defenses against and representations of sexual affects, i.e., exhibitionistic, masturbatory impulses.

This study along developmental lines of an autonomous function —motor activity—led us to comprehensive diagnostic clarity. Speech (also play and work) could be studied similarly as nodal points, intersected by various developmental lines. In the same way, we were able to study Eric's fantasies, his object relations, and his dribbling and other symptomatology. Taking into account his early separation anxiety, we could now appreciate how fixation and regression, in the line of development of maturational patterns, generally undermined ego capacities for control and for rhythmic integration of bodily functions. All of this contributed in various ways to interferences with sleeping, eating, speech, bladder control, activity and affectivity patterns, play patterns, and social relations. Separation anxiety and bodily anxiety led to hyperactivity and to motor awkwardness. The latter, which was also related to hyperactivity and anxiety, became reactive and later symbolic. Early visual stimulation enhanced dramatic exhibitionistic activity trends.

Hyperactivity was connected on ego levels with disguised, displaced, defensive, exhibitionistic masturbatory activity. Related to this were games involving hiding, sudden surprising of the object, chasing, teasing, sudden naughtiness—all designed to obtain help, to provoke prohibitions, to establish external controls, or to be punished. Similarly, these activities, he said, felt good, felt exciting inside. They constituted a phallic equation, as described. Jumping and flying were related to trying to be big, masterful and active—to be superman, to be strong, as against feeling ovehwhelmed, unworthy, helpless, dirty, and expendable. Jumpiness reflected tension, both his own and his mother's. Climbing and jumping represented identification with the aggressor, the daily or weekend activities with the family, such as skiing, and his exhibitionistic display of strength and size.

At the same time, all this was a denial of weakness, of bodily defect (flat feet), and of affect. He was also defending himself thereby against fear of the pain of affect, of painful, depressing thoughts, and forbidden ideas. He would jump, hide, chase, and generally run about, instead of thinking, recalling, and feeling—thereby risking the loss of control over mysterious threatening inner forces. He would become that which frightened him. He could verbalize a fear if the pertinent affect was hidden by being acted out. Magic play helped overcome separation expectations and castration anxiety. His jumpiness both expressed and denied his fears of illness, pain and passivity, as in association with surgery, and of being forced, i.e., having unpleasant things pushed into him, like affects.

Shouting his rude words along with these activities meant that he was shouting commands, as omnipotent parents might. They also served to deny his fears and to master his trauma actively. Yet he libidinized his attempts at mastery, in such passive situations as being at a doctor's office. Passive masochistic behavior appeared, but the clownish silliness that got him into trouble at school, also represented TV figure identification and identification with the aggressor; at the same time, they showed his excellent dramatic imitative abilities.

Some activity was the physiologic expression of the phallic phase of development and was therefore psychologically phallic. Jumping up and down and climbing emphasized how big and breathlessly excited he could become, yet, by the activity, denied that he was able to feel any excitement in phallic areas. At the same time he denied that he had defective organs, such as flat feet. Some action was counterphobic to falling and to passivity; some was clearly related to mechanisms of doing and undoing. This vague and increasingly disorganized or destructive activity revealed his conflicts over liking to soil, yet also enjoying cleanliness.

Some of his negativism reflected attempts to push himself away from an overwhelming mother, as well as from wanting to rub and touch. It also reflected a need to be reassured by and close to his mother, thereby fending off rejection. Yet it expressed his fear of seduction on a higher phallic level, as well as his phallic aggression. Repetitive hyperactivity, such as climbing play, contests of strength, and jumping, were also defensive, obsessional attempts to control excitement. Naughty behavior in school was correlated with hiding activities, and with such secret activities as urination and masturbation. They served as defenses against, and attempts at, mastery of these exhibitionistic, seductive home activities. Tantrums, like his early panic-appearing behavior, alternated with clenched stubborn angry silences (for control of affect, including feelings of being hurt). Hiding, finding, running away also reversed the situation of a threatening aggressive mother, of anxiety at separation.

With this acting-out, he sought to master surgical traumata, helplessness, frightening parental arguments at home, and separations. This led to regressive hyperactivity, which further represented his attempts to gain help and control. With treatment, these elements could easily be connected, ego-wise, with conflicts over separation, tension states, wishes to be both clean and dirty, to be strong and big. Regression stimulated symbiotic orality, intensifying separation anxiety; it stimulated as well anal-sadistic impulses, leading to regressive expressions of love, such as "I'll kill you," which inflamed both teachers and parents.

The function of speech was slightly affected, but not in a primary way. For example, he identified with his mother's tight, breathless, halting and controlled compulsive speech. Her tic-like cough was another manifestation of this speech inhibition. Inhibition and regression were tied in with his traumatic tonsillectomy at 3½ or 4.

His precocious ego functions and his great intelligence rebelled against these primitive regressive id-manifestations, producing intense conflict, along with depression and guilt. His ambivalence also reflected the parents' ambivalence toward him. Regressive animistic thinking trends enhanced infantile omnipotence and narcissism, interfering with his development and with the use of abstract symbolic thinking. The latter impeded his progress in the development of comradeship and play. His controlling, distant mother allowed no aggression, yet at the same time accepted his regression, thus contributing to a poor self concept. The ego mechanisms contributing toward furthering socialization, i.e., imitation, identification, and introjecting, were disrupted by ambivalent, rejecting, separating, poorly controlled parental behavior.

Drive intensity was enhanced by illness, upsetting external events such as parental fights, overstimulation, frustration, and chronic emotional strain. Social relations regressed from cooperative partnership to irritable egoism. Play was no longer goal-directed and constructive, so much as it was impulsive, confused aggression.

Eric was engaged in a struggle that is characteristic of the phallic phase, although he had not altogether consolidated his position on various lines of development. Thus he manifested secondary regression in primary-process activity, speech, play, and peer relations. He had not progressed completely into the appropriate stages of bodily independence; yet he was impelled by a thrust toward development, notwithstanding his fixations. Some disharmony arose out of lack of consonance in developmental lines and much from environmental trauma and early mother-child relations; but little of it was derived from innate constitutional developmental incapacities.

His great castration anxiety, fear of aggression, problems in control, his difficult family situation, uneven precocity in intellect, and some phases of maturation led to a diagnosis of: "Tension-Discharge, neurotic personality disorder." The acting-out, repetitive behavior problems were of unconscious symbolic significance; they did not merely represent discharge. There was evidence of superego development, manifested in guilt, depression, and anxiety. An unconscious wish for having limits set and for punishment was also manifested in his behavior. There was warmth in his relations, despite his ambivalence. In the overall balance, despite the regression, the behavioral difficulties, the difficulties in organizational controls, and the regressive defenses, progressive forces still dominated his personality.

His relatively lower performance could be compared with his high verbal intelligence and environmental demands for achievement, and with his immaturity in developmental lines toward emotional maturity, body management, and companionship. This developmental disharmony made his somewhat atypical behavioral problems in aggression and sexual acting-out more understandable. As a result, his fantasy life was upset and his control of anal and urethral tendencies was unreliable. The whole picture was one of difficulties in the later stages of development; the ability to play and to progress from play to work, to social development and to bodily management.

On page 157 we presented a profile using the GAP (1966, pp. 293–296) Dynamic-Genetic Formulation, with the following variations. In our condensed coordinated profile, the data are organized along five specific themes, including, however, a Traditional Clinical Descriptive Formulation, and an Assessment of Lines of Development, all of which contribute to the final Therapeutic Recommendation and Prognostication. Our case illustration demonstrates the difficulties, some perhaps impossible to overcome at this time, in establishing nomenclature, classification, and diagnostic formulation, without a specific etiological basis.

REFERENCES

[Note: *The standard edition* refers to *The standard edition of the complete psychological works of Sigmund Freud* (London: Hogarth Press and the Institute of Psycho-Analysis).]

American Psychiatric Association. Diagnostic and statistical manual of mental disorders. Washington, D.C., 1952.

American Psychiatric Association. Diagnostic and statistical manual of mental disorders. (2nd ed.) Washington, D.C., 1968.

Breuer, J. and Freud, S. *Studies in hysteria, neurosis and mental disease* (1895). Boston: Bacon, 1936.

Cramer, J. *Common neuroses of childhood*. In *American handbook of psychiatry*. New York: Basic Books, 1959.

Erikson, E. H. *Childhood and society*. New York: Norton, 1950.

Fenichel, C. *The psychoanalytic theory of the neuroses*. New York: Norton, 1945.

Finch, S. Nomenclature for children's mental disorders. *International Journal of Psychiatry*, 1969, 7, 6, 414.

Fish, B. Limitation of new nomenclature for children's disorders. *Innational Journal of Psychiatry*, 1969, 7, 6, 393–399.

Fish, B. and Shapiro, T. A descriptive typology of children's psychiatric disorders: II. A behavioral classification. In R. Jenkin and J. Cole (Eds.), *Diagnostic classification in child psychiatry*. Psychiatric Report No. 18. American Psychiatric Association: Washington, D.C., 1964.

Freud, A. *The ego and the mechanisms of defense*. New York: International Universities Press, 1946.

Freud, A. Assessment of childhood disturbances. *The Psychoanalytic*

Study of the Child, 1962, **17**, 149–158. New York: International Universities Press.

Freud, A.   Assessment of childhood disturbances. *The Psychoanalytic*

Freud, S.   Types of neurotic nosogenesis (1912). *Collected Papers.* Vol. 2. Pp. 113–121. London: Hogarth Press, 1950.

Freud, S.   Neurosis and psychosis (1924). *Collected Papers.* Vol. 2. Pp. 250–254. London: Hogarth Press, 1950.

GAP Report No. 62. Psychopathological disorders in childhood: theoretical considerations and a proposed classification. New York: Group for the Advancement of Psychiatry, 1966.

GAP Report No. 38. Diagnostic process in child psychiatry. New York: Group for the Advancement of Psychiatry, 1957.

Glover, E.   *Psychoanalysis and child psychiatry.* London: Imago, 1953.

Gruenberg, E. *International Journal of Psychiatry,* 1969, **7**, 6, 368–374.

Hartmann, H.   Psychoanalysis and developmental psychology. *The Psychoanalytic Study of the Child,* 1950, **5**, 7–17. New York: International Universities Press.

Hartmann, H.; Kris, E.; and Loewenstein, R.   Comments on the formation of psychic structure. *The Psychoanalytic Study of the Child,* 1947, **2**, 11–38. New York: International Universities Press.

Jackson, B.   The revised diagnostic and statistical manual of the American Psychiatric Association. *American Journal of Psychiatry.* 1970, **127**, 1, 65–73.

Jackson, B. Reflections on DSM-II. *International Journal of Psychiatry,* 1969, **7**, 385–393.

Kaplan, E. B.   Panel report: Classical forms of neurosis in infancy and early childhood. *Journal of the American Psychoanalytic Association.* 1962, **10**, 571–578.

Kraepelin, E. Psychiatrie. Leipzig: Barth, 1904.

Menninger, K.   *The vital balance.* New York: Viking Press, 1964.

Menninger, K.   Towards a unitary concept of mental illness. In *A psychiatrist's world.* New York: Viking, 1959, Pp. 516–528.

Menninger, K.   Sheer verbal mickey mouse. *International Journal of Psychiatry,* 1969.

Meyer, A.   *British Medical Journal,* 1906, **2**, 757.

Neubauer, P.   Panel report: Psychoanalytic contributions to nosology of of child psychic disorders. *Journal of the American Psychoanalytic Association.* 1963, **11**, 595–604.

Rangell, L.   In N. Ross, Panel report: An examination of nosology according to psychoanalytic concepts. *Journal of the American Psychoanalytic Association,* 1960, **8**, 535–551.

Rapaport, D. and Gill, M.   Points of view and assumptions of metapsychology. *International Journal of Psychoanalysis,* 1959, **40**, 153–162.

Ross, N.   Panel report: An examination of nosology according to psychoanalytic concepts. *Journal of the American Psychoanalytic Association*, 1960, 8, 535–551.

Schilder, P.   *Brain and personality*. New York: International Universities Press, 1951.

Settlage, C. F.   Psychoanalytic theory in relation to the nosology of childhood psychic disorders. *Journal of the American Psychoanalytic Association*. 1964, 12, 4, 776–801.

Spitzer, R., and Wilson, P.   A guide to the American Psychiatric Assotion's new diagnostic nomenclature. *American Journal of Psychiatry*, 1961, 124, 1619–1629.

Stengel, D.   Classification of mental disorders. *Bulletin of the World Health Organization*. 1959, 21, 601–663.

World Health Organization. Manual of international statistical classification of diseases, injuries and causes of death. Geneva, 1957.

World Health Organization. International classification of diseases (8th revision). Adapted for use in the U.S. Public Health Service Publication No. 1693. U.S. Government Printing Office: Washington, D.C., 1968.

Zetzel, E. R.   In Panel: Psychoanalytic contributions to nosology of child psychic disorders. Reported by P. Neubauer. *Journal of the American Psychoanalytic Association*. 1963, II, 595–604.

4

HUMBERTO NAGERA

Social Deprivation in Infancy: Implications for Personality Development[*]

S ocial deprivation is a somewhat vague and perhaps too encompassing a term. Thus, social deprivation in childhood can be taken to mean a variety of things such as insufficient contact with other human beings, cultural deprivation, stimuli deprivation, economic deprivation and its sequeale of malnutrition, etc., or a combination in different proportions of all these elements in any given case. For this reason my comments will be very narrowly focused on a specific subject.

* A slightly different version of this paper was presented at the December 1969 meetings of the American Psychoanalytic Association. The paper is the product of wide ranging discussions on the subject at the Child Psychoanalytic Study Program, Department of Psychiatry, University of Michigan, Ann Arbor. Dr. Nagera is the Director of the Program.

Deprivation can take place at any time during the child's life, and it will have different effects according to the stage of development. I am concerned here only with deprivation in the earlier stages of life, when lack of appropriate stimulation (or lack of protection from excessive stimuli) may distort or stunt the growth of the brain structures, or in psychoanalytic terms, distorts the growth of the somatic and psychological ego apparatuses.[1] There are, of course, many other aspects to the problem here considered that I am not discussing. They are indeed of as much or more significance than the one I have selected.

Functions and functional capacities, in ego terms, are predicated on the existence of the organic structures of the brain that make them possible. Behind any given ego function or set of functions there is a somatic ego apparatus in Hartmann's sense to sustain it. Naturally, we have always assumed that there are significant qualitative differences between these organic structures from one individual to another. These qualitative differences were generally considered as "innate givens" and were partly explained on the basis of congenital, constitutional, or genetic differences among different individuals. Though I do not dispute the existence or significance of original, innate distinguishing characteristics, recent data is inclining child analysts to conclude that much that was considered innate can be shown as having been acquired during the first year of life, having added to the inherited constitution (James, 1960).

An enlarging body of information from various fields of science (to which I shall refer later) is making it increasingly clear *first*, that the genetic potential, in terms of the development of the anatomical structures of the brain, is not reached at birth. Many such structures are, in fact, far from complete at that time. *Second*, it is becoming apparent that the blueprint of that genetic potential (determined by the chromosomes and genes) is such that in order to be unfolded to its fullest, organic, anatomical-maturational processes of the brain structures must continue after birth. But such continuation is not only dependent on internal, embryological maturational forces but—and this is what I want to highlight—on the interaction of such forces with different forms of external stimulation without which interaction the embryiological maturational blueprint will not unfold to its full potential. Reception of such stimuli, as contained in the ministrations of the mother to

[1] See H. Nagera, "The Concept of Ego Apparatus in Psychoanalysis: Including Considerations Concerning the Somatic Roots of the Ego," *The Psychoanalytic Study of the Child*, Volume 23, pp. 224–245.

her baby in the mother-child relationship, seems absolutely necessary. Furthermore, this kind of external stimulation seems to influence the internal, anatomical-maturational processes by at least three different mechanisms:

1. It may favor progressive complex arborization of dendrites during the first few months of life. The significance of this in terms of function will not escape anyone.
2. It increases the degree of vascularization of certain anatomical structures of the brain.
3. It increases and furthers the process of myelinization. Myelinization and function are closely related as we know.

The importance of all this may be further highlighted if we remind ourselves of the condition of the brain structure at birth. Richmond and Lipton (1959) noted that the "brain of the human newborn infant is comparatively large, but *it is histologically and biochemically quite immature.* Its weight of 300 to 350 grams is nearly that of adult primates (chimpanzee, 350 grams; gorilla, 450 grams; orangutan, 240 grams). Within two years the brain weight nearly trebles, and by six years of age 95% of the mature weight (that is, 1200–1300 grams) has been attained" (p. 80). They remark too that since "water content decreases after birth, future comparative studies should include data on solid tissue weight" (Ibid).

Conel's (1939) studies of the cerebral cortex of young infants have shown that though cellular endowment is fixed at birth, complex morphological changes continue for long periods of time. Thus, we find progressive arborization of dendritic processes during the few first months of life without any evidence of a quantitative cellular increase. Richmond and Lipton (1959) commented that "since it is now generally accepted that neurons are connected in a network and not merely in a linear series, and that nerve impulses pass about the connections in a circular, more or less continuing fashion, the potential significance of this growing arborization of dendrites for the development of the infant may be appreciated" (p. 80).

The relationship between function, functional capacity, and vascularization (amount of oxygen available to the organ) is well established. There is a direct relationship between an organ's capacity to perform its function and the state of its vascular system. We are all familiar with senile arterioesclerotic syndromes where the arterioesclerotic damage to the brain's vascular system leads to poor oxygenation with the consequent deterioration in the functions of the brain.

As was to be expected, comparative anatomical studies of the brain of different species and their specific functional abilities seem to show that there is a direct correlation between the degree of vascularization of a certain area of the brain and the excellence of the function that such area performs. Thus, for example, Craigie (1955) in his paper "Vascular Patterns of the Developing Nervous System" states that the "more acute sense of hearing of snakes probably is reflected in vascularity of the cochlear nucleus notably in excess of that in other reptiles, and the mobility of the tongue is suggested by a capillary supply in the hypoglossal nucleus about twice as rich in snakes and lizards as in the turtle and the alligator" (p. 28).

Such facts seem to me of extreme importance to the subject under discussion. We have to consider that present day information demonstrates that the process of vascularization of multiple brain areas is far from finished at the time of birth. It takes several months after birth to be completed, and what is more important, *there seems to be a direct correlation between external stimulation of specific areas of the brain (after birth) and the final degree of vascularization that such areas will reach.* Thus, Rao (1955) for example, removed the eyes of rats at birth and studied the capillary beds in the visual centers of these rats at maturity. He found that the length of the capillaries in a unit volume of tissue was significantly reduced in the visual correlation centers by about 19% in the superior colliculus and by about 10% in the dorsal nucleus of the lateral geniculate body, but was unchanged in the striate area of the cerebral cortex. He concluded that there had been "an even more marked retardation of development of the contained blood vessels than the percentages mentioned suggest as a result of the removal of the eyes some time before they would normally have begun to function. Such an effect is most easily explained as due to the absence of that portion of the functional activity in visual correlation centers of the brain which would normally have been stimulated by impulses coming through the optic nerves. Presumably the activity in the cerebral cortex was not significantly reduced in amount by the absence of visual stimulation." The same seems to apply to the human infant. Mali and Räihä (Craigie, 1955) examined premature infants at birth, concluding among other things that the density of the meshes in the cerebral capillary beds is considerably less at birth than in later life.

Other examples where experimental evidence indicates that environmental stimulation has some effect upon ultimate structure and function follow. Langworthy's (1933) studies of kittens have revealed that myelinization can be significantly influenced by neuronal function. He blindfolded kittens from birth and could demonstrate histologically that the optic nerve of the blindfolded eye showed less myelinization than that of the contralateral, stimulated eye. Similarly, Le Gross Clark showed a failure of development of retinal cells in animals restricted from birth to an environment of blue light.

According to Sontag (1941), "animal experimentation suggests that the myelinization of specific nerves can be accelerated by stimulation of the nerves, and there is, of course, considerable relationship between the function of a nerve fiber and its state of myelinization" (p. 1001).

Kennard (1948) has apparently found that human premature infants whose eyes were exposed to light since birth show more mature optic nerve development than full term infants of an equivalent age at the time of death. Richmond and Lipton (1959), concluded that these "types of studies seem to give support to the contention that even after the fetal stage, environmental stimulation (or lack thereof) can modify developing structure in the central nervous system" (p. 82).

It seems to follow that these modifications of the developing structures may lead to important qualitative differences in the ability to perform all those ego functions associated with such structures. It seems possible too that there are critical periods for these developments to take place or that certain time limitations exist. Therefore, if the right kind of stimulation is not forthcoming during the critical time, the result may be a structure that though not necessarily *"damaged"* has certainly not developed to its full potential. If we consider the possibility of cumulative effects of this type, concerning multiple areas of the brain, it is conceivable that the total result may be a much poorer endowment of equipment for those unfortunate children whose fate it is to grow under conditions of deprivation. We might mention here, to make the final links, that the studies of many workers such as Provence and Lipton (1962) have demonstrated through direct observation, the appalling damage to ego development that results from growing under conditions of deprivation of human contacts (human contacts considered here as the vehicle of stimulation of the newborn).

It has been demonstrated too, that many such developmental

lags can be undone by proper placement of such children, at the appropriate time, in more suitable environments (Richmond and Lipton, 1959). Yet, it seems to me, that in another sense many such children are irreversibly and permanently damaged. I mean now that though they will catch up to the levels of the normal, at least in many areas such as language and motility, normality has such wide variations that we may have a "normal" human being who is permanently condemned to perform, in terms of his intelligence, at the lower end of normality. To be graphic, it is the difference between somebody digging holes in a road and somebody with the intelligence necessary for a university education. Thus, though "normal," our deprivational child rearing practices may have blunted his genetic potential to such a point that his best is an I.Q. of 80, while genetically, and given more favorable circumstances in babyhood, he might have reached an I.Q. of 120.

Spitz (1945), too, has shown quite clearly the tremendous differences between the children of professionals, growing up in their parental homes, and children raised in institutions. The first group showed a Developmental Quotient of 133 as the average for the first four months of life, an average that was maintained towards the end of the first year of life. In contrast, the children from the institution (Foundling Home) showed an initial Developmental Quotient of 124 as the average for the first four months of life, a figure that deteriorated to 72 at the end of the first year of life. His limited follow-up studies showed this change and its behavioral manifestations as irreversible once a certain period of time has elapsed.

Obviously, we still need to learn to sort out what may be due to permanent impairment in the somatic ego apparatuses (as such irreversible) and what may be due to poor opportunities to learn and practice the skills of which these apparatuses are capable, whatever their basic quality, once its somatic development has been completed.

It is clear that the amount of stimulation that a baby is subjected to during the first weeks or months of life is largely dependent on the mother's cathexis of her baby, on the type and quality of the mother-child relationship, and on her patterns of child rearing. What is described as a good mother, or "good mothering," in contrast to bad or inadequate mothering, is a very complex pattern of behavioral interaction that contains in it all those elements—in terms of different forms of stimulation (and otherwise)—that may be necessary for the ideal unfolding of the infant's blueprint for genetic neurophysiological-psychological development.

It is most unfortunate that such terms as good or bad mothering have moral connotations that are not only undesirable but that detract attention from the central issue.

I wish to end by quoting Richmond and Lipton (1959).

Though strikingly immature, the central nervous system of the human infant has within it infinite and unique potentialities for development. Whether these potentialities are fulfilled will be determined by its interaction with stimuli in the form of life experiences. The direction and pattern of behavior will be determined not alone by the quality and quantity of these experiences but by their timing as well. As clinicians, called upon to influence the direction of the development of behavior more effectively, a deeper understanding of this brief, but developmentally significant, period is needed. In part, this understanding will depend upon research in neonatal neurophysiology and its implications for later child development (p. 102).

REFERENCES

Conel, J. L.   The brain structure of the newborn infant and consideration of the senile brain. In *Association for Research in Nervous and Mental Disease, Research Publications*, **19**. The inter-relationship of mind and body. Baltimore: Williams & Wilkins, 1939.

Craigie, E. H.   Vascular patterns of the developing nervous system. In H. Waelsch, *Biochemistry of the developing nervous system*. New York: Academic Press, 1955.

James, M.   Premature ego development: Some observations upon disturbances in the first three years of life. *International Journal of Psycho-Analysis*, 1960, **41**, 288–294.

Kennard, M. H.   Myelinization of the central nervous system in relation to function. In *Problems of early infancy*. New York: Josiah Macy, Jr. Foundation, 1948.

Langworthy, O. H.   Development of behavior patterns and myelinization of the nervous system in the human fetus and infant. *Publications 139–43*. Carnegie Institution, 1933.

Mali and Räihä.   In E. H. Craigie.

Provence, S., and Lipton, E.   *Infants in institutions*. New York: International Universities Press, 1962.

Rao, L.   In E. H. Craigie, pp. 46–47.

Richmond, J. B. and Lipton, E.   Some aspects of the neurophysiology of the newborn and their implications for child development. In L.

Jessner and E. Pavenstedt (Eds.), *Dynamic psychopathology in childhood*. New York: Grune & Stratton, 1959.

Sontag, W. L. The significance of fetal environmental differences. *American Journal of Obstetrics and Gynecology*, 1941, 42, 996–1003.

Spitz, R. Hospitalization. *The Psychoanalytic Study of the Child*, 1945, 1, 53–74.

PART II

TREATMENT METHODS

5

SALLY PROVENCE

Psychoanalysis and the Treatment of Psychological Disorders of Infancy

M y acceptance of the editor's invitation to write on psychoanalytic treatment in infancy involved me in trying to define what is meant by the term. Much of the period with which we are concerned is preverbal, and a psychoanalytic treatment process as usually defined does not apply. Furthermore most of the treatment of the psychological disorders of infancy is carried out not by analysts but by nurses, pediatricians, parents and other adults who give care to children. Still psychoanalysis, to my mind, plays an enormously important part in the planning and carrying out of effective treatment of early childhood disorders. This chapter, then, reports on a way of treating psychological disorders of infancy which relies heavily upon psychoanalytic theory. It is based upon experiences that my colleagues and I at the Yale Child Study Center have had in the diagnosis and treatment of developmental disorders of infants seen in outpatient, day care, nursery school, and hospital settings. The focus will be on the treatment of those disorders of the first two years which arise primarily not from defects in the biological equipment, but occur in infants with presumably normal innate capacities. I have excluded entirely the infantile psychoses, since I share with others the opinion that in most instances the psychotic infant suffers from a biological deficit or predisposition to deviational development.

PSYCHOANALYTIC RESEARCH

The interest of psychoanalysts in the earliest years of life has increasingly involved them in direct observations of infants and very young children, especially since Kris (1950) and Hartmann (1950) emphasized the contributions to psychoanalytic developmental psychology that might be made when such studies are conducted by psychoanalytic investigators. Moreover, direct work with infants and their parents has a long tradition in psychoanalysis. Anna Freud's nursery, begun in Vienna for very young underprivileged children in the 1920s, accepted children when, as she described it in a talk in 1967, they could pass the entrance requirement of being able to walk. Later, during World War II, the studies of Miss Freud and Dorothy Burlingham in the Hampstead Nurseries extended and sharpened our knowledge about infants separated from their parents (Freud and Burlingham, 1944). Margaret Fries' (1953) work with mothers and neonates, begun in the 1930s in this country, was a pioneering study of earliest infancy which focused upon motor activity of neonates, with implications for future personality development. And, of course, the studies of René Spitz and of Katherine Wolf, both in collaboration and individually, have not only contributed to theory and practice, but have stimulated other investigations (Spitz 1945, 1946, 1951, 1955a, 1955b; Spitz and Wolf 1946a, 1946b; Wolf 1953).

The Rooming-In-Project at Yale, conducted by Edith Jackson and her colleagues from 1946–1951, was a very significant action-research project, guided by an experienced psychoanalyst who was very involved in on-going contacts with parents and children, beginning prior to the birth of the child, in which help was given while the study of the children's development and parental behavior was carried on (Jackson and Klatskin, 1950).

These studies at Yale overlapped with the longitudinal study at the Yale Child Study Center directed by Ernst Kris and Milton Senn, involving a multi-disciplinary team of psychoanalytic observers in a services-centered investigation of the development of a small group of children. In this study, which had as a major objective the refinement of psychoanalytic propositions, using a normal population, major attention was given to providing services to children and parents which would facilitate the child's normal development or alleviate problems. Selected aspects of the data have been reported by various members of the study staff (E. Kris 1955; Coleman, Kris and Provence 1953; M. Kris, 1957; Ritvo and Solnit 1958).

Sibylle Escalona's meticulous studies of infant behavior conducted over an extended period have contributed much to our knowledge of infancy, of the significance of styles of mother-infant interaction, and of the development of individuality (Escalona, 1953; 1968). While these studies are not focused upon clinical applications, they provide data that are enormously helpful in devising therapeutic interventions.

Selma Fraiberg and her co-workers, in a study of blindness and its effects on various aspects of early development, have worked out therapeutic programs for blind infants which are noteworthy for their sophisticated use of developmental concepts and for their importance to the child and his parents (Fraiberg, Siegal and Gibson, 1966; Fraiberg, 1968). Margaret Mahler and her colleagues have contributed much to psychoanalytic theory and to the treatment of severe emotional disorders through their studies of the infantile psychosis and the normal separation-individuation phase (Mahler, 1965; 1968).

J. D. Benjamin (1961a, 1961b, 1963), Sylvia Brody (1956), Bibring and Huntington (1961), Louis Sander (1962), S. L. Lustman (1956), J. Richmond and E. L. Lipton (1959) are others in a growing list of psychoanalytic observers whose research on some aspect of infant behavior or on mother-infant interaction has enriched the field. The concern of psychoanalysts with the care of infants has been most recently illustrated in two publications, one dealing with day care (Chandler, Lourie and Peters, 1968) and the second with group residential care in the kibbutzim (Neubauer, 1965). Brazelton's (1969) book for parents is a current example of the application of child development knowledge to the practice of pediatrics, written by a psychoanalytically trained pediatrician.

No attempt will be made to cite even a few of the many studies of infancy which have been done in the past and those now being conducted by investigators from theoretical backgrounds other than psychoanalysis. The relevance of Piaget's work and its interest for psychoanalysts is widely acknowledged. Infancy has been rediscovered in recent years, and the investigators ranging from those concerned with physiological or biochemical characteristics are sources of new information, much of which is relevant to psychoanalystic developmental psychology.

CLASSIFICATION OF MENTAL DISORDERS

Psychological disorders of infancy cannot be understood without considering the particular closeness of the mind and body in this period of early development. The tendency of the infant to react with transient disturbances of some aspect of development in the presence of bodily illness is a regular occurrence. Furthermore, deficits or noxious elements in the psycho-social experiences that promote development interfere in the child's object relationships, his cognitive development, his ability to solve problems, or in his instinctual development. Further, there may be concomitant disturbances of body function, among them motor delays, gastrointestinal, skin or respiratory disorders, failure of growth in height and weight, and others.

Infants tend to react quickly to stress with deviations in several areas of function. These quick and multidirectional reactions make the infant look seriously disturbed. However, the infant whose symptoms are due to deficits or adverse conditions in his psychosocial environment is usually also much quicker to respond to more favorable circumstances as corrective experiences than is the older child. Thus, symptomatology and functional competence may change rapidly in the very young child, in one direction or another.

Spitz, as early as 1951, proposed a classification of psychogenic disorders of infancy which was an important effort to systematize what was then known. He categorized deviant and disturbed object relations as quantitative and qualitative disorders and proposed the terms *emotional deficiency disease* to designate the quantitative disorders, and *psychotoxic disease* the qualitative. He link etiological factors provided by maternal attitudes with the infant's disease.

The classification of psychophysiologic and psychological disorders of infancy has been approached in other ways. I will give two examples. Prugh (1963), in an excellent essay on psychosomatic concepts in relation to childhood illness, has classified the symptomatic reactions of infants and very young children to psychological or interpersonal stressful stimuli. (The following direct quote appears as an uninterrupted paragraph in Prugh's article):

1. *Disturbances related to bodily functions,* such as eating (as in food refusal, rumination, pica, vomiting, and failure to thrive); sleeping; bowel and bladder control; speech; patterns of motoric activity; rhythmic patterns (such as rocking, head rolling, and head banging); various habit patterns (such as thumb sucking, nose picking, and masturbation); and sensory disturbances.
2. *Disturbances related to cognitive functions,* including learning failure of various types, distortions of perception, and disorders in thinking.
3. *Disturbances in social behavior,* as in overaggressive patterns, negativistic or oppositional behavior; disturbed sexual behavior; isolated or withdrawn behavior; and overly dependent or overly independent behavior.
4. *Disturbances in emotional behavior,* as in chronic anxiety, marked fears, acute panic states, depression, and feelings of inadequacy.
5. *Disturbances in integrative behavior,* as in repeated tantrums, impulsive behavior, or disorganized behavior (pp. 286–287).

In proposing this classification, Prugh describes behavior which should be visible to the observer as spontaneous behavior or elicited through history-taking or tests of various kinds. It is useful as a first step in classification. It does not profess to suggest causative factors.

Nagera's (1965) approach is oriented toward a designation of psychic disturbances according to psychoanalytic concepts of early development. His emphasis is on internal events. He speaks, in the age group with which we are concerned, of developmental interferences, developmental conflicts and, toward the latter part of the second year, of neurotic conflicts. He approaches the problems from the viewpoint of the predominant characteristics and vulnerabilities of developmental periods or phases, and provides a useful classification of infantile disorders.

In this paper, I have chosen to remain primarily descriptive— both in the case material to be presented and in discussing treatment. I have reasoned that psychoanalysts will have no difficulty in translating the descriptive case material or in relating statements about therapeutic experiences to psychoanalytic theory. Before the consideration of treatment, a brief discussion of diagnosis is necessary.

DIAGNOSTIC METHODS

The diagnostic picture is built up from the evaluation of the child along a number of dimensions and concurrently from the evaluation of relevant influences in his environment. Those aspects of the child's physical environment which either support or interfere with his development directly or indirectly are usually relatively easy to become aware of. However, the evaluation of the child's environment as defined by what he actually *experiences* may be more difficult. During infancy, of course, a great deal of our information about what the child experiences is inferred from the evaluation of parental attitudes and behavior as they report it to us. Here the emphasis is not primarily upon understanding the personality of the parents, though this is always relevant and helpful, but specifically upon the ability of the parents to nurture the child in a way that facilitates his development. There are enormous variations in the ability of mothers to provide reasonably adequate care, and except for the most severe neurotic, character, or sociopathic disorders, the assessment of adult personality alone is of little immediate value in coming to an opinion about the quality of a child's daily experiences and whether they promote or impede his development. I assume that there is no need to go further than to state that sensitive and skillful interviewing is an absolutely indispensible part of diagnosis.

In the evaluation of the infant himself, one begins with the total developmental picture, i.e., his growth, nutritional state, vegetative functions, and his developmental achievements. These developmental achievements may be expressed as quantitative and as qualitative capacities. Methods of study that include a detailed assessment of physical factors with all the means at our disposal, developmental testing, and the description of behavior under varying conditions are basic to the careful delineation of the developmental picture of the child. Decisions about etiology rely heavily on the assessment of the child's behavior combined with an equally careful evaluation of environmental influences.

There are various ways in which the child's development may be expressed. Levels of functioning as measured on one or more of the standardized infant tests are helpful and are often relied upon. Assessments of special aspects of development such as the child's cognitive development, his progress in the development of object permanence, for example, or DeCarie's objectal scale (1965) may be used to organize some of the observations. Lois Murphy's Vulnerability Inventory (Murphy, 1968) may be helpful in constructing a meaningful diagnostic picture of the child. The Hampstead Baby Profile (W. E. Freud, 1967) is another method which can be fruitfully utilized. Whatever method is chosen, the description of the infant should include (1) his physical growth and nutritional state, (2) the quantitative levels of functioning in those areas that can be quantified, and (3) careful descriptions of the infant's behavior not included in the testing proper. Among these observations, those of the child's play are often very revealing. Just as play provides an important avenue to the child's mind when he is slightly older, so it does in the first two years as well. The differences are developmental ones; the principle is the same.

In building up a dynamic developmental profile, we at Yale University have found it useful in many instances to organize the data from the above sources into the following categories: Activity-Inactivity; Perception; Cognitive Development; Affective Behavior and Development; Interaction with Toys; Interaction with People; Language; Coping Behavior and Reactions to Stress; Aggressive Behavior; Capacity to Delay; Self-Stimulating Behavior. Organized in this way the information gained forms the basis for further inferences about the state of psychic development and the pervasiveness of the pathogenic process.

Another method of collecting data that is helpful in arriving at a diagnosis is the observation of mother and infant together. As a centrally important aspect of data collection for research purposes the usefulness of this method is well established. While some have also used it in the diagnosis of clinical problems it has, to my mind, not been sufficiently applied in a systematic way. True, for the infant, especially under a year, it often forms an important part of the basis of reports of nurses, social workers, pediatricians and others who in their daily work visit homes to give child rearing advice. It has also been used in hospitals as an approach to both the diagnosis and the formulation of plans for helping the mothers of infants who fail to thrive. Leonard and Rhymes (1966a, 1966b), for example, have employed this method quite successfully in their work with such infants and mothers. Interviews with parents, of course, provide one important source of data for diagnosing the factors that have brought about a disturbance in development. However, important parts of the picture that may be missing, can be filled in when one sees the mother and the child together. A skillful observer who has an opportunity to see how a mother feeds, holds, bathes, communicates with and restrains her infant, how she provides stimulation or tones it down may derive important data, indispensable for the understanding of the genesis of a child's problem. At times the value of interviewing is limited by the fact that a mother may deliberately withhold some information about her relationship or care of the infant out of guilt and fear of disapproval. She may also unconsciously repress significant information.

One is impressed by the number of situations in which highly relevant aspects of maternal behavior cannot be reported by the mother because she is unaware of them; she has never perceived them. For instance, a mother may report quite accurately her child's behavior in a fight around feeding but may be totally unaware of how her own behavior during feeding incites him to do battle with her. It is also not unusual that complaints parents bring to the attention of the doctor or nurse or someone else are often only a small part of the picture. They may be the most dramatic or worrisome symptoms to the parents, but one will often have to look beyond this to arrive at a diagnosis that leads to an appropriate plan of treatment. Additional problems become visible when one observes mother and child together.

In trying to understand infantile disorders we are very much at the mercy of what we can make of the child's symptomatic behavior. Hopefully, as we have more frequent and earlier access to the infant with problems, prescriptions for treatment can increasingly be individualized and coordinated with formulations of the state of internal affairs in the child's psychic life. However, it should be acknowledged that, for needful infants, much that is therapeutic goes on largely unguided by prescriptions based either on general child development principles or on knowledge of a specific child. The foster mother who takes in an infant who has been neglected or abused and nurtures him is doing, she will say, "what comes naturally." Many other sensitive and skillful caregivers upon whom we call to provide a therapeutic environment for disturbed infants do so with minimal help—or need of help—from professionals. The fact that we count upon their availability does not diminish the need to understand more and to be able to individualize care, for there are infants who do not respond with the desired improvement and whose mothers or mother substitutes require specific prescriptions in order to provide the kind of help needed by the child.

THE THERAPEUTIC ENVIRONMENT

To be most effective, treatment plans should be based upon knowledge of a specific infant's current state of health and development. An evaluation of his environment, especially of the quality and quantity of the nurturing, and knowledge of antecedent experiences are particularly useful. A specific prescription aimed at alleviating his disorder, both symptomatically and fundamentally, should result from such a diagnosis. True, improvement often comes about when, relying upon general knowledge, we can bring about some modification of the infant's experience which shifts the balance from disease toward health. Sometimes, as we all know, improvement occurs for reasons we cannot identify. The drive toward survival and health that is a part of the biological heritage of most infants has saved the perplexed clinician and reassured the worried parent more than once. Nonetheless it is important that we strive toward greater precision in diagnosis and treatment and try to evaluate carefully the results—favorable or unfavorable—that ensue when we intervene. This then is a plea for precision in method, specificity in prescription, and meticulous record keeping in regard to results. While an outcome is not necessarily assured by the specificity of a prescription, it is through an accumulation of such experiences that we shall make progress in the treatment of early disorders.

In what follows, the therapeutic environment is conceptualized in a series of statements which attempt to condense much of what has been learned about the conditions for normal personality development in infancy. Psychoanalytic developmental psychology implicitly and explicitly acknowledges the importance of biological factors in both healthy development and illness, and the importance of the body to the development of the mind. At no time is there greater interdependence than during the earliest years of a child's life. Psychoanalytic propositions about the central importance of the child-object relations, the importance of his early experiences around the care of the body, the interaction of innate and experiential factors, the importance of the balance between comfort-discomfort, gratification-frustration experiences, the phase concept, the importance of antecedent experiences—all will be recognized. Further, the complexity of the determinants of maternal behavior, and ultimately of the child's development as well, is acknowledged.

Because of the unique importance of the human relationship in the child's development and because of the prolonged period of helplessness of the human infant, it appears that the most significant, and at the same time the most practical approach to discussing the therapeutic environment, is to speak of what the environment—mainly, the adults who give care—should provide. What are the necessary and sufficient conditions to promote development? What modifications of the plan or what special conditions must be created for the infant whose development is impaired because of adverse conditions or deficits in his care? Hopefully, formulating the material in terms of important environmental characteristics will lead us more directly to a discussion of individual prescriptions for specific children.[1] How much of what kind of experience should be provided to influence what kind of symptomatic behavior?

The Central Role of Object Relations in the Child's Development

The most urgent and continuing provision is for a nurturing adult who responds to the child's need for comfort, for relief of tension, for stimulation of various kinds, and for a social partner with whom emotional communication can be established. This acknowledges the central role of object relationships in determining the course of development. We assume that it is vitally important to many aspects of the infant's development that he form close relationships to one, or at most to a very small number, of specific care-givers; that in the absence of such relationships many aspects of his emotional and cognitive development will surely suffer; that his physical health and well-being may also be impaired. The most

[1] Some of this material is a modification of recommendations made in two previous publications (Provence 1967; 1968).

favorable conditions are likely to be created when the child's mother —biological or de facto—is or can be helped to be the person to whom the primary attachment can be made. As his development proceeds during the first year, he increasingly develops the capacity to accept care from and to establish meaningful relationships with others. Experiences with substitutes benefit him most when his relationships are firmly anchored in a tie to the maternal figure.

In some situations, however, this primary attachment to the mother cannot be or has not been accomplished, and the therapeutic plan must include assiduous attention to the creation for the child of conditions that foster the development of ties of trust and love between the infant and his nurturers. A plan that fails to acknowledge the importance of this relationship between infant and adult cannot qualify as therapeutic.

The Importance of Acknowledging Innate and Experiential Factors As Codeterminants of Development

This proposition might appear so obvious to those familiar with psychoanalytic thinking that it hardly seems necessary to repeat it. Yet, its application to the development of treatment plans has been insufficiently appreciated. Careful attention to what is innate and what is experiential, and especially their interrelationships, is of considerable significance if one expects to intervene effectively in those situations we label as problems of mother-child interaction. Obviously, infants who are born with frank defects in some aspect of the innate apparatus that serves the autonomous functions of the ego or some deviation in drive endowment will begin life with a vulnerability and a need for special conditions of care or experience. There are some who are permanently handicapped in cognitive or personality development because of more or less severe biological defects which cannot be overcome. These are usually not difficult to recognize. However, of more significance to our topic are those with less severe, often unrecognized biological deficits which make it difficult to make them comfortable or to anticipate how they will react to various components of care. For example, an increasing number of young children are diagnosed as having mild impairments of the central nervous system—structural or possibly biochemical—which interfere with selective aspects of perceptual, cognitive or synthetic mental activities, or with the development of impulse control. In infancy many of these children have disturbances in feeding or sleep. Activity may be heightened or diminished. They tend to tolerate frustration and other tension states less well than other babies. Their ego development often proceeds in an uneven manner, with some functions markedly in advance of others, a condition which predisposes the child to anxiety or other psychic stress beyond that usually expected. They are often experienced by their care-givers as quick to tears and difficult to satisfy. They may be difficult for even the most perceptive and skillful mother, and may present overwhelming problems to a less experienced or less mature or troubled mother.

In addition to the children with severe or mild biological deficits there are a far greater number whose congenital characteristics simply do not adapt well to the mother's style of mothering. If the usual mutual adaptation does not occur either from the infant's side or from the mother's side, trouble ensues. If it is more than a transient problem, disturbances in various aspects of development may occur. To give a simple example: most young infants, we say, should be held for feeding. Yet there are some who when held, squirm, startle, wriggle, cry, and lose the nipple repeatedly. Such infants can often feed not only more successfully but with much more evidence of satisfaction and pleasure in the experience when fed on a soft pillow. Imagine such an infant being the first born of an insecure, tense mother, and you have the makings of a problem in mutual adaptation which, if unsolved, may lead to long-standing difficulties. Other examples of the relevance of this factor will be found in the case material to be presented later.

Importance of the Affective Atmosphere

This refers to the need of an infant for contact with an adult who expresses interest through communication of feelings and in action. This may seem to be implied in the first recommendation, yet it is important enough to be singled out for emphasis. It is impossible to imagine that the variety of affective expressions we recognize in the child of three or four years could develop without experience with and the model of a similarly feeling adult. The affective atmosphere at a given time has much to do with how an infant acts, what he perceives, what he learns, and presumably how he feels. It makes a difference, for example, whether a care-giver tones up or tones down the stimuli in the environment through variations in the zest or energy (or conversely, the indifference) with which she presents them. We assume, moreover, that variations and shifts in psychic energy are reflected in the observable behavior of the infant in interactions with people, toys, and other aspects of his environment. One aspect of this concerns the amount and kind of psychic energy available for attention to and investment of transactions with people, for problem solving, for action, and for play.

Perhaps the most easily visualized of the common situations in which such psychic energy would appear to be unavailable, or at least not directed, is the apathetic behavior of the severely deprived infant or toddler. He may make minimal or, in extreme cases, no effort to initiate contact with another person or to play with toys, or even to solve problems that might help to satisfy his need for food or comfort. In many such children the underlying equipmental potentials for such actions have matured or developed but are not put to use; ego development is delayed or deviant. But remarkable changes can often be brought about, in a short time, when an interested adult, able to give to a child in a spontaneous animated way "energizes" him to attend and to act. The deliberate use of metaphor here accurately conveys the contrast between the apathetic, minimally interested infant who, after a few days may be actively, purposefully, and energetically directing himself toward people and other aspects of his environment. Care-givers are encouraged to stimulate such an apathetic infant in a variety of ways, e.g., through physical handling; through speaking to him about himself and what he is doing or looking at, or feeling. It is clearly possible to increase the child's level of interest and activity and ultimately his level of performance on a more sustained basis through such measures. We assume that such visible changes in external behavior are concomitant with heightened cathexis of the mental representations of persons, of his perceptions of the qualities of environmental stimuli, of his ideational processes, and of actions. Such transactions appear to assist the child in his awareness of himself, of other persons, and of things in his environment.

One of the practical advantages of utilizing the idea of the importance of variations in the affective atmosphere and the concept of cathexis is that even the least sophisticated care-giver—if she has some access to her own feelings—understands immediately when one speaks of the importance of presenting something to the child with animation or zest or at other times of toning down the intensity of communication. The importance of the "charge," the effects of differences in intensity upon the child's responses, are within the everyday experience of most care-givers and are accepted as common-sense aspects of the prescription.

The Importance of the Care of the Infant's Body

This has two major aspects. If the child's psychogenic disorder includes bodily symptoms such as failure to grow adequately, gastro-intestinal disorders, respiratory, skin or other somatic difficulties, it is essential that symptomatic treatment of these problems be instituted. Because children with such symptoms are usually identified by nurses and physicians in clinics and hospitals, it is rare that close attention to these problems is overlooked. The provision of an adequate diet and nutritional supplements, the treatment of illness, immunization against preventable diseases, provision of shelter and adequate clothing are implicit in the expectations of parents and the responsibility of the healing professions. However, there is another aspect of the care of the infant's body which is of major therapeutic importance: the meaning to the child of the adult's concern for the comfort and integrity of his body. As a factor in early infancy good care of the body affects the development of the body ego, including both the infant's progressive awareness of his body self and his ability to initiate actions which bring him into touch with people and things in his environment. The tactile and kinesthetic stimulations which are implicit in the experiences of being touched, held, lifted, cuddled, bathed, moved, etc., are of basic importance to these events. In addition, there is the communication of interest, tenderness, and protectiveness in the way his body is handled or held to produce comfort, supplemented by the pleasure and energizing effect of body contact which asks for a motor or social response from the child. Prohibition of activity by necessary restraint in protecting him from danger or greater pain are essential elements in his learning. There is really no effective substitute for the opportunities for communication provided by the interactions between child and adult that center around the care of his body. When care is given mechanically, without rich affective concomitants or is done without relation to the cues and responses from the infant, singularly important experiences are lost which can only partially be supplied through other experiences. Advice about the importance of the care of the body is usually not difficult for the mother or other care-giver to accept if the infant is very young or if he has specific somatic symptoms. However, they may need reminding of this when the need is less apparent. For example, a well-nourished two-year-old who appears independent and does not ask for, or actively rejects, the adult's attention to his body may not easily be recognized as needful. The isolation of many such children and the hidden hunger for such contact are realized when one sees the response to care and attention patiently and repeatedly offered.

The Importance of a Speaking Social Partner

It is not likely that language can develop adequately if the infant is not spoken to by an adult who is emotionally involved with him. The verbal communications of an adult to whom the infant is an important person is one of the vital experiences through which he learns. Information comes to him in this way, for example, about who he is, how he feels, how others feel about him, about things he encounters, and about what he is doing. One influence is exerted by the adult's responding to the child's babbling, from very early, with affectively charged verbalizations. The adult, in reinforcing and interpreting the infant's vocalizations, joins with intrinsic maturational forces, with the result that the infant's repertoire of sounds having specific meaning steadily increases.

It is also believed that the verbal communications of the adult, especially from the last quarter of the first year onward, provide important elements in the development, differentiation, and organization of the infant's inner world of thought, imagery and feeling. Interference in the development of the infant's speech in the absence of such adult communication is not difficult to recognize and is a frequent symptom in psychological disorders. Delays or confusion in the organization and development of thought are more difficult to discern, but can often be identified and appear to be favorably influenced by the verbal communications of an unconfused adult who is emotionally significant to the child.

The Importance of Consistency and Repetition
Punctuated by Variety and Contrast

Quality and timing of care received from the familiar adults are involved in producing such an atmosphere. Consistency and repetition in the child's experience help to create in him a physical and psychic state conducive to learning; that is, significant periods of time when he is free from major discomfort and excessive tension

and is able to give attention to people and things in his environment. Disturbed infants often have experienced too little consistency and continuity of care. If a child has had several "mothers"
either simultaneously or in rapid succession, or if his mother is
highly inconsistent in her behavior for any reason, the benefits
that come from consistency and continuity may be sadly lacking.
Infants and young children who live in disorganized chaotic house-
holds are often disturbed by the inconsistency of care that usually
characterizes such settings. Conversely, some infants, especially
those reared in group care settings with too few care-givers, often
experience excessive routinization, rigidity, and monotony in the
environment which tends to stifle the child's budding interests.
This routinization should not be confused with the continuity of
care represented by consistent care-givers.

Within the atmosphere of consistency and continuity, it is important, however, to introduce variety and contrast. Infants will
show interest in novel stimuli very early, a response which continues throughout life. Variety and contrast, it is believed, sharpen
perceptions and create in the child mild tension states that call
for an adaptive response. As long as a tension state is not so
massive as to be disorganizing or paralyzing, it can serve as a
stimulus to further development. This concept has its practical
applications in such things as the introduction of new people, new
activities, and variety in toys and plays experiences.

The Importance of Toys and Other Playthings

Toys provide a variety of stimuli, challenges, and satisfactions because of their structure, texture, color, configuration, and other
physical qualities. Thereby, they enhance perception and intellectual development. In recent years, many child psychologists have
been led, by their interest in the infant's cognitive development,
to study the ways in which toys can stimulate various aspects of
his budding intelligence. Early childhood educators have long been
aware of the role of toys and other materials in the education of
the nursery school age child. There is no doubt that such materials
can help to stimulate the infant's learning as well. Toys are also
important as objects upon which an infant can actively discharge
feelings of aggression or pleasure and excitement without evoking
a response. While a responsive partner is essential to the infant's
development, he also needs experience with materials and other
inanimate objects in which his independent actions and manipula-

tions allow him to discover causal relationships, qualities of matter, and his own capacities for exploitation, experimentation, and self-regulation. Play, both with toys and with people, adds an important dimension to the child's life. The importance of the mother's role in sponsoring the use of toys has been recognized. There are many examples of infants with normal endowment whose play with toys has not developed or becomes disturbed at some point. The severely deprived infant is well known, but there are others. The nine-month-old or the toddler who can find no pleasure in play and usually does not play unless it involves the mother, father, or another emotionally significant person is not rare. There are many infants whose parents for whatever reason have not created the atmosphere believed to be conducive to the use of toys and playthings. Its major ingredients are libidinal interest in the child and his behavior combined with the availability of toys, experiences in which adults invest these toys for the child, and with periods in which he is allowed to use them in his own way without competition.

The therapeutic environment for the deprived or disturbed infant or toddler includes introducing him to toys and creating an atmosphere in which he can make use of them in some of the ways indicated above.

The Importance of Exploration, Self-Initiated Activity and Solitude

Opportunities to move about, to play, and to utilize emerging skills in a supportive and safe atmosphere create a beneficial combination of freedom and protection which is increasingly important by the end of the first year in the child's development toward independence and self-determination. Opportunities to enter actively into the possibilities afforded by the surroundings influence the child's development of the sense of self as distinct from others. They are important also in enlarging his awareness of his environment since he now can actively seek new experiences. He can use his emerging skills to explore things more fully or to regulate, within certain limits, the amount of stimulation he wants. He needs, also, to be provided with quiet times when no demands are being placed upon him by the adult, and those that may be imposed by internal strivings or conflicts are at least not heightened by the environment. In our zeal to correct the deficits in his experience, to provide needed human and nonhuman stimulation, we should not forget that solitude can be beneficial and should not be confused with loneliness.

The Importance of Limits and Prohibitions
Appropriate to the Age of The Child

We most often deal with children who have experienced excessive tension and stress, when parental controls and education have either been too severe, highly inconsistent or discontinuous. However, we also recognize situations in which a young child's development is impeded because his environment has not encouraged and required of him the skills, controls, and adaptations of which he is capable, when he has, it might be said, encountered too little frustration. The normal process of education and socialization fosters tension and conflict within the child by requiring him to adjust to some of the expectations and demands of society. Experiences of tension, inner conflicts, and frustrations, it is recognized, are as essential to the development of the child as are the experiences of gratification and comfort referred to earlier (Hartmann, Kris, and Lowenstein, 1946).

The infant is born with the capacity to develop the ability to tolerate tension, to delay discharge of impulse, and to postpone gratification. These inhibitory mechanisms are a part of the infant's endowment, and their antecedents are seen from the early days onward. However, these capacities are influenced in very important ways by the learning process and, of course, by the parents as the child's first educators. They may be seriously impaired by what the child experiences at the hands of his care-givers. It should be emphasized that in infancy, at least, the necessary education and training of the child should take place in an atmosphere of loving attention. Two aspects are worth restating: First, the environment should provide appropriate limits and prohibitions in a supportive atmosphere. Second, the child himself brings a varying capacity—partly innate, partly learned—for self-regulation. Therapeutic plans must include experiences which enhance the child's ability to gradually establish controls over his own behavior with a reasonable degree of pride and self-esteem. In terms of timing for many of the children of two and under who come to our attention, the importance of this aspect of treatment becomes visible while the psychological nutriments referred to in the previous recommendations are being supplied. The infant who has been deprived, abused, neglected, or confused by parent figures may not reveal the incapacity for self-regulation until his delays in development are at least partially corrected. The child of whom little has been required and who may have been excessively gratified in one area may experience significant delays in intellectual development, speech, or the ability to play. While he may appear unusually impervious and controlling and have a much lower than normal capacity to tolerate tension or frustration, he may need a considerable period of judicious and considerate giving from the therapist before the controls, limits, and frustrations—also therapeutic —are added to the picture.

In the foregoing eight points, the "therapeutic environment" for infants has been outlined mainly descriptively. The following cases have been selected because they illustrate typical psychological disorders of the first two years. The therapeutic needs of the infants described will be apparent.

CASE ILLUSTRATIONS

Matthew

Matthew, age ten months, was referred to our hospital for diagnostic study because of rumination of four months duration and failure to gain weight for one month prior to admission. His parents had been concerned for two or three months that he had a serious physical illness, and his pediatrician had become worried when he failed to gain weight. As a very young infant he had been healthy, but somewhat hypertonic and jittery and given to spitting up a mouthful or two of formula after most feedings. His mother, though repelled by this, had managed to feed him adequately for about the first four months, and he had grown normally and seemed healthy. At about this time the mother's patience wore thin, anxiety and anger mounted, and feeding times became fraught with tension on both sides.

At the time of admission Matthew was a fair-skinned baby boy with scanty, wispy, blonde hair and large brown eyes with which he continuously scanned his surroundings, looking prolongedly into the faces of the adults who came into his room. Thorough physical evaluation revealed, besides a slightly below average weight, only a mild nutritional anemia. He ate willingly enough when the nurses fed him, but could usually be counted on to regurgitate, with the classical tongue and mouth movements of a ruminator, when they left him. His play with toys was desultory. He sucked his thumb and played with his hands and feet. He sat alone with good trunk control, but made no effort to creep or crawl. Interviews with the mother, besides eliciting the information given above, resulted in the opinion that she was, in many ways, a devoted mother in her attitudes and behavior, but the particular symptom chosen by Matthew was one she found especially disturbing. It was decided to give her a few days of relief from feeding and taking care of Matthew, so we encouraged her to visit and to be with him in whatever way seemed comfortable, but not to feel responsible for his care. Matthew obviously recognized his mother, was relieved to see her, though he often whined in a dissatisfied way when she was with him and usually vomited when she left the room. Meanwhile, the nurses and other staff carried Matthew up and down the halls when they could or pushed him in a walker. He obviously enjoyed this, and became more active, animated, and playful. On about the sixth day of his hospitalization, responding to what we knew at that point about his tendency to vomit when people left him, I suggested to the staff that they help Matthew learn to creep, which he seemed close to doing. Their enthusiasm for his efforts and his willingness to tackle a small space between himself and a favored adult, culminated in his ability to creep on all fours after another three days. Concomitant with his mastery of creeping, the vomiting disappeared. Along with this, most of the unhappy tension between mother and child was replaced by more mutually satisfying experiences. He began to gain weight normally and concern about his physical health vanished. He left the hospital after two weeks, free of his chief complaint.

EVALUATION   Obviously, one cannot say that they all lived happily ever after, but a major disturbance had been alleviated and the prospects for a vastly improved situation between mother and child seemed good. The most significant therapeutic elements were the exclusion of some life-threatening or disabling physical disease; the understanding and empathy for the mother; the period of respite for both of them from the heightened feelings around feeding; the provision of interested nurses, willing to involve themselves personally as substitute care-givers without having to compete with the mother for the child's favors; the stimulation to play with toys and to have opportunities for untroubled contact with care-giving adults. I believe that the infant's mastery of creeping was both an evidence of general improvement and an indication of a healthier adaptation. It gave him a better way to cope with the threat of the mother's disappearance; he could now control the distance between them by creeping after her when he wished or experimenting with excursions away from her.

The virtual disappearance of the vomiting, concomitant with the mastery of creeping, was a happy event which greatly facilitated the mother's recovery from her own traumatic experience. Symptomatic improvement of the child is at times essential before parents can use help and participate in a therapeutic plan.

Ann

Ann, an infant in the Yale longitudinal study mentioned earlier, was deprived early, by her depressed mother, of many gratifying experiences, especially around feeding. The mother's problem in giving to the child, her need to be given to, and her sadistic tendencies resulted in a noxious combination of neglect, screaming at the child, and spanking her when she cried.

The child's problem was first apparent at age four months on a routine developmental examination, done as part of her regular monthly visit to the center. A decrease in vocalization, a lessening of voluntary motor activity, and a slightly diminished interest in toys were the first signs. Shortly later there was a deceleration in physical growth followed by a slowing in all sectors of development measured by the developmental tests. Language development showed the greatest delay. By age nine months she was a small infant who slept long hours at night, had an anxious, vigilant expression when awake, cried at the slightest disappointment or frustration, and was not playful. The mother could not accept our recommendation that she herself receive psychotherapy; this, she said was for people who could not handle their own problems. Nor could she accept the idea that she work part time at the profession which she had previously enjoyed and have the baby cared for by a regular sitter. Her conviction was, "Mothers should take care of their own children." Still, a few things helped her: she enjoyed the weekly visits to the pediatrician which were instituted to help her with child care. She seemed to benefit from the interest of and support of a new social worker who joined the staff when the child was a year old. Visits with her sister-in-law who lived in a nearby town always made her feel better, and in her presence she was more reasonable in her demands upon Ann.

When her husband's busy schedule lightened, her mood improved and the spanking episodes and scolding were less frequent. Fortunately also, when Ann was in her second year and her mother could formally begin to teach her to talk and to name objects, she was more satisfied with the child. Ann, in her second year, made a remarkable adaptation to the mother. She learned how to get along with her by becoming compliant and "good," no doubt enhancing the relationship, but at the expense of some other aspects of her development.

EVALUATION   The reason for this brief sketch of Ann, condensed from a very large amount of data, is to illustrate that her disturbance was visible quite early, and that in spite of our concern we did not develop the most effective therapeutic plan. Mrs. M. we believe in retrospect, might have responded had we made a plan to ask her to come in to our center with Ann an hour or two several times a week. It would have given her another contact which she needed, and we could have assumed some of the care of Ann in a way that she could have permitted. A nurse or an experienced mother could, we believe, have helped Mrs. M. very much in this way. We had psychotherapists we could not use because Mrs. M. rejected the idea, but our setup did not include a person who might have provided care to the child in a way that was supportive of the mother. Moreover we made an error in not making more effort to involve the father both in the care of the child and, by his presence, in alleviating his wife's loneliness. While there was the reality of his strenuous work schedule, there was some evidence that he could have been more helpful to his wife and child had we emphasized their need for nurturance from him. This leads me to what I believe is a very important point: A variety of services are needed in assisting young mothers with child rearing, and very few are available.

Cindy

An affluent young couple with two older children conceived a third child as a replacement for a lost parent. The mother, an attractive, intelligent, articulate young woman who felt unloved and unlovely during her pregnancy, could hardly wait to get back to her pre-pregnancy way of life and could not mobilize interest in her infant daughter. She employed, in succession, three live-in care-givers during the first year, one of whom was around long enough to become emotionally significant to Cindy, before she left. Cindy was seen in our clinic at sixteen months of age because of delayed speech and motor development of several months duration, resulting in her parents' and pediatrician's fear that she might be mentally retarded. The parents, quite interested and involved in the lives of their older children, were shocked at our diagnosis of delayed motor, emotional, and intellectual development due to deficits in her experience and expressed the wish to exert every effort to help her. Belatedly, it appeared, they had taken note of her presence in the family.

With the expert help of a member of our social work staff, Mrs. H. was able to work on some of her own problems and to become more involved with Cindy in an appropriate way. Cindy's responses to her mother's efforts and to her father's participation in her care, along with suggestions from us about appropriate experiences, encouraged the parents. Improvement continued, and when Cindy was three years of age, additional help was arranged through a good nursery school experience. At age five years, she did not look retarded, and was obviously attached to her parents and siblings, but not in a deep way. She was, to our minds, somewhat pallid rather than robust in her general behavior, and we questioned how healthy she really was psychologically. However, there were no overt symptoms of disturbance, and her parents were quite satisfied with her.

EVALUATION   My impression that Cindy, as an adult, will not have the qualities of motherliness needed to nurture her own young children, may be an unjustified assumption. But one wonders how she might now look if the signs of delayed development visible in the first year had been heeded earlier. If her mother could not then have been helped to be immediately nurturing, could she have provided a more constant substitute, for example? The experience of repeated loss of the care-giving person could not be overcome entirely, and is unfortunately a very common phenomenon. The many young children who go from one foster home to another because our society has not provided a better solution are subjected to repeated trauma of this kind.

Elsa

Elsa, age twenty-one months, and her parents were referred to our clinic for evaluation and counseling by their physician in a city from which they had recently moved. In a series of contacts we learned that Elsa had been a difficult baby to take care of from the beginning. In the newborn nursery her mother had recognized her shrill, piercing cry as distinct from all others, and as she recalled the first year, she said it felt as if Elsa had cried almost continuously. Although she was free of illness, she was difficult to comfort, often irritable and not at all a satisfying infant to the mother who felt helpless, concerned about herself as a mother, and angry at the infant for inducing these feelings. The crying had lessened appreciably at about a year, but the parents came to us because they were concerned about Elsa's delayed speech and what they called "her shyness." She would often play in her room when she and her mother were home alone, but she would not leave her mother's side when they visited or were out of doors in the apartment house play yard with other young children and mothers. Her parents shared a picture of Elsa as a child who at times could be a charming, gratifying companion, but was often "whiney," hard to please, and easily frustrated.

When we first saw Elsa, her passivity and anxiety were conspicuous. Over a few play and test sessions it was possible to understand that if one could create conditions of comfort and provide toys, Elsa could be energized to play and to interact without undue anxiety. It was possible to exclude organic factors as contributing to the problem. From a rather large amount of information gained from Elsa's insightful if troubled mother and from seeing Elsa, it seemed plausible to us, to formulate the problem as follows: Elsa, as a neonate and young infant, was a baby who suffered, more than most, from internal distress and heightened organismic tension, possibly also from external stimuli. We reasoned that she would not have been easy for any mother. For her own mother, who was far away from relatives who might have been helpful, who was disappointed that her first child was not a boy, who felt inept and unfulfilled as a mother, Elsa was impossible. Regrettably, in the several places they lived during the first year, there was no physician, nurse, or wise neighbor who could help this young mother with child care and aid her in establishing a more comfortable relationship with her baby. Her husband, feeling equally helpless, reacted by participating minimally in the care of the child and tried, for as long as possible, to avoid acknowledging that a problem existed.

The story of Elsa has a happy outcome, for both she and the parents were ready for help. We arranged that one of our nursery school teachers would see Elsa individually. She was a gentle, sensitive young woman, able to understand and go slowly with such an anxious, fragile child. At first the mother was in the room with Elsa and her teacher, but after six to eight sessions she was able to leave and join the social worker in a nearby office for her own appointments. While she worked to some extent on her feelings and problems, she did not wish to look closely at them. Further, while she eagerly sought help for Elsa and wanted the child to change, it was not easy for her to allow the teacher and Elsa to establish a relationship. Gradually, however, as the child became more active, more verbal, less uneasy, more competent, better able to cope with frustration and stress, the experiences of satisfaction and pleasure between parents and child increased. The balance had been shifted in the relationship, to a predominance of interactions that supported Elsa's development.

EVALUATION   By the time she was three, Elsa, still appearing as a sensitive, somewhat anxious child, was able to cope with and benefit from a regular nursery school program. Her increasingly apparent high intelligence became both a pleasure to her parents and a source of strength and satisfaction in her own economy. In every way she appeared more robust, much more trusting of her parents and others, increasingly resilient in coping with stress, and possessed of a larger repertoire of useful modes of adaptation.

Michael

Michael, age eighteen months, was examined because of an intractable sleep problem that had finally exhausted his indulgent mother and had led his father to insist that something be done. He was the youngest of four children, the oldest of whom was in psychotherapy because of a school learning problem. Michael's mother sought help with the sleep problem only because her husband insisted. During the process of evaluation, it became clear that she was struggling with her feelings of disappointment that she could not have more children—a strong medical recommendation she was sensible enough to accept for reasons of her own health. She was aware to some extent that she infantilized Michael but seemed unable to acknowledge the degree to which she did so. He was the kind of child who is not easy to test. He chose the few things he would utilize, was adamant in his refusals, imperious in his demands, and raised the roof if the adults were at all out of harmony with his wishes. He could not be appealed to by the usual pegboards, formboards, blocks, and simple games usually attractive to children of his age. Equally significant was the meagerness of his play. He seemed bound to his mother's possessions or to her body as his "plaything."

EVALUATION   I felt that the sleep difficulty was only one part of a pervasive interference with development, induced by the mother's indulgence and the intensity of her appeal to him for a relationship that excluded others and, indeed, allowed for few activities apart from direct involvement with her. She accepted some suggestions about the sleep problem which alleviated it sufficiently that her husband no longer complained. But she could not accept my offer for help with other areas, and clearly thought I was overconcerned about this emotional and cognitive development. While she could, to some extent, recognize that he was babyish and uncontrolled, it was clear that her pleasure in his behavior and her need to keep him close to her prevented her from participating in a treatment plan.

THE THERAPEUTIC PROGRAM

The setting in which treatment of infants is carried out and the people who most often act as therapists warrant a little more attention. The threapeutic program may be instituted in the child's own home, in a hospital ward, in a group residential institution, or in a foster home. These settings may be supplemented by the use of day care services, therapeutic groups, or individual visits to the therapist's office or agency. A small group home or a professional foster home in which the infant's responses to carefully documented therapeutic efforts can be noted is a valuable resource and is usually preferable to observation in the hospital, once the necessary physical diagnostic studies have been done. Such a period of observation of the first phase of treatment can be quite effective in further clarifying the role of some of the many complex factors that often exist. In some hospitals, wards have been modified to permit parents to room in, and efforts have been made to provide carefully selected personnel, playrooms, yards and other resources which make it possible to create a psychologically therapeutic milieu for child and parent.

The infants' therapists are usually, but not exclusively, female.

The child's own father, a foster father, or an older boy can provide important therapeutic experiences not only through the traditionally recognized provision of psychological support to the mother, but through participating directly in the care of the child as an emotionally significant object. More should be done to involve fathers or father substitutes in such plans. Still, the large majority of infants' therapists will continue to be the mothers, mother substitutes, nurses, social workers, nursery school teachers, and paraprofessional care-givers who are affiliated with clinics, hospitals, day care settings, welfare departments and other agencies which give service to families and to infants. They most often look to pediatricians, child psychiatrists, and clinical and developmental psychologists for assistance in understanding the infant with a severe problem. Such consultants vary widely in their ability to provide adequate leadership.

The psychoanalyst, especially the child analyst, is likely to become involved with problems of the very young occasionally in a private practice, but more often in his role as consultant to agencies, as an investigator, or as a teacher of other professionals. He is increasingly aware of the thousands of badly nurtured, deprived, traumatized infants whose plight has been accurately and eloquently described in the Report of the Joint Commission on Mental Health of Children (1969; 1970). Many concerned citizens and professionals, including psychoanalysts, participated in its preparation. The absence of a unified national commitment to children, reflected by insufficient and fragmented services delivered to only a few of those in need, by poverty and racism, by the discrepancies between knowledge and practice, and by the failure to establish and protect basic rights for all children is made clear. The psychoanalyst of the 1970s who is concerned with the treatment of infants will inevitably be drawn into a larger arena, where he will be asked to participate, not only in planning for the treatment of individual infants, but also in influencing society's institutions and attitudes.

REFERENCES

Benjamin, J. D. Some developmental observations relating to the theory of anxiety. *Journal of the American Psychoanalytic Association*, 9, 1961a, 652–668.

Benjamin, J. D. The innate and the experiential in development. In

H. W. Brosin (Ed.), *Lectures in experimental psychiatry*. Pittsburgh: University of Pittsburgh Press, 1961b. Pp. 19–42.

Benjamin, J. D. Further comments on some developmental aspects of anxiety. In H. S. Gaskill (Ed.), *Counterpoint: Libidinal object and subject*. New York: International Universities Press, 1963. Pp. 121–153.

Bibring, G. L.; Dwyer, T. F.; Huntington, D. S.; and Valenstein, A. F. A study of psychological processes in pregnancy and of the earliest mother-child relationships. *Psychoanalytic Study of the Child*, 1961. **16**, 9–72.

Brazelton, T. Berry. *Infants and mothers*. New York: Delacorte Press, 1969.

Brody, S. *Patterns of mothering*. New York: International Universities Press, 1956.

Chandler,C.A.; Lourie, R. S.; and Peters, A. D. In Laura L. Dittman (Ed), *Early child care: The new perspectives*. New York: Atherton Press, 1968.

Coleman, R. W.; Kris, E.; and Provence, S. The study of variations of early parental attitudes. *Psychoanalytic Study of the Child*. 1953, **8**, 20–47.

DeCarie, T. *Intelligence and affectivity in early childhood*. New York: International Universities Press, 1965.

Escalona, S. K. Emotional development in the first year of life. In M. J. E. Senn (Ed.), *Problems of infancy and childhood*, New York; Josiah Macy, Jr. Foundation, 1953.

Escalona, S. K. *The roots of individuality*. Chicago: Aldine, 1968.

Fraiberg, S. Parallel and divergent patterns in blind and sighted infants. *Psychoanalytic Study of the Child*. 1968, **23**, 264–300.

Fraiberg, S.; Siegel, B. L.; and Gibson, R. The role of sound in the search behavior of a blind infant. *Psychoanalytic Study of the Child*. 1966, **21**, 327–357.

Freud, A. In H. Witmer (Ed.), *On rearing infants and young children in institutions*. Children's Bureau Research Report No. 1, 49–55. Washington, D.C.: U.S. Government Printing Office, 1967.

Freud, A. and Burlingham, D. *Infants without families*. New York: International Universities Press, 1944.

Freud, W. E. Assessment of early infancy: problems and considerations. *Psychoanalytic Study of the Child*, 1967, **22**, 216–238.

Fries, M. E. and Woolf, P. J. Some hypotheses on the role of the congenital activity type in personality development. *Psychoanalytic Study of the Child,*, 1953, **8**, 48–62.

Hartmann, H.; Kris, E.; and Lowenstein, R. M. Comments on the formation of psychic structure. *Psychoanalytic Study of the Child*, 1946, **2**, 11–38.

Hartmann, H. Psychoanalysis and developmental psychology. *Psychoanalytic Study of the Child*, 1950, **5**, 7–17.

Jackson, E. B. and Klatskin, E. H. Rooming-in research project. Development of methodology of parent-child relationship study in a clinical setting. *Psychoanalytic Study of the Child*, 1950, **5**, 236–274.

Kris, E. Notes on the development and on some current problems of psychoanalytic child psychology. *Psychoanalytic Study of the Child*, 1950, **5**, 24–45.

Kris, E. Neutralization and sublimation: observations in young children. *Psychoanalytic Study of the Child*, 1955, **10**, 30–47.

Kris, M. The use of prediction in a longitudinal study. *Psychoanalytic Study of the Child*, 1957, **12**, 175–189.

Leonard J. Rhymes, J. and Solnit, A. J. Failure to thrive in infants. *American Journal of the Diseases of Children*, June 1966, 3, 600–612.

Lustman, S. L. Rudiments of the ego. *Psychoanalytic Study of the Child*, 1956, **11**, 89–98.

Mahler, M. S. On the significance of the normal separation-individuation phase. In M. Schur (Ed.), *Drives, affects, behavior*. Vol. 2. New York: International Universities Press, 1965.

Mahler, M. S. On human symbiosis and the vicissitudes of individuation. Vol. 1. *Infantile psychosis*. New York: International Universities Press, 1968.

Murphy, Lois. Assessment of infants and young children. In C. Chandler; R. S. Lourie; and A. Peters. In L. Dittman (Ed), *Early child care: the new perspectives*. New York: Atherton Press, 1968, Pp. 107–138.

Nagera, H. *Early childhood disturbances, the infantile neurosis, and the adulthood disturbances: Problems of a developmental psychoanalytic psychology*. New York: International Universities Press, 1966.

Neubauer, P. B. *Children in collectives: child rearing aims and practices in the Kibbutz*. Springfield, Illinois: Thomas, 1965.

Provence, S. *Guide for the care of infants in groups*. New York: Child Welfare League of America, 1967. Pp. 88–99.

Provence, S. The first year of life in C. Chandler; R. S. Lourie; and A. Peters. In L. Dittman (Ed), *Early Child Care: the new perspectives*. New York: Atherton Press, 1968. Pp. 27–39.

Prugh, D. Toward an understanding of psychosomatic concepts in relation to illness in children. In A. J. Solnit, and S. Provence (Eds.), *Modern perspectives in child development*. New York: International Universities Press, 1963. Pp. 246–367.

Report of the Joint Commission on Mental Health of Children. *Crisis in child mental health: challenge for the 1970's*. New York: Harper & Row, 1969, 1970.

Rhymes, J. Working with mothers and babies who fail to thrive. *American Journal of Nursing*, 1966, **66**, 9, 1972–1976.

Richmond, J. B. and Lipton, E. L. Some aspects of the neurophysiology of the newborn and their implications for child development. In

L. Jessner and E. Pavenstedt (Eds.), *Dynamic psychopathology in childhood*. New York: Grune & Stratton, 1959.

Ritvo, S. and Solnit, A. J.   Influences of early mother-child interaction on identification processes. *Psychoanalytic Study of the Child*, 1958, 13, 64–85.

Sander, L. W.   Issues in early mother-child interaction. *Journal of the American Academy of Child Psychiatry*, 1962, 7, 1, 141–165.

Wolf, K.   Observations on individual tendencies in the first year of life. In M. J. E. Senn (Ed.), *Problems of infancy and childhood*. New York: The Josiah Macy Jr. Foundation, 1953.

Wolff, P. H.   The causes, controls and organization of behavior in the neonate. *Psychological Issues*, vol. 5, no. 1, Monograph 17, 1966.

6

PETER B. NEUBAUER

Psychoanalysis of the Preschool Child

C hild analysis is by now a well-established discipline, and there has been considerable experience in the analysis of the prelatency child. There are a number of major differences between child and adult analysis; it may be useful first to review these and to show their relevance to treatment during the first years of life.

There is, to begin with, the absence, in child analysis, of any evolvement of a transference neurosis. As a result of the child's dependency on the primary object—the parent—full transfer of the central conflicts onto the analyst is usually not observable. There are some writers who have felt that one can occasionally see a transference neurosis in children and that, therefore, this difference is not without its exceptions. One can assume that the prelatency child is even more dependent on the parents, and thus we shall see even less clearly transference phenomena and transference neuroses.

If neurosis is defined as a pathology that stems from unresolved Oedipal conflicts, one may even question whether one could ever find in prelatency a crystalized, full neurosis. It is clear that one can often find neurotic symptomatology: established fixation points at the phallic-Oedipal level of development; phobias and a variety of pre-Oedipal deviations, such as obsessive-compulsive symptom formation, psychosomatic disorders, and so forth. At the same time, full internalization and stable character formation emerge only as a consequence of the pressure of the Oedipal conflict, which is in turn due to increased superego participation.

A minimal requirement for transference experience is the child's previous achievement of a sufficient degree of object differentiation. In Mahler's terms, separation-individuation has to have taken place in order for object representation to be attained and for its transfer to a new person to be possible. Thus the transference phenomena, and with them the usual psychoanalytic situation, will not be able to occur with children in treatment who are still in the symbiotic relationship, or with those who have been unable to achieve a sufficient object constancy to have an interchangeable relationship with any available object.

Another difference between adult and child analysis is the absence of suffering on the part of the child—at least to the point at which the child will ask for help. It is the parents, therefore, who have to bring the child for treatment, whereupon the analyst is confronted with the task of slowly drawing his patient into the treatment process, in spite of the fact that the patient is not seeking help for himself. Again, this is a point that is of even greater significance in the treatment of the prelatency child. Here too there are exceptions, for one can find children who do express their complaints very early, and who do ask for help. A five-year-old boy stated, at his first interview with me, that he "is afraid of his bad feelings," and that he "doesn't know why he has them." At a later moment during that same appointment, he spoke of the "bad man who wants to destroy" all of his toys and possessions. Then, looking straight at me, he asked, "How can you help me with this?" and requested detailed answers.

These few introductory remarks are designed to show that child analysis addresses itself to complex problems, with many individual variations. In order to follow clinical procedure, it may be advisable to discuss this topic by reviewing: (1) indications for child analysis during prelatency, (2) technical considerations, and (3) termination.

INDICATIONS FOR ANALYTIC TREATMENT

At times it is not very difficult to find indications for psychoanalysis as the treatment of choice for the prelatency child. The criteria are the usual ones: a diagnosis that implies the existence of internalized conflicts; the capacity of the child for some degree of verbal expression; the minimal participation of the parents in the treatment plan, and their ability to accept an improvement in the child's development. We may add here that, for this age group, we must have some evidence that the child is able to establish an object relationship and a transference experience. As has been mentioned before, one can see children of preschool age who show an already developed obsessive-compulsive neurosis, or quite fully established phobic manifestations. We may see characterological disorders that are based on pregenital fixations, as well as many other personality disorders that give clear indications for psychoanalytic therapy. One may here apply the measure that, when the disorders interfere more seriously with the further development of the child, the *need* for treatment is established thereby; but it is the level of fixation and the degree of internalization of conflicts that will decide the *choice* of treatment.

There are many other cases in which it is not easy to arrive at a clear decision on these questions. In order to achieve some degree of certainty as to the meaning of a symptom or of a personality deviation, one very often needs to have a longitudinal view; only then is it possible to decide on the degree of interference with development. Often children adapt to an abnormal environment by showing abnormal characteristics that are appropriate to the conditions of their lives. These may be only reactive—they may change as soon as the child has been exposed to a new environment. Today, this can be tested when the child enters nursery school, and the impact of new influences can be used to determine whether the child's problems are reactive or only transitional in nature. The term "transitional" here refers to those problems that appear to be phase-specific and which will disappear as soon as a new stage in development has been reached.

Early development is characterized by continual changes of the internal psychic forces, marked by the appearance and disappearance of symptoms, as well as by innumerable variations of problems and conflicts that can be in continuous interaction. One has to add to this picture a variation, based on the individual developmental style, that may be at times significantly different from the model of normal development. There may be delay or accelerated development; or there may be uneven development in various areas of ego function. There may be an imbalance between drive, ego, and superego influences. Some children may go through the stages showing distinct differences in each stage; in others, we may see a great deal of overlapping of phases. These different modalities will influence the role of the symptom and the points of fixation.

An assessment of samples of children in the community, a nonclinical population, indicates that up to 30 percent of the children show signs of emotional disorders. In a study of children in a community nursery school, undertaken by the Child Development Center, we found about 30 percent of these children suffering from more serious interference with development, while another 30 percent showed various forms of conflicts and symptoms, though at the same time remaining able to maintain their development. These latter children present a more difficult problem regarding indication for treatment. If they were to come into our clinics, there might be some professionals who would prefer to wait— that is, until further development of the child made the decision for us. On the other hand, there might be some who would consider early treatment an appropriate prevention, and, depending on the other criteria for indication of psychoanalysis, would take these children into treatment. Thus, there does exist an area in which a clear decision cannot be made, and there may not, therefore, be full agreement as to indication and choice of treatment.

When one searches out indications for treatment by child analysis, one has to include an assessment of the parental attitude toward treatment. As has been mentioned, very often the child does not suffer overtly from his disorder, or, if he does express discomfort, that expression is often not connected with any desire to explore the problem. The child may be more inclined to expect that the outside world will be able somehow to relieve his symptom and restore his lost happiness. The younger the child, the greater this dependency on the outside world will be, it is therefore particularly significant for the prelatency age.

The treatment decision thus has to rest on the understanding of the parents, and on their readiness to bring the child for treatment, as well as to sustain the treatment program. At times, it may be comparatively easy to assess the developmental conflicts of the child; but in the initial interviews, one may not obtain sufficient information to be able to assess the parental attitude well enough to feel sure of their relationship to the treatment. In order to do this, one would need to explore the family dynamics, i.e., the interlocking of the health and pathology of every member of the family. One has to be able to evaluate the capacity of the parents to permit changes in the child—particularly such improvement that may, at times, interfere with the parents' unconscious wishes.

However complicated may be the interaction system within the family, one would at least like to know whether there is sufficient assistance to the treatment to ensure regularity in the keeping of appointments. Aspects of the family constellations may be substantially changed by the mere fact that the child is brought four or five times a week for treatment, or by the effort required to arrange schedules, or by having to make financial resources available to cover the child's treatment. Other children in the family, for example, may come to feel less privileged. Indeed, at times there may be a certain neglect of the other children, and reactions may set in during the treatment that will have to be recognized if we wish to avoid their negative influence. These factors will also have to be evaluated as part of the indications for treatment. There is no doubt that they will have a continuous effect on the course of treatment; furthermore, they may prove to be factors in the termination of treatment.

Frequency of Appointments

One part of the determination of choice of treatment is obviously connected with the question of the frequency of therapeutic sessions. There has been a general exposure to psychoanalytic psychology, as well as to certain aspects of psychoanalytic treatment technique. The contributions of psychoanalysis to casework, to psychiatric procedures, and to various forms of psychotherapy have made it possible for many to apply psychoanalytic thinking in their treatment of their patients or clients, whether these are seen quite infrequently or a few times every week. Thus, there have been some who feel that the distinction between analysis and psychotherapy has become blurred and is now often only an academic question. In recognition of the resistances of some parents, or of their financial limitations, the therapist at times makes an adjustment that consists of reducing the frequency of treatment.

There is a developing tendency to apply this same practice to children, and more often to the prelatency child. If the therapist is not convinced that analysis is the treatment of choice, and that frequent analytic sessions are necessary, he will very often find that there are only a few children "available" for psychoanalysis. It is interesting to note that when the conviction for analysis is strong, one will more often see children in analysis than in therapy. Those who have established at least four sessions a week as the minimal requirement for the analysis of children have done so because they have recognized the significant difference between psychotherapy and analysis. There is not only a quantitative difference (of frequency), but along with that there is a different approach to the child which makes possible a much more careful view of the intrapsychic forces at work and a more careful application of those interventions that at any given time will have the greatest influence on the treatment process.

Language of the Child

There is one aspect of the psychoanalysis of prelatency children that needs to be emphasized. It has to do with the language of the child, or, better, with the form of communication during this period. Language development has not at this point fully acquired a logic that is based on concepts, abstractions, and causality, operable from latency on. The time sense, and even the concept of time, has not yet been established. Thus, we often get verbal statements that resemble primary-process thinking. Free association is necessary for the analysis of adults; but children are not able to "free associate," to permit thoughts and feelings to follow one another. Nevertheless, they do bring memories and connections as one part of their experiences belonging to various past experiences.

Furthermore, children at this age will often seize on words that they have just acquired and use them in the context of their earliest experiences. These words may therefore have meanings very different from the ones that are generally attributed to them. This is particularly true of children who are exposed too early to a wide vocabulary, to abstraction, and to concepts that are, in fact, beyond their mental grasp. It is important to remain alert to the need for exploring the "meaning" that the child has given to various words. Similarly, the therapist has to learn to express himself in such a way that the child can grasp his meaning, at the level of his own development and experience. It is this mixture of concreteness of the child's memories with condensation, of screen memories with wish fulfillment, that makes communication between child and analyst different. It requires that the analyst learn about the child's language, and that he be sufficiently flexible to "tune in" to the feeling, tone, and early forms of his expression.

The "language" of the child cannot be limited to his verbal statements; it must also include both nonverbal and preverbal communication and expressions. All these components are even more operative at an early age than they are in latency.

Nonverbal forms are seen in the child's gestures, his posture, and in his activity pattern as observed in play. The therapist has to learn to differentiate between language that is *meant to be* a form of communication, and behavior that can be observed and then *given meaning* by the observer. This difference will have an effect on the technique of treatment.

In order to read this nonverbal language, one has to become an observer during the analytic process. It is not enough to listen; one has also to observe the Gestalt of body expression, the pattern of movement, and the style of the gestures. As the therapist takes note of the totality of the situation, he will also perforce increase his self-observation, taking note of where he located himself in the room in relation to the patient, of how he himself acted in the play, and so forth, aside from his verbal interventions or responses. The arrangement of the treatment room, therefore, has to be considered: How close are the chairs? How much space is there for running? Is the material in reach, or does the young patient have to turn to the therapist for help? Relationships are therefore created with a much longer activity interplay than with older children or adults.

The ability to learn *this* language is based on training and experience.

Preverbal expressions are of a different nature. Here, what is to be observed are earlier modalities of feelings and function that stem from the psychic organization of the preverbal phase of life, These may be sounds or body postures; gestures, or a way of looking; or an expression of affect that seems to indicate a regression to this earlier stage.

Therapeutic Alliance

One of the initial tasks in the analysis is the establishment of the therapeutic alliance, or a working relationship that will permit the therapeutic process to occur. There are many variations in this alliance, and therefore many techniques of achieving it in pursuit of the treatment aim. The term "alliance" indicates that one is here referring to a complex *dynamic interplay* between patient and analyst. This has to do with the child's relationship to his problems, his wish for help, the analyst as a person, the patient's ego functions, as well as with the analyst's "alliance."

The prelatency child will often bring specific features to this beginning phase of treatment that will make the establishment of the therapeutic alliance a rather complex undertaking. The child's dependency on the parent, his limited insight and self-observation, and his wishful thinking are among the characteristics that make this stage difficult. "A great amount of work is needed to arrive at a point where the child is able to face the fact that the disturbance and suffering in his life are created within him, and not in the external world only." This statement by Frankl and Hellman (1962), who have proposed various considerations and explorations of the therapeutic alliance, stresses the fact that these factors —externalization and projection by the child—must be recognized and modified in order to establish an alliance.

The therapeutic alliance must be differentiated from the educational phase and the transference aspect of the child-analyst relationship. The need to educate the child toward the therapeutic process implies that a child has to "learn" about the setting, to be made acquainted with the "basic rules," and to be taught to recognize feelings. Here one addresses oneself not only to those ego aspects that will respond to examples, to encouragement, but also to forms of expression that the child has either never learned or is, for one reason or another, unable to bring into this situation. It may be actually the first time that the child is meeting an adult who is willing to listen, who has the patience to wait, or who permits the child to follow his own thoughts and feelings—in short, someone who does not give him directions, as he has known that experience from his home or nursery school.

One must be aware of the possibilities that one may be seeing a child who is responding, above all, to this newness in the situation and that what one is observing is therefore not the child's own "pattern." The younger the child, and the more inexperienced he is, the stronger may be his initial reaction to the therapeutic situation. This reaction will then become linked with his response to a new and very different object—the analyst. The evolvement of the transference aspects in this relationship has its significance for the therapeutic work, and is often possible only because the therapeutic alliance has taken place. It is this alliance that permits the treatment to continue, whether the transference is negative or positive in nature. The achievement of a therapeutic alliance, then, has these two components: forming a relationship, and making it work for the therapeutic aim.

There are children who need treatment yet are not able to separate from the mother, who therefore has to be present in the treatment room. Her presence has obvious implications for the beginning phase of treatment. To untie the child from the mother may be a central issue, involving an understanding of many unconscious feelings and conflicts which need to be interpreted. Since these conflicts will most likely be linked to the mother's unconscious problems with her child, the therapist is here in an unusual position. At times, the young child may be able to leave the mother soon enough, and the exploration of the separation problem can then be approached by way of the usual analytic situation. But there are instances where this does not occur for a longer period of time.

Whether the mother is physically present or not, however, the achievement of separation-individuation is a necessary developmental step, in order to proceed with the analytic work, as well as to achieve object constancy and the internalization of the conflict. The analyst's task, then, is to assist in achieving this developmental step, if indeed the separation problem is based on this developmental lag. Since it may be due to many other factors—phobic elements, aggressive strivings against the mother, oral conflicts, etc. —an evaluation of the basic dynamic condition and its effect on development is necessary. It is often difficult to arrive at an early assessment, and it is by way of the analytic work that the diagnosis reveals itself best. Thus, the ability or inability to reach a therapeutic alliance will itself have diagnostic significance.

Another form of the problem of arriving at a working relationship has to do with the five-year-old girl who comes for treatment in order to play. In each session, she sets up an elaborate family scene with the dolls—including punishing the children for their misbehavior by sending them away, the frequent medical treatments they receive, and their fears of getting an injection. To the analyst she assigns the role of the punishing father. She does not allow any discussion of her "real" life experience, or any deviation from the roles she assigns in the play. Her control has to be complete: the analyst is seen only as one provider of the play's possibilities.

This inflexibility actually lasted for many weeks—until her mother left for vacation. Then, for the first time, she allowed herself the expression of sad feelings upon being separated, and she listened to at least one sentence by the therapist who explained that mothers at times do leave, and one is entitled to have such feelings about it without suppressing them. This was the beginning of a loosening of the repetitive play material. But it was only when her aggressive wishes could be interpreted, and her sexual fantasies and wishes exposed in her plays about "doctor examinations and treatments" could be revealed to her, that she was able to enter into the therapeutic alliance.

TECHNICAL CONSIDERATIONS

Despite the many differences between child and adult analysis, and particularly those that hold true for the prelatency child, the analytic goals are the same: to bring about the resolution of unconscious conflict; to enable the ego to emerge where there was id; and to make it possible for development to proceed, where there had been interference with and fixation of development. The means for achieving these aims are the general analytic techniques of reconstruction, affective reliving, and the attainment of affective and cognitive insight. There are some variations of technique, based on the child's psychic organization at different stages of development. Just as we have learned to modify the analytic approach with the adolescent, so we do it in still earlier stages, particularly in the prelatency phase.

Object-Relations

The child is still in a state of dependency on the primary object. He expects the parent to be able to fulfill his needs, that is, he assumes that any problems or difficulties he experiences can be resolved by means of outside intervention. Externalization of conflicts—aggressive strivings, with the aim of changing the environment—are only partially counteracted by the evolvement of superego and guilt.

But then again (once more to caution against generalization) there are those prelatency children who show precocious indentification with the adult and a too early independence; there are those whose ego restriction is due to severe superego influences and low

self-esteem; and those with early obsessive-compulsive mechanisms, indicating structure-formation with corresponding behavioral rigid patterns and symptoms.

When the child is able to bring to the analytic situation a capacity for a secure object relationship, as the result of his having
achieved object constancy, then the analytic technique can proceed
in accordance with our intention. Many children are unable to rely
on the primary object long and securely enough for their relationship to the therapist to reflect that experience.

The Analyst as a Primary Object

It may be that the analyst is, for the child, his first continuous object. Reliable, and therefore always available for identification, the
analyst may then serve in many ways as a primary object. The
analytic relationship will thus be providing the young patient with
ego-building experience, in addition to the analytic work, with its
influence on the correction of earlier defenses. The child may have
had a history with his mother of such character that a cathexis of
the object was not possible—she having been insufficiently available, as the result of illness, physical absence, or emotional detachment, resulting from depression or other conditions.

Thus, we may find many different varieties of past experiences
with the object that will affect the child's relationship with the
analyst and with it the analyst's technique. It takes experience and
tact to differentiate the various forms of needs and wishes that the
child has for the analyst. The latter will respond to expectations
that are developmentally legitimate differently from the way in
which he would respond to those that are repetitions of earlier
patterns in the analytic relationship and have their basis in fixation.

Transference

Recognition that transference phenomena are among the essential
requirements of psychoanalytic treatment makes it important that
we discuss these phenomena as they occur during the prelatency
period. We should like here to define the term "transference" in a
narrower sense: taking in those experiences that come from the
past and are now "transferred" to the analyst, while proving to be
irrational in this new relationship. This definition, therefore, does
not include the repetition of patterns of behavior in the analytic
situation, even if these repetitions are nonrealistic. It includes only

those transference phenomena that are expressed directly in the relationship with the analyst.

Furthermore, transference can take place only when the child has already established a significant relationship with the parent, which can then be shifted to a new person. The child must have been able to internalize the parental image, he must have achieved object constancy to a certain degree; he must also have been able to differentiate external reality from internal wishes, and to have established sufficient structure-formation. When a child who comes into treatment expects that the therapist will behave in as rejecting or as gratifying or as seductive a fashion as the mother, he must first have achieved a certain degree of patterned relationship with the mother, in order for him to be able to transfer this expectation to others. But it is important to realize that, as long as the child has not yet had sufficient experience to know that different people will act differently, he will expect any new person to behave similarly to his mother. This implies: (1) that the child is able to differentiate people from each other in his expectations of their function, and (2) that the child has had a long enough experience with the analyst to know that, in fact, his behavior is different, although he still insists on his fantasy and on an emotional experience that equates the therapist with the mother.

It is for this reason that there are those who insist that one should speak about transference only when it emerges during the ongoing therapeutic process, so that the patient will have had the chance to experience the newness of the relationship, before one can define that irrational component that is essential for the transference. Another factor, then, that contributes to the child's ability to develop a transference is his capacity for reality testing.

When we take all these qualities into account, we are not surprised to discover that there are many children who are not as yet able to form a relationship that includes transference expressions. This will be so, for example, with the child who is still in a symbiotic relationship, and is thus neither sufficiently differentiated from mother, not yet exposed to different relationships than the one he had with her. We may then see children who have been unable to cathect the primary object with sufficient strength and who are therefore condemned to go from object to object, seeking mothering but without having a clear representation of the image of mother, or an object representation.

There are other children who regress to an earlier stage of development: they insist on direct need-gratification, being unable to accept any substitution, therefore, at a higher degree of relationship, with verbal expression or understanding of his need. Some degree of postponement of gratification, that is, of the capacity to accept frustration, is a necessary prerequisite for psychoanalytic treatment. To the degree that the analyst is a primary object, we shall find interference in the transference evolvement, and we shall have to modify the technique of treatment to include parameters or substantial modifications.

I have referred to a number of examples to highlight those situations that are clearly indicative of the problems the child may have in object relations and that may therefore affect his transference experiences. It is clear that we find, as usual, clinical pictures that indicate a variation of functions at various developmental levels; or else we find that, in certain areas, the child is able to function on a higher level, while in others he stays at a lower level, or regresses to still lower levels of functioning. It is, therefore, very important that the child analyst who treats children during the prelatency period be well aware of these various levels, so that he can make the proper choice of which conflict or experience he wishes to address himself to, in order to strengthen the child's ego and with it his development.

Transference and Special Life Condition

There are many special situations that have their impact on the transference evolvement. There are young children whose father is absent, as the result either of death or of abandonment, or when, because of divorce, he has moved far away from the child's place of residence. When these children have a male therapist—particularly during their phallic and Oedipal period of development—they will use him for imitation, identification, and working through of the Oedipal conflict, thus using him as a primary object. This will raise quite a number of complex technical questions at the point at which the analyst comes to recognize these developmental needs, while at the same time having to maintain the degree of detachment necessary to proceed with the analysis of those conflicts and symptoms for which the child has come for treatment.

What we see here is an interesting variation of transference phenomena. The child may have an image of a father that has been formed by his wishes and his needs, and he may transfer these to the analyst. Thus, the transference does not move from a primary object relation to the analyst, but instead stems from a fantasied object relationship. The irrationality, in this instance, arises out of the child's wish, rather than out of any interplay between his needs and his past realities. The interpretations of the transference thus have a different accent and impact on the reorganization of psychic life.

It may well be that the magic image of the absent father is an idealized one, as can be seen so often, or the child may see him as forever punishing, in order to satisfy his own sense of guilt for his dependency on and sexual wishes for mother. This constellation will give the Oedipal conflict special characteristics, for the problem has to be worked through without the aid of a continuous reality-testing provided for by an intact family.

Variations of this situation can also be seen with children in adoptive or foster homes. In such situations, fantasies about the real parents take on the features of an unchecked projection of wishes. At times, it is an intriguing situation to see a child forming a true object relationship to the therapist, and then bring this back to his family, to work through his relationship with them at a different level of function and with different possibilities of solution. I do not mean this happens during the usual course of interpretation—that is, the unlocking of unconscious mechanisms so that the ego can integrate them in a better form—but rather by means of the child's primary identification with the analyst. One could further assume that this new relationship to the therapist, if sufficiently consolidated, may then be transferred to the parental relationship, so that one sees the transference taking place *from* the analytic situation *to* the home situation, and thus constituting a reversal of its usual course.

As a consequence of the child's fluidity of structure, his developmental flexibility, and his dependency on the primary object, there are a great number of variations, as has been indicated, in the interplay between the child's relationship to the parents and his relationship to the analyst. The child's ability to differentiate various persons from each other and to understand the different positions they hold in relationship to him is the prerequisite for the therapeutic alliance. It is the ego of the child—that is, its reality-esting, self-observation, and understanding of the function and position of the analyst—that makes it possible for this alliance to be established between the patient's ego and the therapist, so that the therapeutic task can be undertaken. We see here that transference and object relationships based on reality can coincide. One might say that they must coexist, for without the knowledge that the analyst is not in reality a parent, the transference (that is, the projection of wishes onto the analyst that stem from the primary love object) could not take place.

The child who is continuously engaged in responding to and integrating new experiences will produce transference phenomena that will often mix present relationships with the parent with those from the past. In addition, we may see elements in the transference that belong to the earliest aspects of the child's feelings and needs, before the appropriate differentiation and ego structure have taken place. This mixture, in addition to the fluidity of function, necessitates a much more careful approach to reconstruction and to other therapeutic interventions. The child may, in one session, refer to the mother as being bad, because he recollects a disappointing situation from the past; at the next moment, he may speak about her in positive terms, because he thinks of something pleasurable she did or may do during the day. This changeability may not be based on the inherent ambivalence that we may see in older children or in adults, where patterning of relationship has already occurred and where the changes between libidinal and aggressive strivings remain in an ambivalent position. These fluctuations may be further increased during the Oedipal phase of development, in which the alliance with mother may shift to an alliance with father, in order to cope with the internal conflicts. At times we do see polarization and a more specific interplay of forces, particularly when we examine specific symptoms.

Transference-Neurosis

Over the years, there have been a number of discussions about the establishment in child analysis of a transference-neurosis. Whether it is found to exist in the same form as it does in older children or adults depends on one's definition of the term. If we mean by transference-neurosis that the central neurotic conflict emerges, during the analytic treatment, in relation to the analyst, then we may have difficulties finding such a complete crystallization of the conflict in the transference. It is exactly for reasons of developmental change, the openness of interplay, and the lack of stable psychic structure-formation that such organized transference may not take place in prelatency.

If, on the other hand, one is satisfied to define transference-neurosis as the occurrence of a neurotic symptom in relationship to the analyst, one can often enough observe that. Thus one can see phobic elements in the transference, or an attempt to repeat a real or fantasized traumatic sexual event, as it is projected in relation to the analyst; or else the analyst may stand for the punishing figure, and we are able to see the projection onto him of superego and drive conflicts. These may occur at certain periods of the analytic treatment, and they are usually not as prolonged as we see them to be in the analysis of adults.

Furthermore, some of these transference phenomena may relate to part of the analyst's environment, for example, the office or the house in which the treatment takes place. If we were to stay within a strict definition of transference, these would not be included; but if we look at the clinical phenomena, we can see very often a fusion of the object with part of his environment. The noises that the child may hear in the room, or the specific arrangement of the room (that is, of inanimate objects in it), or other people who may live in the house—all these may set off transference reactions, or else the transference response to the analyst may spill over to the things and people in his environment.

The technique of transference interpretation is the same as with adults. Because we are also relying on some of the child's appropriate ego functions—as seen in the therapeutic alliance—we are able to interpret the child's conflict, whether he is in a positive or a negative position of transference.

Developmental Factors

REPETITION-COMPULSION   Very young children continually repeat experiences. One has to learn to detect whether these repetitions are serving as an exercise on the road to mastery; whether they contain the element of changing a passive experience into an active one; or whether they are following the repetition-compulsion, that is, a repetition that does not lead to any solution. During the pre-latency stage, it is often difficult to determine at any given time which of these factors is at work, nor does the psychic experience connected with these functions permit an immediate differentiation of behaviors that may look alike in so many ways. Often enough, we are unable to learn what the child is experiencing, unless it is clearly played out, or unless we know of the original experience that is now being repeated, with the child assigning himself an active role.

The young patient may continue his usual modes of behavior in the analytic situation, particularly those that have become patterned, that is, those that are by now expressions of a more stable structure, or of developmental fixations. Some may be due to the formation of secondary autonomous character-formation and are therefore ego-syntonic.

That is to say, we have to view the child's behavior from the developmental point of view as well. We have made a number of earlier references to the developmental aspect, for example, in referring to the questions of diagnostic assessment, indication for analysis, and the role of transference. We are defining development here in terms of a process of unfolding, including changes over time, and the establishment of sequences in structure formation. We are referring to the process that governs the emergence of differentiation, that is, of integration of function into more and more complex units. In one way, this refers to drive development, i.e., to libidinal phases of development and their concomitant aggressive components, to corresponding ego and superego organization, and to the maturational sequences. We do not mean by development the sum of all psychic functions as such: the most important changes occur during prelatency, and more rapidly than during any other period.

When we treat a child during this period, we are therefore continually confronted with a changing psychic system, which affects every aspect of the child's functioning. Treatment is indicated because the child's development has been interfered with to a substantial degree. At the same time, in certain areas, development continues. There may be points of fixation or symptoms that have become stable, or even permanent. There may also be pathological manifestations that change their mode of expression, as the result of the developmental influence or, better, of the changes in psychic organization that are due to development.

Since we want to bring about change, it is important for us to know whether it takes place because of therapeutic intervention, developmental reorganization, or environmental influences. It is very often difficult, if not impossible, to know with certainty which of these factors is operative, because they may conjoin or each may affect the other.

The Longitudinal View

In recognition of these problems, we may assess the child by creating a profile, that is, by studying all the aspects of the child's outer and inner life. In that event, we are not satisfied to evaluate symptoms alone, or the ego's pathological defenses, but rather consider the *interplay* between health and pathology and the degree to which development is proceeding. This implies that we have to know the past development of the child, and also that we need to follow the ongoing developmental process for a long period of time. Another approach is to attempt to formulate the dynamics of the core of the child's psychic constellation. While various other forms of conflict may come and go, we shall be directing our interest to this main psychic organization and to its relationship to the developmental task.

Developmental Variations

In certain functions we may see the developmental forward pull, while in others we may see various forms of regression. At the prelatency age, we can therefore observe a wide progression-regression swing, particularly if we focus on the libidinal-aggressive organization. We assume that normal development proceeds from phase to phase, that is, that we can expect some discontinuity of older organizations, as new hierarchies are established. This is not always seen in such distinct form. There is at times an overlapping of phases, which means that we can find, at certain times in development, that both the old and the new psychic functions are present.

There are also many other variations in developmental sequence. There is the question of precocity, that is, the emergence of phases or functions *before the expected time.* This may be due to early stimulation or to a strong developmental *retardation,* the slow unfolding of phases over a longer period of time, in which phase-specific conflicts emerge later than expected, and often in a less intense form. From the standpoint of psychic structure-formation, there may be normal progress to phallic dominance and later, an Oedipal unfolding. In some variations, oral-anal manifestations may coexist with phallic-Oedipal conflicts, that is, libidinal phase development is continuing, but without either dominance or discontinuity.

The reasons for these variations may be many, but since they may also include a maturational constitutional factor, they must be recognized as having a special role in conflict-formation and in treatment. A longitudinal view of the child's development is needed if one wishes to observe these variations and their influence on ego development, on indications for, and limits of treatment.

The following case will illustrate some of these factors.

CASE ILLUSTRATION

Summary of Six Developmental Assessments

Assessment	Age
1	3.6
2	4.2
3	4.7
4	5.2
5	5.7
6	6.2

Possibly Significant Environmental Circumstances

The mother's history is one of some degree of maternal deprivation and of chronic depression (including suicidal attempts) for which she was hospitalized in her early twenties, before her marriage. Throughout A.'s early childhood, the chronic depression continued, and apparently the mother had long periods of lying in bed. The history indicates that the mother has strong symbiotic needs with regard to her babies. The tendencies were both to need A. as a person who would cheer her up, and on whom she could herself depend, and also to seduce her back into a symbiotic relationship. The mother has a tendency to idealize A., and thus to instill narcissism, as well as a fear of negative affects and aggressive expressions. Both parents are, on the one hand, solicitous of A., as well as idealizing of her. On the other hand, they can withdraw from her in pursuit of their own needs, sometimes accompanying this with outbursts of anger. The depressive and symbiotic characteristics of the mother were noted in the first profile; what became clearer later on was the mother's seductive aspect, and the extent of her withdrawal in general from object relationships. In the first profile it was observed that both parents were contributing to A.'s self-idealization and to her fear of aggressive interaction; it later emerged that the father got into violent rages, despite his solicitous qualities, about the demands made upon him by his wife and children.

A.'s History

The history is one of a rather idyllic babyhood, in which A. received abundant attention from both her parents, as well as from an old lady who lived in the same house. She slept and fed well; she preferred the bottle to the breast, and established a regular routine; teething was early and rather painful to her. Mother took A. with her everywhere, including having the baby in her bed and strapping her in a sling on her back. She was very happy with A. as a baby—up to her "no phase," when she was 1½. The parents would avoid aggressive interaction with A. by distracting her through singing, games, etc.; they encouraged and admired her developing skills.

At 1½ there was a sudden change of circumstances: the parents moved away from the maid; at the same time, A., for the first time had to sleep in a separate room. She was made to give up her bottle, and to begin toilet training, and the mother began to react with anxiety to her "no phase." There were also marital problems, with threats of desertion and separation. At age two, A. began to insist on sleeping with her mother—this was one of the referral problems—and she continued to have difficulty going to sleep on her own until profile 5.

One can speculate on how this environment may have contributed to A.'s development, particularly to her longings for a gratifying and symbiotic relationship with her mother, and the mutually seductive characteristics of that relationship; the lack of verbal communication; A.'s difficulty in establishing realistic self-object representations; her wish for a fully satisfying environment and the idealization of self and objects, whom she also wishes to be omnipotent. There is also the lack of aggressive interaction. At the age of 1½, in terms of the sudden change referred to above, A. lost one gratifying object—the maid—and she suddenly had to face the problem of controlling oral and anal impulses. She developed a fear of anal impulses in particular, and of separation from her mother, along with a need to placate and an attempt to regain oneness. This included the wish to sleep with her mother (an effort to regain a symbiotic relationship) as well as a lack of development of the processes of individuation.

Fixation Points and Their Effects on Personality Development

ORAL-RECEPTIVE AIMS   It would seem that an oral-receptive aim has persisted in A., and that she has regressed to this under the impact of her mother's pregnancy and the birth of her brother. This aim is shown toward mother and toward other female objects in general, although the frustration of her wishes has also led her to withdraw from objects into gratifying fantasy relationships. However, the oral wishes directed toward objects persist, together with a longing for merging and fusion, and a lack of internal regulation on this score. While oral-sadistic impulses are felt, they cause conflict, which leads to regression to passive aims. This contributes to her defenses of flight from frustrating objects and to her lack of verbal communication, as well as to her rejection of help and her feelings of helplessness and vulnerability.

The self-representation is based on the need to be an ideal and good girl. (This involves denial of aggressive feelings.) The object representations are either of ideal-gratifying objects or of frustrating and therefore hostile ones. The oral aims combine with the narcissistic ones, i.e., needing to be the favorite and the center of attention, to be exempt from any criticism or failure, to be constantly praised, etc.

In her ego development, what is apparent is A.'s need to please, to comply with and identify with objects in order to remain the center of their attention, and thus to control them. Although she has excellent ego skills and functions, their development appears to have been too greatly motivated by the need to please objects and to support narcissistic wishes, so that lack of pleasure in them for their own sake is evident. (This became clearer in the later profiles.) The assimilation of knowledge, which is highly developed, is largely motivated by attempts to control the world and her objects, and to regain a kind of unity with them. For example, in profile 4, teachers comment on "her use of materials and food as a vantage point for observing the outside world, as if satiating herself with this," and they make constant references to her attempts to ingratiate and adapt herself to objects, instead of interacting with them.

In the later profiles, an increasing fear of loss of the mother is seen, as a consequence of the latter's pregnancy and the birth of the brother. This intensifies, as well as frustrates, A.'s oral-symbiotic wishes and the terror that her aggression may succeed in alienating her objects—which then further intensifies the aggressive wishes. Her anger breaks through toward other childern in particular, from whom she becomes increasingly alienated. There is also a narcissistic withdrawal into more gratifying fantasy relationships, in which the object is under control. With the loss of the idealized situation, come increased feelings of helplessness and depression.

In her therapy, she seems to wish to regain this ideal situation: she shows enormous anxiety over aggression between herself and her mother, attempting to deny affects of disappointment and loss.

ANAL IMPULSES   On the anal level, there would also seem to be incorporative and possessive aims which are shown toward objects, together with powerful wishes to control and dominate them. The rather abrupt toilet training demands seem to have led to fear of anal-aggressive impulses, which are largely externalized and projected. Her destructive and sadistic wishes are rather shakily controlled by reaction formations; that is, they break through into sadism toward other children, and in her fantasies her death wishes come very close to consciousness.

After her brother's birth, the parents allowed A. to displace her aggression toward him without adequate control; this in turn increased her fear and guilt. A. is caught between the need to submit to and placate objects. Angry attempts to control them coexist with enormous fear of her own omnipotence. A.'s superego appears to be based on a need for oneness with objects, stemming from her symbiotic wishes, together with fear of talion reprisal for oral- and anal-sadistic impulses. Yet, she still seeks object reassurances, rather than developing internal sources of approval. This heightens her need to be good, by denying both negative affects and feelings that she is a helpless infant and an anal product (for example, her description of herself to her therapist as "a nice thing").

One consistent theme in her profile interviews had to do with her death wishes toward mother, at the same time as she felt that "she couldn't live without her." Simultaneously, there was her search for another mother. There is also the theme of her need to be "Superman," defending the witch, i.e., she needed iron control over her own sadistic impulses.

PHALLIC ORGANIZATION What looked in the first profile like phallic-Oedipal organization, revealed itself later on, as was anticipated, to be a mixture of pre-phallic and psychic organization. Her oral wishes largely determine a negative Oedipal constellation, in which she seeks love from women, while the father is, for the most part, an alternative object, toward whom she has very ambivalent feelings. Good ego skills seem largely motivated by her wishes to attract and please female objects.

Her competitiveness and penis envy appeared to have been

determined mainly by a need for omnipotence and completeness: it was only after her brother's birth that she had to face the reality of boy-girl differences and her own castrated state. She has always been quite castrating and critical of others' performances; boys were sought after only as long as they could gratify her narcissism. The therapy sessions indicated her absorption with this and with her wishes for her mother. A.'s intelligence and curiosity seem largely motivated by attempts to control objects in the world; they do not have the autonomy that one would expect of true phallic organization.

The essential features of A.'s personality development were observed in the first profile, although they became better understood in later profiles, when more detailed observations became progressively available. The therapy sessions to date appear to confirm the essential picture. It would seem, then, that A.'s development by 3½ forecasted her later development, up to 6½. It is true that she was faced with the particular circumstance of her brother's arrival in the family, but her reaction to this did seem to be, on the whole, predictable, if one considered her already established ways of relating to and regulating her objects and her own drives, the self- and object-representations already established, and her narcissistic position.

Core Constellation

These assessments are presented to illustrate some of the factors outlined earlier. We see here a core constellation which was observed at the first profile. This does not mean that it had not been established before, or even that one could not have seen some of it during the first month of life. But the fact is that between three and four years of age, we were able to outline such a basic constellation. We are not referring here to a core pathology, but to a certain coordination of factors that is specific to a given child and that has the tendency to remain consistent during prelatency. Symptoms may persist or they may change; many ego functions may expand; and still we find certain features continuing. They may influence further development, and they may in turn be influenced by developmental progression, but without giving up their chief characteristics. We are not implying that this core is to be reduced to the constitutional segment; it may, as a matter of fact, be the result of the interplay between constitutional and environmental factors. Similarly, it may represent the results of healthy as well as pathological forces; for each particular child, one would have to determine where the emphasis is to be placed.

Moreover, these assessments of A. demonstrate her individual variation in libidinal phase development, in the form of a coexistence of all three stages of development, without the achievement of phase primacy or of phase-specific conflicts, distinct and separate from previous conflicts. Thus, what appears to be coexistence is often an interlocking of conflicts from different phases.

It is interesting to pursue such a core constellation with regard to its relationship to secondary autonomy of ego function or to the fate of the infantile neurosis. However, the more we are able to outline in detail this basic constellation, along with the developmental mode of progression, the more we become aware of the actual task of analysis, as we come to realize what has to be analyzed beyond the symptoms or other internalized conflicts, as well as what the analytic limitations may be, at least for this period of development.

CASE ILLUSTRATION

The following sections from an analysis will illustrate other aspects of technique.

John had finished lunch when I went to pick him up in the nursery. We got to my office with a minimum of difficulty, although he did insist on walking down one floor and catching the elevator to go the remaining floor.

Once in my office, John took the chair near the toy table and, speaking out loud, but more to himself, commented that he was hot; no, he was cold; no, he was hot today; and maybe he should turn off the air-conditioner. He got up and began to fidget with the air-conditioner; then, turning to me, he asked that *I* turn it on (the plug was pulled out). I commented that he never seemed able to make himself quite comfortable, and that while I knew he tried very hard to change things around, nothing ever seemed to really work. John told me to be quiet.

Then he noticed a book of matches pushed up under the toy cabinet. John went to get them and then put them into my pocketbook; I thanked him for calling them to my attention. John suggested that perhaps the cleaning people had dropped them there, and then he launched into a somewhat rapid stream of talk about fires. It was frequently difficult for me to understand him.

John said that the matches could light up all by themselves, if the room got hot enough, and then he went on to enumerate how each thing in the room would burn, with the fire getting larger and larger, e.g., the cabinet would burn, and then the chairs would catch fire, and then the desk, and soon the whole room would be on fire. Then he would run out of the room and, using a rope like the one window cleaners use, he would go down the floors to the street. He then said that window cleaners went *across* floors and not *down* them. Consequently, he felt he would have to run down the stairway, and he asked whether it too would be on fire. With a sort of mock menacing laugh, John said that I would burn up in the fire but that *he* would get out safely.

This led him to think about what would happen if there was a fire in their trailer camp. He said that the fire door there was currently jammed, but there was another door they could get out through. Also, there were two fire extinguishers. He would give one fire extinguisher to his father and the other to his mother. He then began to demonstrate how they would spray the whole place; while the whole room would get wet, the fire would be put out. This would complicate the sleeping arrangements, since there were only two sleeping bags. He first thought that he and his brother should have the two sleeping bags, and again, with his mock menacing laugh, he said that his parents would have to sleep on the wet bed. Then he reconsidered: maybe they would make fires and dry out all the clothing and the bed, or maybe he and his brother would let the parents have the sleeping bags, or all four of them might end up sleeping in the car. He felt that his father should sleep in the front seat and his mother should sleep in the back. He would sleep in the front on the floor with his father, and his brother would sleep on the floor in the back with his mother. It was important that his father be in front, in case the car began to roll down the hill, since he was the one who could stop it.

At this point, John began to want to throw things at me, and he did throw a crayon. I commented that talking about fires had made him very excited, and he replied that he was not talking to me. He then went to the door, as though to go out, whereupon he came back, having apparently decided that he would throw another crayon at me. Abruptly this stopped, and he decided he would build a barricade in the office, using all the chairs as well as the toy cabinet. He crawled into his barricade, commenting. "You are not to look; you can't see me." Later on: "Maybe mother will come in and join me; father is away. My brother too. We are safe here. I will take care of things."

Evaluation

I am presenting part of this session in order to show how a child can take a theme and within one session "try on" different solutions, of which none seems to be sufficiently satisfying. In previous, as well as in later sessions, new variations were found, and old ones repeated.

I shall not discuss the meaning of the interest in fire-setting and John's need for rescue, but I do want to highlight his attempt to find an arrangement within his family. This child had not yet entered the Oedipal phase, in spite of the sexual references in his interest in fire. He had by this time reached phallic organization—but without achieving phallic primacy over earlier libidinal and aggressive strivings. His play with water, the wet bed, the fire extinguishers—all these point to what are still pre-Oedipal conflicts. But then he brings the parents together, and allies himself with father in front of the car, because the father was able to protect them. In the end, however, it is with mother that he barricades himself.

We see here variations on a theme: his role in the family is still open, as can so often be observed at this age. It is striking how, during this period, the child tries continually and creatively to solve the problems that arise between his drives and the environment by experimenting with innumerable solutions, while being unable as yet to find a lasting, successful one. It is enough if the solution satisfies the demands of a momentary compromise. If one were to assume that throughout, the child holds one recognizable, stable position, that is, to eliminate father and to gain mother, then one would be surprised to see to how great an extent the impact of guilt and the reality of the family situation, as well as the need to adapt to it without losing either parent, are capable of bringing about rapid changes until, later on in development, a solution can be arrived at and maintained.

The technical approach to this, at the prelatency age, is to find the main theme; but it is not at all easy to know which is the dominant theme at any given time. Thus, one can address oneself instead to an essentially undirected struggle, under difficult circumstances, to find solutions by bringing to light the various wishes and conflicts that are involved. In addition, this session demonstrates once again that material from different developmental levels can coexist, or that one single behavior can have a meaning that still contains the echoes of various levels; that is, we observe its multiple determinants.

The complex interplay of forces, the changeability, the forward and backward movement—all these imply that the task of analyzing prelatency children is more difficult, but it is often more interesting and rewarding.

In the next session, John began as he had in the previous one. He complained about the room itself, the air-conditioner, and the size of the room. He couldn't seem to find anything in it that he was able to like. When this was pointed out to him, he asked how old the therapist was and, without waiting for an answer, said that he knew what her age was. He did not want to reveal what he knew, but rather wanted to strike a bargain, in which he would make an exchange of information. When this attitude was explored with him, namely, that he does not ever want to give anything before he has received something from a grown-up, he said that he wanted to get full information about who else was coming for treatment and whether they left anything behind that they made during their sessions. He admitted that he wanted to be the only one coming. He then said that the analyst was twenty-six years old; even if she were to correct this, he still would not believe it. She could not be any other age.

Then John requested that the treatment room be made into a bedroom, assigning the corner where the double bed should be, where the chairs should stand, the table, and so forth. By doing this, he realized that the room was much too small for his needs, because what he really wanted was to combine a bedroom with a playroom. When it was pointed out to him that this was perhaps one of the reasons why he had been dissatisfied lately with the size of the room and what was in it, he agreed that this was what bothered him. He wanted to make sure in his arrangement that he would be moving in with the therapist not only for the night, because he wanted to live with her all the time. He avoided any sexual, that is, phallic-Oedipal, fantasy expressions, but stayed within the orbit of general living and sleeping arrangements. Still, at the end of the session, he requested that there be a dart set. He had seen one at his friend's house when he visited there and said it was very important to him that there be one at his next appointment.

Here we see a continuation from the point at which he had ended his previous session. It has to do with the alliance with the woman. What is of interest here is that his wish is expressed, not in the form of play, but rather in reality. It did not offer the therapist the opportunity to play out a fantasy situation with him, but she had to be aware of this difference, namely, that this was a direct appeal to her to take him in.

Naturally, John knew about the difference between his wish and his reality, and therefore these forms of expressing his wishes take on a special significance. In his case, this was seen not only as a wish for a primary relationship with the analyst, in which she would take over his care, but also, since his mother was ill during this period and separated from the children, it was a wish for a substitute mother. Thus we see reality needs, fantasies, and transference phenomena, all mixed together in on, as we see in prelatency.

TERMINATION

In general, the same criterion holds for termination of analysis of the prelatency child as for the older child or adult patient: the resolution of the internalized conflict that has significantly interfered with the child's functioning and/or with his development. As has already been noted in the section on indication for treatment, some aspects are specific for this age group. Often enough, the adult patient will join in deciding on the termination of his analysis, just as he joins in deciding on the beginning of his treatment. The younger the child, the more dependent he is on his environment, the more we have to take into account his environment with regard to both indication and termination of treatment.

The relationship of the parents during treatment and its termination must play a significant role. If they think that the therapy has achieved a sufficient change with regard to those particular problems for which they have brought their child for therapy, they may not continue to support the treatment for other conflicts which may not be disturbing to them. The analyst, on the other hand, may assess the change that has taken place in the child as constituting only a modification of the conflict, not its solution, or he may feel that the improvement has not reached the core constellation that will, unless it is reached, continue to affect further development. He is then forced to evaluate the parental attitude and to decide whether the continuation of the therapy is possible even without their support.

Furthermore, what may have been disturbing to the parents may not be the actual disturbance in the child. The mother who considers the child's dependency disturbing may be satisfied, for instance, with the fact that the child has become less dependent, without recognizing that other symptoms or malfunctions of the child may be syntonic to her own psychic life. Similarly, a feeding or sleep disorder may be disturbing to the mother, while she may consider other disorders in the child insignificant. There are many variations in the family dynamics that will conjoin in determining the success of treatment, as well as the timing of its termination.

We must also include here the relationship of the parents to their other children. They may feel that it would be unfair to support the needs of one child financially, while depriving the others thereby of the rightful fulfillment of their needs. In addition, the attention that has to be paid to the child in analysis, i.e., bringing him to the daily session and spending an inappropriate amount of time with him while the other children are cared for by others or are left alone, may become more and more unacceptable to the parents. The effect of the treatment situation on the other children, and how the parents respond to that, has to be kept under continuous scrutiny.

The analyst will have, to begin with, to answer the question of whether he has achieved his original treatment aim, or the one that he has evolved during the analysis, and whether it was indeed realistic to expect to reach it.

In order to judge whether the pathological conflicts have been sufficiently eliminated to permit development to proceed, the analyst may wish to see the child during the succeeding stage of development to study the new psychic organization and the new levels of integration. At the same time, he will not want to prolong the analysis for that reason. The patient will know that a sort of "waiting period" is involved and he may feel that the analyst is "holding onto him" beyond the working-through period. If the analyst does indeed keep the patient longer, he may find that this will lead to new problems that he would wish to avoid. The child may respond to this with increasing reluctance to keep his appointments; or else he may feel that the analyst has a liking for him beyond his therapeutic interest, and he may, as a result, assume a wrong role.

The analyst may, however, consider tapering off, decreasing the frequency and later the regularity of the sessions, as one way of "standing by" and following the child's further development. Some think that such a procedure may not be advisable, because it does not offer the opportunity to explore fully the internal condition and thus defeats its own purpose. Furthermore, if such a diminished contact continues for too long, it establishes a therapeutic pattern that changes the analytic milieu from one of exploring internal conflicts, of insight and self-observation, into a relationship of reporting.

There is another difference here between the prelatency child and the child at later stages; namely, the absence of the "working-through" period. With adult patients, who have a more structured psychic system, there is need for this part of the analysis, in which the defenses have been modified and the conflicts resolved, yet the new alternatives that are now open to the patient have to be reinforced so that the regression to the old pattern may be avoided. In the young child, we see instead that the analysis now permits the development to proceed, and thus *new* psychic functions emerge at higher levels of organization. At times, one has to be aware of the possibility that the developmental pull is already engaging the child in latency attitudes and functions, before earlier conflicts have been sufficiently resolved.

Considerations with regard to termination of the analysis will have to take into account the vicissitudes of the developmental process, that is, the individual style within which the progress is to be judged. Furthermore, the degree of progress that is possible depends not only on the analyst and on the patient's capability for change, but also on the condition of his environment. Since the prelatency child continues to be dependent on the parents for identification, for the interplay between his own sexual and aggressive strivings and the parents' position toward him, one has to assess what the reality prospects are for the child's achieving his health, given his life circumstances. At times one has to be satisfied with the fact that the child has achieved an optimal adaptation to a pathological home situation, at this present stage of development, without achieving appropriate functioning. One may expect that, in the future, when there is a higher degree of independence, a further analytic period may be able to lead to a real termination.

Our ability to predict is severely limited by our inability to foresee the many unusual events that may occur and exercise a regressive influence on our patients. This is even more important for the younger, more vulnerable child. Thus, one should keep the door open for the child's return for further analytic therapy.

For these reasons, it has been recommended that one should terminate the analysis at a time when the relationship to the child, as well as to the parents, is positive. It is not being implied here that the transference relationship should be positive; what we are speaking about is the general relationship to the therapist, as well as to the therapeutic process. One would thus have to differentiate termination, which usually constitutes reaching the therapeutic aim, from a kind of interruption of the treatment, under circumstances in which one is aware of the fact that, while significant pathological components are still present, the conditions are not present for further therapeutic intervention. There is a third possibility, namely, that the analysis be discontinued because geographic, economic, or other circumstances make it impossible to continue it.

Thus, one is not always able to determine the timing of the termination in any simple fashion. Where one is able to set the time, one would prefer to do it in such a way that a return to therapy is still possible. When one sees children in follow-up, one can quite frequently observe the large aspects of prelatency analysis falling victim to the repressive forces of the latency period. Some details or screen memories may emerge, but the living experience of the internal struggle to master conflicts does not remain conscious. Still, there are children who will ask to return to the analyst during latency or later, since they harbor a positive feeling toward that experience—one that is connected with a sense of comfort and a feeling of being understood, even if the memory of the past conflict is no longer present.

If one leaves open the possibility that the child may return in the future, one may have to decide whether one is considering a continuation of the analysis, or whether a shorter contact will suffice to support the child's development. One will wish to avoid exposing the child to analysis, and then later to a short psychotherapy, which may again lead to analysis. This would mix techniques and thereby interfere with the analytic task.

REFERENCES

Abbate, G. McL. Notes on the first year of the analysis of a young child with minimum participation by the mother. In E. R. Geleerd (Ed.), *The child analyst at work*. New York: International Universities Press, 1967. Pp. 14–23.

Bornstein, Berta. The analysis of a phobic child. Some problems of theory and technique in child analysis. In *The Psychoanalytic Study of the Child*, 1949, 3–4, 181–226.

Burbaum, E.   Technique of child therapy. In *The Psychoanalytic Study of the Child,* 1954, 9, 297–333.

Flapan, D. and Neubauer, P. B.   Issues in assessing development. *Journal of the American Academy of Child Psychiatry,* 1970. To be published.

Fraiberg, S.   A comparison of the analytic method in two stages of a child analysis. *Journal of the American Academy of Child Psychiatry,* 1965, 4, 387–400.

Frankl, L. and Hellman, I.   The ego's participation in the therapeutic alliance. *International Journal of Psycho-Analysis,* 1962, 43, 333–337.

Freud, A.   *Normality and pathology in childhood.* New York: International Universities Press, 1965.

Freud, A.   *The psychoanalytical treatment of children: Lectures and essays.* New York: Schocken Books, 1964 (orig. pub. 1946).

Freud, A.   Indications and contraindications for child analysis. In *The Psychoanalytic Study of the Child,* 1968, 23, 37–46.

Geleerd, E. R.   Intrapsychic conflicts as observed in child analysis. In E. R. Geleerd (Ed.), *The child analyst at work.* New York: International Universities Press, 1967. Pp. 288–310.

Harley, M.   Transference developments in a five-year-old child. In E. R. Geleerd (Ed.), *The child analyst at work.* New York: International Universities Press, 1967. Pp. 115–141.

Kestenberg, J.   Problems of technique of child analysis in relation to the various developmental stages: Pre-Latency. In *The Psychoanalytic Study of the Child.* 1969, 24, 358–383.

Kolansky, H.   Treatment of a three-year-old girl's severe infantile neurosis. In *The Psychoanalytic Study of the Child,* 1969, 15, 261–285.

Kramer, S. and Settlage, C. P.   On the concepts and technique of child analysis. *Journal of the American Academy of Child Psychiatry,* 1962, 1, 509–535.

Neubauer, P. B.   The one-parent child and his oedipal development. In *The Psychoanalytic Study of the Child,* 1960, 15, 286–309.

Neubauer, P. B. and Flapan, D.   Developmental assessment and grouping of the pre-school child, 1970. Unpublished.

Weiss, Fineberg et al.   Technique of child analysis, problems of the opening phase. *Journal of The American Academy of Child Psychiatry,* 1968, 7, 639–662.

7

MAX GOLDBLATT

Psychoanalysis of the Schoolchild

nna Freud and her coworkers at the Hampstead Child Therapy Clinic in London developed the concept of *developmental psychoanalytic psychology*. This chapter will focus on this concept by presenting the major aspects of Anna Freud's book, *Normality and Pathology in Childhood* (1965). Miss Freud's book demonstrates how present-day child analysis is dependent essentially on the assessment of normality and pathology in childhood from a *developmental* point of view. It shows us why child analysts are now able to make their own contribution to metapsychology and the theory of psychoanalytic therapy of both children and adults. The book deals inter alia, with the historical basis to the present status of child analysis; compares the problems of child analysis with those of adult analysis; and indicates the therapeutic possibilities open to the child analyst, providing him with a rationale of a psychoanalytic therapy for children.

THE PSYCHOANALYTIC VIEW
OF CHILDHOOD:
LONG-DISTANCE AND CLOSE-UP

In this first chapter, the object is to show how child analysis grew out of the experience and knowledge gained from the analysis of adults. From the beginning of Breuer and Freud's work, when it was found that "hysterics suffer mainly from reminiscences" (Breuer and Freud, 1893), analysis was concerned more with patients' past experiences than with their present ones. From what was learned of early happenings in the lives of patients, it seemed that the analyst would come to know all about the psychical life of the child as well, even though the analyst was working with adults only. The main facts that were mentioned related to the sequence of the libidinal phases (oral, anal, and phallic), the Oedipus and the castration complexes, infantile amnesia, etc. Out of these grew the method of "reconstructing" childhood events, which produced the data that have come to form the central part of present-day psychoanalytic child psychology.

After a decade or two, some analytic writers applied this new knowledge to child-rearing, with the hope that by enlightening parents about the dangers inherent in such matters as sexual dishonesty, demanding moral standards that were unrealistically high, being overstrict or overindulgent, frustrating the child's needs, punishing him or employing seductive behavior, etc., a "psychoanalytic education" could be devised which would prevent neuroses. These educational attempts consisted of a long series of trials and errors. With each fresh psychoanalytic discovery, a fresh educational idea arose; but it was not possible at the time to have sufficient insight into the complicated and interrelated structure of personality, which had to be learned gradually, one small finding having to be added to the next, which is more characteristic of our present-day approach. As a result, at that time, psychanalytic education failed as a preventive measure. We know now that because of the division of the personality into an id, ego and superego, and because these agencies are at cross-purposes with one another, inner psychical conflicts are inevitable. There are cases where an "analytic upbringing" assists the child towards an adequate solution of these conflicts, but there are many others where inner discord cannot be prevented.

With the advent of child analysis, in addition to the reconstruction of childhood events from adult analyses, reconstructions were added from the analyses of older children as well as findings from the analyses of the youngest. But child analysis did more than this. Not only did it study the "interaction between the concrete environment and the development of the child's capacities," but it also opened up "a host of intimate data about the child's life." As a result, "his fantasies as well as his daily experiences became accessible to observation . . . only the child analyst provided a setting in which daydreams and night fears, games and productive expressions of the child became understandable . . . in a much more concrete sense than the secret parts of a child's experiences . . . had ever before become accessible to adult understanding" (Kris, 1950, p. 28). Moreover, in the psychoanalyses of the young, the agitations created by infantile complexes were more accessible to view.

This "close-up view" of childhood provides the child analyst with an approach to the development of personality which is subtly different from that obtained from adult analysis. As Anna Freud later demonstrates, child analysts now "make their own contribution to metapsychology and the theory of psychoanalytic therapy."

It took some time for analytic theorists to "come to the conclusion that psychoanalytic psychology is not limited to what can be gained through the use of the psychoanalytic method" (Hartmann, 1950). However, many analysts, analyzed school teachers, and people working with adolescents, delinquents, and young criminals, were observing and reporting either the behavior of their own children or the young people under their care, concerning the details of infantile sexuality and the Oedipus and castration complexes. Such work became systematized only after the Second World War. Anna Freud, in this sub-chapter, reviews the relations between psychoanalysis and direct observation as they have developed over the years, taking into account the misgivings the analyst has to overcome "before he can extend his interest to surface behaviour."

In the early days of psychoanalysis, and long before child analysis began, several factors prevented analysts from even wanting to consider the relations between analysis and surface observation. The first analysts felt it their task to emphasize the differences between outer behavior and unconscious impulses, not their simi-larities. It was felt as particularly important to demonstrate the prime significance of unconscious motivation, the more so because of the public hostility to the idea of an unconscious which was inaccessible to consciousness. Even the younger generation of analysts tended to confuse the content of the unconscious with its overt derivatives, e.g., the differentiation between the mani-fest and the latent contents of dreams was not easily learned. And because many young analysts, in their eagerness to go beyond the confines of consciousness, tried to "spot" specific unconscious drives from their patients' overt behavior or thoughts, students were warned against these attempts at surface observation, and were advised not to bypass the slower work of unraveling the repres-sions. The analyst's main task was that of perfecting the technique of analysis itself.

At the same time there were factors which lessened the analyst's hostility toward surface observation. It became increasingly evident that the derivatives which the analyst was exploring "broke through" in many ways other than through the transference situa-tion and relationship. This could occur outside the analytic situa-tion. For example, in adults, there were symptomatic and faulty actions, slips of the tongue, etc., which indicated preconscious or unconscious impulses. There were also "typical dreams" and dream symbols which revealed their unconscious meaning without the need for interpretative work. We can see in analytic work with children how straightforward fulfillment dreams reveal uncon-scious wishes; and there are daydreams which indicate the stage of libidinal development with a minimum of distortion. Anna Freud points out that there have always been those analysts who are particularly adept at guessing the unconscious content from such manifest indications. The danger here lies in the possibility of turning "a correct analytic therapist into a 'wild' analyst." Never-theless, this flair can enable the analyst to "turn otherwise arid and unrewarding surface manifestations into meaningful material."

Here we see another factor which lessened analysts' hostility toward surface or manifest behavior. As analysts began to turn their attention more toward the methods whereby the ego warded off unconscious psychical activities from consciousness, it became apparent that certain defense mechanisms were readily observable as surface manifestations. This is especially true in the case of *reaction formations* (e.g., the qualities of shame, disgust, pity come about only as consequences of internal conflicts with exhibitionism, messing, cruelty), *sublimations,* and *projections.* In the case of *repression,* it is true that there is no overt behavior to signify its existence; nevertheless, it is readily inferred through the absence of overt trends which, "according to the analyst's conception of normality," are essential ingredients of the personality. For example, an undemanding, uncomplaining little child may be noted by the analyst not to display the greed and aggression usually seen in childhood.

Apart from the defense mechanisms there were also the *character traits* and personality types which were readily observable and from which valid deductions about unconscious psychical activity could be made. For example, the first discovery of this kind concerned the insight into the genetic roots of the obsessional character, where outward orderliness, cleanliness, obstinacy, punctuality, parsimoniousness, indecisiveness, hoarding, collecting, etc., indicated the unconscious anal-sadistic trends from which they stem. In 1932 Freud noted that it was reasonable to expect "that other character traits as well will turn out similarly to be precipitates or reaction-formations related to particular pregenital structures." Since 1932, this expectation has been fulfilled, particularly in the case of the oral and urethral type, seen especially in children. For example, the oral fixation point which may threaten a child's progress may reveal itself in the child's attributes of insatiableness, greed, and craving. It may also emerge in relationships which are clinging, demanding or devouring; or in fears of being poisoned, refusing food, etc. A urethral fixation point may be indicated where impulsive behavior is linked with burning ambitiousness.

Analytic writers felt encouraged to collect further items where there were fixed and unchangeable connections with specific id drives and their derivatives. Conflict in the phallic phase, e.g., can be seen in a number of childhood behaviors. *Shyness* and *modesty* can be seen as reversals of exhibitionistic tendencies; *buffoonery* or *clowning* is seen to be a distortion of phallic exhibitionism, with the "showing off displaced from an asset by the individual to one of his defects"; *exaggerated manliness* and *noisy aggression* overcompensate underlying castration fears; complaints of being *maltreated* and *discriminated against* are defenses against passive fantasies and wishes; complaints of excessive *boredom* are related to strongly suppressed masturbation fantasies or activities.

The child's behavior during illness also reveals aspects of his inner mental state. When ill, a child may either look to his environment for comfort, or turn away from it seeking solitude and sleep. The choice indicates something of "the state of his *narcissism* measured against the relative strength of the *attachment to the object world*." The ill child who submits readily to doctor's orders, etc., and who appears to be reasonable in so doing, may be obtaining "regressive pleasure in being positively cared for and loved," or his behavior may be the result of *guilt feelings*, e.g., where the child feels he is being punished by, or is responsible for, being ill. Hypochondriacal behavior in an ill child may reflect his feeling of being badly mothered, inadequately cared for or protected.

There are typical play activities which also reveal aspects of the child's inner mental state. The sublimatory activities of *painting, modeling, water and sand play* indicate anal and urethral preoccupation. Sexual curiosity is seen in breaking up toys in order to discover what is *inside*. The various predominant ways of playing with trains are revealing: crashing them may be a symbol of parental intercourse; building tunnels and subway lines may express interest in the inside of the body; heavily loaded vehicles may be symbols of pregnancy of the mother; speed and smooth performance may be symbols of phallic efficiency. In all these modes of play it is the *main pleasure* which is derived from them which is symbolically significant.

The school boy's favorite position on the *football field* may reveal, in symbolic terms, his relations to his peers, in terms of attack, defense, the ability or inability to compete, to succeed, to adopt the masculine role, etc. The small girl's *horse-craze* may reveal several things: if her enjoyment is due predominantly to the horse's rhythmic movements, primitive autoerotic desires are indicated; if her special pleasure is looking after or grooming the horse, she may be identifying with the caretaking mother; identification with the animal's large size and power, treating it as an addition to her body, reveals her penis envy; the ambition to master the horse, to perform well on it, etc., is indicative of phallic sublimations.

The child's behavior toward *food* tells us much more than its "fixation to the oral phase" aspect, with regard, e.g., to food fads and greediness. And since the disturbances of eating are developmental ones, and are linked to special phases and levels of id and ego growth, "their detailed observation and exploration fulfill the sign- or signal-function of behavior details to perfection." (This refers to Hartmann's concept, 1950.)

In the area of *clothes*, it is known that exhibitionism may be displaced from the body to clothes in the form of vanity. It may appear in the form of neglect in matters of dress where exhibitionism is repressed or acted against. Excessive sensitivity to stiff and "scratchy" clothes indicates repressed skin erotism. The girl's dislike of her feminine anatomy may take the form of avoiding feminine clothes.

Despite the fact that there is so much to be learned from these many examples of childhood behavior, as Anna Freud points out, "child analysts have to be warned not to be led astray by them." The deductions made from them are "useless therapeutically." It would only increase the child's anxieties to point them out without proper analytic interpretation of the ego defenses built up against the unconscious content. To bypass analytic interpretation proper, results in a heightening of the child patient's resistances. Moreover, there are so many items of childhood behavior which could be derived from more than one underlying source or impulse.

Direct (as distinct from analytic) observation has improved since ego psychology has been included in psychoanalytic work. Especially in the conflict-free area of the ego, observations outside the analytic situation do not conflict with the analyst's observations, particularly with regard to the various *ego apparatuses* serving perception and sensation. Of course, the outcome of their action is of the greatest importance for identification, internalization, and superego formation (which processes are accessible only through the work of analysis); nevertheless, they can be estimated outside the analytic situation, as can their degree of maturation. The same can be stated for ego functions. For example, the child's *ego control over the motor functions,* his development of *speech,* can be verified by nonanalytic observation. The range and efficiency of *memory* can be measured by tests; however, it requires analysis to assess how it is dependent on the pleasure principle, e.g., remembering what is pleasurable, forgetting what is not. Overt behavior reveals what is intact or defective in *reality testing.* This is not so with the *synthetic function;* only where it is most severely damaged is it obvious; otherwise, only with analysis can its damage be assessed.

Primary and secondary processes of mental functioning can be observed at different developmental stages. Their discovery was due to analytic work, of course, but once their different qualities were understood they became easily observable outside analysis. For example, in infants in the second year of life, and in preadolescents and adolescents with delinquent trends, it is easy to see rapid alterations between the two modes of mental functioning. In the latency (school) child, where there is a lessening of the intensity of the drives, secondary process functioning is predominant. When an impulse suddenly becomes urgent or overwhelming, primary process functioning can be seen to take over.

It is in the preverbal period of development that direct observation has been so important and helpful, e.g., with regard to the mother-child relationship and the consequences of environmental influences in the first year of life. Separation anxiety in its various forms was first noted outside the analytic situation, in hospitals, residential institutions, creches, etc., though only by observers who were analytically trained.

But to get the fullest information concerning the preverbal period of development, it is best if early detailed recordings of the infant's behavior are complemented by analysis in later childhood and a comparison made of the results. Or, following the analysis of a young child, a detailed longitudinal study of manifest behavior could be made. It is clearly advantageous where analysis and direct observation are employed to check-up on each other. (Anna Freud refers in this respect to the studies undertaken by Ernst and Marianne Kris in the Child Study Center, Yale University and in the Hampstead Child Therapy Clinic.)

THE RELATIONS BETWEEN CHILD ANALYSIS AND ADULT ANALYSIS

The Therapeutic Principles

In the early days of child analysis, child analysts tended to emphasize the similarities between child and adult analysis and to feel committed to the same therapeutic principles as in the analysis of adults.

Following the pattern of classical analysis, they chose to analyze first the ego resistance before the id content, allowing the interpretive work to flow freely between the ego and the id. Material closest to consciousness is dealt with first. The analyst represents a transference object, facilitating the revival and interpretation of unconscious fantasies and attitudes. He attempts whenever possible to analyze impulses in the state of frustration, in order to prevent their being acted out and gratified, for he endeavors to relieve tension, not through catharsis but through shifting material from the level of primary process functioning to secondary thought processes, i.e., to turn id into ego content (A. Freud, 1965, p. 26).

The Curative Tendencies

If the concept of the "curative tendencies" (E. Bibring, 1937) is taken as an area of comparison, we can see how children differ from adults in the treatment situation. The adult patient shows an innate urge to complete treatment, to achieve drive satisfaction, to repeat emotional experience. He prefers to be normal rather than abnormal. He has the ability to assimilate and integrate experiences and to externalize parts of his own personality onto objects through transference.

It is very different with child patients. For the child, "getting well" may feel like having to adapt to a reality which is far from pleasurable, by having to forego wish fulfillments and secondary gains. The child does not wish to *repeat;* his aim is a hunger for *new experience* and new objects. In the child there is the age-adequate stress on mechanisms opposite to those of assimilation and integration, such as *denial, projection, isolation, splitting of the ego.* The very powerful impulse to obtain *drive satisfaction* in children is not an asset in analysis. The one exception which restores the balance is the immensely strong urge in the child to *complete development.* The child's personality is in a fluid state, so that symptoms which serve as solutions to conflicts at one developmental level are useless on the next, and are, therefore, discarded. Libido and aggression are more ready to flow into new channels opened by analysis than is the case with adults. All this being so, it is not difficult to appreciate the child analyst's query (where the pathology has not been too severe) as to how much the improvement has been due to analysis, and how much to maturation and normal development.

Technique

Because of their immaturity, children differ from adults with regard to those qualities considered essential for analysis. Children tend to have no insight into their abnormalities; they do not display the same adult wish to get well or the same kind of treatment alliance; their ego is on the side of their resistances; it is not *their* decision to begin, continue or complete treatment; they relate to their parents as well as to the analyst, the parents having to stand-in for or supplement the child's ego and superego in many ways. The history of child analysis is really about the efforts to deal with these difficulties.

THE ABSENCE OF FREE ASSOCIATION   Whether it is because they do not have sufficient trust in their own ego strength, or whether they feel unable to trust adults sufficiently to be quite honest with them, children all show an uncompromising resistance to free association. In Anna Freud's opinion no remedy for this has yet been found. Numerous activities have been introduced into the analytic situation and hopefully accepted as substitutes for free association (e.g., play with toys, painting, drawing, fantasy games, acting in the transference); but they are in no way valid substitutes for free association. They are even disadvantageous: they tend to produce symbolic material only, which introduces into child analysis "the element of doubt, uncertainty, arbitrariness, which are inseparable from symbolic interpretation in general"; moreover, because they lead to *acts* instead of talking, the analytic possibilities become limited. Especially where the child puts himself or the analyst in danger by his acts, attacks property, or tries to seduce or be seduced, the analyst is compelled to interfere. The child, therefore, cannot be given the license to *do* as he wants (Cf. the adult patient being encouraged to *say* whatever he wants).

Anna Freud stresses another difference between the two techniques. She feels that while free association tends to liberate the sexual fantasies of the patient, relatively free action seems necessary in order to facilitate the liberation of aggressive trends. Therefore, in transference, the child acts out his aggressive feelings through, e.g., hitting, kicking, scratching the analyst. This behavior is time consuming, requiring that the analyst check the very behavior that his initial tolerance has allowed to emerge. Theoretically this connection between aggression and acting out tends to distort the assessment of the proportion between libido and aggression in the child.

This phenomenon is complicated by the difficulty in interpreting aggressive impulses in children and the belief that catharsis leads to change; a belief which while dismissed, for the most part, among adult analysts, still persists among child analysts (pp. 30–31).

INTERPRETATION AND VERBALIZATION   The young children who come into analytic treatment, have, for various reasons, pathology which has delayed (or prevented the completion of) secondary process functioning and therefore of verbalization. These are essential if the ego is to be able to master orientation in the external world and the chaotic emotional states of the inner world. Anny Katan (1961) has emphasized the importance of verbalization for early development. As she points out, the date when the super-ego develops is dependent to a certain extent on the child's ability to replace primary process thinking with secondary process thinking. Verbalization is essential for secondary process thinking; verbalization of the perceptions of the outer world comes before that of the inner world; verbalizing the content of the inner world makes reality testing possible, so that the ego can control the id. Freud's insight into this important role of verbalization was made as far back as 1893 (Freud, 1893, p. 36).

Children differ from adults: in adults, analysis deals first with secondary repression, analyzing defenses against id (primary process) derivatives; only then do the "not remembered" primary process experiences come to be relived in the transference. In older children the process is similar, but in younger ones, and this may apply to children of school-going age, the ratio between these two elements is reversed, as is the order in which they appear in analysis.

RESISTANCES   There is a common misconception that resistances to the upsurges of id derivatives into consciousness are less strong in children than in adults, that the defenses have not yet had time to consolidate. The opposite is the case, and the child's resistances are, if anything, stronger.

Besides those resistances which the child's ego shares with the adult's, Anna Freud (p. 34) lists seven further difficulties and obstacles which occur in a developing, as opposed to a mature, individual.

1. The child does not choose to be in analysis, and so "does not feel bound by any analytic rules."
2. The child, unlike the adult, has no long-term aim in view; hence the difficulties experienced as caused by the analysis in the present outweigh the idea of future gain.
3. Except in the case of obsessional children, "acting out" dominates the analysis.
4. The child's defenses are more rigid since he feels so much more threatened by analysis than does the adult. This is particularly so at the beginning of adolescence.
5. Throughout childhood, very primitive defenses occur along-

side the maturer ones; hence, "the ego resistances based on defenses are increased in number, compared with the adult."

6. All children want to run away from analysis when unconscious material threatens to become conscious, or when the negative transference becomes too intense. They attend analysis then only because of the parents' support.

7. In certain phases of developmental transition, the urge to move away from earlier states to more mature ones results in a strong resistance to allow analysis to uncover or revive the former. This occurs in the early latency child who is moving away from the Oedipal period and in the adolescent who is moving away from his childhood objects, when analytic revival of infantile relationships may result in treatment ending abruptly.

All children prefer "environmental solutions" for their inner conflicts rather than "internal change." This is because they "externalize their inner conflicts in the form of battles with the environment." The child's unwillingness to come to analysis when such externalizations predominate should not be misinterpreted as "negative transference."

TRANSFERENCE   Anna Freud remarks (p. 36) that while she has modified her former opinion that transference in children is restricted to single "transference reactions" (i.e., that it does not develop to the complete status of a "transference neurosis"), she is "still unconvinced that what is called transference neurosis with children equals the adult variety in every respect." This is because of two characteristics of child analysis, already discussed: the absence of free association prevents much of the transference from appearing in the material, and because of the tendency to act instead of talk or associate, the aggressive transference is more apparent than the libidinal one.

According to Anna Freud, the manifestations of transference are evident from the outset of analysis and must be interpreted as such. Since transference phenomena are believed to be of prime importance, they often becloud all other sources of psychoanalytic material and become the "royal road to the unconscious." Sometimes the analyst becomes so involved with this aspect of the treatment that he may forget "that transference is a means to an end, not a therapeutic measure in itself" (p. 37).

These views on transference seem to be based on three assumptions that:

1. anything that occurs in the patient's personality structure can be analyzed in terms of his object relationship to the analyst;
2. all levels of object relationships can be affected by interpretation;
3. figures in the environment serve only as recipients of libidinal and aggressive cathexis (pp. 37–38).

The Child Analyst as a New Object   The analyst is used by the child in a variety of ways. The child uses the analyst as a new object, i.e., for a *new experience,* as well as for *repetition* (transference); and the double relationship is not easy for the analyst to handle. "To learn how to sort out the mixture and to move carefully between the two roles which are thrust on him are essential elements of every child analyst's training in technique" (pp. 38–39).

The Child Analyst as the Object of Libidinal and Aggressive Transference   This section deals with "transference proper," where the child, like the adult, transfers onto the person of the analyst object constancy, ambivalence, oral, anal, and phallic-Oedipal are those of narcissism, unity with the mother, need fulfillment, object constancy, ambivalence, oral, anal, and phallic-oedipal stages. They come into treatment at one or other time, not necessarily in the above order; the type of disturbance will present its own "depth of regression" at the time treatment begins. Withdrawal from the object world will relate to narcissistic self-sufficiency, standing in the way of analytic effort; the wish for total merging with the analyst is indicative of symbiotic attitudes (cf. the adult's plea for hypnosis); the "wish to be helped," which puts the onus on the analyst, stems from the return of the anaclytic dependence; oral attitudes are seen as demandingness and dissatisfaction with what the analyst offers; anal trends are presented as stubbornness, withholding material, provocations, hostility and sadistic attacks (acted out, not presented through verbal associations). Where the child is compliant and easily suggestible, one sees the need to be loved and the fear of loss of the object (here the analyst must guard against seeing these signs as improvement). Where the analyst observes secondary process functioning (in the form of insight, coordinated self-observation, object constancy and the attitudes indicative of the Oedipus complex, positive and negative), he can reasonably hope for the cementing of a treatment alliance which can weather the difficult aspects of analysis.

As Anna Freud points out, the above indicates the need to interpret pre-Oedipal aspects of the transference before Oedipal ones, rather than at the point, as Freud suggested early on, where transference is used as resistance (pp. 40–41).

It can also be seen why deprived, homeless, motherless, and concentration camp children cannot comply with a therapy based on voluntary cooperation with the analyst; they have never achieved the object constancy necessary for an enduring treatment alliance (see Edith Ludowyk Gyomroi, 1963). This applies also to the older child whose development is arrested at a pre-Oedipal level.

The Child Analyst as Object for Externalization   The analyst may become the "representative of the child's *id*" (where he "seduces" the child through tolerating his freedom of action, thought or fantasy). He may become an "auxiliary ego" by verbalizing and helping against anxiety, the child then clinging to him for protection. The analyst may be treated as an "external superego," as a judge of the id derivatives he has uncovered. All these are very useful in understanding what is going on in the child's internal life, but it would be wrong to interpret them as transference manifestations. This applies to the analyses of adults as well.

Infantile Dependency as a Factor in Adult and Child Analysis

From the beginning of analysis, adult patients were treated as independent beings. The therapy which evolved from this attitude resulted in the patient giving the material himself, about himself; the environment was to be seen not objectively, but as the patient saw it, subjectively. The relations between patient and analyst were private and exclusive and the past and present relationships of the patient were reenacted in this privacy.

The child analyst, however, deals with the child's tendency toward independence as an ongoing process. But he can assess the *state of the child's dependency* or independence, whether or not it is in accordance with the child's chronological age. This can be seen in the following consecutive uses the child makes of his parents:

1. for narcissistic unity with the mother during the period at which the child is unable to distinguish between the self and the environment;
2. for gratification of bodily needs and drive derivatives through environmental manipulation;

3. as figures upon whom narcissistic libido can be attached and thereby converted into object libido;
4. to lend support to the child's ego in its efforts to master the id;
5. to serve as figures with whom the child can identify, helping him to build up an independent structure (p. 46).

It is particularly important not to see a mother's disturbed behavior, which could be the result of the child's illness, as being the *cause* of it (as is done easily in the case of autistic children). The simultaneous analysis of parents and their children (as carried out in the Hampstead Child Therapy Clinic and in other places) makes it possible to assess the interaction between them in an objective light. The following findings have emerged.

Parents may require the child to represent "either an ideal of themselves or a figure of their own past." The child, in order to be loved, lets his personality be "molded into a pattern which is not his own and which conflicts with or neglects his own innate potentialities" (p. 47).

Some parents transfer onto the child a role related to their own pathology and so fail to relate to the child on the basis of his real needs. There are mothers who pass on their symptoms to their young children, acting them out together as a *folie a deux* (see Dorothy Burlingham et al, 1955). It requires the parent's own analysis to loosen such bonds in order to help the child, especially when the parent expresses the abnormal relationship in action rather than in fantasies.

Some parents *maintain* the child's disturbance; the child keeps up symptomatic behavior (like phobias, food avoidance, sleeping rituals) only in collusion with the mother, e.g., especially where the mother dreads the child's anxiety as much as the child does.

Because of the need for the parents' cooperation, the child analyst is placed in an unenviable position. His techniques for dealing with the parents will range from excluding them from the treatment situation completely, to "keeping them informed, permitting them to participate in sessions (with the very young), treating or analyzing them simultaneously but separately, to the opposite extreme of treating them for the child's disturbance in preference to analyzing the child himself" (p. 48).

The Balance Between Internal and External Forces as seen by Child and Adult Analyst

The different experiential attitudes of adult and child analysts are discussed in this section. The adult analyst "is in no danger of becoming an environmentalist." The child analyst is. Nevertheless, as Anna Freud states, "nothing should convince the child analyst that alterations in external reality can work cures, except perhaps in earliest infancy" (p. 51).

THE ASSESSMENT OF NORMALITY IN CHILDHOOD

The adult analyst has "little concern in his clinical work with the concept of normality, except marginally, where functioning . . . is concerned" (p. 55). The child analyst, on the other hand, because he "sees progressive development as the most essential function by the immature, is deeply and centrally involved with the intactness or disturbance . . . of this vital process." The study of normal development is central to the problem of the *early spotting of pathogenic agents,* i.e., of prediction or prevention. The theoretical extrapolations from clinical findings made by Heinz Hartmann and Ernst Kris, have considerably increased knowledge of the normal in recent years.

Now while the analyst can assess the child's development and indications for the need for treatment (through studying the libidinal and aggressive sides of his personality on the one hand, and the ego and superego sides on the other, for signs of age-adequateness, precocity, or retardation [A. Freud, 1945]), the emerging indications are more useful for diagnosing pathology and the child's past than for assessing the normal or predicting his future.

The child analyst is consulted not only to treat pathological states but also to advise on matters of normal upbringing. Only by translating external events into internal experience is this possible; since there are no general answers that fit all children, only particular ones to fit a given child. A practical difficulty lies in the way the parents see problems (logically, reasonably, practically), and the way the child experiences them (in terms of his psychical reality). The child analyst has the task of pointing out these discrepant attitudes and explaining to the parents the child's understanding of events.

Four Areas of Difference between Child and Adult

The infant's *egocentricity* leads him to see the mother as providing for his needs and wishes, rather than as a person in her own right.

(The disturbed, regressed schoolchild may display a similar attitude to a greater or lesser degree. This applies also to the other three areas referred to below.) As a result of this egocentricity, whatever happens to the mother, or whatever she does, is seen in terms of satisfaction or frustration of the child's needs. For example, the child may feel rejected or deserted because of the mother's concern with others, with her work or outer interests, her illnesses, depressions and even her death. The birth of a sibling is felt as a hostile act, (indicating the parents' unfaithfulness, criticism of the child, etc.).

Second, the *immaturity of the infantile sexual apparatus* forces the child to "translate adult genital happenings into pregenital events" (p. 59).

Third, the *relative weakness of secondary process* thinking compared with the strength of fantasies and impulses, leads to misapprehensions due not only to a lack of reasoning but also to economic factors. For example, a child at the phallic phase may well understand the significance of illness, the role of the doctor, yet be overwhelmed by fantasies of castration, mutilation, or violent assault when he has to visit the doctor or enter the hospital (pp. 59–60). Having to lie in bed is felt as imprisonment; the diet is felt as intolerable oral deprivation. The parents who allow all this to happen are felt to be horrible, arousing the child's anger, rage, and hostility against them. (See also Anna Freud, 1952, and Joyce Robertson, 1956, in this respect.)

Finally, there is a different *evaluation of time* at different age levels, which can lead to the child's feelings of the parents' insensibility to his sufferings when he has to wait (in various situations) for periods of time which seem short or of little consequence to the parents.

The Concept of Developmental Lines

This concept arose out of the problem of how, usefully, to answer the parents' questions concerning developmental issues. The external decisions had to be "translated into their internal implications." Previously, there were selected developmental scales valid only for isolated parts of the child's personality. What was required were "the basic interactions between id and ego and their various developmental levels, and also age-related sequences of them which, in importance, frequency, and regularity, are comparable to the maturational sequence of libidinal stages or the gradual unfolding of the ego functions." This could be applied, e.g., to studying a line of development leading from the "infant's complete emotional dependence to the adult's comparative self-reliance and mature sex and object relationships, a gradated developmental line which provides the indispensable basis for any assessment of emotional maturity or immaturity, normality or abnormality" (p. 63).

Several other lines of development could be studied as well, "always contributed to from the side of both id and ego development." These include: the line "from the infant's suckling and weaning experiences to the adult's rational rather than emotional attitude to food intake; from cleanliness training enforced on the child by environmental pressure to the adult's more or less ingrained and unshakable bladder and bowel control; from the child's sharing possession of his body with his mother to the adolescent's claim for independence and self-determination in body management; from the young child's egocentric view of the world and his fellow beings to empathy, mutuality, and companionship with his contemporaries; from the first erotic play on his own and his mother's body by way of the transitional objects (Winnicott, 1953) to the toys, games, hobbies, and finally to work, etc" (pp. 63–64).

The various developmental stages through which each of these lines can be followed are then detailed beginning with a "Prototype of a Developmental Line: From Dependency to Emotional Self-Reliance and Adult Object Relationships," which has eight stages. The latency period is characterized by a lessening of oedipal urgency and a transfer of libido from the parents to contemporaries, community groups, teachers, leaders, impersonal ideals, and aim-inhibited sublimated interests.

CORRESPONDENCE BETWEEN DEVELOPMENTAL LINES   When one finds disequilibrium between developmental lines in the "normally endowed" child, it may be necessary to look to "accidental environmental influences," for forces "embodied in the parents' personalities, their actions and ideals, the family atmosphere, the impact of the cultural setting as a whole." To take just one example: depressive moods in the mother in the first two years of the child's life may create a tendency toward depression, which may appear only several years later. This is not a "developmental" achievement; rather, the child produces the mother's mood in himself. Where disequilibrium between developmental lines is produced in this way, it is not to be regarded as pathological as such, but rather as one of the *"many variations of normality"* which account for the endless differences among individuals (p. 87).

Brief mention will be made here of the practical *applications* of these lines of development. The most important of these is that the chronological age of the child is not the sole criterion of the behavior and attitudes that can be expected from him. For example, a child who is regarded from the point of view of his chronological age only, to be old enough to enter nursery school, but has not reached the age-adequate level in the developmental line "from dependency to emotional self-reliance" (i.e., *object constancy*), will legitimately express protest and suffering. On the other hand, if he has at least reached this stage, separation from the mother is much more bearable, though the change still has to be made gradually.

What is discussed next, in the context of the child's normal "regressive rate" (Ernst Kris, 1950; 1951) is "the fact that no young child should be expected to maintain his best level of performance or behavior for any length of time."

Regression as a Principle in Normal Development

Sigmund Freud, in an addition to the *Interpretation of Dreams* (1900), made a distinction between three types of regression, a topographical, a temporal, and a formal type (1914, p. 548). Anna Freud restated Freud's thinking about these in current metapsychological language and maintained that the regressive process can take place in all three parts of the personality structure, and it may affect both the psychic content and the methods of functioning. Regression can occur in regard to aim-directed impulses, object representations, and fantasy content.

REGRESSION IN DRIVE AND LIBIDO DEVELOPMENT   The interdependence between *fixations* and *regressions* is considered here, but in the light that regression (e.g., *sexual* regression) may occur in one or more of the three forms (related to object, aim, and method of discharge). These have to be distinguished separately. It is not enough to say, e.g., that a boy under the stress of castration anxiety "has regressed to the anal or oral phase." What has to be described additionally is the form, scope, and significance of the regressive movement that has taken place. For example, the above statement could simply mean that the boy's regression has reactivated his preoedipal conception of his mother (in clinging, demanding, torturing), but that otherwise he regards her as a whole person in her own right and goes on discharging the anal and oral excitations linked with her in the act of phallic masturbation. Or it could mean that the level of object-relatedness has also been affected by the regression (object constancy being given up and past object attitudes revived—a relationship normal for the toddler but at later stages making for shallowness and promiscuity in object-relationships). Or the regression could include the method of discharging sexual excitement (so that phallic masturbation disappears and is replaced by impulses to eat, to drink, to urinate, or to defecate at the height of excitement). The position is most serious where all three forms of regression occur simultaneously.

REGRESSIONS IN EGO DEVELOPMENT

Temporary Ego Regressions in Normal Development   Anna Freud quotes the popular saying that "children take two steps forward and one back." She gives several examples of the backward moves which occur in every child's normal development of functioning. Such regressions are taken for granted as a common characteristic of infantile behavior. Sudden steps forward are viewed with suspicion. "According to experience, the slow method of trial and error, progression and temporary reversal is more appropriate to healthly psychic growth" (p. 99).

Other Ego Regressions Under Stress   The subject was taken up by some analytic writers only at a later date. Ernst Kris, after observing young children's behavior in nursery schools, introduced the term "regression rate." He showed that the younger the child, the shorter his period of optimal performance. Anna Freud points out that whatever the causation factor, there is one distinguishing factor characteristic of ego regression; the regression is not a move back to previously established positions; instead it retraces, step by step, the line pursued during the course forward. Invariably it is the most recent achievement which is lost first.

Ego Regressions as the Result of Defense Activity   Although maturational and adaptational forces move toward the increasing, and reality-governed efficiency of ego functioning, the defense against painful (unpleasurable) experiences works in the opposite direction, and interferes with ego functioning. *Denial* interferes with accuracy in perception of the external world by excluding the unpleasurable. *Repression* affects the inner world in the same way. *Reaction formations* replace what is unpleasurable with the opposite. These three mechanisms interfere with memory. *Projection* interferes with the synthetic function by attributing anxiety-arousing elements to the object world.

DRIVE AND EGO REGRESSIONS, TEMPORARY AND PERMANENT   It has been seen how regressions of the drives, ego, and superego are normal aspects of the flexibility of the immature individual. On the other hand regressions often become permanent, especially following traumatic distresses, illnesses, etc. When this happens, regression becomes a pathogenic agent. Unfortunately, there is no way of knowing clinically whether a regression is already permanent or whether spontaneous recovery can be expected.

REGRESSION AND THE DEVELOPMENTAL LINES   Having seen regression as a normal process, we are faced with the unevennesses in the various lines of development due to regressions of the various elements of the structure and their combinations. Hence the so frequent deviation from straightforward growth and from the average picture of the hypothetically "normal" child. We have to recognize that the *variations of normality* are innumerable.

ASSESSMENT OF PATHOLOGY: SOME GENERAL CONSIDERATIONS

The line of demarcation between illness and mental health is more difficult to draw in the child than in the adult because of the "constantly shifting internal scene of the developing individual," as a result of which "the current diagnostic categories are of little help and increase rather than decrease the confusing aspects of the clinical picture" (pp. 109–110). Descriptive assessments of current diagnostic categories contradict essential psychoanalytic thinking by emphasizing "manifest" symptomatology, instead of the underlying pathogenic ("metapsychological") factors. As examples of this confusing state, certain terms (such as temper tantrum, truancy, wondering, separation anxiety) each contain several analytic categories, each requiring a different therapeutic approach.

To take a *temper tantrum*, for example, three possible pathogenic situations are considered. The tantrum may be the young child's "direct motor-effective outlet for chaotic drive derivatives"; or it may be an outburst in which aggressive tendencies are turned away from the object world and deflected onto the child's own body; thirdly, it may be seen to be an anxiety attack (in a phobic child, e.g.) when the environment disturbs the child's protective mechanisms. In the first example, it is not treatment that is required: the symptom should disappear when an ego-syntonic channel of discharge (e.g., speech) has been established; in the second case, it is necessary to elicit the anger and reconnect it with the offending external object; in the third example, either the defense must be reinstated, or the original source of the displaced anxiety must be traced, interpreted, and dissolved through analysis (p. 112).

With regard to *truancy*, or vagrancy, or wandering, there is a similar variety of quite different states. Children may run away as a result of being maltreated, or they may not be "tied to their families by the normal emotional bonds"; they may be afraid of their teachers or schoolmates, or be afraid of being criticized or punished for various actual reasons. Here the causes are external or environmental. But in other cases there are internal reasons: the child, though appearing to run *away* from the environment, may really be "running *toward* the fulfillment of a fantasy," such as a lost object belonging to the past. Only analytic "tracking down" of the unconscious wish can remove the latter type of symptom.

Separation anxiety is less dynamic than descriptive in the way the term is used. It is applied both to the states of distress due to separation (e.g., in infants), and to the mental states causing school phobias (the inability to leave home) or homesickness (a form of mourning) in latency (school) children. Only analytic insight can cure the second group of symptoms.

It will be clear at this stage that what is lacking in this "static" type of terminology are questions of age and the stage of development of the child; moreover it fails to differentiate between symptoms due to the "delay or failure to attain and perfect specific personality traits" and those which are due to "breakdown of function or transgression against it" (p. 114). For example, behavior such as *lying* and *stealing, aggressive and destructive attitudes, perverse activities*, etc., cannot be assessed pathologically unless a "timetable of developmental sequences" is taken into account.

In the case of *lying* (pp. 114–116): it is normal in the infant to *deny* or ignore persistent painful impressions. What the child analyst has to do is to decide at what stage of development (in a particular child) the transition has taken place from primary to secondary process mental functioning, the ability to differentiate the inner from the outer world, reality testing, etc. "Delinquent" lying is reserved for those children of advanced ego development who have "other than developmental reasons for avoiding or distorting the truth," with motives such as obtaining "material advantage, fear of authority, escape from criticism or punishment, wishes for aggrandisement, etc." A middle group is that of the so-called "fantasy liars" who cannot tolerate painful realities and regress to infantile forms of wishful thinking. A clinical case of lying may contain factors applying to all three groups: it is essential for the analyst to differentiate one from the other.

Stealing in children can be related to oral greed, anal possessiveness, urges to collect and hoard, and overpowering needs for phallic symbols. Whether or not he steals, however, depends upon educational coercion, superego demands and gradual shifts in the id-ego balance toward the development of honesty.

The diagnostician has therefore to assess whether the act of stealing is due to incomplete or arrested growth in terms of individual status, object relations, empathy, or superego formation or whether there has been a temporary regression in any of these areas; or if there has been a permanent regression with the stealing representing a neurotic symptom; or finally if the stealing is a delinquent symptom of insufficient ego control over normal, unregressed desires for possession.

Here, too, the problem of mixed etiology must be taken into account.

The criteria used in the case of adults (existent symptomatology; the suffering they cause; resultant disturbance of functioning) have to be considerably modified if they are to be valid for children.

Symptom formation does not necessarily have the same significance in childhood that it has in the adult. They may, for example, be due to stresses and strains associated with normal development in the child and may disappear when, e.g., adaptation to the particular developmental level has been reached.

Mental distress in the child is not a reliable guide to the presence of pathology or its severity. This may not be true in the case of anxiety attacks, but phobic and obsessive states "successively serve the avoidance of pain and unpleasure" rather than cause it (p. 120). What children *do* suffer from is the "inevitable by-product of the child's dependency and of the normal developmental processes themselves," such as frustrations; helplessness; separations, disappointments; Oedipal jealousies, rivalries, and castration anxieties. "Even the most normal child may feel deeply unhappy for one reason or another, for long or short periods, almost every day of his life." It is the child who does *not* complain who arouses "our suspicion that abnormal processes are at work in them" (p. 121).

Impairment of function.   In the child there is normally an unceasing fluctuation in the level of performance. Anna Freud points out in this connection that on the whole "it is safe to insist that children of all ages should be permitted at times to function below the level of their potentialities without being automatically labelled as 'backward,' 'regressed' or 'inhibited' (p. 123). She has previously indicated (A. Freud, 1945) that there is one factor alone, concerning impairment of activity in childhood, which compares with adult impairments (such as interference with love, sex life, and the capacity to work), and that is the interference with "the child's capacity to move forward in progressive steps until maturation, development in all areas of the personality, and adaptation to the social community have been completed" (p. 123).

What can be seen is that the usual adult criteria for assessing severity of illness fall into diagnostic categories which are generally rigid, static, and descriptive. In place of these, Anna Freud discusses three groups of criteria which enable child analysts to examine the clinical pictures in quite a new way and to assess them "according to their significance for the process of development." Symptomatology is now related to the child patient's position on the developmental scale with regard to drive, ego and superego development, to the structuralization of the personality (stable borders between id, ego and superego), and to modes of functioning (progression from primary to secondary thought processes, from pleasure to reality principal), etc." The analyst has thus to ask himself such questions as, has the child reached levels of development adequate for his age; has he gone beyond them or remained behind, and in what respects; are maturation and development present as ongoing processes, or are they affected by the child's disturbance; and, finally, have regressions or arrests intervened, and, if so, to what depth and on which level.

What is needed in order to answer these questions is "a scheme of average developmental norma for all aspects of the personality." Miss Freud discusses the scheme with a view to showing that the more complete is such a scheme, the more successful will the evaluation of the patient be, in regard to "evenness or unevenness of progression rate, harmony or disharmony between developmental lines, and temporariness or permanency of regression."

DISHARMONY BETWEEN DEVELOPMENTAL LINES   If the imbalance between these lines is excessive, the child presents as a "problem." He is either disturbed in himself or is disturbing to others. When investigated clinically, the child does not fit the usual diagnostic labels. If we use the stages along the various developmental lines as an approximate measuring scale, we find that the child's levels of achievement are quite disproportionate. A common example is the case where the child has an unusually high verbal I.Q. and a low performance I.Q. (suggestive of organic damage), as well as unusual backwardness on the lines toward emotional maturity, companionship, and body management. Here the case may be diagnosed as "borderline" or "prepsychotic".

The child who is usually described as "lacking in concentration," having "a short attention span," or as "inhibited," may show the following combination: he is unable to reach the last stages along the line from play to work; but is age-adequate regarding emotional and social development, body management, etc. Here it is necessary to look for the prerequisites of the right attitude to work: e.g., control and modification or pregenital drive components; effective reality-principle functioning; and pleasure in his ultimate results of activity.

PERMANENT REGRESSIONS AND THEIR CONSEQUENCES   If regression is not spontaneously reversible, its effect is not beneficial. Permanent regressions may have their beginnings in any area of the personality. If they begin in the ego and superego, both of these may be reduced to a lower level of functioning, the damage then spreading to the id derivatives. Impulsive behavior, a break-through of affect and aggressive tendencies, frequent breaches of id control, and erruptions of irrational elements then result from a weakening of "censorship" due to a lessening of controlling power brought on by ego and superego regression. Clinically, this may be traced back to traumatic shock, internal or external events arousing anxiety, separations, severe disappointments in the child's love objects, severe disillusionment with his objects of identification, etc. (Jacobson, 1946).

Regression may begin on the side of the id derivatives, in which case the ego and superego are affected by either *condoning* the lowered drive activity or by *objecting* to it. In the former case, the internal id-ego conflict is avoided and the drives are *ego-syntonic*. Or the total personality may be affected, with a reduction of the whole level of maturity: here, many puzzling clinical states result, often described as infantile non-typical, delinquent or borderline behavior. This occurs more frequently in children because of the comparative weakness and immaturity of the infantile ego, but it is not wholly absent in adults.

When the ego and superego are better organized, they "object" to lowered drive activity. Internal conflicts then result, with the emergence of the various infantile neuroses with which we are familiar, such as the anxiety, hysterias, phobias, pavor nocturnus, the obsessions, rituals, bedtime ceremonials, inhibitions, and character neuroses.

Anna Freud presents a detailed account of the difference between ego-syntonic and ego-dystonic drive regressions in the case of regressions from the phallic to the anal-sadistic phases as they occur in boys at the height of the castration fears associated with the Oedipus complex (pp. 130–131).

Assessment by Type of Anxiety and Conflict

The "external" refers to the conflict where the child and his environment are at cross-purposes with each other. The conflict has not yet been internalized. The associated anxieties take different forms according to a chronological sequence: fear of annihilation due to a loss of the caretaking object; fear of loss of the object's love; fear of criticism and punishment by the object; castration fear.

The "internalized" conflict occurs after identification with the external powers and introjection of their authority into the superego have occurred. The resultant anxieties are brought about through fear of the superego, i.e., guilt.

"Internal" conflict is derived exclusively from clashes between id and ego and is seen in the opposite qualities in drive representatives and effects, such as love and hate, active and passive, and masculine and feminine trends. During the period when the ego is immature, they cause no conflict, but become incompatible with each other and cause conflict once the synthetic function of the maturing ego is brought to bear on them. They arouse enormous amounts of guilt in the child, but can be identified only during analysis and not at the diagnostic stage.

The above classification helps considerably in assessing the severity of childhood disturbances due to conflict and determines the nature of therapy. External conflict can be improved by the management of environmental conditions; internalized conflict can be resolved by psychoanalytic therapy of average duration. Internal conflict may require analytic treatment of long duration and unusual intensity, presenting the analyst with excessive difficulties (see S. Freud, 1937).

Assessment by General Characteristics

There are certain personality characteristics (mainly ego, usually innate) which act as "stabilizing factors," and which give the analyst some indication of the child patient's chances of future mental health. These are: high tolerance for frustration; good sublimation potential; effective ways of dealing with anxiety; and a strong urge toward completion of development.

FRUSTRATION TOLERANCE AND SUBLIMATION POTENTIAL   Clinical experiences reveal a close connection between the child's ability (some at an early age) to tolerate drive frustration and his chances of remaining mentally healthy. Where tolerance of the unpleasure of unsatisfied drive derivatives is poor from early on, the child is endangered. Primitive defenses like denial and projection predominate in the ego's precarious check over undiminished amounts of tension and anxiety; or the latter find periodic outlets in the form of chaotic outbursts of temper. There is a short path between these devices to pathology, such as displaying neurotic, delinquent, or perverse symptoms.

MASTERY OF ANXIETY   As has previously been stated, anxiety is inevitable in all stages of the child's development. What is significant is the ego's ability to deal with anxiety, and this differs considerably from one child to another. The children who cope best show an early ability for "active mastery" of anxiety rather than a retreat from it. This they do by way of ego resources (intellectual understanding, logical reasoning), changing of external circumstances, aggressive counterattack, etc. Active mastery has to be distinguished from counterphobic tendencies in children, where the ego defends itself secondarily against established phobic tendencies.

REGRESSIVE VERSUS PROGRESSIVE TENDENCIES   Both tendencies exist in all children, but their proportionate strengths vary from one child to another. The clinical distinction between the two tendencies can best be seen in the child's reactions to such taxing life experiences as bodily illness, the birth of a sibling, etc. Where the progressive tendencies outweigh the regressive, the child reacts to long periods of illness with a maturing of his ego rather than by becoming more infantile. In the case of the birth of a sibling, the stronger progressive forces are seen in the child's response by claiming the status of the "big" brother or sister, rather than by giving up his achievements and wanting to be the baby himself. Where regressive forces predominate, there is a greater likelihood of arrests between developmental levels, the establishment of fixation points, and the recourse to symptom formation.

A Metapsychological Profile of The Child

The large mass of information collected during the process of diagnostic assessment can be organized into a comprehensive metapsychological profile of the child, which gives the analyst a picture which includes dynamic, genetic, economic, structural, and adaptive data. This enables the analyst to synthesize otherwise disparate or confusing findings. Profiles of this kind can be drawn up at different stages, e.g., at the preliminary diagnostic stage, during analysis, at the end of analysis, or at follow-up investigations. The draft of a profile which could be employed at the diagnostic stage is outlined below:

I   Reason for referral

II   Description of child

III   Family background and personal history

IV   Possibly significant environmental influences

V   Assessments of development

    A.   Drive development (Here both libido and aggression are assessed; libido with regard to phase development, libido distribution, and object libido; aggression, with regard to quantity, quality and direction.)

B.   Ego and superego development (Here we have assessments of the ego apparatus and of ego functions—the examination in detail of the defense organization; and finally any secondary interference of defense activity with ego achievements.)

VI   Genetic assessments (regression and fixation points)

VII   Dynamic and structural assessments (conflicts—external, internalized and internal)

VIII   Assessment of Some General Characteristics (Frustration tolerance, sublimation potential, overall attitude to anxiety, and progressive developmental forces versus regressive tendencies).

IX   Diagnosis

The diagnostician integrates the various aspects of the child's behavior in such a way as to make a clinically meaningful assessment. He will have to decide between a number of categorizations such as:

(1) that, in spite of current manifest behavior disturbances, the personality growth of the child is essentially healthy and falls within the wide range of 'variations of normality;'

(2) that existent pathological formations (symptoms) are of a transitory nature and can be classed as by-products of a developmental strain;

(3) that there is permanent drive regression to previously established fixation points which leads to conflicts of a neurotic type and gives rise to infantile neuroses and character disorders;

(4) that there is drive regression as above plus simultaneous ego and superego regressions which lead to infantilisms, borderline, delinquent, or psychotic disturbances;

(5) that there are primary deficiencies of an organic nature or early deprivations which distort development and structuralization and produce retarded, defective and nontypical personalities;

(6) that there are destructive processes at work (of organic, toxic, or psychic, known or unknown origin), which have effected, or are on the point of effecting a disruption of mental growth. (p. 147)

ASSESSMENT OF PATHOLOGY: SOME INFANTILE PRESTAGES OF ADULT PSYCHOPATHOLOGY

The assessment of the child's disturbance serves more than one purpose for the child analyst. There is the practical problem of deciding for or against therapy and then deciding on the treatment of choice. Then there is the wish to learn more about the developmental processes themselves. Perhaps even more important is the attempt to obtain clearer insights into the early or initial stages of mental disorders which are usually known clinically in their later phases and to distinguish between transitory and permanent psychopathology.

The Infantile Neuroses

Here the child analyst feels most at home, seeing that the infantile neuroses have, from the beginning, been considered on a par with their adult counterparts, even as their prototype and model. But discrepancies between the two soon became apparent. Instead of symptoms forming part of a genetically related personality structure as is usually the case in the adult, in children, symptoms may occur in isolation, or are linked with other symptoms and personality traits which are unrelated and have different origins. Then it was seen that there was no certainty that a particular form of infantile neurosis would lead to the same form in the adult. In fact clinical evidence often points to the opposite happening. This may be due to alteration in ego attitudes during maturation and development, delinquent traits might turn as a result to compulsive traits. The field of mental disturbances in childhood is much wider than was expected from a knowledge of adult pathology. Till recently the formulations of these varied childhood disturbances were descriptive rather than dynamic, and certainly not dynamically detailed.

The Developmental Disturbances

Childhood disturbances are so frequent and so varied because of the child's dependence, and because of the stresses and strains of development itself. Infants have to accept whatever care is given them. If this care is not appropriately sensitive, a variety of disturbances occurs, usually around sleep, feeding, elimination, and the wish for company.

While external stresses are avoidable, internal stresses are inevitable. Ego and drive progression, which either cures or causes the developmental disturbances, is best shown "at those transition points between phases where not only the quality but also the quantity of drive activity undergoes a change." A dramatic change occurs when the "Oedipal" child becomes a "latency" child. At the height of the phallic-Oedipal phase, one sees in the child extreme castration fear, the death wishes and fears and the defenses against them, and the resulting inhibitions, masculine over-compensations, the passive and regressive moves.

Just the opposite occurs in the transition from latency to preadolescence. Here we have changes both in quality and quantity of the drives, as well as an increase in primitive pregenital trends (oral and anal particularly). This results in "a severe loss of social adaptation, of sublimations and, in general, of personality gains . . . achieved during the latency period." Thus the preadolescent appears to be less normal, less mature, and apparently delinquent. But this picture changes when the entry into adolescence proper occurs: the genital trends which emerge act as a transitory cure for any passive-feminine leanings resulting from the negative Oedipus complex; they also remove the diffuse pregenitality of preadolescence. Adolescence also creates its own symptomatology, as described by Eissler (1958), and Geleerd (1958), which, in the severer cases, has a quasi-dissocial, quasi-psychotic, borderline quality. Once adolescence has run its course, this pathology disappears.

FAILURES OF SOCIALIZATION   The multiplicity of factors in the socializing process is matched by the multiplicity of disorders which affect it. There are very considerable differences between individuals with regard to chronology, consistency, and scope of superego development, it is thus more useful "to think in terms of variations of superego formation rather than in terms of deviation from a hypothetically fixed norm." Anna Freud discusses many factors and constellations which to dissociality, such as: *failure in higher ego development* (in delinquents and criminals who are discovered to be of primitive, infantile mentality, retarded, deficient, defective, with low I.Q.'s); *dissociality and criminality* on the part of the *parents* (which are incorporated into the child's superego; *identification* with the parents which is *disrupted* (through separations, rejections, and other interferences with the emotional tie to them). Qualitative factors (in the child's struggle for socialization) receive more attention than *qualitative* factors in the literature. She points out that it is normally the components of infantile aggression (rather than of infantile sexuality) which are stressed in the literature as being a threat to socialization. In fact, aggressive strivings if "fused in the normal way with the libidinal ones, are socializing influences, rather than the opposite" (p. 180). It is only when aggression occurs "in pure culture" (i.e., either unfused with libido or defused from it) that it menaces socialization. The cause of this is in the libidinal processes and not in the aggressive drive itself, where the former may not have developed to the point of "toming down and binding aggression," or may have lost that capacity during the child's development at some point, owing to object loss, rejections (real or imagined), severe disappointments in object love, etc. The anal-sadistic phase is a special danger point for defusion, a phase when the social usefulness of aggression is particularly dependent on a close tie with equal quantities of libido. This is illustrated in the toddler's behavior: where diffusion frees sadism in a purely destructive form, the toddler's "half-playful, provoking, self-willed attitudes" become "fixed in the personality as quarrelsomeness, ruthless acquisitiveness, and a preference for hostile rather than friendly relations with fellow beings" (p. 181). Moreover, defused aggression is uncontrollable, externally and internally. If this state persists and fusion is not re-established, the destructive attitudes become a major cause of delinquency and criminality.

MOVING FROM FAMILY TO COMMUNITY STANDARDS   The moral norms on which family life is based result in "initial privileges" for the child, such as "benefit of age," the benefits of his specific personality, and his specific position in the family; result from identification with parents whom the child loves, and from the positive narcissistic identification of the parents with the child. When the child moves from home to school he retains only a few of these privileges, which may result in difficulty in achieving a successful transition from home to school standards. Success in identifying and complying with home standards is not necessarily a guarantee of similar success with school standards. If the child likes, loves or admires a teacher (and uses the latter as an object for identification), then school rules still have a "personal flavor." But school rules usually "take less or no notice of individual differences." Then again, within the child's age group, all children "are expected to conform to a common norm, whatever sacrifice this may mean to their personalities."

When the adolescent child leaves school to enter the adult community, "the legal norms finally become impersonal." Although legal codes (which are of a complex, impersonal and formal nature) do not become part of the individual's inner world, "what a functioning superego is expected to ensure is . . . his acceptance and internalization of the existence of a governing norm in general." The delinquent or criminal carries on in the style of the child who "ignores or belittles or disregards parental authority and acts in defiance of it." There are also those types of people who succeed in becoming once more what individuals set out to be as infants, namely a "law unto themselves." There are individuals whose "moral demands on themselves are higher and stricter than anything which the environment expects from them or would impose on them." Their standards result from identification with an *ideal* image of the parents, which they enforce via an excessively severe superego.

Homosexuality as a Diagnostic Category in Childhood Disorders

Some of the arguments applied to dissociality can be employed in the case of childhood homosexual manifestations. It is difficult to determine at what age the term homosexuality can be used because homosexual behavior is at times appropriate to normal development. Moreover in the case of adult homosexuality it is difficult to connect certain preliminary stages which can be seen in childhood and the final adult manifestation (p. 184).

The phenomena which are of relevance for the child, (as distinct from those which relate only to the behavior of adults), deal with three subjects: *object choice;* the *reconstruction* in adult analysis and their significance for the prognosis of homosexuality in childhood assessments; and the general question of *causation* of homosexuality by weighing inborn against acquired elements.

OBJECT CHOICE: THE AGE FACTOR   Object choice is discussed here as it relates to *infants; to pregenital component trends;* to the *phallic phase* and Oedipus complex; to the *latency period; to preadolescence* and *adolescence.*

Although the whole developmental line needs to be considered for a proper appreciation of the significance of any one phase, we shall discuss here only the aspects of object choice which relate to the *latency period.*

The child's behavior during the *phallic Oedipal period* "foreshadows more closely than at other times his future inclinations regarding sexual role and choice of sexual object." This aspect of the libidinal life disappears once more from view when the child enters the *latency period;* although, in neurotic children, who have not solved and dissolved their Oedipal relationships to their parents, there are "unmodified remnants of the Oedipus complex which determine the attachments." But apart from these, there are also "the phase-adequate aim-inhibited, displaced or sublimated tendencies for which the sexual identity of the partner becomes again a matter of comparative indifference."

Diagnostic assessment at this period is further confused because "object choice with regard to contemporaries proceeds on lines opposite to those usual in the adult." The boy who despises girls and seeks male companionship exclusively is not the future homosexual. This behavior is rather the hallmark of the normal masculine latency boy (the future heterosexual). Choice of playmates of a similar age in the latency period is based on "identification with the partners, not on object love proper, that is, on equality with them, which may or may not include equality of sex."

PROGNOSIS VERSUS RECONSTRUCTION   Although there is in the literature a mass of relevant data reconstructed in the analysis of adult homosexuals which trace the different manifestations of overt and latent homosexuality back to their infantile roots (e.g., inborn endowment; narcissism; links with oral and anal pregenital phases; overestimation of the penis in the phallic phase; influence of excessive love for and dependence on either mother or father, or extreme hostility to either of them; traumatic observations of the female genitalia and of menstruation; envy of the mother's body; and jealousy of rival brothers who are subsequently turned into love objects), these reconstructed data cannot be used as a means of the early detecting of homosexual development in children. A different or even opposite outcome cannot be excluded, even if the same childhood elements are known to have led to a specific homosexual result in others. It is not the major infantile events and constellations in themselves that determines the outcome, but a variety of accompanying events and circumstances which make it difficult to determine both retrospectively in adult analysis and prognostically in the assessment of children. These events and circumstances included external and internal, qualitative and quantitative factors. For example, the boy's movement toward mature heterosexuality through his love for his mother or his repression of his aggressive masculinity for her is not entirely up to him. The mother's personality and behavior, the amount of satisfaction and frustration that she gives him, both orally and anally, the degree to which she either hinders or promotes independent behavior, and the attitude she adopts concerning his phallic advances toward her are of the utmost importance to his sexual development.

There are more factors in various other etiological situations, and A. Freud states that what has to be considered finally are the purely chance happenings, like accidents, illnesses, seductions, object losses through death, the difficulty or ease of finding a heterosexual object in adolescence, etc., which are unpredictable, and which may encourage development in one or another sexual direction.

HOMOSEXUALITY, FAVORED OR PREVENTED BY NORMAL DEVELOP-MENTAL POSITIONS   On the assumption that during the child's development, leanings towards homosexuality compete and alternate regularly with normal heterosexuality, and that "the two tendencies make use in turn of the various libidinal positions through which the child passes," what favors homosexual development are the following factors:

1. The bisexual tendencies which are part of the inborn constitution. This innate bisexuality is intensified in the pregenital period and remains the constitutional basis for any later homosexual inclinations.
2. The child's primary and secondary narcissism, i.e., the libidinal cathexis of his own self. If later childhood object choice follows the original narcissistic pattern, the child chooses partners as identical as possible with his own self, including identity of sex. This is characteristic of latency, and certain stages of preadolescence and adolescence.
3. The anaclitic object attachment of the infant, for which sex is of secondary importance. This is specially significant for female homosexuality, since the girl may become fixated to this stage as to a "homosexual" one.
4. The libidinization of the anus and the usual passive tendencies of the anal stage which are the normal bodily basis for the boy's feminine identification.

5. Penis envy which is the normal basis for the girl's masculine identity.
6. The overestimation of the penis in the phallic phase which may make it difficult or impossible for the boy to accept a "castrated" love object.
7. The negative Oedipus complex which is a normal "homosexual" phase for both boys and girls. (pp. 195–196)

Factors which protect against homosexuality are: the quantitative increase in heterosexuality in the phallic and positive Oedipal phase which automatically reduces residual homosexual inclinations from the anal period; the very intensity of castration fear may act as a counterforce against the negative Oedipus complex and a barrier against homosexuality; reaction formations against anality (in males), especially disgust, blocks the path to homosexuality effectively; the "tendency to complete development" and the "biological reasonableness" (E. Bibring, 1936) which make individuals prefer normality to abnormality, count as factors against homosexuality.

THE THERAPEUTIC POSSIBILITIES

The experience at a psychoanalytic clinic for children, such as the Hampstead Child-Therapy Clinic, is that the entire spectrum of childhood disorders come for treatment. One extreme are the most common developmental difficulties, educational failures and upsets, delays and arrests in mental growth. Then there are the more serious pathological instances such as traumatized and seduced cases, and the infantile neurosis proper, and the other extreme— atypical grave ego defects, borderline disturbances, autistic and psychotic states, delinquent or neat-schizophrenic adolescents, etc. (p. 213).

The therapist is thus faced with a dilemma. Within the area of the neuroses proper, (i.e., where there are permanent regressions and fixed neurotic symptomatology) "nothing will change the child except analysis which works for alteration in the balance of forces within the structure" (p. 232).

Usually the child's inner disharmonies, which are normal by-products of structural development, are dealt with by the child's ego itself, together with parental support, comfort, and guidance. When the father is inadequate, analysis might help to reduce anxieties (through clarification, verbalization, and interpretation) before they lead to pathogenic consequences. Nevertheless, the analyst is likely to feel that a therapeutic method has taken over a task which belongs by right to the child's ego or to the parents.

The decision to employ psychoanalytic treatment is directly related to symptom formation: if an ego withstands the drives sufficiently to enforce neurotic compromises on them, such an ego thereby proves the intention to maintain its position; and that indicates, in theory at least, its willingness to accept external help for doing so.

Many neurotic children want therapy because of their suffering; e.g., where bodily discomforts and pains are caused by the psychological upsets of stomach and digestion, the skin eruptions, asthma, the headaches, sleep disturbances, etc.; in the phobias of school, street or animals, by the loss of freedom of action, the inability to do what other children can do, and being excluded from other children's pleasures; in the rituals and obsessions, by the feeling of being at the mercy of an unknown and compelling force which prescribes senseless actions; etc. (p. 220).

Occasionally these feelings are openly verbalized. A boy patient aged four and a half years said to his analyst after an attack of his compulsive ritualistic behavior. "Now you can see at least what my worries force me to do," thus expressing the utter helplessness felt by his ego in the situation. A girl of six who suffered from a severe school phobia said to her mother, "You know, it isn't that I don't want to go to school, I just can't." A latency girl, the eldest of a large family, with character difficulties caused by penis envy, jealousy, masturbation guilt, sang to herself, "All the other children are good and only I am bad. Why am I so bad?" Like the others, she was thereby expressing the gulf she felt to exist between her ideal of herself, her superego demands, and her helpless ego, together with the puzzlement as to why, on her own, she could do nothing to remedy the situation (see also Bornstein, 1951).

But such insights will not provide the child with more than an initial approach to treatment. The kind of sustained introspection, which is a normal ego capacity in the adult, is not present in the child. Children do not scrutinize their thoughts and inner events, unless they are obsessional. But even in the latter cases, introspection serves pathological rather than constructive ends (e.g., the urge to exploit self-criticism and guilt for masochistic purposes, etc.).

Children do not tend to observe themselves objectively or to "take stock honestly of the happenings in their own minds. Their natural inquisitiveness is directed away from the inner to the outer world," and it is only at puberty that self-examination and excessive introspection may be seen to occur as painful aspects of adolescence in certain juveniles, other than the delinquent type, of course.

In the pre-Oedipal, Oedipal, and latency stages the child is not willing to experience any conflict consistently as intrapsychic. The mechanism of externalization comes in to play here, when the child escapes from guilt feelings by provoking the parents (or analyst) to assume the role of a punishing or critical authority. It is this externalization of conflict with the superego which results in otherwise unexplained acts of disobedience in the child. This is seen especially in latency children who have an active masturbation conflict: after each eruption and satisfaction of their sexual needs, they do their best to turn the adult world against themselves by provocative behavior. "In the realm of dissociality as well, it is a familiar fact that a guilty conscience not only follows the delinquent act but very often precedes and motivates delinquency" (p. 222). Relief from the internal conflict with the superego is obtained by being criticized, accused, or punished by an external agent.

The same thing happens with drive conflicts. Dangerous pre-Oedipal or Oedipal impulses (such as the oral and anal; unconscious death wishes against siblings; hostility against the rival parent) are displaced and externalized or projected onto figures in the external world, who are thus turned into persecutors or seducers with whom the child is then able to enter into an external battle. The mechanisms which are used here are well-known from the infantile phobias (school, street, animals), where, through displacement and externalization, the internal background is converted into an external one.

This tendency to externalize internal conflicts has a bearing on the child's expectations regarding therapy: he hopes that the analyst, through his superior powers, will change the environment for the better. For example, the child who fears a dreaded teacher expects help by a change of school (to obtain relief from what are really his guilt feelings: He expects separation from a "bad" companion in order to end temptations (the child ignores the fact that the latter arise from his own impulses and sexual-aggressive fantasies) or removal from bullying classmates (to remedy what in reality are the child's own passive-masochistic inclinations). The analyst who, correctly enough, refuses to accept the role which his child patient thrusts on him, easily becomes, in the child's estimation, an adversary rather than a helpmate. Often enough, the parents, too, prefer environmental to intrapsychic changes.

It must be understood that lack of introspection is a characteristic ego attitude of childhood and is employed as an effective protection against mental pain. Only if the child can identify with an adult he trusts, and is therefore in alliance with him, is it given up, and "reluctantly replaced by a more honest viewing of the inner world."

This denial of the intrapsychic nature of conflicts is used as a defense by many adults as well; but these individuals do not usually choose to enter psychoanalytic treatment. "It is a special difficulty, reserved for the child analyst, that his patients have to submit to a procedure and meet demands which they have not chosen knowingly or of their own free will" (p. 224).

A SUBSPECIES OF THE INFANTILE NEUROSIS IN ANALYSIS

Where, in the child, the conflict with the drives is not solved by means of an infantile neurosis proper, but instead by removing the "disagreement," by lowering ego standards completely (as occurs in infantilisms, the nontypical disturbances, and certain dissocial reactions), the child is content with his deterioration, just as in the case of adults who are perverse, delinquent, or criminal. Like such adults, child regards analytic treatment as undesirable since it disturbs his peaceful state. If the analyst is to treat such children he needs to "foster" the kind of id-ego conflicts as occur in the (treatable) infantile neuroses. Specific technical parameters have been described twice (in the literature) to deal with this problem. August Aichorn (1935; 1923–1948) has described how he changed the ego standards of children with dissocial leanings, who rebelled against the environment and himself, thus making analytic treatment impossible. He fostered a (narcissistic) tie and identification, first with himself as a person, and then with his value system. In this way he introduced disharmony into their psychic structure. The delinquent was thus changed into a neurotic who could then respond to analytic treatment. Anna Freud suggested an "introductory phase" (1926) with a similar motive in mind. The aim of this was to alert the child to his inner disharmonies by effecting an ego state favorable for their perception; although many colleagues misunderstood this as an "educational" intervention to bring about transference improvements, and was therefore unjustifiable. As she points out now (1965, p. 226) in "present-day work the consistent interpretation of defenses serves the same purpose of id-ego confrontation."

With regard to all childhood *conflicts*, "disturbance and analytic therapy are closely matched." Real improvements (as distinct from initial transference improvements, e.g.) result from "consecutive interpretations of material, resistance (defenses) and transference repetition, i.e., to analytic work in its strictest sense."

In the *developmental disharmonies and difficulties*, by clarifying and interpreting anxieties, distress is diminished and arrests are counteracted, regressions are undone (kept temporary), and progression is brought back by analytic clarification of the danger situation which enforced them. In the *infantile neuroses*, anxiety attacks, bedtime rituals, and daytime ceremonials are reduced or overcome by the interpretation of their unconscious content; touching compulsions disappear where their connection with masturbation, or with the underlying aggressive fantasies, have been revealed; phobias disappear after the analysis of the Oedipal displacements which have caused them; fixations to repressed traumatic events are loosened when the trauma is brought back to consciousness in memory, or relived and interpreted in the transference.

Finally, in the symptomatology of the infantile neuroses, damage is done to both the drive derivatives and the ego. The "double action" of the analysis reflects the therapeutic counterpart of this: defense interpretation alternatives with interpretation of content; as a result, relief is given first to the hard-pressed ego and then to the equally hard-pressed drive, until what is unconscious in both is brought up to the surface, verbalized, clarified, interpreted, and so becomes part of the child's integrated personality.

THERAPY OF THE NON-NEUROTIC DISTURBANCES   The further we move away from diagnostic categories I–IV (i.e., the conflict-based neurotic disorders) to categories V–VI (the arrests, defects, and deficiencies of development), so does the therapeutic process change its nature; though analysis is still applicable and helpful in effecting improvements.

All writers on the subject agree that there are more elements in the psychoanalytic method then *interpretation* of transference and resistance, the *widening of consciousness* at the expense of the unconscious parts of id, ego and superego, and the resulting increase in *ego dominance*. Miss Freud details these other elements, pointing out that they are unavoidable even when unintended. The elements she refers to are *verbalization* and *clarification* of the preconscious (which play an important role, especially in children, by preparing the way to interpretation proper, and by diminishing the impact of the anxiety associated with the latter); *suggestion* (an inevitable consequence of the analyst's temporary position of power and emotional importance in the child's life, and represented by the "educational" side effects of analytic therapy); *reassurance* (which is inseparable from the presence and intimate relationship with an adult whom the child trusts). The greater the child feels the role of the analyst as a "new" object, the more he will tend to misuse the transference relationship for *"corrective emotional experience,"* the last nonanalytic factor mentioned here by Miss Freud.

Although analysts are taught to guard against using these analytic ingredients, it is their patients who in the last resort determine the "choice of therapeutic process."

Ferenczi (1909, p. 55) quoted Sigmund Freud as saying with regard to the neuroses: "We may treat a neurotic any way we like, he always treats himself . . . with transferences," i.e., by repeating his neurotic constellations rearranged around the person of the analyst.

K. R. Eissler (1950) with regard to ego pathology, stated similarly that every patient reacts to psychoanalytic technique in his own way; and that the patient's ego deviation from the norm can be deduced from the parameters which he enforces on the analyst.

Selection of Therapeutic Elements According to Diagnostic Category   The *borderline* child shows a negative therapeutic reaction to interpretation of the unconscious proper; the "very wording of the analytic interpretations is taken up by the patient and woven into a continued and increased flow of anxiety-arousing fantasy." What does help him is "verbalization and clarification of internal and external dangers and frightening affects which are perceived preconsciously but which his weak and helpless ego, left to itself, cannot integrate and bring under secondary process dominance" (p. 230).

Children with grave *libido defects* relate on the low level of object relationship at which their arrest has occurred (e.g., they transfer onto the analyst symbiotic or need-fulfilling attitudes, absence of object constancy, etc.). In order to assist a move forward to more appropriate levels of libido development, experience indicates that "the child may answer to the intimacy of the analyst-patient relationship, which is favorable for the proliferation of libidinal attachment . . ." (p. 231). This "corrective emotional experience" has to happen "approximately within the same developmental phase in which the damage to the libidinal process has taken place. Once such time limits have been overstepped, it is too late for correction."

Intellectually retarded children suffer intensely from their archaic fears as a rule. The therapeutic element which is responsible for improvement in these children is "the analyst's reassuring role, not his analytic one."

REFERENCES

[Note: *The standard edition* refers to *The standard edition of the complete psychological works of Sigmund Freud* (London: Hogarth Press and the Institute of Psycho-Analysis).]

Aichhorn, A. *Delinquency and child guidance: Selected papers.* (1923–1948). New York: International Universities Press, 1965.
Aichhorn, A. *Wayward youth.* New York: Viking Press, 1935.
Alpert, A. Reversibility of pathological fixations associated with maternal deprivation in infancy. *Psychoanalytic Study of the Child,* 1959, 14, 169–185.
Bibring, E. On the theory of the therapeutic results of psycho-analysis. *International Journal of Psycho-Analysis,* 1937, 18, 170–189.
Bibring, E. Psychoanalysis and the dynamic psychotherapies. *Journal of the American Psychoanalytic Association,* 1954, 2, 745–770.
Bornstein, B. On latency. *Psychoanalytic Study of the Child,* 1951, 6, 279–285.
Breuer, J. and Freud, S. On the psychical mechanism of hysterical phenomena: Preliminary communication (1893). In *The standard edition.* 1962. Vol. 2. 1–17.
Burlingham, D.; Goldberger, A.; and Lussier, A. Simultaneous analysis of mother and child. *Psychoanalytic Study of the Child,* 1955, 10, 165–186.
Eissler, K. R. Ego-psychological implications of the psychoanalytic treatment of delinquents. *Psychoanalytic Study of the Child,* 1950, 5, 97–121.
Eissler, K. R. The effect of the structure of the ego on psychoanalytic

technique. *Journal of the American Psychoanalytic Association,* 1953, 1, 104–143.

Eissler, K. R.   Notes on problems of technique in the psychoanalytic treatment of adolescents: With some remarks on perversions. *Psychoanalytic Study of the Child,* 1958, 13, 223–254.

Ferenczi, S.   Introjection and Transference. In *Sex in psychoanalysis.* New York: Basic Books, 1950.

Freud, A.   *The psycho-analytical treatment of children.* London: Imago Publishing Company, 1946; New York: International Universities Press, 1955.

Freud, A.   Indications for child analysis. *Psychoanalytic Study of the Child,* 1945, 1, 127–150.

Freud, A.   *Normality and pathology in childhood.* New York: International Universities Press, 1965.

Freud, S.   On the psychical mechanism of hysterical phenomena: A lecture. In *The standard edition.* Vol. 3. 25–39.

Freud, S.   The interpretation of dreams. In *The standard edition.* Vols. 4 and 5.

Freud, S.   New introductory lectures on psycho-analysis. In *The standard edition.* Vol. 22. 3–182.

Freud, S.   Analysis terminable and interminable. In *The collected papers of Sigmund Freud.* London: Hogarth Press, 1950. Vol. 5. 316–357.

Geleerd, E. R.   Borderline states in childhood and adolescence. *Psychoanalysis of the Child,* 1958, 13, 279–295.

Greenacre, P.   Considerations regarding the parent-infant relationship. *International Journal of Psycho-Analysis,* 1960, 41, 571–584.

Gyomroi, E. L.   The analysis of a young concentration camp victim. *Psychoanalytic Study of the Child,* 1963, 18, 484–510.

Hartmann, H.   Psychoanalysis and developmental psychology. *Psychoanalytic Study of the Child,* 1950, 5, 1–17.

Jacobson, E.   The effect of disappointment on ego and superego formation in normal and depressive development. *Psychoanalytic Review,* 1946, 33, 129–147.

Katan, A.   Some thoughts about the role of verbalisation in early childhood. *Psychoanalytic Study of the Child,* 1961, 16, 184–188.

Kris, E.   Notes on the development and on some current problems of psychoanalytic child psychology. *Psychoanalytic Study of the Child,* 1950, 5, 24–46.

Kris, E.   Opening remarks on psychoanalytic child psychology. *Psychoanalytic Study of the Child,* 1951, 6, 9–17.

Mahler, M. S. and Gosliner, B. J.   On symbiotic child psychosis: Genetic, dynamic and restitutive aspects. *Psychoanalytic Study of the Child,* 1955, 10, 195–212.

Panel: Psychoanalysis and dynamic psychotherapies: Similarities and differences. *Journal of the American Psychoanalytic Association,* 1954b, **2**, 711–797.

Robertson, J.   A mother's observations on the tonsillectomy of her four year-old daughter. With comments by Anna Freud. *Psychoanalytic Study of the Child,* 1956, **11**, 410–433.

Symposium: The theory of the therapeutic results of psycho-analysis. *International Journal of Psycho-Analysis,* 1937, **18**, 125–189.

Symposium: The widening scope of indications for psychoanalysis. *Journal of the American Psychoanalytic Association,* 1954, **2**, 567–620.

Symposium: Variations in classical psycho-analytic technique. *International Journal of Psycho-Analysis,* 1958, **39**, 200–242.

Winnicott, D. W.   Transitional objects and transitional phenomena: A study of the first not-me possession. *International Journal of Psycho-Analysis,* 1953, **34**, 89–97.

Winnicott, D. W.   The theory of the parent-infant relationship. *International Journal of Psycho-Analysis,* 1960, **41**, 585–593.

Zetzel, E. R.   Panel report: The traditional psychoanalytic technique and its variations. *Journal of the American Psychoanalytic Association,* 1953, **1**, 526–537.

8

MAURICE R. FRIEND

Psychoanalysis of Adolescents

P sychoanalytic treatment of the adolescent, sixty-five years after the publication of Sigmund Freud's *Three Essays on the Theory of Sexuality* and a *Fragment of an Analysis of a Case of Hysteria* (the Dora case), is probably one of the most moot topics of clinical psychoanalysis. There are many psychoanalysts (e.g., Zetzel), who questioned the application of this technique to the adolescent period of life. There are others, e.g., Blos, Erikson, and Pearson, who regard the technique, theoretical, and clinical considerations as belonging within the total framework of psychoanalysis. For many years little attention was paid to the topic of psychoanalysis of adolescents. But since 1957, in the proceedings of the American Psychoanalytic Association, there has been increasing panel consideration devoted to this topic.

From the beginning of psychoanalytic investigation, attention has been paid to the biological and chemical hormonal influences of growth during puberty. In no other phase of human existence beyond the infancy period do these influences play such a vital part in somatic and personality behavior (Cf. GAP, Vol. 6, No. 68, 1968).

These factors tend to obfuscate psychological considerations for many therapists. The biological influences of drive (id) energy are so forceful and there are so many diverse behavioral possibilities, that the stability of not only psychoanalysis, but any treatment modality of the adolescent is overwhelming to consider and systematize. It is felt by many psychoanalysts that psychoanalytic technique is intrusive and that it tends to provoke the discharge of mental energy in such a way that psychoanalysis of adolescents is impossible.

Psychoanalysts find it difficult to reach a consensus on both what adolescent process is, and when adolescence begins and ends. Simple chronological reference to menarche in girls and seminal emission in boys does not give an index to psychological considerations of adolescent mental operations. Moreover, the different manifestations in the male and female further compounds evaluation.

Historical accounts of mankind have always alluded to behavioral difficulties at this time of life. Not only do these pertain to individual function, but also to group formation and processes of adolescence in the evolution of civilization, e.g., the use of drugs, political activism and violence.

Psychoanalytic educators affiliated with the psychoanalytic member institutes of the American Psychoanalytic Association are presently experimenting with the training of analysts who wish to specialize in adolescent analysis, requiring that they receive only minimal training in work with younger children while still receiving thorough training in adult analysis.

The child and/or adolescent psychoanalyst has studied the biological and social and psychological aspects of child and adult psychiatry. Yet, institutionalization of such training has led to iatrogenic transference and counter-transference problems. The psychiatric training in child and adolescent psychiatry often "fixes" in a descriptive and intellectualized way the regard for the subtle internal potentiality of this period. Frequently, adolescents are referred to residents and young practitioners who, without adequate supervision, have inextricable problems of counter-transference. Sometimes, the demands of society influence the choice of the therapeutic situation so that motivations for psychological change will be grossly affected. The resultant evaluation of efficacy of change in personality becomes secondary, as a scientific procedure influenced by social group adjustment.

These prefatory remarks indicate difficulties in considering the psychoanalysis of adolescents. All psychoanalysts who practice are aware of the importance of understanding the psychological manifestations of this period. Yet, the developmental process itself, thought to be universal, is particularly subject to repression by the therapist and the adult generation. The difficulty of reconstruction of adolescent developmental pressures in the psychoanalysis of adults must stem from this factor.

HISTORICAL TRENDS

Historical trends in the evolution of theory, technique, research, and education are basic to the topic of technique. Technique or technical methods, when viewed apart from the historical evolution, isolates and oversimplifies considerations which are nevertheless important to a handbook of child psychoanalysis.

The historical trends in child and adolescent psychiatry must be considered in relation to trends in child and adolescent psychoanalysis. Historically, the development of psychoanalytic technique took place in Vienna and London. However, in the United States, various clinics devoted to the treatment of children represented common offshots from Kraeplinian psychiatry of the nineteenth century and related the development of educational theory and methods, the development of psychological testing, and the growth of academic psychology to the theory of the development of children and adolescents.

First must be mentioned the development by Healy and Bonner of the Child Guidance Movement in Chicago and then in Boston as part of the humanistic encouragement to the mental hygiene concept and movement prior to World War I. This humanistic trend intertwined with the evolution from the Kraeplinian concept of disease of the mind to social and more psychological concepts of growth of personality in a fluid interaction conceptualization. The concept of help evolved by degrees from relief of poverty, from moral condemnation, to ideas of psychological reactions, as individual treatment relationships gradually extended to group process. Hospitals for training evolved from descriptive classifications and custodial isolation and care to more dynamic aspects. Children in families were seen as units of detection, prevention, and care. Professional disciplines such as sociology, political science, psychology, and social work appeared to converge with medicine and psychiatry. Psychiatry itself developed as a specialty, and child psychiatry was recognized in the United States only recently, i.e., 1959. Yet it was the development of child guidance clinics in the United States that led to similar developments in Great Britain and other parts of the Continent.

One of the most neglected areas of child psychiatry, psychology, and social work was the study of dynamic social interaction. It was in this particular area that psychoanalytic contributions, led by Anna Freud in Vienna and later in London, and by many of the psychoanalytic refugees who fled to the United States and South America before World War II, vitalized treatment. They reinforced the impact of Sigmund Freud's 1911 Clark University lectures on psychoanalysis. Later visits by Otto Rank and Alfred Adler produced therapeutic personality concepts in the fields of social work and education. The cross-fertilization of biological and psychic determinants of personality and social determinants of behavior led to a growth of psychoanalysis as a medical specialty in the United States far beyond what Sigmund Freud could have imagined.

The popularity of psychoanalysis during World War II influenced resident training in psychiatry, as an outgrowth of applied psychoanalysis to military stress problems (W. Menninger, 1948; Grinker and Spiegel, 1945). This led to an enormous development of psychoanalytic education in the United States (Lewin and Ross, 1960).

Extension of the concepts in child psychiatry led to the formation of Specialty Boards (1954) and the growth of certain organizations for standards of training such as the American Psychiatric Services for Children (Rexford) and the American Academy of Child Psychiatry (Berman).

In the present decade there has been a change of medical and psychiatric services, i.e., extension of such services for detection, prevention, and amelioration, and the provision of services for various segments of our social classes. Community mental health centers serve catchment areas of socially disadvantaged population groups. Broadened and differing concepts of medicine and the specialty of psychiatry emerged as a result of increased socialization of government. No longer does the field of psychoanalysis and psychoanalytic education appear to enjoy the regard of those interested in psychiatry. Group therapy (Slavson, 1947) family therapy (Ackerman, 1958), and crisis intervention (Kaplan, 1961) are some of the techniques featured in current psychiatric education. Social implications of psychiatric nomenclature have been extensively investigated by Hollingshead and Redlich (1958).

An important historical influence for child psychiatry, and later for psychoanalysis, occurred when childhood schizophrenia was accepted as a syndrome (Kanner, 1943, Bender, 1947) and later genetically, by Spitz (1945) and Mahler (1949) (Cf. Friend, 1967). The prevalence of severe child and adolescent mental disturbance leading to adult schizophrenia focused attention on ego variations in childhood.

These historical trends were significant because they influenced the climate and background of the child and adolescent psychoanalyst. Moreover, systematization of concepts derived from practice and technique of adolescent analysis (Blos, Fraiburg, Belmont, Geleerd, Harley, Furman, Anna Freud, Klein and Pearson, and Josselyn) extended technical knowledge.

THERAPEUTIC AND
THEORETICAL CONSIDERATIONS

Freud emphasized three psychoanalytic aims: therapy, research, and the formulation of a general theory of personality. Separation of these elements is not possible. The close interrelationships of psychoanalytic theory and practice are nowhere more vital than in the consideration of therapeutic relationships in the psychoanalysis of adolescents. Differences between adult and adolescent psychoanalysis on the one hand, and between adult and child psychoanalysis on the other, are more reflective of modality differences than of differences in the basic approach. For purposes of teaching, it is necessary to help the student develop a common "psychoanalytic stance." This is a frame of reference which consists of listening and utilizes verbalization between the partners in the psychoanalytic situation (Stone, 1961) which leads to a conviction, on the part of the analyst, that there are multiple determinants of psychic functions affecting the vicissitudes of behavior and expression in the adolescent. These psychic functions are subject to interpretation, growth, and evolution, as part of the acceptance of the treatment situation which in itself leads to re-education and greater access to internal and external responses of the adolescent. It goes without saying that the conviction maintains itself apart from the current form of social expression on the part of the adolescent.

It is this therapeutic conviction and the maintenance of inquiry and curiosity within the investigation of the relationship of present psychic functioning as related to past maturation and development that is essential to psychoanalytic practice. Moreover, empathy and tolerance rather than therapeutic zeal provides an atmosphere that is necessary for the many disappointments and social yearnings of the adolescent.

The specific contribution of psychoanalysis of adolescents is that it deals with a human psychic developmental phase which has biological and social correlations. Extremely labile and regressive potentials are very characteristic. Integrations of psychic and somatic components with sublimation of sexual drive are a developmental task and are never smooth. Image representations and various syntheses of them emerge with changing affects and moods. The capacity to test old object representations with those of new ones is afforded at this period. Idealistic (superego and ego ideal) capacities, reaction formations, and sublimations of ego functioning are in precarious equilibrium. Fantasy formation and disturbances of ego attention, i.e., daydreaming, are noteworthy. Changes in bodily tension discharge occur continuously as at no other time in human life. Changing mental representations of parental figures in the very presence of the physical parents affords a unique opportunity for reconstituting the Oedipal constellation. The adolescent, as it were, coexists with infantile pre-Oedipal derivatives, Oedipal derivatives and post-Oedipal derivatives on his way to assuming parenthood.

It is understandable that constant parental demands which are unrelenting, persistent, and frequently inconsistent, are attributes of any civilization which evoke reactions of aggression or passivity from the growing organism. These problems do not lend themselves to psychic distance from the acting ego, so characteristic of the adult psychoanalytic situation.

Moreover, successful mastery or the rapidly changing successful competitions amongst friends and the peer group afford changes in the moral values of the superego aspect of personality. Thus, it is obvious that the psychoanalyst who works with the adolescent must interact more intently and be capable of variation and more flexibility than is usually demanded in the psychoanalysis of the adult.

Basic to the selection of adolescents who may be analyzed is the recognition of conflict, symptom formation, and the capacity for verbal communication of both inner and outer reality representations. These capacities are vital to progress. Without the theoretical genetic anlage of developmental lines and needs (Anna Freud, 1965) one cannot differentiate normality from pathology. One cannot select suitable adolescents for even trial periods of psychoanalysis. Assessment is not merely practical but theoretical and is an unending process in the therapeutic functioning. (For further details, see Chapters 1, 2 and 3 of this volume.)

In summary, the following points have been emphasized: (1) Adolescence is viewed as a human developmental phase of biological, and social existence. (2) Psychoanalysis is a special situation utilizing free association, delay in discharge, and demanding reflection and a tolerance for anxieties of which all youths are not capable. (3) The medical psychoanalyst of the adolescent is himself a product of historical traditions, generationally far removed from the adolescent. He, himself, has to bridge the conceptual understanding of personal phases of childhood and the resulting personality integration on the way to adulthood. (4) The psychoanalyst also has to differentiate, through experience and education, the use of psychoanalysis as a procedure of choice from the therapeutic aspect and correlate this with its potentiality for research.

AIMS OF PSYCHOANALYSIS
OF ADOLESCENTS

The psychoanalysis of adolescents must be correlated with the concepts of adolescence as a developmental phase (Blos, 1962 Erikson, 1959). Its goals have remarkable similarities to those of psychoanalysis of adults. Psychoanalysis has basically the fundamental goal of personality change from both *within* and *without* the "persona." From the social context, choice of adaptations becomes possible rather than fixity of responses, and moreover, the individual may better live up to the basic potentialities of his native mental endowment and constitution in the varied social context of a changing society. The capacity for sublimation and the ability to achieve, marry, reproduce, and work have been stated as goals by Freud and constitute the necessary perpetuation of civilization.

Psychoanalysis utilizes language communication with delay of discharge, in its efforts to gain access to affects, behavior, and ideation. Through the consistency of relationship in the psychoanalytic situation (Stone, 1961) the viewing of ego functions of the personality is increased. Ultimately, through access to the many aspects of personality function, a sense of historical continuity, a reduction in the level of disorganizing anxiety, and a utilization of signal anxiety (Freud, 1926) constitute the benefits of this therapeutic method. The aim of psychoanalysis is not to eliminate conflicts of drives and desires, nor is it to produce "happiness," but to increase awareness and tolerance of conflicts, (conscious and unconscious) and to reduce but not to eliminate primitive responses to stress. The aims of psychoanalysis do not include restructuring of society, although it is vitally concerned with value judgments of the society within which mankind operates (Heinz Hartmann, 1960). It is a time-consuming procedure, and since it deals with multiple psychic determinants of social behavior, has as a process its own termination, which may not be conducive to social approval or sanction, Psychoanalysis has the task of changing "points of fixation" which is akin to the modern child analytic dictum which proposes that child analysis is indicated where there is interference with progression of mental development, at the appropriate "normal" stage of development of the mind and personality. With the above general framework of psychoanalytic goals in mind, adolescence as a developmental phase presents specific differences and challenges.

It is the period of development characterized by a tremendous rate of change in both physical and hormonal influences of growth. Mental ego disturbances and changes in inner self-representations, i.e., psychic body image representations are frequent. It is the period of ultimate sexual, physical and psychic organizational togetherness, identity (Erikson, 1959) or consolidation (Blos, 1963). There is involved change in consideration of self and of mental object representations of others and their attitudes. It is a period of lability, of regression to an "undifferentiated phase" of development or a "flux" (Anna Freud, 1958; Geleerd, 1964) with adaptive as well as nonadaptive functioning.

The group appeal, functioning or dysfunctioning, tends to "collectivize" the adolescent in order to rid the self of internalized experiences of anxiety and conflict. This necessarily produces resultant subjective experiences of depression, fear of loss of control, and externalization of internal dangers. Fears of intimacy, "engulfment," make for torturous individual therapeutic relationships. The tendency to discharge early nonverbal experiences in order to avoid the intimacies of the psychoanalytic situation results in both adaptive and nonadaptive patterns of "acting out." Older individuals such as parents and others in society are stimulated to react to these threats of disorganization which they, the component "older generation" have repressed. These reactions are characterized by aggression and punishment which invariably seek to curb behavioral deviation.

To expect to systematically carry through a joint reflective process such as psychoanalysis without threat of parental transference reactions is untenable. Identification problems with parental figures in the past as well as in the present become difficulties in the analysis.

There is a vividness of "reality" to the above phenomena coupled with the individual's lack of experience with newly emerging psychic derivatives of drives. This lends a continual "inner crisis quality" to the analytic situation of the adolescent in contrast to the psychoanalysis of the child or adult.

Psychoanalysis is an economically costly and time consuming procedure. Since the psyche in its unconscious aspects deals with limitless time variations, the "insights" which must be relearned *and* re-experienced are over a long period of time.

Psychoanalysis deals with what Freud (Schur, 1946), termed the repetition compulsion principle. Essentially, the human personality may be considered as a complex equilibrium of psychic drives, energy, and affects which influence thoughts and ideas dealing with an interpsychic and reality representation "system," and which are manifested by behavioral responses. Flexibility of response is a cliché. Psychoanalysis has learned that the psychic equilibrium maintains a constancy which Cannon used to term "homeostatic equilibrium" in physiology.

Despite the fact that many social phenomena evolve as a result of mankind's collective scientific accomplishments, it is doubtful that biological and psychic species mutations have occurred. Similarly, adolescent change in group activities, either of passivity or violence or withdrawal cannot be considered new in the sense of evolutionary phenomena, nor will they in themselves produce some discernible species role differences. At the risk of being subject to generational criticism, psychoanalysis provides an opportunity to

help the continuation of individual growth within a social framework. Although family functions and modalities vary from the
past, they seem to exist for the purpose of large and small group
functioning. One finds this whether in Israeli collectives (Neubauer, 1965,), in Russian governmental experiments, or in political
socialization of former family functions in the United States which
have resulted in varied social institutionalization of family, school,
and government formations. While "freedom" and "liberty" are
common utterances, Freud and many others have repeatedly
stressed that civilization has inexorable demands for the sacrifice
of these psychological freedoms. The only exception to this rule
appears to be the stage of early infancy, and even this freedom is
quickly given up for purposes of individuation, growth, and survival.

As part of a human developmental phase, adolescence functions
to enable the individual to individuate socially and to create a place
for himself in the matrix of social existence as a means of survival.
It is exactly this period with its extremes of behavior that are incompatible and unfused that has been so well-described by Anna
Freud in "Ego and the Mechanisms of Defense" (1946). In the
middle of the twentieth century, when mankind has been forced
to contemplate threats to its own biological and social existence by
the development of group means of annihilation, it appears that
values of civilization undergo an increased rate of change and
psychoanalysis and its contributions are themselves subjected to
change.

On the one hand, the outward social efforts to change society
and governmental policies and controls become new ideals. Individual reorganization and psychic change, always slow and difficult, are not appealing. To delay the discharge of mental energy
by trial thinking coupled with restraint of action—an inevitable
resultant of psychoanalytic technique—renders psychoanalysis increasingly unpopular, in marked contrast to its earlier historical
popularity.

Since the technique of psychoanalysis is uniquely structured and
does not lend itself to the modification which would render it socially useful, once modified it evolves into some other kind of
therapeutic technique. Opponents of psychoanalytic technique have
much to make themselves popular and to help them mobilize
others.

Dealing with the same phenomena, but with different goals,
shorter and more direct techniques of therapy involving body communication and groups may be less time consuming and costly and
may appear more practical. But invariably they are associated with

decreased systematic consideration of mental phenomena and become linked with freer discharge of drive energy. Intellectual acceptance of psychoanalytic research without the intellectualized convictions gained from personal and therapeutic practice abound, and they generally serve mankind to repress and maintain unconscious defenses.

Adolescence lends itself to most varied therapeutic approaches and may always lean on various political movements. Probably, analysts who have worked with adolescents have also contributed the technique of "free verbalization" rather than "free association" of ideas, thoughts, and feelings, which is in effect more applicable to the adolescent. I will later indicate, under "Technical Considerations," that preparation for later analysis may itself be termed psychoanalysis proper.

Despite all these considerations, the aims of psychoanalysis of adolescents are discernible and clear. They are more limited than those in adult work, yet they do comprise effective psychoanalytic effort. These considerations can be enumerated as follows:

1. In the psychoanalytic situation, a given adult (therapist) may be perceived by the patient as a person in his own right and as a significant object representation within the family, both Oedipal and pre-Oedipal. These considerations may be systematically examined.
2. Genetic connections. The historical approach of individual personality development may be shared with consequent "revivications" of visual and affective memories. This leads to a constant revision of these historical events and memory screens.
3. A consideration of values. The ego ideal and conscience (superego)and their resultant derivatives may be expanded.
4. Various ego problems such as learning, use of memory, feelings of sexual inadequacy, and other severe inhibitions of functioning in addition to symptom formation may be resolved.
5. Various significances of group relationships and their utilization by the adolescent, together with the representation values of various ego images may be realized.
6. A consideration of the nature of anxiety and the phenomena of regressive pulls with associated differences in thinking, feeling and behavior inevitably becomes a part of the therapeutic aim.
7. A maintenance of feelings of closeness, understanding, and

trust with another person coupled with an opportunity to individuate and not merely identify with the analyst will result in accomplishment of increased mastery of self expression and a more tolerable psychic relationship within the self and in other social settings, i.e., in family and peer groups.

In adolescence, the phenomena of love and depression cannot in themselves be analyzable (Cf. A. Freud, 1958), but physical and psychic function may be better understood. A direction of inquiry and a more tolerant attitude of self and others may be effected. Most vital is the relinquishment of infantile narcissistic and omnipotent self-attitudes and the acceptance of the phenomena of regression and progression and the utilization of interests (sublimation) by activities and attitudes which involve much more than the self.

The psychoanalytic situation is maintained and supported in most instances by the parents. At the same time, the psychoanalyst of the adolescent must, in my opinion, modify his technique to enable parents to participate from time to time in the psychoanalysis of their child, with his consent. This in itself is unique for it allows the manifestations and use of parental reactions to regressive behavior of their own children. Where significant "binds" or traumata may occur, the parental reactions themselves may enable referral of parents for resolutions of their conflicts. This approach could be included or could be thought of as a modified working out of the generational differences.

The psychoanalyst of the adolescent has the task of undertaking a "piece of psychoanalysis." His psychoanalytic work cannot resolve all the transference manifestations to the degree that he may wish. His analytic work is frequently interrupted rather than terminated. The interruptions are most frequently not to be understood as a resistance or acting out, but as an inevitable need for functioning apart from family and analyst. Of course, this is not always as clear as the above wording may sound. The psychoanalyst who has the opportunity to see the adolescent subsequently as a young adult may have the task of doing another "piece of psychoanalysis," or he may consider the work sufficient yet allowing occasional contacts in the future. There is considerable difference in the young adult who is not within the "psychic bosom" of the family.

Finally, the psychoanalyst of the adolescent should realize that his selection of adolescents is skewed in terms of the total adolescent population. He must be careful to know that much more research and collective study would be necessary in order to extend the concepts of adolescent psychology derived from his own clinical work into the framework of a generalized psychology of this period (Blos, 1963).

TECHNICAL CONSIDERATIONS

Assessment of The Adolescent for Psychoanalysis

Both Sigmund and Anna Freud have utilized the term "assessment" for what in clinical psychiatry had always been termed "the diagnostic or evaluative study." When used by colleagues, it generally connotes that the study or assessment is performed by the professional and that the adolescent patient or client is the object of this study. Since so much of the collaborative nature of psychoanalysis, particularly at this time, rests upon a "therapeutic alliance" I would emphasize that it is wise to think of assessment as a mutual assessment procedure, particularly when considering the complex aspect of *motivation for treatment.*

I would also emphasize that the mutual assessment is an ongoing process for both analyst and analysand. Where resistances or acting out become inevitable, it is obvious that the analysand is only able to view his situation subjectively. Early introduction of mutual participation in the analysis is necessary for differentiation of the analytical function as separate from the parental function and role. At the same time, the parental point of view may be ascertained from the onset and utilized as an objective consideration within the analysis, provided there are not such over-regressive manifestations of indulgence or rejection that make it impossible to establish meaningful communication. As with the psychoanalysis of children, parental reactions of guilt, frustration, and failure, associated with the need for a therapist have their own guilt-producing functions in the adolescent. Depending upon the nature of initial assessment, the sharing of these conclusions, not the technical work and its details, may be conveyed to both the parents and the adolescent.

One of the understandable clichés that has impressed me is that the adolescent must be accorded individual freedom and responsibility. Carried into practice, I have found that many analysts invariably will discourage parental visits and, in a sense, tend to identify with the adolescent against the family. In many instances, where the level of psychic regression within the adolescent renders him much younger than his chronological expectations, this makes for an unnecessary hardship. Similarly, independence of the family may in itself be immature, and family communication regarding the patient's behavior may be helpful to the analyst's basic task of viewing the adolescent's percepts of his significant psychic representations of parents and others.

At the same time, there are situations where this is not necessary, particularly where the parents may have had their own experience in personal psychoanalysis. Yet, I have even found that these parents tend to differentiate the goals and techniques of adolescent analysis with their own therapy which may have occurred in young adulthood or in early marriage.

Furthermore, in contrast to the psychoanalysis of adults the initial assessment must generally depend upon parental sacrifices of functions, time, and money and not just those sacrifices of the adolescent.

Conversely, when parents are not included early in treatment, many subtle regressions of jealousies and resistances, serve to support the resistances of the adolescent. Regression itself is fostered and the psychoanalytic situation is needlessly overendowed with the magic and omnipotence of the priest plus the doctor rather than the more rational acceptance of help from an understanding therapist.

Since the psychoanalyst of the adolescent inevitably becomes a meaningful, real figure to patient and family, just as in child psychoanalysis, occasional visits of parents merely allow for this experience to become a part of the psychoanalytic situation and not vitally interfere with it.

HISTORICAL INFLUENCES—THE PAST AND PRESENT   While the actual interviews for assessment proceed spontaneously and with no fixed form, historical influences play an important role in the analyst's mind. The historical influences operate within parents to promote identificatory roles which are unconscious or preconscious in the adolescent. For example, a seventeen-year-old son, referred for assessment following the ingestion of sedatives and an acute suicidal "crisis" which resulted in a few days' hospitalization, had severe feelings of unworthiness following a series of costly mishaps to a second-hand car and the cancellation of a high school prom. In addition, he was still awaiting college acceptance. The misunderstandings and irate outbursts of the father seemed to produce intense struggles within the boy. Upon an interview with the father and mother it was learned that the father's history indicated intense aggressive outbursts in his own adolescence which necessitated staying away from home with a paternal uncle for a year. The same identificatory struggles of the father and their reappearance in the son's crisis became apparent. In a sense, there appeared, unconsciously inevitable, the father's participation in his son's particular responses. It became obvious that the boy wished to remove himself from the closeness of the father relationship. This had the father's unconscious sanction and would not allow for the possibility of psychoanalysis at the time of assessment.

Another example is the referral at the age of fourteen of an older son because of apparent passivity, lack of friends, and mediocre work in school. Historical influences revealed that since the boy's birth the intelligent, striving foreign-born mother was unwittingly pressing the critical competitive strivings of an unfulfilled, frustrated displaced refugee's existence onto her son. He identified with the phallic mother and it became his mode of existence to internalize the aggressions and to accede to the mother's unconscious needs to both dominate and inconsistently indulge the boy.

SOCIETAL STATUS AND PEER INFLUENCES   The societal status of the adolescent is pertinent to the assessment for psychoanalysis. While the role of class structure is not readily apparent, it does, with upward or downward mobility of the generational influences, play a part in the familial expectations of the adolescent. For example, a thirteen-year-old boy was referred for consultation by his psychoanalytically oriented therapist because the boy wished to discontinue his treatment. Moreover, the therapist felt the boy to be resistant. Actually, he presented the interesting problem of wishing to free himself from the gentle yet insistent therapeutic demand of the therapist which unwittingly served as reinforcement of the boy's father. The father was in psychoanalytic treatment and had severe, depressed, and narcissistic disturbances as a result of severe mourning reactions and guilt on losing his wife. The father expected the son to have exactly the same reactions to the loss of his mother as he, the father, did to his wife. Allowing no personalized differentiation of reactions of grief, and occurring at the beginning of the boy's adolescence, it became evident that the father's identification with his own therapist led to an intolerable series of family group psychotherapy experiences in which the father could aggressively release his new found knowledge and share it with his son. The unconscious homosexual relationship was more than any boy at this age could endure, and it was being reinforced by the therapeutic situation. Upon the recommendation that psychoanalysis was not indicated at this time in the boy's development, and that the boy's sensitivities were present despite their dissimilarity to the father's expression, relief was afforded to both the boy and his disappointed therapist.

More common is the reaction of the adolescent to peer influences and the reaction of parents to these same influences. For example, a chronologically young adult at twenty-three had been referred by his mother for assessment at the age of fourteen and then again at twenty-two, the last referral being after a long history of drug ingestion, hospitalization, and constant association with delinquent aggressive boys. It soon became apparent that not only was the boy impulse-ridden but so also were both his parents. Following the death of his father, severe inhibited sexual functions became related to the mother's failure to separate from the boy. Moreover, the relationship of her own paranoid projection system and the boy's intertwined closely. This pathology had been present throughout the boy's life, and it appeared impossible for separation and individuation to ever occur. It was principally through identification with severely disturbed and protesting peers that the boy was trying to defend against essentially psychotic identifications with a psychotic but successfully socially compensated mother. If the boy could discern differences between himself and disturbed peers and yet coexist with them, he could both maintain his own self security and repeat the traumatic experiences he had been subjected to. Obviously, such a situation would not be conducive to psychoanalysis.

SEXUAL DIFFERENCES   Sexual differences of the patient and his analyst are not too vital when one deals with adults because the transference phenomena and the transference neurosis develop. In early adolescence, the presence of a woman analyst at the time of beginning sexual emissions and masturbation conflicts may not lend itself to unfolding. The seductive relationship would be felt as too threatening by the adolescent. It is only when the psychoanalytic situation has started in the latency period and extended through the beginning adolescent development does this situation seem to be endurable.

However, not only does the sexual role play a part, but so also does the age of the analyst. When the analyst reaches the vintage of apparent grandparenthood both the sexual and erotic drive components of the patient seem less threatened, and it is as though a "great all seeing GRAND mother or father person representation" with tolerant understanding, and yet a "with it" attitude, provides removal from the parental role itself.

DRIVE CONFLICTS It is in the assessment of drive conflicts that the psychoanalyst contributes a great deal of wisdom. In instances of isolated masturbatory group experiences, occasional homosexual experiments by both boys and girls frequently disguised as close friendships or being, from the parental point of view, unduly influenced by the friend rather than their own child, problems of bisexuality can with difficulty be assessed. Predictions of actual outcomes can rarely be made. Many parents unconsciously dread this necessary experimentation and will wish for premature closure of this manifestation of adolescence.

The concomitant attachment to and persistence of desires for certain inanimate objects, fetishes, related to the young child's need for imaginary companions, may lead to severe characterological assessment problems in impulse-ridden adolescents who have evolved from impulse-ridden childhoods with many different traumata. These are quite different situations than those of the adolescent who finds himself involved in rituals, acts of undoing, as obsessional defenses or atonements for severe masturbation guilt.

The assessment will reveal many carefully ill-concealed exposures of parents' intimacies, which provide a continual source of heightened eroticism.

The psychoanalyst of the adolescent is familiar with the phenomena of intrapsychic drive conflicts, as well as with the fact that drives are not manifest as such in undisguised form. He is theoretically convinced that there are constitutional variations in aggressive and libidinal endowment and that ego and superego defenses play a vast role in their externalization. Repressions both in the adolescent and in his parents have interacting roles, and the conflicts become readily displaced both psychically and socially.

An example of a weakened defense against libidinal drive manifestation is illustrated in the following vignette. A fourteen-year-old well-developed boy had been dating for a number of years and finally "went steady" with an attractive partner. Ultimately, she was ready for the crucial moment of penetration in a bedroom situation. While petting and foreplay was acceptable to the boy, when the ultimate moment came, he rushed out of the bedroom in great excitement, stripped off his clothes, donned a tracksuit and sneakers and ran around his high school track until he exhausted and drained himself of this drive manifestation. What becomes outstanding is the stark subjective terror engendered in some adolescents when the libidinal drive coupled with the realities of penetration become possible rather than remaining parts of a masturbation fantasy. It is probable that this phenomenon takes a derivative function from compulsive masturbation conflicts in earlier adolescence, when repeated libidinal drive urges and repetitive ejaculations are coupled to the point of physical exhaustion. Under the influence of both denying the superego and at the same time complying to the point of exhaustion, the pleasurable effects are nullified, yet the ego experiences a reality of existence and a type of personal experience of "rebirth," or at least "not death."

A twenty-year-old girl, extremely well-developed physically, could only permit foreplay above the "waist." She had engaged in masturbation with clitoral orgasm since the age of four. She had a close mystical experience for a number of years with one boy whom she had to feel in love with and with whom she finally consummated the sexual act. It was in therapy, rather than in psychoanalysis, that she could acknowledge that she had always felt it was "sinful" and that despite the experience, she still subjectively felt like a virgin, though she knew realistically she wasn't. Under the pressures of the reality, rather than the fantasy experience, she wished to separate from her "beloved," to know whether she was truly "in love." She then began to ruminate about marriage, sexual precautions, and about using the pill. She practiced withdrawal and obsessed conflicts about the danger of becoming pregnant. While these clinical phenomena are not unusual, how infrequently does one view the phenomena as instances of drive conflicts. Further defenses lead to symptom formation.

With this patient, one may have approached the problem from the nature of biological drive endowments in conflicts, because for years the girl had used her mental endowment to deprecate both herself and her friends, by exhibiting herself and then withdrawing from promiscuous males. This definitely appeared to be related to exhibitionistic conflicts. She incurred unconscious satisfaction from recurrent depressive mood swings which were, I believe, not only intersystemic, i.e., superego conflicts, but were fed with aggressive and libidinal energy that was manifested in physical emulation of males. This was evidenced by her pleasure in riding horses and, later, motorcycles. In her late adolescent therapy, she could share some of her physical terror of regression which had not been possible earlier. She could also view her functions with more equanimity, based upon other ego accomplishments such as working, writing poetry, and taking voice lessons. She could almost become more feminine rather than regress to a more infantile level.

PUBERTAL CONSIDERATIONS Probably no period is more difficult for psychoanalysis than late prepuberty or early puberty. I have often found that because one has treated latency children through prepuberty to adolescence, that one tends to underestimate the technical problems. For the youngsters who are referred initially for psychological assessment for psychoanalysis at this time in their lives (eleven to twelve in girls and twelve to thirteen in boys), I believe the problems are technically too great to consider psychoanalysis proper. To be sure, a goodly number are referred because of parental discomfiture. The problems are generally in relation to social immaturity in school, lack of sociability, lack of competitiveness with boys, "impossible" behavior toward the parents, and lack of interest in learning. But in whatever terms the referral may be couched, the youngster, while sometimes interested in a challenge and curious about the psychoanalytic situation, soon evinces resistance to the process. He complains about the excessive time taken away from social activities and that it seems to be much too long a process.

Most vital is the inability, due to the strength of repression, to relate the erotized conflicts of mastery of libidinal and aggressive drives accompanied by their most devastating psychic states. Furthermore, there seems to be a tremendous need to identify with older peers or indeed with an entire peer generation, to lose oneself in music, to exhibit and to retreat, to participate in drug experiences, i.e., anything, but to remain free of psychic energy discharge. This is also accompanied by severe internalized fears of being different, of being insane. Further, the prospect of actually seeing a psychiatrist seems to confirm the conviction that one is not only insane but helpless and subject to the ostracism of his peer group. Or, indeed, one can become preoccupied with intense interests in hobbies, such as photography, stamp collecting, dance, music and need to share this even vicariously through television (the "boob tube") as well as telephone conversations, or simply withdraw from peer contacts.

For example, Robert, thirteen, oldest and only son of parents who both had psychoanalytic experiences, was not living up to the expectations of his private school parents. They expressed wishes that he transfer from a more progressive private school to one similar to his father's private school background. He did not study consistently, and for the past few years the school reports brought out that he had not been living up to his intellectual potentials. In the assessment interviews, including some with the parents and several conversations with the referring psychoanalyst, I concluded that Robert had only experienced ejaculation in the past six months. He previously had been exhibitionistic and tried to surpass his male classmates socially, using girls as his audience. He suffered from daydreaming and inhibitions of attention while studying. He "wished to see if he could progress on his own."

In the assessment, the father had severe obsessional problems, particularly with money, and had severe aggressive outbursts. Physically, he was a very large man. The mother, despite her analytic treatment, had greatly impaired reality testing, was immature, and maintained a dependent relationship with the father at best. I concluded, despite the referring analyst's opinion that Robert should enter psychoanalytic treatment, that (1) the boy's wishes to "wait and see" should be granted; (2) this was an early pubertal struggle; and (3) the boy himself could always contact me if he chose, supported by the parents' permission. A year later, the parents reported that Robert was doing better, and this was corroborated by the referring psychoanalyst.

INFLUENCES OF PAST TREATMENT EXPERIENCES   Many psychoanalysts have experiences with adolescents who have had either psychotherapy or psychoanalysis at an earlier period of life. Sometimes these have been the psychoanalyst's own experiences with the child; in other instances they represent change of psychoanalyst by the parents or direct referral by the child psychoanalyst.

At times the referral is from the psychoanalyst of one of the parents and is an outgrowth of the interchange in the psychoanalytic situation between parent and psychoanalyst. In marital situations, the adolescent is able to enter individual psychoanalytic treatment first, sometimes last, and sometimes not at all. At other times, the adolescent enters psychoanalysis because the partner of his heterosexual cathexis is in psychoanalysis or psychotherapy.

One of the common experiences of adolescents in psychoanalysis who have had past treatment is the repression of the earlier treatment. Despite the fact that years may have been spent in psychoanalysis, there is surprisingly little recall of meaningful transference and interpretative work that must have transpired. It is as though the adolescent phase is uniquely of the present, and the nature of the therapeutic situation of the past is prehistoric, foreign, and ego alien. It is different from the continuity of contact with representation of the parents and/or siblings. There appears to be a "self-alienation" akin to the social group alienation of the adolescent. This phenomenon of repression is most difficult to share and is generally uncovered when the analytic treatment is terminated.

A boy who was a moody, seriously depressed, guilt ridden, and passive adolescent with capacities for panic and disorganization, recalled his woman therapist only as "an old white-haired lady" with whom he played and improved. Why he did not continue was never ascertained, although it was inferred that the improvement of his social behavior developed from the influence of a supporting "good mother transference relationship," in contrast to the severe reality problems of his biological mother who was seriously depressed when he was an infant and had had shock treatments. His mother, despite her talent, ability, and later good social adjustment, still projected her critical, hostile, and despairing feelings onto her son. It was in adolescence that the boy had his own despondency and inertia and unconscious feelings that, in a masochistic way, were trying to provide mothering he had never been able to experience.

Another example was a boy whom I had seen in late latency for periodic supportive visits and who subsequently entered psychoanalysis with me following college drop-out and severe drug experiences. He was ten when initially referred to me, his father was in psychotherapy with a psychoanalyst, and his mother was undergoing psychoanalysis with a second psychoanalyst. Robert was short, very intellectualized, and at the time of referral appeared sophisticated. He had a professional knowledge of psychoanalytic language, wished to become president of the student body, and was also interested in profiting financially from complicated philatelic trading and speculation. In the early assessment, there were considerable castration fears linked up to urinary withholding, masturbation conflicts, and marked exposure to an aging father who projected his own potency problems onto his son.

Robert's visits were always preceded by declamative, introspective, analytical letters from his mother, revealing the disparaging projective mechanisms of her disappointment in herself, her husband, and in the high hopes she had placed in Robert who could never fulfill her conscious aspirations. In his twelfth year, a stormy divorce occurred and he denied extreme guilt and insecurity. He prospered until he went to the college of his choice, as far away geographically as his psychic distance from his very narcissistic parents.

When he returned for psychoanalysis, drug activities were readily given up and he was able to master heterosexual fears and diffuse anxiety. He was able to correlate this anxiety to withholding manifestations of his body and mind. On completion of this phase of his analysis, he was able to gain a perspective on his need to become a revolutionary to satisfy both his mother's unconscious aggressions and his father's liberal humanitarian aspirations. He was able to marry and to overcome some of his unconscious ties to a severely sadistic projective mother.

It was in the terminal phase of his analysis that he was able to recapitulate, in the transference, his early contacts with me as a realistic older person, supportive and thinking better of him than he of himself. His wishes and desires for me to be his father and advisor were carefully analyzed and he became able to differentiate himself from the infantile, jealous, and anxious little boy who could never have his dependent, passive wishes gratified. What was interesting to me was the opportunity to see myself as an object manipulated to satisfy narcissistic needs, to defend against great insecurities, and to maintain Robert's intellectual facade and distance from his own emotions—a prominent mechanism of isolation. These phenomena were in marked contrast to the bewilderment of not being able to intellectualize the analysis, either from its inception to its termination phase. It did not appear to correspond to his idea of "Freudian." The capacity for tenderness and affection increasingly emerged. This had been so importantly missing in his boyhood, when being helpless or ill were the means to obtain solicitude.

While some of the same intellectual defenses were observable in latency and in adolescence through young adulthood, an ability to experience and tolerate anxiety became possible. Moreover, he was able to expect less of himself and to endure uncertainty. Transference and identification reactions which did not seem possible at the time of the first evaluation interviews became evident in the analysis. Certainly, his therapeutic gains could not be measured in terms of the expectations of his divorced and remarried mother. Her values appeared unchanged despite many achievements.

The more experienced and older psychoanalyst of adolescents also has the opportunity to therapeutically treat patients whom he had analyzed as children. I can recall one of my first children whose treatment had to be interrupted at about eleven to twelve because I went into the military service. This child then transferred to an experienced woman analyst, who worked further until the beginning of adolescence. Upon my return I had occasion to see Charley while in college and to follow the situation through psychotherapy of the mother. First the father died and then later the mother, of a malignant disease. Following marriage and the birth of three children, there was a period of vocational uncertainty and, I believe, an unconscious need to experience object constancy with me which had never been internally or externally possible.

He recounted his early latency defenses and struggles with me and how he kept his sexual conflicts a big secret from me, his child analyst and his parents. But he suddenly and vividly depicted, as an adult, his basic characterological dependency: "It was all right as a boy for me to leave you, but for you to leave! Never." While, obviously, this was related to his own guilty death wishes, it was also clearly related, by unconscious identification, to his anxiety-ridden over-solicitous mother. The knowledge of the child analysis by the analyst and patient, plus the reality representation of a constant, nonleaving (immortal) therapist, unlike the parents, became a necessary source of continuity for the boy who had immense needs to be rescued from the vicissitudes of life and death.

EGO CAPACITY CONSIDERATIONS   With all that has been written on ego considerations by Anna Freud, Geleerd and others, much has to be synthesized by the adolescent analyst's education, personal therapeutic analysis, and supervision. To remain empathic, patient, persistent, and lonely in this work and to endure restraint within oneself, while verbal and interactive with the patient, and to endure colleagues' criticisms of passivity, activity, or simple non-understanding is the fate of anyone who analyzes adolescents.

Which of the many ego considerations appear most pertinent in this labile, developmental phase of adolescence? I would simply consider a capacity for verbalization of utmost significance! While I do not intend to convey that silences, intellectualizations, and defensive use of language are to be decried, I do mean that capacity for use of language for truthful sharing with the analyst is the most valuable asset. This ability to verbalize is not at all simple and obviously is limited to language in various guises—that of the uncontrolled primitive schizophrenic thinking, the "word salad" where the words become "thing representations," to the obsessional valuation of words for other body representations such as the flow of excrement, milk, or semen. But with all the various meanings of language to the individual, the adolescent must have some degree of verbal facility to express relationships of meaning of the self and object world to another human being and to delay discharge. While I believe there are gender differences both in onset and use of language, I am far more impressed with the use of language not merely for accuracy (secondary process thinking), but for the conveyance of affect and the ability to break away from the confinement of language (Tarachow, 1965) to utilize various modalities in conveying nuances and variations of thinking and feeling. No other form of therapy depends so closely on mutual exploration of language meaning than does the psychoanalytic process. Where inhibitions are too severe, where there is aggressive utilization of language or its abuse, i.e., "a breathing silence," one may ascertain that the defensive agents of language provide an index of disorganizational panic. The defenses should be accepted as possibly occurring in a psychotic ego.

One case comes to mind of a fourteen-year-old adolescent boy referred for problems of learning, lack of friends, and morbid distance from his parents. Obviously intelligent, he presented in a perseverative pattern, his ignorance of what was said, passivity in reaching-out relationships, and a need to conceptualize in mathematical symbols. In self-defense, I utilized couch technique. The defensive use of his language, a pseudoliteral quality, and a need to withdraw attention from more primitive visual representations became gradually understandable. Words become devices to drone, to get one's attention off disagreeable sexual conflicts and fantasies. Dreams were to be faithfully reported but not to be utilized. It would cause little wonder that such particularized utilization of language was overdetermined by factors such as identification of language with feminine traits of a disturbed childhood image of a voluble, angry, demanding mother and a detached, distant, philosophical, nonspontaneous father. There were obsessional problems of handling severe sado-masochistic fantasies and urges associated with possible perversion. It would not surprise one to learn that intellectual functions were severely inhibited. It would not be difficult to contemplate that learning of a foreign language appeared almost impossible, for one would have to abandon one's "mother tongue" (Buxbaum, 1949). Despite all the contraindications, the analysis proceeded well therapeutically. Although technically slow, it seemed to proceed on a basis of assimilation by the patient of an amelioration of superego censure and continued use of language as utilized in various stages of several mental states. I would hardly recommend such experiences to a candidate for adolescent psychoanalysis.

Another consideration is the capacity for cathexis to an interest or an activity, with some indications of talent, to the partial exclusion of narcissistic concerns. Whether the activity is utilized for sublimatory or defensive purposes matters less than that there is a mobilization of energy into some socially recognizable pattern. I think there should optimally be some persistence in the pursuit of an interest, whether it be photography, mountain climbing, bird watching, athletics, reading, or socially organized recreation. There should be some enjoyment and satisfaction in this activity. This ego consideration is obviously a constellation or cluster of psychic derivatives resultant in a social process. But complex as this is, it remains as some kind of index of object cathexis with motivation that augurs well for synthesis of many psychological potentials. If patterned, it indicates a system of effective discharge of some potential. Without it, one is left with worries of inner aridity, desolate affects, and lack of sublimation potential to utilize the therapeutic interplay of psychoanalysis. By its absence, there may be indicated the significant absence of genetic progression of needs that become object directed in the sense of Anna Freud's developmental lines.

Another ego consideration is the ability to acknowledge fantasy formation, daydream, and dream phenomena. There are adolescents who are so loath to acknowledge the presence of this kind of mental life that one is beset with disorganizing primitive anxiety or primitive discharge systems so that delay in thinking appears minimal. While this ego consideration appears too simple to mention, its absence may indicate severe disturbance in object relationship and not merely phenomena of resistance or acting out.

One hopefully thinks that promiscuity in its sexual and aggressive drive aims is not too severe. To be fondled, caressed, loved or to be the same object of attacks and criticism if beyond certain normal limits, makes for irreparable characteriological disturbances to warrant psychoanalysis. To differentiate these problems under the stress of assessment for psychoanalysis of the adolescent may be impossible initially, but inferences may be ascertained and provide for indications of continuance beyond a trial period.

When I summarize these various ego considerations, they invariably show themselves as manifestations of a range of normality which seem to be necessary for a therapeutic alliance and a meaningful joint psychoanalytic endeavor. They do not presage success but are a modicum for an analyst's "working stance" and lend to the objectivity and selection of case beyond which countertransference pulls become too great. Essentially, they depend on many clues and inferences from observation, utterances, and historical evidences linked with parental interchanges, which possess the same qualities. It is in the setting of the analytic situation of the psychoanalyst, structured or unstructured but in keeping with the personality of the analyst, that the nuances are weighed jointly by the analyst and the analysand.

The analyst, in a theoretical frame of reference which is not only clinical but human, must perceive (1) the capacity for some object constancy, (2) the capacity to undergo and experience anxiety without it becoming disorganizing and lasting, (3) intellectual capacity for language and problem solving, (4) a capacity for ego viewing which may align itself with that of the analyst, (5) the historical evidence for progression to development along lines which attain a semblance of genital primacy, and (6) the absence of concretistic, disordered thinking which is too laden with the primitive thinking and affect of the psychotic. These criteria are not too dissimilar from those used for the adult, but take into account changes, a lack of concomitant identifications (which is characteristic of the adolescent phase of development), a yearning for consistency without premature fixity of patterns, and attainments.

AUTOPLASTIC VS. ALLOPLASTIC TRENDS   Some authors, particularly Josselyn (recent AAPSC), tend to emphasize "autoplastic," a descriptive term, in contradistinction to "alloplastic," with the connotation of discharge of psychic energy away from self. Both terms, to me, represent a way of describing what Freud viewed as object cathexis *vs.* narcissism and, of course, can be used to describe what has already been covered. Heightened and persistent narcissism may, when coupled with aggression and diminished guilt, make for a characterological disorder of the impulse-ridden type.

Whether in childhood, adolescence, or adulthood, it may be difficult to cope with in the absence of the maintenance of conflict and tolerance for anxiety.

REGRESSION POTENTIAL   I know of no developmental phase where the potentials for regression are greater and are so difficult to distinguish from psychotic functioning. Clinically, behavior changes of mood from apathy to enthusiasm, object relationships from adulation to intense antipathy, and thinking of a high order of perceptivity to inability to conceptualize are all evidences of this phase of development. But within the variation and reversals there is basically (Blos, 1963) an adaptive goal of freeing oneself from childhood representations and aims with painful affects of loss and differentiation, the attainment of mastery of one's individual and group identity, and eventually the attainment of personal and social change. The important technical consideration is to be able to recognize regression, because one does not interpret from the objective level of the adult when the mental and emotional comprehension is not sufficiently neutralized. One remains constant, accepting, and not punitive in the face of these powerful aggressive or self-destructive impacts during regression. The regression in the analytic situation repeats early patterns of dyadic equilibrium where one must steer between the Scylla or Charybdis of seduction and aggression of the parent rearing figures.

TRANSFERENCE READINESS   In contrast to adult psychoanalysis, there is transference readiness rather than fixed transference reactions. Regression may occur at the most disorganized phase and seemingly not affect the relationship capacities. The difficulty in acknowledging "transference love" appears to be a developmental pull necessary to combat the infantile periods of life which are frightening. As a result, it is only later that one can infer and integrate the transference. Despite the fact that the behavior appears to reduplicate the reactions to parental attitudes and representations of the past, they can be so evanescent and variable within the same sessions, that it is impractical to interpret for a long time the unconscious aspects of the derivatives. Indeed, where it appears evident, the experienced adolescent analyst may well guard against premature interpretations, just as the modality of the relationship is not identical with precarious unconscious identification derivatives of the adult.

DEPRESSION, THINKING DISORDER, ARRESTS, AND FIXATIONS   The aim of dedifferentiation of old object representations and values is in itself akin to mourning and loss. The affect is one of insecure loneliness. Each adolescent faces the problem of endurance of his own self-images, his potentials on a comparative realitive base in a competitive striving with the peer group and the older generation. Whether by profound withdrawal, alternation of moods or affects, or by an overcompensated sociability, there appears to be a painful capacity for experiencing the uniqueness of self in a cosmos of pantheistic or monotheistic theology. The contemplation of self, either as an enormity or a microcosm, is so common that one readily may perceive this as part and parcel of self-viewing ego introspection. Indeed, there develops a group phenomenon of this very thinking process—a glorification of, and a dread of excessive use of this modality. It is this same quality of thinking that may project or perceive parental attitudes, but is not tempered by the restraint, judgment, and renown that will come later.

Despite the universalities of adolescent thinking, and despite the dangers of casting characterological predictions which are not of great value (Cf. Anna Freud, 1958), the analyst, in his assessment, must render value judgments as to the desirability of psychoanalysis for some adolescents. While acceptance was once a distinguished mark of achievement, it no longer holds this appeal and is perceived by many adolescents as temporizing, conservative, and leading to an acceptance of intolerable unchanging institutions of society.

It may well happen that psychoanalysis may become an outlet for an escape from hospitalization or social ostracism—an unpopular last resort amongst a peer group devoted to change and action. It certainly bears a "conservative" connotation. Yet, it would appear that for some adolescents the connotations will have an exhibitionistic and intriguing magic appeal. Despite its costliness and the need for parental support and active participation from the adolescent, the psychoanalytic situation has an omniscient, magic, omnipotent appeal. Other therapeutic, and often primitive, approaches have always failed the adolescent. The professional parents, colleagues of the helping professions, have always been a source of patient referral.

The analyst must then make the best selection possible, maintaining the conviction that the therapeutic affectiveness is not suited to those who are psychotic or too traumatized or have too severe levels of fixation and arrest.

Psychological Prerequisites of Analysts

COUNTER-TRANSFERENCE   This difficult topic—the problems of incapacitating counter-transference capacities, is the subject of every training program in psychoanalysis. The educational process of becoming an analyst of children and/or adolescents is in transition. Our experiences are limited to a few trial experiments of training analysts who have little to no systematic experience with patients other than adolescents.

I believe that the personal psychoanalysis of many who work with children reveals the overdeterminants of their personal motivation. To mention only a few, are the opportunities to defend against the incompletely analyzed infantile-parental problems of the analyst, the omnipotent need to maintain a nurturing feminine identification or a powerful, authoritative masculine identification with the adolescent as a figure for projective identification. There may be unconscious seductive erotic determinants of unresolved infantile components and a desire for leadership or omnipotence that extends the analyst into areas of interaction that he himself would never individually narcissistically enjoy. The painfulness of an individual's adolescent reactions may temper the unconscious aspects of one's own reactions and substitute for unresolved aspects of this developmental phase.

Certainly it appears that in the analysis of adolescents, one must be careful of ego distance and be neither too remote nor too intimate. There must be a cognizance of one's own adolescence, whether in one's personal historical development alone or in the evolution of one's own phase of family development. Just as it is helpful to have children of one's own, it is helpful to have had understanding and misunderstanding of one's own adolescent children, not that the biological evolution is the only prerequisite, or its absence a disqualification.

One of the most frequent supervisory experiences I have encountered is with analysts who have had parental losses in their adolescence. This phenomenon, occurring in such a developmental phase, serves to reinforce a narcissistic aim to undo loss reactions of the normal vicissitudes of the ego in adolescence and secretly to undo the traumatic personal reactions. Counter-transference identifications, with increased sense of frustration and aggression in response to the adolescent's lack of acceptance of this altruistic idealized concept, appears inevitable unless this is clearly dealt with in supervision and extended in the process of self-analysis.

There is also necessary, as previously described, a flexibility in dealing with the adolescent's family from time to time. One should utilize this as part of the adolescent's changing object representations and not as a means of unconscious identifications of the analyst with the adolescent. To know the innate ambivalence of a regressed adolescent is a wise admixture for judging mental views of parents.

The constant necessity to reconstruct past events with relevance to the present, with all the opportunities for displacement and amnestic resistance, is a feature of both adolescent and adult psychoanalysis. The adolescent may cling with passionate conviction to screen memories and family myths as though they were his own recollections, yet also have the capacity to experience contradictory recollections which tend to make reconstruction possible by its very contradictions. There is also, sometimes, an intense cathexis to these recalls which is not so characteristic of many adults and is of definite assistance to a therapeutic alliance.

It is a prerequisite of the analyst of adolescents not to indicate, subtly or grossly, his own judgments of societal change. While one recognizes this is largely or entirely impossible, I mention it as basic to viewing material as it emerges only under the tolerance of the analyst's objectivity toward the analysand. This must remain the primary focus, not the societal evolution that the analysand is part of. By that, I do not mean that the analyst is part of a closed, static system, but rather that his focus is the world as the adolescent perceives it—a world of many mental representations rather than the conventional cliché of "manipulable environment" or "milieu." The former is metapsychological; the latter is simplistic and manipulative.

AGE CONSIDERATIONS   One of the truisms of psychiatry, at least in the United States, is that young psychiatrists and young psychoanalysts generally see adolescent patients. That this is a cultural corollary of our regard for the young and our difficulty in venerating the aging seems possible. It also is a possible corollary that "when one is young, one has 'little problems' and when one gets older. . . ." This axiom does not seem to be true psychologically, and with the growth of knowledge of child development, we may only note that childhood communication is limited and ego growth is necessary for the phenomenon of ego-viewing functions so characteristic of adolescence and adult phases of development. Since parents support the treatment of children and adolescents in our society, whether private or clinic, their own attitudes become invidious to younger psychiatrists. It is only in the course of psychiatric and psychoanalytic education that the complexities of the adolescent phase are studied in depth and the problems of goals, limitations of treatment consideration, and technical prerequisites, including one's own personal didactic analysis and supervision, as well as analytic styles, become the focus of therapeutic investigation and research. One of the problems of the adolescent phase is its general inaccessibility to psychoanalysis of candidates unless it is appreciated by the training analysts themselves. More and more training analysts in the past two decades have been trained in child as well as adult psychoanalysis, so that the conceptual framework of psychoanalytic education has been extended beyond the earlier framework of Freud.

In the early days of psychoanalysis and when the pioneer analysts themselves were younger, age considerations for psychoanalysis were younger. Understandably, it was felt that psychic changes could be effected more easily than when patterns of behavior become codified or "ossified." This viewpoint must in part have reflected the cultural influence and generational problem of the pioneers as well as their patients. Nevertheless, it was a tradition in the United States that the child psychoanalyst would not for long work with children, that he would gradually end up supervising others and would, in his fifties, see chiefly parents and possibly grandparents.

With the passing of the generations, the above expectation was not borne out. Ernst Kris, in his fifties, contributed vitally to the longitudinal studies of infants at Yale. Neubauer, Escalona, Galenson, Solnit and Mahler, when they were in advanced middle age, contributed vitally to studies of young children, and Anna Freud has continued her rewarding and active clinical and theoretical investigations in her seventies. As a result of this generational influence, there was fully emerged a specialty of child psychiatry and psychoanalysis, and the practitioner or research investigators practice it from the time of their training throughout their careers. There is one difference in the clinical practice of child and adolescent psychoanalysis from that of the practitioner dealing with adults. No child analysts in my experience, and few child psychiatrists, limit their practices solely to the young. I believe that the reasons for this are the complexity, strain and, communication problem of treating this group, which would place too much stress on the adult, just as a mother might have too many children to take care of personally, and must delegate some of the mothering to the other children.

Another aspect of the age factor is that many of the older figures in the field are, of course, better known by students, patients and publications, so that a great amount of consultation and assessment for treatment is done by the "senior citizen group" in private practice.

For the adolescent himself, the phenomenon of age of the analyst is itself a subject of reflection. From the initial testing confrontation throughout the psychoanalysis, the phenomena of life and death, illness and health, play important frames of reference for identification of the analyst as parental or grandparental figures with the accompanying comparisons to the actual parental representations and to the obvious transference wishes and fears of the adolescent. I contrast this relationship to a difference in age of the adolescent-therapist relationship where the span is less than a decade. In these situations, the reality aspects lend possibly to initial identification with older sibling figures, but it is doubtful that this phenomenon, unless fostered by a counter-transference problem, does not give way to parental identifications.

My own later experiences lend some credence to a relief factor in the adolescent when he perceives the "generation gap" is not unencompassible and that understanding is a human phenomenon, not a product merely of peer communication. Relief in being understandable to others is a therapeutic phenomenon that affords a uniqueness in psychoanalysis and, with older psychoanalysts, adds a quality of reinforcement or "awe" in the sense of Greenacre (1956). That this phenomenon must be taken up in the analytic situation goes without saying.

The psychoanalyst of an older vintage must, however, be in good health. To be burdened with physical illness and to have it intrude into the awareness of the adolescent adds a needless strain and interferes with the emergence of aggressive components of the narcissistic problems. I have seen adolescents who have nurtured their infirm analysts, and only upon transfer have they been able to reveal their mixed forgiveness and contempt for lapses of memory and concentration which is not characteristic of younger analysts.

There is a phenomenon with which all therapists are familiar— many older patients seek younger psychiatrists as a kind of insurance for help when they become infirm. This, of course, cannot apply to senior, aging psychoanalysts. One, in a sense, trades wisdom and experience for the inevitability of loss, which must be part of the psychoanalysis of the adolescent as with everybody else.

Research Potentials

Every psychoanalysis is an instance of clinical research, and the problems of organization and presentation of work experiences are as great a problem now as confronted Freud in the presentation of his five clinical histories. There is no doubt that when the psychoanalyst has particular interests, he will find evidences of this in his clinical psychoanalytic work. Indeed, his patients may unconsciously wish to contribute to his psychoanalytic writings, if they have read them. His "aura" will be shed over the adolescent if there is popularization and use of public media by the psychoanalyst. This may apply even to the selection of psychoanalysts who were writers on various topics such as creativity, talent, youth, and child rearing or education. Ernst Kris used to say that when there was a discussion coming up at a psychoanalytic meeting, one was liable to find material from patients that would lend itself to the discussion. Or vice versa, following a meeting, a psychoanalyst may find influences operating upon him to make interpretations based upon some clarification that ensued at that particular meeting, due to complicated identifications and transference phenomena with one's colleagues. Certainly this phenomenon operated in Freud as he was involved in his development of psychoanalysis and is not too different from any piece of clinical research.

The technical problem of the psychoanalytic situation and subsequent reportage, memory loss, and revelation of patients' identities present a unique, puzzling problem. Most of the clinical reports are vignettes and may come from supervisory situations, second-hand, where the student sends in reports. Few senior psychoanalysts review or write notes on daily sessions. The flood of recollections present a problem in the use of time alone. Attempts to obviate this by audio-visual means (Gill et al., 1968) have come into trial, and group discussions have revealed some of the same distortions as any other clinical research technique would show. Another problem in the research is how to share, document, and present the connection of both patient and analyst in the unfolding and flow of the material at the various stages of psychoanalysis. The study of supervision, notes by students, or in rare instances by supervisors, leave a host of problems that are unsystematized.

That this is basically true of any clinical psychiatric presentation
is accepted, but not verbalized frequently. So at best, psychoanalysts are placed in the position of illustrating certain theoretical postulates, conclusions, and inferences that they have derived from the research potentials of every given patient. Much
more will be gathered in the field of adolescence (Blos, 1963) and,
in a sense, will be grouped by the analyst as by any clinical investigator, hopefully in an objective and unbiased fashion, but with
a recognition that ultimate truth is to be gained by experiences
of many psychoanalysts of adolescents.

Other Technical Considerations

TECHNIQUE OF ASSESSMENT INTERVIEWS   The assessment interview actually has its own preparation long before the face to face
confrontation with the psychoanalyst. It basically involves the adolescent in a triadic relationship at its simplest breakdown. Few
arrangements are simple, and the metapsychological aspects may
never have been clarified through the course of the analysis.

Obviously, the psychological situation is being established before
the psychoanalyst is aware of it. The psychoanalyst, therefore, is
in a natural position to assume a humble, enquiring position, and
the adolescent is beset with conflicts about the simplest communication, but is also, despite this stress, in a realistic situation of
knowing more about himself than any observer. To set this into
a matter-of-fact framework would seem natural and understandable, but it is nevertheless beset by many factors which would obviate the presentation of this "shared" fact. The psychoanalyst may
be young, in supervision, or needful of a promising adolescent for
his training. Despite his theoretical training, his own needs will
place him in the role of a magical or medical authoritarian source,
or will render him in a seducer's role. His natural style of verbal
communication in a face to face situation may become a cover
for his own anxiety, may preclude his own straightforwardness
which is vital in a mutual endeavor to get at facts. He may talk
too much, give too much advice, or he may be relatively silent
with the image of the supervisor or the idealized teacher in mind.
He may be involved with his hitherto unsuccessful search for getting suitable cases. He may think of his previous experiences or be
going over what had been brought up in supervision previously.
He may, indeed, feel that everything that is to transpire must be
recalled and presented to a supervisor, institute, or some higher

type of body. These are some instances of what may be playing in the assessment interview—anything but the hopefully neutral human relationship to be established and technically called a "therapeutic alliance."

From the time of the first contact, whether by letter or telephone, it is important for the analyst to note who telephones—the adolescent himself, the mother or father, or a friend. Conversation over the phone may early establish a relation or disestablish it. The sound and the content of the verbal contact is meaningful, as is the name, place, age, and sex of the analyst. The urgency of parents or adolescent, the need for a here and now appointment, the length of time and delay in seeking the appointment, the source of the recommendation, whether it be patient, colleague, friend of the family, school educator, or social agency is important and to be taken into account. Sometimes, the actual location of the residence is important in concepts of travel time, shared living accommodations, etc. Information given by one's telephone answering service, promptness or delay in answering initial communications, the time of such communications all play their role in the preparatory contact.

A modest attitude of enquiring who wishes to be seen first, some reference, if the adolescent is not calling himself, as to his proximity to the person telephoning, is of value in setting up the family situation. Do the parents wish to include the adolescent and his preference to see the psychoanalyst before or after the parents? The psychoanalyst can be an initial help in leaving this to the adolescent and his family or, without cues, he may set it arbitrarily. In back of most parental minds is a considerable amount of anxiety, aggression, insecurity about their role, and some wish to meet the psychoanalyst who is going to consult and possibly work with their child. They want to know his office arrangement and what his personality is like. Is he going to assuage or increase their own feelings of despair; how does this "talking method work"; how will it continue, and what frequency is involved; how will they afford it; and in what way will this affect their own living—the introduction of a nonfamily member into the close interpersonal relationships hitherto kept from societal scrutiny. A frequent question is, "Where did we go wrong?" and this is correlated with dismay at the change in their adolescent's relationship to themselves and fears about his own adjustment as viewed from their standpoint.

Another problem that is one of the inevitable accompaniments of parenthood, particularly during adolescence and earlier childhood, is the vital sharing of responsibility or its relinquishment in contrast to the blaming and deprecating of one parent by the other.

Unwittingly, parents are frequently unaware of how they have been involved by the Oedipal constellation and by young Oedipus himself. Changes in former relationships may cause pain, anguish and feelings of loss and tend to cause parents to reassess their own marital involvements. Previous adjustments, whether as a result of psychoanalysis or therapy in the past, seem threatened by the crisis of their own adolescent's difficulties.

There is no one set pattern for an "assessment situation" and the family experience to determine it, even if it demonstrates the various struggles that now emerge to be assessed. One frequent procedure is not to see adolescent and parents together. The objective attitude of getting the family's and the adolescent's points of view separately is obviously more neutral.

The adolescent may come alone, initiate the request, or, because of reluctance, he may be accompanied by one or both parents either voluntarily or by severe moral persuasion. Once the analyst and adolescent are alone, facing each other, the verbal interchange follows the visual and other cues that have preceded. If the adolescent's reluctance to verbally describe is marked, and if he does not respond to statements of confidentiality, there is some obvious disappointment in the referral, and it is unwise to have more visits. But in these visits, which are preponderantly the case, with encouragement, expression of curiosity about the setting of analysis, the process, and the anxieties about the process for oneself may be initially ventilated.

But of course, there must be some self-recognition of conflict or disturbance for which help is needed, and indeed one visit is rarely enough to lay the groundwork for consideration of psychoanalysis of the adolescent. The second and third visits afford an opportunity for observation of change, reflection, and a certain continuity in meaningfulness of communication which must be present. A first visit which piques and challenges the adolescent may be followed by loss of interest, ennui, and other attitudes which make for no therapeutic agreement. The analyst's preliminary formulation of the goals of psychoanalysis, paraphrasing much that the adolescent has thought about, is sometimes possible without appearing authoritative—it is couched as it appears at this period. Recognition of anxiety and fears of insanity may be verbalized early and dealt with as recurrent thoughts rather than taken as questions of fact or fancy.

Social immaturity, fears of sexual intimacy, interferences with learning all appear as problems that previous efforts to master or even to share with friends have continually failed to solve. The eventual derivation of these experiences of conflict and level of maturation are too varied to even tabulate. But some initial formulations need to be shared with the adolescent and parents; the silent, listening attitude of the oft caricatured psychoanalyst should not be followed.

CONCEPTS OF THE TRIAL PERIOD   In some instances, increasingly so, I have discussed the start of psychoanalysis as a trial period—both for the adolescent and the analyst. The parents are "in the wings" with regard to this aspect, and it is up to the adolescent to decide whether or not he wishes the psychoanalyst to participate in informing the parents of a mutual decision to not continue at a given time. Assessment may change due to many factors in the motivation of the adolescent. An example is a seventeen-year-old junior high school student, bright, curious, and intelligent who was distant from her family, unhappy and depressed about her relationships with boys, and severely self-conscious about obesity problems. She was referred by an adult psychoanalyst who had assessed her himself and had stated in the first visit that she should plan to undertake psychoanalysis in the city and that she must, under no circumstances, go away to college.

In my own assessment, I expressed the idea that much understanding had to be shared and that at this time I could not honestly come to such advice. It was necessary for us to see what these conflicts were about, and we would do a piece of work together provided that she agreed. This was infinitely more acceptable, and indeed, she eventually came for psychoanalytic treatment in her senior year. To have given up a prestigious college away from home would have been to accept a humiliating position in her social and home sphere that would have been devastating. This piece of psychoanalysis done, it led to understanding of loss and separation aspects of her life and aided in finding psychotherapeutic help while in college. It helped her, too, to accept a series of interviews after graduation to seek psychiatric help in a city of post-graduate study choice. Indeed, the initial psychoanalytic treatment fostered a growing understanding of severe tendencies to estrangement and depression. The persona of myself, identified and introjected, became a stabilizing influence in itself to both the girl and family until some point would be reached when she attained her career choice and could better come to grips with her narcissistic problems.

A use of the trial period of analysis has been present in psychoanalytic literature for many years. It has been in and out of vogue. I tend to favor it, provided that when an opportune moment comes, the trial period is concluded on a mutual basis. If the analytic procedure seems unendurable, if the psychoanalytic procedure doesn't appear to be worth the sacrifice, these feelings must be discussed with the patient (despite unconscious feelings of rejection) with understanding of the severity of his condition, and efforts should be made, with the adolescent's consent, to finding a suitable psychotherapist, preferably with a psychoanalytic training. In such an instance, I prefer the use of referral so that the painful hostile expressions of rejection, loss, and failure may be ventilated more easily and a more reality based relationship be assured of a better therapeutic start.

GROUPINGS OF ADOLESCENTS SUITABLE FOR PSYCHOANALYSIS
While I have positive convictions about the use of psychoanalysis for adolescents, I am impressed that the stability necessary for its maintenance, even physically, is not common and that moves away from high school to college plus experimentation with drugs, military service demands, responsibilities or evasions make it unseemly to have the same requirements as for adult psychoanalysis. I have the impression that those children who are in child analysis through late puberty years and then go through early and middle adolescent phase development comprise the group most suitable to be considered as adolescent analyzands.

The next group in the population are the young college freshmen and sophomores who experience severe alienation reactions, in a descriptive sense, while away from home and their childhood group. Here it is possible, provided there is sufficient consultation with parents and adolescent, to allow him to combine his educational achievement problems with psychoanalysis. Indeed, this is a modality of psychoanalysis related to the educational opportunities of certain urban areas such as Boston, Philadelphia, and San Francisco, where some of the more prestigious learning institutions are situated.

Another referral group is from families of colleagues and other helping professionals in the field of mental health where, with family support and encouragement, delays in choice of vocation or marriage may occur. In this circumstance, a period of psychoanalysis may be ushered in with eventual resolution for transfer to another colleague in another city.

It is in this college population group and for those taking advanced degrees that our concepts of the adolescent phase merge with those of young adulthood. To those of us who are older, it is hard to conceive of young adults as much differentiated from phase developments of adolescents. Yet, I believe that we do the psychological phenomena a grave injustice because the severe strains and incongrous apposition and opposition of drives, defenses, and adaptations are not so pervasive as in the adolescent and without the perspective of the young adult. Regardless of the value (superego) systems adopted, the young adult is more patterned and consistent, though not more secure, whereas the adolescent is so "surely unsure" that for a period of growth, he truly lacks the consistency of anything but an "impersonator in search of his person." He is unique, different, and no one knows better his variegated untrustworthiness than himself. This, of course, is different from the group of adolescents who actively maintain their dependence and fear change even at the cost of maintaining infantile aggressions and sexual autoerotisms as part of their narcissistic characterological problems.

CONCEPTS OF PREANALYTICAL PREPARATIONS   Early in child analysis, there is the concept of a stage of "preparation for analysis," based upon the need to establish a working relationship with child and family, and to develop a continued assessment. After this early stage, the frequency of the visits is increased to four times a week, and the parents are seen once a week in those instances where kindergarten and early latency-age children are being treated. This also serves to prepare and condition child and family to the fact that although psychoanalysis was most important in the child's life, it did not prevent his school and social participation, which is often the modality of resistance on the part of the parents. Another form of difficulty is the effect of psychoanalysis of one sibling upon the other. Thus, the concept of preparation for psychoanalysis of children deals with preparation and strategy for a close involvement with the child and family, leading to the optimal therapeutic working relationship necessary for the technique.

There is generally an interesting effect upon the young student of child analysis. Geared to a frequency of visits once or twice a week plus occasional contacts with the mother, he has difficulty in developing an inner conviction that frequency as in adult analysis is necessary for continuity of psychoanalytic work. Indeed, he often found it difficult to deal with parental problems of resistance to the procedure. Without the inner conviction of differences rather than similarities between child psychoanalysis and psychoanalytically oriented psychotherapy, the psychoanalytic technique suffered severe impairments.

The psychoanalysis of adults never had the same problem concerning frequency of visits, because students were well-able to observe differences of tempo as well as the effects of frequency upon the free associative trends and the impact of the "week-end crust" in contrast to the more active aspects and less systematic investigation of psychotherapy. Since the child's play and observations and interpretation of behavior differ in terms of the manifest content (plus the fact that there is such a distance between adult and child), it is harder to "therapeutically negotiate." Yet this difficulty gradually lost prominence as more child psychoanalysts became trained and recognized.

Adolescents have always presented unique problems for any type of therapeutic approach to deal with the maintenance of a relationship. Indeed many papers are still written on the topic of how to maintain contact with the adolescent. Thus, the effect of suggesting four or five visits a week to the adolescent led the therapist to believe that he would be regarded as one so intimate, and either seducing or punishing, that an adolescent could not accept this stipulation of a working relationship unless he were so overwhelmingly threatened by his problems as to be virtually psychotic. This kind of approach also seemed to be opposed to the adolescent's need to individuate himself once again from family and to maintain his identity (Erikson, 1959). Yet, these are the same rationalized or intellectualized objections often used for denial and resistance to establishing the optimum working conditions of any psychoanalytic situation.

In the instance of adolescent psychoanalysis, I believe that there is distinct need to prepare the adolescent so that he may mobilize his efforts to participate more frequently and in a positive manner rather than on the basis of fear and symptom exacerbation. For the adolescent, considering a frequency of four or five times a week is often a submission to authority—to a parent—and is unconsciously a return to various infantile phases which lead to seductive genital strains or erotic excitement, homosexual wishes and defenses, or to more provocative oppositional stances of earlier lines of development. In these instances, it seems desirable to direct one's efforts to the working, observing ego of the adolescent, to assess together the manifestations of difficulties in understanding the flow of associations as phenomena of mental activity and the relationships to present responses in varied situations, before significant interpretive comments are made to tie up past recollections. Such a preparation, which necessarily enjoins a description of experiences of the relationship (not designated as transference) and the difficulties of the psychoanalytic joint endeavor, can be handled in such a way as to be reasonable to the narcissistic aspect of the ego. Suggesting and allowing the adolescent to move from a schedule of two or three visits weekly to four or five must be predicated upon a sense of mutual cooperation and should allow time for the ego to make adjustments. For the adolescent, if handled too forcibly, will relate with dismay that he does not have time to work at his studies or sports or to participate in family functions and will feel that this objection is solely reality oriented. When, however, it can be mutually demonstrable, that fantasy, day-dreaming, and conflictual wishes play a great role in the ineffective use of his or her time, the efficacy of increased visits gradually can be acknowledged.

Another phenomenon, of course, is the feeling that once shown how, the adolescent can, in effect, do "self analysis"—for example, already proficient from his analytic contacts, he can be helpful to his friends—unconsciously identifying with the positive aspects of his analyst. Or in other instances, the giving up and sacrificing his urges to discharge energy by engaging in compulsive hobby activities means relinquishment of his concepts of "free will and self-determination," in contrast to the discovery that there are many psychic determinants and that his rationalized ideas of causal relationships of the meaning of phenomena are much too oversimplified and, indeed, intellectualized. Then, too, by the time these discoveries are shared and mutually checked, not only by his observing ego, but also with the psychoanalyst, he can gradually understand that regardless of the parental wishes for change within himself, this change is something that he, himself, not only wishes but needs the time to work on, through and *with* the psychoanalyst. Only in such a fasion can psychoanalysis of the adolescent occur, and it is for this reason that the early concept of preparation for psychoanalysis appears to be a necessary part of the treatment of the adolescent.

SEPARATION FROM THE ANALYST   Most psychoanalysts take vacation during the summer, take time off for professional meetings during the year, and perhaps take other time off for personal reasons. A rough working schedule seems to approach forty-six to forty-eight weeks a year. In the instance of child analysis, the working schedule must be flexible since the school schedule involves nine months and there are vacations and holidays when families as a group plan to travel. For the child analyst, then, there is more difficulty than with adult patients in maintaining continuity and yet there is recognition that the child is a growing individual within a family and that the psychoanalytic situation is not to be construed as a rival for these family nurturing functions. It is important that the child realistically consider his family functions and no child analyst would regard these interruptions per se as resistance phenomena, although they could be vehicles for the expression of resistance. Unlike the adult in analysis who soon learns to have his time correspond as much as possible with his analyst's schedule, the adolescent must demonstrate his own phasic developmental needs, of which his use of analytic time and scheduling represents a natural part of the psychoanalytic situation.

An unconscious linkage of psychoanalysis with school seems natural and subject to varied interpretation, i.e., substitute parental role of teachers and analyst, time for work versus play, pleasure versus displeasure, a time for being awake rather than asleep, a time for controlling fantasies and conflicts rather than eliminating them by destructive devices.

Weekends are times for "going barefooted mentally," like the Saturday bath, and consist of telephoning, dating, television, sports, and certainly as little study as possible except under strain of examination times. Psychoanalysis is soon identified as depending upon the setting of resistance or working through of the complicated transference reactions, a form of internalized pressure of viewing conflicts and opposed to complete denial, discharge, and idealized elimination of conflicts. Infantile aspects of pleasure-seeking cannot be gratified or overindulged at the cost of masochistic suffering, and it takes time to understand that this is an internalized problem and not within the province of any psychoanalyst to grant immunity from consequences of conflict.

Yet the psychoanalyst of the adolescent also must realize that summer travel, study and relaxation, plus variation of schedules, allow for opportunities not only to regress but to master aspects of what has been learned in the analysis and also to express the developmental pushes of progression from childhood. The differences in attitude may vary with the analyst, but for a group of adolescents there must of necessity be modication of what is appropriate for adults or children. Opportunities for work experience both in camp, away from the analytic setting, or in other settings are a necessary part of this period. For some adolescents who indeed are obsessionally bound up in their strivings, relaxation and the opportunity to observe oneself alone as well as to observe the development of an analytic process of thinking that has become internalized and a way of life is necessary.

Because adolescents are not adults and because their society also recognizes these differences, psychoanalysis must take the normative phenomena in this society into account, and will modify its conceptualized approaches to vacation time, other time schedules, and the other needs of this period. Mutual agreement rather than a feeling of getting special attention is necessary, and many an adolescent psychoanalyst has to curb his own envy of this aspect of adolescence. The reality background of economic payment will be dealt with in another section, but suffice it to say that the psychoanalyst must be free of conflict over these working conditions and must realize the inevitable differential uses of this aspect of the analytic situation. This frequently comes up in supervision of one's first cases of adolescents.

With this background, one then has the opportunity to view the adolescent's varied uses of time lapses from analysis and may bring them into consideration. There are opportunities to interpret phenomena of leaving, rather than of being left, of feelings of helplessness and wishing the analyst to come along, fears of increased loneliness and responsibility, jealous reactions over the limitations of choice as to where to go and with whom, in contrast to the fantasies of the psychoanalyst as one who can take off in regal, luxurious style with mate and children. These feelings provide an opportunity to observe basic transference phenomena brought up by the phenomenon of loss in the past. Death of parental figures, friends, pets, may all enter into complicated contemplations of projected wishes of death to others or inwardly directed with unconscious narcissistic ideas of punishment and accompanying depression. Fears of change of routine may lead to reexperiencing anxiety, masturbation conflicts, and the disheartening realization that narcissistic desires of "cure" are not observable. Wishes to hear from and maintain contact or communication with the analyst may reassert themselves. A return to manifestations of starting the psychoanalysis with exacerbation of old symptom formations may prove helpful to the implied need to continue treatment and ensure return, which is in conflict with the desire to be terminated and to never again recognize the problem.

Separation phenomena also include a familiarity with different levels of functioning, of coping and planning, and reality-based operations contrasted to some of the more regressed modes of behavior thinking in the analytic situation. It is as though the "real" separation even in leaving after an hour becomes forcefully viewed in contrast to the fantasied mental representations. Often, there is pleasurable excitement as well as anxiety present.

Generally, each separation is attended by a return and resumption of the analysis. Narrative accounts quickly subside and work continues which may bring into focus changes in operation and increased confidence. Contrasts to previous experiences may give a perspective of better utilization of insights than had hitherto been possible. There also are opportunities for the analyst to assess his predictions of his patient's mental equilibrium away from the analysis, and the effect of his patient's experimentation, in contrast to other periods of the analysis. It gives him an opportunity with adolescents to predict loosely when the particular problems of this phase have been "worked through" sufficiently so that a longer separation, transfer, or termination of analysis may be mutually considered. Little has been reported of the resumption of the analytic work and the effect of this upon the analyst's inferences and assumptions. I think it is important to contrast the organization of patients as they are after being away and their reliability as the analytic situation renews.

The following is an example. A twenty-year-old severe obsessive young college student with particular learning and thinking difficulties utilized his approaching summer vacation to study a foreign language in the specific country. This involved his theory that if he identified as a member of that country, he would overcome his particular difficulties in learning a language necessary for an advanced degree. Before he left, he was also beset with unhappiness over lonely social relationships with girls and his inability to form relationships with them that would lead to intimacy. The need for maintaining a hostile dependence was an aspect of the transference, and indeed, marked at the time his growing efforts to emerge out of this conflictual struggle. Before his separation, his need to masturbate, with fantasies which would shield him from socializing was interpreted. His conviction that girls would have nothing to do with him was almost delusional. His own preoccupations with this problem, in addition to his ability to withdraw mentally when he could not master problems (as exemplified by his difficulty with language), contrasted to great abilities in math. As he contemplated departure, he wondered if he would not succeed and be finished with the frustrations engendered in his analysis. Upon his return, it was learned that he had, as predicted, become constricted, experienced the same frustrations with girls in his foreign student setting and, similarly, had difficulty in identification as a foreigner. *But* he had experimented purposefully with the idea of desisting from masturbation, and he came back with a notation system, characteristic of this obsessive symptomology, of the influence of his masturbation conflicts upon his social behavior. I questioned mentally, at his departure, whether he could endure the anxiety of his severe sadomasochistic, perverse fixations. Upon his return, it was evident that he had carried the difficulty within him, and arrived at interlocking hypotheses. I learned, indeed fortuitously, that the entire trip and attempt to find a foreign setting was independently conceived and carried out to the satisfaction of his parents. I had had no access to this aspect of his life from the analytic setting before he left.

VERBAL AND NONVERBAL COMMUNICATIONS   One important consideration in the psychoanalysis of adolescents is the use of verbal communication, particularly the role of language as used by the psychoanalyst. From the time of the initial phone contacts, the psychoanalyst is aware that his own restrained use of language, geared particularly for interpretation in the adult free associative technique, must undergo modification in dealing with the adolescent. Many interpretations of the analyst's silence have been made, but in the assessment interviews and beginning phases of psychoanalysis of the adolescent, it may prove in itself to be overwhelming and unconsciously perceived as hostile, castrative, punitive, superior and reacted to with severe anxiety and opposition. The inevitable analytic response to have the analysand continue, reflect, and pursue his own investigation of what is occuring in the field of his mental operations is beset with the phenomenon of the adolescent developmental phase, which itself is characterized by subjective heightening of this very process and is often regarded by one aspect of the ego as ill, disordered, or just plain "crazy." Very frequently, the adolescent projects this onto the analyst if the external communication system of the analyst is geared to that for the adult— the psychoanalytic situation or analyst is termed "crazy," or the adolescent makes no response to the simplest inquiry.

If one is mindful that in the assessment interviews the needs to have verbal interchange are present and that its relative absence in a sitting up situation places undue strain on most adolescents, there is opportunity for a transition to the more structured psychoanalytic situation of the couch and free association. Also, the assessment interviews themselves afford much opportunity for clarification by such comments as "It's not clear to me, would you explain?" or "For example," rather than the much more unstructured situation with the adult. The adolescent, in my opinion, needs more verbal educational approaches, although piecemeal, as the opportunity lends itself, than does the adult patient. The adolescent is much too close and protective of his own fantasies and daydreams than is the usual adult who, at least initially, can give a more structured account of himself and what he regards as relevant to his history and its difficulties. The adolescent, almost like a paranoid patient, is keenly aware of what is illogical and almost delusional and is geared to more immediate considerations of the present fluctuation of mood and recall than is the adult. Instead, the adolescent, if given instructions about "the fundamental rule—free association" will take this as an order and an affront. The same goal may be attained by the suggestion to speak as freely as possible and then utilizing the interferences with friendly consideration that gradually differentiates speech as used in the psychoanalytic situation from that in everyday usage. Attention to the phenomenon of reexperiencing emotions by recall helps give a normal frame of reference to the adolescent which he sorely needs. At the same time, one still adopts the same analytic attitude of reflection, consideration, and attention to the nature of the communication which invariably produces nonverbal responses as well as verbal. It may well occur that it is not what is said, but what is not said, the absence of the unusual commendation or hostile response, that leaves its imprint.

By the above modification of use of language, I neither advocate conversation for itself or silence for observational purposes. It is important, for purposes of rapport, that the analyst differentiate himself from an involved parental image on the one hand and a condescending adult image on the other, as well as from the "pal response." At times, even some personal reflection may not be amiss and will not interfere with the analytic work. It may even jar some fixed preconceptions of the generation gap and may individualize the concepts of the particular psychoanalyst. It is vital for the psychoanalyst to be regarded, in part, as human and real, capable of emotions and feelings and leading some kind of existence other than seated in a consultation room. This may readily be conveyed by numerous references and slight queries in the fields of endeavor in which the adolescent is interested. Differences of opinion and view can be encouraged and certainly not disagreed with. Most important, of course, is not to agree with the images and feelings expressed in the initial phases—this is true of all analytic methodology.

Preliminary regrouping of what has been said in order to suggest other views of the same phenomenon described, affords opportunity to note the capacity of the given adolescent to be flexible rather than to hold adamantly to fixed convictions and defend altruistically one aspect of phenomena. One may use humor, kindness, and express in cryptic ways an appreciation for the problems of existence in this developmental phase.

Repeated questioning is to be regarded with disfavor, as it has the unconscious hallmark of nonacceptance and accentuation of difference—indeed, it generally connotes too probing an approach to secret mental life, generally drive derivatives which ego operations of the adolescent maintain a control of. Inescapably, the demands for communication are inexorable and for those adolescents who cannot endure this compact, there cannot be some mysterious magical system of communication which the analyst insists upon. Every adolescent, despite the assessment, can later utilize the analytic technique. Recognizing this is one stage of the adolescent's life may make it possible for him to contemplate this at a later date when more "consolidation" ensues. The psychoanalyst of the adolescent knows that he may be ill-distinguished from the punitive or martyred parent—no matter how he conducts himself, certainly not in a role-playing manner to deliberately offset the parent—and if one can agree that the situation is not now conducive to understanding, but that he can see and return if he so wishes, future continuance is possible. While this seems so reasonable as to be banal, it never appears this way in the actual experiences. Too often, the impulsive nature of interruption, missed appointments and the like are apt to be misconstrued by the analyst as reactions to his technique, when frequently they may be aggravated or directed toward other objects of the adolescent's life and are better displaced and acted upon the analyst. Some of the experiences can never be pointed out to either the analysand or his parents.

PSYCHOLOGICAL AND SCHOOL ACHIEVEMENT REPORTS The usual adolescent presenting himself for psychoanalytic consideration has an extensive experience with being psychologically tested in the school systems as well as repeated testings for scholastic aptitude for college entrance.

The psychological test results and evaluations are generally invisible to the adolescent, while the actual scores in college achievement and aptitude testing are well known. They, in themselves are aids in the assessment of the mental operations and certainly may be utilized if cooperation is maintained. It is possible that these are not available and may be wished for to assist in assessment as well as to have some kind of reality consideration for the adolescent and his parents to cope with. Both genius level and retarded functioning are rare for psychoanalytic functioning, but interferences and inhibitions in the exercise of such functioning may be objectively utilized for cooperative performances in the analysis and can serve as a baseline for achievements in the future course and stages of the psychoanalysis.

From the reality aspects of ego functioning, it is, of course, obvious that ignorance of oneself is far from bliss, but rather a source of tormented ill-satisfied wish fulfillment. The intelligence test scores themselves may be regarded with magical wishes and dreads, and they require careful cooperative understanding between analyst and adolescent. The adolescent who has undergone projective tests as well, group or individual, may have had these administered by teachers rather than by qualified psychologists, or by student psychologists and all kinds of inferences may have had lasting imprints upon the family, teachers, and adolescent himself. How often do we hear, "I have always been told that I don't live up to my *intellectual potential*," whereas little has ever been conveyed about the interferences that may appear evident in the hidden interpretations of the psychologist. In many instances, the level of functioning of the intellectual operations has been utilized by teacher after teacher so that the child has been unwittingly "typed and cast" in a fixed academic performance role in a manner similar to stage casting, and the adolescent's further development cannot fully grasp the implications of limited expectations in the given succeeding teacher. Or in other instances, the child has been grouped in various levels of classes as Math II section, Language III section, which he fully grasps, and has no idea that in some instances he adapted to the reality expectations of teachers with no cognizance of his conflictual problems and the crippling anxiety consequences of conflicts.

Utilization of psychological and achievement test results within the analytic assessment or treatment situation may be helpful, but only when they are utilized and shared with the adolescent himself. In most instances, the family may be extremely curious, but I have generally found that the essential aspects may or may not be discussed with the parents depending on the adolescent's wishes. In few instances have I been overwhelmingly astonished, but have been gratified in later analytic work to find detailed corroboration of ego operations which have been helpful to be less conflictual and certain defenses which have been made available to the awareness of the adolescent ego. In many instances, I have referred the adolescent analysand for testing with the definite understanding that we will mutually discuss this, including scores, potential functioning, and anxiety potentials. I have always shared, though often translated into more understandable terms, the psychologist's summary and sometimes the clinical recommendations.

I believe it self-evident that psychologists vary as do psychoanalysts. It is important to have a psychologist whom one has relied on for long standing, a psychologist who has considerable testing experience with children and adolescents, and best of all, a psychologist who is utilized by other psychologists for teaching and evaluating the various personality and intelligence test items. I personally find that psychologists who are more apt and interested in child therapy rather than observation are not as reliable for analytic assessment purposes. There is a tendency to intertwine the behavioral interview responses of the subject of the psychological testing in a therapeutic frame of reference which interferes with the appraisal of the reactions to the objective presentations.

What then is most meaningful to the analyst and adolescent? My experience has shown that discrepancy in scores between Performance and Verbal Scale of the WISC invariably point to a disorganizing anxiety potential akin to the proportions of panic. In most instances, they are not good indications for neurotic conflicts, but rather borderline psychotic or impulsive characterological disturbances. Certainly, the evidence of superior intellectual performance in a stress situation helps one to know a reality performance separate from the anxious experience and subjective attitudes. This in itself may be useful for sharing the inner feelings of guilt and self-criticism despite performance on the test. A third value has been the exemplification of mood disturbance and/or depression which may be very difficult to pick up initially in assessment and which the adolescent can acknowledge in a framework that would make this significant rather than the framework of the usual "adolescent variation of moods." I find that the libidinal conflicts, the level of developmental lines and personality organization as expressed in various parts of the test are not as pertinent for the adolescent as for my own later reference.

There is occasional need and value in discussing some of the responses to the Thematic Apperception Test picture items. The adolescent's approach to these stories convey: (1) an expression of making utilizable something about the self which one has passively experienced and yet never shared the knowledge of—an indicator of what to expect in the analytic process itself, (2) certain factual results which can be utilized, or objective resultants of what mental apparatus in conflict discharges, and (3) that any test situation, of which the psychological situation is but an example, stimulates stress. The results indicate functioning under difficulties and as such may be divested of such interferences, with the inference that with understanding plus effort, rather than with fulfillment, change may be achieved in the field of recall and synthesis. (4) The therapeutic alliance is one essentially between the participants. The family and parental influences upon the analytic work can rest upon the adolescent's own participation rather than a situation where the analyst must assume the protective role toward the child. This is exemplified by the sharing of the testing with the adolescent at the risk of displeasing the parents. This, of course, is not true of more seriously disturbed adolescents where knowledge of the serious pathology is to my mind best shared with the family at some time during the course of a nonanalytic therapy.

Prerequisites for the "The Psychoanalytic Situation"

TIME AND FREQUENCY   Despite many views on this subject, after assessment and a preparatory or nonpreparatory phase and the mutual acceptance of trial analysis as a process of communication, the method needs an optional frequency of visits on the part of the patient. While one grants that there are fluctuations in the ability to free associate, depending on a myriad of elements such as character formation, anxiety manifestations, symptom formation and complexities of unconscious motivation, a minimum of three visits weekly extending to five is conducive to the best interchange. Analytic students are advised to develop trial use of four to five times weekly from which one can proceed to cut down or increase with mutual participation of the patient and his own evaluation. Certainly, the time factor and the continuing theme of mental content has a certain rhythm and flow which is always observable, and interferences such as resistance and acting out phenomena may be optimally interpreted. Certainly, this aspect of the working alliance should be primary to economic fee considerations for pursuance of this technical method. The analyst and adolescent must share the knowledge that what they are technically setting up is psychoanalysis in a Freudian approach and cannot be equated with what one's friends, parents or teachers, or popular writing may term psychoanalysis.

There is the mutual understanding that the aim of such a technique is not to eliminate or cure, but to increase "access to oneself" and to allow for greater choice and hopefully more efficient means of performing socially, i.e., the large goals of work and love.

COUCH REQUIREMENTS   There is the understood and shared acceptance of the principle of free association with the emphasis on verbalization of thoughts, ideas, and feelings as they are primarily perceived, regardless of the value judgments of the adolescent. Also, the content as such is not to be regarded as disagreeable, whether it concerns the analyst or anyone else. There is the gradual development and acceptance of this stipulation, as evidenced by the many experiences of refuting it, with the knowledge that this is an ideal to be approximated. It is not to be understood as a "fundamental rule" for the specific reality of the adolescent connotation of rules.

This then leads to the use of the psychoanalytic couch. The psychoanalytic method technically best utilizes the couch for adolescents regardless of much grumbling on this aspect. The effect of visualization of the analyst by the patient with all the attendant cues and distractions and the difficulty of approaching defenses is such a parameter, that without the couch technique I would offer the opinion that the technical method cannot accomplish its goals though its therapeutic efficacy may be praised by both patient and therapist. It can well be that many adolescents can abide this requirement for only different periods of their treatment, yet this may serve as an adolescent experience for future analytic work as an adult.

However, by using the couch, introduction may be experimented with in many ways, provided that the couch be utilized actively rather than passively by adolescents. Frequently, they will notice and inquire as to its use, and at the same time can be informed that it has many advantages, thus discussing the various fears and dreads as they occur. They can be encouraged to assume a facing position on the couch, and gradually turn around. Invariably, I have found that if there is a patient, tolerant conviction about the use of the couch by the analyst, this can be tolerated—granted that there may be circumstances when this is interfered with as any other aspect of the relationship may be.

In contradiction to the analytic use of the couch, many borderline and severely disturbed personalities will utilize the couch situation only to enter severe trance-like, withdrawal states which remain persistent despite acceptable interpretative utterances. This points to the underlying passive threat of regression that is present in many adolescents and which makes the psychoanalysis of these adolescents an impossibility and an absurdity. There is also a danger that the couch and apparent cooperation in analysis does not unconsciously indicate a regression, nonetheless, to the mystical union with mother and couch, indulge the narcissistic aspects and, despite verbalization and intellectualization, result in little ego change, but rather a positive transference phenomenon not conducive to ego interpretation. Yet, we have a sufficient body of cases in our psychoanalytic institutes where adolescents assume the couch position and participate in this procedure satisfactorily.

FEE REQUIREMENTS   Fee requirements of psychoanalysis is a topic that has been part of the literature of psychoanalysis since its onset. Early concepts were based upon the meaningfulness and symbolic significance of money to the patient in his search for access to his unconscious strivings and conflicts. Further, it became evident that money was related to the motivation and sacrifice along with the expenditure of time to resolve conflicts and secure psychic change. Very little has been published on the needs of the therapist, and many distortions of the psychoanalytic fee have crept into common parlance.

In the field of child work, fees for private practice have received little study compared to various fee studies for child guidance clinics and social agencies. General comparisons of psychiatric and psychoanalytic fees compared with increasing medical costs of other specialties, medical education, to say nothing of hospitalization and health insurance costs, are not available for most practitioners of psychoanalysis.

In the field of adult psychoanalysis, money and fees have been discussed from the onset. Indeed, the psychological attitudes involved in the acquisitive and spending uses of money are closely linked to the infantile attitudes of many drive components. In child analysis, this has also been the subject as dealt with by the child analyst in terms of gifts and presents of objects, food and the like.

In the field of adolescent psychoanalysis, one has heard little about fees for a number of reasons. The adolescent is himself in a transition period of economic individuation and accomplishment on the one hand and dependence on parental maintenance on the other. Societal provisions for employment and job security as part of vocational aims afford little economic opportunity to have accumulated money for the purchase of medical and psychological provisions. High school students, largely in the middle class social structure, depend on parental resources and various types of health insurance which provide little for outpatient economic aid. In the college age group, the health resources of college clinics include mental hygiene facilities, but do not include psychoanalytic treatment.

As seen from the adolescent viewpoint, the psychic aspects of money seem future-oriented rather than real. Further, the derivatives of drive aspects of the meaningfulness of money and object are delayed in accomplishment in the middle class culture that partakes of psychoanalysis. Thus, the usual sacrifice of and meaningfulness of money for psychoanalysis is not one of the significant aspects of most analysis of adolescents. It is true there are problems of self-esteem, wished for accomplishments, and daydreams, but little actual interchange between patient and analyst.

In these situations, at the time of assessment, it is wise to share with the adolescent what has transpired with the parents. Frequently, the amount of the fee becomes meaningful to the adolescent in terms of the equation of the parents' financial sacrifice, to say nothing of the equation of desired material objects the adolescent would and does wish for. Concepts of narcissistic overevaluation of money, power, aggression, and greed become then a part of the analytic interchange.

As part of the technical methodology, it is recommended that the adolescent be given the statements for services rendered so that he can be familiarized with the arrangements that have been established for the payments of such services. Further, this becomes part of his sharing and differentiating his own attitudes about money as distinguished from the parents. One example comes to mind of a situation where the adolescent's family always allowed the analyst's bills to accumulate. Considerable tension was incurred which became important to consider in a supervisory situation. When it was suggested that this problem be shared with the patient, severe characterological problems of the father as contrasted with the mother emerged. Involvement of the adolescent's Oedipal attitude as this related to his own attitudes and varied protective attitudes of distance from it in the analysis were also brought to light. Finally, it became much more evident that identificatory problems as they related to money could be linked to other problems that needed understanding.

Finally, it is not to be denied that arrangements with parents for psychoanalytic treatment of adolescents depends on needs of the psychoanalyst. That the analyst be seen as a person with needs to provide as any other parent should be taken as a textual realistic framework for the adolescent to consider in terms of his own eventual attainment of functioning.

CASE ILLUSTRATION

This case portrays the implementation of assessment early in life, a period of child analysis, and then psychotherapy for both parents. It also demonstrates the continued valuable services of the analyst as a consultant during two phases of adolescence—pubertal or early adolescence and adolescence proper (Blos, 1963, pp. 52–128).

Julie, an only son with a sister three years his junior, was born of professional parents. The father was twenty-nine, foreign born, but with schooling and professional training in the United States and a few years out of his career training. The mother was twenty-eight, born in this country, and was the daughter of professional parents. She gave up her interest in teaching and mutual formal support of the family to raise her children.

The father secured my name from a professional colleague, a psychiatrist who had undergone psychoanalysis. It was the father who telephoned initially and despite my encouragement that he seek someone else for assessment, he waited three months until I had time available. I have come to learn that his waiting for the consultation indicated in itself a tendency for loyalty, an infantile insecurity, and a respect for reputation that represented narcissistic problems for his family relationships, including his relationship with Julie.

The precipitating cause for referral occurred when, during a visit to the maternal relatives in the country, the father was teaching Julie how to play ball, and he related that the boy "hung on to me like a leech," and finally "in some anger I asked him to leave me. Julie left disconsolately, walking down the road, sucking his thumb and dragging his bat behind him." There was little doubt that this paternal fantasy of Julie as an emasculated male haunted the father and probably was a projection of his own sado-masochistic images. This has recurred to the present time, and the boy is pictured by the father as not superior, easily led, someone who will do what the other boys wish, is not a leader, and will never make it to college.

In several interviews with the mother, it was revealed that the boy slept in the parental bedroom until his sister was born, when Julie was three. They then moved to a larger apartment. At thirteen months, he developed a mild coeliac disease which subsided with dietary restrictions of fat intake. The father felt that his wife pampered the boy, that his eating habits were "bad" and he might be regarded as a "spoiled brat." Julie sucked his thumb from seven weeks of age, but this did subside. He was attached to his baby blanket until it became a disintegrated "piece" when he was four. He also had been a severe bed-rocker, but not a head banger.

At three, his sister was born and he spent a month with the maternal grandparents. He was jealous of his sister and there were frequent arguments with her when he was four and she was one. When Julie was five and a half, the family moved to a suburban home where he shared a room with his sister. He had occasional nightmares of "gorillas" and some ritualistic problems of not wanting things moved from his desk.

His speech started late and was somewhat immature, so that his mother and father could not understand him. (Indeed, this seemed their wish, and it was part of the ambivalent closeness in their relationship to each other and to Julie.) He started kindergarten and on the advice of a speech therapist his speech was evaluated. The parents were told he was a late developer, and since that time he has progressed in speech.

When he was first seen, Julie was frightened. Initially, he clung to his mother but eventually separated. It was four days before his seventh birthday, and he had wanted to go swimming at day camp. Contrary to his parents' description of hyperactivity, he showed no evidences of this as we talked over milk and cookies. I had mentioned that mother and father had consulted me about his growing up, and that I helped boys of his age. I wanted to get his point of view. His speech *was* immature and not always intelligible. His principal problems were that other, larger boys teased and beat him up, and in school he was blamed unjustly by the teachers for talking, when in fact the talking was started by other boys. He was also blamed by his mother for fooling around at the table. He loved to play make-believe games of "good cowboys and bad Indians." He related that when he has troubles, he cries, goes to his mother and then returns to play. He hoped to get a cap rifle for his seventh birthday because his cap guns were broken. I indicated my sympathy and stated how tough it feels not to have a good gun.

He appeared immature and not very bright, considering his membership in this very verbal, professional family. Yet, he was serious and could verbalize well with me.

On his second assessment visit, which followed his birthday, he was at ease and friendly, despite the fact that he and his mother had traveled through a summer thunderstorm. He was pleased not only about receiving his wished-for rifle, but that he had mastered diving off a ten-foot springboard, a feat which his mother smilingly confirmed. We then inspected the cap guns in my play equipment, and I learned that only until recently Julie had been frightened of caps with his guns. This fear had ceased when he began playing with the long rifle. He went on to tell me that his sister liked to play with him and his guns. But when he gets rough, she tells mother and he gets punished. He told me that when he gets upset, he goes to his mother, which in turn upsets his father who blames mother. When I utilized this material as a means of testing him on ability to communicate, by saying, "and you and your sister quarrel sometimes like your folks," he nodded in firm assent. He told me that his mother does not like him to suck his thumb and that he has taken to biting and picking his nails. I assured him that this was a hard thing to stop and that it may be one of the problems he needed help with.

My impression at this time was that Julie was a pathetically immature, possibly dull boy, who was not so much in internal conflict, but who became the center of excessive parental demands (especially the father's), and who remained infantile in order to compete for the attention given to his three-years younger sister. I had the impression that he was not mentally gifted enough for psychoanalysis and suggested psychological testing. I felt that both parents needed psychotherapy and that the boy's reactions were reactive to them.

I should also state that I had learned from one of the mother's visits that her husband's father was the dominant, foreign-born master of the household. The paternal grandmother was under the grandfather's sway, and he had had several coronary attacks. The maternal grandparents had both been professionals and shared responsibilities, and the mother had had an equable child rearing atmosphere. She had vowed to herself that she would never allow what had happened in her husband's upbringing to happen to her son, and indeed, had wishes for an aggressive, athletic son, as she herself had always been athletically inclined.

In our first joint discussion, I brought out that Julie was able to communicate and relate well with me, and that he had mastered some boyish activities such as diving and cap pistol play. He had been straightforward with me. Yet, there seemed certain immaturities which might show up on psychological examination and these immaturities might play an important role in Julie's attempt to satisfy their aspirations for him. There was no doubt that he needed help, but I was not sure whether this type of help should be psychotherapy or psychoanalysis. Nor did I tell them that the father was in need of psychoanalysis and that both mother and son could profit from psychotherapy.

I should mention that I had, for purposes of assessment, secured Julie's school reports from his first grade teacher. These reports indicated that although he was slow, he had made good progress in reading and his enthusiasm for numbers helped him to control his excitement in class. Socially, he was able to share with others and he was not outstanding in his needs for attention. However, he had placed in the fourth quartile of his class on the California Achievement Test.

In the fifth week of assessment, the psychological testing was performed by a most competent psychologist who has tested many of my patients. I have always shared my own recorded impressions with her. In summary, the test results revealed pronounced immaturity closely associated with "aggressive and sexual conflicts and possible traumatic experiences." ". . . His negativism towards growing up and toward learning result in a not too successful babyish facade. His fantasy life, though often phobic, is indicative of superior imaginative capacity. . . . This is an intense, easily troubled child, who is struggling toward a defense of the inconspicuous average. . . . There is something in the home situation that is quite entangled and not conducive to this child's development. . . ."

He achieved a verbal scale of 106 and a performance scale score of 122, with full scale of an I.Q. of 115 on the WISC scale for children. On the Rorschach, however, he showed rich fantasy and superior interpretive ability and demonstrated a superior potential in contrast to his overt passively negativistic responses.

I discussed these results with both parents, highlighting the boy's minimal intellectual functioning despite evidences of a good creative imagination and that, despite their own personality make-ups and differences, the boy's basic personality was intact. I reminded them that it was the father who felt the boy had only average intelligence, while the mother had felt it was far better. There was no evidence of psychotic functioning or mental retardation, but rather inhibitions resulting in passivity, fearfulness of aggression, and immaturity.

I told them too, that the psychologist had had her dog present during Julie's testing, and the seven-year-old had looked intrigued at the sleeping dog, but made no move to pet or ask about her. He stated that he has goldfish, but when he "gets older his mother will get me a dog." As I related some of this interchange with the psychologist in a preparatory way to discussing the role of parents with a child in psychoanalysis, I learned that for the past year Julie had wanted a dog. In front of a pet shop with his mother he had told her he didn't think he could stop from crying because he "wanted a dog so much." It came out that both parents did not wish for a dog because it meant continual care and responsibility which they weren't prepared to give (to a dog or child). Characteristically, the mother said she felt guilty because Julie needed affection from a dog that he wasn't getting from his parents. She reasoned that she would not give the dog as a substitute for this affection. When I responded that the dog might be looked at by Julie as a gift from beloved parents, the mother responded that she had never considered this viewpoint. There were cues in the assessment that both intelligent parents could respond, and which indicated a capacity for reflection with an impartial, objective psychiatrist. This interchange had occurred in the parents' visit, after they were considerably relieved of guilty fears as to their responsibility for an unchangeable psychological condition of their son.

I then indicated that Julie needed child psychoanalysis four times a week, and that mother and father would participate in weekly visits—mainly mother, to allow the child analyst to know the realities of the family life and historical aspects as they would come up. The aim of the analysis would be for the child analyst to discover how Julie viewed things, and changes would occur as a result of his sharing his viewpoints with the analyst. Changes would necessarily occur within Julie and the members of the family. I addressed myself to the father, stating that the possibility of his psychoanalysis had occurred to me, but that this could be ascertained better after a period of child analysis of Julie. In the meantime, I told the father to feel free to discuss this possibility from time to time. The father's conscious attitude was one willing to make whatever sacrifices were necessary and, when offered some choice of a consultation fee, he selected the higher fee which indicated his confidence in me. In the same breath, he revealed that he had not discussed the assessment with his own mother in contrast to the fact that his wife's parents had been informed and were helpful.

Julie would be in second grade, and travel considerations, time for school, and transportation (by mother by automobile) were discussed. They agreed that the principal factor would be their own assessment and participation with the child analyst I would help them secure—not the geographical closeness to the exact site of their residence (within reason). I furthermore indicated the approximate fee, the working months of the year, and my own practices in vacations, illnesses, and charges for missed hours. I told them that, although few qualified child psychoanalysts were available, I felt confident I could find one who had time available, but he, of course, would be entitled to his own impressions. I said that I would send him my assessment studies.

I felt, at the time of the assessment, child analysis might not need the participation of the school, but depending on many things, this question would better be left to the discretion of the child analyst. I indicated that there would be times when Julie might not like treatment, and it was obvious that he was initially going in order to please his parents. That was why it was so important that they both have strong convictions to pursue this treatment approach for their son. I indicated that they should tell Julie he had done very well on his psychological tests. Mother then told me she had already informed him. (I had spoken briefly and positively to her by telephone before their final assessment visit.) I brought out that Julie might utilize this as a resistance. I told them they would hear from me in the early fall, and if there were further questions, they were free to be in touch with me.

A student child analyst (and graduate psychoanalyst of adults) who was quite gifted and for whom I had great respect, was contacted, and Julie started child psychoanalysis that fall, four times weekly for two years. The father was referred for psychotherapy to a qualified psychoanalyst. There was supervision of the analysis by a training child analyst regularly.

Two years later, I received a telephone call, again initiated by the father, for reassessment of Julie. I indicated my lack of understanding about their wish to see me, and they said that the child analyst had been agreeable to this request. They had just returned from a vacation and, though intending to see the child analyst, had delayed this until they talked with me. They had greater confidence in me and thought that the doctor might be more prejudiced to continue treatment of Julie than I would be. The father had been in psychotherapy eight months and on leaving said, "I have been going a year and I don't feel anything, though Dr. X is very nice." The mother had given up an academic position and was prepared to enjoy her increased leisure. They both appeared more relaxed, at ease with each other and with Julie.

The father still showed impatience and anger at Julie's "lack of intellectual drive" but was able to see that the boy was ready for fourth grade. Julie's own drives became manifested when he insisted that the mother verify and correct a parapraxis of the teacher, who had written on his report, "Promoted to third grade" (instead of fourth). He was interested in playing baseball as well as a musical instrument. His younger sister had become jealous of all the attention paid her brother and wished to visit Julie's doctor herself.

I assured them that they had every right to reassess the situation. I would be glad to get in touch with the child analyst as well as the father's analyst. The mother indicated that in the past few months she had been discussing her own problems with the child analyst. This surprised me, and I suggested that if interruption at this time were contemplated, it might be wise to consider tapering off visits for the boy with the possibility that Julie could see him later, whereas the mother could have a separate therapist. In a telephone conversation, I learned from the child analyst that he had definitely planned to discontinue with Julie in the fall, and at the suggestion of his supervisor, was trying to build up a relationship with the mother when Julie discontinued. At this time, in Julie's mid-latency period, I had the impression that growth had been achieved and some of the inhibitions were lessened. The parental interchanges of a severe, interlocking characterological type were subtly, but persistently traumatic and made for difficulties in the development of more transferentially neurotic relationships to the analyst. I also learned that the father's therapist was extremely dubious about analyzing the father. I then concluded this parental visit by stating that they should proceed to discuss the situation with the child analyst and alluded only to the fact that everyone appeared to be in basic agreement. I also stated that it was not necessary for me to see Julie at this time.

When Julie was thirteen, the mother, for the first time, called me for consultation, and I learned that, when he was eleven, Julie had returned to see his analyst on a once a week basis for six months. In spite of my verbalizing that Julie's analyst knew more of the situation than I, they wished to see me. The reason for this consultation, occurring a few months after the father had changed therapists (again, to someone whom I knew professionally), was that the father felt that Julie would develop better if he attended boarding school the following year, thus avoiding exposure to the father's frustrated rage reactions with him. The mother felt differently.

In this visit, the father immediately commented on my loss of weight and made an interesting and envious allusion to some object in my office. His accurate observations and high level of intelligence contrasted to his capacity for rage. Both parents expressed disappointment with the personality makeup of the child analyst and the father's first therapist. Julie, according to the father, was not utilizing his potential and in frequent arguments, would tense up, appear "stupid" and cry. In other words, the behavioral picture of this interchange closely confirmed the seven-year-old psychological test findings. Julie, in the meantime, had grown tall, slim, and showed secondary sex growth characteristics. He was shyly, but definitely interested in girls. The father's new therapist had brought out that Julie might feel going away to school was a rejection. At one point in this interview I attempted to understand what images of the boy occurred in the mind of the father while enraged. The only response I got was an obsessive thought, "Julie is mentally retarded." Realistically, the father knew this was not appropriate, as the boy had received one A and four B's. He also had received fine reports from camp, but no longer wished to attend. In the meantime, the mother commented that taking Julie to analysis for two years had been a chore, as I had mentioned. She now was enrolled in a Ph.D. course in a new profession and her husband was pursuing his professional activities. I discussed with the parents that Julie would probably recall little of me since the age of seven. It would be desirable to convey that I would like to discuss with him his viewpoints about going to residential school, and it would be important not to see him after an acrimonious family quarrel or fatherly "scene." I considered the possibility of a private day or residential school within the city, but did not convey this to the parents.

When Julie came to see me, he indeed appeared grown up, was definitely in puberty and recalled nothing of his early consultation visits. On the other hand, he had heard of me from his parents on many occasions. He related to me easily and expressed the idea that it was his own desire to go to private school away from home. Friends of his were going away and he had heard that the high school in his area would not prepare him to attend college. He also would not be too homesick because he had already gone away to camp. He did not have any close friends, girls or boys whom he would miss much and there would be holidays when he could see them. Behind the structured intellectualized statements appeared a persistence and a strong desire to excel in school and sports which belied a conscious agreement with his father's aims. He knew that his father "blew his top," but he had respect for the attainments in his profession and thought he could "double this." He did not have any feelings that he was being punished. He indicated that he would be glad to be away from his sister who was always "envious of him."

I mentioned that I could understand his wishes, but that he would need educational advice, as I was not myself familiar with the many private residential schools. I would recommend an educational consultant, someone who himself was a headmaster of a private school in the city. Also, his capabilities and attainments would require that he be tested again by the psychologist he had once seen at my recommendation at seven. But this time I would discuss the results of the test situation with him first, and then we would see what the advice of an "education person" would be. He and his parents would, of course, have interviews at the schools and he might experience disappointments by not being admitted to the school he liked best. He accepted these introductions to what awaited him and that it was possible that he might change his mind.

His parents arranged for visits with an educational consultant who advised me that he felt it would be helpful for Julie to go away. He recommended various schools to the parents. He felt that the boy had maturational needs which could be developed away from home. Julie was not retested until some months later— in the spring, when he was 13:8.

The psychologist noted that he was a handsome, appealing adolescent. His plodding pedestrian seven-year-old bent to demonstrate mediocre intelligence was gone; but so also was the creative excitement of the early Rorschach. On the intelligence tests, he was lively and interested and showed more appropriate verbal scale I.Q. responses. On the projectives, he was tense, depressed, with subdued rage behind a surface compliance. He scored in the superior verbal range and bright normal in the nonverbal range. "The obsessive devices retain a borrowed, not thoroughly assimilated quality that may relate to attempts at identification with his father . . . are geared also to defense against his own repressed rage and sadomasochistic pattern." Julie, in early adolescence, had developed conceptual and verbal expression, but at considerable psychic expense. The boarding school experience would create powerful separation phenomena from intense narcissistic family relationships. I commented that he would have much to contend with in his competitive sibling experiences, and it was to be hoped that he would begin to have heterosexual experiences.

What ensued was a period of two successful years at boarding school, with the opportunity for a summer work experience in a foreign country. He became more peer-related and provoked considerable excitement within his family when he indicated that he had smoked marijuana. His parents panicked before his return from that summer experience, and only upon consultation with me, and again with the boy, did this quiet down.

I saw some of the letters that he wrote to his parents. These indicated his own expectations of failure (to still please the father), and the realities were never that bad. His teachers thought well of him and despite tension interfering with his scholastic aptitude test, he was able to manage successful academic grades as well as succeed in some of his athletic aspirations.

I had occasion to see him when he was in love. He was most idealistic and fearful; his hopes did not materialize when he had to return to school. He seemed like a young Herman Hesse, but finally he recovered from his initial "crush" experience.

His relationships to continued psychiatric consultation with me during his adolescence only pointed to a need for emancipation before he was ready to be considered for a further period of psychoanalysis. By this time, the family strains and continual traumata became clear and served to illustrate that while he had been helped enormously by his early child analytic experiences, the interlocking family conflicts had by no means been resolved. I definitely had the impression that considerations for psychoanalysis would have to await further growth and inevitable suffering on his part.

REFERENCES

[Note: *The standard edition* refers to *The standard edition of the complete psychological works of Sigmund Freud* (London: Hogarth Press and the Institute of Psycho-Analysis).]

Arthur, H. A.   A comparison of techniques: Psychoanalysis vs. psychotherapy. *American Journal of Orthopsychiatry,* 1952, **22,** 484–498.

Ackerman, N.   *The psychodynamics of family life; diagnosis and treatment of family relationships.* New York: Basic Books, 1958.

Bender, L.   Childhood schizophrenia. *American Journal of Orthopsychiatry,* 1947, **17,** 40–56.

Berman, S.   Epilogue and a new beginning. *Journal of the American Academy of Child Psychiatry,* 1970, 9, 193–201.

Berman, S.   Alienation: An essential process of the psychology of adolescence. *Journal of the American Academy of Child Psychiatry,* 1970, 9, 233–250.

Blos, P.   *On adolescence: A psychoanalytic interpretation.* New York: Free Press, 1962.

Blos, P.   The concept of acting out in relation to the adolescent process. *Journal of the American Academy of Child Psychiatry,* 1963, **2,** 118–136.

Blos, P.   The second individuation process of adolescence. *Psychoanalytic Study of the Child,* 1967, **22,** 162–186.

Blos, P.   *The young adolescent.* New York: Free Press, 1970.

Brown, S.   Clinical impressions of the impact of family group interviewing on child and adolescent psychiatric practice. *Journal of the American Academy of Child Psychiatry,* 1964, **3,** 688–696.

Buxbaum, E.   The role of a second language in the formation of ego and superego. *The Psychoanalytic Quarterly,* 1949, **18,** 279–289.

Caplan, G.(Ed.), *Prevention of mental disorders in children.* New York: Basic Books, 1961.

Caplan, G.   Community mental health services for adolescents. In G. Caplan and S. Lebovici, (Eds.), *Adolescence: psychosocial perspectives.* New York: Basic Books, 1969, 372–386.

Eckstein, R. and Wallerstein, R.   *The teaching and learning of psychotherapy.* New York: Basic Books, 1958.

Erikson, E.   Identity and the life cycle. *Psychological Issues,* 1959, No. 1.

Fraiberg, S. A comparison of the analytic method in two stages of a child analysis. *Journal of the American Academy of Child Psychiatry,* 1965, **4,** 387–400.

Frankl, L. A specific problem in adolescent boys; difficulties in loosening the infantile tie to the mother. *Bulletin of the Philadelphia Association for Psychoanalysis,* 1963, **13,** 120–129.

Freud, A. *The ego and the mechanisms of defense.* (1936). New York: International Universities Press, 1946.

Freud, A. Adolescence. *Psychoanalytic Study of the Child,* 1958, **13,** 255–278.

Freud, A. Four contributions to the psychoanalytic study of the child. *Bulletin of the Philedelphia Association for Psychoanalysis,* 1961, **2,** 80–87.

Freud, A. Regression as a principle in mental development. *Bulletin of the Menninger Clinic,* 1963, **27,** 126–139.

Freud, A. *Normality and pathology in childhood. Assessments of development.* New York: International Universities Press, 1965.

Freud, S. *Fragment of an analysis of a case of hysteria* (1905a). In *The standard edition.* Vol. 7. 3–122.

Freud, S. *Three essays on the theory of sexuality* (1905b). In *The standard edition.* Vol. 7. 125–245.

Freud, S. *Beyond the pleasure principle* (1920). In *The standard edition.* Vol. 18. 3–64.

Freud, S. *Inhibitions, symptoms and anxiety* (1926). In *The standard edition.* Vol. 7. 77–175.

Friend, M. Psychoanalytic psychology of childhood and schizophrenia. *Journal of the Hillside Hospital,* 1967, **16,** 85–93.

Friend, M. Youth unrest: Reflections of a psychoanalyst. *Journal of the American Academy of Child Psychiatry,* 1970, **9,** 224–232.

Geleerd, E. Some aspects of psychoanalytic technique in adolescence. *Psychoanalytic Study of the Child,* 1957, **12,** 263–283.

Geleerd, E. Some aspects of ego vicissitudes in adolescence. *Journal of the American Psychoanalytic Association,* 1961, **9,** 394–405.

Geleerd, E. Adolescence and adaptive regression. *Bulletin of the Menninger Clinic,* 1964, **28,** 302–308.

Geleerd, E. *The child analyst at work.* New York: International Universities Press, 1967.

Gill, M.; Simon, J.; Fink, G.; Endicott, N.; and Paul I. Studies in audio-recorded psychoanalysis. I. General considerations. *Journal of the American Psychoanalytic Association,* 1968, **16,** 230–244.

Greenacre, P. Experiences of awe in childhood. *Psychoanalytic Study of the Child,* 1956, **11,** 9–30.

Greenacre, P. Regression and fixation considerations concerning the development of the ego. *Journal of the American Psychoanalytic Association,* 1960, **8,** 703–723.

Grinker, A. and Spiegel, J.   *Men under stress.* Philadelphia: Blakiston, 1945.

Group for the Advancement of Psychiatry (GAP), Committee on Adolescence. *Normal adolescence: Its dynamics and import.* Vol. 6, Report No. 68, February 1968.

Harley, M.   Some observations on the relationship between genitality and structural development of adolescence. *Journal of the American Psychoanalytic Association,* 1961, 9, 434–460.

Hellman, I.   Observations on adolescents in psychoanalytic treatment. *British Journal of Psychiatry,* 1964, 110, 406–410.

Hartmann, H.   *Psychoanalysis and moral values.* New York: International Universities Press, 1960.

Hollingshead, A. and Redlich, F.   *Social class and mental illness: a community study.* New York: Wiley, 1958.

Holmes, J.   *The adolescent in psychotherapy.* Boston: Little, Brown, 1964.

Josselyn, I.   *The adolescent and his world.* New York: Family Service Association of America, 1952.

Josselyn, I.   Observations concerning child development and psychological terminology. *Bulletin of the Philadelphia Association for Psychoanalysis,* 1961, 2, 136–138.

Kanner, L.   Autistic disturbances of affective contact. *Nervous Child,* 1943, 2, 217–250.

Kestenberg, J.   Phases of adolescence. *Journal of the American Academy of Child Psychiatry,* 1967, 6, 426–463, 577–614.

Koff, R.; Anthony, E.; Haug, E.; and Littner, N.   Transference in children; a panel discussion. *Bulletin of the Philadelphia Association for Psychoanalysis,* 1962, 12, 127–129.

Kramer, S. and Settlage, C.   On the concepts and technique of child analysis. *Journal of the American Academy of Child Psychiatry,* 1962, 1, 509–535.

Lewin, B. and Ross, H.   *Psychoanalytic Education in the United States.* New York: Norton, 1960.

Mahler, M.; Ross, J. R.; and De Fries, Z.   Clinical studies in benign and malignant cases of childhood psychosis. *American Journal of Orthopsychiatry,* 1949, 19, 295–305.

Menninger, W.   *Psychiatry in a troubled world.* New York: Macmillan, 1948.

Neubauer, P. (Ed.)   *Children in collectives.* Springfield, Ill.: Charles C. Thomas, 1965.

Offer, D.   Normal adolescents. *Archives of General Psychiatry,* 1967, 17, 285–290.

Pearson, G. (Ed.)   *A handbook of child psychoanalysis.* New York: Basic Books, 1968.

Raush, H.   The preadolescent ego, some observations of normal children. *Psychiatry,* 1961, 24, 122–132.

Rexford, E.   Child psychiatry and child analysis in the United States today. *Journal of the American Academy of Child Psychiatry,* 1962, 1, 365–384.

Schur, M.   *The id and the regulatory principles of mental functioning.* New York: International Universities Press, 1966.

Serrano, A. et al.   Adolescent maladjustment and family dynamics. *American Journal of Psychiatry,* 1962, 118, 897–901.

Settlage, C.   Adolescence and social change. *Journal of the American Academy of Child Psychiatry,* 1970, 9, 203–215.

Silber, E.   The analyst's participation in the treatment of an adolescent. *Psychiatry,* 1962, 25, 160–169.

Slavson, S.   *The practice of group therapy.* New York: International Universities Press, 1947.

Solnit, A.   Ego vicissitudes of adolescence. *Journal of the American Psychoanalytic Association,* 1959, 7, 523–535.

Spitz, R.   Hospitalism: An inquiry into the genesis of psychiatric conditions in early childhood. *The Psychoanalytic Study of the Child,* 1945, 1, 53–74.

Stone, L.   *The psychoanalytic situation: an examination of its development and essential nature.* New York: International Universities Press, 1961.

Tarachow, S.   Ambiguity and human imperfection. *Journal of the American Psychoanalytic Association,* 1965, 13, 85–101.

Toolan, J.   Depression in children and adolescents. *American Journal of Orthopsychiatry,* 1962, 32, 160–169.

van Amerongen, S.   The psychoanalysis of a young adolescent girl. *Journal of the American Academy of Child Psychiatry,* 1971, 10, 23–52.

Williams, F.   Alienation of youth as reflected in the hippie movement. *Journal of the American Academy of Child Psychiatry,* 1970, 9, 251–263.

Wise, L.   Alienation of present-day adolescents. *Journal of the American Academy of Child Psychiatry,* 1970, 9, 264–277.

9

SAUL SCHEIDLINGER AND ESTELLE RAUCH

Psychoanalytic Group Psychotherapy with Children and Adolescents

In view of the recent proliferation of varied group treatment measures within the mental health field, the term *group psychotherapy* will be used in this paper in its narrowest sense, connoting ". . . a method within the broader realm of psychotherapy wherein a practitioner (usually psychiatrist, psychologist, or social worker) utilizes the interaction in a small, carefully planned group to effect 'repair' of personality malfunctioning in individuals specifically selected for this purpose. A clinical orientation, which includes a diagnostic assessment of each member's problems, is part of this picture. Furthermore, the patients are cognizant of the psychotherapeutic purpose and accept the group as a means to obtain help in modifying their pathological mode of functioning" (Scheidlinger, 1970).

All extensions of group psychotherapy as well as the many more broadly conceived group intervention measures will be termed "therapeutic" group approaches—allied to and yet different from group psychotherapy.

GROUPS FOR LATENCY-AGE CHILDREN

The significant role of school and peer groupings in the ego development of latency-age children is well known. As Erik Erikson (1959, p. 81) stated so well: "At no time is the individual more ready to learn quickly and avidly, to become big in the sense of sharing obligation, discipline, and performance rather than power . . . and he is able and willing to profit fully by the association with teachers and ideal prototypes." The child's school and indigenous peer groupings offer not only a sense of belonging and of emotional support, but also an opportunity for the sublimation and redirection of aggressive and libidinal impulses. The provision of this opportunity is particularly important in view of the urgent need of latency-age children to deal with the sexual and aggressive drives carried over from their Oedipal conflicts; they also have the related need to emancipate themselves from earlier dependency on the parental figures.

An observation of Bornstein's (1951) has important implications for the education and treatment of the latency-age child. She argues that free associative productions and attempts at promoting introspection constitute a massive threat to the latency-age child's strong need to maintain his newly gained ego organization. This is especially true during the second phase of latency (ages eight to ten), when some measure of equilibrium is likely to have been established.

Thus, except for instances of neurotic suffering, latency-age children tend to resist treatment measures based solely on verbal communication. They may even resist any encounter with adults in which the expression of subjective feeling is elicited directly. In contrast, when it comes to manual activities or sports, they respond eagerly.

Activity Group Therapy

The predilection of latency-age children for group experiences which deemphasize verbalization was first exploited for therapeutic purposes in the early thirties, with the development of activity group therapy (Slavson, 1943) and "diagnostic groups" (Redl, 1944). Activity group therapy, as its name implies, stresses the expression of fantasies and drives through play and action. A permissive group climate promotes benign regression in which earlier and current conflicts can be relived in the context of a stable and accepting environment. The basic therapeutic elements accrue from the interaction of the children with each other and from their relationship to the therapist. An activity group consists of about eight members of the same sex and similar age, carefully selected with a view toward achieving a favorable group balance. Thus, there are apt to be aggressive individuals, infantile or overly dependent ones, or shy and fearful ones. The physical setting of such a group comprises a large room, equipped with simple furniture, including a kitchen corner to prepare food, tools, crafts supplies, and games. These are chosen from the standpoint of their therapeutic effectiveness. The following excerpt from a group session illustrates the process in general, highlighting also a group's reaction to the arrival of a new member.

CASE ILLUSTRATION

In general, up until about this point, the boys had been working relatively much more quietly than they had in previous sessions. There was little verbal interchange and what there was occurred in whispered tones, the only noise being from hammering and sawing, and the latter in moderate tempo. Charles continued painting; Melvin was sawing on wood when not talking to Thomas; Errol continued working by himself, hammering together what seemed to be a box-like structure; Joseph had taken a piece of plywood and was drawing the side view of a man's head and doing pretty well at it; Melvin had gone back to the second work bench and this time was followed or trailed by Thomas.

At about 4:15 P.M. there was a knock on the door and Wayne, a planned visitor, entered, escorted by his mother. I met them in the middle of the room with Mrs. L. handing me a letter of introduction from her caseworker. She was a slender woman, pleasant looking and quiet spoken. She got confirmation that the club meeting would end at 5:30 P.M., informed Wayne that she would be back for him at that time, and left. I introduced myself to Wayne, who was already beginning to peel off his clothes and looked at the coat rack. Wayne is a small youngster of slender build, about the same size as Charles and Melvin. He wore a bright yellow long-sleeved T-shirt and dungarees. Wayne was hanging up his coat as I invited him to meet the other members, and I proceeded to introduce him to Charles, who looked expectantly, standing aside from his work, and more or less ducked his head in a nod. The boys did not shake hands, Wayne responding to my introduction with an uncertain smile, Charles reciprocating pretty much in a like manner. I then introduced him to Errol, who also stopped working, turned away, and seemed uncertain whether or not to reach out his hand to shake, though he did not in the end. He also ducked his head in response to the introduction. As I approached Thomas and Melvin, introducing them, they ducked their heads in an abrupt nod, with watchful expressions of Wayne.

There ensued a hasty whispered discussion between Melvin and Thomas, with Thomas calling to me and asking if Wayne was going to be a club member. Charles, Joseph, and Errol had more or less gone back to their work, but I had the impression they, too, were listening behind me, as the room was silent. I had the letter of introduction in my hand and, glancing at it, replied that I understood from the club department that Wayne was visiting with us. Thomas and Melvin again engaged excitedly in a whispered discussion, with Melvin eventually going back to his work while I proceeded to show Wayne about the room. When I had done this, I returned to some work I had been doing, Wayne trailing me and remaining in close proximity. He watched as I put some pieces of wood together and asked me what I was doing. I told him I was working on a shoe shine kit. He asked if I was making it for one of the fellows or if it was for myself. I replied myself. Wayne remained close by, watching me for another few minutes. Only occasionally would he sneak a glance at the others.

Joseph had finished drawing on the plywood, placed it on a tool shelf, got into the supply closet and now was working with leather and gimp. Wayne finally drifted over to watch Joseph who moved away from the supply cabinet and then wandered over to watch Charles. Thomas was leaning on a large table watching Charles too. Again, he called Melvin over and they seemed to be in some discussion which I believe had to do with school, as I heard that word mentioned and something about Melvin being in a certain class. Wayne stood off to the side listening to the conversation between Melvin and Thomas, but not joining in.

At about 4:25 P.M. I began preparation for the meal, putting the water on and then returning to the vicinity of the tool cabinet. Errol had painted the roof of his box structure red and was now also in the vicinity of the tool cabinet, examining the bird feeding station I had placed on it. Errol had asked at the last meeting if he could have it, but had left early without taking it with him. At a point where I was close to Errol, I remarked that he could now have it if he wanted it. As I moved away, Errol, who had at first been listening more or less impassively, nodding as I finished speaking, now turned about, striking the palm of one hand with his fist happily, and whirling in another direction once or twice, again examining the feeding station and moving back to his work. I put my work away and replaced some tools I had used in the tool cabinet, then returned to the kitchen area to resume preparation of the meal. As I worked there, the tempo of the group's activity seemed to pick up in terms of hammering, talking, moving about. Wayne, Melvin, and Joseph initiated a game of ping pong, with Wayne and Melvin starting. Melvin appeared the better of the two players and won the game. He then engaged Joseph in play. Thomas, at the large table, moved in closer to Charles who continued painting away. Errol worked alone at the second bench. A couple of times Charles came over to the kitchen area to clean the paintbrush, glancing at what was cooking. Over at the ping pong table the game had turned into a three-sided exchange with Joseph, Wayne, and Melvin batting the ball amongst each other. I should have mentioned that originally it was Wayne who appeared to have initiated the idea of the game, asking Melvin and Joseph if either one of them knew how to play. The boys batted the ball around the room yelling at each other. Thomas moved in crying out, "Who wants to play tag?" There was a concerted dive on the part of all but Errol to get under the table, for the last boy "under" was supposed to be "it." I did not get to observe whether Errol participated in this game or not. There was, however, a good deal of running around with shouting on the part of all.

I should mention that just about the time the game of tag got under way, Joseph had taken off his glasses and put them on the tool cabinet. As I began laying out the food at about 4:55, Melvin and Thomas broke away from the game, somebody yelling "time out." They came over to the sink, beginning to wash up. Wayne and Joseph locked themselves in the bathroom; Charles on the outside, with his back to the door, seemed to be half-heartedly kicking at the door. After a few minutes the boys came out, but

Charles did not enter, rather, he trailed them to the table. Thomas and Melvin were the first ones to take seats with Thomas announcing that he was going to take his old seat. Wayne took the seat that I had normally taken in earlier sessions. I heard Thomas whispering something to Melvin, but I did not quite pick up what. I believe it was in reference to the seat that Wayne had taken. Errol, as soon as he was seated, began eating, followed by Melvin and Thomas. The meal consisted of franks, beans, chocolate milk, and cupcakes. There was a bottle of ketchup and a small jar of pickles on the table. I should mention that Wayne was the last one to sit down. Seating arrangement was: Wayne on my immediate left, then Charles, Errol, Joseph, Thomas, and Melvin on my immediate right. Melvin and Thomas struck up a conversation about camp. Both had been there. Joseph chimed in and there soon was a three-way conversation among Joseph, Thomas, and Melvin, while Errol, Charles, and Wayne listened silently. The conversation centered around Melvin and Thomas at first wanting to know when each had been to camp and to make sure that they were both talking about the same camp. They talked about their counselor, Tony, at which point Joseph chimed in, and then Melvin announced that there were two counselors named Tony. They talked about the group in which they had been with Melvin, asserting that neither of them could have been in group four because they were not old enough. They talked about the various activities they participated in and about the physical features of the camp. At one point, as Melvin was describing the lake, the therapist accidentally coughed and there was a sudden silence. After a couple of moments of silence, Thomas and Melvin seemed to look around the table, then at each other. They grinned briefly, with Melvin resuming talk, carrying on about the physical features of the camp and about the lake, canoeing, swimming . . .

Play Group Psychotherapy

For children under the age of seven years, a modified form of activity group therapy, termed "play group psychotherapy," has been in use. The approach here is akin to that encountered in psychoanalytically-oriented nursery schools. Besides setting definite limits on the amount of impulsive activity, the therapist offers interpretation of behavior patterns in order to promote self-understanding. There have been instances where the children's parents received simultaneous group treatment.

Foulkes and Anthony (1965) described a group approach for latency-age children in which each group session is divided into a discussion phase and an activity phase. During the discussion phase the children are encouraged to talk about their concerns, such as sexuality, and about various fantasied and real fears. Following the discussion period the children are free to choose an activity for the day.

Barcai and Robinson (1969) reported on the use of discussion group therapy with a group of fifth and sixth grade children in two slum neighborhood schools who were referred because of difficult classroom behavior or poor academic performance. The authors concluded that conventional group psychotherapy was considerably more effective than supervised art classes offered to the same kinds of children.

Traditional activity group therapy has been found uniquely suited to the treatment of children with mild character and neurotic disorders (Coolidge and Grunebaum, 1964; Scheidlinger et al, 1959). A modified version of it, which made it possible to reach severely disturbed and atypical children, was also developed (Scheidlinger, 1960). Ego deficiencies, such as poor reality testing, difficulty in perceiving the difference between inner and outer sources of tension, inadequate impulse control, poor peer relationships, low self-image, and a confused identity were generally characteristic of all these children. There was, in addition, a primitive oral greediness coupled with the hostile expectation that such needs will never be gratified.

The activity group treatment measure adopted to help these severely impaired children contained three major therapeutic elements: The first was *guided gratification* in both a real and a symbolic sense. This involved restitution for past deprivations as well as minimizing current frustrations. As might be expected, it was around the theme of food, the purchasing, cooking and serving of it, that the most dramatic and meaningful interactions occurred. The second element referred to a *guided regression* wherein the child was enabled to relive, with different actors and with a different ending, conflicts from early fixation levels. The final and perhaps most decisive treatment element involved a *guided upbringing and socialization*. Building on the earlier climate of gratification and the ensuing attachment to the adult and to the group, demands for controls and socialization were posed. A channel for identification, for internalization, and for learning was thus opened. As in the upbringing of young children, genuine socialization required a climate of constancy and a steady and gratifying adult object suitable for internalization.

The amazing readiness of these groups to accept children who are markedly "different" and vulnerable as "one of the family," is touching. Such an acceptance is usually followed by well-timed demands on the part of the group members that the individual in question "stop acting crazy." It is only on rare occasions that protective restraint has to be employed, at which time it is perceived by these vulnerable children with relief and relaxation as a renewed guarantee that the adult will not permit overwhelming psychological or physical threat to anyone.

CASE ILLUSTRATION

Carl, 9½, moody, sullen and withdrawn, is characteristic of one of these severely disturbed children. His moods seemed unrelated to external factors. He had no close relationships with anyone and gave the surface impression of passivity. Suspiciousness and shyness with adults were noted. There was a twitching of the face, and both fear and fascination at the theme of death. At school Carl stood out as different and aloof. He worked far below his capacity, and was markedly retarded in reading. The psychotic mother was in and out of mental hospitals for years. During these periods the children (including an older brother and a younger sister) were neglected, often without any adult in the picture for a number of days. Later on, an aunt, a sickly woman seventy years old, would assume care of the children until her niece's return from the hospital.

During the first period of treatment, Carl related to the group with extreme caution. He was very suspicious toward the adult. In spite of the fact that he spent most of his time at a corner table away from the others, he was the first boy to announce, during the eating, that the group should meet more often than once a week and for longer periods. Of particular significance was his voracious manner of eating; he grabbed food and stuffed it into his mouth, using the fingers of both hands. This behavior was so much more exaggerated than that of any of the other boys, also deprived, that they quickly dubbed him "Greedy." This would always cause Carl to glower at them, but in no way deterred his grabbing for all extras. The boys rather quickly accepted his tremendous needs and could usually, by tacit agreement, allow him the extra food without overt competition.

While there was a gradual improvement in the boy's relationship to the others by the second year, there was little change in
his attitude toward food, or toward the therapist. By the third year,
Carl became friendlier with the therapist, and showed an increasing dependency on him for help with tools and materials. Concurrently, there was a dramatic change in Carl's consumption of food.
At times he would pass up seconds, or would be slow enough in
reaching for them so that other boys began competing more actively and directly. Carl did not seem to be upset if they got ahead
of him. His table manners had by now become quite acceptable.
The mood swings were hardly in evidence. The summer camp
noted, for the first time, a marked gain in impulse control. In contrast to the previous year, Carl would become realistically angry
without "flying to pieces" or appearing to have to "sit on himself"
to keep from blowing up. During the fourth year the therapist
noted a definite relationship between Carl's attitude toward him
and his food consumption. When he was particularly hostile to
the adult, he did not even take his basic portion. During this same
year Carl brought some candy for the therapist after the latter
had kept a chocolate rabbit for him from the Easter party, which
the boy could not attend.

Despite the numerous successful demonstrations of activity group
therapy as depicted above, outpatient group treatment for latency-
age children has, in general, failed to flourish. This is especially
regrettable since for many children group treatment is probably
the most desirable and efficacious method of therapy available at
present. The failure of activity group therapy to keep pace with
the rapid development of group treatment for adolescents and
adults is probably related to the prevailing modes of training in
child psychiatry and the resulting preference of therapists for
verbal and dyadic approaches. The need for special physical facilities for group therapy for children may be another factor.

As noted by Frank and Zilbach (1968), however, there has con-
comitantly been a marked increase in modified kinds of groups
(paratherapeutic) for latency-age children in school settings as
well as in residential treatment centers.

Para-Therapeutic Children's Groups

Among the pioneers who applied the techniques of activity group
therapy to children's play groups in elementary schools is Schiffer

(1969). Begun in 1950, his groups included six- to nine-year-olds and were led by school guidance counselors. As in activity groups, the counselor's stance was essentially permissive and nondirective, promoting limited regressive behavior and transference reactions. However, there appeared to be with these younger children more stress on a balanced composition of members and on more frequent leader intervention so as to prevent uncontrolled emotionality in these groups.

Most treatment groups in elementary schools today are regrettably devoid of the systematic approach and the pretraining of practitioners which characterized Schiffer's approach. Nevertheless, as was noted by Frank and Zilbach (1968) such groups in schools tend to be relatively successful wherever the method reflects an awareness of the reality of the school setting and of the unique psychology of the latency-age child. For example, in one school a "reading club" was devised for eight-year-old boys with behavior problems and reading disabilities. The boys were supplied with food and a variety of reading materials and word games. In the absence of any "push" from the adult, the youngsters gradually chose to engage in reading rather than in play, asking the worker for help with it. At the end of the year, the teachers reported marked improvement in the boys' behavior and several of them had gained a year in their reading level.

A modified kind of activity group approach was applied to a sample of about forty disadvantaged latency-age children with superior intelligence, in an educational project (Scheidlinger, 1965). The design called for a ready possibility of replicating this group intervention measure in schools, under the direction of guidance personnel. In addition to the usual tools and craft supplies characteristic of traditional activity groups, special materials such as science sets, educational games, musical instruments and maps were provided. In contrast to the regressive climate encouraged in group psychotherapy, reality considerations were planfully injected from the start by limiting the amount of food available, by not allowing visitors to attend, and by permitting only completed projects to be taken home. The worker's role was quite different from that of the activity group therapist. Along with the role of accepting adult went that of active stimulator, guide, and teacher. Realistic praise and support were offered, together with confrontation in regard to undesirable behavior patterns, such as undue dependence. The major focus was on strengthening the relatively unconflicted ego functions through individual interventions and group discussions. These were evoked from the very beginning as a means of enhancing the group's cohesiveness and of helping it to resolve its conflicts as well as to make plans for the future.

It was impressive how ready these groups were not only to absorb the small number of severely disturbed children in their midst, but also actively to help bring about improved functioning in them. This was accomplished through direct intervention by the leader regarding undesirable behavior patterns, coupled with enlistment of the group's understanding and help.

Diagnostic Groups

Short-term diagnostic groups for latency-age children represent yet another adaptation of activity group therapy. As depicted by King (1970), these groups contained five boys and girls aged 7–11½ years who met for a total of four sessions with a female social worker. In contrast to some other similar programs (Redl, 1944; Churchill, 1965), these diagnostic groups were utilized as an integral part of the casework study and planning process in a family service agency. The unique advantage of these groups resided in their flexible character. They could thus accommodate children of both sexes about whom almost nothing was known, as well as those where specific diagnostic questions were being posed. Control of impulsivity presented no undue problem in these groups once the traditional nondirective stance of the activity group therapist was modified. Immediate adult intervention coupled with a role of benign authority worked best. As might be expected, the worker had to have a wide variety of interventions available. The need to exert limits for the benefit of the weakest child was balanced by the desirability of allowing sufficient freedom for the emergence of spontaneous behavior. Availability and use of tools and materials were managed with a view to the short-term diagnostic purpose of the group as well as flexibility in controlling the amount of regressive behavior.

As noted by King (1970), certain aspects of the children's developmental levels and functioning emerged more clearly than others in this diagnostic group experience. Each child's current ego functioning was most clearly demonstrated, especially in regard to object constancy and relationships, reality testing and judgment, impulse control, frustration tolerance and characteristic defenses. There was, in addition, much useful data pertaining to levels of psychosocial development, to aspects of self-concept and of sexual identification. Also revealed were such areas of functioning as the degree and quality of energy as expressed in motor activity and outward-directed interests and curiosity and the child's span of attention and ability to concentrate. There were in addition, some indications regarding withdrawal and excessive fantasy.

As might be expected, children's residential treatment settings abound in group treatment modalities. These range from milieu groupings encompassing the whole institution or living-in units, to small socialization or recreational groups (Konopka, 1970). There has been little systematic utilization of activity or discussion group therapy in institutions, largely due to the difficulty of combining the permissive role characteristic of these approaches with the need for authoritative handling of the generally impulse-ridden patient population.

In general, as has also been concluded by MacLennan and Levy (1969), despite the fact that the need for the treatment of children has approached the character of a crisis, the literature on group therapy of children fails to reflect this fact.

GROUPS FOR ADOLESCENTS

There are as many ways to go through adolescence as there are people—but the core issues to be dealt with and the ultimate goals to be achieved are universal. The adolescent must deal with his still powerful, dependent tie to parents, at the same time that he must learn to cope with the anxiety about trying to manage on his own and learn to find security in himself and in extra-familial objects. He must permit himself some socially acceptable gratifications of his aggressive and sexual drives, and resolve the bisexual identity characteristic of preadolescence in order to arrive at a firm heterosexual orientation. He must ultimately achieve some clear sense of himself and along with this, of his values. He must select a career and follow through on training for that objective. A tall order—and all to be dealt with against the background of tremendous physcial upheaval, and a difficult social reality.

The management of adolescence is to a large extent determined by the way the child's ego development progressed through the earlier stages, but, according to Blos (1962, p. 10): "Adolescence often affords spontaneous recovery from debilitating childhood exigencies which threatened to impede his progressive development." Blos goes on to describe the importance of latency as preparation for adolescence: as we already noted, within latency much sexual and aggressive energy is channeled into sublimated activities, there is normally considerable broadening of the conflict—free spheres encompassing perception, memory, thinking, etc., and superego functions are fairly well secured. Thus, the increase in instinctual pressure in early adolescence does not normally undermine most aspects of reality functioning.

Early adolescence, brought into existence by dramatic physical changes, is characterized by a fairly chronic state of emotional lability. Conflict is everywhere: in the home the issue is to separate from parents or remain "safely" a child; at school he will either be popular with the opposite sex and make it with his peer group or be a failure; and we must not forget the necessity of meeting academic requirements, a task often providing a basis for conflict. The one-sex peer group gradually gives way to intense heterosexual curiosity, then dating, as both girls and boys move away from the primal love object and alter the overwhelmingly narcissistic orientation normal for the earlier period. Devaluation of parents occurs and considerable open conflict with them is usual and perhaps even necessary to facilitate ultimate separation. The emotionally healthy individual will have repressed his sexual wishes toward the opposite sex parent by late adolescence, and will have identified with the same sex parent, thus permitting a resolution of the childhood ties. This ultimately will allow for selection of an extra-familial heterosexual object. With diminished pressures internally and within the home, the sixteen- to eighteen-year-old can more readily invest his energy in intellectual and career pursuits.

Breakdown can occur at any point in adolescence. Studies have suggested that often the onset of schizophrenia takes place within the adolescent period. In terms of the less pathologic symptomatology, we note that most often girls are brought for treatment because of intense mother-daughter conflict, unwanted pregnancy, or depression. Boys are often referred by the school due to truancy, school failure or unduly aggressive behavior. In recent years youths of both sexes are frequently using drugs. One often encounters teenagers who are friendless, or who are neither feminine nor masculine, but asexual, or those who are in fact already beginning to act like and appear as members of the opposite sex. Almost invariably these are youths who are suspicious or even hostile to adults since they have failed to deal with the adult world both at home and at school. Many of them have turned almost frantically to their peer groups. This reluctance to depend upon adults, coupled with the natural inclination toward peer group formation, are two major reasons why group therapy is often considered the treatment of choice for many adolescents (Torda, 1970). There are, in fact, adolescents who from the outset make it clear that they are unwilling to work on an individual basis with the therapist, or who agree to come and do so only to remain totally silent within the one-to-one treatment setting. Common concerns among these youths are that they will be thought of as crazy or that the therapist could read their minds. On a deeper level, they frequently fear the attachment to the therapist. For many of these adolescents, the comfort of a group permits sufficient anonymity and distance from the adult so that thoughts and feelings can be shared more naturally.

There are adolescents who cannot readily fit into the usual therapy groups. Those who exhibit overt psychosis or psychopathy are accordingly excluded from group therapy except where special groups are set up to treat individuals with this type of psychopathology. Similarly, there is agreement in the field that youngsters who are intensely jealous of peers, and those who have practically no social relationships, are not ready for the therapy group. For them, the primary object is not the peer group but the adult, and until they work through some of these dependency problems in individual therapy, they cannot manage in the peer group. Slavson (1950) emphasizes the importance of careful selection of group members; he suggests that adolescents should be grouped according to their general level of psychosexual development, believing that such homogeneous groups would help the members be more attuned to each other's unconscious, and thus be more able to make astute observations concerning one another. He also stresses the need for group balance, as between "talkers" and "silent" members, the acting out and the withdrawn, and in relation to levels of pathology and hostility. It should be noted that therapy groups which call for verbal communication can absorb people from different socio-economic backgrounds and with a wide range of intelligence, providing all members have at least low average intelligence.

The setting for the group is of crucial importance; thus, it must have a regular place available for meetings. The room should be large enough to permit a sense of spaciousness, but not so large as to make people uncomfortable (MacLennan and Felsenfeld, 1968). Most teen group meetings are held around a table, which facilitates discussion. Often, adolescent groups have soda served and at the beginning they frequently need supplies, such as drawing materials, to help the more anxious members to physically drain off excessive anxiety, which might otherwise drive them away. The group therapist makes it clear from the outset, however, that the expected means of communication is primarily verbal.

During the initial part of such a group's life, absenteeism is often so high that many a leader has wondered whether the group will fall apart. Some authorities recommend a brief individual contact with each adolescent prior to his admission to a group. It is believed that the relationship thus formed will hold the adolescent in the group during the initial period of high anxiety. Early group sessions are frequently characterized by spurts of chatter, especially by girls, followed by painful silences which cannot be tolerated by most teenagers. The group therapist must come across from the outset as a warm and interested person who will not take over, who can tolerate some regression as well as contempt for authority, and who will maintain total confidentiality. Once the level of intense anxiety related to the adult is reduced, the natural tendency toward peer group formation will take hold.

The above noted developments are illustrated by an all girls' teen group conducted at a family service agency. The girls had been interviewed individually at least three times each by the group therapist before the decision was made for placement in the group.

CASE ILLUSTRATION

The group consisted of eight girls, six of whom had been present from the outset. Two other girls withdrew after one session so that two new members were added after six sessions. Anne, sixteen, white, Catholic, pretty and articulate, an only child, was having severe difficulties with her mother and was extremely reluctant to be seen individually. Jill, sixteen, a bright black girl, the youngest of five in a middle class family with high aspirations, was failing in school, cutting classes, fooling around with drugs, and while still very tied to mother, hated her father intensely. She appeared to be making a predominantly masculine identification and showed little evidence of femininity. We suspected from the beginning that she was also quite depressed, but overtly she only showed an almost paranoid suspiciousness of adults, coupled with a hostile flippancy. Rose, white, Roman Catholic, and at fifteen, the youngest in the group, was precariously close to dropping out of school; she also was having serious problems with her foster parents. When approached with an offer of help, Rose rejected individual contact but reluctantly accepted the idea of the group. Phyllis, 17½, white, Protestant, and a gifted musician, was an only child living with her disturbed single mother. She became depressed during her senior year in school and asked the guidance counselor for a referral to a treatment setting. Janet, sixteen, white, Roman Catholic, living with her parents and several siblings, was intensely hostile to her mother and very jealous of a younger sibling. She had taken to cutting school and was failing in her subjects. Elaine, nearly seventeen, a lovely looking black Protestant girl of clearly above average intelligence, had been seen briefly in family therapy focused on her problems with mother. Out of that experience Elaine had indicated her interest in getting further help, admitting that she was truanting; she also had some history of stealing and was under-achieving at school. The late comers were Kathy, sixteen, Protestant, shy and depressed, prone to excessive involvement with school work and no social life, and Lola, an attractive, sophisticated seventeen-year-old, who was doing extraordinarily well at school but already was quite promiscuous and heavily experimenting with drugs.

The girls had all met Mrs. Jones several times prior to that first group meeting, and in fact had seen the observation and the group therapy rooms. While all were "willing to give the group a try," which was what was asked of them, Ann and Janet were clearly very reluctant. Phyllis and Elaine seemed very interested, while Jill was suspicious. In several individual sessions and in the first group meeting, the group therapist told the girls that they shared common concerns, that she felt they could help each other, that she, too, would like to be helpful, and that they would be experiencing anxiety which was to be expected in a new situation. From the outset, the girls joked about similar experiences which they had read about such as marathon groups or nude groups, describing these as places where everyone tells all and where promiscuity abounds. They clearly were asking the group therapist, "What will happen here?" The anxiety level was high and very much connected with the group therapist's presence. Before Session 1, a girl who eventually dropped out telephoned the worker four times, each time to change her mind about whether or not she was coming to the meeting. Several girls kiddingly "locked" the group therapist out when she briefly left the room to show some late-comers in. Ann and Jill were quite open in agreeing that the girls shouldn't tell anyone they're coming to this place because "if other people know you're coming here, they will think you're crazy or something." As already noted, another common fear early in therapy is that the group leader can read minds. Thus, one girl who dropped out after one session told Mrs. Jones that while she might have a problem, "You mean some place down in my deep, dark, unconscious—if I do, I'm really not going to be able to find it and I don't think anyone here is going to get that far either." The other girls agreed completely. They also agreed while briefly chatting about drugs, that adults could never understand anything about this subject. Not infrequently the girls spoke indirectly of their fears of Mrs. Jones, when they described their expectations or experiences with other adults: Ann was critical of her mother for "inspecting her work"; Jill's mother screams, demands and criticizes; Elaine's mother worries constantly, talks a blue streak, will not listen, and thus Elaine clams up. Will Mrs. Jones be like any of these people?

The word "problem" is out of bounds for such teenagers: to them it means that they are either out of control or crazy. Jill told the girls that it was too hard for them to talk about problems since they all had different ones and were from different backgrounds. She suggested that they talk about "something else," and if something came up naturally they could discuss it "without concentrating on problems." At times the girls relieved their anxiety by giggling at everything the group therapist said. When one of the girls found a session too anxiety-provoking, she sometimes missed the following week's session, offering as an excuse her need to study or a minor somatic complaint. The girls used the early sessions to identify themselves as to where they go to school, what their interests are, whether they have boy friends, and very superficially, about why they're in treatment. By Session 4, the separateness which was marked from the outset had changed so that there was now a warm friendliness amongst the girls. They drank the Cokes without any hesitation and asked each other what happened about something one of the girls discussed last week. On the other hand, superficial facts having been shared, the girls were more prone to anxious silences as they were not yet sure whether or what to share. The big issue was "can we trust each other?" but also and most particularly "can we trust her?" meaning Mrs. Jones. The group leader offered support, noting how hard it was to talk, especially with her there, and reassured them that all groups go through this.

If no one offers a subject for discussion, which is not uncommon, the therapist usually introduces a theme, as in the following illustration, for the girls cannot tolerate silence and are ever ready to run. Phyllis, wanting badly to please Mrs. Jones and really in need of nurturance from her peers, reached out to the group with the first "problem" concerning a boy she was interested in. The others grasped at this straw: Jill, who was vieing with Mrs. Jones for the group's leadership, quickly offered a pat solution in a domineering way, leaving no place for opposition; Elaine, intrigued with the problem, asked a few questions, and then there was silence. Mrs. Jones picked up Jill's comment, remarked on it as an interesting possible solution, noted that Elaine seemed to be pursuing another idea, and asked if she or anyone else wanted to take it further. As the girls appeared to have gone as far as they could with this, the therapist picked up on Jill's comment and soon the girls, led by Janet and Ann, both so hostile to their mothers, began contemptuously to speak of mothers in general: they're ignorant, jump to conclusions and blame teenagers for everything. Naturally, the group therapist was sympathetic and did not question their reasoning, but she also did not agree with this. As might be expected, mothers, and the girls' problems with them, represent the first subject that all of the girls are usually willing to talk about. Speaking about mothers, but clearly about her anxiety as to whether the group therapist could be trusted, Elaine stated in this group that she would never tell her mother if she were ill. Lola remarked that she kept almost everything from her mother who she felt really did not want to know anyway; Lola did voice a not uncommon concern that her mother might be upset about Lola's sharing here in the group what she wouldn't ever share at home.

Often, in the midst of this kind of discussion, Jill would accuse Mrs. Jones of wanting to force the girls to talk too fast—Jill would then order another girl to talk and when that girl, often Elaine or Janet, actually began a story, Jill would stop them with, "that's enough," clearly demonstrating her own as well as the group's ambivalence about moving ahead. Although Jill at that point seemed almost overwhelming to the other girls, Mrs. Jones had to avoid direct intervention; to do so with Jill would have set Mrs. Jones up as a very threatening adult, something which could have jeopardized the further progress of the group. It was also clear that Jill was terrified of Mrs. Jones and was doing most of her attacking or intervening with the other girls because of this fear. Mrs. Jones became acutely attuned to the possible danger of premature attempts to limit Jill; when the following week after she did in fact a few times gently stop Jill from taking over, the whole group was utterly silent, betraying their anger and fear of Mrs. Jones. When they next spoke, Janet warned Mrs. Jones by telling the others that it took her a long time to make friends because she's been hurt so often. Others in the group, most particularly Jill and Phyllis, wanted Mrs. Jones to tell them what she thought of them, demonstrating a sharp, though temporary increase in their anxiety about the group leader. It was only when Jill, the girl who was most fearful of Mrs. Jones, was calmer, that the girls could become a group. She then would not need to take over so much and the others would be comfortable enough to handle her, if necessary.

While this group was not beset with many absences (which often occurs in teen groups), it did lose two members, which was felt keenly. It also had to deal with the late admission of two new members. This was timed at the point when the members were beginning to feel comfortable with one another so that they could accept the newcomers and help them get oriented. The few early absences which did occur were very much noticed by those present and served as sources of disturbance as the girls moved toward coalescing as a group. Thus, Janet and Jill questioned whether Rose's absence was for a good reason, and in another session Ann was told outright that she could not make a date on a group night. Underlying these expressions of concern seemed to be a beginning commitment to each other. During this early period, probably commencing with the fourth or fifth session, the girls were also acutely attuned to whether a story sounded honest, though they accepted anything that was shared and rarely asked questions of one another that could be considered personal. In fact, when Lola gave some information on birth control to the girls which made it fairly obvious that she had had sexual experiences, while failing to describe these experiences, the others dropped the subject, agreeing that they had no basis on which to discuss such a subject. Not only were they not yet sure what they could ask Lola, but they were also not ready to discuss sex in front of Mrs. Jones. Of great help at this stage, when they are struggling with how much they may ask of each other, could be comments from Mrs. Jones remarking on their interest and wish to help one another, but recognizing their natural reluctance to push; there should be talk of their concern about whether sharing can help, and where sharing has helped within the group, certainly Mrs. Jones would be picking up on this, encouraging the girls to think about it. The group was certainly concerned about how sharing with Mrs. Jones would be received. Thus, when Mrs. Jones, in Session 7, made a comment to Kathy which Kathy clearly did not want to pick up on, and might have felt awkward about, Mrs. Jones's reassurance that "it's okay to take your time," was the most enabling response. These remarks, plus careful, sensitive handling of Jill resulted in Jill's approaching Mrs. Jones individually for help, which led to her sharing much of her depression. The girls moved from their separateness into a cohesive group, a step which usually signals the termination of the first phase in the group's life.

An all boys' group may discuss different issues but actually goes through the same struggles around trusting the adult, characteristic of the girls' group described above.

Thus, a group of seven 13½ to 14½ year old boys met for a period of about two years during which time there were two dropouts. There were five white boys and two black boys, one of the white boys being Puerto Rican. Problems for the most part related to rather serious school difficulties and some delinquency. One boy seemed to be developing along homosexual lines, while another was felt to be very disturbed and possibly in need of more intensive therapy. Most of the boys were seen in some individual treatment prior to admission to the group, and a few of them continued with it during the life of the group. (Such a use of combined treatment is not unusual and was in fact true of a few of the girls who attended the group described earlier.) The boys initially were very shy and awkward and not able to talk too much, needing considerable help from the group therapist to involve them. When they could talk, their complaints were very similar to the girls', involving their hostility to teachers and school and their general feeling that "adults pick on kids and don't like children." The boys, unlike the girls, went into graphic detail describing all of the adventures in the school setting and out, and participated in some rather dramatic physical acrobatics in the group therapy room. It is characteristic of boys that they use their bodies to express feelings much more so than do girls who may appear restless but generally remain in their seats. One boy in this group, when describing a serious event which might have led to his expulsion from the school, said it was important for him to talk in the group because "at least people can hear my misery." This was a youth prone to acting out and not used to articulating his feelings. This group's early sessions were characterized by talk of dramatic adventures, seemingly to test out how the group therapist would take to some of this. They described shop classes where people cut their fingers off, adventures on the outside with purse snatchings, and truancy. They went on to talk about girls and what they liked to do with them, but this kind of talk didn't go too far. What they were freer to express was a totally negative attitude toward school. Nowhere in the early sessions of the boys' group were there really serious complaints about parents; instead, almost all of the anger was displaced onto the school setting. They seemed to admire all types of fighting and giggled as they described all such dramatic fights and near fights. When the group therapist asked if they could say in words what their giggling meant, they laughed more, as they were unaccustomed to using words to the extent to which adolescent girls are. It took a while for them to get down to talking openly about whether they could trust each other, something which the girls did much more quickly. But interestingly enough, after they talked about this, they seemed to move more readily into closeness and came and went together earlier than did the girls' group. The attendance in this particular boys' group was very good as they "had a ball" in group, and following the meetings they enjoyed running down nineteen flights of stairs together. They were so active outside the sessions that the agency personnel utilizing nearby offices had to be fairly tolerant. If they came early they kidded around some, flirted with the secretaries, and occasionally tried to peek in to see their therapist or some other people whom they had met. They at times also followed some girls whom they had seen in the waiting room, and in general caused much more stir than does an adolescent girls' group. The boys also said quite openly that "outside teachers and counselors spoil the fun." What will the leader do? Does she believe in fun? With a female leader there is likely to be even more bragging and flirting.

Socially deprived youths share the psychological struggles of their more advantaged peers, but have the additional burden of their reality deprivation and of their not uncommon verbal poverty. Unused to expressions of feeling through language, these youngsters often resort to action, sometimes of a destructive nature. MacLennan (1968) makes note of the special difficulty such a teenager has in utilizing the group initially: he finds it difficult to trust, much more than the average middle class child, and cannot readily identify with the therapist whose background is so different from his own; he has no faith in goals for the future for he has seen little success around him. Practitioners working with these youngsters generally agree that a much longer period of testing could be expected, and that the group therapist may need to involve himself with the group in an activity or even go outside to help these youngsters individually with their pressing reality concerns.

John, age fourteen, in the group described above, fits this description. A black boy from a broken family on welfare, John was not only beset with emotional problems that at times resembled a schizophrenic picture, but also by the reality of not having proper clothing or food, and of almost never having had stable family members within the household. His father, when he saw him, was frequently drunk. Most often, he was absent, almost never working. An older sister who was fooling around with drugs and quite promiscuous was threatening to leave the house. His mother was either angry and drinking or depressed and unavailable. She alternately leaned on John and rejected him, seeing him as representative of the men who used her. When John came to the group he was caustic and hostile, openly suspicious, and raised questions about how the group therapist could possibly relate to him since he was black. He wondered from the beginning about the issue of racial prejudice, and told the group therapist in another session that what was on his mind was that he was poor. For a very long time it appeared that John never felt that talking would solve his reality problem, and the question had to be raised as to what held him in the group so long. It undoubtedly was the relationship which the group therapist was able to establish with him by reaching out and by consistently offering herself as a nurturing object: she would not push herself on the boy but was available for crises, was not critical of him when he described some of his semi-delinquent activities, but also did not encourage him to follow that direction and in fact showed him new constructive possibilities for the future. It took much longer for John to learn how to utilize the group setting than for some of his more advantaged peers. The type of activity the group therapist undertook with this boy is clearly different from the traditional psychoanalytic group psychotherapy offered to middle class teenagers. For example, there were a number of individual contacts outside the group which were not psychotherapy sessions per se, but rather meetings to solve concrete problems which threatened to overwhelm this boy and his family. There were many school visits and contacts, calls to the

YMCA and to job placement settings, and often several times a week brief "chats" in the hall as the boy turned up when anxiety threatened to overwhelm him or he just couldn't take school that week.

Magary and Elder (1970), in describing a group of inner city girls, stated that the lower class Negro girl with an absent father cannot "play out her conflict in the usual way. She lacks the reality of the stable masculine figure against which to correct her shifting fantasies. Unlike the middle class girl, she cannot choose to be a part or aloof from the father since she has no opportunity to be in contact with him at all. Achieving independence from the mother is complicated by long overdependence on her as (frequently) the sole important adult, and also by the fact that the mother's way of life is often that which the adolescent consciously rejects. There may therefore be no adequate adult models, in contrast to the middle class patterns of a "mother with whom I identify," in order to win "father-as-a-good-husband" (p. 41). They go on to note that achievement does not serve the same function for the lower class Negro girl because the fantasies of succeeding cannot be supported by their observation of people in their environment, so that under the slightest pressure the fantasies crumble and the goals are given up.

Although all adolescent groups in the beginning phase can cause the new group therapist great anxiety, it is certainly true that a group of disadvantaged youths can be even more taxing. For these often hostile and suspicious teenagers may act out considerably, absent themselves for weeks on end and then turn up unexpectedly in serious trouble requiring dramatic intervention. If the group therapist is able to hold such a youngster in the group this is likely to change, but the first ten to fifteen weeks in the group's life are crucial, often determining the outcome of the treatment.

The aim of group treatment with all adolescents is to support the ego in its struggle to cope with instinctual pressures and with external reality. Within this general framework adolescent groups have in common specific themes characterizing the beginning, middle and end of treatment, which reflect the adolescent's own basic conflicts during these years. We have already seen how the initial struggle within the group revolves around trust of the leader and of each other. The content around which this is worked out involves their common hostility toward and contempt for parents, the unfairness and incompetence of school authorities, and the external, superficial facts about each of their life situations. We see emerging clearly the dependent-independent struggle fought out at home, at school, and with the group leader. Once this major issue of trust is resolved, the individual member moves into the group while the group as a whole moves into the middle phase within which more intensive treatment can occur.

Fried, in her article "Ego Emancipation of Adolescents Through Group Psychotherapy" (1956), notes that often behavior of the adolescent is more related to the conscious and unconscious parental demands than it is to environmental reality. She describes for example, how an unconscious need on the part of a parent to have a particular child reject his masculine identification might result in his doing so, or on the contrary in his dramatically acting out to prove he is a boy. She notes that where two parents are coordinated in their conscious or unconscious conviction, there is even more danger that he will respond in a pattern connected with these parental demands. The ego in adolescence has a limited capacity for organization and integration so that very wide fluctuations in behavior, aims, and symptoms occur. Group treatment, while at times heightening the adolescent's tendency toward disorganization because of the presence of multiple stimuli and varied models of identification, may at the same time force the adolescent to examine what *he* wants and needs so that his gratification will be *self-determined* rather than "a parent-servicing ego" (p. 367). For the adolescent, emancipation can be a frightening desertion of the parents, since he lacks certainty concerning his capacity to care for himself; thus, he often is conflicted about whether he should indeed attempt to ascertain his own wishes and feelings or follow through, without thinking, on parental demands. The treatment group offers the teenager a chance to consider where his feelings are taking him, where his behavior follows environmental reality and where it diverges. Group members often ask each other such questions as: "Why are you truanting? How did it happen that you stole that purse? You were depressed last December and this May; what do those periods have in common, if anything?" In the middle phase the group leader can encourage the members to look at these issues and when they fail to do so, can periodically suggest that there's something going on within the group or within a particular member which is causing resistance. The group therapist can explore with any particular member the basis of some of the behavioral manifestations either within the group or without, as described to her by this member.

An example of the middle phase of treatment in an all girls' group follows.

CASE ILLUSTRATION

Margie, a fifteen-year-old in a group of five teenage girls, had been consistently failing since junior high school, and was involved in a chronic battle with her mother around her poor performance. She had been in this group just a few weeks when she came in one week reporting a grade of 85% on an examination. She then stated that her mother still was not satisfied and had not lifted any of the unfair restrictions placed previously due to the girl's failure. Barbara and Lois picked up on this immediately and told Margie that she had done quite well and that she should be proud of herself. They were very sympathetic to her plight, as far as the restrictions were concerned, and both indicated that Margie could do something about these restrictions. They thought she shouldn't mess herself up in school and that she could win her mother over eventually. They proceeded to describe some ways wherein she would not antagonize her mother and still win out in the end. Lois, seventeen, said that her mother had been just as restrictive in the past, which seemed to make Margie feel much better.

On another occasion this particular group was discussing "teenage rebellion" in a very intellectual fashion, all agreeing that it was normal but not always necessary. One of the girls remarked that "some rebellion is silly—you should get educated." The two under-achievers in this group exchanged glances and Margie remarked that she "was very hung up on this in the past year" but is beginning to feel better. The group therapist noticed that Margie's tone of voice, usually very hostile when talking about her mother, was calm. In another session, Barbara, seventeen, who was having a very hard time separating from her mother, turned to the group therapist and asked her if she thought a child should stand up for her views or go along with the parent. When the group therapist threw this question back to the group, Lois remarked that she didn't have the strength to stand up to anything since she couldn't get along without her mother. Although nobody picked it up in this session, weeks later Barbara pointed out how competent Lois was and there was a consistent interest in the independent activities that Lois demonstrated. She was given great credit when she was able to travel to the group by herself, something which had not been possible in the first few weeks of the group's life. Similarly, when the issue of independence was examined in relation to the question of job hunting, Margie, listening to Barbara's joking about her interest in taking a summer job in the country, remarked on the girl's anxiety about this, saying, "You were certainly scared of a job." This took the girls into a discussion about jobs, how one approaches them, and what people are worried about. While they kidded a lot they were ultimately quite supportive and encouraging of each other and offered the suggestion that "when you earn your own money you're more your own person." One girl, who had been working for some time, shared a number of her positive experiences and recalled her own initial anxiety, noting that this was something everyone goes through and gets over. Later on within this group there was an increasing ability to share important feelings. One day Barbara started the session by telling the girls that she had been extremely depressed after seeing her former boy friend at a party the previous weekend. This boy had suddenly dropped her during the summer and she had never really gotten over this or, in fact, the unexpected earlier divorce of her parents. The girls were extremely sympathetic, understanding why she would feel this bad and then they began to ask some questions. The group therapist picked up on what Barbara was saying and remarked on her affect, saying it seemed that seeing the boy in a party situation and recalling all that had occurred was a serious blow to her self-esteem. Lois remarked on the inevitability of changing patterns of relationships in adolescence, and went on to describe her own severe depression the previous December after she had broken up with her boy friend. The girls moved from this subject to a discussion of their parents' relationships, especially those which were either unstable or had actually ended in divorce. They spoke about how their experiences of being left by adults often made them feel that there was something wrong with them. They considered whether their depressed moods meant they were crazy, but immediately reassured themselves, saying all teenagers get depressed and "kooky" and that they had good reason to feel sad sometimes. Although Barbara in particular reported that after "opening up," (telling the girls about how depressed she was), she had felt quite sad in the group, in later sessions she noted that she didn't quite feel the same about the experience, and was not as depressed; we saw Barbara gradually move into activities which she had heretofore avoided, such as joining a soriority at school and attending dances outside of the school setting. Her breaking the silence about a subject as frightening as depression resulted in the other girls' being able to grapple with the question of whether there was a hereditary predisposition to messing up one's relationships. Several jokingly suggested that prostitution or out-of-wedlock relationships might be a better way to deal with men and sex, both subjects having been avoided in the early phase of the group.

In this second phase of the group's life, the girls tend to select seats, and to keep them; they come regularly and are furious when one of them cancels for a minor reason; they are quick to pick up on each other's feelings, and are capable of exploring problems, confronting a peer with her avoidance, and, by now some members can even criticize the group therapist. There is a feeling of solidarity here which one could sense immediately upon entering the room. Individuals offer advice to each other in all areas and seem to feel a responsibility for each other's progress. an attitude which greatly influences the group members' behavior. We note that members' interventions are generally sensitive, well-timed and astute, and often deal with another's unproductive be-havior either within the group or outside. At times, they are terri-bly moralistic, more demanding in their expectations than any adults.

In a mixed group (boys and girls), there is an additional group process issue in this middle phase, as after the initial period of discomfort. There is often considerable flirting to establish sexual adequacy; it is during this phase that some dating outside of the group might occur.

Although it is true that there is a significant lessening of kidding around in the group in the middle phase of treatment, we do see in almost every session interspersed with the work, short periods of chatter, giggling, or intellectual conversation. The group leader must have some tolerance for the recouping effort which the chat-ter or discussion of world affairs represents. If, however, the main work is thwarted, the source of resistance must be identified. The girls' group described above had to be transferred to a different therapist after about fifteen sessions due to the first therapist's leaving the agency. For months afterward, there were periods of depressed silence, interspersed with irrelevent chatter. Then, once the group was solidly reestablished but preparing for the summer break, the old pattern reappeared. When the group therapist questioned the basis of the blocking, one girl remarked that she felt sad that the group was going to break up for the summer. This eventually enabled other girls to voice what seemed to be a common fear: would the second group therapist leave? Any feelings such as these, left unexpressed, invariably lead to blocking.

Individual Therapy

Individual sessions with group members are used selectively by most group therapists, but there is a wide diversion of opinion here as some therapists always do combined individual and group psychotherapy while others recommend using the group as the primary treatment modality.

Lois, of the second adolescent girls' group described, was seen in individual and in group treatment. The decision was made to offer her individual treatment after a year within the group. Prior to this she had declined individual contact after having had three sessions in preparation for entrance into the group. She was very tied to her mother and seemed fearful that individual therapy would threaten this relationship. When Lois again became depressed and fearful that he mother's second marriage was about to break up, she reached out to the group therapist and requested individual sessions. Lois continued to utilize the group effectively but needed much more at this particularly critical time and recognized herself that she was going to have to work intensively on her anxiety about separating from her mother. While Lois's acute awareness of her core conflict added markedly to the level of her anxiety and depression, it also made it possible for her to recognize her need for help and to seek this and utilize it. She was therefore seen in combined individual and group treatment on a more intensive level.

Another girl in the group described above, Barbara, was also offered individual treatment when it became clear that she was suffering from depression from which, at times, she seemed unable to emerge. Her work in school was suffering and her outside relationships were very poor, but Barbara was extremely reluctant to be involved with the group therapist, especially as she had been very attached to the first therapist who had left her. It was only after a year and some months of group treatment with the second therapist that Barbara was willing to enter into a time-limited and focused individual contact with her.

There are times, such as summer breaks or personal crises,

when the group member must be offered something supplemental to the group. (This may be particularly true in once-a-week group psychotherapy.) In the case of work with Lisa, who had been seen for 2½ years in intensive individual treatment prior to admission to the group, one aim of the group therapist was to utilize the group to help Lisa relinquish her need for individual therapy. Since the group experience was felt to be a crucial part of the termination process, after the first few group therapy sessions no individual appointments were offered Lisa on a regular basis, but when she occasionally requested them, they were granted.

Termination of the Therapy Group

The final period of a therapy group tends to focus on the working through of the sexual identification process. In the girls' group there was great interest in relationships with boys and a moving away from the special connection to father and hostility to mother characteristic of the earlier period. While the interest in the father is there, as is love for him where he exists as a nurturing figure, the extrafamilial heterosexual object is firmly the choice at this point. In the last phase, girls and boys are apt to bring in vivid descriptions of their outside peer relationships, and in mixed groups we see a use of one another to test out their facility in dealing with the opposite sex. Some of their fantasies about the opposite sex, including their fears, are aired, and the group is again used supportively as an opportunity for these young people to test out reality as far as sexuality is concerned. Although there is at times acknowledged sexual experimentation within the group, members often encourage each other to limit such experimentation to activities short of intercourse, pointing out the possible complications, i.e., pregnancy, depression, guilt.

The treatment group, in effect, is a substitute family enabling the members to utilize it as a transitional support while separation from primary objects takes place, and to test themselves out in a small, still protected setting before venturing forth in a world outside. We find that each member at times reacts to other group members and to the group therapist in part as he does to his own family. As a group member's perception of his reality is altered by his own growth and by others' observations and challenges, increasingly we would expect him to perceive the group members and the group therapist more as each really is. Slavson (1950) delineates this, the dissolution of the transference, as the ultimate task in the life of the group.

Para-Therapeutic Groups for Adolescents

Traditional psychoanalytic group psychotherapeutic technique must be altered in treating delinquents and addicts. Some of these groups are held in closed settings, such as hospitals, prisons or reform schools, and are not totally "voluntary," while others are taking place in environments not primarily considered clinical in nature. These members have something special in common which separates them from the professional group leader and brings them into closer relationship with their peers. For this reason, addicts' groups, for example, often have used a former addict as leader, with the co-leader being a trained group therapist. This is at least in part due to the addicts' natural tendency to trick the unsophisticated leader, who is not a part of the addicts' world, into believing he is off drugs. Underlying this, too, must be the fact that the group therapist often has considerable anxiety about working with such clients, and may, on another level, be fascinated by drugs himself so that he either could stimulate the use of drugs, or, as reaction formation, need to act restrictively and critically with group members to cope with his own unconscious wishes. Because of the special difficulty inherent in leading such a group, co-therapists are frequently utilized, and the groups often also have outside observers. (While there are many problems inherent in the co-therapy situation, including the very real problem of staff shortages, with this type of group there may be good reason to seriously consider such an approach.)

Groups for addicts and for the seriously delinquent were utilized initially after fairly conclusive evidence showed that individual therapy was generally unsuccessful. Several short-term groups were offered institutionalized delinquents, often aimed at facilitating adjustment to the institution and motivating the boys for further (individual) therapy. Feder (1962) noted that both these aims were served. In the long-term treatment models, Epstein and Slavson (1962), Blos (1961), and Shulman (1957) all remarked on the necessity of altering techniques during the beginning phase of the group. This is primarily due to the absence of basic trust which the severe non-neurotic delinquent brings to the group experience. Shulman (1957) describes the delinquent as grossly intolerant of anxiety, impulse-ridden, externalizing his conflicts, often in physical aggressiveness, and as having considerable impairment in time perspective (so that past and future are meaningless, only what is important for now counts). He further states that group sessions with delinquents must be structured, or the group will indefinitely remain focused on sexual and aggressive activity, and frequently scapegoat the group leader; on the other hand, the group leader cannot be too powerful, or even ask group members to confront each other—for they will view this as an attack. Instead, Shulman suggests that the group therapist point out how their silence is not helpful to their own aims, i.e., leaving the institution. He defines his ultimate therapeutic aim as character synthesis, not analysis. Epstein and Slavson (1962) described their first several months with a boys' group in a residential treatment center as similarly characterized by distrust, much physical movement (in and out of the group), and boasting of sexual and aggressive exploits. With this group, it appeared to be essential that the group leader be cued in to the boys' interests so that he could capitalize on some random comment made by one of them and get the rest of the boys curious. This particular group appears to have ultimately been able to go on in a more traditional fashion, but most of the groups reported in the literature have emphasized the long-term need for more controls, for special environmental manipulation, including at times the giving of food and presents; all have stressed the importance of attempting to help the boys become connected with their feelings as they pertain to the need to continue delinquent behavior (Heacock, 1965).

Blos (1961) sees treatment of the delinquent as aiming to transform the delinquency into a neurotic symptom, which can then be treated traditionally. Viewing delinquency as a symptom of ego pathology, Blos describes the delinquent as suffering from a lack of basic trust, probably connected with his early sado-masochistic power struggle with mother. In his configuration, the delinquent failed to master his environment, so instead settled for control, where the fantasied position of infantile omnipotence is maintained, and the underlying feeling of helplessness, of dependency, is very great. All conflict is externalized. In girls, this generally takes the form of sexual delinquency, and/or drug addiction. Blos views female delinquency as often connected with one of two issues: either an intense clinging to the pre-Oedipal mother, or, in the more mature girl who does have a foothold on the Oedipal level, an inability to give up the Oedipal struggle so that the delinquency is actually a continuous revenge on the mother. In both cases, a pseudo-heterosexuality may exist, but underlying this is very much the pre-Oedipal connection. In the boy, there usually exists a continuation of intense castration anxiety which may lead to considerable acting out in order to cope with the constant fear of damage.

The addicted young person appears to be seeking a direct gratification of his oral needs which have either never been adequately met, were prematurely disturbed, or were overly indulged, providing the ego with little help to develop the capacity to tolerate tension. Very frequently we see in addicted young men a strong homosexual underpinning which they are fighting off by frequent heterosexual behavior, bragging, and other delinquency. Thus, often, these young men and women need the group milieu to offer the nurturing and support toward healthier adaptive patterns before they can begin to tolerate the tension connected with giving up their behavior. This group experience would aim at enabling the young delinquent or addict to perceive reality differently from his usual perception of the environment as a hostile, ungiving, dangerous place existing only for him to take advantage of and to desert.

FUTURE DEVELOPMENT

Experience has shown the therapeutic group to be an exceptionally responsive approach to the treatment of children and of adolescents. This fact, plus the tremendous upsurge in interest in all types of group approaches, has resulted in more professionals being trained to do group therapy, which ultimately will mean many more adolescent group programs. Whether true therapy groups for children will prosper as well, remains an open question. In addition to the most common mono-gender adolescent group, we anticipate an increase in the mixed type of boys' and girls' group as the few studies reported in the literature have not borne out the widely held concern that boys and girls in a group invariably are stimulated to act out sexually (Ackerman, 1957; Kraft, 1968; Shulman, 1957).

In addition to the long-term intensive group treatment models described in this paper, we expect to see many more short-term groups offered to persons who might benefit from a combined therapeutic-educative approach. One such short-term model is the multiple family group, a relatively new technique which combines theoretical concepts developed within the family therapy field with those of traditional group therapy. Kimbro, Jr. (1967) found that such a group, within twelve sessions, was able to move to examine destructive patterns of each family's interaction as well as to discuss the more universal inter-generational anxieties. The advantage of the multiple family group may lie in the greater likelihood of nonfamily members being more able to cut through another family's strongly held system. This technique does not pretend to replace separate therapy plans for individual family members where needed, but may loosen some destructive patterns and increase communication within the family. It is of paramount importance to evaluate these newer short-term methods in the face of the staggering need for mental health services and a recognized lack of sufficient resources and staff to meet these needs.

REFERENCES

Ackerman, N.   Group psychotherapy with a mixed group of adolescents. *International Journal of Group Psychotherapy,* 1957, **2,** 249–260.

Auerbach, A. B.   *Parents learn through discussion: principles and practices of parent group education.* New York: Wiley, 1968.

Barcai, A., and Robinson, E. H.   Conventional group therapy with preadolescent children. *International Journal of Group Psychotherapy,* 1969.

Blos, P.   Delinquency. In S. Lorand, and H. I. Schneer (Eds.), *Adolescents—Psychoanalytic approach to problems and therapy.* New York: Harper-Hoeber, 1961. 132–151.

Blos, P.   *On adolescence, a psychoanalytic interpretation.* New York: The Free Press of Glencoe, 1962.

Boenheim, C.   Group psychotherapy with adolescents. *International Journal of Group Psychotherapy,* 1957, **3,** 398–406.

Bornstein, B.   *On latency. The Psychoanalytic Study of the Child,* 1951.

Carrothers, M. L.   Sexual themes in an adolescent girls' group. *International Journal of Group Psychotherapy,* 1963, **1,** 43–51.

Churchill, S. R.   Social group work: a diagnostic tool in child guidance. *American Journal of Orthopsychiatry,* April 1965, **35.**

Coolidge, J. C., and Grunebaum, M. G.   Individual and group therapy of a latency age child. *International Journal of Group Psychotherapy,* 1964, **14,** 84–96.

Duffy, James H., and Kraft, I. A.   Group therapy of early adolescents: an evaluation of one year of group therapy with a mixed group of early adolescents. *American Journal of Orthopsychiatry,* 1965, **35,** 372.

Epstein, N., and Slavson, S. R.   Further observations on group psychotherapy with adolescent delinquent boys in residential treatment. *International Journal of Group Psychotherapy,* 1962, **2,** 199–210.

Epstein, N. Brief group therapy in a child guidance clinic. *Social Work, July,* 1970, **15,** 3, 33–38.

Erikson, E. *Identity and the life cycle.* New York: International Universities Press, 1959.

Feder, B. Limited goals in short-term group psychotherapy with institutionalized delinquent adodescent boys. *International Journal of Group Psychotherapy,* 1962, 4, 503.

Foulkes, S. H., Anthony, E. J. *Group Psychotherapy.* Baltimore, Maryland: Penguin Books, 1965.

Frank, M. G., and Zilbach, J. Current trends in group therapy with children. *International Journal of Group Psychotherapy,* 1968, **18,** 447–460.

Fried, E. Ego emancipation of adolescents through group psychotherapy. *International Journal of Group Psychotherapy,* 1966, 6, 358–373.

Heacock, D. R. Modifications of standard techniques for outpatient group psychotherapy with delinquent boys. *American Journal of Orthopsychiatry,* 1965, **35,** 371.

Kaufman, P. N., and Deutsch, A. L. Group therapy for pregnant unwed adolescents in the prenatal clinic of a general hospital. *International Journal of Group Psychotherapy,* 1967, 3, 309–320.

Kimbro, E. L., Jr. et al. A multiple family group approach to some problems of adolescence. *International Journal of Group Psychotherapy,* 1967, 1, 18–24.

King, B. L. Diagnostic activity groups for latency age children. In *Dynamic Approaches to Serving Families,* New York: Community Service Society.

Konopka, G. *Group work in the institution, a modern challenge.* New York: Association Press, 1970.

Kraft, I. A. Some special considerations in adolescent group psychotherapy. *International Journal of Group Psychotherapy,* 1961, **2,** 196–203.

Kraft, I. A. An overview of group therapy with adolescents. *International Journal of Group Psychotherapy,* 1968, 4, 461–480.

Lorand, S., and Schneer, H. I. (Eds.). *Adolescents—Psychoanalytic Approach to Problems and Therapy.* New York: Harper-Hoeber, 1961.

MacLennan, B. W. Group approaches to the problems of socially deprived youth: the classic psychotherapeutic model. *International Journal of Group Psychotherapy,* 1968, 4, 481–494.

MacLennan, B. W., and Felsenfeld, N. *Group counseling and psychotherapy with adolescents.* New York: Columbia University Press, 1968.

MacLennan, B. W., and Levy, N. *The group psychotherapy literature,* 1968. *International Journal of Group Psychotherapy,* 1969, **19,** 382–408.

Magary, L., and Elder, V. Group therapy with adolescent girls; two models. In *Dynamic Approaches to Serving Families.* New York: Community Service Society, 1970.

McCormick, C. G., D. Ed.   Objective evaluation of the process and effects of analytic group psychotherapy with adolescent girls. *International Journal of Group Psychotherapy*, 1953, 3, 181–190.

Redl, F.   Diagnostic group work. *American Journal of Orthpsychiatry*, 1944, 14, 53–67.

Scheidlinger, S.   (Chairman) Symposium on the relationship of group psychotherapy to other group modalities in mental health. *International Journal of Group Psychotherapy*, October, 1970.

Scheidlinger, S. et al.   Activity group therapy for children in a family agency. *Social Casework*, 1959, 15, 193–201.

Scheidlinger, S.   Experiential group treatment of severely deprived latency age children. *American Journal of Orthopsychiatry*, 1960, 30, 356–368.

Scheidlinger, S.   Three group approaches with socially deprived latency age children. *International Journal of Group Psychotherapy*, 1965, 15, 434–445.

Schiffer, H.   *The therapeutic play group.* New York: Grune & Stratton, 1969.

Shulman, I.   Modifications in group psychotherapy with antisocial adolescents. *International Journal of Group Psychotherapy*, 1957, 3, 310–317.

Slavson, S. R.   *An introduction to group therapy.* New York: The Commonwealth Fund, 1943.

Slavson, S. R.   *Analytic group psychotherapy.* New York: Columbia University Press, 1950.

Spruiell, V.   Counter-transference and an adolescent group crisis. *International Journal of Group Psychotherapy*, 1967, 3, 298–308.

Torda, Clara.   A therapeutic procedure for adolescents with emotional disorders of functional origin. *Pathways in Child Guidance*, 3–4, Bureau of Child Guidance, Board of Education of New York, 1970.

Whitaker, D. S., and Lieberman, M. A.   *Psychotherapy through the group process.* New York: Atherton Press, 1964.

PART III

DIVERSE APPROACHES

10

HANNA SEGAL

Melanie Klein's Technique of Child Analysis

T he controversy which existed between Anna Freud and Melanie Klein in the beginnings of the techniques for child analysis is probably well known, and by now many issues have become less controversial. Therefore, there would be no point in restating the arguments here. Nevertheless, in order to present the Kleinian technique of child analysis one has to go back to the papers she wrote at that time and to the introduction to *The Psycho-Analysis of Children*. In those papers she describes most clearly the basic principles of her technique, and those principles remain unaltered in their essentials in our procedure today. I want to take up three basic points that Melanie Klein makes in those papers: transference, the analytic situation, and the play technique.

Transference

According to her observations, children, like adults, develop a real transference on the analyst. It had been argued that children could not develop a proper transference because they were still, in reality, attached to and dependent on their real parents. Nevertheless, the transference occurred, and it could be seen that it developed on the basis of the child's projection onto the analyst of internal parental figures. Since the child's object relation already had a long history in which parental figures were both internalized and distorted, it is those figures pertaining to the internal world and to the past which form the basis of the transference. Just as in adult analysis, it is not the current parental figures but the internal ones which are projected onto the analyst. Furthermore, since splitting is an important mechanism, particularly in small children, the child would readily transfer onto the analyst split-off aspects of his parents.

The Analytic Situation

Melanie Klein aimed at establishing with children an analytic situation as strictly as it could be done. Unlike other workers in the field at the time, she found that such an analytic situation could be established and maintained with children however small, if one relied on the interpretative work and kept an analytical attitude uncontaminated by moral, educative or reassuring attitudes. These two aspects of the situation were, according to her, interdependent: one could not observe the transference if one did not establish a proper analytical situation, and a proper analytic situation could not be established if one did not analyze the transference. Reassurance is derived by the child in the course of the analysis, but it results from the analytical situation itself: the child derives a basic and more lasting reassurance from the analyst's uncritical understanding, from his reliability and his capacity to relieve anxiety, than he would from any reassuring attitudes or maneuvers. As with adults, reassurance coming from the analytical process itself proceeds in depth, through real changes in the child's inner world and the nature of his internal objects. The educative process as well is affected by the analysis, through relieving the vicious circle between anxiety and aggression, and through increasing the child's tendency toward introjection and identification with the analyst and the parental objects in their good aspects; the analytical work lessens destructive processes in the mind which interfere with education and learning.

The Play Technique

The specific technique that Melanie Klein introduced for the analysis of children is the play technique. She understood the child's play as a symbolic expression of his conflicts and anxieties and used it as an analytical tool. Since small, or even older, children cannot be asked to free associate, their more natural mode of expression being play, Melanie Klein treated the child's play, as well as his verbal communications, as free associations, and used their symbolic content for purposes of interpretation.

THE PLAY TECHNIQUE SETTING   Since the time she introduced the play technique, the use of toys for child analysis, psychotherapy, treatment in child guidance clinics, etc., has become commonplace. The setting and the toys used, however, vary enormously. It may therefore be worthwhile to describe the kind of room and equipment recommended by Melanie Klein, as this is an essential part of the technique. It is important that every child have his own individual drawer, if there is a chest of drawers in the room, or his own individual box. The toys he uses become very much his own. (This is often not followed in child guidance practice, where the toys are often shared.) In the individual drawer or box the child gets the following kinds of toys: small bricks, fences (possibly), a few small cars and/or trains, one or two balls, a few animals of various sizes, a few human figures, preferably in two sizes, to be used easily as adult and child figures, and small containers. All these toys are small, to make them easy for the child to handle, and as far as possible nondescript so that they do not suggest games. Nonrepresentational materials are also provided, such as paper, pencils, possibly glue and plasticene; if the child is not too small, scissors, and string. The aim of this material is to provide the child with toys which leave maximum scope for his imagination. Apart from the individual toys, it is better if running water is available and some equipment common to all the children, such as rags for cleaning up, soap, etc.

The room should not contain anything easily breakable; electric fires, lights, etc., should be well out of the child's reach. Life is also made easier if the walls are washable and if there is a good floor covering. The room should be so organized that the child is free to express quite a modicum of aggression without danger to himself or actual damage to the surroundings. There should be a table and at least a couple of chairs. A couch is desirable, which the children can use for play but which they may gradually start using to lie down on when they feel like free associating. The analyst himself is an important part of the setting: As I have suggested, the analyst in his therapeutic relation to the child should maintain the proper analytical role; nevertheless, as long as the child is in the consulting room, the analyst, unlike his position vis-à-vis the adult patient, is also an adult in charge of the child, that is, he must take the ordinary adult responsibility in relation to the child's safety. He must be able to stop an action of the child that is dangerous to the child himself as well as putting a brake on any actual aggression in relation to the analyst's person. He may also have to restrain the child from destructive behavior in the room which would lead to lasting damage and prevent the room being used by other patients.

The children are very quick to grasp the difference between the toys in their individual drawer which are for their use only and the room itself and such equipment as belongs to the room, an attack on which is an interference with the analytical setting and the analyst's other child patients. While they are free to do what they please with their own equipment, and what they do with it is an object of interpretation, what they do to the room has quite a different character and sometimes has to be restrained as well as interpreted.

This setting naturally has to be altered somewhat according to the age and the degree of illness in the child. With psychotic children or aggressively psychopathic latency or puberty children, one may, for instance, have to remove sharp or hard toys when they are used primarily as weapons.

THE INTERPRETIVE TECHNIQUE   Basically, however, with the use of the play material and the child's other communications, the analyst aims from the start at establishing contact with the child's unconscious. There is no attempt at "taming" the child or "getting him used to the situation," nor appealing to his good behavior. There is no particular catering to his wishes or interests, like providing him with the particular kind of toys he might be interested in, etc. From the first contact, the analyst tries to understand the child's communication and relies on the fact that his interpretation relieves unconscious anxiety to maintain the child's interest and cooperation.

I can give as an example a first session with a child of 2¾. When I came to collect her from the waiting room she was clinging to her mother, obviously anxious, and refused to follow me into the playroom, the door of which was open so that she could see it from the waiting room. I started interpreting to her in a very general way, suggesting that she was afraid of me because she did not know me; knowing that she suffered from nightmares, I went on to say, after a little while, that she was afraid of this unknown room and unknown person rather in the same way as she might be afraid of the dark and the unknown things happening in the dark. When I said that, she looked at me with evident interest. After a little while she started throwing covert, curious glances at the playroom. I then said that she was also very curious about the unknown things in the room and that maybe during the night she was not only frightened but also curious about what was going on in the dark. At that point she let go of her mother and shyly advanced into the playroom. The mother stayed just outside the door so that the child could still see her. She inspected the room and looked into the drawer with the toys, while I explained to her briefly and simply that as her mother had probably told her before, she would now come to play with me every day except on the weekend; and I indicated that the toys in the drawer were for her to use. She inspected her toys quite contentedly until she discovered a little toy lion among the animals; she immediately showed signs of anxieties and stopped playing. I interpreted to her that she seemed to be afraid of the little lion, as at the beginning she was afraid of me and the room; and was she maybe afraid that I was like a lion and would eat her up. Soon after, she ran out to her mother, showing some signs of anxiety, but mostly becoming very possessive and demanding in relation to her mother (this being one of the things the parents had complained of in her behavior). She insisted on opening her mother's bag, demanded sweets, etc., and her mother was obviously annoyed and irritated.

I interpreted to her that she felt she was now, like the greedy lion, making demands on her mother, and that this made her afraid of her mother being angry and of me being like an angry mother who would be punishing to her, which I thought explained why she was afraid I would be like a lion. She came back to the playroom and started sorting out the animals into families. When the end of the hour came she was reluctant to leave.

Between the first and the second session the mother rang me

to tell me that several times during the day the child asked to be brought back to the playroom. When the time for her session came, however, she clung to her mother, with her back firmly turned toward me. I interpreted to her the resentment at not being allowed to come when she wanted to come and her punishing me now by not wanting to play with me and turning her back on me. After a time she laughed and followed me into the room. She took out a cow, which she said was a "nice milky cow," and a little pig, which she called "nasty piggy." I interpreted to her that after I kept her waiting she was not sure if I was going to be like the nice milky cow or like a nasty piggy, because she had been so angry with me. She looked at me for a long time; then said "you talk very funny, but go on talking." And a little later, while still playing with the animals, when I was silent, she turned to me and repeated "go on talking . . . tell me." I think from that moment the analytic relation was established. She perceived my "funny talk" as a different kind of communication from what she was used to—an analytic language that we were beginning to develop, she and I, and she obviously appreciated it as such.

I think those sessions can also be used to illustrate what I meant by saying that children transfer onto the analyst split-off aspects of parents, internal figures from the past, already a part of the child's internal world. The little girl had a clinging, loving relationship to her actual external mother: she saw in me the lion-mother; that lion-mother was split off from the external idealized mother (probably seen as the nice milky cow). It was also a figure introjected at an earlier stage of the child's development, when the relation to mother, or to the breast as a part-object, was predominantly oral. One could also begin to see how this lion-mother contained the projection of the child's own biting impulses.

There are of course as many beginnings as there are children. Sometimes the first contact will be made with hope and expectation rather than anxiety. A latency boy, for instance (not a case of mine), in his first session drew toys which he liked, and the analyst was able to interpret the child's hopes and expectations of the wonderful things his treatment would give him—in his case it was primarily potency. Only later in the session did anxiety supervene, linked with the thought of the rivalry and jealousy of the other children at the wonderful gifts he would be getting in his session.

Those are the easy beginnings. With more withdrawn children, or with latency children well armed with their latency defenses, one may for a long time have to interpret rigid and defensive attitudes, while always looking for clues to the underlying unconscious anxiety.

With adolescents one has to be particularly careful to be able to establish contact with their infantile anxieties, without offending the susceptibilities of their young-man or young-woman image of themselves, so touchy in adolescence.

Here is an example of a session which I thought was well-handled by a candidate in training. The patient was a foreign boy of fifteen who had had some psychotherapy in his own country. He was brought to his first session by his mother: she started explaining to the analyst that as the boy had a partial organic deafness he might not hear the buzzer opening the door. (This in spite of the fact that in the original consultation with the analyst his deafness had of course been discussed.) She went on to say that he had a cold, and would the analyst phone for a taxi to collect him at the end of the session. Then, as if afraid that she was making her son appear less clever than he was, she added that on other days it would not be necessary as he was most expert about finding his way about. The analyst made a noncommittal answer, saying that all this no doubt would be discussed with the boy in his sessions.

When they went into the room the boy said, rather defensively, that in fact he heard the buzzer very well, but did not push the door because he was interested in watching some cars in the street. He then started inspecting the analyst's room, comparing it with the room of his psychotherapist in his own country, and saying with some relief that he could not see any toys like the ones he had had during his childhood psychotherapy.

At that point, the analyst interpreted that he was wondering how she would compare with his previous psychotherapist, and particularly whether she would try to make him feel small and childish, the way he felt maybe his mother made him feel small when she was so protective of him at the beginning of the session. The boy relaxed visibly, sat down, and said that he thought maybe it would be best if he told her about his interests. He went on talking for a time about his interest in football, how good he was at table tennis, etc. He was interested in which team his analyst would support in a forthcoming football match between his country and Great Britain. Throughout this, the analyst made only a few comments, among them about his anxiety ("whose side would she be on?"). Then gradually he started talking about his country, its warmth and beauty compared with England, his family left behind, and his friends. She was able to interpret to him his longing for his own home and country and his anxieties about separation, relating it also to separations in the past. (The boy's father being a diplomat, the child had been subjected to a great deal of changes of country and environment).

He moved on to talking about his sister, who was left behind, being pregnant, and how much he looked forward to having a nephew. When the analyst asked him why he was so sure it would be a nephew, not a niece, he said he was sure of it, and only a nephew would do, as he could then teach him things like football, etc. As he went on talking about his nephew, it became clear that he was shifting between seeing himself as the father of the child and identifying with him: "only a nephew would do" because the new baby was to be himself. After a time he started drawing a star, saying he wanted to make a beautiful star—a five-pointed star (he was to have five sessions a week), but he was afraid that from her side it looked messy and absolutely terrible. As this followed on the material about the very idealized baby nephew, the analyst interpreted that he wanted to be her star baby, like the little baby still inside mother—his nephew—and how afraid he was that she would see him quite differently, as quite terrible and messy. He then started looking around the room and asking her if she had many other children patients, and were they older or younger. She interpreted to him his curiosity about her other babies and his jealousy of them. He then resumed his talk about football, and she interpreted to him how the part of him that wanted to be the baby star inside her was felt by him as a great threat to the part of him that wanted to be the big boy playing football and very masculine.

This I thought was a good handling of the session; the analyst was able to see the conflict in the adolescent between his masculine genital position and his infantile self longing to be the "star baby," and the anxieties ("it will look terrible to you") belonging to this infantile position.

The problem of communication with children of various ages presents, of course, difficulties slightly different from problems in the psychoanalysis of adults. The small child communicates primarily by movement and play. The latency child can alternate between communication through speech, and sometimes true free association, and communication through play and behavior. The adolescent is capable of free association, but more prone than the average adult to express himself by behavior, acting in and acting out. It is the task of the analyst to accept all these modes of communication, and whenever possible communicate back to the child by his interpretations.

Unlike the analyst of adults, however, the analyst of the child, particularly of a small child, must up to a point also cooperate in the child's play. He must occasionally perform services which the child cannot do himself, such as sharpening a broken pencil, tying a knot, etc., and must, up to a point, participate in the child's game when the game necessitates two partners. This is particularly important when the child wants to express something by personification, and expects the analyst to take on a role. To what extent the analyst should participate in the child's play is an extremely knotty technical problem and one requiring a lot of experience to gauge accurately. The main principle should be that the analyst should participate as little as possible in action and cooperate only to the extent to which his cooperation is necessary for the child to express himself or herself fully. From the viewpoint of the analyst, the child's play is a communication that has to be understood and interpreted, and all his actions should be directed only at furthering this communication. To give a typical example, a little girl of six wants to play at being teacher and wants the analyst to be the child. As the child, the analyst is to be stupid and ignorant, and the little patient playing the teacher is relentlessly mocking and attacking, humiliating her and punishing her. The analyst accepts this role, though being very careful not to introduce anything of her own into the play, and accepting only to act exactly on the child's instructions. Once a game is in progress the analyst starts interpreting how the little girl got rid of the unbearable feeling of being an ignorant and stupid child into the analyst and how she identified with adults experienced as cruel and mocking. (It is interesting to note that that particular little girl went to a liberal and progressive school and that she was never punished at home. The cruel punishments seemed to be of her own invention.) As is frequent in this kind of situation, the child resisted the interpretation, screaming and shouting the analyst down. It could be interpreted to her how she needed to put herself in the role of the teacher because she felt it so unbearable to be little and not to know, but also how in doing that she stopped herself from learning (this being one of her important symptoms). After a time, the child changed the game, making the analyst be the teacher, while she as a child secretly mocked her and attacked her, the second game coming closer to her real feelings of inferiority and anger. In this game the analyst's interpretations did effectively deal with the child's projective identification and the game changed, with the child giving up the reversal.

Often, however, particularly with latency children, the child will insist on going on with the game because of the gratification derived from the position of control and from sadistic attacks. The game becomes not a communication but a repetitive "acting-in." In such situations the analyst may have to stop acting the role that the child demands and confine himself to interpretations—often directed at the child's rage and distress when he finds out that he cannot control his object. Repetition-compulsion is what the patient aims at; this may express itself in the repetitive play. The analyst's task is to modify the repetition-compulsion by understanding. This of course is as in the analysis of adults, but since the analyst of adults uses only verbal interpretation, he is less likely to be a partner in the repetition-compulsion. Here, the task of the child's analyst is technically more difficult because he must participate in the child's game to understand what the child's pattern is, but by doing so risks becoming a partner and colluding in the repetition-compulsion. We always have to watch the patient's response not only to our interpretations, but also to our behavior. A cough, a squeaking of the chair—all actions are experienced by the patient as a communication. The analyst of the child has to be active to a far greater extent and must therefore watch the child's response very carefully. The apparently most innocent actions become imbued with meaning. For instance, a small child breaks a pencil in drawing and asks the analyst to sharpen it. Soon it happens again. And again. A look of sly triumph begins to appear on the child's face. What has started as a reality-situation, i.e., the pencil must be sharpened if the child is to draw, becomes a situation of gratification in terms of getting control over the analyst, getting an endless supply of goods, castration of the analyst, etc. Any situation in which the analyst participates can be easily used for purposes of repetition-compulsion and/or direct gratification of instincts.

Often the question is raised: how much can little children really follow and understand verbal interpretations, particularly complex ones? It has invariably been my experience, both in analyses and in supervisions, that provided the interpretations are put in simple language, and provided they are correct and close to the child's experience, the child can follow the interpretations, on the whole more easily than a sophisticated adult, who tends to mobilize intellectual defenses much more readily.

As illustrating this point, I remember particularly well a session with the little girl whose first session I reported above, when she was just under four. I was then having supervision on this child with Melanie Klein and, being in a hurry to present some rather difficult sessions at the end of the week, I wanted to summarize for her very briefly the sessions at the beginning of the week. I said that on Monday it seemed the little girl was preoccupied with a fantasy of my pregnancy over the weekend, and then, taking a deep breath, I said "And I interpreted to her that an introjection done under a preponderance of envious greed leads to the fragmentation of the internal object, fragmentation of self, internal persecution, confusion, a loss of identity, and particularly sexual identity." I saw then that Melanie Klein looked at me with a really shocked expression, and she said, very quietly, "I think I would rather like to see this session: I do not quite see how you interpreted all that to a child under four." I then told her the session in detail and she agreed with the line of interpretation.

The little girl came into the room. She looked at my abdomen and said "You've got fatter over the weekend." She then showed me a little purse, of which she was obviously very proud. She then went to the drawer and pulled out a brown paper bag, which the previous week she had filled up with little toys. She looked at the bag and said, with real fury, "Your purses are always bigger than my purses." I interpreted then that she thought my tummy was always bigger than her tummy and she thought mine was full of babies, like the paper bag, and that was why it was so fat. She then filled the basin with water, tore the paper bag into shreds, and put the torn bag and all the animals into the basin. She also put her own purse there, saying, "Anyway, they're not *your* toys —they're *my* toys." She started swirling the water around angrily and putting in bits of soap, making the water cloudy. As in the past, putting things into this water basin often represented introjection, and as she accompanied it by saying "They're my toys," I interpreted to her that she wanted to take my tummy and my babies inside her tummy to make it into her babies—but she was so angry that it was mine to begin with, that in taking it in she tore it all into pieces. Then she looked at me less angrily and said that on Sunday she had had a nasty tummy ache. I related the nasty tummy ache to her having fantasied that she had torn off bits of my tummy and babies inside her, and the bits were angry and making her hurt. Then she looked at the basin and said, "Oh, what a muddle" (feeling muddled is something she occasionally insightfully complained of). I interpreted to her that she put the bits of soap in to make the water cloudy because she did not want to know which bits inside her were hers and which she thought she had stolen from me; and then she felt muddled inside about what was her and what was me, and that she felt this muddle both as a tummy ache in her tummy and as a muddle in her thoughts, not knowing which thoughts were hers and which came from me. She then started looking for her purse in the water and became very anxious and angry when she could not readily find it "in the muddle." I then interpreted that when she so much wanted to have my insides inside her and all muddled up with her and was also so angrily tearing them into bits, then she became very frightened that she could not properly feel her own body. She went on looking in the basin with one hand and with the other she started looking between her legs for her genital. I said that this feeling of not being able to find her own things made her feel sometimes that she could not find her own "baby-hole" because in her mind she felt it was so muddled up with mine. After this interpretation she readily found the purse, took it out of the water, and showed great relief.

At no time in the session did I have the feeling that my interpretations were too complicated for her or that she could not follow them. And though she verbalized little in this session, in the next she spoke quite freely of her anxieties that either I or her mother would go on producing new babies and of her envy and wish to be a "mummy full of babies" herself.

One can well see, however, that in summarizing one's interpretation one may sound as though one were talking a language which would be complete gibberish to the child.

The problem of language can sometimes present difficulties with adolescents who are using an "in" language. The problem arises, how far should the analyst use the patient's own language and how far should he respond in his own, "common usage" language. One has to steer between the Scylla of using the adolescent's language with an unconscious implication of "I-am-one-of-you" and a collusion against the adult world, and the Charybdis of rejecting the adolescent's mode of communication and being experienced as a rigid and un-understanding superego figure. I have always used the patient's own language—"groovy" or "high" or whatever the current "in" word is, when referring to what the patient has said himself. When interpreting, however, I use the current ordinary English. The patient's language itself should also become an object of analysis. Often those slang words, consciously meant to describe vague and undefined feelings, such as "groovy," when analyzed yield rich unconscious fantasy content. If one can analyze the patient's language itself, one can make him experience that one does indeed understand his language and does not reject it, but that one is not oneself involved and identified with the patient's unconscious processes as expressed by his language.

A particular problem present in child analysis is the relation to the parents. When we analyze the adult, as changes occur in his internal world the patient himself can materially affect his external circumstances. Not so with the child: the child's external environment is largely determined by his parents. Sometimes, as the child's treatment progresses, vicious circles in the interaction between the child and parent are resolved, and the parents may respond to the child's improvement by a better relationship to him. Often, however, the environment whose pressure contributed to the child's illness continues exercising some pressure and, as is well known, sometimes the parents even react adversely to the child's improvement if the child's illness was necessary to the family. We can enable the child to deal better with his environment by strengthening his good internal figures and his ego, but we cannot alter the environment itself. It is always a great temptation to the analyst to try to influence or educate the parents. It has, however, been an almost unvariable experience that this does not lead to favorable results and is liable to interfere with the psychoanalytic relation between the patient and the analyst. If the parents seek help and advice, it is always best to find suitable help for them from a person other than the child's analyst.

Whether, and how often, one has contact with parents I have found varies with the individuality of the analyst and the needs of the parents. I do not think that in all my experience of analysis and supervision there have been two situations in which I would deal with the parents in the same way.

Often the question is raised, What is the aim of child analysis, and in what way does it differ from the analysis of an adult? Nowadays, when psychoanalytical findings have become the basis of many psychotherapeutic techniques, one has to be particularly clear about the nature of the psychoanalytic process and the aim of psychoanalysis in the treatment of a child. I think that essentially the aim of psychoanalysis is the same whatever the age of the patient: it is always to get the patient in touch with his psychic realities. The analysis of defenses and of object relations in fantasy and reality should help him to differentiate between external and internal realities, and to foster the process of psychic growth.

REFERENCES

Klein, M. *Psychoanalysis of children.* London: Hogarth Press, 1932.

Klein, M. Infant analysis. *International Journal of Psycho-Analysis,* 1926, 7, 31–63.

Klein, M. Personification in the play of children. *International Journal of Psycho-Analysis,* 1929, 10, 193–204.

Klein, M. The importance of symbol-formation in the development of the ego. *International Journal of Psycho-Analysis,* 1930, 11, 24–39.

Klein, M. *Narrative of a child analysis: The conduct of psycho-analysis of children as seen in the treatment of a ten-year old boy.* London: Hogarth Press, 1961.

Meltzer, D. *The Psychoanalytic process.* London: Heineman Medical Books, 1967.

11

RUDOLF DREIKURS

The Individual Psychological Approach

Every therapeutic or corrective approach is based on a certain premise about the nature of man. Consequently, the model of man which one has chosen as the theoretical basis will determine the therapeutic procedure. However, various approaches may have certain aspects in common despite a theoretical divergence; and, conversely, therapists who share the same or similar assumptions may differ in their practice. To illustrate this point, we may compare theoretical and practical approaches as they appear in divergence or similarity to our Adlerian position. The model of man which Adler has developed and which we accept as our own frame of reference is relatively close to the concepts of Carl Rogers; but our practical procedures differ sharply. On the other hand, many of our therapeutic procedures are similar to those used by behavioral therapists; but our theoretical assumptions are at variance. To stress this point even further, most Adlerians accept the theoretical foundations of Individual Psychology, and yet everyone uses slightly different approaches.

As a consequence, when we present the Adlerian approach, it has to be kept in mind that we can only present what we are doing. It was Adler's constant admonition that we should not try to mimic what he was doing with his patients; each one of us has to develop his individual approach; and yet, we all can be identified as Adlerians.

Another qualifying statement is in order. Not only do I consider my approach as not being "psychoanalytic"; what is even more serious, I have reservations about the term child psychoanalysis, or even child psychiatry. While I do not agree completely with Szasz (1961), who rejects the concept of mental illness, I am convinced that the majority of children seen by child psychiatrists are not really sick and are, therefore, not in need of either therapy or analysis. They need education, guidance, but not what one generally understands as psychotherapy. This opposition to the medical aspect of disturbances is presently greatly supported by a general tendency to use ancillary personnel in dealing with the problems of children, such as occupational and music therapists, psychologists, counselors, play therapists, etc., and in many cases without involving either psychiatrists or analysts. According to our experience the professional group which can and should exert the greatest corrective effectiveness is none of the above mentioned professional groups. They are the teachers. Teachers who know how to influence children—which presently only very few are trained to do—can undo much of the harm done to the child by his family and by the community. And the involvement of parents, which is essential for any corrective attempts with young children, can be accomplished without professional help. They, like many groups of disturbed people, such as alcoholics and drug addicts, can help each other often more effectively than by receiving personal therapy.

In this sense, the Adlerian approach in therapy has its own characteristic elements (Dreikurs, 1956). However, while there is some overlapping between the approaches used by Individual Psychologists and those of other schools, in regard to the "treatment" or, better, education of children, our approach seems to be rather unique and in its fundamental aspects different from any other.

One has the impression that the present tendency of prolonged therapy is not sufficiently effective and constitutes an unnecessary expenditure of time and money. Before long, it will probably be replaced by far less time-consuming but much more effective methods to bring about change and improvement (Shlien, Mosak, and Dreikurs, 1962). As far as children are concerned, this change in therapeutic procedures is already taking place. While no method and approach can claim 100 percent effectiveness, it is our experience that even very serious problems of children can be dramatically resolved. This occurrence is so frequent that one can assume that more improved techniques will bring about reorientation and adjustment relatively quickly. This statement is prone to evolve considerable doubts for as far as children are concerned, our whole generation of adults is affected by a deep sense of pessimism. This therapeutic pessimism, becoming increasingly pronounced with the rising frequency and seriousness of disfunction and misbehavior of children, seems to be the inevitable result of the prevalent confusion and ignorance about how to influence children. The most pathetic example of this pessimism is presented by a mother who comes to get help with her child. Being advised how to cope with the problem, she comes to the next session with an expression of utter surprises: "It really worked!" Whoever heard about anything that can really influence the child? And, unfortunately, this doubt and pessimism is shared by many highly qualified professionals; they cannot imagine that simple procedures can really achieve deep and lasting results.

THERAPEUTIC OPTIMISM

The therapeutic optimism of the Adlerians is proverbial. Adler stated very clearly his opinion, based on his considerable practical experience. According to him every criminal can be rehabilitated if one can win his confidence. "I am convinced that we could change every single criminal" (Adler, 1931). "We can do absolutely nothing unless we succeed in winning him for cooperation . . . everything is secured if we can win the interest of the criminal for human welfare, for other human beings; if we can train him for cooperation and set him on the way toward solving the problems of life by cooperative means" (Adler, 1935). The many cases where even inveterate criminals were rehabilitated prove that it can be done.

Similarly, we are no longer impressed with the often apparent hopelessness of psychotics. We are beginning to "understand" them. The psychotic appears to be irrational only to those who do not understand his private logic. "Meaningful therapeutic inter- change begins when the patient is able to receive from the therapist a message that shows understanding. . . . When the therapist understands the patient's private world well enough to formulate a meaningful statement in return, a useful interchange has taken place" (Shulman, 1968).

So much for the most "pathological" and therapeutically difficult cases of adults who are already deeply entrenched in their position. The belief in the possibility to reach patients is even more appro- priate when we are dealing with children. Adler stated bluntly that no child should be considered hopeless (Adler, 1931). This opti- mistic therapeutic outlook is in stark contrast to the pessimism, or at least doubt, found in most professional circles. What is the basis for our optimism?

Here the significance of our theoretical orientation becomes clear. Certain basic premises are difficult to understand and to accept by those who do not share our frame of reference. Although we witness a certain tendency toward similar concepts, particularly since the new developments in theoretical physics have changed the basic epistemological premises in science, the general accept- ance of these principles still seems to be far off. What are they?

There is first the recognition of man as a decision-making organ- ism. In his first book, *Study of Organ Inferiority and Its Physical Compensation* (Adler, 1907; 1917) Adler realized that the effect of organ inferiorities depends on the response of the child. When he experiences a physical weakness, he will either be discouraged and develop a lasting weakness, or he will over-compensate and develop a special skill in the area where he had encountered diffi- culty of function. But what makes one child give up and the other over-compensate? At this point Adler recognized the creative power of the individual. Nothing "makes" a child decide what he will do— it is his own conclusion, long before he can have any conscious awareness of what he is deciding. Similarly, the influence of the environment depends on the child's perception of it. In this light, the child is not the victim of forces to which he is exposed; it is less important with what a child is born than what he does with it afterwards.

TELEO-ANALYTIC APPROACH

This realization of man's ability to decide what to do is a crucial aspect of Adlerian theory and practice. Heretofore, man has been considered a victim of forces from within and from without converging on him. Now a new concept emerges of man as the master of his fate. This "discovery" of man's power, heretofore hardly recognized, is of similar importance for the history of mankind as is the discovery of the tremendous power within the atom, which had been regarded as a negligible entity. Nuclear energy and human energy are the two pillars on which a new society will be based. While man's personality was assumed to be formed by hereditary and environmental factors, we realize now that he is not merely responding to stimulation but selects the stimulation to which he decides to respond (Ferguson, 1968).

For this reason, our understanding of all patients and our therapeutic effort is concerned with the here and now, since the individual has the power to change at any moment. The past merely serves to understand the direction and attitude which the person has chosen. All his actions are based on cognitive processes, ideas, and goals. This is the second basic assumption on which we operate. Behavior is purposive. The American Pragmatists long ago realized that the significance of behavior lies in its consequences. All assumptions of causes are speculative. We have no scientific tools to validate any personality theory. Some believe in the significance of heredity, others in environment, most in a peculiar mixture of both sets of forces which "form" the individual's personality; some consider instincts and the psychosexual development as determinant factors, others, particular traumatic events, etc. It seems that personality theories depend less on scientific research than on political and cultural factors. In an autocratic society one had to assume that personality was determined at the moment of conception. This assumption was necessary to justify the importance of birth, being born high or low, in a particular class or caste. Scientists afterwards provided the "proof" for such assumptions, particularly through the study of identical twins. As society became democratic, the emphasis shifted to environment. As the German psychiatrist Lange supported Hitler's concept of racial superiority, so the American Watson and the Russian Bechterev used Pavlov's conditioned reflex to support the influence of environment. Freud's concept of man expressed the rebellion of rugged individualism, claiming the repression of instincts by a hostile society is responsible for maladjustment. Adler's model of man seems to fit into the needs of a democratic society when he regards man as a social being who tries to find his own place in society, who is free to decide, but must learn to use his freedom with responsibility, for the common good of all.

The teleo-analytic approach deals with the goals of man and with the correction of mistaken goals which are responsible for social maladjustment. Clinically, it may be difficult to distinguish normal and abnormal behavior. In a sense, every behavior, regardless of how deviant it may be, appears logical and "normal" from the point of view of the patient. Even the delusions and hallucinations of the psychotic are far less "abnormal" than we think. The content and the process of psychotic thinking are exactly the same as the normal person experiences in his dreams, i.e., the uninhibited expression of his private logic. What distinguishes the psychotic from the sane is that he "dreams with open eyes," so to speak. Actually, deprivation of dreams often leads to a psychotic-like condition where the person, who is deprived of the dreams during his sleep, compensates with "dreaming" while awake.

NORMAL—ABNORMAL

The distinction between what is abnormal and what not is usually made on the basis of symptomatology. Anyone who has symptoms which prevent him from functioning adequately can be considered as clinically abnormal. But then we find that many maladjusted people share the same abnormal condition with other members of their society. Sociologists are inclined to consider society as the last instance to set normative values governing behavior. Whoever conforms to these standards can be considered as normal, while everyone who negates them is deviant. In this sense, anomy, the lack of social standards, may produce behavior which may be considered as socially acceptable although it is not in line with outwardly accepted values (Merton, 1957). Thus, it becomes normal for people to behave in an abnormal way. Therapy, then, means correction of faulty social values which are generally accepted (Dreikurs, 1957).

This holds particularly true for our whole generation of children. They are at war with adult society, subtely or openly, at home, in school, and in the community. As a consequence, we have a high degree of behavior problems in almost all families; they often begin every morning with a fight. Kvaraceous (1959) recognizes a "continuum of norm-violating behavior of our children." On the one end of the continuum are the children who do not want to get up in the morning or go to bed in the evening, who eat too much or too little, fight with their brothers or sisters, refuse to do chores or their homework, etc., etc.—in other words, the average American child; and on the other end of the continuum are the juvenile delinquents. There is no qualitative difference between them, only a quantative difference, i.e., the degree of open rebellion. Kvaraceous did not recognize that this general defiance is an expression of a war between adults and children; he attributes it to the penetration of low class social morals into middle and upper class society.

We can see that the present formulation of what is adequate human behavior and what constitutes mental health does not help to distinguish what is normal and what is abnormal. For example, is conformity desirable, both for mental health and for social adjustment, or not? It can bring about useful contributions; but it also can be a deterrent to improvement and a means of covering up a sense of inadequacy. Adler proposed a basis for evaluating normality and mental health. It is "social interest," a poor translation of the German term *Gemeinschaftsgefuel.* Only where one truly feels belonging as an equal can one be sure of one's place and utilize one's tremendous inner resources. Social interest thus is the basis of normality. Only where a person feels belonging will he find effective means of coping with people and life problems (Dreikurs, 1969). We are born with the capacity to develop it. It is not a static quantity. If we are successful, we enlarge the radius of our social interest; when we feel defeated or discouraged, we restrict it. The psychotic has none. Social improvement of the psychotic means establishing a small area of being understood. "Social interest is a normative ideal, a direction giving goal. . . . Everything we call a mistake shows the want of social feeling" (Adler, 1938).

Social interest is for Adler the criterion for normality. It is the basis for overcoming difficulties, for concern with the welfare of others, and for a task-oriented attitude. "Social interest is the barometer of the child's normality. The criteria which needs to be watched by the psychologist and by the parent is the degree of social interest which the child or the individual manifests. As long as the feeling of inferiority is not too great, a child will always try to be worthwhile, and on the useful side of life. It is almost impossible to exaggerate the value of an increase of social feeling. The mind improves, the feeling of worth and value is heightened, giving courage and an optimistic view" (Adler, 1938).

THE CULTURAL DILEMMA

Here we are confronted with a cultural dilemma, which has to be recognized when the problems of therapy and guidance are considered. The majority of our children are deficient in one or another way, academically, socially, or mentally. This is a consequence of our ways of raising children, or rather, our inability to raise them properly. We almost systematically deprive our children of the feeling that they belong, that they are worthwhile as they are (Dreikurs, 1968). Our methods of raising children present them with a sequence of discouraging experiences. Consequently, children refuse to act as they know they should. This general rebellion of children leads them to a distorted view of how they can belong. The degree of discouragement, of fright and hostility, of a lack of belonging, is responsible for the seriousness of disturbing behavior.

This similarity of all misbehaving or deficient children is matched by another even more dangerous cultural factor. Our parents do not know how to raise children—they are no match for them. Few realize the enormity of this cultural predicament. There was never any living being on this earth who did not know what to do with its young—except our parents. The reason for this dilemma is the lack of tradition. Raising children was always based on tradition. One generation learned what to do with children from its preceding generation. Margaret Mead (1949), in her study of the South Sea Islands, observed the difference of raising children in various primitive societies. These differences brought about different personality types, characteristic for each tribe. One can be reasonably sure that in each, the children were raised in the same way for hundreds of generations, and every adult and every child knew what to expect from the other.

The dilemma of our parents is due to the fact that the traditional methods of raising children, effective and necessary in an autocratic society, became futile. The pressure from without, particularly through punishment, is insufficient to promote cooperation and adjustment. But most parents and teachers are not aware of the fact that punishment no longer produces the desired effect. The only children who respond well to punishment are those who don't need it, whose cooperation one could secure without punitive retaliation. There are those who remember for the rest of their lives the one time they were punished. The rest of the children shrug it off, as part of the spoils of war. One can—and usually has to— repeat punishment which, at best, brings only temporary results. What is worse, a child who is punished will, out of his own sense of equality, respond in a characteristic way. "If you have the right to punish me, then I have the same right to punish you, too." Acts of mutual retaliation fill our homes and our classrooms. The old fashioned methods of pressure from without will have to be replaced with stimulation from within. Some parents and some teachers know that; it is their sense of empathy which enables them to understand the child and to motivate him. However, the vast majority of adults do not know it and will have to learn the methods which are effective in a democratic setting.

Since most parents suffer from the same predicament, their reaction to any deficiency or misbehavior of their children is usually the same. No two mothers are alike in education, background and personality; but they all behave in the same way. They either fight or give in, in any conflict situation, which precludes a satisfactory solution of the conflict. All mothers do the same in the moment of a conflict—they talk. They simply do not know that in a conflict talking is the worst thing to do. Words become weapons and nobody listens. Before one talks with a child, one should make sure that he wants to listen—which eliminates a great part of all the talk within the family. Most mothers have an extreme sense of responsibility which frustrates them since they do not know how to discharge it. It is the idea of what a good mother should be, enhanced by professional advice about the needs of children, which makes them the victims of the manipulation of their children, and hinders them from giving up their idea of "control," which they no longer have over the behavior of their children. The greatest obstacle in helping parents is their idea of their own responsibility which prevents them from sharing the responsibility with their children, a prerequisite in a democratic setting.

These considerations of the general situation, and of the precarious relationship between parents and children, are essential if one wants to understand the problem of the disturbed child. As we said before, there is only a quantitative difference of antagonism which distinguishes the "good" child from the "bad." Even the good child rebels, makes demands and challenges the authority of adults, and, therefore, operates on the same level as the most disturbed and "sick" children. The same principles apply to the minor and the major disturbances. Without understanding the child's private logic, the goals which he has set himself for coping with adults, one is in no position to really help the child in his process of readjustment.

PARSIMONIOUS EXPLANATION

At this point one has to mention the tragic role which counselors and therapists play. Due to their lack of effective ways in stimulating children, they raise objections to our approach. First of all, we are accused of over-simplification. They say that we do not realize the complexity of the problems which does not permit a simple answer or solution. It is our experience that things appear complex only if one does not understand them. The basic rules are always simple. When Newton discovered the first general principle in physics, he found out that all the complex movements and relationships between stars and all the movements on earth depend on one simple principle of gravity: on mass and distance. And suddenly, order came into the universe and the movements of the stars became predictable.

This is the first reason why we cannot accept the assumption of complexity emphasized by everyone, with the result of an inevitable pessimism. The objections to our presumed superficiality are slowly diminishing since the rediscovery of the old law of parsimony. If there are several explanations of observable events, the one which is more simple has a greater probability of being correct. We are witnessing today a proliferation of assumed "causes" for the difficult child, the slow learner, the "sick" child, etc. We cannot accept the explanation that a disturbing or disturbed child is "emotionally sick." We find nothing wrong with the emotions of such children, only with their intentions. The emotions always support the intentions of a person. If he is for someone, he develops conjunctive emotions; and if he is against someone, his emotions are disjunctive (Adler, 1927). The emotions are like the gas which drives a car; it is the driver who uses the gas in line with his intention to move.

We find today an abundance of theories to explain the problems of children. So-called "scientific research" provided and still does provide a variety of reasons to explain the inability of our teachers to teach children how to read and write. There was first the low

I.Q., an assumed indication of the child's intellectual ability. Then came the slow development of boys, the danger of early toilet training which was supposedly responsible for maladjustment. Recently, we are confronted with a host of organic explanations for learning difficulties. There is the minimal brain damage, the cerebral disfunction, the perceptual disadvantage, the inadequate physical development with all its variations, dyslexia and now, cultural deprivation. It is a safe assumption that all of these "proven" handicaps will disappear before long when parents, teachers, counselors, and therapists will demonstrate their ability to rehabilitate the child.

It is evident from what has been said so far that we consider some basic steps necessary in correction and therapy of children. While the symptomotology may vary with each child, the basic problems are the same for all. We find in children the same type of disturbance as in adults, from slight disregard of order to neurotic malfunction, the behavioral problems, juvenile delinquency, and psychoses. In all of them, we find a lack of social interest, a faulty life style, discouragement and/or withdrawal. "If we can shed light on the fundamental structure of all psychiatric disorders, if we can come to understand psychoses and psychopathic personalities as well as we understand neuroses, much confusion will be avoided in our own thinking and in the field of psychiatry as a whole" (Dreikurs, 1945).

All conflicts with a child are social conflicts, resulting from a disturbance or strain in the social relationship between adults and children, impairment of his integration in the community, and obstruction of his participation and social function. Our inability to deal effectively with the conflicts created by children is the result of our inability to solve conflicts in a democratic transaction. Conflicts will always exist when people live together, conflicts of opinions and interests. In the past autocratic order they were resolved through a contest: the stronger decided the outcome of the conflict, and the weaker had to accept his terms. Today, this is no longer possible. All victories—if they occur at all—are short-lived. Neither fighting nor giving in will resolve any conflict. If one fights, one creates rebellion, and if one gives in, one creates anarchy. Our parents and teachers will have to acquaint themselves with effective means of solving their conflicts with children. When they learn this, there will be relatively little need for individual therapy and counseling. Let us give a few examples.

EDUCATIONAL APPROACH

The Viennese Adlerian teachers established an Individual Psychological Experimental School in 1931 in the worst slum district of the city of Vienna. Its educational success brought experts from all over Europe to visit it. It ended with Austrian fascism and started again in 1946, with twenty-nine classes with about 1100 children. It was again in one of the worst districts. Seventy-six percent of the students shared their flat with 2 to 11 persons, 30 percent had no father, and 28 percent of the mothers worked. It was a typical "culturally deprived" environment. And, yet, the school soon was recognized in its success with difficult children. There were no truancies and no failures. During the school year 1952–1953, children from the whole city of Vienna were transferred to the school, "because they did not fit in any school, were aggressive and a danger to their comrades; most were neglected children and some were mentally damaged. There were some legasthenics, post-meningistics, pseudodebiles and depressive neurotic personalities. Some had been stealing, some had been sexually abused, some had been caught by police as vagabonds. Of the 63 children with clinical records whom the police or social workers sent to our school, 60 could be kept and restored to normality. Three had to be turned away because they endangered other children, and were sent to "special institutions" (Spiel, 1956). The details of how the Experimental School could achieve these successes can be found in Oskar Spiel's book, *Discipline Without Punishment* (1962).

Grunwald (1966) gives an example of a boy who was both a behavior and learning problem. His teacher reported that he was an emotionally disturbed child who had been expelled from kindergarten, a parochial school, and a military school. He had been seen by a psychiatrist for a year with no improvement, and it was felt that he would have to be placed in a special class for emotionally disturbed children. The boy insisted that he wanted to be "the biggest, the scariest monster that ever lived, . . . more famous than Frankenstein." He taught himself to walk and talk like a monster, and spent all his money on "monster pictures, masks and other monster paraphernalia." At times he would dress up like a monster and jump at children from behind a door. Sometimes in his efforts to frighten them he would scratch them, and several parents threatened to take action.

One day, as this child was telling the class of one of his monster experiences, another boy got up and told the class how tired and bored he had become of these monster stories. I asked the children of a show of hands who of them felt as bored as he was. All hands went up. A few days later, I noticed that the monster pictures and stories which the little "monster" had always pinned on the bulletin board were gone. One day he announced to the class that he had burned all his monster pictures as well as all the monster things. This was the end of the problem.

The enthusiasm of the class is something that I will never forget. They almost carried this boy on their shoulders. He had never received so much attention nor appreciation from anyone as he had when he changed his behavior. This just shows how we can make so very wrong interpretations; we could have marked this child for life. (Grunwald, 1966)

Here we have the two cardinal features for the teacher's ability to influence even very disturbed children in a class. One feature she described—the influence of the group. It is a fact that a teacher is a group leader, which permits her to change the attitudes and values of children. The second point she did not mention. It was her unwillingness to respond to the child's provocation, the quietness which she maintained and which made his destructive approaches useless. He obviously wanted special attention which she refused to give him, and she did not let herself be drawn into a power conflict with this most provocative boy.

From our point of view, dealing effectively with the disturbed child requires work with the family, the school, the social agencies and, of course, with the child. These optimal conditions do not always exist. While they are desirable, they are by no means necessary, in contrast to widely held opinions where one party in the case refuses to take on responsibility if the others do not cooperate. Any one person can exert a beneficial influence, if he understands the child and helps him to change his concepts and motivation. By and large, the cooperation of the family, especially the mother, is most desirable because a change in her attitude and behavior almost with certainty brings about a change in her child's behavior. This is the reason why Adler and his co-workers began to work with the whole family as far back as the beginning of the twenties (Adler, 1963). While we maintain that anyone who understands the child can help him, the question arises as to who has the best chance to exert a corrective influence, the mother, the teacher, the counselor, analyst, the priest or social worker? In our experience the teacher has the best chance to effect a change in the child because she can utilize the group. In our present society with its diminishing authority of adults, the peer group is one of the strongest influences to which the child is exposed, not passively, but by choice. Each child chooses his reference group with which he identifies himself. And most disturbances in children are group phenomena. The slow learner, the under-achiever, the rebel, the criminal, and the drug addict, they all are part of a group process; and, therefore, individual therapy and counseling is the least effective approach. This holds true also for the isolate and even the psychotic whose isolation is part of his specific role in his group. For this reason, group therapy and music therapy are methods of choice in dealing with severely disturbed children.

Our corrective or therapeutic approach is the same regardless of the kind of problem the child may have. Some Adlerians have a more structured approach than others. We have developed a very definite procedure, partly because it permits a more dramatic and, therefore, effective impact, and partly for didactic purposes. In this way, the student has a very definite plan of action.

FOUR PHASES IN THERAPY

As in all forms of depth therapy, one can distinguish phases which overlap and yet require the recognition of specific dynamics. The first phase is the establishment of a proper relationship. The second is the exploration of the nature of the problem, its analysis. The third is confrontation, providing insight, and the fourth is reorientation. While this scheme can be observed in many forms of uncovering therapy, each school has its own explanation for its procedure and its success. The Adlerian approach gives each step a definite and characteristic significance.

Phase 1   Establishing of a Therapeutic Relationship

From our point of view, this requires more than warmth, interest, friendliness, important as they are. Since we are teleo-analytic oriented, the crucial factor in a relationship is the ability to bring the goals of the therapist and of the client in line. Wherever and whenever the goals of the therapist and of the client clash, we observe the phenomenon of "resistance." Many therapists who do not recognize their own role in the conflict with the client blame him for his resistance, which actually is only a breakdown in an agreement about procedures. This resistance may start at the beginning or it may develop at any point during therapy. The first duty of the therapist is not only to recognize the impasse, but to resolve it. Whenever a client, be he adult or child, fails to cooperate, one has to understand him and his goals and help him to overcome the obstacle, instead of blaming him. The prime factor in establishing a relationship is providing the client with the feeling of being understood. This crucial element in therapy is only too often overlooked.

We have specific tools which enable us to be more effective in providing our clients with the feeling of being understood. It is the concept of the private logic. We operate on the assumption that behind any action lies a definite idea, a concept, a goal. When we can show the client his goals, he may begin to recognize the significance of what he is doing, i.e., "understand" it. We recently developed a special technique of guessing what went on in a client's mind when he did or said something, which we call "the hidden reason." When a patient does or says something which is rather unusual, one has to guess what went on in his mind at the time. It is most striking how reliable the patient's response is. When he says "no," one can be sure that the guess was incorrect; when he says, "it could be," then one came very close. And if one can say the words which went on in his mind, then he compulsively says, "You are right." This has been found to be true in *all* cases, even in juvenile delinquents and psychotics, who heretofore were completely unreachable. In this moment the whole expression of the patient changes—he drops his defenses, because he feels understood, often for the first time.

Here is an example of two fourteen-year-old girls who behaved in a similar way. They sat immobile, without any reaction, while they and their parents were interviewed. In one case, all the girl did was to complain about what people had done to her. We asked if she wanted help. She shouted, "No." Then we asked her why she doesn't want help. Psychologically speaking, there may have been many reasons for it. She may be a pessimist who doesn't believe she can be helped; she may not want to give up her particular form of fighting with people and life, or there may have been another psychological reason. It would not have made much difference anyhow at that time to explain it to her. But then we had to guess her immediate reason or rationale for declining any help. A number of guesses were made without any reaction. Then it was suggested she may feel that *she* did not need help, but all the others were all wrong and needed it. To that she immediately responded, "Yes, that's what I think." And, as usual in such incidents, her facial expression changed with her attitude and she was willing to discuss the matter.

On another occasion, a fourteen-year-old girl acted in a rather similar way when her problems were discussed with her and her parents. It was an extremely ambitious family where every member was a success except this girl who failed in school. She hardly responded to any question and sat there sullen and silent. When asked why she behaved that way, she did not answer. My guess was that she just wanted to be left alone and wished I would stop questioning her. She did not respond. Therefore, I was sure I was wrong. But what did she think? I ventured several guesses without any response, until I asked her whether she did not participate because she was sure she would not be able to give the right answer. And again, she agreed, and like a flash, her posture changed and we could discuss her extreme doubt in her ability to ever satisfy adults.

The crucial significance of these interactions is the development of confidence through the feeling of being understood. In our experience, this is a most powerful means for establishing and maintaining a therapeutic relationship.

Phase 2   Exploration of the Situation

To understand our method of analyzing the dynamics of a case, one has to keep in mind that we are holistic. We attempt a rather quick perception of the situation as we see the pattern of relationships and of transactions. Traditionally, one tries to gather enough material before one can venture a diagnosis. It is a process which can be called factophilia (Winthrop, 1959). We oppose such reductionistic procedure which usually leads to a situation where one cannot see the forest for the trees. We are training counselors and therapists to listen actively to whatever a patient says, trying to see his pattern, of both personality and behavior.

With younger children we always talk with the parents first; teenagers are usually given the choice whether they want to be interviewed first, or after their parents. In most cases it leads to a session with the parents.

Contrary to an accepted practice, we listen to the mother or parents only for a short while. If one would let them do so, they could talk about their problem child for hours on end. Very soon it becomes a variation on the same theme. At this point, the trained therapist can already guess the situation and the transaction between child and adult. To make sure, one always asks a mother, when she mentions some transgression of the child, what she is doing about it. Only when one knows the reaction of the adult can one recognize the meaning of the child's misbehavior, his mistaken goals. Before long it becomes obvious that almost every mother reacts exactly as the child wants her to react, i.e., in line with his mistaken goal, which only becomes reinforced by the reaction of the adults.

Our ability to recognize the child's goal is greatly enhanced by our description of the four goals of misbehaving children (Dreikurs, 1948). The child, like any human being, is a social being who wants to belong. As long as the child is not discouraged, he will act in line with the needs of the situation. Every child knows what he should do—he just may choose not to do it, especially if he is discouraged and does not believe that he could have a place in the group through useful contributions. Since we discourage children systematically, very few children grow up with confidence in their ability to have a place through useful means. Our way of raising children presents them with a constant series of discouraging experiences, either by pampering or spoiling them, grossly underestimating their abilities, or by scolding, humiliating, threatening, and punishing. In this way, we deprive children of the realization of their worth and ability, and this is also true for those who seemingly are successful and yet, cannot relax in the knowledge of being worthwhile.

Out of this situation, the child derives a mistaken notion of how he can belong. The child acts by trial and error; he will attempt innumerable forms of behavior and continue that which will get him the desired results. And this is usually much easier to get through disturbing behavior than through accomplishment.

FOUR GOALS OF MISBEHAVIOR   We observed four goals of the child's misbehavior, all directed toward adults. These four goals can also be found in adolescents and even in adults. But there they are no longer exclusive. The four goals are the means by which the child expects to benefit from adults, because they provide him with his status. Later, the child's desire to belong and have significance and status depends more on his transactions with his peers; therefore, besides the four goals, other behavior patterns seem to bring status, through excitement, personal power, "independence," through deviant behavior, etc. All so-called forms of abnormal behavior, even psychoses, reflect the above goals which the child has set for himself.

The recognition of the four goals and their significance is only possible when one no longer is concerned with "causes." Our psychology is one of use and not of possession or inventory. We are less concerned with what the child is or has than with what he does, how he uses whatever quality, asset, or deficiency he may have. For us, it is less important with what the child is born than what he does with it afterwards, how much intelligence he has rather than how he uses whatever intelligence he possesses, what advantages or disadvantages he has, culturally, perceptually, cerebrally, etc. Unless one knows the child's goals and how he utilizes whatever he possesses for obtaining them, one does not understand the dynamics on which he operates.

To repeat: The four goals which we encounter are goals of the disturbing or deficient child, his mistaken ideas about how to belong, how to be significant. Goal (1) is to obtain *attention* from adults. If the child cannot get it through pleasant means, he receives attention through disturbing. He prefers to be scolded, threatened, and punished than to be ignored. If he does not get the attention he wants, he feels lost, and the fight between adults and children begins. Adults, parents, and teachers want to stop him from disturbing and to make him take on responsibility; and in the ensuing war, the child moves to goal (2), *power*. He often will openly say, "If you don't let me do what I want, you don't love me." The child feels justified in doing what he wants, and an increasing number of children are in a power conflict with adults. Tell them what to do, and they will refuse to do it; tell them what not to do, and they feel honor bound to do it. And most parents and teachers do not know how to cope with such children. The more they try to subdue them, the more violent becomes the power conflict, until the child moves to goal (3). He feels he can have significance only when he pays back to the adults what they do to him. *Revenge* is goal (3). These are the most vicious children, who succeed in evoking utter despair in adults. Then we observe goal number (4), i.e., the attempt of a very discouraged child to belong. As long as nothing is demanded of him, it does not become apparent how deficient and dumb he is. These children usually succeed in convincing adults of their *hopelessness*.

The first objective of our exploration is toward an understanding of the field of action in which the child operates. We can see the same transaction between adults and the child in the wide variety of unresolved conflicts. We usually explore a typical day in the family, from getting up in the morning to going to bed in the evening, with all the conflicts of a disturbed relationship in which the children manipulate the adults.

Then we try to understand how this particular disturbed relationship evolved. It is the consequence of a characteristic family constellation, in which each child develops his notions about himself, about life, about his chances to find a place. Whatever the children of a family have in common reflects the family atmosphere. The children do not experience society at large directly, but only through the transaction between the parents. The differences between the children are the result of competitive strife. The behavior of all children within the family is coordinated. The greatest difference in character, personality, and abilities is usually between the first and second child. Wherever one succeeds, the other gives up, and vice versa. The children decide amongst themselves, although without conscious awareness, which role each one is going to play, and the parents afterwards, reinforce their decision. The parents make the good child better and the bad child worse by their reaction to them. An only child will find his own way of manipulating the parents, often playing out one against the other, i.e., provoking father so that mother should feel sorry for him and side with him. When the third child is born, the second becomes a middle child, who either feels squeezed out because he does not have the rights of the older nor the privileges of the younger; or he succeeds in pushing the other two down. The first and the third child usually are more alike and allied because they have a common enemy. All possible alliances and competition can be observed. From the personality development of each child, one can see the kind of transactions he has with all the other members of the family. When parents are helped in bringing about the adjustment of the difficult child, one always finds that the good child is getting worse. Only when the parents learn to treat all children alike "as one group" can they diminish the competitive strife between them and help each child to recognize his responsibility, i.e., that each one is his brother's keeper.

In young children, the observation of the way in which each child moves within the family constellation is sufficient to understand the concepts and goals of each child. The immediate goals of each one's behavior can be recognized by mere observation. With older children and with adults, one needs additional exploration. First, one has to reconstruct the transactions up to the age of eight or ten. Adler provided us with the tools to preceive the personality holistically, to recognize each person's life style through his early recollections. For many years the early recollections were disregarded because they were considered as insignificant screen memories concealing the real traumatic childhood events (Freud, 1915). Today, it is becoming generally recognized that one remembers from the multitudes of childhood experiences only those incidents which fit into one's outlook on life. The early recollections are so reliable that they are not only needed to assess the pattern of personality, the patient's life style; they are the only reliable basis for evaluating therapeutic and corrective results. When the early recollections have not changed, then there was no improvement of the basic problems even though the patient may have lost the symptoms and showed marked clinical improvement. When a change in the mistaken life style has been achieved, then the recollections will change also. The patient may bring up new, and structurally different kinds of recollections. He may remember the same incident as before, but with entirely different details; and most dramatic—the client will deny ever having had an experience as it was noted in his record. Dealing with adolescents makes the use of early recollections imperative. Besides an understanding of the transactions of the youngster at home, in school and in society, one has to understand his basic concept of himself, his life style. Without the use of early recollections, one cannot achieve that, although one may be able to get interesting unconscious material. But all observations are peripheral in comparison with the fundamental dynamics revealed by early recollections.

Phase 3   The Confrontation of the Patient or Client with his Goals

This is the most characteristic aspect of Adlerian counseling and therapy. The Adlerian approach can be described as teleo-analytic, as the Freudian approach is psychoanalytic and the Existential approach ontoanalytic. We are exclusively concerned with recognizing goals and changing them. In contrast to behavior modification, we are concerned with motivation modification. And the self-set goal, be it the long range goal of the life style, or the immediate goal in a given situation, are the decisive factors in adjustment or maladjustment.

The insight which we offer to our clients is exclusively insight in the goals which they have set for themselves. However, these goals do not become a causal factor, a causa finalis, as some assume. Even within the frame of a given life style, a great variety of immediate transactions are possible. We can help people to function more adequately without changing their life style. All mothers can learn how to cope with their children, regardless of their own personality; and children can change their immediate goals as soon as they become useless, without changing their life style. Changes of life style are only necessary when a wrong concept of oneself and life makes it difficult to function.

We have developed a definite technique of confronting children with their goal. The child does not know it; when the disclosure is done in a proper way, the child begins to recognize his goal and responds with what has been called a "recognition reflex" (Dreikurs, 1948). We found that a certain sequence of well-formulated questions is necessary to get the recognition reflex. Counselors, using a foreign language, have to find the specific translation of the words used, otherwise they do not get the recognition reflex. First we ask the child why he is doing what he is not supposed to do. He either will say he doesn't know, or he will use a rationalization. We know that he doesn't know; but the question "why" is a prerequisite to the next question. "Could I tell you what I think?" And then we can come with the disclosure, but always in a tentative way, never throwing it at the person or accusing him. The key phrase is, "Could it be that. . ." This phrase has become our trademark. It leads to an explanation of the child's behavior. "Could it be that you want to keep mother busy?" (goal 1). "Could it be that you want to show that nobody can stop or make you?" (goal 2). ". . . that you want to get even? . . . Or to hurt?" (goal 3). ". . . to be left alone?" (goal 4). Most children will respond with a recognition reflex when the correct goal is mentioned Some have a poker face, and some find it impossible to believe that they would do something like that to their mother. The latter group will have less difficulties in recognizing what they do to their teachers. Usually, one can come to one particular transaction with the adults where the child can easily see what he was doing.

The recognition reflex is a rather dramatic experience for the child and for the counselor. Sometimes the child may take a few seconds of intensive thinking before the quivering lips and a certain expression of the eyes indicate that he is beginning to catch on. This procedure is not only of extreme value as a diagnostic tool, identifying the child's goal, it also has considerable therapeutic implications. When the child recognizes his goals, he begins to see alternatives. Until he is confronted with his goal, he is unaware of what he is doing, and, therefore, pessimistic about his chances to be different. He is convinced that he is either stupid, lazy, bad, or mean—he was told that often. There is little he can do about it. Becoming aware of his goal actually has a considerable corrective effect. Despite the fact that what is revealed to him is not "good" or pleasant, this revelation is actually the first encouragement for the child. Now he *can* do something about it—he does not have to continue either to demand special attention, to show his power, to get even or to give up .

As the child is not aware of the role he plays in every conflict situation, neither do the parents know theirs. It is most difficult for them to realize that their reaction to the child's provocation is in line with his intention. This general predicament of our time is to a large extent brought about and intensified by prevalent professional opinions. According to them, the child is the victim of all the forces converging on him, from heredity, environment, and primarily as the result of parental influences. Consequently, mothers are mostly blamed for the maladjustment and deficiency of their children, when they actually are manipulated by them. In the past, such manipulation on the part of the children was limited because adults had the authority to enforce parental control. Today, in a state of general equality, everybody is unwilling to submit, and the child in turn exerts a strong and often overlooked influence on those who try—mostly in vain—to dominate him.

For this reason, it is difficult for parents as well as for society at large to realize the power of even very young children. The child tries an unlimited variety of behavior, always in pursuit of his hidden goal; and whatever is effective he will continue. We find infants of four weeks old who have already discovered how they can tyrannize the family. And since the parents are not aware of such manipulations, they are helpless victims, reinforcing all the mistaken goals of their children.

As we have to confront the children with their goals of which they are not aware, so we have to reveal to the parents the role which they play. As long as the purposiveness of the children's behavior is universally unknown, one assumes that parental deficiency is primarily due to lack of love, interest and time, and neglect. Confronting parents with such accusations has the same consequences as blaming children for their deficiency or maladjustment. The basic dynamic factors are thereby overlooked. Once they are recognized, they lead to a completely different form of confrontation and suggested corrective steps.

FEAR AND JEALOUSY   Some of the most striking differences in approaches concern the problem of children's fear and jealousy. One assumes that they result from neglect, insecurity, unmet dependency needs. Actually, the so-called dependency of dependent children is a misnomer. The parents depend on the children's demands, and the dependent child can become independent almost instantly when the parents refuse to be provoked by real or assumed deficiencies and weaknesses. The situation is similar with fears. Children develop fears only if there are adults who are impressed with them. It is difficult to make a harrassed mother realize that the child develops his fears for her attention and sympathy. Children can have a shock reaction, either by sudden noise, falling down, or a threatening experience. But this reaction will not lead to continued fears if the parents do not try to make up for the "shock." Because this is so difficult for a loving mother to accept, we prefer counseling parents in a group. Then some of the other mothers will report how the child's fears instantaneously disappeared when no fuss was made over the incident. Here is an example.

> Gilbert was nine years old when his mother came with him for help. He was a fine boy, obedient and kind. But for about a year he had suffered from terrific fears. He had seen his grandfather die, and could not overcome the shock. Since then, he had lived in constant fear that something might happen to his parents. He woke up during the night screaming and running to the parents' room to see whether they were alright. He was especially worried about mother. When she leaves the house, he is terror-striken: something might happen to her. She must call home every hour. If she is five or ten minutes late, he gets frantic. The parents are very sympathetic. They do not fight or scold him, but they don't know what to do with him. Medicines do not quiet him down. Once they sent him to his grandparents' farm. For a few days Gilbert was alright. Then he woke up one night terror stricken, waking his grandparents. He was convinced that his mother was dying. They had to call home in the middle of the night to reassure him. After that he couldn't stand it there any longer and was sent home.

A short examination of his past development revealed that while he had always been very close to mother, prior to his grandfather's death he had been well adjusted at home and in school. There were no significant difficulties. He was affectionate and conforming, almost a model child. He even made a good adjustment when a little sister was born three years ago, and he was affectionate and friendly towards her. All that had changed when the grandfather died.

At this first interview, no definite conclusion was reached. However, it seemed that the grandfather's death had become important only because of the extreme sympathy and concern which the parents showed about the shock which Gilbert had experienced. The event had occurred at a period in Gilbert's life when he probably felt insecure in the competition with his little sister, who was very cute and attracted considerable attention. Gilbert, not trained for open rebellion and antagonism, undoubtedly capitalized on this new opportunity to gain the limelight and to keep mother even closer to himself than she had been, certainly closer than his age and development would warrant. He was, of course, unaware of this mechanism, as were his parents and other relatives. Mother was advised to stop being impressed by Gilbert's fears; the sympathy which he received only aggravated his condition. But she was also warned that it might take some time to give Gilbert a feeling of independence, so that he would not have to resort to these fears.

During his interview, the boy appeared very frank and intelligent, sincere and kind. We had a brief talk with him, asking him first whether he knew why he was so afraid that mother might die. He shook his head. "May we explain it to you?" we asked. He was eager. So we told him that apparently he used his fears to keep his mother concerned with him and close to himself, because he might be afraid of losing out to his little sister. Could it be? He grinned with a characteristic "recognition reflex." He had never thought of that before, but he admitted that it might be so. We asked him whether we should, perhaps, help him to overcome his feeling of insecurity. After all, he was a good boy and did not need mother so much any more. He was quite agreeable.

An appointment was made with mother and son for two weeks ahead. A few days before the appointment the mother called to cancel it. Gilbert's fears had completely disappeared. (Dreikurs, 1948)

One can well imagine the extent to which our children show fear when they realize how timid and afraid the adults are, particularly when dealing with their children, being unable to cope with them effectively. For this reason, we find an inordinate extent of jealousy and, thereby, encourage the child to experiment with it. When the child tells his mother that she does not love him, then this too is well designed for its effect. He knows that it is not true. But he also finds out how it upsets a loving mother who then tries to make up for this apparent lack of love and attention. No child will continue his jealousy if it does not impress the adults.

Similarly, when children fight, they do it for the mother's response. One child usually does it for attention to get mother's help and support, particularly when he is weaker and smaller. Many fights are instigated by such a child just to get mother against an older sibling, who usually fights to defeat mother, who cannot stop or prevent him from beating up and abusing the younger one. It is dramatic how the children's fights diminish when mother sincerely stays out of them. But it is her sense of responsibility and her fear of what may happen which prevents her from taking the only effective step. A temper tantrum would be silly if there is nobody to be impressed with it—so the parents provide the necessary audience.

In order to understand the situation, we have to change our concept about young children and infants. They are not parasites; they are not irresponsible and unreasonable as is often assumed. But in our mistaken evaluation of them, we treat them as if they had no intelligence, and they take advantage of our misconceptions by outsmarting the adults. A typical example for the ability of infants to size up the situation is provided by children of deaf parents. It is a wierd experience to see a six-month-old infant crying. The tears stream down his cheeks, the face is in grimaces, the whole body shakes—and no sound comes out. He already knows that his voice would not get him any response, so he does not use it. Everything an infant and child is doing is well designed; but unfortunately, this design is not perceived by the adult. We were told that it takes a new born infant of deaf parents one to two months before he stops making any sound. This, of course, is different when a grandmother or another hearing adult is in the house. Later these children show their anger by stamping their feet—the parents can perceive this vibration.

These considerations are essential to understand our therapeutic and corrective efforts. They make little sense to those who are causalistic-deterministic, who look for partial phenomena as explaining the whole, who consider feelings as motivating features, rather than ideas, concepts, and goals.

Phase 4   Reorientation

The goal of counseling and therapy is to effect a change in the child's concept of himself, or life, and of his chances to be significant. It implies an increase in the child's social interest, a feeling of belonging as a worthwhile member of the group. The main factor behind inadequate social interest is doubt in oneself, and in one's ability to find a place through useful contribution. The greatest obstacle to growth and development, to learning and to increased ability to function, or even to continued functioning on the level already reached, is discouragement, doubt in one's own ability. One cannot use one's inner sources if one is convinced of having none. Prejudice against oneself, which is rampant today, deprives child and adult alike from recognizing and utilizing abilities, skills, knowledge and—most of all—one's innate creativity (Dreikurs, 1968, pp. 80–92).

ENCOURAGEMENT   This essential process is almost absent in our homes and in our schools. As a matter of fact, it seems that discouraging children is an essential aspect of all our educational efforts. Everybody believes in the need for encouragement, but few know how to give it. We deprive children and each other of the realization that we are good enough as we are, that we have a significant place by our mere existence. The child who fails has lost faith in himself (Adler, 1930). Our schools too are mistake-centered, making learning a chore instead of an adventure. The less the child wants to learn, the more unpleasant we make it for him.

While encouraging children is essential for their improvement, nay, for their functioning, our effort to help parents and teachers —and counselors and therapists—to exert an encouraging influence must first be directed toward elimination of the present interactions which take place between children and adults. Before one can learn what to do, one has to clearly recognize what one must avoid doing.

The child will have no chance to improve or to adjust as long as he will continue to experience all the advantages of deficiency and misbehavior. Before a mother can cope with a child, instead of contributing further to his deficiency, she has to extricate herself from his manipulation. The greatest obstacle for a mother in letting the child assume responsibility is her notion of what a good mother is and what she has to do. She thinks she has to single-handedly take responsibility for each child. Mothers, like many teachers, still believe that one can force a child, as they did in the past in an autocratic society, that punishment can still bring good results. It is most difficult to extricate oneself from a power conflict with a child, particularly if the mother is overwhelmed by her "duty" to control the child. However, as long as she is involved, as long as her power and status is at stake, the children will capitalize on her weakness. Children know very well what mother can't tolerate, and for many that is the green light. Regardless of what the child is doing wrong, most mothers respond in the same way—they talk. It does not make any difference whether they advise, scold, threaten or "explain"; it is still the same interaction of giving special attention and of fighting a losing war.

The therapy and counseling of the young child requires, therefore, that the mother learn what to do and what not to do. She is no longer prepared by tradition, and she has to know new methods to stimulate the child from within. A new relationship of understanding and trust is required, and the therapist and counselor has to know what a mother can and should do. Many object to such an assignment. They may consider it manipulative and gimmicky. Actually, these accusations are correct, if one does not understand the meaning of our procedure. We give advice to parents as to what to do, because they don't know it. But our advice does not consist of cook book recipes; every bit of advice is directed toward a change in relationship, freeing mother from the service and tyranny of her children. In a sense, there is a manipulative process. But this is inevitable if the parents want to be a match for the children who are masters of manipulation.

In our form of therapy, all members of the family are included, since they all contribute to the development of conflicts and problems. The "good" child often induces a sibling to get his place through misbehavior. And when the difficult child improves, his "good" and competitive sibling usually begins to misbehave. The problem of each child has to be understood within the setting of the whole family. None is the victim of the other; each one contributes to the interaction which takes place among all. The methods which are used for correction are identical with the principles of democratic education. When parents learn to establish a democratic family, then they discover means by which they can influence all children, regardless of their difficulties. We found that the same methods are effective whether we are dealing with the so-called normal range of disturbing behavior found in almost all children, or with the slow learner, the culturally or perceptually handicapped, with the juvenile delinquent, as well as with the autistic and psychotic child. The last group needs perhaps one approach which is different from all other disturbances, i.e., a firmness which may include physical restraint.

We found that all generalizations are ill-advised, e.g., the mother should show more love, be more patient, etc. Regardless of how justified such recommendations may be, mothers may not know how to apply them even if they want to. Then one assumes that she may need personal therapy to develop these desirable qualities. We don't agree with this assumption. Regardless of how much the mother may love her child, if she does not know how to cope with a tyrant and feels constantly defeated by him, she has little opportunity to show him how much she loves him. Others believe that the mother needs a proper attitude. If she has it, she does not need advice, and if she does not have it, no advice will help her. This is not true. The experience of love and the development of a proper attitude is a consequence of mother's ability to cope wtih the child, not the prerequisite.

There was a time when we assumed that about 75 percent of all mothers can learn what to do with a child, while about 25 percent may be so disturbed that they may need personal help with their own problems. We no longer assume that. Since we have refined our techniques we can help *every* mother to become a better mother even if she is disturbed or psychotic.

THE "BATHROOM-TECHNIQUE"   One of the most effective means to extricate mothers from the manipulation of the child in the so-called *bathroom technique* (Deikurs and Soltz, 1964). It was evolved first from the advice that the mother, in a conflict situation, bring a door between herself and the child. Then we suggested that the mother retreat to her bedroom whenever a conflict arises, or—if it gets worse—that she take a walk around the block. It was a mother who brought to our attention that the bathroom is much more effective as a means of disengagement. It has a dramatic effect on the children. It is the most powerful method of bringing harmony in the family. The bathroom retreat is a declaration of mother's independence. Every mother, including the psychotic mother, can become more effective, since everyone can go to the bathroom.

To understand this technique one has to understand our premises. In a democratic family nobody has the right to dictate to others what to do. But when we consider pressure and punishment as obsolete, we are not in favor of permissiveness either. People may say that the mother "gives in" to the children when she goes to the bathroom. The opposite is true—she deprives them of their power over her. And children will try every means to prevent her from going to the bathroom, threatening with dire consequences, upsetting furniture, etc., because they realize that mother no longer is their servant and slave. Naturally, this is only the first step among many other methods mothers can use. It is essential that the mother has some literature and a transistor radio in the bathroom, otherwise she remains involved by hearing what is going on.

Since mothers are intimidated and fearful anyhow, they may worry about what might happen between the children while she is in the bathroom. They can hurt each other as well while she is in the kitchen.

We described thirty-four principles which mothers can apply in influencing and correcting the children (Dreikurs and Soltz, 1964). These principles can be learned by any mother and form the basis of a democratic education, replacing traditional pressure from without with stimulation from within. We already have mentioned one of the most essential techniques parents have to learn: the technique of encouraging children (Dinkmeyer and Dreikurs, 1963). The encouraging process is very complex. It has a prerequisite of mutual respect, of recognizing the tremendous ability of the child, even if he uses it in his fight against adults. Whatever one does with a child, regardless of how justifiable it may be, its effect will depend largely on whether the child has been encouraged or further discouraged. Most of our corrective methods at home and in school imply discouragement, further loss of self-esteem and self-confidence.

THE APPLICATION OF NATURAL AND LOGICAL CONSEQUENCES
This is the most important method of teaching children responsibility (Dreikurs and Grey, 1968; 1970). While the authority of adults as a motivating factor has diminished, parents can utilize real situations from which children can learn. Many adults find it difficult to distinguish between logical consequence and punishment. Punishment is retaliation and warfare, and evokes rebellion. Logical consequences permit the parent to remain a friendly by-stander. We distinguish between so-called natural consequences

which take place without any action on the part of the parents and logical consequences which are initiated by the adults. Natural consequences means that when a child does not come for dinner on time, there is nothing left for him to eat. When a child comes with dirty hands to the table, the mother has no right to send him back to wash, but neither does she have the obligation to serve him when he has dirty hands. This is a logical consequence. It seems that this technique holds great promise for parents to learn how to influence children without fighting with them. Opportunities for their application constantly arise. And parents have to learn how to spot them and utilize them.

FAMILY COUNCIL   These are three of the most important principles. Another equally important, but more difficult to master, is the arrangement of a *family council*. We can no longer run schools or homes for the children—we can only work with them. That is the sense of the revolutionary movements all over the world. It has been compared with the revolutions of 1848 whcih spread from one European country to another. At that time, people were striving for their political freedom; today they are striving for participation in decision making. No conflicts can be resolved anymore without it; but most of our institutions are not yet democratic, and therefore fail to recognize the need for it. This is the reason why we have almost insolvable conflicts between men and women, between blacks and whites—and between parents and children. In a sense, child guidance (or if one wants to call it counseling and therapy) establishes methods which are effective in all human relationships, wherever a democratic society emerges. In an autocratic setting, we do not need new methods; the old were effective for many thousands of years of autocratic control.

The family council should meet once a week at a given time. Its first obligation is that every member of the family listens to the others. At the present time, nobody listens. As soon as someone says something he doesn't agree with, an argument ensues without any reconciliation. Instead of talking every day about the conflicts which exist with children, such talk is restricted to the meeting of the family council. Parents have to learn how to be group leaders, neither imposing their ideas on children, nor giving in to what they want. No problem is so urgent that it cannot wait until mutual agreement has been achieved. In the meantime, parents are free to act, to apply logical consequences, to encourage, etc.

These four principles are the backbone of our new approach to children: (1) disengagement of the parents from the conflict, (2) encouragement, (3) applications of logical consequences, and (4) the family council. Here are some of the other principles that we recommend (Dreikurs and Soltz, 1964): Avoid reward and punishment; be firm without dominating; show respect for the child and help him to respect order and the rights of others; avoid criticism and minimize mistakes; take time for training; win cooperation; act instead of talk; don't shoo flies; have the courage to say "no." Do the unexpected; don't over-protect; stimulate independence; don't get involved in arguing between children; don't be intimidated; treat them as if they are all in the same boat instead of playing one against the other; listen to the child; be careful with your tone of voice; have fun together; talk with the children, not to them. One principle is difficult to recognize: the need not to feel pity for the child, regardless of what is happening to him. The pity of well-meaning relatives and friends often does more than the cause of the pity. Another point which encounters opposition is to treat all children alike. This violates our sense of justice according to which everyone should be treated in line with his merits. Doing so, we make the good one better and the bad one worse. But when parents learn to make them all responsible regardless of who did what, then the children can actually learn that each one is his brother's keeper and not enemies as brothers and sisters so often are.

The application of shared responsibility and participation in decision making applies not only to parents and teachers who usually make decisions for the child, but also for the counselors and therapists. Whatever goes on has to be based on mutual agreement; and the trained therapist has to know how to reach it. Too many of our children are exposed to counselors and therapists who either try to manage them or are manipulated by their charges, often because of mistaken identity with those who rebel against society, often under the misunderstood idea that democracy means permissiveness where everyone can do what he wants.

The Seriously Disturbed

One may be inclined to believe that all these principles apply only to "normal" problems which adults have with children. It is our experience that the same principles apply also to most seriously disturbed children. In any case, where a mother comes for help, one must be able to understand and help immediately. When clients leave the office without having derived any benefit, then the counselor or therapist has failed. Regardless of the severity of the case, some concrete suggestion or helpful information can be given. One does not have to wait until the "proper" relationship has been established, or until more extensive study of the case has been made. In other words, all four phases of therapy which we have enumerated can take place within the first interview. One can establish a valid relationship, one can analyze the nature of the problem, one can confront children and their parents with what they are doing to each other, and one can start to use principles of conflict-solving. All this requires, of course, proper training in our method; it also requires a change in our general adult-child relationship in which it seems only children have the right to be clever. We have to help adults to become a match for children.

Here is a typical situation with a disturbed teenager. You ask him why he came, and he answers that he doesn't know—his parents sent him. "Why did they send you?" "I don't know, ask them." Then you ask a few questions about how he functions. And he always answers in the same way, "Everybody does it," meaning skipping school and not studying, now perhaps some drug abuse, etc. So, one asks whether he wants any help. Of course not; there is nothing wrong. What now? We usually ask him whether he expects to get married. "Why not?" "Do you expect to have children?" "Probably." "What would you feel if you had a boy of your age who was exactly like you are?" "That would not be so good." "Why not, if there is nothing wrong with you?" Some smart kid may say, "But he wouldn't be like me!"

Despite all the bravado and the defiance of order, our youngsters know very well how they endanger themselves—they just don't care. And you cannot treat any one of them alone. We are confronted with group problems. The drug problem will not be solved and will only take on more dangerous dimensions until the whole problem of adult-child relationships and the mistaken value system on which our adolescents operate has been recognized and changed. Behind the increasing use of drugs are three main problems which begin in early childhood and reach a peak during adolescence. There is first the over-concern with excitement—boredom is intolerable. Overcoming it justifies the most violent and hazardous acts. The second factor is defiance, striving for so-called identity, which means being different from adults and rejecting their values. Defiant youth chooses acts which adult society cannot tolerate; and drugs are the most frightening to adults. The third factor is temporary insanity. As the psychotic disregards reality and its demands, through delusion and hallucination, so does the drug addict escape from reality and the demands of society. No plan can be made by representatives of society for the delinquent or for the drug addict. Solutions can only be found by participation, and some of the addicts, like alcoholics, receive much more help from each other than from those who are supposed to treat and correct them.

The newly found group of deviations attributed to cerebral disfunction deserve our scrutiny. Minimal brain damage and perceptual handicaps are assumed to be responsible for slow learning and reading difficulties, for dyslexia in all its various forms of physiological deficiencies. The voices of dissent are drowned out by the propaganda of the cerebralists. Of course, there are children with brain damage; there is a peculiar form of aphasia. But these disturbances are rather rare and do not produce behavior problems like hyperactivity, low interest span, etc.

Money and others (Money, 1966) have suggested that the methods in perceptual training and visual motor coordination have not yet been proved to have any direct effect on the learning of reading. Competent investigators have been led to contrary conclusions about the role of handedness, heredity, perceptual handicap and the like. "It is fashionable today to talk of minimal brain damage in relation to reading disability" (Money, 1966). In the majority of cases, no kind of brain damage can be demonstrated by today's technique. EEG anomolies are not different from similar findings of "normal" children. Hyperactivity as such may effect the EEG.

Our experience indicates that children with these "conditions" respond well to our approach. Characteristic for hyperactive children is their determination not to accept any control. But they can learn quickly to accept it, if firmness and friendliness are used instead of fighting and yielding.

> A five-year-old girl was brought to our office because her parents were utterly defeated. The girl did not talk, and ran around incessantly, like a tiger in a cage, touching everything she was not supposed to touch, and at the same time looking at her parents with a frightened expression as to what they would do next. The parents were asked to remain completely quiet, which was difficult for them to do because they felt responsible and tried to exert control. I took

the responsibility that nothing would be broken by removing all breakable objects from her reach. The girl still ran around without any reaction to what was said or done.

I put her in a chair and stood in front of her so that she could not get up. She began to scream hysterically, looking at her parents for help. It was hard on them not to be permitted to console her in her predicament. I continued to talk with the parents, showing them what the girl was doing. She was determined to get out of the chair, but her force met an immovable object. I did not say anything to her and completely ignored her screaming. It lasted for perhaps ten minutes. When she realized that nothing would help her, she settled down and became completely quiet. Her hyperactivity was gone for the rest of the interview. She sat in the chair quietly for about half an hour. The parents did not know what happened. Never before was the child "able" to sit quietly, even for a few minutes.

Contrary to a widespread opinion, these children can tolerate and usually respond very well to a quiet firmness. The girl became very affectionate and gave me a kiss before she left. Obviously she was relieved by being free from being a bad girl.

A six-year-old boy had been in a private sanitarium for three years. He was completely unreachable and always violent and had to be kept most of the time in a padded cell. Since, by that time, the financial resources of the family were exhausted, the mother was advised to commit the boy to a custodial institution.

Before she accepted this solution, she came for a consultation. She was told to respond firmly but quietly. Since this was difficult for the parents to do, we found a foster home where parents were able to use quiet control, of course, without beating or harshness.

The boy needed extensive dental work because it had been impossible to get dental care in the sanitarium. The mother was advised to bring the child back to the hospital for a day so that he could be put to sleep for one day, to permit the dentist to work on him. After a week in the foster home, the child was so quiet and manageable that the mother could take him to a dentist's office where he cooperated and had his teeth fixed. His medication was actually far less than he had received at the sanitarium, and there without any effect.

Organic Cases

Most children who really are autistic and mute need considerable retraining. There can be no doubt any more that such retraining is possible. We found music therapy together with effective relationships to be a method of choice. Music represents a nonverbal expression of order to which such children do respond (Dreikurs and Crocker, 1955; Dreikurs, 1960). Recent observations indicate that behavioral therapy, particularly operant conditioning, can have excellent results. In other cases where immediate results have been obtained, the pathological condition has been simply a faulty diagnosis.

During a semester at a university, we worked with a group of parents and their children who had been diagnosed as suffering from minimal brain damage. The children sat through the weekly discussions with their parents; and during the two hours almost all sat quietly in their chairs without disrupting.

In one of the sessions, the parents of Jim, five-years-old, discussed an event which had taken place the day before the interview. The boy wanted ice cream after dinner and the parents refused. Whereupon, he took his food, threw it on the floor and smeared it all over. The father told him to clean it up, but the boy disappeared. The father went after him and saw him getting away on his tricycle. The father called him, he looked back, but did not respond when he was asked to come back. On the contrary, he went in the opposite direction. Eventually, the father reached him and dragged him back home, telling him to clean up the mess. Whereupon the boy declared he would go up to his room and he would start a mess there. And so he did. When father went upstairs asking him to pick up everything that he had thrown on the floor, the boy ran out of the door, not without arranging that the door would lock as soon as father tried to catch up with him. The door could only be locked from the inside, and he was now unable to get into his room. The father still tried to get him to clean up his room. In order to do so, the father had to take a screwdriver to unlock the door. In they went together, but the boy still refused to pick anything up and eventually again left the room, arranging the door to lock. Again, he was locked out, and again he asked the father to open the door for him, so that he could clean up. But again, he refused to do so, and for the third time, he went out, locking the door behind him. This time father remembered what he had learned from our class, to let the child experience the consequences. And consequently, he refused to unlock the door for the boy. The mother felt sorry for him and read to him. Eventually, she asked him to go to bed, and felt badly that her husband persisted in not opening the door. Consequently, the boy had to sleep on the floor, with scarcely a blanket to cover him.

So far, this was the story. A profound change had suddenly taken place between father and the boy. He was told by several physicians that the boy was very sick and could not be influenced; the parents let him do whatever he wanted. Occasionally, they got provoked too much, and entered into a power conflict like the one described above. It was obvious that the boy defeated the father all the time, doing just the opposite of what he was asked to do, until the moment when he found the door to his room locked against his will. This broke the ice.

The next week father reported the events. He had begun to catch on and no longer attributed the child's misbehavior to his brain damage. He began to see what went on.

After returning from the session the boy began to cry. The father had already cleaned up the mess in the kitchen; but there was still the mess in the boy's room. He refused to clean it up, and then began to look for excuses. He complained that it was too big a job and that it would take him the whole day. He asked father to clean it up for him. But father refused. Whereupon the boy tried to open the lock with a screwdriver. But this was a little too difficult for him, so father helped him to open the door. And the boy picked up everything from the floor, although it was not in perfect order. What impressed father the most was not that the boy was willing to cooperate, but that he was extremely happy about it. This was probably the first time that the boy had real enjoyment for accomplishing something that was useful. Previously, all his victories and accomplishments were on the useless side. In picking things up from the floor, he removed many things which had been on the floor for a long time.

The change became apparent at the dinner table. Usually, he did not eat, he just picked at things. This time he wanted to have part of the meal saved for later. Father objected. So he sat down and cleaned his plate. It was the first time that he ate everything. Usually, he and his brother got up from the table to go to the toilet. In the past, parents did not object. Now they did. If anyone went, he was excused and did not get the rest of the meal.

After the mess in the room was cleaned up, the boy did not mess it up again.

Here we have a typical example of how certain changes in behavior by the parents change the whole relationship and the child's function and behavior. Children respond very quickly when they see that the "jig is up," so to say, that the adults no longer fall for their manipulations. In many cases, such an experience means a change in the whole family. In other words, it does not always require long term therapy and analysis to correct faulty concepts of the child. What we are doing is not behavior modification, but motivation modification of the child. Here is another dramatic incident:

As a consultant to a major pediatric institute in Chicago, I saw a five-year-old boy who seemed to be completely out of touch with reality. Despite three months of testing, no definite diagnosis had been made. It was not clear whether he was autistic, brain damaged or perceptually handicapped, or severely retarded. He did not talk or respond visibly to any environmental influences. He had to be fed and kept from doing any damage to himself and others. An emergency had occurred: the boy walked around during the night and had been found swinging from a light fixture. Institutionalization was considered.

I decided to leave the boy in the counseling room, advising the staff not to respond to whatever he would do. There was no danger requiring any restraint. The boy ran around and made horrible noises.

Two observations made me dubious about the diagnosis of severe disturbance. First, mother related that he behaved like that almost from birth on, completely out of control. But she also reported that she was very apprehensive before he was born because her sister had a brain damaged child.

Second, observing the boy who supposedly was out of touch with reality, I was struck by how well he responded to reality and to the situation. When I stopped talking, he was quiet too. As soon as I began to talk, he began to shout as if to drown me out. At one point he went up on the stage facing the audience, making horrible noises while "conducting" the audience, actually with the movements of a conductor. He certainly was not oblivious to the people, but related himself perfectly well, and from his point of view, logically, to the audience, demanding their full attention.

I was so sure of my correct interpretation of the situation that I predicted what would happen: if nobody would pay any attention to him and his antics, he would not continue them, and before long, settle quietly in a corner. None in the audience believed that possible for such a disturbed hyperkinetic child. But it happened. After half an hour of his futile harangues, he retreated to a corner, talking quietly to himself.

It was explained to the mother how her anticipations were self-fulfilled. The child lived up to them. She would have to learn to withdraw from his provocations, which, of course, was impossible as long as she was convinced—and supported in her conviction by the staff—that he was hopeless and unreachable. Despite the danger of doing harm during the night, she should trust his ingenuity for not going too far. She should stop protecting him and serving him.

Instead of feeding him, she should put the food in front of him and let him eat by himself. But, most important, she should not make any fuss over whatever he does, and declare her independence, acting firmly but quietly. She began to see immediately how she was intimidated and controlled by the boy, and was willing to change her own attitude and behavior.

She could not understand why nobody ever before had told her what was going on and what she should do. She began to read my book (Dreikurs and Soltz, 1964) and joined a mothers' study group. The boy's behavior changed immediately and drastically. After two days, he stopped waking up during the night since mother stopped responding. One month later she came for a follow-up with the boy, who was now quiet and manageable. One year later, she called just to say that she was leaving the country and that the boy, no longer a behavior problem, had begun to speak, not yet too clearly, since she probably had not completely disengaeged herself.

Similar mistaken diagnoses are often made about dyslexia, cerebral disfunction, and perceptual handicaps. While our experiences are limited, so far, in each case which we saw, the diagnosis was faulty. In each case, we have seen the perceptual handicap disappear instantaneously when it was demonstrated to parents and professionals that these children merely pretended to be stupid, with all the special attention and care they get in this way.

This has not always been as obvious and dramatic as in the following case:

During a workshop for counselors, a mother was interviewed. Fortunately, the interview was video-taped and can be seen. Otherwise one may doubt what happened.

Her main problem was her twelve-year-old daughter who had a perceptual handicap. In the third grade she was reading on fourth grade level. But since then she remained on the same reading level, with some indication that she now may regress to the third grade level. What happened when she was in the third grade? Her brother was born. Now it was clear why she refused to progress in reading. Mother, a highly sophisticated and ambitious woman, suffered from her daughter's inability to read. The father was a professional, well-known in the community, and both felt humiliated and hurt. Little did they realize that that was their daughter's goal, to punish and hurt, especially the mother, for being dethroned by a little boy. She rebelled in a passive way while the little brother responded to the pressure and anxiety of the parents in an aggressive fashion.

At this point I suspected that she could read on the fifth and sixth grade level, although she was being tutored by a special teacher, to overcome her perceptual handicap. When I expressed this opinion to the mother, she exclaimed, "Yes, she is reading novels and mystery stories." During my interview with the girl, I asked her whether she can read, and she answered, "Only what interests me." And the fourth grade level material certainly did not interest her. We explained to her how she developed her deficiency in order to hurt mother, and she responded with a recognition reflex. All that was left to do was to take the girl out of the special reading class, put her in the regular class, and let her shift for herself. The mother could not believe that her problem was so simple. But after a little discussion she recognized what went on, and was willing to accept our advice for a solution to the problem. There was a follow-up contemplated, helping the girl to overcome her anger against her parents. But since she was a "good" girl, the probability is that she could not continue her behavior once she recognized its purpose.

Severe Neuroses

The following case shows how the relatively easy changes in a mother's attitude can resolve some of the most severe disturbances of a child. A severe compulsive neurosis in a child is relatively rare nowadays. And its prognosis is usually considered to be very poor. Here we see not only that this assumption is incorrect; by the luck of circumstances, we had the occasion to see that the result of a short therapy was lasting.

Present situation: Eight-year-old Sharon had been a "normal," healthy child until one month ago. She was charming, obedient and kind, and performed equally well in school and at home. Suddenly she developed fears of blindness, of infantile paralysis, of dyptheria. She could not breathe and was terrified of death. She repeatedly asked mother whether she would die or become sick, demanding reassurance and sympathy. For the last four days, she had been afraid her food was poisoned, and mother had to taste all foods before she would eat them. She drooled because she could not swallow her saliva, afraid of the germs in it. She lived in constant expectation of disaster. She had many compulsive symptoms, counted the steps or other objects when she walked on the street, and developed new symptoms each day. When she was not concerned about her symptoms, she was impertinent, mocked her mother if scolded, and demanded continual reassurance that she was loved. One day she pointed a knife to her mother, and on another occasion she threw a ball violently at her parents when they were together. The parents always carefully avoided a demonstration of affection between them in the child's presence. At school, however, Sharon behaved well, was exceptionally advanced for her age, was liked by the other children and played well with them.

Past history: Three years ago the patient had a disturbing episode when she enrolled in school. She did not want to leave mother, was afraid mother would not be home when she came back from school. Mother had to go through a ritual of promising that she would be home, crossing her heart and repeating the same assurance many times. The child was taken to a psychiatrist who arranged play therapy for once a week. She went for nine months and was completely well when discharged.

Her parents were divorced when she was 2½ years old. Since then she lived alone with her mother. They had been constantly together, although the mother remarried three years ago. Her second husband has been in the service until 2½ months ago.

During the interview with the girl, she maintained that she was happy, not at all sick, and denied any fears. She said she did not need nor want help. She denied ever having seen another doctor, but spoke of a playroom in a hospital, drawing pictures, and eating candy. Upon further insistence she stated that she did not want to talk, that she didn't like the doctor and stalked out of the office.

The following impressions were related to the mother at the first interview. It seemed that Sharon had been completely dependent on her mother and wanted to possess her exclusively. Her first disturbance was directed against entering school, and against the mother's remarriage. Apparently, the play therapy induced her to accept a temporary separation from the mother and prepared her for school. The present episode seemed to be caused by the return of her stepfather and by her fear of losing her monopoly of her mother. Her symptoms were the expression of her rebellion and were her tools to occupy mother constantly, not only forcing uninterrupted attention, but also concern and worry. As she never was openly rebellious and seemingly wanting to please her mother and be a good girl, she could never admit her rebellion to herself, nor express it overtly. Furthermore, we suspected from her symptoms, that the girl had been subjected to much pressure. The pressure of a compulsion is usually the response to some pressure from the outside.

Mother was perplexed about this explanation. Her husband had expressed similar ideas about Sharon's using her symptoms coersively, but she had not accepted this explanation. However, now she could see that our impression might be correct.

She was advised to ignore the girl's behavior, although doing so would probably increase Sharon's violence and symptoms. However, mother should not permit herself to be intimidated or dominated by the girl's behavior. On the other hand, she should not become angry or impatient, she should not show any annoyance, but be affectionate and play with her. As a first step, she would have to overcome her own apprehension and distress and would have to establish a new relationship with the child. (At that time we did not know yet about the bathroom technique; otherwise, that would have been our main recommendation).

Three days later, the mother reported the following development. She was capable of maintaining an attitude of neutrality. The girl first pleaded, then raved, then attacked her with a pair of scissors and a knife. She wrote on the wall, "Mother is a stinker." She was destructive; she cut mother's nylons and threw objects around. She begged mother to kiss her when she was in bed in order to keep her from falling asleep as she was afraid of her dreams. Mother told her she was willing to kiss her because she loved her, but not after she had been bidden goodnight. Last night she wanted to get into her mother's bed because she had been alarmed by a fire siren; but mother refused and the girl went to sleep on the floor. When mother paid no attention, she arose in half an hour, asked for a phenobarbitol and retired to her own bed without any coaxing or persuasion.

Sharon told mother how angry she was at us; she protested that we had changed mother's personality. She asked mother why she did not get angry when she was destructive. She said, "I don't know what makes me so bad. God didn't make me like this. How can I be good?" Her mother advised her to talk it over with us.

We commended mother for her attitude and for her ability to retain her composure in the face of the child's provocative behavior. She was advised to continue in this same way. The mother had come alone without the girl.

She came again one week later to report that Sharon was recovering from a mild case of measles. Prior to this illness, her aggressiveness had subsided, now, in her convalescence, she once again became hostile, kicking her mother and others. Her compulsions also had increased; she counted steps and spat her retained saliva on the floor. She placed an ash tray on mother's head when mother was sleeping. She went into her parents' room after they had retired, turning on the lights. She followed her mother everywhere about the house, wanting to hold her hand. Sharon was now afraid of contracting polio, and if mother was not with her all the time, she was fearful that she would die in mother's absence. She did not want to listen to the radio because she might acquire new fears. Her eating habits also changed. After our first interview, Sharon had decided not to eat the same food as the parents, but to have something special. Now she decided to take nothing but milk. On the other hand, she had asked mother to have us telephone her at home because she wanted help in overcoming her worries.

At the next interview, Sharon was willing to talk about her problems. She was quiet, friendly, cooperative, attentive. An attempt was made to give her some understanding of the reasons behind her behavior—that she was accustomed to having mother to herself and had rebelled against her father's return because she did not want to share her mother with him. She used her fear to make her mother become concerned about her without being aware of it, as she probably was not aware how angry she was with mother, and that she annoyed both parents not only to get their attention, but to punish them. She listened attentively and responded several times with a recognition reflex.

The next week the stepfather came to our office with Sharon because mother was sick. He reported much improvement. Sharon lost her temper only once a day. However, she continued to swear at mother and father and to expectorate all over the house. But for the first time, she went with her girlfriend for a ride, leaving the house without her parents. It was still difficult to get her out of the house to play with children; she generally followed her mother from room to room. She ate better and did not demand that her food be tested. For the first time she went to bed by herself without fussing.

The next interview with the mother, a few days later, indicated additional progress. The mother had learned to let Sharon experience the consequences of her actions. If Sharon became angry, mother simply left the room. When she returned, the girl generally was quiet and accepted the necessary rules of order. Previously, the selection of the daily wardrobe had been a major problem. Now, after a short discussion in which the mother expressed her opinion but left the decision to Sharon, she accepted mother's choice without remonstrance. When mother succumbed to the temptation to coax her, Sharon stopped her, saying, "That is none of your affairs." Mother did not feel hurt, but smiled inwardly. She recognized how much pressure she had exerted before. It was still difficult for her at times to restrain herself; but she accepted increasingly her new role and relationship, and no longer became upset by the child's coercive activity, which she now recognized as a reflection of the forcefulness she had previously exerted. When Sharon started to demand reassurance about her symptoms and fears, mother referred her to the doctor and encouraged Sharon to seek advice there. The previous evening Sharon had telephoned us, and asked what she could do about her fears. Our answer was a reference to their purpose—that she wanted to absorb her mother's attention by demanding sympathy, consolation, and assurance. She was praised for her cleverness and determination and was told to continue her scheme. (Such anti-suggestion is often very effective.) The girl seemed to be satisfied with the answer and ended the call with friendly thanks.

The principal remaining difficulty, discussed at the next interview, was Sharon's "inability" to swallow saliva. Sharon volunteered the information that she was bad and did not deserve to be happy. It was pointed out to her that perhaps she could not swallow her saliva because she considered everything in herself to be bad, including her saliva which was full of germs. But regardless of what the cause may be, her expectoration was an expression of her contempt for order and regulations. It was an expression of her anger, since she no longer could manifest it through her tantrums.

During the discussion with the mother, a policy was established in regard to Sharon's spitting. It was suggested that mother tell her that she should go up to her own room if she wanted to spit on the floor instead of using a cuspidor.

Two weeks later mother reported that the spitting had stopped. Mother and daughter spent much time playing together, and there was little disturbance in the family. Only once during this period did she have a relapse, shortly after Sharon had visited her own father. Coming home from this visit, she berated her mother and struck her several times. (Apparently the girl was unwilling to forgive her mother for all her sins, the worst of which had been her remarriage.) Sharon did not like to have her hair combed and sometimes became very angry on such occasions. It was still her rebellion against being overpowered and managed.

During the next few weeks, Sharon occasionally became moody as an appeal to mother for special consideration. Occasionally she struck her mother who managed to ignore the abuse completely.

After three months of treatment the case was closed as "recovered." Sharon became her old self, but on a different basis. Not only did she make peace with sharing mother with her stepfather; she caught herself whenever she became angry at mother and stopped her anger rather than expressing it with symptoms. Several months later, mother reported that Sharon had continued well and happy without a recurrence of any difficulties.

The question now was: Was the improvement only temporary or lasting? Did we deal with the real underlying dynamics or not? For many years I could not respond to critics who said that such brief therapy could not be lasting. We had no way of follow-up. But eight years later, when Sharon was sixteen, mother approached me in one of our guidance centers just to tell me that Sharon is volunteering her service in another center because she wants to become a child psychologist. There had been no recurrence of her difficulties.

The Question of Prognosis

This case illustrates all the major points in our approach to therapy. Naturally, one cannot expect 100 percent success in all cases.

The parents and the children are free to continue their disturbed relationship. But one can say that every child and every mother can learn what to do; every child and parent *can* change, although one never knows in any case whether they will.

This assumption is of far-reaching consequences. One of the most powerful psychological influences is anticipation. We all move toward what we anticipate. It may not always happen as we expect, influences out of our control may change the course of events. But we are always moving in the direction which we expect. To what extent teachers influence children by their anticipation has been convincingly demonstrated (Rosenthal and Jacobson, 1968). In this light one can visualize the tremendous harm which is done by our present correctional pessimism, reinforced by the new "discoveries" of brain pathology, of handicaps and deprivation, be they cultural, perceptual, or physical.

For this reason, making a prognosis impedes progress. If the prognosis is good and the patient does not make the expected progress, it produces deep discouragement in the therapist and patient alike. And if the prognosis is poor, the expectation of the therapist becomes an obstacle in his therapeutic facility. Making a prognosis is justified in medicine, where the course of therapy may depend on the statistical evaluation of various procedures. Dealing with individual human beings does not permit prediction. Even in severe cases, one cannot predict whether the individual will respond, although the odds are against him. The counselor and therapist are obliged to do the best they can, without having a stake in it. This was the chief advice which Adler always gave to his students, "Man muss seine Sache auf nichts stellen," which means, let the chips fall where they may.

In summary: the outstanding feature of the Adlerian approach is its emphasis on "teaching" parents and teachers how to cope with each child and how to change the child's motivation. This is a cultural problem. Understanding the child is a prerequisite for exerting a corrective influence. For this reason, we are organizing, in the States and abroad, study groups for parents. They are the first line of influence. Another Adlerian approach serves both the preventive and corrective purpose; Parent's Education Centers are needed in each community and eventuality in each school, where parents and teachers together learn how to understand the child and how to influence him regardless of the kind of difficulties he may have. We cannot solve the increasing problems of children and youth without such general educational efforts. Adler (1963) began his guidance work with the teachers in Vienna before he and his followers developed guidance centers in the community where each family was interviewed in front of teachers and other parents. We need such general projects of instruction. It seems that the Adlerian approach lends itself particularly well to provide it. As long as the necessary group procedures are not established and available, one may need individual counseling and therapy. But its effectiveness is limited in comparison to the group approach.

REFERENCES

Adler, A.　Study of organ inferiority and its psychical compensation. *Nervous and Mental Disease.* New York, 1917.

Adler, A.　*The education of children.* New York: Greenberg, 1913.

Adler, A.　Understanding human nature. New York: Greenberg, 1927.

Adler, A.　The criminal personality and its cure. *Internationale Zeitschrift für Individuelle Psychologie,* 1931, 321–329.

Adler, A.　The prevention of delinquency. *International Journal of Individual Psychology,* 1935, 1, 3–16.

Adler, A.　*Social interest: A challenge to mankind.* London: Faber & Faber, 1938.

Adler, A.　*The problem child.* New York: Capricorn Books, 1963.

Dinkmeyer, D. and Dreikurs, R.　*Encouraging children to learn: The encouragement process.* Englewood Cliffs, N.J.: Prentice-Hall, 1963.

Dreikurs, R.　Psychological differentiation of psychopathological conditions. *Individual Psychology Bulletin,* 1945, 4, 35–38.

Dreikurs, R.　*The challenge of parenthood.* New York: Duell, Sloan & Pearce, 1948.

Dreikurs, R.　Adlerian psychotherapy. In F. F. Reichman and J. I. Moreno (Eds.), *Progress in psychotherapy.* New York: Grune & Stratton, 1956, 111–118.

Dreikurs, R.　Psychotherapy as correction of faulty social values. *Journal of Individual Psychology,* 1957, 13, 150–158.

Dreikurs, R.　Music therapy with psychotic children. *Psychiatric Quarterly,* 1960, 34, 722–734.

Dreikurs, R.　The developing self in human potentialities. In H. A. Otto (Ed.), *Human potentialities.* St. Louis: Warren H. Green, 1968.

Dreikurs, R.　Social interest: The basis for normalcy. *The Counseling Psychologist,* 1969, 1, 45–48.

Dreikurs, R. and Crocker, D. B.　Music therapy with psychotic children. In *Music Therapy,* 1955, 62–73.

Dreikurs, R. and Grey, L.　*Logical consequences: A new approach to discipline.* New York: Hawthorne Books, 1968.

Dreikurs, R. and Grey, L. *Parents' guide to child discipline.* New York: Hawthorne Books, 1970.

Dreikurs, R. and Soltz, V. *Children: The challenge.* New York: Hawthorne Books, 1964.

Ferguson, E. D. Adlerian concepts in contemporary psychology: The changing scene. *Journal of Individual Psychology,* 1968, **24**, 151–156.

Freud, S. *Psychopathology of everyday life.* New York: MacMillan, 1915.

Grunwald, B. Is the teacher a psychotherapist? In R. Dreikurs (Ed.), *Education, guidance, and psychodynamics.* Chicago: Alfred Adler Institute, 1966.

Kvaraceus, M. C. *Delinquent behavior.* Washington, D.C.: National Educational Association, 1959.

Mead, M. *From the south seas.* New York: W. Morrow, 1949.

Merton, R. K. *Social theory and social structure.* Glencoe, Ill.: Free Press, 1957.

Money, J. et al. *The disabled reader.* Baltimore: Johns Hopkins Press, 1966.

Rosenthal, R. and Jacobson, L. *Pygmalion in the classroom: Teacher expectation and pupils' intellectual development.* New York: Holt, Rhinehart and Winston, 1968.

Shlien, J.; Mosak, H.; and Dreikurs, R. Effects of time limits: A comparison of two psychotherapies. *Journal of Counseling Psychology,* 1962, **9**, 31–34.

Shulman, B. H. *Essays in schizophrenia.* Baltimore: Willman & Wilkins, 1968.

Spiel, O. The individual psychological experimental school in Vienna. *American Journal of Individual Psychology,* 1956, **12**, 1–11.

Spiel, O. *Discipline without punishment.* London: Faber & Faber, 1962.

Szasz, T. S. *The myth of mental illness.* New York: Paul Hoeber, 1961.

Winthrop, H. Scientism in psychology. *Journal of Individual Psychology,* 1959, **15**, 112–120.

12

MICHAEL FORDHAM

A Theory
of Maturation

I n this essay I shall outline a theory of maturation and child care based on theories developed
largely by myself, but derived from Jung's conceptual model. As this is not always familiar, I
will first present a brief definition of the main
terms used and introduce my own application
and elaboration of the self concept.

Jung worked on a structural model using three
main entities: the ego, the archetypes, and
the self.

THE EGO   The ego was defined at the center of
consciousness, though Jung recognized the existence of unconscious parts of it in the "shadow"
(Jung, C.W. 9, ii).[1] However, once the ego con-

cept is extended to include parts of the psyche which are not conscious (and cannot easily achieve consciousness), it becomes **necessary** to define the attributes ascribed to it. The following list will suffice in the present context:

1. Perception
2. Memory
3. Organization of mental contents
4. Control over motility
5. Reality testing
6. Speech
7. Defenses. These may be divided into those that rely on exclusion of a mental content, e.g., repression, and those that rely on their distribution, e.g., projection, and introjection.
8. Capacity to relinquish its controlling and organizing functions.

THE ARCHETYPES   The archetypes are theoretical a priori structures of the unconscious. Though most studied in their complex but typical symbolic forms, i.e., in dreams, fantasies, mythology, folklore and religion, the essential core of Jung's theory is as follows: an archetype is a psychosomatic entity having two aspects, linked closely with physical instincts, the other with unconscious psychic forms. The physical component is the source of libidinal and aggressive "drives"; the psychic one is the origin of those fantasy forms through which the archetype reaches incomplete representation in consciousness. Whereas the drives are object-seeking and capable of relatively few though developing applications, fantasy can expand in many ways, use various objects, and sometimes, especially in pathological cases, display relatively unlimited variety.

Since the imagery through which archetypes express themselves is very varied, it becomes important to distinguish between the archetype as a theoretical entity and the empirical imagery and behavior which the concept organizes.

THE SELF   In Jung's view, the self is a concept embracing the wholeness of man represented in a number of symbolic forms. These seem to refer to an organizing system which includes not only the ego but also the archetypes. Understanding the meaning of these forms leads to progressive self-realization, termed individ-

---

[1] C. W. refers to *The collected works of C. G. Jung.*

uation. At first individuation was thought to occur only in adults, but my observations showed that symbols of the self occurred in dreams and fantasies of small children.

It was clear that the fantasies I, and later others, observed were related to the child's self-feeling, his sense of self-esteem and of identity, all feelings which could attain consciousness and so must be linked to the ego. Hence, there must be some particular dynamic relation between the ego and the self.

Analytical psychologists tend to conceive of the self as a stabilizing, centralizing, and even closed system. However, exclusive emphasis on stability and organization is not suitable when applied to the changing and developing periods of infancy and early childhood. The idea of the self as an integrator alone leaves no room for the emergence of part systems brought into being by the dynamic patterned drives and environmental stimuli.

It is assumed in this essay that the integrated self system is primary and so the infant or fetus is looked on as a unitary self, out of which the archetypes and the ego are derived. Aim-directed behavior, fantasies, thoughts, feelings, perceptions and impulses, all of which can be described separately in dynamic terms, do not grasp the child's nature as a whole unless it is realized that each group of experiences is linked to others not being cathected at any particular time. Recognition of these interrelations does something toward expressing the organic wholeness and individuality of the child in which his sense of identity is founded, but it requires modification to include an unstable, unintegrated status.

The idea of the self as expressed in steady states of integration alone, therefore, requires supplement, for during maturation unstable states of the self recur, sometimes involving part and sometimes the whole of the self. They last for a short or a long time, yet the whole self continues in being. An unstable state is not, in health, a disintegration, a term used to refer to splitting of the ego, and are therefore termed deintegrates, which are changes in orientation involving the whole person at first and later parts of it as maturation proceeds.

The stabilizing entity is conceived at first to be the self only, but soon the ego contributes and ensures that the dynamic sequences in the self do not prove unproductive and circular, but are changed by ego activity which in turn increases its strength. Thus, the structuring of the psyche is brought about to a major extent by the ego. Without the ego, only repetitive archetypal deintegrative-integration sequences would occur, and these, though adaptive, would not lead to permanent interacting structures, represented in symbols.

MATURATION

Intra-uterine Life

The fertilized ovum and the fetus is a unit bounded by but separate from its mother's body. Her function is to protect it and to provide raw materials for growth. She thus provides the necessary conditions through which genetic inheritance can control the form the infant's body will take at every stage in development.

While in utero, there is minimal exteroceptive sensory stimulation. Increase in knowledge of intra-uterine behavior reveals, however, that some of the activities in which the fetus engages are responses to stimuli, such as noise, reaching it from inside (defecation and heartbeat, for instance) and from outside its mother's body. There are also signs of muscular activity, besides arm and leg movements: thumb-sucking, swallowing amniotic fluid, and breathing "exercises" take place during intra-uterine life. All these show disturbances in the unitary state occur, whether they be stimulated by sensory stimuli or by discharges from within the nervous system. But in spite of them all, the predominant state of the embryo and fetus is quiescence and something very much like sleep.

Birth violently interrupts the protected aquatic life of the infant. It is widely held that the event gives rise to prototypic anxiety reflected later in birth and rebirth themes of archetypal fantasy. Yet the baby appears singularly unaffected by this drastic event: apart from a cry that accompanies the first inspiratory act, there are few or no signs of distress; soon the baby seems comfortable, and he re-establishes the essentials of his intra-uterine existence by sleeping. Once again unity is re-established. If we take the infant's intra-uterine life as the prototype of sleeping and his emergence into the world as the prototype of waking, the cycle repeats through life.

The Nursing Couple

The momentous event of birth is followed by others which derive from the infant's need to be fed, to be nursed, held, and to perform all those acts which lead to his developing with his mother the relation expressed in the phrase "the nursing couple."

Much study has been directed to the impulses, reflexes, and chemical systems which operate in the infant in the first few weeks and months, but though a healthy mother may know something about these, she does not relate to her offspring as if he were a bundle of impulses and reflexes in a complex of chemical systems. She senses and relates to him as a person. In my view, she thus grasps and respects the potentialities within her baby and his wholeness, which she will progressively get to know as development proceeds. At the same time she recognizes his independence from her. Birth has been a loss to her, which is only partly made up for by fulfilling her part as one of the nursing couple, and so a transitory depressed feeling is frequent till her relation with her baby is established.

The first feed is initiated by the mother. She picks up her baby, holds him and in doing so changes the infant's position, to initiate approach behavior (Cf. Call, 1964). Her facilitating acts provide the conditions for infant behavior that will culminate in taking the nipple into his mouth and starting to suck.

In establishing the feeding situation, the unity of a baby is disturbed by deintegrative discharges which are partly due to neurophysiological innervation. However, the theory of deintegrates presupposes a directed pattern intimately connected with the whole self, and carrying with it psychic features of the primary unity. Each response is total in the sense that it is felt to be its own world; there can be no other. There is no breast "out there" and the baby can only experience his mother, or rather the parts of her that he contacts, as a self representation.

Once breast feeding is established, the activity of approach behavior followed by feeding and perhaps by regurgitating air or food, leads to comfortable, relaxed play and sleep. It is the deintegrative drive in this sequence that brings the sensory-motor systems into operation, and so material for ego growth is provided in the first feed and all subsequent ones as well. Although some hold that ego activity can be observed during the first few feeds, their observations on perception are difficult to believe because there seems to be an enormous disparity between the complexity of the sensory input and the absence of a perceptual apparatus adequate to record their impact. Thus it seems that though the first motor activities are well-directed, the perceptual ego functions lag far behind in organization. Spitz (1965) suggests that first perceptions are vague and global, and only at about three months can the infant recognize "pre-objects." The smile of a baby depends upon his being presented with a schema composed of the forehead, eyes, and nose; it is not till seven months, he claims, that personal recognition takes place, and so only then have libidinal object relations been established. His ideas, based on observation and experiment, might lead to the conclusion that no object exists before three months. This cannot be the whole truth because it is known that the shape of the nipple determines whether a baby will feed from it or not. However, Spitz's observations are valuable in helping to date significant stages in maturation.

There is much evidence to suggest strongly that object relations begin very early, though are not clearly perceived in consciousness. It thus becomes necessary to postulate unconscious processes lying behind perceptual development, which simple observation and experiment have not yet grasped. Only observation combined with analytically informed inference have done much to fill in a gap.

In the first weeks and months the self deintegrates further. Simple drive discharges divide up into opposites, and this enables the baby to organize his accumulating experiences into "good" and "bad" objects. The objects producing satisfaction, and the breast does so during and after a good feed, are experienced as "good" objects; they lead to sleep and so to re-establishing the primary unity of the infant. Those that do not satisfy, because they do not meet the infant's needs, felt as hunger or other bodily discomforts, are experienced as "bad" objects.

At the start, the "goodness" and "badness" of an object is determined by satisfaction or dissatisfaction. The resulting nature of the object is "all or none": satisfaction is blissful, dissatisfaction catastrophic. But soon the baby starts to develop ways of managing his objects. Some can be turned "bad" and manipulated. For instance, an absent but needed object is treated concretely as a thing—a bad object. Thus if the breast is not available at once when needed, hunger can absorb the baby altogether. As the absent breast is understood concretely, it is treated as the origin of distress, and so it is felt as a bad breast which can be pushed out by defecating, for instance. Because this experience is total, there cannot be a good breast anywhere, and so the baby cannot relate his hunger to a potentially nourishing one when it is presented to him. The observation that only repeated stimulation of a baby's lips will lead to his accepting the nipple at all refers to this state of affairs.

The establishment of good and bad objects is a deintegrative step to which innate mechanisms and sensory experience contribute; each object represents a part of the self and so may be conceived as a part object which, in a primitive way, is adapted to the realities of the mother's behavior in relation to the infant's needs.

All this occurs before part objects are represented in the ego, and in this period everything depends upon the mother's sensitive provision of care for her baby (to be considered later, Cf. infra p. 473).

DEVELOPMENT AND MANAGEMENT OF PART OBJECTS   The existence of good and bad part objects creates a situation in which a number of ways of dealing with them gradually emerge. A bad object can be projected into the breast, and then it seems that the breast is attacking the baby by biting him, though the baby has in reality bitten the breast himself. On the other hand, as the example given above of the bad breast implied, the objects can be introjected. The same processes take place with good objects: they can be projected into the breast which becomes idealized and can produce not only satisfaction but concurrently a feeling of bliss. The good breast can also be taken in, introjected, and this gives the infant more good objects inside and increases the experience of himself as good through identification of himself with the good object.

All this implies that good and bad part objects have become representations, and when this happens a field of consciousness has developed. At first the two kinds of objects are not connected because the infant has no means of relating them to each other, but soon the ego starts to struggle with them so as to keep the good and bad objects separate. The intensity of anxiety can be very great, and has the "all or none" quality of any omnipotent and ruthless object.

The development of the processes referred to as projection, introjection and idealization, in later life so easily recognized as essentially psychical processes, are much more primitive and "physical" to an infant. They are the descendants of the mother-infant unity and result from its partial resolution and from the development of a sense of external and internal reality. Thus projection can only be perceived when affective experience can be compared with reality and seen to be incongruous with it. What this step means can be seen by reflecting that in the first place the equation of mother and self leads to states that in the adult would be called delusions. These are often called projections though, at this stage, projection is implied rather than existing, for it is only when ego growth has proceeded far enough for there to be boundaries between the infant and mother that we can speak of the ego projecting, introjecting and identifying with objects; each of these mechanisms implies the existence of two frames of reference, i.e., subject and object.

But inasmuch as all these processes seem to take place apart from ego activity and are therefore unconscious, they must first be based on archetypal structures that have deintegrated out of the self in the early stages of maturation. Each of these structures has boundaries and so can project or introject parts of themselves into others.

It is tempting to try and anatomize these early stages of maturation in a detail which can easily become misleading, because they presuppose ego structures that are improbable. The introduction of combined terms for intermediate states has, however, proved useful; for instance, projective and introjective identification have achieved increasing recognition.

Before leaving this attempt to conceptualize a primitive, unintegrated, prepersonal and ruthless period which corresponds with primitive identity in Jung's writing, it is worth trying to formulate, in living bodily metaphor, the nature of two of the three dynamic processes as they are experienced by babies: introjecting *is* eating, hearing, seeing, and breathing in; projection *is* excreting, spitting, regurgitating, vomiting, and breathing out. Identification by contrast has no such correlate, being a development of the first vestigial experiences of the self leading to the unity of the mouth and nipple and other parts of the nursing couple.

TRANSITIONAL OBJECTS   The first months have so far been directed to the deintegrative archetypal aspects of the mother-infant unit and the rudimentary efforts of the ego to control good and bad part objects on the basis of patterns derived from the dynamics inherent in the nature of the self. The description has lately been extended by Winnicott in a way that is significant for analytical psychologists.

It has long been known that small children become attached to objects which seem to be essential to their well-being. These may be anything from a bit of rag or stuff to a doll, particularly a soft one. They are treated as possessions and attempts to remove them are vigorously, even violently resisted, as if children's existence in some sense depended upon them. That the object itself is needed shows that it is not part of the child's inner world, nor does it represent a part of the mother or other libidinal object in the external world, for it is, in reality, controllable.

The transitional object, as Winnicott calls it, is conceived to originate during periods in which the mother is around and the baby is secure and comfortable. Then the baby may use the breast, or a bit of cloth that gets into his mouth, to play with and to create illusions (or delusions) which become meaningful. Thus the transitional object links with part objects, the nipple, skin, etc., which can be used to produce satisfaction in terms of libidinal need, but which are not so doing. The transitional object is not a substitute for libidinal and aggressive objects but is rather, in my view, an early attempt at self representation and so may be the first symbolization of all. In its development, the transitional object acquires archaic characteristics, and in it are found all kinds of part object (i.e., oral, anal and phallic) representations. These are, however, drawn into the object in an attempt to extend the self representation by the ego and the integrative action of the self during quiet and secure periods between deintegrative activity. Here it is apparent that the early stages of psychic objectification are to be found and the "spiritual" role of the archetype is being used and developed; indeed Winnicott locates the source of cultural processes here.

WHOLE OBJECTS   At about seven months, simple observation and experiment combine to show that a radical change takes place: the infant recognizes his mother as a libidinal object (Spitz, 1965) and he shows more explicit evidence that separation from her is distressful. Before this time it seems easier to substitute another woman for her, but now the baby can show signs of anaclitic depression (Spitz, 1946) if his mother is absent for too long, and especially in crisis periods. Independently, psychoanalysts have also dated changes at about this time. Klein formulated a theory of the depressive position, which is largely followed here; she held that it began at four to five months and culminated at six months. Winnicott called it the stage of concern but cautiously refused to date it.

It is not all that important at what precise age this change comes about, but it is necessary for it to occur if the personality is to develop well. The change is like one from madness and unintegration to sanity and integration; it is a step from part object life to living with whole objects; i.e., persons. During it, the sense of reality increases to make recognition of the infant's dependent situation clearer. Concurrently the inner world, already made possible partly by perceptual developments, but also by earlier introjection of sufficiently good omnipotent objects which have ensured that they will not be overcome by the bad ones, is given increasing definition.

The change from part to whole object relations is especially significant because it means that objects previously felt to be either good *or* bad, blissfully satisfying or catastrophically frustrating and persecuting, can now be recognized as the same object. Consequently the baby becomes concerned lest, in his angry or greedy attacks, he damages or destroys his mother's good breast when he feels it is bad. And he can now feel that this had happened and recognizes his need for his mother's continued existence.

At this point he may mobilize some of the old feelings and, by denying that the breast is good *and* bad, make an illusion that it is only bad, and so apparently make it safe to triumph over. But this illusion does not really work, and so his triumph does not bring comfort, but restless and excited exaltation.

The defense by triumphing (manic defense) is made against another sequence which derives from the infant feeling concern and a prototype of guilt, which leads to his being overwhelmed by a kind of depression, not however to be confused with its adult equivalent. But if he does so feel, he has yet to make the next step in discovery: he can repair the damage. He can feel that there is a cavity or hole that he has made in his mother during his greedy attack on her and that this can be filled up, and his mother restored. When he does so, he begins all those feelings that go on later to being sorry and wanting to make better, harm that has occurred as the result of some accidental or deliberate damage of which he has been the cause. Feelings of guilt, sadness and the capacity to make reparation all originate in this period.

SYMBOL FORMATION   Here also, symbolic images increasingly replace concrete object representation. The increase in the baby's sense of reality runs concurrently with the formation of his body image and so his capacity to build up his inner world. His objects are no longer mother-self objects, but his own, and his self images are distinguished from external object representations. This important step is an essential part of the formation of whole objects. Concurrently the baby's feelings about his mother and himself become distinguished in the formation of external objects and symbolic images in his inner world.

The progression to symbolic representation has however a different aspect brought about by the formation of transitional objects. They do not belong to the inner world nor to the outer, but refer to or combine both. They are therefore between the two and make room for symbolism of a different kind which bridges reality and the inner world. In the first place they participate in the concreteness of the part object, but it is known that they are important in learning processes, in play, fantasy and in the development of transpersonal cultural life. Therefore, in the symbolizing processes they probably become less attached to objects and more to plastic forms of expression.

CONCLUSION   Enough has now been said to draw a conclusion relevant to the general theory of analytical psychology. The self in which interrelated omnipotent objects have developed has become represented in an organized central personal ego which reflects its wholeness and contains good and bad objects. Though there is an essential imbalance, in that the good objects are sufficient to predominate over the bad ones, the structures have been developed which can render future steps in separation sad but rewarding.

The primal unity of the self has through deintegration led to primary identity with the mother, and out of this has arisen a situation out of which psychic structures developed. They have become integrated into a whole in which the ego has become established and has taken a leading part in the organization of its parts. The state which Jung described as identity, or alternatively *participation mystique* with the environment, has been dissolved for the first time.

Ego Growth

Maturation has so far been thought of as taking place during the oral (nutritional) phase, when the baby is primarily concerned with his mouth as a source of excitement, satisfaction, frustration, anxiety, and the focus of his growing perceptual world. His deintegrative drives, reflected in hunger and greed, were focused on feeding and his ego was occupied in gaining progressive mastery over them. But much more has gone on than feeding; greater control has been progressively achieved over skeletal musculature, whose often violent activity was at first uncontrollable—biting and scratching were a major source of destructive fantasies. Further, anal and urethal activities have played a part which has been touched on but not developed. As in feeding, the interplay of libidinal and aggressive energies have given rise to anxieties about the effect of excreta on the infant's mother and on himself. On the one hand there has been pleasure and satisfaction in the release of internal tensions: feces and urine were felt as parts of the self which can be good objects, gifts given in gratitude for the love and care resulting in comfort when distress and pain threatened to become intolerable. On the other hand there have been fears of drowning, poisoning and destroying his mother and himself with their imagined violence, which at first plays ruthlessly on her and his own body and then, as the objects become recognized as both good and bad, feelings of concern, sadness, guilt, and wishes to make reparation develop, and symbolization begins to take place.

The importance of control over excreta takes its place in relation to control over feeding and the expansion of the infant's perceptual field, his reality sense, and especially his inner world located inside his body. His excreta take a special place in expressing his being a person with a skin surface that defines what is inside and what outside. Though he can exert little control over his internal bodily functions, he can increasingly decide what he takes in and what he extrudes. His sense of self is increased as his body becomes established, and it may be abstracted, imagined, symbolized or broken up and apparently dissolved. But in health it persists once control over excreta, feeding and musculature has been mastered.

The essentials of a self representation in the ego are well-given in this simple paradigm of the body image. To complete the significant dynamism of its life, other activities need to be added: crying, screaming, spitting, at first release activities, become communicative; incorporative activities, like holding and clinging, are now increasingly recognized as essential to infant well-being and so, as self-feelings.

Vision occupies a special place in preception and in establishing object constancy upon which depends the feeling of being one and the same person in space and time. As the distance percept, which starts to function at the first feed, it explores the external world and forms the basis for recognizing that objects continue to exist in their physical absence. But object constancy is not only visual, it applies both to objects outside the skin surface and to the person of the infant himself, who in the setting of his mother's care and empathy discovers his own continuity of being; it is there in the first place as the self, but is unrepresented and has to be discovered by the ego gradually, piece by piece.

The next steps in self-mastery are arrived at by exploring the external world. An infant has up to now been dependent upon parts of it being presented to him directly or indirectly by his mother, except with respect to seeing and hearing. To be sure, he can start putting food into his mouth when it is put near enough to him, and he has learned that expressions of rage and pining will result in objects being provided for him; he can fantasy magical omnipotent control over them, but it is only when he can first crawl that he can in reality increase the accuracy and range of his discovery in which up to now only his eyes and ears were of much use.

One other motor activity has still to be mastered; it is speech. Once achieved, the infant becomes in all essentials viable—a fully communicating and basically independent person.

Individuation

When a child has become mobile, first by crawling and then walking, he has reached the toddler stage. From now on he becomes physically far more independent of his mother: he can play with toys of his own choosing, he can get those that he wants without having them brought to him, and he can manipulate a wide variety of objects with a skill that rapidly increases.

Normally a toddler plays on his own for a restricted period and cannot tolerate his mother's absence for long without signs of distress. If he plays on his own he will tend to return to her from time to time, clamber onto her lap and then climb down to continue his play. Soon mother's absence can be tolerated, and the presence of a substitute will do, until at nursery school age he can happily join a group.

These manifestations of progressive independence are also due to the child's use of toys as symbolic representations of ideas and fantasies which facilitate independence and develop social relations by providing an objective medium of communication. The developments at the toddler stage have been referred to as the separation-individuation phase by Mahler (1963) and are so called because they end the "symbiotic phase" of identity between mother and infant. Her formulation draws attention to the increased capacity for mobility, as cogently expressing individuation in action. There is also clear evidence that the infant is developing his ego functions in his independent activities which in themselves will soon no longer need his mother's presence. Certainly there are many signs of identification besides individuating processes, and the need of the infant to reunite with his mother is still evident between his exploratory activities, but in this period there can be no doubt that primary identity, or as Jung called it alternatively *participation mystique,* is progressively dissolving, that the infant's symbolic life is becoming better established along with his greater mastery of reality. It is a period of increasing stable integration. Early on, deintegrative processes predominated in growth; gradually they did so less, and then with the development of an inner world, true symbolization began and the reality sense became greater; separation-individuation processes were well under way. By two years, it may be said that ego growth has gone far enough through integrative-deintegrative sequences. The individuation processes that first began when whole object relations developed are now clear for all to see. Jung's definition that individuation is "the process of forming and specializing the individual nature . . ." and "the development of consciousness (the ego) out of the original state of identity," clearly applies.

The use of the term individuation in relation to infancy has led to protests that this is not the same as Jung's usage and, so as not to cause confusion, Henderson (1967) proposed that it would be better to refer to "the individuating processes," reserving the single word to indicate the processes that Jung worked on so much in the later part of life. The only objection I have to Henderson's proposal is that it makes for cumbersome nomenclature and implys that the dynamic processes in each case are essentially different—this is not my position.

Oedipal Conflicts

The next critical phase in maturation centers in the Oedipal situation. It is the period during which the basis for subsequent heterosexual life is laid down and in which genital feelings, impulses, and fantasies mature and make themselves conscious.

The aspect of this period to which I want to draw attention is its importance in the child's growing sense of his identity. The earliest identity conflicts begin in the pre-Oedipal period; they become increasingly evident during the toddler stage and they culminate in the Oedipal phase because the child's feelings about himself as male or female are thrown into relief.

A boy or a girl, given tolerant and trustworthy parents, will have realized the existence of sexual differences before this time; penis envy in the little girl and penis pride in the boy allied to castration anxieties in both will have become conscious so long as the parents' attitude is perceptive and tolerant. If it is inadequate, the discoveries may be withheld or made secretively and indirectly. In the Oedipal period, the establishment of genital primacy and the rivalries with and jealousies of the parent of the same sex become central. Increasing weight and poignancy is given to fantasies, feelings, and impulses related to the physical relationship between the parents. The primal scene, first believed to record the child witnessing his parents during sexual intercourse, was later recognized as representing not only the real event but also the child's fantasies about sexual union. This discovery means that the situation is an archetypal one. It corresponds to the conjunction that has been studied intensively by Jung (*C.W.*, 14) as a central feature of individuation. The union of opposites to which it leads has, according to him, almost endless representations, abstract, archaic and sexual. To a child the primal scene comprises almost any situation in which his parents are in reality or fantasy exclusively occupied with each other to the exclusion of himself. He adapts himself to this situation either by attacking them and trying to separate them or by putting himself, either in play or in fantasy, in the position of one or another or both of them.

If maturation proceeds normally the situation leads to conflicts centering around a genital position. Alongside progression there are periodic regressions in which earlier experiences revive and lead to fantasies and speculations based on them: parents may be conceived as feeding each other or enjoying sensory pleasure in excretory activities, and frequently bizarre combinations are imagined. As with earlier sexual "discoveries," the child's conflicts may be largely unconscious; indeed, whether they become conscious or not depends to a large extent on whether his parents are aware of what is going on and understand it too.

The satisfactory outcome of this frequently complex situation is brought about by a realignment of identifications. Those with the parent of the same sex, if earlier maturation processes have gone forward smoothly enough, are firmbly established. Masturbation anxieties and guilt are increased and this leads to the repressive mastery of the libidinal drives.

The importance of this period for identity formation is crucial. By identification the child's sexual affects are organized into patterns of behavior and accompanying fantasies which accord with his body image and his physical inheritance. Furthermore, these patterns are allied through his parents with the collective matrix, conscious and unconscious, in which the family lives. In this process earlier identifications with the opposite sex remain, but they are built into the child's inner world. The Oedipal conflict strongly reinforces the establishment of anima and animus figures (Cf. Jung, *C.W.*, 7) which lie ready as it were to be projected in the love relationship of adolescence. It is here that the main trends henceforward are directed toward social adaptation, on which Jung laid so much stress when he emphasized the sexual and adaptive aims of young people. He was justified in doing so because of the intensity of his study of the introverting processes of later life. But there are really no grounds for believing that the social implications in the identifications that resolve Oedipal conflicts are the whole picture. The increase in the child's sense of his own identity is indeed witness to the activity of individuating processes at work, or, to put it in another way, the alignment of his sexual behavior and fantasies with his impulses and his body image increase his capacity for true self-expression. If the ego is strengthened, the underlying wholeness of the self is not necessarily made inaccessible.

In aid of the idea that one-sided development is necessary and inevitable, the theory of repression can be evoked. However, this defense belongs to the Oedipal conflict and leads to sexual latency which, optimally, continues till adolescence. So long as it is brought about internally and its internal function is not masked by personal and social pressures, it becomes part of the individual's means of development during latency. Defenses originate when deintegration of the self brings opposites into being and when the infant ego's struggle to establish his good objects against the bad ones starts. The conflict develops into castration anxiety when the Oedipal phase is reached. Repression is therefore one way of managing internal conflict. It does not apply so much when sexual maturity is reached. However, if one defense is going to be evoked to support a questionable theory, what about all the other ones? If they are all included, then individuation would mean doing away with essential ego functions, which is not how it is conceived.

Latency and Adolescence

With the passing of the Oedipal conflict, all the essential structures of later development have been laid down; each develops further in intensity and richness, and becomes increasingly complex; each enters into new combinations and is applied in different fields.

From now on the extent of consciousness grows and is consolidated in the development of activities outside the family, most of all in school. During this period the personal differentiates, and the child discovers how to take greater part in society and find his level in it.

At adolescence this relative stability is disrupted by the maturation of the child's sexuality. Its effects will be discussed later, for a significant impact of adolescent turbulence, which does not belong properly speaking to childhood, is on the social aspects of family life and on society itself.

THE FAMILY

Maturation can only proceed fully in a good environment, and that means a family life based on a good enough marriage. There is no room for perfectionism here, and the inevitability of conflict in marriage is well expressed in the symbolic formula that male and female are opposites. Where there are opposites there is conflict; a marriage without it is suspect. Everybody understands that conflict between parents and children is inevitable, but those between parents, if worked out, are equally an expression of vitality in the marriage relation.

It would be mistaken to claim that *any* conflict is desirable; it is rather its nature that is important both quantitatively and qualitavely. Open destructive conflict between parents is bad for children, but absence of conflict in so-called happy marriages can be damaging as well, especially if the happiness is unreal, idealized, and kept up at the expense of instinctual life.

It was Jung's thesis that the unlived life of parents becomes the burden of their children or, in more technical terms, the psychopathology of parents becomes introjected by their children. The formula has many facets, for it makes a great difference at what stage in development the baneful influence of parents is most felt. The examples in the literature of analytical psychology mainly stem from post-Oedipal identifications when the solution of the parents' conflict situation brings relief to the child whose ego has developed sufficiently to resolve the trauma once its cause is removed. But the damage begins earlier in infancy; if an infant is inadequately held, fed, cared for, the result is far more serious and even catastrophic.

The negative formula about parents and children can be related profitably to another proposition: in nursing an infant and bringing up a child the parents recapitulate their own infancy and child-hood. In doing so opportunity is provided to relive and resolve, with their child, developmental failures or deviations resulting from their own past. It is only when this redevelopment fails that it brings about impingements or damage to a child because no mod-ification is possible in the parents' affective life, and a traumatic situation persists by reinforcement over and over again.

Marriage can be achieved for varying motives, but the ones of most concern are those that stem from the identification of the couple established in the course of their own maturation. They derive from various levels but the way in which the Oedipal situa-tion of the potential mother and father has been worked through is the most important. To put it briefly, it is necessary for a hus-band and wife to reflect sufficiently the characteristics of the grandparents of the opposite sex. Too great a similarity creates infantile reactions just as too much difference makes mutual adap-tation excessively difficult. The special reason for taking up this idea derives from Jung's formulations about the meaning of mar-riage customs in primitive tribes. He claims (Jung, *C.W.* 16, p. 224 ff.), following Layard, that they are structured to ensure a proper compensatory interchange; they are a compromise between endogamous and exogamous tendencies. The former consolidate family ties; the latter lead to group solidarity and "ongoing spir-itual life." Too much of one and too much of the other lead to undesirable consequences, because either the family will become an anti-social unit (because it is satisfying in itself), or it will not receive sufficient libido to make it stable.

Jung's thesis (ibid., p. 225 ff.) includes in it the idea that mar-riage depends largely upon the mutual projection of unconscious archetypal forms, the animus and the anima. Besides identifica-tions with the personal parents of the same sex, which takes place during maturation, Jung held that they represent an archetypal substrate into which the identifications are built. The archetype is expressed in typical fantasies of what men, in the case of a woman, or a woman in the case of a man, ideally ought to be like and assumes that human beings are functionally bisexual. Marriage is consolidated by each partner carrying enough of these archetypal projections which only gradually get withdrawn as each partner needs to form more and more realistic appreciation of the other. This simple statement about marriage is sufficient for present pur-poses. In reality it is a combination, relatively simple in biological terms, rendered extremely complex by the range of personal and social factors influencing and combining in it. For the present, its effectiveness will be taken for granted and so the following discussion assumes a good enough marriage for children to be raised in. Its aim is to indicate the effects children have upon, and the benefits they receive, from their parents.

Family life begins when a wife becomes pregnant. Then she starts to withdraw some of her libido from the outside world and concentrates it on the changes in her body and the baby that is growing inside her. At first she pursues her day-to-day activities as before, but as she becomes more and more dependent and in need of so becoming, the stability of her relation to her husband is tested.

The increased demands made on him derive from her need for him to participate in the pregnancy by doing what he can to make her physical burden less. But just as she becomes physically dependent so does she also become emotionally vulnerable and in need of his care and protection. All this will be well enough understood by a couple who can trust each other because they have come from good enough families themselves and have memories of how their own parents behaved and how they themselves reacted to their mothers' pregnancy and the birth of another baby. Under these conditions their own built-in instincts will be reliable.

When labor begins, it was often customary to exclude the father till birth had occurred. It was reinforced by medical care which aimed to make birth safe for mother and baby and so the father, as a complicating person, was kept out of the way so that full medical care could be provided. Nowadays, however, antenatal care has made labor increasingly safe, and if parents want to be together there is no reason why they should not be and so reserve continuity of experience between them. There are techniques of "natural childbirth" which include the father and show that in a good marriage labor can be made easier.

Infancy

Once the baby is born, the mother is instinctively prepared to meet his needs, given the support of her husband, and she relates to her infant through primary maternal preoccupation. Winnicott used this phase to describe the capacity of a mother to become absorbed in her infant during the last weeks of pregnancy and the first weeks of extra-uterine life. In this way she becomes sensitized to the absolute needs of her baby and indeed at once starts not only satisfying but also anticipating them. It is a period during which the baby has virtually no means of conscious orientation, so the failure to meet a need easily becomes catastrophic.

The last weeks of pregnancy, continuing through the first weeks of life, are thus crucial for the baby's further development. There is a natural sequence here: the mother's increasing focus on the baby inside her, leading to birth followed by primary maternal preoccupation. Clearly a mother who has carried the baby inside her is the best one to manage the formation of true self-representations in her baby. Much can be done to make up failures by what is ordinarily called "spoiling," but it cannot be truly remedied. A mother is predisposed to treat her baby as a person—so she relates to the self—whom she can empathically know. She also needs to reestablish the feeling that he is part of herself; her capacity to react on the basis of her own life when she too was a baby is important here. Inasmuch as her unconscious "memories" are good enough, she can, as a separate person, not only provide, but she can also put herself into the infant's position. Thus by anticipating, she creates a situation in which disturbance in her baby is made not merely tolerable, but in the first place is completely matched through her behavior and empathic feeling. The unity of the self is thus replaced by the mother-infant unit.

The baby treats his mother as a part of the self to which she gives physical and psychical reality. By providing reliably and empathically, a mother thus creates the basis for feelings of trust from which grows a sense of individual identity in a secure and reliable environment—the two being co-extensive.

A consequence of primary preoccupation is that the father is further deprived of libido previously invested in him. It is usual to think that how he responds is not particularly important, but this is not so, and therefore he has been included all through my account. Of course there are other primary and secondary gains for him: pride and satisfaction in his wife and the baby and new motives for exertion in his work to keep their material existence secure. He can also draw on maternal identifications and become motherly when providing security for his wife and baby and leaving them to find out more about each other without interference. Perhaps so little attention has been paid to what he does because it seems so obvious and because his seems so much the lesser achievement, but all the same his emotional reliability and stability are tested through and through, and so the family undergoes stress when the first baby arrives which will not be repeated in the same way again.

Once the early phase has been worked through, the mother can recognize that her baby is established in relation to her. From now on she can safely begin to frustrate him, for the baby will be able to grasp what this means and react with increasing reliability by crying and other expressions of rage, thus giving signs that he is hungry or suffering from other forms of discomfort. Based on her own early experience she has acquired a reliable basis for knowing what emotions her baby can begin to manage and what becomes destructive; at the same time she can get to know the length of time that her infant, when awake, can tolerate her absence. All this seems at variance with the baby's inability to distinguish his mother from a substitute one; his perceptions are vague and generalized, and when objects get represented they are part objects; only by the rather arbitrarily chosen date of seven months does his mother become a true libidinal object. But the difficulty may not be so resistant to understanding if it is the baby's self that his mother first gets to know. Rudiments of an ego, however, are soon clearly perceptible and it rapidly grows, particularly in early play between feeds and through successful management of tolerable frustration.

This attempt to describe in outline only, how a mother establishes the nursing couple set-up, implies a degree of necessary regression. Through this she can empathize with her baby and develop herself if necessary, but it does not include the medley of affects to which her baby will subject her. She will need to participate in feelings of being sucked dry, bitten, eaten up "cannibalistically," rejected, insulted, assaulted, as well as loved, adored, and ravished. All this rich variety of experience must evoke hate as well as love in her, and her own infantile feelings will be roused and earlier management crises in her life are liable to be evoked.

This picture of mothering is intended to introduce an aspect of a mother's nature, instinctive, non-rational, half-conscious, yet reliable. It is an aspect of what Jung called eros, whose praises he sang in such glowing terms, especially in *Memories, Dreams, Reflections* (p. 325 f.). His praise tends, however, to obscure the realistic and nonmythological eros which a mother lives. The stresses to which she is subjected make it understandable if she needs help. Some mothers require more, others less, so if she cannot achieve maternal preoccupation there is no point in refraining from finding substitutes. Idealization of motherhood cannot be justified; if breast feeding is not tolerable, a bottle can be used and helpers can be introduced in such a way that mothers are not prevented from doing what they are able and fitted to do.

Just as women have varying capacities for adapting to their babies so also fathers differ in their ability for providing the support and care of their wives—for taking over the baby for a time, cooking, helping to get feeds ready, and so forth. If a mother's own instinctual and infantile life is tested, so is the father's. For him, this period can evoke envy and jealousy which he needs to know about and if necessary allow for by actively recognizing his limitations and getting the support and practical help for his wife which he may not be able to provide.

Oedipal Conflicts

So far the father has necessarily been in the background—a sort of essential participating observer—but as maturation proceeds he can do more and more. If the baby is not the first and there are other children, he has already performed a useful part in developing his relation with them as they find their mother occupied in loving another baby. It is an opportunity which has needed all his skill and understanding. However, assuming that the baby is the first, he is to some extent out on a limb. This is by no means so as the Oedipal conflicts begin to emerge, for with the shift to the triangular situation, both parents necessarily participate with equal status. The drives mobilized in the child with particular intensity are ambivalent, actively sexual and aggressive, and can rouse comparably intense responses in the parents. Knowledge about the jealousy and rivalry which children feel toward parents of the same sex and also guilt over genital excitement with concurrent castration anxieties can go some way toward helping, but in affective crises intellectual knowledge is unfortunately a broken reed.

Jung's position on infantile sexuality has often been much criticized and with some justification, because his ideas on how to understand the facts vacillated within wide limits. Occasionally he went so far as to say that he viewed the subject from the position of the parents, as if infantile sexuality was an introjective phenomenon. He never elaborated this position, so it is not known what he really meant. However, his exaggerated statement is valuable because it includes parents' affective life in the Oedipal situation and probably refers to the observation that conflicts between them can lead on the one hand to compulsive sexual manifestation in their children or on the other to virtually complete suppression in the child of direct sexual feelings, impulses or fantasies.

Anxiety on the parents' part is common because children can

rouse sexual feelings in them by their behavior. If Jung's position cannot be sustained, still, much too little attention is given to the parents' part in Oedipal conflicts and surprisingly little has been recorded about it. It is not discussed openly, no doubt because of the incest taboo which presupposes that parents act out their sexual wishes if not supported by social sanctions. But if sexual maturation means anything, it could be taken as a sign of maturity if the children can succeed in exciting their parents. Far from leading to perversions, it would be an indication of health so long as it were recognized as part of the Oedipal conflict pattern, in which libidinal drives are inherently checked by castration anxieties and guilt. It takes a strong ego to manage the drives, and it can only be done if the sexual life between parents is healthy and they have participated in their child's libidinal life, recognizing that frustration of it has an essential part in maturation. Any infantile anxieties on the parents' part can be ruthlessly sought out by their children. From this stems often distressing infantile jealousy which can be overlooked, and so leads to recrimination between the parents.

The Oedipal situation is the culmination of a child's development and so cannot be thought of in isolation. The form it takes depends on earlier vicissitudes of the parent-child relation, and its successful resolution depends once again on the instinctual health of the parents. This is the important element in Jung's overstatement.

Alongside the libidinal developments at this period, aggression toward the parents of the same sex expressed in rivalry and death wishes comes to the fore. To this also, the same principle applies. Their management is perhaps more important because it is essential that the parent behave in such a way as to support the child's concurrent admiration and trust, and so foster the identifications which will lead to instinctual repression and to the child's ongoing development.

Adolescence and After

The loosening of identifications and the growing independence of the adolescent places strains on the parents and once again tests the durability of the marriage. Ideally, a couple should be equally matched and so complement each other, but this is never the reality. At the beginning of this chapter the importance of similarities and differences in the history of the parents was stressed, and many changes will have taken place in the course of bringing up children, especially if it is understood that they themselves will need to change progressively as maturation proceeds.

Under favorable conditions, a father's manliness will be reinforced, as will the wife's motherliness. However, this can only happen if projections have taken place concurrently. In a mature personality, aspects of the self are deintegrated into archetypal structures which, in the context of a family, are defined as the child archetype (Jung, C.W., 9, i), the anima in the father and the animus in the mother. Each of these archetypes is a system of relationships to the opposite sex and children, and the degree to which and the form in which they are projected depends upon the maturity of the adult. The less mature, the more idealized and omnipotent will they be, so the more conflict-work will be necessary to sustain the marriage, because more infantile trends need to be worked through and resolved.

Many years ago Jung (C.W., 17, p. 189 ff.) introduced a useful formulation. He laid emphasis on inequalities in the personalities of the married couple: one can be more complex and differentiated and gifted than the other. He noticed that the more complex of the pair was the less satisfied by the other, who was content if fascinated and contained. If this disparity is not worked on, it provides a basis for disturbances in the marriage which start from the more complex person. He or she will look elsewhere for the satisfactions not supplied by the mate. A particular tendency is for the anima or animus to become projected, and this leads to extra-marital love affairs.

His formulation tended to leave out the degree of maturity which means, in terms of maturation as conceived in this essay, the stability of the inner world and so of inner resources. While complexity and richness of personality is one element, the other is the capacity for stability and deployment of abilities in a profitable manner. In other words, the more stable and complex personality need not be a disruption to family life.

The frequency with which one partner is partially contained in the other is often emphasized by adolescence and its sequelae, which will throw differences more clearly into relief. The parents are progressively thrown back on each other, and their relation changes from a biological to an increasingly psychological and personal one. The change increases the necessity for the parents to withdraw projections that may have worked perfectly well up to now and will involve alterations in libidinal interests of quite an intense kind. Perhaps this applies more to the mother than to the father, but this is not always so, and in any case leads to a renewed testing of inner resources and the development of abilities.

However, though adolescence marks a change in family life, it is by no means the end of it. Parents are still required from time to time, and when their children marry they will become grandparents and so instinctual satisfactions are still available.

Adolescence, however, ends intimate and continuous family life and starts a process to which Jung paid particular attention, and during which he noted particularly strong individuating processes. He studied this period of middle and old age, to which, classically, individuation belongs. Certainly the second half of life had been given insufficient attention when he wrote, and to give it meaning he was fully justified in almost confining individuation to it. However, individuation, in the sense of developing consciousness by paying attention to and activating inner resources, and so making projections flexible and capable of being integrated, is a continuous process.

So far the need for further individuation has been considered in terms of the need for parents to gain a more realistic understanding of each other's needs by withdrawal of aspects of the animus and the anima. In addition, however, there is the child archetype which is a more complete self representation. As children grow up, the withdrawal of the group of structures and functions expressed in this archetype will evoke further individuating processes. Functions that have become specialized will need revaluation in the light of the needs of the personality as a whole. For this reason, family life can be understood as a means not only of satisfying biological (instinctual) needs, but also as a way of realizing individuating processes in the personalities of the parents. The adolescence of children is a testing time for how far the parents have been able to use their combined life for maturation of their own selves, how far they have adapted parenthood to the growing needs of their children, and how far they will be able to continue to make their lives meaningful when family ties cease to be the center of their libidinal investments.

THE SOCIAL SETTING

As part of group life, society has developed ways of representing archetypal functioning in myths, religious observances, art, politics, and the law. In all these the archetypal patterns are relatively conscious and contribute to forming culture patterns. But no society has represented all the needs and aspirations of its individual members and those not represented remain primitive and largely unconscious. In the aggregate it is they that form the shadow of the group and comprise the collective unconscious.

The unrepresented archetypes do not appear in ordinary social life, and so the majority are not aware of them. If, however, the prevailing culture pattern is unstable, and today this state of affairs predominates, then the unconscious archetypes become active and will become vaguely apparent in social discontent. They can lead, if their import is grasped by enough individuals, to the formation of groups advocating social reforms, religious change, new developments in art, and the like. In the course of time, and if circumstances are favorable, the groups grow and the ideas they represent, whether religious, political, intellectual or aesthetic, get assimilated into the community and some change in the culture pattern results.

Jung was particularly interested in the dreams and fantasies of individuals expressing incipient collective change (C.W., 10) and, combining these with his theory and his knowledge of the history of religions, he set the dreams of his patients in their mythological context. His very elaborate research led him to make interpretations of major trends in civilization, and he spotlighted self symbols as indicating a sort of group individuation process going on at the present time (cf. C.W., 11, p. 355 ff.).

Not until adolescence are children sufficiently independent to make much impact on society; then it is their identity conflicts that become dynamically acute as they struggle to find their place in society. The increase in their often distressing rebelliousness arises in part from ongoing trends and as such is valuable. New alliances are being formed and in the process the boy or girl can come into relation with the shadow of social life, and so the outrageousness of adolescent behavior sometimes becomes a scandal. In this state of affairs regression is apparent and the relationship patterns between infant and mother are revived to become expressed in confusion and disorientation.

The regressive element is not only negative, as this account might suggest, for it establishes continuity in impersonal life and, when integrated, contributes to establishing the identity feelings of the adolescent in the expanding social context, away from his family, toward which he is moving. An adolescent has a long development behind him which does not disappear. He has, it is true, acquired socialized experience, mainly in school, but this is only partly an adequate introduction to the larger world which makes many impersonal demands on him. The roots of the adolescent's uncontrollable turbulence lie, then, in infancy, when his mother and later other members of the family comprised his "society"; it was in relation to them that the prototype of later patterns of behavior were laid down.

In all the early periods, maturation processes pressed him away from personal ruthless drives toward forming perceptions of himself and his mother as a person about whom he has felt concern; now at adolescence the prepersonal structures revive in response to the less personal roles he is expected to fulfill. So the infantile roots are needed if he is to find his identity in new patterns of living. Omnipotent fantasies result in attacks on parents and on society that stem from the manic defenses of infancy, the source of heroes and heroines. Depressive episodes, depersonalizing, hysterical and splitting processes in the ego are not at all infrequent and often constitute a kind of "normal insanity." The ruthlessness characteristic of these states is proverbial, and when they predominate an adolescent needs support and a kind of indirect holding such a mother provides for her infant, rather than the direct control of discipline which only provokes more rebellion.

An adolescent comes into direct contact with the culture pattern and the collective unconscious. In a very different way and right from the beginning, when an infant, he had been influenced indirectly by the society in which his family lives. His parents expressed collective attitudes to infants and infancy, accepted methods of child-care, and later on, education reinforced them. Then he did not grapple with them directly as he does now, and will in later life, but much of the outcome depends on whether early influences are related to how he is expected to behave now.

The predominating customs surrounding birth and early infant care were not determined by his or his parents' needs. It was and still is widely—almost universally—held that the relationship between mother and father must be interrupted by the birth of the baby: either the mother goes into the hospital, from which her husband is excluded, except as a visitor after the birth, or else, if the birth takes place at home, doctor and midwife take charge to the exclusion of the father. The next step in a common regimen is to remove the infant from his mother immediately after birth, wash him and put him in a cot; only after a period of separation is the baby brought to her for feeding and then taken away again.

Thus the baby's intra-uterine adaptation to aquatic life is rudely interrupted, not only by birth but also by custom. Protective skin substances are removed by washing and the relation to his mother broken just when a more empathic understanding of the baby would feel it to be undesirable.

Infant feeding is likewise controlled to a large extent by custom. Regular feeding techniques and methods of habit training were based on custom rather than knowledge of the kind of handling that an infant needs, and other examples could be multiplied from every day experience.

Their significance cannot, however, be easily grasped because they are commonly accepted without much or any reflection and are too near at hand to be seen in perspective. Studies made of primitive tribes by social anthropologists show more easily, because they are less imminent and less laden with potential affect, how the customs of infant management relate to the culture in which the infant will one day live. The studies are made in relatively small societies and are easier to envisage than the large Western ones which in any case comprise a variety of differing subcultures.

Comparative studies show clearly that radically different customs can be successful. By contrast with ours, other cultures give far greater importance to a father's usefulness, in that he may participate in birth. Turning to the baby, infants may first be suckled by a "wet nurse" because the colostrum is conceived to be bad for them; alternatively, mother may take sole charge and feed her baby, not for the short period current in our society, but for up to three years. During this period the husband is excluded as a sexual partner, for his wife is expected to devote all her libido to her infant.

A prominent feature of all these researches is that varying methods of infant care are intimately related to behavior that will be required of the child, adolescent, and adult in society. Applying this idea to our culture, the revolutionary change that has today begun to emerge in infant care and the upbringing of children must be socially significant. Indeed, whereas before the mother first and later other adult members of the family were the center of the scene, today the satisfaction of the infant's developing needs is becoming more and more central. Concurrently new attitudes and methods of education are being introduced which diminish the importance of discipline and seek to meet the developing needs of children. Sometimes the changes are determined by scientific knowledge, but not often, and it is far more likely that they are part and parcel of the idealization of democracy. Since this is supposed to require more sense of responsibility from the individual, it is thought desirable to foster it as early as possible. Therefore to ask what an infant needs from his mother so as to develop himself, not how he can be made to conform to specified requirements, acquires extra significance.

The relatively new attitude has not, it is true, arisen from sociological reflections. It has rather derived from investigating the psychopathology of patients and discovering the causes of mental illness. Nonetheless the breadth as well as the depth dimensions from which new ideas and techniques of infant care derive are worthy of consideration. They lead us to realize that, if we know the conditions under which babies, children, and adults will remain healthy, application of this knowledge will cut across longstanding cultural behavior patterns. These need to be changed if any particular mother is to receive manifest support in using such a technique as demand feeding of her baby, or for the father to participate in his wife's pregnancy, labor and infant care. In other words, it is not only knowledge of infant welfare that is needed to prevent mental disease, but also personal and social knowledge. Necessary changes in attitude that seem revolutionary may be vigorously resisted and can indeed make it impossible to implement what is patently needed for an infant's mental health in any particular case.

The next complementary question to ask is what capacity has the child—an infant has none—for meeting collective behavior patterns from within himself? When does he begin to relate directly to the culture pattern, its shadow the collective unconscious, and the stream of history which lies behind each? It is obvious that he is not immersed in them from the start; quite the reverse, he grows toward them, and may only confront them directly at adolescence.

Jung laid particular emphasis on the essential independence of the ego from the collective unconscious. The unconscious, he found, was expressed in forms of creative imagination which take on the character of being objective. At once many children's fantasies and statements spring to mind as analagous. When a child asserts that he has a brother or sister who does not exist in reality, he can develop his fantasy as if it were objective and feel it to be true. He may say during a thunderstorm, "He's angry," and when a simple rational explanation is given he waits until it is finished and then reasserts, "There's people up there and he is angry." Such communications which adults conceive as subjective or magical thinking are still experienced by the child as objective because they stem from a level at which the inner subjective source of them is not differentiated from the outer realities. Such occurrences are common in infancy and have been elaborated in the study of early object relations. It has been shown that the probable age at which the infant can experience his mother and himself as whole persons with any degree of stability is at about seven months; at about that age an infant's personal life begins; before that time there are only relations between part objects. Until seven months, the ego has not developed far enough for a whole person to be represented; there can be no subject and object in the later sense, and there is much experience of their fusion and unity. All experiences in the period before seven months are thus prepersonal and objective, and the unity between and fusion of subject and object is also relevant because in the collective unconscious fusion between individuals is an essential requirement. Without it there would be no collective unconscious and no mass psychology.

It would appear, therefore, that the early origins of impersonal elements which develop into the collective unconscious in later life are to be sought for in this very early period; it is necessary to assume that the prepersonal ruthless part objects persist and develop to create a nonhuman environment. It is during this early period that transitional objects are formed.

Winnicott held that they form the root of cultural life because they are intermediate between the inner world and the outer world of real objects. He worked out a series of stages in the development of transitional phenomena—they acquire a meaning and texture; they show vitality and have a reality of their own; later they become thoughts, fantasies and, it may be added, dreams, by a process of diffusion. When this has gone far enough the original objects are "relegated to limbo." It may therefore be conjectured that transitional phenomena are an ontogenetic root of the "objective psyche": they are archetypal in nature and so contribute in essential respects to artistic, religious and other spiritual experience.

A volume, *Children and their Religion*, by Lewis, contains much relevant material, especially the interaction between the child and his religious environment. She studied the objective elements in children's play and fantasy related to religious instruction, which could be furthered or obstructed according to the way and time it was given. She also wrote an interesting study on group activity in which she shows how objective fantasy forms a factor that sustains group coherence. The children formed gangs as it were around these symbols whose significance died away as the purpose for which the group seemed to have formed no longer continued to operate.

The persistence of the objective nature of objects is maintained and their development facilitated by periodic regressions. Thus there is a positive place for regression which ensures that ongoing personalizing trends do not dissociate the personality from earlier and more primitive modes of response needed for social adaptation.

In early childhood, access to the non-ego is easy, but later on, as the ego becomes stronger and self representations get more firmly established, defense systems are built up and it is only possible to contact them through controlled regression. In periods of crisis, such as occur frequently in infancy, acutely at adolescence and subsequently in the later-life crises studied by Jung, regression is required to maintain continuity of being. In this process a deintegrating-integrating sequence is at the same time time reached which creates the conditions for ongoing change.

By considering early infantile psychodynamics it has become possible to understand how parts of the psyche are separated off so as to form a relatively permanent non-ego, composed of impersonal objects, and to understand how they may be made accessible to consciousness when necessary. There is a further state of affairs that needs assessment. During maturation the infant's anxiety about his aggressive drives is especially significant: aggressive objects tend to be excluded from the main body of the self because of the need to form self representations in the infant that are felt to be good. The bad objects are not only extruded but are also shut out of the self integrate. These projected bad objects, at first felt as parts of the child's own or his mother's body, are progressively displaced into a non-human object. That this mode of managing bad objects may be common is supported by infant observation, reconstructions, and by the early dreams of children. It is probably the close relation of pre-personal, and later impersonal, forms to aggressive and destructive drives that has given rise to the belief that the archetypal contents are dangerous for children.

In Jung's conception, however, the collective unconscious contains not only dangerous destructive components, but good and potentially creative ones as well. Is there then a known mechanism by which good objects can be extruded and kept separate from the individuating processes in infancy? The answer is easy to find: good objects are idealized and kept separate from the personal self representation when the internal world is felt to be overwhelmingly dangerous, and when destructive processes seem to be threatening the infant's good objects. To protect them they are projected into the mother, idealized, made omnipotent and so preserved. The dreams of small children reflect this state of affairs, for in them their mothers, with very few exceptions, *only* take a positive and helpful role, often with complete disregard for reality.

PSYCHOPATHOLOGY

Analytical psychologists have not contributed much to the psychopathology of childhood, but have mainly used researches by psychoanalysts and also Adlerian principles (Cf. C.W., 17). Since the development of ego psychology in psychoanalysis the earlier interest in Adler has waned.

Special emphasis has, however, been paid to the influence of the actual parents on the formation of pathological structures in their children; indeed Jung and Wickes both conceived that, because of these, analysis of parents was usually—but not always—indicated. If successful, then the child's capacity for maturation would correct any deviations that might have occurred in the past. This thesis is, however, only true in part, since it is known that children can develop mental disorders during maturation without their parents being the cause of them.

Some work has also been done on autism and schizophrenia in childhood by applying the theory put forward in this essay (cf. Fordham, 1966). Using the division of autism into primary and secondary, it has been suggested that primary autism, which starts from very early on in an infant's life, is due to failure in establishing the mother infant relation. Whether this is due to failure on the mother's part, innate failure in the infant, or a combination of the two is undetermined.

Whichever it be, it is assumed that there is a dislocation in deintegration and so, whereas the physiological discharge systems operate, the psychical systems tend to remain integrated. Autism would seem, therefore, to be a disorder of integration, which makes communication in a sense irrelevant. The conception does not require the formation of a boundary behind which the child constructs his inner world because the distinction between inner and outer is not yet made.

However, it is not usual to find a child who is purely autistic in this sense, for the class of children commonly diagnosed as autistic comprise a large spectrum of cases ranging from predominently autistic through infantile schizophrenia, ending up with the schizoid-obsessional syndrome.

ANALYTICAL PSYCHOTHERAPY

The Analytic Method

Analysis means elucidating complex structures and reducing them into their simpler, ultimately irreducible components. In practice it means listening to and observing a patient so as to find out what complex structures are causing anxiety and need intervention to relieve distress or, if this is not possible, at least to make sense of it.

Interventions may be of several kinds. First and foremost the analytical therapist aims to elucidate the situation in the here and now; but because much of what is made clear does not apply to the present situation, i.e., it is transferred from another one, it is necessary to explain what is going on. The data are then interpreted in the light of their origins in the present family situation, in the past, or in the inner world of the child. To be effective analytic procedures must be used with concern for the patient: the timing and grading of the insights provided is therefore important, and an analytical therapist needs to use sympathy and tact, as well as his knowledge, in all that he does.

Analysis is the essential element in psychotherapy, but does not comprise all that goes on. In working through his anxieties a child may become violent, and his aggression may have to be restrained, even though he has been shown that his fears are not justified by reality and refer to a long time back. Again, it can be desirable for the therapist to enter into the child's play activities so as to help his patient to express himself.

In the process of making analytic interpretations, synthetic processes are of necessity also involved. Linking unconscious with conscious elements means modifying defenses so that different and beneficial new combinations can take place. When this happens the analyst will be led to show his patient what has happened and will intervene verbally in this and in other ways that are not analytic. Because more than analysis goes on in any treatment, the term analytical psychotherapy is more appropriate than simply "analysis."

Jung classified his treatment techniques into analytic-reductive and synthetic. Objection can be taken with some justification to this division on the grounds that each process occurs in the patient anyway. However a technique represents only the attitude and method of the therapist towards the patient's material.

In child therapy the analytic attitude is most suitable because synthetic processes are very active. There are: first, satisfactions in developing new skills, emotional and physical; second, the overriding urge to grow up based on small physical stature and the real and imagined pleasures that grown-ups enjoy by reason of their size; third, the unconscious maturation processes themselves. For all these reasons it is better to aim at elucidating by analysis and providing conditions for the synthetic processes to come into operation on their own as far as the child himself is concerned.

Transference

The most important and therapeutically valuable event is the development of a transference in which projections are made by a patient on to the analytical therapist. The projections create a dynamic situation and ensure that analysis becomes an affective as well as an intellectual procedure.

Because of the transference it is necessary for an analytical psychotherapist himself to have submitted to a training analysis so that he may be able to empathize more easily with his patient. But there is also another reason for including analysis in the training of analytical psychotherapists. The transference projection from the patient tends to evoke a counter-projection, suitably termed counter-transference, which was at first seen in a negative light because it was a frequent source of misrepresentation and mismanagement of patients in the early years of psychotherapeutic practice. A training analysis is the best method of making the counter-transference manageable and of converting it into a useful indicator of the patient's transference, which recent research has shown that it can become in the hands of a skilled practitioner.

There has been much discussion about the relation between counter-transference and empathy, which on occasions are difficult to distinguish, particularly with regressed patients who may not be capable of analysis at all and who need something more akin to primary maternal preoccupation from their analysts. Then analysis becomes secondary to care of the child. To enter into this difficult subject, which is still in need of clarification, does not come within the scope of this paper.

Special Techniques of Child Therapy

This introductory outline of the core of analytic psychotherapy applies to adults or children, but there are special techniques of child therapy which need consideration. They derive from the size of the child, his inability to produce verbal associations, and his dependence upon his parents.

1. A child is brought to a clinic or consulting room by his parents, and he may, therefore, not be a willing participant in the undertaking. Indeed this can present serious difficulties, especially when a child's hostility to his analyst is being worked on. But except for special situations, being brought is an expression of his inability to transport himself.
2. Next, the symptoms of which his parents complain are not necessarily the same as the ones for which a child feels he needs help. A child in an intense conflict with his parents may indeed refuse help altogether—usually this applies in behavior disorders and delinquency. On the other hand, children develop anxiety like adults, and can, like them, wish to be rid of it. This applies to physical pain, depression, and to physical symptoms causing distress. So there is a wide range of symptoms of distress for which a child may clearly want help in the same sense as his parents.
3. A child's distress is closely related to his parents' anxieties, and indeed the cause of them can often be more in them than himself. This situation is essentially a matter of diagnosis and of providing help for the parents who need it. For this reason a child analyst can need to work in conjunction with an adult therapist to whom parents may be referred if their anxieties are too great for him to manage.
4. A more important problem arises from a child's restricted ability to make verbal associations, but in their place play serves, in a rather different way, to provide clues to unconscious processes at work. Naturally the treatment room has to be accommodated to give greater freedom of movement.

For all these reasons child analytic psychotherapy is a technique which necessitates special training. The expertize that a child analyst has to acquire centers round: starting therapy, since this involves making a family diagnosis; the use of play techniques; and the continuing need to look for times when parents need help.

STARTING THERAPY: FAMILY DIAGNOSIS   When a child is brought to a clinic or consulting room he usually has some idea why, though he may not have been told about it, and so the child's idea about the interview may be differently expressed or at variance with that of his parents. Therefore, it is often useful to see a child with his parents when he first comes. Under favorable conditions the procedure will clear up uncertainties on both sides, but more important, the therapist can observe parents and child together and make observations about how they behave under the stress of a first interview. A further advantage of this procedure is its familiarity. The situation is like others that the child has met before, when, for instance, he went to see a doctor with his mother and father.

To conduct the first interview with as many of the family present as can come is also useful because it starts the treatment off as a family affair, and an understanding of the family situation and its varying motivations is all-important. It is, for instance, fruitless to suggest treating a child unless it is clear that the parents are sufficiently ready and willing to accept and cooperate in the treatment. Often they are not motivated for therapy and this can become apparent at the first interview, when they make clear their wish to obtain help in managing their child. While this situation maintains, any treatment for the child himself has to be approached with great care, for it is extremely important not to undermine parents' feeling of responsibility for their child. Only when they have reached the end of their capacity as parents in particular respects and have decided that their child requires help that they cannot give is the way to analytic treatment open. In such cases they may have worked this out with the child, and so his need for help has become conscious before the interview begins. This situation is not as rare as might be expected, and is best illustrated by parents who have themselves been analyzed.

Another situation arises when parents bring their children along because they are near understanding that they want help with their own personal or interpersonal conflicts. The child has become the vehicle for them, and consequently therapy for him is not indicated —all he needs is to get his parents off his back so that they do not make him into a scapegoat for their own anxieties.

Leaving, on one side, the grossly deteriorated family situations when there is nothing to do but remove the child from the home altogether, these are the main diagnostic problems whose implications need to be worked on first.

DIAGNOSIS OF THE CHILD'S CONDITION   Concurrently with understanding the family situation goes investigating the child's state and its relation to his parents' management of it. In this the diagnostic classifications of child psychiatry are useful but insufficient. To decide that a child is autistic, schizophrenic, mentally retarded, hysterical, obsessional, phobic, suffering from an anxiety state or from a behavior disorder, indicates that the conflict situation has gotten built into the self. To understand its significance it is necessary to know the origins and structure of the disorder. Observation and history-taking are often, but not always, revealing, and to penetrate further it may be necessary to manage the anxieties of the parents: a diagnosis cannot be arrived at without initiating a therapeutic alliance between therapist, child and parents. Therefore, interpretations and other interventions are useful from the beginning, because therapy and diagnosis cannot be completely separated. In a sense, indeed, details of diagnosis are not obtained until the end of analytic psychotherapy.

Nevertheless, good indications of where the source of conflict lies can be elicited early on. Hence the concept of the actual present is useful. It is not enough to discover that crisis situations have arisen in the past; it also needs to be decided whether they are active in the present or no. The term "actual present" used by Jung (C.W. 4, p. 166 f.) refers to this amalgam of present and past, and also to possibilities for change in the future. To illustrate what is meant: suppose a gifted child is in a regressed state because of traumatic situations in his early life, and suppose his mother is not good with small children and babies but can relate to a child who can communicate verbally or can play with toys and imagine ingeniously. If her child can, with analytic help, develop out of his regression, then an ongoing relationship can be established and the prospects for the future are good. The actual present here contains a disturbed child whose trauma can be treated and a mother who can adapt to a healthy child of his age.

MANAGEMENT OF PARENT-CHILD PSYCHOPATHOLOGY   The situation just described is a favorable one. There has been a traumatic situation earlier in the child's life; it may have been an illness at an unfortunate time when family conflicts were destructive, but his parents will be ready to accept him when he has worked through a situation that no longer maintains. But there are less simple causes for disorders in maturation, and particularly those in which the traumatic incident is not located in time but is continuous because of persisting attitudes in parents operating in the present. While it is possible for a child to influence his parents or behave so differently that he no longer focuses their psychopathology, and while parents sometimes change through the transference that they make to the therapist when their child is being treated, neither can he be relied upon. When they do not the child will be unable, or will find it very difficult, to develop, because he comes up against the same situations which caused his neurosis in his everyday life. The significance of persisting neuroses in parents varies from child to child, from age group to age group, from family to family, but by and large if therapy is not to be slowed down or obstructed in the preadolescent period, concurrent change in parents is desirable and sometimes necessary. For this reason a child therapist needs to discover what in the parents' attitude is obstructing maturation and if possible to draw it to their notice and provide help for them as well as for the child, when they are able to use it. With older children, some analysts will use a play room. In my view an ordinary room such as that used for adults is quite suitable for older children so long as the child is not schizophrenic in the sense that he will sometimes urinate or defecate on the floor, or need a room where destructive activities can be accommodated. It is possible, but not desirable, to treat parents on principle, for many parents get on better and function better if they are not induced to submit to a therapy for which they are not motivated. The fact that a mother is ill, and knows it, may indicate that analysis is desirable for her, but in spite of this she may very well know that her child needs therapy for himself and will not let her need come before his. Not until her child's distress is tangibly met and therapy is begun, or in marginal cases until he has recovered, will she become motivated to get help for herself.

PLAY TECHNIQUES   To treat a small child, i.e., before latency, a playroom and toys are needed. In the playroom, which should be able to accommodate rough play (water being thrown on the floor and paint on the walls), a couch, chairs, tables, a rug, and a cushion are usually provided, as ordinary and familiar furniture. So as to keep the relation personal, the analytic therapist needs to keep a stock of toys in a box or a bag so that the child can then keep it clearly in view that these are for his use during the session, and that they belong to the therapist. To this store can be added others for which a particular child has a predilection, or he may bring his own to the session as he feels inclined. In this way the tendency of children to confuse issues in diffuse activity is reduced, this particular defense thrown into relief, and the underlying anxieties more easily brought into the open.

Besides the store of toys it is useful to have such materials as water, jugs, a sink, and plasticine generally available. Sand and a sand tray are of dubious value, since it can create the kind of mess that is unhelpful, particularly when the substance gets thrown about. If used, the therapist may have to intervene or even exclude it, particularly in violent episodes. Such interventions are best reduced to a minimum.

The question of how far the therapist should allow his body to be used is variable. In this context important factors are the kind of clothes worn and the care taken to keep the playroom as clean and attractive-looking as possible.

With suitable play facilities and the preliminary investigations completed, it can be assumed that a good enough therapeutic alliance has been established between the analytic therapist, the child, and his parents, and that the disorder in the child has been well enough located to warrant proceeding with analytic therapy.

REFERENCES

[Note: Only authors specifically referred to in the text are cited. For more detailed sources cf. Fordham, M., *Children as individuals* (London: Hodder & Stoughton, 1969) from which this essay is extracted.]

Call, J. D. Newborn approach behaviour and early ego development. *International Journal of Psycho-Analysis*, 1964, **45**, 286–295.

Fordham, M. Notes on the psychotherapy of infantile autism. *British Journal of Medical Psychology*, 1966, **39**, 299–312.

Henderson, J. *Thresholds of initiation*. Middletown, Conn.: Wesleyan University Press, 1967.

Jung, C. G. *The collected works of C. G. Jung*. Edited by Herbert Read, Michael Fordham and Gerhard Adler. Translated by R. F. C. Hull. No. XX in Bollingen Series, Princeton, N.J.: Princeton University Press and London: Routledge and Kegan Paul, 1953.

Jung, C. G. *Memories, dreams, reflections*. London: Collins and Routledge and Kegan Paul, 1963.

Klein, M.   The psycho-analytic play technique: Its history and significance. In *New directions in psycho-analysis*. London: Tavistock, 1955.

Lewis, E.   *Children and their religion*. London: Sheed & Ward, 1962.

Mahler, M. S.   Thoughts about development and individuation. *Psychoanalytic study of the child*, 1963, 18, 307–324.

Spitz, R. A.   Anaclytic depression. *Psychoanalytic Study of the Child*, 1946, 2, 313–342.

Spitz, R. A.   *The first year of life*. New York: International Universities Press, 1965.

Winnicott, D. W.   *Collected papers*. London: Havistock, 1958.

Winnicott, D. W.   The location of cultural experience. *International Journal of Psycho-Analysis*, 1967, 48, 368–372.

13

GERALD T. NILES

Karen Horney's Holistic Approach: A View of Cultural Influences

orney's holistic theory develops the concept
that the relationship between the culture
and neurosis is a qualitative one. Cultural trends and neurotic conflicts are related to each other. Horney proposed that Freud's
view was one sided; since instinctual forces were
central, he could only see how the natural forces
influenced the instinctual forces. Through his
dualistic mechanistic theory, Freud did consider
the influence of cultural factors in neurosis, but
in a mechanistic, quantitative way. The main external factor is frustration engendered by restrictions on libidinous and destructive drives. Horney
(1937; 1939) on the other hand dealt with the
complexity of the interrelatedness by considering
three main sets of factors:

1. the matrix out of which neurosis may grow;
2. basic neurotic conflicts and attempts at solution;
3. the factors in the facade that the neurotic shows to himself and to others.

For example, she points out that sibling rivalry may be determined more by the competitiveness in the culture than as the result of a natural human phenomenon.

The libido theory was thus rejected when Karen Horney became aware of the decisive role that cultural elements played in the production of neurosis. Yet one of Freud's basic contributions was that conflicting forces operate within the mind. Applying this to children we can see that they can be unaware of conflicts and yet the conflict can have a profound influence on the structure and function of the personality. The conflicting forces are compulsive neurotic drives which are developed as defensive measures against anxiety rather than being libidinous in origin. These defenses involve basic attitudes toward others and the self, and so conflict becomes the dynamic center of the neurosis.

Another crucial contribution by Dr. Horney to the treatment of children is the concept that at the core of each human being is a dynamic force—the real self—whose natural impulse is to move toward self-realization, i.e., fulfilling basic human potential. Healthy development is predicated on the authenticity of love, respect, guidance, and fair treatment. When these are present, a child develops feelings of inner strength, freedom, and self confidence. He has the courage to experience himself spontaneously as having both love for others and healthy independence from others. The forces from which confidence springs are the constructive forces. For when the analyst is able to contact the patient's unconscious constructive forces, he develops confidence in the patient which is crucial for the therapeutic process.

Because medicine and psychiatry have been more concerned with disease prevention than health promotion, we can more easily describe what is harmful to growth than what is beneficial. When we approach a patient, we begin with the basic concept that we cannot fight illness with illness and we must use healthy forces to counteract the pathological ones. This is not a moralistic good or bad concept but one related to an integrative morality of evolution. What are some of the elements we look for?

1. Parents. Without them there is no patient; we underline this as perhaps the most constructive force in therapy. The parent

does not necessarily have to be a biological one, but there must be some significant adult in the child's background who has made a difference, be it a teacher, grandparent, policeman, etc. Our experience at the clinic has taught us that without a previous relationship with a respected authority figure the prognosis is poor.

2. Capacity for psychological thinking. A child who can translate a bellyache into worries and troubles is easier to work with than a child who rigidly holds onto a symptom in a concrete way. It is more arduous to work with a child who refuses to go to school because of somatic complaints than with the child who can refer to his fears.

3. Intellect. The lower the intellect the more difficult it is for the analyst to use his usual analytic techniques. This does not imply the reverse, i.e., that a higher intellect makes therapy easier, but a good intellect is a source of strength. At the end of this chapter I shall refer to a special psychotherapy project conducted with mildly retarded people at our clinic.

4. Trying. "It is better to have loved and lost than never to have loved at all." The patient who goes to the plate and strikes out has the same .000 batting average as the fellow sitting on the bench, but he gives himself the opportunity to experience himself in action and to learn about himself. In helping the patient to try, we make therapeutic use of the therapeutic situation. After all, why should a child with a school phobia try to go to school just because he is in therapy? In the shifting of focus from success and failure to feelings about himself, with the analyst's encouragement, the patient may be more willing to take a risk. One young patient said; "My father said I could try therapy but if I fail I will get it." I told him that if he made a really good try I see no reason why failure would have to be an issue. By a really good try I told him it was important for him to tell me as much as possible, anything that was meaningful to him. This was stated in conjunction with evaluating his assets.

5. Perceptual ability. Internal and external—taste, smell, hearing, seeing, touching, awareness of inner feelings.

6. Memory—psychological and organic. Through unconscious process we become unwittingly aware of the sense of continuity. This sense will be heightened in therapy.

7. Sense of humor. It has been said that if one looked in on a therapy session with an adult he would usually find a heavi-

ness many times bordering on oppressiveness. This mood cannot and should not be sustained in working with children. It is also important to be able to see more than one side of a situation and not to be rigidly bound by one-sidedness.

8. Gifted children (looks and talents). These children's indiscretions are more easily tolerated by society and they are given more chance before punitive measures are taken.

9. Judgment. Of course, intellect has to be considered here. In children, where poor judgment may interfere with the therapeutic process, e.g., getting in trouble with the law, the therapist has to take an authoritative attitude in the relationship and toward the purpose of the work so that therapy may continue.

10. Reality testing. Does the patient know the difference? Can the child distinguish reality from fantasy? Can the child play superman without having to be superman and jump off the roof? A schizophrenic child walked around with a rag cleaning the germs in the air in the playroom; when she walked out into the waiting room she put the rag away. She explained that this is the waiting room, and she can't do things like that here. This was an important factor in my deciding to work with her on an outpatient basis.

11. Control of motility. The appropriateness, the degree, and the nature are considered also. Whether or not speech and language development are adequate to substitute for acting out behavior is also important.

12. Can the child accept substitute gratification? If a child wants something concrete from you, can he accept a piece of chalk or must he have the blackboard to take home.

13. Nature of his relatedness. How does he relate to you, to others? At what expense to himself? How much control is required?

14. Tolerance for frustration. As there are frustrations in the therapeutic process, without the ability to postpone gratification and find outlets for excessive tensions, therapy can be tenuous.

15. Affectivity. Here again we have to evaluate the degree, kind and appropriateness.

16. Sense of curiosity. Not only about the outside, but especially inner curiosity—an interest in what makes him tick.

Parents should be involved in the therapeutic situation. For example, a parent may ask, "If I do or say that might it hurt

Johnny?" I reply, "While Johnny is working with me don't be afraid to hurt Johnny for I shall take care of the effects of the hurts. Should, however, an effect threaten to be irreversible, I will let you know. This gives the parents not only a chance to share their guilt feelings about their aggressiveness but gives them a chance to identify with the therapeutic situation. Most important it gives them permission to be as natural as they can be. In therapy we do not work directly on patients, only surgeons do. We work on the effects, the results of what goes on inside of people. In lectures to social workers, I tell them that casework may be more difficult than good analysis. For in casework, they have no access to unconscious forces which are perhaps one of the strongest motivating forces in therapy.

When a child's healthy needs are not satisfied, when he is smothered with affection or ignored, worshiped or disparaged, dominated or indulged, treated with disrespect and unfairness, when the timing of responses is off, when the climate of the home is severe, he then feels isolated, helpless and hostile in a menacing world. Instead of basic confidence he feels basic anxiety. He is then compelled to adopt strategic defenses to achieve safety. Feeling helpless he may move toward others and look to love as the solution to all his problems and so become compliant in his orientation. He may move against others if he feels the world is hostile, in an attempt to control and dominate them for his sense of security. He may also move away from people looking to complete self-sufficiency and independence as a solution. Underlying all these moves are relationships to people. Each of the moves is compulsive, rigid, indiscriminate and insatiable, since anxiety underlies all of them. His habitual patterns become compromises among the various conflicting tendencies. It is in this way that neurotic character structure is formed. Aside from the unnecessary loss of energy in the neurotic character structure, the shifting from one solution to another can also be draining.

Sooner or later the child comes to adopt important elements of all three neurotic orientations. While one may be predominant the others continue to exist and exert their influence. The picture then is one of intensive conflict between three sharply opposed, irreconcilable sets of drives upon which the person's inner sense of safety depends. This is the basic conflict—relationships to others. It will be discussed again in the section on interpreting to children.

Just as basic anxiety made adopting of defensive measures necessary, the basic conflict makes it necessary for the child to adopt further ways of coping with this new crisis. In his inner being this threat to a sense of unity, the need for integration, requires a more comprehensive solution which he finds in the construction of an idealized image, fantasy creation which embodies the absolute fulfillment of all his neurotic needs and values. It is thought that at about three years of age the more complex structures of self-effacement, expansiveness, and resignation are added to the moves of toward, against, and away. When there is enough of an idealized image then more direct analysis of the child may be attempted.

For this image represents an urge to be godlike, a state which can magically lift him above conflict. Yet the image is so absolute, so perfect, that it is not humanly possible for him to mold himself completely into this state of perfection. Inevitably he turns against himself with hatred and contempt. He is now confronted with the need to blot out the hated self. The child is now caught between two compelling forces—self-idealization and self-extinction. Here is a new major conflict within the pride system, an intrapsychic conflict involving primarily the child's attitudes toward himself, just as the basic conflict involves attitudes toward others. It is necessary to say a word here to clarify the often used word alienation as distinguished from detachment in the Horney frame of references. Alienation refers to how far the individual is from his real self and so is an intrapsychic concept, while detachment again is connected to relations with others. A man in prison is detached from society but not necessarily alienated.

So while the pride system with its compulsivity is undermined, the child is becoming more aware of his aliveness and his constructive forces. Many times, early in treatment parents will ask why their child takes after only the "bad parts" of them and not the "good parts." I indicate that the child, by getting to know himself better will be able to evaluate better these "good parts" the parents are offering and make good use of them. Conversely, he may avoid the bad and not be so adversely affected by the ill winds of the family.

As with many good theoretical frameworks Karen Horney's theory easily lends itself to be extended, amplified, and used in child development. The modifications were developed by the author in his experience at the Karen Horney Clinic. While there are basically three moves, we can speak of five phases of development. The first one, protective autism and autonomic reflex, is the essence of being. During the first three months of life, the rhythms of involutionary processes are being ordered and developed. As described by Spitz and named by Glover, we do believe in critical phases at which time the interaction and response to and with the child must be necessarily encouraged by the environment—especially by the parents. Just as we look for the smiling response of the infant, we should question parents as to when they last smiled at their child. The first phase may correspond to the last or fifth phase of life when a person may be in coma and there is a decompensation of the autonomic processes. Corresponding to the moving toward people is the dependence on the mother where the child is given permission to be himself in a safe, boundary-setting atmosphere. This is a time of complete acceptance and nourishment. If the child is a male he is then permitted by the mother to identify with the father. There is some thought that this underlies the recommendation for male homosexual patients to work first with a woman therapist and then move to a male therapist. The female child may play out a tomboy role with the father and then return to the mother for further identifying. With the father the children are licensed to expand. Yet when so licensed one must be able to do things, such as use his muscles, etc. He is more than being; he is becoming. He is learning skills and is developing many ways of doing things. After this period of identifying, he moves toward independence which is not necessarily independence from his parents but more specifically dependence upon himself. Here he has to learn and know what there is in him to depend on. He may become independent from his neurosis. While this is progressing, the child is constantly evaluating and reevaluating what is in his best interest.

Any one piece of behavior may contain all three moves. In one of the annual Karen Horney lectures, Frederick Allen (1956) mentioned that a child may move toward the mother, attack her breast, and then move away with complete satisfaction.

Schematic Developmental Theory

Evaluating and Reevaluating

Autonomic	Mother	Father	Independence	Coma
Reflex Protective autism	Boundaries Permitting Accepting Dependence (Love)	Licensing Aggressiveness Growing Expanding (Mastery)	Dependence on self and constructiveness in environment. From effects of harm- ful environment.	

The introductory children's course in the analytic school is made more meaningful to the therapists by explaining to them that while the therapist works with one person, he actually works with the entire family. The basic question about the patient and his attitude to himself is what kind of a parent he is to the child within. The child in him refers to his total past, all that has gone on in his life until the present. No matter what school of thought the therapist uses, whether it be that of Horney, Freud, Sullivan, or Adler, there are two basic questions he must answer:

1. What does the patient have in terms of assets and liabilities and how does he use them?
2. How does the patient relate to himself? The team approach in therapy, encouraged by Horney's concept of "we," when used in child guidance, lends itself to analytic treatment of all people. The basic parent-child relationship has to be seen in a working dynamic way to develop this attitude.

The following is a schematic representation of what will be discussed.

Parent	Feel, Relate, Experience	Child
1. Do about it	Working-processing	1. What have
2. Subject		2. Object
3. I		3. Me (myself)
4. Conscious		4. Unconscious
5. Thinking		5. Feeling
6. Secondary process		6. Primary process

We cannot work at a relationship; we relate by doing good work. Each one has to resolve for himself what good work means. So it is with a parent-child relationship and the working relationship one has with oneself. The child has the problem and what is done with the child depends upon the parents. By directing ourselves toward the child we help him become a better parent to himself than the parenting to which he was exposed. While with parents we cannot dissociate ourselves completely from unconscious forces; in practice, however, it is a matter of focus and we relate to them mainly on the conscious level. We do not encourage dreaming and free associating. The reverse is true with the children; we do encourage dreaming and free associating, many times via play. I do not know of any words that can adequately describe the relating process. We use the words balancing, experiencing, yet he who is absolutely perfectly balanced is dead. The same goes for the homeostatic approach. I like Dr. Martin's rhythmical concept of the relationship, which refers to it as pulsating. It is not one or the other, but a constant interplay of forces similar to the systole and diastole of the heartbeat. The thrust or systole refers to the parents, and the filling or diastole, to the child. We know that when the analyst can get the feel of the pulsating relationship he can allow himself to do play therapy with his adult patients on an unconscious level.

So when the question, "how do I feel myself?" is asked this brings up many possibilities. Is the patient accepting himself? Is he relating to himself in a constructive way? What is his approach to his childhood, all that has gone on in him up to and including this moment? Is he being a good parent to himself with a realistic appraisal of his assets and liabilities and acting in his own best interest?

Sometimes for teaching purposes I compare the team approach to a baseball team. The first and third base coaches are the mother and father respectively. The batter is the patient. The doctor is the manager whose job is to help develop the patient so that even if the coaches give wrong signals, the patient can score. Of course the parents are "coached" not to give wrong signals and hopefully to be able to work together. A coach can be an adequate coach in spite of personal problems.

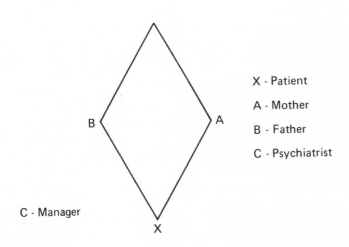

X - Patient

A - Mother

B - Father

C - Psychiatrist

C - Manager

There are three areas in which we can relate to our patients when interpreting: (1) the patient-doctor, (2) the interpersonal, and (3) the intrapsychic relationships. The relationship which is most available to the patient should always be used. It is important to be aware of the kinds of positions the patients will try to put the doctor in, in an effort to solve his problems. A child may scream in the play room, knowing his mother is in the waiting room, to give the impression that the doctor is hurting her child so she can rescue the young one from what the "terrible" doctor is trying to accomplish. Of course the doctor must never work from a defensive position, such as letting himself get tied up or closing his eyes. He should have all his facilities available at all times so that he can be of help to his patients. Since children grow through relationships (as discussed in our three moves and basic conflict), the interpersonal interpreting is used especially with younger children. If a child builds with blocks and then knocks them down we may personalize the blocks, but at all times remembering they are blocks. One may then say, "The poor block couldn't run to his mommy and say, " 'See what that bully did to me.' " However, in the spirit of holism, I try to interpret as much as possible in a universal frame of reference which I call an organismic framework. This is a natural life situation that includes the biology of a person. For example, a pre-adolescent girl came into the therapy session complaining about the weight of a load of books she was carrying. This gave us a clue to investigate the possibility of any pregnancy fantasies. In our clinic we use a family approach to our children. In the intake, after the families are seen in whatever combination deemed necessary by the intake worker (singly, couples, conjoint), a routine psychological test is given the child as well as any other necessary procedures such as neurological exams. Before the family is accepted for treatment at the clinic I will see them in conjoint session, mainly to firm up the family approach and to delineate and clarify the problems. Family therapy also gives us a very good opportunity to work on the cognitive elements in a family. As described previously my framework in working in a dyadic relationship with a parent is in essence a triadic one. With our emphasis on constructive forces we hope that the family leaves with a feeling of hopeful expectation.

Initially in therapy we emphasize the constructive forces and pick up anything in the authority system that relates immediately to therapy. I once worked with a mother who knew that my own wife was pregnant with our first child. As she was leaving one session, she said with an admonishing finger, "You'll soon know what it's like." I replied, "Then we will have more to share." The daughter, after the third session said, "I'm afraid we're ganging up against my parents." I told her, "Yes it is true we are forming a gang, and I hope that in time your parents will see the wisdom of what we are trying to accomplish and may want to join us." If I hear from the child that he told his parents, "I don't care what Dr. Niles says to you"—I discuss this with the parents mainly in terms of the ineffectual light in which a statement like that puts the parents. We do leave a good part of the treatment of choice up to the comfortableness of the therapist, and we do not feel that every family has to be seen in conjoint sessions at all times. If it is felt that a definite approach is necessary—single, conjoint or otherwise, and there is a reluctance on the part of the therapist, we then discuss it and try to help eliminate whatever the obstacle may be.

As can be seen, the therapist's attitude is of utmost importance to the therapeutic approach. The therapist is a participant observer —always actively using himself. We not only look, we observe. We regard therapy as an experience—hopefully a constructive and mutually gratifying one. Especially with a child, we hope to become an important adult in his life, one who makes a difference. Of course, we never replace his parents. We feel that when a message is sent to the brain it is not simply filtered, but there is a reaction and something new is being transmitted. Our therapeutic approach is similar; there is interaction and experience between two people. Throughout therapy it is hoped that here is an identifying process going on by the patient. The therapist is at all times identified with the patient's constructive forces, and if the patient wants to be like him there is no objection, especially if he is identifying with his constructive forces and his ways of using them for his best interests in the realities of his living. Initially in treatment if a patient tries to please me I am delighted because what really pleases me is his growth. This is mentioned because it is sometimes said that the patient should not try to please anyone but himself, including his parents. In the process we are concerned with helping to convert a punitive superego of the past into healthy disciplining forces that serve the patient in the present. We are continually on the alert for any identifying phenomenon, especially that which implies consideration for another human being. If a child runs away from home and does not leave a note, it is quite different from the act of a child who does leave a note. If an adolescent calls me on the phone when he is in trouble and says, "Don't sweat it, Doc, I can manage things," I am impressed with this kind of communication more so than if he were simply in trouble.

In the course of treatment we feel that as the child becomes more acceptable to himself, and his family becomes more accepting of him, he is then more able to move toward realizing himself. Compared to an adult in a schematic three year period, the child would take one year to the adult's one and a half years, once the way is cleared.

Doing therapy with families, we must be aware of the "negative therapeutic reaction." This appears many times when the child is improving and the family appears to be worse. This reaction certainly underlines our need to work with the parents for our patient to continue progressing. There are many explanations for this— parents losing spheres of influence, shift in family equilibrium, etc. It seems that health has certain demands and that, at times, these demands may be too much for families to sustain. In our framework, while we are extending, supporting and developing the constructive forces, we are also undermining the retarding forces. The retarding forces are divided into blockages and obstructive forces. Blockages are regarded as anything that is at cross purposes with the work. If this is not looked into then what may follow will not "take." For example, an adolescent boy put a magazine over his head and pretended he was sleeping. My response was that he thought his father should have unlimited resources to sustain him while he wasted his time. We were then able to examine the patient's resources. This young boy subsequently went to my college, joined my fraternity, and at present is a graduate psychology student. It is therefore a dictum that we handle blockages first. The therapeutic challenge can then be directed toward the obstructive forces or the neurosis.

The Oedipus complex or situation is not thought of as natural or instinctual. All attachments intense enough to justify the term "Oedipal" are caused by excess anxiety and due fundamentally to a severe home climate—an absence of attitudes essential to growth— and/or hostility. In a lecture at the New School, it is said that Dr. Horney was asked how penis envy fits her theory. She simply said it didn't. Of course there can be envy and at times penis envy, but again not as a natural phenomenon and certainly not as a determinant of character structure.

Concerning sex and children, we do feel there is a healthy curiosity. When there is compulsive sexual behavior the child is expressing his anxiety. For the child has to approach sex from a feeling of inadequacy, at least anatomically and functionally.

Horney's constructive theory has lent itself well to an area that is generally shunned and neglected by psychiatrists. At present in the Karen Horney Clinic we are working on a federally funded project treating mildly retarded people using the family oriented child guidance approaches described in this review. We have been very encouraged by the remarkable increases in the human movement responses that the Rorschach records for these people. These young people are beginning to feel that "I am a person who can take the initiative to—." There have been corresponding changes in their self concept, interpersonal relationships, work, and school attitudes. The human movement response may change without the IQ changing. In fact at a recent meeting with the referring agencies, this result was accepted with so much enthusiasm that one of the participants felt that this was an important index to be followed along with the IQ.

The basis of the character structure developed in childhood is a result of the totality of relationships, not simply a repetitive phenomenon. In working with adults in the here and now, childhood may also be viewed in terms of temporal depth and distance. Horney's human, holistic, open-minded theory lends itself well to the growth process, and I know of no more fertile area than the growth process in children.

REFERENCES

Allen, F.   Horney's conception of basic conflict applied to child psychiatry. *American Journal of Psychoanalysis,* 1956, 16, 99–111.

Horney, K.   *Neurotic personality of our time.* New York: Norton, 1937.

Horney, K.   *New ways in psychoanalysis.* New York: Norton, 1939.

Ivimey, M.   Childhood memories in psychoanalysis. *American Journal of Psychoanalysis,* 1950, 10, 38–47.

Kelman, N.   Child analysis and Horney theory. *American Journal of Psychoanalysis,* 1949, 11, 38–47.

Kelman, N.   Character development in young children. *American Journal of Psychoanalysis,* 1950, 10, 5–7.

Martin, A. R.   The oldest and the youngest child. New York: ACAAP Bulletin, 1945.

Mullan, H.   Fathers and children. New York: ACCAP Bulletin, 1952.

14

MAURICE R. GREEN

The Interpersonal Approach to Child Therapy

t is paradoxical to write of a "Sullivanian approach" to child therapy, for Sullivan never treated children nor is there any evidence that he even consulted in the treatment of children. Nonetheless, through his writing and teaching, Sullivan had an enduring influence on many practices and ideas in child therapy today. He was one of the first clinicians in psychoanalytic psychiatry to recognize the importance of the work of Jean Piaget for the theoretical understanding and practical treatment of the disorders of infancy and childhood. From a careful study of the literature of the 1920s and 1930s in child development and in child psychopathology, together with his own observations of adults and inferences drawn from his experiences in treating the disorders of adolescence, young adulthood, and adults, he developed a detailed theory of maturational processes in infancy and childhood, with particular emphasis on those vicissitudes of failure or warps in personality growth that contributed to the more serious disorders in later life.

Sullivan was not interested in developing an epistemology as Jean Piaget was doing, nor was he interested in developing a comprehensive, consistent theoretical system as Freud, Jung, and others were doing. Sullivan was primarily a clinician interested in treating very sick people and trying to understand the difficulties and obstacles that one encountered in pursuing this goal. The theory that he developed came out of that context; his purpose was to clarify what actually went on between people, to facilitate therapy in enhancing the maturational processes intrinsic to personality growth and fulfillment.

EMPHASIS ON COMMUNICATION

Sullivan focused more than anyone else of his time on the subtle details of the communicative process between the patient and the psychiatrist. Two of the most important contributors to communication problems today have acknowledged their great indebtedness to Sullivan—the late Don Jackson and Jurgen Ruesch. Because he emphasized what was actually going on between people—that is, between a significant person and the patient, as well as patient and psychiatrist—Sullivan found that he had more in common with the discipline of social psychology than with the traditional, neurologically oriented, medical neuropsychiatry of that time. For this reason he was not particularly interested in the generalizations that a person might offer about himself as a distinct, separate entity. Sullivan preferred to be informed as to what actually happened in one's life and what was actually communicated between a patient and other persons; in other words, he wanted to know how the patient was actually living his life with others.

Sullivan discovered that it was difficult to get accurate statements. He described these difficulties in terms of the distortions that the individual experienced not only in perceiving what was going on but also in communicating what had happened and receiving the communications of others.

Sullivan used the term "anxiety" in a very specific way to refer to the chief obstacle or the principle disjunctive factor in human perception and communication. He likened the effect of severe anxiety to the effect of a blow on the head. A child, who was very anxious with his father, said that when his father entered the room where he was writing or reading his mind would go blank. Another child who did very well in creative writing with a warm, empathetic teacher, froze up, as he put it, in his regular English class where the teacher had a certain sarcastic edge that this boy was particularly sensitive to. Children are not fully conscious of the interpersonal significance of their anxiety and may believe there is something wrong with their "head." *Anxiety,* therefore, refers to this disjunctive signal of a loss of one's self-respect, dignity, value, and worth as a human being. When the danger of such a loss threatens, a tension of mind and body occurs that can actually block the individual's awareness of it. The tension itself, then, to a varying degree, prevents the individual from recalling and communicating significant information. Sullivan's view of maturational processes, then, centers on communication, the skills of communication, and the factors that contribute to anxiety in a way that interferes with the development and use of these skills.

Sullivan pioneered in describing a series of developmental stages that were characterized by specific achievements in human communication and relationship, in understanding and in perceiving, beginning in earliest infancy and progressing through adolescence into adulthood. Erik Erikson, who was familiar with Sullivan's work, must have been influenced by it in his own *later* description of a similar series of developmental stages.

In the Bulletin of the Washington School of Psychiatry for 1944–1945, Sullivan wrote a summary of a course he was teaching in Washington and in New York City entitled "Basic Psychiatry." This summary, written by Sullivan himself, is the most succinct description of his loosely woven theoretical system that I have seen:

The considerations which lead to defining psychiatry as the study of interpersonal relations are outlined. The subject is then amplified along three principal lines: the developmental history of the person's living; the dynamisms which are useful abstractions in organizing one's participant observation and thought about another's personal problem; and the reasonably probable influence on subsequent life of various situations of personal interaction. The genetically given developmental possibilities of the infant and the time-pattern of their maturation is coordinated with the cultural influences that makes the human animal a human being. The system of dynamisms making up the self and its functional activity are outlined, and the origin and role of anxiety made clear. There follows a consideration of alertness, awareness, attention, and the peculiarities of recall and recollection; of the gamut of implicit symbolic operations in and outside of personal awareness; of sublimatory, substitutive, and dissociated processes; and the establishing of the relatively durable pattern of interpersonal relations which may be said to characterize the person. The parataxic elements in the person's relations with others are shown to imply the type of recurrent difficulties he experiences, the way he thinks and speaks of them, the foreseen and unnoticed goals towards which his behavior will be addressed as an approach to intimate acquaintance develops, and the course of events that can reasonably be expected to relieve his major difficulties. The proper meaning of many unnecessary technical terms appears, and the rationale of presumptively therapeutic interpersonal activity is formulated.

Sullivan's self-system or self-dynamism refers to a social self that is emergent from human relationships and is separated from the rest of the personality by selective attention and censorship. He conceived of this self as being made up predominantly of reflected appraisals—as the on-going, self-conscious part of the person as he participates and communicates at a particular time in relation to one or more other persons. However, in using this notion of self, Sullivan by no means refers to the whole person or even to the essential character or identity of a person. The self in this limited sense, more or less analagous to the ego and its defense mechanisms, tends to endure and resist change; but through therapeutic or other fortunate experiences in living, a person may achieve an expansion of this self. As for the human personality as a whole, he sees it beginning both within and without the boundaries of the self-system in the symbolic elaboration of events experienced through time by the individual organism; these events are the beginning of its continuity (or experience) as a personality throughout life. Although personality is conceived in much broader terms than the self and includes events and processes which may be temporarily or permanently inaccessible to attention and recall, nonetheless personality is also conceived as a social process, and Sullivan (1953) defines it as follows: "Personality is the relatively enduring pattern of recurrent interpersonal situations which characterize a human life" (p. 110).

The Three Modes

Sullivan defines experience as any event lived or undergone, in other words, any event that, however trivial or significant, enters into the personality's development in time. Drawing on his familiarity and affection for the American pragmatist philosophers, he divides experience into three modes: the *prototaxic,* the *parataxic,* and the *syntaxic.*

The prototaxic, which is the name he gave to the first mode, corresponds more or less to George Herbert Mead's concept of the "I." This first experience can be felt or intuitively sensed but cannot be communicated because it antedates the dualism of subject and object. As Sullivan saw it, the first experience was made up of processes involving the outer and inner factors, the raw materials that made up the living of the human organism—that is, the momentary states and the succession of momentary states. This mode is first, in the sense of being the most fundamental experience of the human organism throughout its life, its necessary ground as well as the main or predominant mode of experience at the beginning of life in early infancy.

For the second mode of experience, Sullivan took the term "parataxic" from Thomas Verner Moore, who first used it in describing early, not quite formed symptoms of war neurosis, symptoms of a very general, vague quality, difficult to describe. Feelings often occur in this mode that may be represented by metaphor, poetry, imagery, and the like as the individual gropes for articulation. In George Herbert Mead's philosophy the mode would correspond to the intuitive aspect of the self-other dialogue. Sullivan (1953) defines it in one sentence: "The generalizing of experience, so that the significant common factors mixed in with the differences are identified or connected with one recurrent pattern of experience" (p. 84).

This would refer to vague stereotyping, the imagery of dream and play, the generalized characters in myth and fairy tale, in superstition and folk lore, in private experience of the "good me, bad me," good other, bad other, and so on. This schematizing or patterning of experience is the foundation of mental life, on which more precisely articulated and validated experience can be built for communication with others.

As Sullivan saw it, the parataxic mode of experience begins early in infancy, perhaps even before birth, predominates throughout early childhood, and to some extent persists into adulthood and even into old age. It is in the parataxic experience that the beginning of self-consciousness occurs; it corresponds more or less to what has been called the preconscious, the intuitive, the presentational, the prelogical—in other words, feelings and thoughts that arise out of incomplete experience and have not yet been tested and validated, not yet articulated for communication. Thus we can see that the parataxic mode covers a very wide range, from the most primitive autistic referential processes to the most sophisticated and rich creative intuition that is not yet ready for realization.

As one can see from the description of parataxic, the degree to which an experience is developed moves it from one end of the mode to the other; i.e., as experience becomes more and more articulated and ready for significant communication to another person it moves out of the category of the parataxic into the third mode of experience, the syntaxic; this term describes the state in which experience can be more or less precisely and reliably shared.

There are many instruments of communication through which one can experience all three modes. There are the eyes, ears, nose, mouth, skin, kinesthetic experiences, etc. However, for most purposes and for most individuals, the predominant mode in which syntaxic experience occurs is in their two great areas of communicative behavior, namely, gesture and speech.

Sullivan believed that a multidisciplinary approach was essential for studying the area of learning: the organization of experience. He believed that the biological basis for learning lies in the serial maturation of the capacities of the human animal coupled with the opportunity for manifesting this ability in the course of time; that is, one must have not only the biological maturation of the capacity, but also the opportunity to exercise that capacity in appropriate and useful experiences. He divided learning heuristically into six types of processes: learning by the anxiety inhibition; learning on the anxiety gradient (which has to do not with inhibition caused by the experience but by the discrimination of gradually increasing from gradually diminishing anxiety that affects one's activity, a process that can lead to the development of sublimination, in which there is some kind of satisfaction of a physiological tension); learning by trial and success; learning by reward and punishment; learning by trial and error; and, finally, learning by eduction of relations. He defines this last process: "A capacity —of the most infinite complexity—of our nervous systems which enables us to get more and more to see relations which endure in nature and therefore are, to a truly remarkable degree, dependable (1963, p. 156)."

Among the many innate tendencies manifested in the activity of the newborn human being, there is the manual-exploratory function, which, together with oral, anal and other zonal tensions, leads to an organization of experience that comes to be eventually personified as *my body*. This is very early affected by learning experience, so that there is a tripartite division of the prehended body personification into a "good me," "bad me," and "not me."

DEVELOPMENTAL STAGES

Childhood

The development of gesture and language is of incalculable significance for the growing child and marks the transition from infancy to childhood. Sullivan (1953) posits an important theorem that characterizes the human being from the beginning of early childhood. He stated:

> Thus from early childhood onward another general statement might be applied to interpersonal relations, which, for want of a better name, I once called the theorem of reciprocal emotion, or reciprocal motivational patterns: integration in an interpersonal situation is a reciprocal process in which 1) complementary needs are resolved, or aggravated; 2) reciprocal patterns of activity are developed, or disintegrated; and 3) foresight of satisfaction, or rebuff, of similar needs is facilitated (p. 198).

Due to this process, the infant is no longer so completely dependent on the mother and is ready for abandoning certain kinds of infantile behavior, such as nursing at the breast. It is in the course of such educative experience that disgust and shame become developed as part of the self-system in relation particularly to the "bad me" aspect of it.

If authority figures are more or less consistent, the child begins to discriminate very early among the variety of authority situations with which it has to cope so that it can begin to anticipate with some accuracy when it is unsafe to violate authority and when there is some chance of "getting away with it." In fortunate, consistent circumstances, this leads to the development of a healthy discrimination which provides useful data for later living. However (and this has more to do with the next section on psychopathology), when the authority figures are confusing, inconsistent, and incongruous, the child may suffer a deterioration in the development of foresight and show inappropriate or ill-timed behavior. With a chaotic authority on the part of the parents, the child cannot foresee the consequences of its behavior. For example, there was a family where the father was a traveling musician. He was frequently away and, when at home, he was very unstable and alcoholic. The mother too was immature, though very bright; she tended to scapegoat her husband and her son whenever she experienced minor rebuffs in her work or social life. The boy, who was also very intelligent, learned to deploy the flak by showing off some particularly abstruse word from his extraordinary vocabulary. This delighted his father, who enjoyed vicarious fantasies of genius, and deflected the mother, who was temporarily overwhelmed by the verbal pyrotechnics. Needless to say, the boy did very well with his teachers and very poorly with his peers who, frustrated at more mundane relationships with him, teased him mercilessly for his "queer" ways. The boy became increasingly rigid, unhappy, and lonely.

Sometimes children are literally taught by one or more authority figures to conceal and to deceive. Sometimes they develop this ability on their own simply by trial and error and by observing and analyzing the successes and failures of themselves and others. There are two especially common patterns of deception which Sullivan described as occurring in mid-childhood, between the ages of one and five or six. In the first case, the child uses words as rationalizations; in the second pattern he dramatizes and play-acts approved behavioral patterns, pretending to be mother or father.

The normal play of children in the make-believe games of the good mother and bad mother, good guys and bad guys, helps them to differentiate by means of these stereotypes the variety of benevolent and threatening figures they must prepare for within and outside of the immediate family. Sometimes this play takes a pathological turn. I saw a three and one half year old girl who on first meeting suggested something of the good fairy godmother in her manner and way of speaking. She was the middle child in a family of five children born to a mother who had married, one after the other, six alcoholic husbands. The mother was on welfare and behaved like an invalid much of the time, requiring the children to wait on her, bring meals to her in bed, and so on. This little girl got some comfort by dramatizing herself as the stereotype of the Good Mother who had never been available to her in real life. In the hysterical development, children learn a variety of such stereotyped roles and can switch rapidly from one to another in an effort to find the role that will capture attention. At the most refined level, such a child appears to be a warm, colorful, and charming person.

Sullivan believed that in the first thirty months of life it was not important whether the child was clear about what was true and real or mixed it up with fantasies and falsifications. However, Sullivan was convinced of the importance of the distinction between actuality and fantasy at the end of childhood.

The Juvenile Period

The vital ability to distinguish between objective experience and fantasy develops at the same time that the child discovers the profound need for compeers, wherein he will have playmates, real or imaginary, but realistic and very much like himself in many ways.

This occurrence marks the end of childhood and the beginning of the juvenile era of development. The juvenile developmental period is one in which the child participates with other children, compares himself with others, learns about himself and the otherness of his compeers, and begins to expand beyond the boundaries of his immediate family. It is the first developmental stage at which the intense influence of the home and the parents can be open to some kind of corrective or remedial change from the school and society: that is, outside of therapeutic intervention. It is a stage in which he is also open and vulnerable, of course, to harmful influences in the school and society.

There are two main categories of interpersonal growth at this time: (1) the experience of social subordination, and (2) the experience of social accommodation. Social subordination describes the range of experiences in which the juvenile person encounters new authority figures in his life, apart from those he is familiar with, such as school teachers, policemen, recreational directors, and, not the least, the leaders and bullies of his own age group. He learns not only to develop further his skill in coping with authority situations but also to understand the different personalities, temperaments, and interests of persons who are in positions of authority. The other major juvenile discovery is what Sullivan calls "social accommodation," that is, cooperation: the contact with and necessity for getting along in some way with a wide variety of people of one's own age and a little older.

By participating in the lives of his playmates and classmates, the juvenile learns to observe how they deal with the same authority figures that he must deal with, and with what results; he learns to compare his own skills, abilities, and competencies with those of others; to discern similarities, differences, and even possibilities that he had never conceived of before. In this respect one's own parents, too, can be compared with the parents of others; the weaknesses and virtues in one's own parents that may have been unnoticeable, simply for lack of opportunity to compare, become manifest.

Compeers in the juvenile period (approximately seven to ten years of age), are essential for the development of social skills, especially here in America where there can be so little reliance on formal manners or etiquette acquired in the home for dealing with contemporaries outside the home. Children who have missed out on the competition and cooperation experiences of these years are confused and awkward with the social occasions of preadolescence and puberty. They are apt to fall back on stylized imitations of behavior they have observed in movies, television, or older youngsters that gives them some semblance of dignity. One young boy painfully imitated a popular young male teacher in his school. Another copied a comical movie actor to win some kind of acceptance through being amusing.

Preadolescence

The next stage of human development occurs between the age of eight to ten and eleven to fourteen, encompassing what Sullivan called "the quiet miracle of pre-adolescence." This is a time of greater independence vis-à-vis authority figures, where one begins to feel that one has some influence in modifying or enlisting collaboration from some authorities. But the most salient characteristic of this phase is that a particular other person, usually of the same sex and age, becomes very important as a companion or chum. There is a tender, respectful affection between two persons in which the other person's interests and needs become truly significant, and through which each individual's horizon expands remarkably through a deep sharing of experiences, feelings, and ideas. They read books together, play together, pursue some hobby. In all that they experience together, the details take on additional meaning because of shared affection and sympathy. Fears and handicaps from earlier years become susceptible to assurance and helpful change under the sympathetic tutelage of a peer who cares and wants to help. This relationship is what Sullivan would call love, and has nothing whatsoever to do with the idolatry of romantic love or with the game-type operations of sexual activities, which may or may not be an accompaniment. His idea of love is close to that of Aristotle (as Patrick Mullahy [1970] pointed out), who in the *Nichomachean Ethics* said that a friend is another self. The discovery of love, in Sullivan's use of the term, is the most important event that can occur in human development; it prepares a person for a kind of education and approach to knowledge that opens the way to the most effective living of one's life with others.

Preadolescence is also the period of life when the phenomenon of loneliness—a major disorder in the highly industrialized, bureaucratic, urban societies of today—reaches its full, sometimes catastrophic extent. Catastrophe can occur when the various components that contribute to the fulfillment of preadolescent love are frustrated in the culmination of loneliness. Patrick Mullahy (1970, p. 362) describes Sullivan's notion of these components as (1) the need for tenderness, (2) the need for adult participation or audience in childhood activities, (3) the need for compeers, (4) the need for acceptance, and (5) the need for intimate exchange with a fellow being.

One category of homosexuals exemplifies this failure to achieve intimacy with a peer in preadolescence. This category is made up of men or women who at the age of ten to fourteen were unable, for one reason or another, to care for another person of their own age with whom they could be in touch and share most intimate feelings. They rationalize their feelings of inadequacy and yearn in terms of a sexual hunger for the ideal athletic, handsome, virile or feminine (as the case may be) person of their own sex with whom they can fuse in ecstatic eternal fulfillment. This is by no means true of all homosexuals.

Adolescence

Adolescence has two main phases that characterize its thrust. One is that of seeking the intimacy of the opposite sex and developing the capacity for interpersonal intimacy or love between oneself and a member of the opposite sex. The other is the development of sexual behavior that is more or less satisfying and may or may not be simultaneous with and directed towards the person with whom one experiences interpersonal intimacy. This era of development poses problems that many adults do not yet seem to have resolved satisfactorily. Even with the most enlightened parents and education, children do turn to their peers for information: adolescent boys first explore the meaning of sex with other boys whom they esteem and regard, and girls do the same. Even the steps towards intimacy with the opposite sex take place with close friends of the same sex. Girls discuss the boys they are beginning to care for, as well as boys per se, with their girl friends; boys do likewise. If no undue warping has occurred, boys and girls both discover a new kind of intimacy with a very special person of the opposite sex. Romantic love or infatuation may then emerge as the chosen person becomes more important than one's friends. Disappointment and disillusion in romantic love may occur as the intimacy deepens and incompatabilities or other difficulties emerge between the two persons. The pain of disappointment may provoke a fearful withdrawal for a short or longer period of time, in which one's friends will again become a great resource. One learns from a series of such experiences, each deepening one's capacity for love and preparing for the challenge of the next relationship, leading, hopefully, to a mature and enduring love between two persons of the opposite sex.

The development described is an ethical ideal in most Western as well as non-European societies. Its consideration leads to problems relating to Sullivan's study of family relationships and kinds of membership in the community at large. But to pursue these would serve no purpose in the present context; here we are concerned only with the concepts that underlie the Sullivanian or interpersonal approach to the treatment of the mental disorders of childhood. Sullivanian conceptions of psychopathology arise from —and contribute to—the foregoing theoretical base.

CLINICAL CATEGORIES

Sullivan was impatient with the traditional categories of mental disorders very early in his professional career. He acknowledged the importance of biological, toxic, hereditary, and other factors in mental disorders, where they play a large or even a predominant part at times. He preferred, however, to concentrate on the difficulties of living that arise mainly from misfortunes in developmental history, where patterns of inadequate or inappropriate interpersonal relations occurred and, to varying degrees and extents, endured.

Although Sullivan wrote a great deal about the patterns of

familial interaction before, during, and after the birth of the child, and especially about the early relationship with the mother, he stressed the implications for the diagnosis and treatment of such adult disorders as schizophrenia and obsessive compulsive neurosis. He never referred, so far as I know, to any instance in which the insights and information gained from his study of childhood were used in the understanding or treatment of children.

In spite of his distrust of fashionable labels, Sullivan did believe in making very detailed and precise descriptions of what went on with the person, so that one might put him in some category (e.g., hysterical personality, obsessive-compulsive, or whatever) in terms of his predominant mode of functioning and presenting distress. He also described each basic clinical category in terms of a style of human relationships. Although he did not apply his conclusions to the vast realm of the disorders in childhood and adolescence, many of his students did take on this task.

Four Types of Childhood Disorders

Barbara Fish, (1965) a former student of Sullivanian psychiatry at the William Alanson White Institute, who was also influenced by the interpersonal formulations of Lauretta Bender and Paul Schilder divided children's disorders into four groups according to the predominant mode of communication and interpersonal behavior. Each category includes the very mild to the most severe of its spectrum.

Type one subjects, the autistic-disjunctive, are absolutely, relatively, or mildly restricted in the capacity to use language and gesture for communication; they range from the most extreme cases who lack intelligible speech, to the most mild, whose speech is self-centered and difficult to understand. The autistic-disjunctive category of children includes, at the most severe extreme, infants and children labeled by other authors as displaying primary autism, symbiotic autism, childhood schizophrenia and pseudo-retardation. Etiological factors vary in weight from one child to another and include genetic, hereditary, prenatal, perinatal, toxic, infectious, interpersonal, intrapsychic, intellectual, perceptual neurophysiological and endocrine. The interpersonal aspect is most clearly seen in the flaccid withdrawn young child who has an overanxious, oversolicitous and overprotective mother. This same mother may have a fairly healthy child in addition to the sick one, but it is hard to determine where circumstances, the child's own responses, or something particular in mother's behavior caused a morbid mother-child relationship. Certainly anything that the doctor might say to enhance her guilt feeling only worsens the sickness between the child and its mother. I saw a nine-year-old girl of this type who was originally referred as a childhood schizophrenic, mute and withdrawn most of the time, retarded at school and isolated from her peers. However, in the course of lengthy therapy and investigation she turned out to be a fairly bright labile young girl with brain damage that caused a motor aphasia which could be compensated for by painstaking training. She bravely fought her tendency to withdrawal and after many years of hard work learned skills and developed lasting friendships.

The second type, the immature-labile, includes individuals who are inadequate or inappropriate in their behavior and communication and unpredictable in mood swings and reactive patterns, from the extreme of a hysterical acting out, psychotic type of flamboyant behavior and dramatic hyperbolic communication to the least extreme, the mildly hysterical and impulsive child.

The immature-labile category may include children classified as hysterical, phobic, hyperactive, or having minimal brain dysfunction or "organic" childhood schizophrenia. For example, a mild case of this type was the young seven-year-old boy who was too impatient with instruction to learn to tie his shoe, clung to his mother when it was time to go to school, hit the other children, and kicked and screamed at minor frustrations. His mother was desperately anxious, guilty and enraged, becoming involved in futile power struggles. In his case a firm, consistent, quiet structure rigorously adhered to at home and at school helped him quiet down. The parent's status injury was relieved by diagnosing him as only temporarily immature—"a late bloomer!"

Type three, the anxious-neurotic, includes children who, at one extreme, are psychotically anxious, panicked, terrified, paralyzed, preoccupied with a fearful withdrawal and hypersensitivity, and at the other end of the scale are only "nervous"—for example, the somewhat hypochondriacal child who is oversensitive to criticism and somewhat overly dependent. The anxious-neurotic type includes all the classic childhood neuroses and represents the largest percentage of patients seen in private offices. Freud's famous case of Little Hans and his phobia of horses fits in this group. At the mildest, they might appear as average middle-class children, eager to do well in the Little League and make their parents and friends proud of them, and worried about their rank among peers. At the most severe, it could include a hypochondriacal psychosis with fearful delusions of little people inside one's body.

The fourth type, the sociopathic-paranoid, encompasses a spectrum that ranges from the psychotic extreme of a full-blown paranoid psychosis with hostile persecutory formulations to the mildly hostile, impulsive, somewhat delinquent behavior, which is inconsiderate, self-centered, and self-seeking beyond the natural self-centeredness of childhood. The socio-pathic-paranoid type is frequently seen in a neglectful lower socio-economic family, and sometimes in very wealthy families. At the mildest, the youngster comes across as a kind of successful, charming, aggressive "operator" who gets away with petty infractions and thoughtlessness. At the most extreme there is the hostile, exploitative, suspicious person with belligerent hallucinations or delusions of a paranoid character.

This typology has been very useful for prognosis and for predicting the usefulness of pharmacologic therapy. For example, it was found that children of the first and second type did not respond to placebo therapy; these children were more specifically dependent on the effectiveness of particular drugs for their improvement. Improvements in children of type three and four, however, were more dependent on environmental factors and were more responsive to placebo. Other factors of importance in considering the course of psychopathology and its prognosis are differences in age and sex, measures of intelligence, socio-economic grouping, specific symptom clusters, and family constellations and attitudes.

Sullivan's formulation of epigenetic critical transition periods for age differences seems to be confirmed by research over the past twenty years. One critical transition period, for example, between infancy and childhood, is the development of intelligible speech and gesture. Three and one half years seems to be a fairly critical point for the prognosis of autistic speech worsening with increasing age. Another critical point occurs around the age of seven, which marks, according to Sullivan, the transition from childhood to the juvenile period, when ordinarily many functions normally become more organized and stable. The third period starts about the age of ten; for Sullivan, this would mark the transition between the juvenile period and the preadolescent period. At this time changes in psychiatric manifestations as well as changes in responses to certain drugs may be observed. Puberty itself, which occurs roughly between the ages of eleven and fifteen, marks another critical turning point, both physiologically and psychologically, in the development of the personality.

Sex differences also are correlated statistically with different manifestations and severity of psychopathology in children and adolescents, just as in adults. For example, it is well established that biological handicaps and psychiatric disturbances are reported to be two to five times higher in boys than in girls before puberty.

Measures of intelligence are also correlated with disorders in children—the functioning of the growing child, as measured by the intelligence tests, is easily affected by environmental and biological insults. As is well known by now, lower I.Q. in children from the lower socio-economic groups may reflect neglect, cultural deprivation, and an increased incidence of both prenatal and paranatal insults, as well as traumatic or unfortunate family and educational experiences.

Autistic Children

Maurice R. Green and David Schecter, who were trained in Sullivanian theory at the William Alanson White Institute, studied the phenomena of autism from a familial, interpersonal point of view in trying to probe beneath the behavioral manifestations into making some inferences about their meaning in the relationships that the three children had to their mothers. They reported (1957) a study of three blind children, confirming the pathological importance of symbiotic activity, first described by Erich Fromm in adult problems and later by Margaret Mahler, specifically in relationship to the autistic phenomena in infancy and early childhood. There was no statistical comparison of the families of the three blind children with the families of other autistic children to determine the importance of defects in triggering or contributing to the complicated relationships that developed. However, there is much in common between the mothers of the three and the mothers described by Mahler and others. Green and Schecter (1957) wrote:

> All three mothers were extremely anxious, with intensely contradictory attitudes toward their children. None sought help on her own initiative, or recognized any serious mental condition in her child, although in all three cases it was very obvious that the child was isolated, severely retarded, and very disturbed. Moreover, each was grandiose in her almost dream-like expectations of the child's eventual performance, though very impatient with his everyday difficulties. The mothers interfered and did many things for the children, thus preventing them from learning through their own efforts. They were all very lonely, frightened women who found overt comfort in

the clinging, infantile behavior of their children, which they sought
—at the same time that they rejected it—out of their guilty anxiety
and frustrated ambition. Unhappy with their husbands, having few,
if any, friends, their time was taken up by their sick involvement
with the equally lonely, even more frightened, and much more helpless children.

The fathers of these families were also less than adequate. Dorothy's father was confused and relatively detached. Robert's father
tyrannized his wife and treated his child with overwhelming permissiveness or with demands for evidence of genius, and blinded himself to the reality of the child's condition. Aldo's father openly resented the child and soon broke up his marriage and abandoned his
child. In no case was the father a source of strength, stability, or
resourcefulness. (p. 10)

The authors raised the question of how the normal and healthy
symbiosis between the infant and his mother becomes unhealthy,
mutually frustrating and destructive to the development of the
infant. Certainly some mothers are unable to encompass the constitutional, hereditary or traumatic defects that an infant may
bring to the relationship, such as brain damage, mental deficiency,
blindness, or other serious deficiencies.

The newly born infant achieves fulfillment of his needs and affords
his mother the opportunity for the expression of tenderness and of
her need to be mothering. Because of the human infant's singular
state of helplessness at birth, this extreme early dependency is quite
appropriate and, in fact, necessary for survival. However, to continue
the early symbiotic relationship much beyond infancy is to ignore
and frustrate the child's growing need for investigation, communication, and contacts with the outer world. In his extreme dependency
upon his mother, there is no preparation for the reality of the outside "public" world; that is, society. The child is kept isolated from
the culture he lives in as long as his mother fails in her role as intermediate "culture-carrier." He is left with a poorly developed or
damaged ego structure whose shape has largely been molded by the
needs of the mothering adult. (p. 15)

Such mothers oscillate in their attitudes from extreme closeness
to extreme distance, from extreme warmth and hovering, smother-
ing attention to extreme hostility and rejection.

This cyclical pattern prevents the establishment of a healthy mother-
child equilibrium, as it continually shatters the frame of reference
upon which the child's ego must grow and, therefore, leads to un-

certainty, panic, and rage. These experiences, if severe and of long duration, may force the child to withdraw in apathy and seclusion, defenses similar to those observed in the schizophrenic. One can, therefore, postulate that much of the autistic behavior observed in the three cases was a defense against this kind of shattering, contradictory, oscillating cycle of experience. Sullivan has described the protective nature of the infantile dynamisms of apathy and somnolent detachment in dealing with the excessive tension of frustrated needs and the anxiety of interpersonal insecurity. Both of these dynamisms are probably similar to the defensive withdrawal that is seen in autism. (p. 16)

Green and Schecter questioned Mahler's postulation of a purely autistic psychosis unrelated to the mother's behavior and attitude. They suggested that it may be more parsimonious to postulate that the appearance of such a purely autistic psychosis is a more severe and incrusted defense against unsatisfactory relatedness wherein the defense masquerades as a total psychosis.

Schecter, in a later paper, distinguished between the defensive attempts at symbiosis and fusion that characterized autistic, schizophrenic disorders and those that characterize neurotic disorders. He contrasted symbiotic and autistic identification with the identification of learning—of imitation for the purpose of further separation and individuation of a more capable and more differentiated personality. Schecter (1968) wrote,

Under conditions of traumatic separation, loss or frustration, identifications may be induced as defenses with varying degrees of adaptive or coping power. Five broad variables contributing to the adaptive outcome are considered clinically and theoretically:
   a. the capacity of the ego to develop intrapsychic structure;
   b. the syntonic versus traumatic nature of the loss or frustration—determined by the "dosage," timing, and quality of the experience;
   c. the underlying affective conditions;
   d. the quality of object relationship between identifier and his model;
   e. the manner in which the identification becomes organized into the total personality; e.g., the selectivity of the identification, the resulting harmony or conflict with other aspects of the personality. (p. 77)

Sullivan (1953), thirty-five years earlier, referred to a similar phenomenon in his notion of the stereotype:

The loss of the primitive mother is a necessary step in personality growth, and the longer it is postponed into childhood by reason of maternal (or relaxed) over-solicitude, the greater a handicap there is imposed on the growth of the child's personality. (p. 102)

The stereotype here would be the conception that the child has, reflected from the mother, of an inadequate, helpless, needy individual; he then identifies with this mother in a pathological way as described above by Green and Schecter.

One sees a healthy symbiosis watching a happy young mother feeding her baby, burping it on her shoulder, and gently but firmly, laying it down. She feels a sensitive confidence in her competence and a pleasant oneness with the baby's activity, satisfaction and quiescence, sometimes moving her own lips as the baby is sucking or eating. The contrast of this with the unhealthy symbiosis is immediately evident in the anxious, impatient intervention of the mother to give the baby the bottle before he cries for it, to get the toy to him before he reaches for it, to say the words before he says them, thus encouraging, if not forcing the child to be increasingly helpless and supplicant. The child's rage reactions are either ignored or treated as an illness.

One can consider many of the disturbances of infancy within this frame of reference, such as the colicky infants who calm down, not when their formula is changed, but when their mothers are given sedatives. There are also the problems of delayed speech, refusal of food, delayed walking, toilet training, night terrors, and other behavioral disturbances of early infancy that one can approach in terms of the family constellation.

Ecological Dimension

The interpersonal point of view has had a profound and widespread influence in communications theory, family therapy theory, and other related fields. Its exponents deplore the individualistic mode of viewing the child out of the context of his family and the prevailing culture in which the family participates. Child psychiatry needs a theoretical framework, like Sullivan's, that would extend the understanding of psychopathology not only to the family constellation but to its participation in the school, the neighborhood, the extended family, and the subcultural groups. Minuchin (unpublished manuscript) wrote:

. . . The family is a behavioral setting which comprises the child. From this point of view, the family is an extra-individual unit with regulatory power over the behavior of its members. At the same time, each member of the family has a separate identity: he is an individual as well as an interacting member of the family unit. The members of a family will exhibit the characteristic pattern of behavior which pertains to that family. At the same time, all the family members will encompass the family rules in their own individual, differentiated ways.

This has important implications for therapeutic interventions (which will be discussed later) in that the therapist is not limited to his transaction with the child alone, but must intervene with the family, the school, and other elements of the child's pattern of interpersonal relations.

Let us look at an example of the ecological dimensions of the interpersonal approach to a particular young boy. He was about eleven-years-old with a long history of immature, labile behavior showing low frustration tolerance, irritability, temper tantrums, and hypersensitivity from his earliest years. There was definite evidence of mild brain damage on neurological examination with impaired coordination of the extremities and later difficulties with reading, spelling, writing, and arithmetic. A program was planned of providing special training for him in athletic activities and in writing and reading so that he was eventually not only completely compensated but had become highly skilled. At the same time the therapist had to be in regular touch with the parents and the teachers to guide him along the proper balance of firm structure and yet allow plenty of outlet for his aggressive energies. In addition, the parents had to supervise his relationships with his classmates and friends so that his weaknesses and tendencies to overcompensate were not exploited by others. Simultaneously with all this, the boy was seen in individual psychotherapy to confront him with his repeated tendencies to deny his difficulties and to scapegoat his teachers and parents. In the course of this he was able to develop genuine self-respect and confidence, built on the competence he had realistically achieved, with an acceptance of the limitations that he eventually corrected.

PREADOLESCENCE

Preadolescence was, for Sullivan, the transition between the juvenile era that encompassed the majority of the years in the primary school, and the adolescent era of sexual maturation and relations with the opposite sex. Preadolescence is uniquely characterized by the emergence of a need for intimacy, usually with a member of the same sex. Sullivan defined intimacy as a kind of closeness which has nothing to do with genital contact, particularly, but is based on a proximity between two individuals who feel that the other person is important enough to permit validating and sharing of their feeling of personal worth in their experience of living. Sullivan used the term "collaboration" to refer to the special feeling of sensitivity that can develop at this age, which is much more respectful and attentive to the needs and feelings of the other person than simple cooperation, competition, and compromise, in which one, so to speak, plays by the rules of the game. Preadolescent intimates tend to cluster and form groups, which sociologists call "gangs." Some adolescents move at an earlier age than others into a more intimate and personal one-to-one relationship. The kind of sharing and communication in these groups leads to the development of opinion leadership, in which an outstanding preadolescent will tend to have an influence over the others in his group.

Sullivan saw this era as a unique opportunity, outside of the intervention of the trained professional, for spontaneous correction of the warps or other unfortunate consequences caused by disturbing, handicapping, and painful experiences of earlier development. Because the preadolescent gets a good look at himself through the eyes of his closest friend, who is apt to be much more honest, straightforward, and direct with him than with the parent (the latter having been a partner in the development of his difficulty). He is able to undergo real expansion of the personality and develop a much greater awareness of who he is and how he is coping with the various aspects of living in the world.

Fortunate experiences in living, particularly in the preadolescent phase from ten to fourteen years of age, can contribute a great deal to the correction of earlier personality warps. For example, there was a young girl, the daughter of an immature, hysterical, depressed mother, and a quietly domineering, seductive and compulsive father, who developed a shy, reserved personality, protecting herself from all sides by a bland virtuous manner, withholding her emotional spontaneity. At thirteen she became involved in a very intense relationship with another girl from an aggressive, exuberant, outgoing ethnic minority, and this led to her participation in a group of girls who expressed their feelings very easily, cried easily, giggled, got angry, swore and so on. As a consequence she herself opened up a great deal becoming more expressive and creative in her academic work as well as in her everyday living.

Sullivan has emphasized, more than anyone else, that there is no necessary correlation between the physiological sexual drive that begins to mature around the time of puberty and the need for intimacy or interpersonal closeness, which also develops about the same time; so that all types of permutations and combinations are possible. For example, an individual can develop great closeness with a member of one sex and yet have no capacity for collaborating or developing a sexual, lustful relationship with that sex. Although the conventional pattern is to be more intimate with one's own sex and more lustful toward the opposite sex after puberty, just the opposite can occur in certain homosexual relationships, where individuals have chums of the opposite sex with whom they can really talk, but relate sexually, often in brief encounters, to members of their own sex, with whom they will then maintain a very distant and sparse kind of intimacy.

Other vicissitudes occur in terms of the wide range of physiological changes that take place. Boys are generally taller up to the age of ten years. Then between the ages of ten and fourteen years, girls have a growth spurt and may surpass boys of the same age. However, by the age of fifteen, the boys again are taller and afterwards maintain that increased height over the girls. There is a wide range of difference, although most boys and girls tend to begin their physiological changes about the same age for their sex, girls, generally, are about two years ahead of boys. However, many youngsters are at one end of the scale or the other. Boys may begin to show pubertal changes as early as ten or eleven, or as late as sixteen or seventeen, and the same is true for girls. The small minority who are at the extreme ends of the spectrum will have emotional problems that are an expression of this difference from the majority of their friends and classmates. Hilda Bruch (1948, p. 229) said that very early pubertal development in girls tended to be related to sexual delinquencies, and very excessive height in girls tended to be related to less stability and poorer capacity to make social adjustments. She also pointed out that small and late maturing boys often suffer from feelings of organic inferiority.

In relation to the development of girls, Clara Thompson (Green, 1964) wrote:

   . . . As puberty approaches, the feeling of difference increases. Since girls usually mature a year or two earlier than boys, the chasm between one-time playmates widens, and a sense of mystery deepens.

All of this sense of difference is usually reinforced by various rules, which are more stringent as they apply to girls. Unless there has been a serious traumatic experience, by the age of twelve a girl is well underway to becoming a woman of our particular social order.

A period of close association with one's own sex usually begins a year or so before puberty and extends into the early part of adolescence. An increasing need for intimacy at this time is responsible for the first close friendships. Often there are groups of girls who may call themselves a club or may just get together. They often have a secret language or exchange secrets. The beginning puberty changes in their bodies are a source of mutual interest, and information and misinformation about sex are frequent topics. One group of grammar school girls met from time to time to inspect the progress of growth of each other's pubic and axillary hair; later the growing breasts were subjects for comparison. This displays an essentially healthy curiosity in the dramatic changes of bodily development. Of course, misinformed groups can succeed in frightening each other quite severely.

Thompson goes on to point out that intimacy between two people of the same sex is very important. Sullivan proposes that the capacity for love develops some time between the ages of nine and twelve. Until this period, what the parents call love in the child has been characterized by considerable dependency. During this period the capacity to care about what happens to another person appears. As the sexual drive begins to mature, confusing emotions concerning boys develop. These emotions are characterized by self-consciousness, a feeling of awkwardness, and sometimes, defensively, a feeling of contempt for the boys. Both these feelings about boys and bodily changes are often discussed in the intimate relationships between girl friends. Sexual experimentation between girl friends may occur, and parents may become concerned that they have a young homosexual on their hands. The healthy girl, however, shifts to an interest in the opposite sex. Moreover, a girl who reaches adolescence having acquired a capacity for healthy companionship with her own sex is well on the way to achieving emotional maturity (p. 296).

ADOLESCENCE

In the last ten years there has been a tremendously increasing interest in the feelings, problems, symptoms, behavior, ideology, and intentions of the adolescent part of our population, which has also increased a great deal in size and in its ratio to the rest of the population. This has placed a much larger load on employment resources and educational resources, with consequent challenges to educators, parents, administrators, and other relevant resources of our society.

In most societies, the adolescents are separated from their parents and immediate family in some kind of institutional group led by their older peers or by some adult figure who is distantly or not at all related to the family. This provides a transitional organization through which adolescents become acquainted with a variety of peer relationships that they will encounter in the larger community and in their adult life; and they also become acquainted with the institutional requirements of adulthood that they will eventually have to meet in order to take their place in the socio-economic order in which they will participate—the crafts, skills, knowledge necessary for social and occupational positions within the community. Opportunity is also usually provided for exploring the erotic and sexual modes of communication with the opposite sex within the structure of the laws, codes, and taboos of the particular society. Thus an adolescent moves from a family-centered childhood through a peer-centered, preadolescent, and adolescent life toward adult life that is centered around his own group of friends and his own family.

America, having a mobile society characterized by waves of immigration and changes of both caste and class structure, has provided shifting sands rather than a stable structure for this transisional experience. Over the past hundred years, one wave after another of adolescents has gone through the syndrome, now familiar, of having parents who, however devoted and loving, come from remote social and cultural backgrounds towards which the children feel shame and contempt in their defensive and desperate wish to become integrated into the newly acquired American culture.

Although a significant section of American youth appears to have taken, in the past decade, a radically new direction toward independence from both parental domination and that of archaic or oppressive social institutions—creating, in effect, an adolescent sub-culture in their rejection of the competitive materialism and status consciousness of the dominant culture, and in their celebration of idealistic, shared ethical and political values in a communion characterized by intense interpersonal relationships—the patterns of the past continue to warp the perceptions and development of the majority.

In a mass society characterized by desperate social and economic competitiveness—and this describes the aggressive culture in which we all live—it is extremely difficult for the adolescent to develop his own genuine potentialities, talents, and personality, without being driven into loneliness and bitter isolation, with its attendant psychological hazards. Obviously, this observation applies with multiple force to the adolescent who comes from a minority culture deemed inferior by the dominant one, e.g., the working class Puerto Rican or black of our swarming urban ghettoes. Hilda Bruch (1948) said, twenty-four years ago:

> Those who are less secure will strive to conform, often at the price of great anxiety and tension. The intimacy and sincerity of friendship and personal relations is sacrificed to the prestige rating within the group. Sex becomes an important coin in this competition. The insecure adolescent girl, fearing the shame of unpopularity, will be more yielding and will grant sexual liberties which are in stark conflict with the ideals of her upbringing. To achieve popularity at this price often means not only conflicts about sex, but also the sacrifice of personal dignity and self-esteem. The insecure boy, on the other hand, in order to prove his masculinity to himself and to his peers, feels obliged to date the girl who has acquired the reputation of being liberal, and he, in turn, counts his success on "how far" he has been able to go with her. In these situations the danger is great that the adolescent will drive himself or herself to earlier and more hectic heterosexual activity than the genuine needs demand. Often, sexual behavior shows sharp divergence in the degree of emotional maturity, independence of thinking, and ability to judge situations. The compulsion to be popular, and the high competitiveness in achieving it, forces upon many young people a facade of maturity before they are capable of making reasonable decisions for themselves. (p. 242)

Today there are many adolescent girls who are compelled to become "free" of their virginity with almost any boy who will suit the purpose, regardless of their interest or capacity for a genuine relationship.

The importance of achieving independence from the family, that is so crucial for the adolescent, highlights the fact that the members of the family are very much a part of his relationship to himself; and that his awareness of this fact is very important in his separating himself for participation with his friends, and with the larger community. Each member of the family has a number of functions and roles, both conscious and unconscious, with every other member of the family, with interlocking patterns of defenses, aims, perceptions, inhibitions, restrictions, and values. Sometimes the struggle for independence leads to negative stereotyping of members of the family in which only the faults are seen and none of the more constructive attributes are appreciated. For the more dependent individual the opposite may be the case, where only the constructive aspects of the parents are seen and idealized beyond all proportion. However, the healthy adolescent moves to an appreciation of his parents as simply human beings among others, with all the faults and virtues that their humanity connotes.

PROBLEMS OF INFANCY AND EARLY CHILDHOOD

Hunger and Appetite

Hilda Bruch, who worked very closely with Harry Stack Sullivan for many years, wrote a number of papers applying Sullivan's ideas to the understanding and treatment of the problems of living experienced by children. Her chapter on adolescence had Sullivan's strong endorsement. More recently she has contributed an interpersonal approach to the understanding of hunger and appetite. She pointed out that the awareness of hunger and, for that matter, of all other biological needs, is not innate but requires learning, in the context of interpersonal experience, in order to become conceptualized for communication.

> . . . the infant must experience, repeatedly and consistently, a definite sequence of events: felt and expressed discomfort, recognition of this signal by the mother, appropriate response and felt relief. Deprivation of this experience, which may vary widely in its contradictory, inappropriate, or neglectful aspects, will render a child deficient in accurate guideposts to his needs. He will grow up confused in experiencing himself as a separate, self-directive unit. . . . (Bruch, 1969, p. 93)

Dr. Bruch studied a large group of children, adolescents, and adults suffering from anorexia nervosa and some developmental obesity, some of whom were, or became, borderline or clearly schizophrenic. She found in her analytic inquiry that food had a great variety of meaning, whether it occurred in the context of a devouring, uncontrollable intake or in the most rigid and fanatic refusal to eat. She found that food might represent symbolically, insatiable wishes for unattainable love, or intense feelings of rage and hatred. It might also represent symbolic sexual satisfaction, or express a kind of asceticism. Further, food may symbolize an envious wish to deny castration feelings and imitate a man who possesses a penis; or, on the other hand, a wish for pregnancy or a fear of it. Food may even serve some sense of grandiose power and pride in taking in more and in dominating others; or it might be a defense against the responsibility of growing up and becoming an adult. It may also be used as part of a helpless clinging to parents; or, conversely, it could be used to reject and express hostility towards them.

Psychoanalytic inquiry, however cooperative and responsive the patient seemed to be, was severely limited in its therapeutic achievement as well as in achieving a full understanding of the problem. The patient suffering from obesity seemed to profit much less and show less change than almost any other diagnostic category in response to psychoanalytic treatment. It has become clear that the resolution of the motivational conflicts was not the issue in the syndrome and did not help them very much because it didn't touch their basic problem of orientation to their body and to their sensations in time and space. Such patients, even at a relatively young age, had begun to mistrust any thought or feelings originating within themselves and were basically confused and uncertain about the behavior of others. Analyses of the transference and the acceptance of such insight were as ineffective as any other interpretive clarification because of this basic position of self-mistrust. The fat person could not exercise responsible control over a function or need that he was not able to discriminate. This was also true of anorexic patients, who at times did not have any awareness of the hunger contractions in their stomachs, and at other times were overpowered by an urge to gorge themselves to the point of vomiting. The fat person suffering this characterological syndrome is a helpless, submissive victim passively overwhelmed by feelings that he does not understand, eating to relieve anxiety, depression, or other distress, or stubbornly and uncritically negativistic.

The interpersonal approach points out that the infant is not utterly helpless or dependent, but rather is an agent of an interpersonal transaction, who gives cues and signals, indicating to the mother his wants and needs. Thus it is very important to differentiate between the behavior that is initiated within the infant and the behavior that is in response to outside stimuli. This, of course, applies to both the biological and the social-emotional field. On the mother's side, one can also distinguish between behavior that is responsive to the child and that which is stimulating to the child. Furthermore, one can rate the response in terms of its appropriateness, i.e., the degree to which it is appropriate and serving the infant's survival and development; or the degree to which it is inappropriate, and thereby distorting or disregarding the requirements for well-being and maturation of the infant.

Naturally, this does not imply that the mother needs to have any special magical powers in fathoming the cues and signals that the infant communicates. This is all at a very simple level and requires no special education, training, or skill except the freedom from emotional handicaps that interfere with the appropriate responsiveness and stimulation. Genetic factors that handicap the infant, paranatal injuries that have gone unrecognized, or some kind of traumatic or confusing early experiences may handicap the infant in communicating clearly the cues and clues to his needs. Because of these factors his needs may then be communicated in a weak, indistinct, and contradictory way, which the mother may find difficult, confusing, and emotionally disturbing to satisfy. Of course, the negative factors would be completely confusing to a mother who is emotionally ill and preoccupied with personal problems, and, for those reasons, insensitive to the expressions of the child's requirements.

There has been much discussion in the literature concerning the balance of overeating and inactivity in the causation of obesity. Bruch and her co-workers have found that *overeating* tends to occur as a developmental problem in infancy and early childhood, whereas *lack of activity* may be incurred at an early age, but it tends to become more of a problem in later life. In both cases, however, a clearly interpersonal phenomenon is involved: overeating has to do with the symbolic meaning of food and the inappropriate activity of a parent who is over-solicitous, over-anxious, inhibiting, neglectful, or indiscriminately permissive, leading to perplexity and confusion in the child. Inactivity can also be caused by the encouragement of passivity, inhibition of motor activity, and the lack of encouragement for activities on the part of the mothering one. It is well known that motor restlessness, hyperactivity, and nutritional need are closely related in humans as well as in animals. In laboratory animals, hyperactivity often precedes increased feeding behavior. In human infants, non-nutritional sucking is often provided for the relief of motor restlessness. This seems to be a congenital mechanism. The wide use of the various types of "pacifiers" is based on this mechanism. Food intake, the post-cibal somnolence, and sedation associated with such food intake can lead to the use of it for appeasing crying and restlessness. This leads to the indiscriminate offering of food, thus depriving the infant of learning to differentiate these states of tension from restlessness, discomfort, and distress apart from hunger.

Thus we see, as many writers have confirmed, how important Sullivan's interpersonal approach to developmental vicissitudes is for our continued progress in psychiatric treatment of all age groups.

Disturbances of Competence

Recent applications of the Sullivanian approach to problems of early childhood were made by Martin Kohn at the William Alanson White Institute in studying the population of four day care centers in New York City. The children were from one to five years of age; one center was predominately white, the others were predominately black. Taking the construct of competence (introduced by Harry Stack Sullivan and developed by Robert White), Kohn and his co-workers developed a seventy-three-item competence scale to asses the functioning of the children in their interpersonal relations to teachers and peers in terms of their activity, productivity, self-help, and other interpersonal processes, including the management of transitional periods. They postulated that since so many of these children came from a socially, culturally, and economically deprived environment, they would find manifestations of the so-called cultural deprivation syndrome in the disturbance of competence, and in the more obviously psychiatric measures of symptoms and behavioral disturbance. They expected, on the basis of this assumption, that these children would receive a compensatory kind of mothering from the highly individualized, warm, nurturant attention of the staff of the day care centers. Further anticipated was a warm, ego-supportive, one-to-one kind of attention, fostering positive relationships with each child's peers and with other teachers, helping the child expand his range of activities, protecting him from massive conflict situations, and developing and fostering a positive regard and feeling of himself.

Although most of the children did respond to this kind of therapeutic teaching with varying degrees of improvement and became more actively involved in the program, more self-assertive, and more self-directive, many of them became extremely provocative and jealous of the teacher's attention, and regressed to infantile dependency, exhibiting clinging and demanding patterns of behavior and low frustration tolerance. They became a disciplinary problem in expressing rage and vituperation. It became clear from further investigation that these patterns reflected the child's behavior at home in relation to those who mothered him.

It becomes clear, then, that just as in adult life, when an individual becomes more engaged in a more intimate relationship, he calls upon the repertoire of interpersonal patterns that have been developed and sustained in previous relationships, so in early childhood, where the repetoire is more limited and more immediate, this is even more true. The child brings from the home to the day care center what it has developed, what has worked for it in achieving self-satisfaction and maintaining security in intimate living with other persons.

Among the many symptoms and behavioral disturbances, two general patterns emerged that were particularly interesting. One was a pattern of anger and defiance that occurred predominantly with children who had suffered from maternal neglect. The other was a pattern of apathy and withdrawal, seen predominantly with children who had suffered from maternal overprotectiveness, oversolicitousness, and infantilizing activity. Therefore, it became clear that any therapeutic approach based upon simply compensating for maternal neglect by providing a kind of substitute mothering would be a gross oversimplification and would only encourage the acting out and transference of behavior patterns that may have been appropriate in the family setting, to the day care setting, where they were inappropriate. A therapeutic program would have to involve changing the family transactional patterns so that there would not be such a gap, and this would include attention, of course, to the parents and other siblings in the family setting, as well as to the child in the day care center.

Family Therapy

Raymond Sobel, director of child psychiatry at Dartmouth Medical School, was an early student of Sullivan's and a graduate of the William Alanson White Institute. Together with Nathan Ackerman, Sobel wrote one of the first papers on family therapy, which is of course, a natural outgrowth of Sullivan's interpersonal theory. However, there are so many schools of family therapy today that the Sullivanian influence is difficult to determine, and the term itself has become almost meaningless. However, as both Sobel and Ackerman very early pointed out and have developed more systematically in their own work over the last twenty-five years, the parents are a very important part of the solution as well as of the problems that the child presents in treatment. There has been more of a tendency among many psychiatrists to put greater emphasis on the treatment of the parents, especially those with very young children, than on the treatment of the child itself. Many prefer to work with mother-child pairs in treating specific problems— such as refusal to go to bed, disturbed eating patterns, and other habit disturbances; these, of course, reflect as much the mother's psychopathology as they do the child's.

Sometimes it is necessary or more useful to see the mother and child as a pair rather than in family therapy or in individual psychotherapy. For example, a young girl was referred by the school because of increasing absences, withdrawal, and anxious, tearful behavior. She lived alone with her mother whom she followed about every minute at home, even not allowing her mother to be in the bathorom alone. The mother was a frightened, lonely woman, estranged from her relatives and abandoned by her husband. With the help of the social worker, relations were reestablished with the relatives eventually. The mother and child were seen together and confronted as a pair with the destructive, constrictive impact they were having on each other. With the ventilation of many heretofore "hidden" feelings, individuation was then allowed to proceed on each side.

In another case, a very tight-lipped, anxious mother who sat on the edge of her seat brought a thin, pale, wan little six-year-old-boy, complaining of his refusal to eat which led to violent fights that, she said, completely exhausted her. I saw the two of them together over a period of several months, during which the power struggles were allowed to take place during the session. It was then much easier to point out to the mother where her guilty vulnerability lay and how she could avoid getting the little boy's back up and could avoid encouraging him to tyrannize her.

Sobel (personal communication) has used the diagnosis of the family constellation as an important part of the diagnostic appraisal in the planning of treatment strategy. He attempts to assess current, on-going, distorted relationships among the members of the family, between the parents and the extended family, with other relatives, and even the important relationships they have out-side the family. He tries to determine the origin of these distortions in the parent's past and to discover how the child adapts and attempts to cope with what is a transference or distortion on the part of the parent in the parent's relationship to the child. For the milder variety of conduct and habit disturbances, Sobel will observe the mother and child together in the playroom and show the mother very directly where she herself reinforces the kind of behavior that she desires to have removed by the psychiatrist. The approach can be used with the larger family, that is, including siblings and both parents in the playroom-treatment situation.

Richard Gardner (1968b) applied a Sullivanian interpersonal approach to the problems of brain injured children in their relationship with their parents. He has shown how the denial reaction, the angry reaction, and the overprotective reaction of parents contribute to the difficulties of the child and, in their turn, provoke reactions in the child of withdrawal and regression. They may also provoke a neurotic exploitation of the organic symptoms, generalizing and interpreting the brain damage itself to mean that the child as a whole human individual is damaged and inadequate. Accurate perception of the transactions between the children and their parents in this instance, as in the others previously described, is necessary for a basis in planning the treatment strategies.

In reviewing the literature and his own personal experience with the conscious fantasies of children, Gardner (1969b) concluded that children, consciously, at any rate, were preoccupied much more with feelings of violence, hurt, misfortune, and separation than they were with the oral, anal, and other libidinal phases of development that Freud described. Freud described these conflicts mostly in terms of unconscious processes. Gardner suggested that findings of the classical Freudian school of psychoanalysis were true but derived from a morbid sample of the population in which these attitudes developed due to the unfortunate attitudes and relationships within the family. Empirical studies of both the waking consciousness of children and of their dreams as reported through EEG awakenings during the night confirm Dr. Gardner's hypothesis. The latency period, in that context, then, would not be due to any repression of sexuality in most cases, because there would be no sexuality to repress.

With older children, the standard play equipment may no longer interest them and various other techniques may be used to invite their production of fantasies, such as starting a picture and having them finish it and tell a story about it. For example, a boy of eleven always avoided making up stories, reporting dreams, or even drawing pictures. But in this case he accepted the invitation to finish the squiggly lines begun for him and he made a flying saucer out of it. With considerable prodding he invented a story of a father and son attacked by an alien being from another planet. The son, through quick thinking, outwits the extraterrestrial entity, rescues the father, and they come back safely to earth. This fantasy helped open up the dissociated rage the boy felt towards the father for preferring a younger sibling. His guilt and fear of this rage and its consequences were symbolized by the alien monster from outer space, a more or less conventional horror-science-fiction character these days.

In another study, Gardner (1969c) showed that the severe guilt reaction that parents often had towards children who had suffered serious physical illness was a complex phenomenon and could not be understood simply as overcompensation or as reaction formation, or even as simple, straightforward guilt; in many instances guilt was a defensive operation that gave the parent a greater illusion of mastery over, and responsibility for, the fate suffered by himself and his child, thus easing the intense pain of helpless injury.

Fear and Anxiety

So far we have discussed infancy and childhood in terms of Sullivan's theory of development and in terms of his students' understanding of the pathological consequences of failures or disturbances in development. We have seen this in terms of interpersonal patterns—of failure to develop communication and intimacy; we have seen this in relation to the dynamism of withdrawal from communication and intimacy to varying degrees ranging from the psychotic to more mild withdrawals; we have seen disturbances and warps of relationships between the child and the parents that endure and persist pathologically; and we have seen, particularly in Bruch's contribution, the importance of a successful development of what Sullivan called the personified self: the degree to which an individual experiences an image of himself, and experiences an awareness of his body and its activity in relation to other people that is valid, competent, and esteemed. This is a terribly important base for future development and for the ability to survive unfortunate experiences.

The communicated, expressed, or implied feeling state that one observes in the child is a useful index of the nature of his personified self at the time and of its activity in relation to other important people. His discussion of the feelings of fear, anger, rage, hatred, discouragement, grief, morbid grief, guilt, of the rationalized anxiety called "guilt," and of pride, conceit, envy and jealousy, are an important contribution to the understanding of interpersonal processes underlying not only healthy development but the various pathological turns it may take. Sullivan is very careful to distinguish fear from anxiety: fear is a self-preservative response widely shared between human organisms and many other living organisms, whereas anxiety is a self-esteem preserving response that is exclusively human. However, he recognizes that subjectively the anticipation of anxiety may feel very much the same as the anticipation of fearful situations. Fear can be called out by the great novelty of a situation, by its danger to the survival or bodily integrity of an individual, by the threat of pain or severe distress, or by confusion among these things. With children, as with adults, the importance of distinguishing between the terror of extreme fear and the terror of extreme anxiety can be far-reaching in the treatment situation. An individual who is frightened by the novelty of a situation—going into a hospital, starting school, having a new person come in as a nurse, moving to a new neighborhood, and anticipating violence or aggression from one source or another—can be helped by probing and carefully discriminating what is going on. The child or youth will feel less fearful and terrified if the danger can be spelled out very carefully or the orientation required for new situations or relationships can be carefully defined. The terror of anxiety, however, can be increased by such probing, particularly when the anxiety is caused by the tendency of a dissociated part of the personality to come into consciousness—some tendency that the individual has developed the capacity for not noticing begins to intrude on conscious attention. Any attempt made to develop clarity and bring the tendency into awareness will be provocative of more anxiety and terror unless the time is taken to build up the context of support and regard in which this can be allowed to happen and the resultant anxiety can be relieved through the relationship with the psychiatrist or some other important person.

Anger and Hatred

Anger, like fear, is also a part of the biological equipment that the human organism shares with a wide range of the mammalian family. Like fear, it is a response to dangerous situations, but its purpose is not to prepare for flight but to enable the organism to destroy the danger or to drive it away. Sullivan believed that very early in life, even before the development of effective language behavior, the young child learns to use anger to cope with anxiety. He postulates that this arises from the parent or other important adult punishing or disapproving of the child by mistake, so that the child justifiably feels abused and angry. When he sees that this anger is the same as the anger of his parents or nurse or other important people, as an expression of their disapproval or punishment of his behavior, it then becomes a part of his social conditioning. Sullivan (1956) wrote:

> At the same time it takes on a very important justification for existence in that it spares one anxiety. The child needs only a very little random experimenting with this new discovery to find that if he gets angry, he does not suffer much anxiety. And so, various degrees of anger, from what is politely called irritation up to a feeling that borders on rage, come to be the most frequent expression, as far as can be objectively detected, of situations that provoke mild insecurity, except when one is in the company of people who are so significant that it is dangerous to be angry with them or—a very much smaller group of exceptions—among people who can be unpleasant that it is not wise to provoke them. (p. 95–96)

Sullivan describes rage as a more extreme and intense expression of anger where its purpose of injuring, destroying, or driving away the threatening object or person cannot be accomplished. Thus we see rage in the struggles of an infant who is restrained, and we see rage in the temper tantrum of the older child who feels unable to use his anger effectively. One sees this dynamism at work particularly in the phenomenon called power struggle, wherein the mother or parenting one tries to "make" the child eat, do, or be something which the child feels threatened by and helpless with, so that his rage calls forth an increased anger and coercion from the parent, which in turn calls forth more rage from the child, resulting in an impasse that can sometimes be enduring and lead to a stalemate or, even worse, a deterioration on both sides. Here it is helpful to clarify parental feelings of helplessness and competence and what can and can't be done at a particular time. Once the pressure is off, the child eventually becomes "reasonable."

Hatred is a manifestation of enduring rage which is aimed at hurting another individual, destroying his self-respect, and making him feel small and humiliated. Sometimes individuals develop the capacity for disparagement in order to avoid noticing the tendencies to anger, rage, and hatred within themselves by becoming hypersensitive to the irritation and anger in other people in a way that derogates and disparages their worth as human beings. One avoids events that might provoke anger in oneself. Naturally the process produces somewhat detached individuals who fend off others instead of coming to terms with them.

Feeling of Inadequacy

Sullivan believed that very early in life, some time after the development of language behavior, the individual comes to avoid inadequacies in himself, and humiliation that he has experienced in relation to these inadequacies, by a denial of inadequacy and by boasting and self-assertion—that is, by an avoidance of humiliation and an expression of pride. Sullivan uses the term pride in the very narrow sense as a kind of morbidity that doesn't work too well at avoiding humiliation. Conceit is related to pride in that it is also a way of avoiding humiliation, but it is a much more dependable one in that it rests upon the exaggeration and overemphasis of essentially correct appraisals of ability, skills, talents, attributes, and so on.

Envy and jealousy, on the other hand, are very important feeling-states that may often trigger the onset of a severe mental disorder. Envy is an acute discomfort produced by the discovery that another person has some attribute or object that one feels one ought to have oneself. Sullivan (1956) said that the people who are at the mercy of envy have learned to see themselves as unsatisfactory, inadequate human beings. Sometimes this learning process has gone on in a simple, direct, and comprehensive way. The home environment and the succeeding school society have taught them that they do not rate, or that they are not the way others want them to be. They are the children who have disappointed their parents' expectations and hopes for them. Sometimes they are people who have rather small gifts, but who have parents who expected them to have larger gifts, and therefore the smallest of their gifts was brought very keenly to their attention.

Sullivan goes on to point out that with other types of envious people the lesson may have taken a different form. These people do not feel inadequate; rather, they have been given an irrational and extravagant picture of themelves as children and young juveniles. From the beginning of the school era onward, they have experienced constant dissatisfaction from others because of their attempts to approximate the extravagant ideals instilled by their parents. "In other words, they have been taught that they are more than can be demonstrated in the world" (p. 129).

This breeds a chronic sense of inadequacy and worthlessness for which the individual seeks protection and relief in acquiring status of one kind or another—Cadillac cars, sexual conquests, a superior supply of marijuana, or whatever—which, however successful, only serves temporarily to distract one from the gnawing, hollow sense of emptiness and worthlessness at the edge of consciousness.

Sullivan particularly emphasized the unfortunate institutionalization of the vain, frantic activities in the American culture of immigration, mobility, and mass production.

> The result is that gadgets—and even such gadgets as money—come with preternatural ease, and commerce has developed fabulously; and, at the same time, the cultivation of that vicious misuse of human credulity—advertising—has become one of the most lucrative of all activities in America. The business of making things as conspicuously different from each other as possible, and grading these differences in terms of cost, has become an extremely successful way of accumulating other people's money. As a result, the material trappings with which one frantically tries to relieve one's envy—and thereby magnifies it—grow apace. (1956, p. 135)

Writers from the early history of our country, such as de Tocqueville, and later Thorstein Veblen, in his *Theory of the Leisure Class,* have pointed to this powerful aspect of the American society. Sullivan has underscored its poisonous influence in human development on the achievement of successful intimacy. Instead of genuine friendship we have the widespread superficiality of "friends" and the preoccupation with "keeping up with the Joneses."

Competition is another problem heightened by American social patterns. There is the very early form of competition which has to do with the desire to hold onto and increase what is possessed and part of me, my and mine, and therefore responding to any attempts at sharing or removing as though these attempts were a deprivation of anticipated pleasure in whatever it may be—food, toys, clothing, or the attention and contact with others. This early kind of competition, which enters into the concept of sibling rivalry, is very different from the later competition that develops in the so-called latency period, or what Sullivan called the juvenile era of the early years of school society. Here the individual has to prove his value in various contests and tests with his peers, whether by physical fighting, athletic activities, or intellectual contests. In an exaggerated form, which tends to be encouraged by the structure of our culture, the individual becomes ambition-ridden and handicapped for intimate relationships or for useful collaboration with others.

In the ghetto and among the lower socio-economic immigrant groups, the prevailing disparaging and derogatory attitudes of middle-class adults and institutions toward the ghetto children in their care promote whatever interpersonal experiences these children have in the direction of facilitating their feelings of worthlessness; and as they enter the school society of the juvenile era, many of these youngsters begin to become impaired in their intellectual skill and emotional equipment for developing self-respect in their relationships with others. Immigrant groups have countered this tendency by developing pride in their subcultures, which, when based on genuine skills and traditions, can be effective.

Many black children who grew up in their early years at home with a good experience of themselves as competent, loveable, and worthwhile children came to experience an erosion of their self-esteem as they progressed through the first three or four years of schooling and were forced to cope with negative stereotyping of their black identity as inferior, unworthy, unloveable, incompetent, and even dangerous. Fortunately there is a trend toward correcting this in the use of mass media, textbooks and attitudes of teachers and the community—so that blacks can take some pride in their identity along with other minority groups in our society. The outstanding current example is, of course, the black nationalist movement, with its defiant slogan, "Black is beautiful."

The word "jealousy" is often used to refer to envy, as described above, or to competition or infantile struggles against unrealistically anticipated deprivation. However, Sullivan uses "jealousy" very specifically to refer to the painful experience of inadequacy in personal relationships, incapacity for intimacy, that he would probably formulate as a feeling of being unloveable. He wrote (1956) that the person has developed a deep conviction of relative unworthiness. He feels that he does not deserve the people whom he has enjoyed; they are better than he is. Moreover, he has a feeling of relative emptiness of value in the interpersonal field (p. 141).

Jealousy and grief do not appear in their full form before preadolescence since they both have to do with the problem of achieving and maintaining intimacy with someone important, wherein there is at least the beginning of a love relationship. Although Sullivan recognized mutuality and reciprocity occurring in the relationship between a child and its parents from very early in infancy on, he emphasized the fact that this relationship was based on a rather fragmentary awareness on the infant's part of what the mother was as a real person in her own life. The natural dependency of the infant and young child weighs this relationship towards its healthy instrumental purposes for the child's own development and for the parents' satisfaction in their competence as parents. The parents therefore are not very important to the child in their own right, with their whole separate spectrum of needs and problems. It is only in preadolescence that the individual comes to the experience of another separate person as an important person in his own right, one whose needs, feelings, and value are as important as one's own. This is what Sullivan meant by love.

Grief

Grief, as Sullivan defined it, is a series of painful processes by which the consciously imagined experiences and ties to a lost loved person are gradually erased as the person recognizes and accepts the painful loss. By this means the integrating tendencies of the whole personality that had been deeply involved in the love relationship, which is now ended permanently, are gradually released for life with others. Thus grief is a very necessary part of our humanity and an extremely valuable and protective one.

> The first day after the loss, since intimacies interpenetrate so much of life, it is almost impossible not to be reminded of the loss by any little thing—even the position of the salt cellar on the table, for instance. But each time this happens, you might say, the power of that particular association to evoke the illusion of the absent one is lessened. . . . Thus, imediately after a loss, the position of the salt cellar may be reminiscent to you of dear John, because it was always placed half-way between you and John. But the next time you see the salt cellar, you might become a little bored; its power to evoke dear John is diminished by the very fact that you have clarified the associational link with him. And so it goes: by erasing one tie after another, and releasing the personality to move on into life, to seek satisfactions by cooperation or collaboration with other people, grief protects us from making a retreat. (Sullivan, 1956, p. 107)

However, as Sullivan was quick to point out, morbid grieving is a very different matter. It is a horrible caricature of the healthy grief in which the releasing and erasing function is lost and grief itself becomes the predominant mode of life.

Hysterical Personality

The hysterical personality begins rather early in life in the childhood era before school and in the early juvenile era soon after school begins. This type of personality pattern grows out of the relationship of the child to a self-absorbed parent who regards the child as something of a toy or a plaything rather than as a growing personality. This parent lacks appreciation or respect for the child and belittles reality extravagantly, setting an example for the child to exaggerate and dramatize every event that occurs. The hysteric is not particularly cautious about his impact on other people. Unlike the schizoid personality who is careful to avoid provoking rebuff, the hysteric is so self-absorbed that he is content to participate in the audience about him as he watches his own extravagant and dramatic movements across the stage of life. In this rather unrefined fantasy world of existence the individual can move fairly comfortably in relatively superficial contact with other self-absorbed people and not notice his lack of capacity for mature intimacy. In the juvenile era they may be mistaken as warm, outgoing, colorful children unless stress leads to specific symptom formation.

Hypochrondriacal patterns of behavior can develop very early in life wherein the individual's physical distress and imagined ailment, or real ailment, become of much more importance than anything else about the personality for the important parental figures that are around. This may or may not continue; to the extent that it does, it sets the stage for the individual to relate to others, and feel most secure and comfortable, in terms of what is ailing him, in predominance over most anything else in the way of living with people.

Sullivan introduced the term *algolagnic* to describe a somewhat comparable failure of self-esteem and interpersonal growth, in which the individual appeals for sympathy or attention in terms of what is ailing the world, expressing his pain and distress at what is happening about him and dramatizing how others are failing or disappointing him, excluding, of course, present company. In childhood, this might come across as a whining, complaining, critical child for whom nothing done can bring much evidence of satisfaction.

Obsessional Disorder

The obsessional disorder dates to the late infantile and early verbal stages of development. The infant and young child suffering this disorder experiences a profound insecurity in their relationships with the parental figures; they do not protect themselves very well with gestures and words that are incomprehensible to others and have no discernible logical order, and with consequences that have no necessary relationship to causes. They try with more or less success to conceal their very low self-esteem by quietly acting the part of a subtle, powerful, magical figure. By tagging his behavior or verbal performance with some ideal to which the parent figures have allegiance—religious, ethical, or whatever—the child is able to avoid punishment and disapproval to a degree that allows him sufficient peace of mind to go on about the business of living. This may come out in the area of toilet training, wherein the individual, by exaggerated display of taking pains in the direction of cleanliness, neatness, and orderliness, puts off any possible criticism or punishment for other activities that might cause rebuff. However, toilet training may be uneventful and still the obsessional dynamism and character structure can develop; there is no one-to-one correlation. Such children are always victims of parents or older siblings who abuse them, use them as scapegoats, and then evade responsibilities by rationalizing their behavior in terms of some ideal: "Johnny did it first;" "It's for your own good." These children generally grow up in homes where there is no genuine affection or genuinely rational behavior. In fact, there may be a great deal of overt aggression, violence, disorder, and at the same time, preoccupation with status, prestige, and the rationalization of a variety of selfish, domineering, and exploitative behavior.

Depression

Although Sullivan had little or nothing to say about the development of depressive dispositions in childhood or the etiology of the manic-depressive psychosis, he did refer to a number of dynamisms that do contribute to what we see clinically as depression in children. He described the angry protest that occurs in infancy, that is, what he called anger at a threat or change in the situation that the infant or young child is not prepared for, and how that can be used by the child to avoid anxiety or humiliation. He also described "somnolent detachment," or what others might call apathetic depression.

> . . . I would like to set up provisionally the term "somnolent detachment" as the protective dynamism called out by prolonged, severe anxiety, in contradistinction to apathy as the protective dynamism called out by unfulfilled needs. (1953, p. 56–57)

Sullivan would use the term apathy to refer to the deprivation and neglect syndrome of institutionalized children described later by Spitz and Bowlby, who really lacked fulfillment of the important biological need for contact.

I have only seen one case of severe apathy in an infant. It was a few months old and had lost all interest in food or drink or any external stimuli. It had not received any warm maternal contact and was wasting away into a dried up, wrinkled mummy-like figure in a classical case of marasmus. However, on proper diagnosis, a warm, maternal nurse was hired who held the baby a great deal, and gradually nursed it back to life again as a blooming, pink cheeked, vigorous infant.

The loss or interruption of the relationship between the child and the one it knows as the mother, after the age of six months, is characterized by a basic movement from anger to a weeping, tearful, sad expression, to a lack of expressiveness and responsiveness. There seems to be some correlation between such experiences and a later hyper-responsiveness to temporary separations or anticipated separations. This type of depressive syndrome should be distinguished from another type in which it is not the anticipated separation so much as a humiliation of some kind to a basically insecure child who has propped himself up with vulnerable defenses of denial and grandiosity. The depression in the latter type of syndrome will have much more agitation and rage in it and be almost a disguised, or not so disguised, temper tantrum. Thus depression based on real loss or neglect could show a mixture of anger, perhaps expressed most frequently as a sullen resentment, and anxiety, expressed as sleepy detachment or as "tiredness." The depression based on repeated failures to win esteem might be expressed in a variety of angry self-depreciatory avoidance behaviors; at its extreme form, even in suicide.

INTERPERSONAL THERAPY

Aim

There has been some confusion about the aims and goals of treatment. Is it for enabling the child to join an elite group of "analyzed" persons? Is it for getting rid of something uncomfortable, like extracting the psychological equivalent of a splinter? Is it to achieve happiness? I suppose for most people it follows the traditional healing aim of medicine which, for thousands of years, has offered help in overcoming or relieving pain and enabling or restoring function to the whole body or its part. However, within the interpersonal approach it seems to me the purpose of treatment is twofold: on the one hand, to facilitate intimacy; and on the other, to restore or improve competence wherever it is restricted or handicapped by interpersonal problems, in the foreseeable future, present, recent or remote past. I see the most important part of my work with children from the earliest age as an enablement and facilitation of the capacity for noticing, articulating, and expressing an increasingly wide range of feelings that they can share with me, hopefully with their parents, and certainly with their close friends as they mature. For the children from two to ten, this means most of the time working with the paernts in one way or another so that intimacy can develop between the child and its parents. After the age of ten the emphasis shifts to a respectful distance, particularly with the parent of the opposite sex, and a greater intimacy with one's peers, one or more best friends, and eventually love relationships. The most important aspect of this sharing is not the mere catharsis of feelings for their own sake, but the sharing with another separate person who by his response shows appreciation, understanding, and foresight. The development of reliable foresight is the *sine qua non* of a successful communication, sharing and intimacy. This foresight makes for a responsible participation in the world according to age and capacities.

To this end, the therapist should have available a wide variety of materials that can be used expressively: doll house and doll families, both black and white, anatomical dolls, hand puppets, toy soldiers, tanks, airplanes, Lincoln logs, blocks, toy animals, crayons, clay, poster paint, and drawing paper. For the older ones I'll also have knock-hockey, dart boards with rubber suction tips darts, playing cards, checkers, and scrabble.

Interpretations are always stated in the most concrete, specific terms of the child's own language, e.g., "Oh, so *you* are the big monster, huh?" Or, "What does your mother say or do that suggests she likes your little sister so much more than you?"

Sometimes the information given by a younger child cannot be used much with the child, but is more useful in helping the mother improve her own situation with the child. Sometimes the child points to some pathology in the mother that needs to be treated quite separately from the child.

My youngest patient was a little girl two and a half years old, who was referred for treatment for pulling out her hair. She had a brother who was two years older. The mother and father were both intelligent, educated, and cooperative. I saw the family shortly after I had returned from a visit in the summer of 1950 to the Tavistock Clinic in London, where I had observed how useful it was as part of the preparation for treatment, to see an entire family simultaneously for a diagnostic impression of how its members related to each other. We began to do this routinely at the child psychiatry clinic at Roosevelt Hospital under the directorship of Dr. Janet Rioch, who had been closely associated with Harry Stack Sullivan. The practice seemed to fit in very well with Sullivan's own orientation. The child to whom I have referred was articulate, with a good vocabulary for her age, was bright and responsive, and engaged immediately in play with the various doll figures, doll furniture, and doll house that were part of the equipment of the playroom in which we treated children.

It became clear over a course of several months of play therapy, observing what the child did with the family of dolls, that she adored her older brother, that she was somewhat distant from her father, and that she was worried about her mother, who was seen at times with the child and at times by a separate therapist. At one point in the course of the play therapy, the child had the mother doll flush herself down the toilet. When this was brought up with the mother's therapist, it seemed to confirm the findings that were emerging in the mother's therapy, of suicidal tendencies associated with a very complex pattern of problems that antedated her marriage and that had brought the marriage into jeopardy. When the problem was resolved, in the course of the mother's therapy, the mother's depression was alleviated and the marriage between the mother and father secured. The child's hair-pulling stopped, and she was soon discharged, with no further symptomatic behavior within a two-year follow-up period.

Although young children relate to the psychiatrist as a parent surrogate in the age group between two and a half to five, six, or even seven years of age, communication occurs in global, affective terms of dependency, gratification, frustration, competition, cooperation, fantasy and play-acting, with the family most of the time experienced as a fairly solid center base of support and reference. Although some insight can be given to the child in terms of pointing out specifically maladaptive or aggressive behavior that is no longer necessary or useful, work has to be done simultaneously with the family so that the insight is realistically programmed for a family situation in which it can be integrated. In some cases we lack family cooperation. Then, a rather intensive, long-term relationship with the child is required, in which the child eventually comes to accept the limitations in his family situation, which may be quite severe, and to find his satisfactions and fulfillments with teachers, peers, and others outside of the family circle.

In one such instance I saw a boy of six who had been rejected by his mother since infancy but had a warm relationship with an uneducated black maid. The maid was genuinely interested in his well-being and provided a basic physical contact and warmth. The father, who was more removed, was also genuinely interested in the boy but felt that he was hopelessly retarded.

The mother was hopelessly isolated—an immature, hysterical woman who could give no warmth or emotional nourishment to the boy; the father was a very defensive, somewhat isolated individual who wanted very much to help his son but had little insight into his own or other personalities.

Diagnostic appraisal showed that the boy was very withdrawn, with a strong negative image of himself and primitive feelings of infantile rage and cannibalistic yearnings for closeness. It was decided that he be taken out of his public school and placed in a special private school where small classes made it possible to give him a great deal of individual attention over a period of many years, during which he continued to receive psychiatric treatment. The treatment moved from a simple play therapy with soldiers and Lincoln logs and other toys toward roughhousing and various kinds of games, and ended up with mostly verbal communication in which the boy became able to formulate, with insight, statements about himself and his family and to make constructive plans for his future. His I.Q. developed with the general growth of his personality and, although he continued to be somewhat schizoid in his adolescence, he was able to develop close friendships and go on to a rich, normal adolescent life in a regular, highly qualified academic school.

Patient-Therapist Relationship

Transference has always been recognized as the most important instrument for psychoanalytic treatment of adults as well as children. The transference-countertransference has, however, been neglected in child psychiatry. Many writers emphasize the importance of the analyst's awareness of his countertransference responses and have urged regular consultations and periodic periods of re-analysis for the child analyst.

The implication is that the countertransference is a hindrance that should be understood in order to prevent it from interfering with the treatment. Such a view fails to recognize and appreciate the importance of the countertransference in understanding the patient and in promoting what Sullivan called participant observation of the patient and analyst together.

Hannah Colm was one of the first people in the literature to apply Sullivan's theories to this issue. In applying Sullivan's field theory to the child-psychiatrist transactional experience, she wrote, "In the field experience there can be only spontaneous acting and reacting to the situation, and countertransference becomes merely one facet of the common humanity of patient and analyst." Thus, the analytic situation is merely a human situation in which the responses of both the analyst and the patient represent the same human involvement with their pasts. The analyst, however, is better able to distinguish from the present involvement. He does not react parataxically; nor is he undefensively willing to be open to the patient's suspicions and accusations that he is not realistically involved; rather, he engages in self-scrutiny. "Thus the analyst's human responses, his countertransference reactions, need not merely be used privately by him, but can, when it is called for, be put at the patient's disposal in order to clarify with him the interpersonal reaction" (1966, p. 96). Given this point of view, the appearance of countertransference does not represent a fault of the analytic situation, but, rather a way to investigate the mutual interaction.

Colm emphasized in her writing again and again the common

humanity of the patient and his doctor, and the effort to meet the center of the other in bringing together all their involvements on a conscious as well as unconscious level, relevant to the issues at hand. She (1956) said that in therapy the patient and analyst work together.

She (1956) said, the analyst must deal with the patient in his whole field while recognizing that, through the analysis, the analyst's own field and that of his patient will begin to interact. Both analyst and patient have new experiences and reactions. They will show new defenses and there will be spontaneous reach-outs. The communication in this goes, for the most part, from unconscious to unconscious. The analyst tries to contact the center area of the patient in order to help him toward "center-area" living in contrast to his defensive "fringe-area" living. Thus field analysis represents ". . . an examination of the common field between the two people, in the course of which, for each person, the unconscious probably has the more permanent impact, and the conscious, the more temporary impact" (p. 97).

Thus from the interpersonal or Sullivanian point of view, the analyst cannot remain a distant authority, narcissistically involved with controlling and withholding an artificial relationship that is supposed to accomplish therapeutic results. On the contrary, as Colm has pointed out, the Sullivanian approach requires a mutuality of spontaneity and openness on both sides. She (1956) wrote that therapy cannot be a one-sided opening up—a relationship which for the one person is spontaneous and open, and for the other, controlled and withholding, growing all too easily into a narcissistic unrelatedness. There must be an inner contact of two human beings who turn to each other,

> with their fields of experience—past and present, conscious and unconscious—and meet, interact, relate. It is true that this is not an unstructured meeting, but has come about in specific pursuit of getting and giving help. In the course of this pursuit, however, the therapeutic situation develops, bringing the life experience of the two persons into one field experience. Through this experience, the comon field can be studied and analyzed on both sides, enabling both partners to get the greatest possible insight into the interaction; when difficulties arise, both participate in determining whether these represent distortions on the one side or the other, or whether they are reality difficulties. (p. 98)

Colm makes it clear that she does not refer to any wildcat analysis wherein the analyst acts out his own problems, conflicts, and feelings, exploiting the patient for neurotic or other kinds of gratifications. Quite the contrary, she refers to a dedicated and responsible involvement in which the analyst uses his most private and intimate resources to enhance the patient's well being.

Spontaneous Approach

Colm feels, and I agree, that the mutual, spontaneous approach is particularly helpful with the latency child, who has moved from the juvenile period of competition and cooperation toward the preadolescent period in which he begins to seek intimacy with another youngster his own age. Latency children are usually resistant to unstructured play activity and are seldom interested in examining their dreams, fantasy life, or intimate relationships with others. They do not want to explore their interpersonal existence for fear of being thrown back to more childish feelings and exposing their newly won maturity to some test in which they may find themselves inadequate. Any attempt to discuss this problem, to relieve their fear and apprehension, embarrassment, need for control, and trust only increases the tendency of such youngsters to withhold.

The therapist may respond with sympathy as well as with despair. Here it may be useful to express one's feelings to the child. For example, I can say to a youngster, "I really feel very unhappy with you. I know you are coming here because your parents want you to come and hope that I can help you. But at the same time, I know that you don't want any help, and you feel burdened by the obligation to be here. You make me feel that I am useless to you and that you'd rather be all to yourself, and I feel a little hurt and rejected, you know."

It is good to have material handy to help with the communication. There may be pencil and paper, a big lump of clay, some checkers, a deck of playing cards—a variety with which the child can reach out and begin to communicate. Such materials can be useful in different ways at different stages of development.

Richard Gardner (1969) has written about the use of the game of checkers at different periods of development. He described three different stages in which the game can be used in different ways to reveal interpersonal problems in the child's life. The average child of five to six is usually able to play checkers.

When he first learns to play:

He is apt to see a magical relationship between the color of the checkers and his chances of winning. He plays a strictly offensive game and is not too concerned with his partner's potential danger to him. He restricts his focus to a small segment of the board, forges doggedly ahead, trying to jump his opponent, regardless of the consequences. He does not devise any traps or grand plans. He sees single, but not double or triple jumps, and has to be told that he can jump further. Deriving great pleasure from kings, he tries quickly to get to his opponent's side. But once he acquires a king, he tends to leave it and tries to get more, rather than to move it out and attack his opponent from the rear. His delight in acquiring kings, along with the inability to use them effectually, is the hallmark of this early stage. Lastly, he frequently interrupts the game to determine whether he is winning by counting the number of checkers that he and his opponent have taken off the board, and tends to disregard the fact that such reckoning fails to take into acount the kings.

When the child reaches the age of seven, he begins to realize that the immediate feat of winning a man can be more than counterbalanced by his opponent's subsequent move. Now, he plays more cautiously, his focus broadens, but he still can see only one step ahead, i.e., his opponent's single subsequent move. He knows that he can use his kings for simple pursuit, and moreover he readily sees double and triple (and quadruple!) jumps and derives tremendous enjoyment from them. "He recognizes that the winning player is determined by the number of men on the board, kings and regular men, and not by what one holds in one's hand" (p. 142). But it is not until the child is ten or eleven, that he can really play a game which requires that he be able to plan further ahead than his opponent's next move. "He can devise traps, sacrifice to gain more in the end, and engage in various gambits" (p. 142).

Against this normal developmental background, one can appreciate the various operations, moves, and remarks the child makes in a psychoanalytic context and interpret accordingly, so that one can call attention to cheating and its significance; countertransference may be manifested by an overzealous ambition or hostility toward the child that can be useful in understanding what the child does to provoke this response in the analyst and in other significant people in his life. The passive child can be urged to take more initiative; the insecure child can be encouraged and reassured to develop more security in terms of genuine recognition and not extravagant and false praise; the "sore loser" can get some insight into the overevaluation of competition as a measure of self-esteem. Masochistic children who *need* to lose can be given some insight into the way the play illustrates what they do in their daily living with their peers and with adults.

Dreams can be very useful in the treatment of children just as they are in the treatment of adolescent and adult patients. However, with children two to seven years of age, play, fantasy, and story telling seem to be much richer and more informative than the dreams they report. With the older children, the same principles apply that one uses with adults. For example, a ten-year-old girl reports the following dream: "My girl friend and I are playing cards by the fire place. Then we get into our beds with big thick quilts on a very cold, very dark night. Suddenly there is terrible thundering and lightning and we get into the same bed together all shook up by the storm." The parents were being seen in conjoint therapy, and it was clear that the child was afraid of a big storm that was actually brewing between the parents. Being with friends and having overnights with them was a great source of comfort which I encouraged for her, as she felt an exaggerated sense of protection toward the mother who was actually in no need of any protection. The young girl used the dream to help separate herself from her parents' struggle with each other, and to make more of her ties with her peers.

In conclusion, it seems clear that the interpersonal approach to child therapy is most demanding on the resources of the therapist. He must be personally present, known and accountable to both the child and the child's family. He must be capable of intimately sharing feelings with a wide range of ages and character structures, and with the sexes of the children he treats, being at ease with laughter, tears, anxiety, fears, irritation, anger, envy, jealousy, frustration, and rage. He must also guide, instruct, inform, set limits, design therapeutic strategies and programs for the family as well as for the child. And above all, he must be accepting of his own limitations so that he, too, can be more simply human with his patients and their worried, anxious, searching parents.

REFERENCES

Bruch, H. The role of the parent in psychotherapy with children. *Psychiatry,* 1948, 11, 169–175.

Bruch, H.   Puberty and adolescence: Psychologic considerations. *Advances in Pediatrics*, 1948, 3, 219–296.

Bruch, H.   Psychotherapy with schizophrenics. *International Psychiatry Clinics*, 1964, 1, 863–890.

Bruch, H.   Hunger and instinct. *Journal of Nervous and Mental Disease*, 1969, 149, 91–114.

Bruch, H.   Psychotherapy in primary anorexia nervosa. *Journal of Nervous and Mental Disease*, 1970, 150, 51–67.

Bruch, H.   Instinct and interpersonal experience. Presented at the Cincinnati Society of Psychiatry and Neurology, Cincinnati, Ohio, January 21, 1970.

Cantril, H.   (Ed.) *Tensions that cause wars.* Urbana: University of Illnois, 1950.

Colm, H.   *The existentialist approach to psychotherapy with adults and children.* New York: Grune & Stratton, 1966.

Fish, B.   Drug therapy in child psychiatry: psychological aspects. *Comprehensive Psychiatry*, 1960, 1, 55–61.

Fish, B.   Evaluation of psychiatric therapies in children. In *Evaluation of psychiatric treatment.* New York: Grune & Stratton, 1964.

Fish, B.   Drug use in psychiatric disorders of children. *American Journal of Psychiatry*, 1968, 124, 31–36.

Fish, B.   Problems of diagnosis and the definition of comparable groups: a neglected issue in drug research with children. *American Journal of Psychiatry*, 1969, 125, 900–908.

Fish, B.   Limitations of the new nomenclature for children's disorders. *International Journal of Psychiatry*, 1969, 7, 393–398.

Fish, B., and Shapiro, T.   A typology of children's psychiatric disorders. I. Its application to a controlled evaluation of treatment. *Journal of the American Academy of Child Psychiatry*, 1965, 4, 32–52.

Fish, B.; Shapiro, T.; Campbell, M.; and Wile, R.   A classification of schizophrenic children under five years .*American Journal of Psychiatry*, 1968, 124, 109–117.

Gardner, R. A.   The mutual storytelling technique: use in alleviating childhood Oedipal problems. *Contemporary Psychoanalysis*, 1968a, 4, 161–177.

Gardner, R. A.   Psychogenic problems of brain-injured children and their parents. *Journal of the American Academy of Child Psychiatry*, 1968b, 7, 471–491.

Gardner, R. A.   The game of checkers as a diagnostic and therapeutic tool in child psychotherapy. *Acta Paedopsychiatrica*, 1969a, 66, 142–152.

Gardner, R. A.   Sexual fantasies in childhood. *Medical Aspects of Human Sexuality*, 1969b, Oct.

Gardner, R. A.   The guilt reaction of parents of children with severe physical disease. *American Journal of Psychiatry*, 1969b, 126, 82–90.

Green, M. R. The roots of Sullivan's concept of self. *Psychiatric Quarterly,* 1962, **36,** 271–282.

Green, M. R. (Ed.) *Interpersonal psychoanalysis: selected papers of Clara Thompson.* New York: Basic Books, 1964.

Green, M. R. Depression in adolescence. *Contemporary Psychoanalysis,* 1965, **2,** 42–47.

Green, M. R. The problem of identity crisis. In J. Masserman (Ed.), *Science and psychoanalysis.* New York: Grune & Stratton, 1966.

Green, M. R. Common problems in the treatment of schizophrenia in adolescents. *Psychiatric Quarterly,* 1966, **Apr.,** 1–14.

Green, M. R., and Schecter, D. E. Austistic and symbiotic disorders in three blind children. *Psychiatric Quarterly,* 1957, **31,** 628–646.

Kohn, M. Early identification and treatment of the emotionally disturbed child in day care. Presented May 8, 1969, Day Care Council of New York, New York, N.Y.

Minuchin, S. Family therapy: technique or theory? In J. Masserman (Ed.), *Science and psychoanalysis.* New York: Grune & Stratton, 1969.

Minuchin, S. The paraprofessional and the use of confrontation in the mental health field. *American Journal of Orthopsychiatry,* 1969, **39,** 722–729.

Minuchin, S. Adolescence: society's response and responsibility. *Adolescence,* 1969, **4,** 455–476.

Minuchin, S. The use of an ecological framework in the treatment of a child. In E. J. Anthony and C. Koupernik (Eds.), *The Child in his family.* New York: Wiley-Interscience, 1970.

Minuchin, S., and Barcai, A. Therapeutically induced family crisis. In J. Masserman (Ed.), *Science and psychoanalysis.* New York: Grune & Stratton, 1969.

Mullahy, P. *Psychoanalysis and interpersonal psychiatry.* New York: Science House, 1970.

Schecter, D. E. The integration of group therapy with individual psychoanalysis. *Psychiatry,* 1959, **22,** 267–276.

Schecter, D. E. The Oedipus complex: considerations of ego development and parental interaction. *Contemporary Psychoanalysis,* 1968, **4,** 111–137.

Schecter, D. E. Identification and individuation. *Journal of the American Psychoanalytic Association,* 1968, **16,** 48–80.

Schimel, J. L. The child who *won't* go to school. *Consultant,* 1961, **Oct.** (Smith, Kline & French Laboratories).

Schimel, J. L. Parents vs. children. *Redbook,* Aug. 1966.

Schimel, J. L. How to stop fighting over money. *Redbook,* Nov. 1967.

Siegel, L. Case study of a thirteen-year-old fire-setter: a catalyst in the growing pains of a residential treatment unit. *American Journal of Orthopsychiatry,* 1957, **27,** 396–410.

Siegel, L. Live supervision in multiple impact therapy: a preliminary report. Talk delivered to graduate study group, supervisory process, William Alanson White Institute, New York, N.Y., Nov. 16, 1965.

Siegel, L.   Big fish, little fish, and medium-sized fish: the adolescent and his family. Talk delivered to Aiona Chapter, Hapoel Hamizrachi Women's Organization, Brooklyn, New York, Jan. 17, 1966.

Siegel, L.   System-changing family experiences in conjoint family psychotherapy: targets and tactics. Prepared for panel on "Family Psychotherapy: Strategy and Techniques," Fifth Biennial Divisional Meeting, American Psychiatric Association, New York, Nov. 17 and 18, 1967.

Siegel, L.   Family psychodynamics of school avoidance in adolescence. Condensed version of paper for presentation at panel on "'School Phobia and School Avoidance in Adolescents,'" Society for Adolescent Psychiatry, May 17, 1967.

Siegel, L.   Prospectus for a program of family-centered mental health services for adolescent & young adult patients. 1965–1970. Maimonides Hospital of Brooklyn, Department of Psychiatry.

Sobel, R.   The child's role in therapy: a comparison of the child's sick role in treatment as seen by four disciplines. *Journal of the American Academy of Child Psychiatry,* 1967, 6, 655–662.

Sobel, R.   Special problems of late adolescence and the college years. In J. Marmor (Ed.), *Modern psychoanalysis.* New York: Basic Books, 1968.

Sobel, R., and Ingalls, A.   Resistance to treatment. *American Journal of Psychotherapy,* 1964, 18, 562–573.

Sullivan, H. S.   *The interpersonal theory of psychiatry.* New York: Norton, 1953.

Sullivan, H. S.   *Clinical Studies in Psychiatry.* New York: Norton, 1956.

PART IV

PREVENTION AND RESEARCH

15

BENJAMIN B. WOLMAN

Prevention of Mental Disorders in Childhood

T he purpose of this essay is not to prove that mental disorders in childhood and adolescence can be prevented, but merely to explore the possibilities and limitations of preventive action.

The lack of clearly stated diagnostic and classificatory categories in child psychopathology is a major block in the study of preventabilty. This difficulty must not be taken lightly. Classification of mental disorders in adults is a highly controversial issue and every edition of the *Diagnostic Manual of the American Psychiatric Association* bears witness to the complexity of diagnostic and classificatory procedures (Wolman, 1966a).

The study of childhood disorders is even more

complex. Halpern (1965, p. 637) noticed the total absence of easily recognizable diagnostic signs. "The multiplicity of factors, innate and environmental, that go into the making of the end product—the child—renders any simple, 'cookbook' approach to diagnostic problems impossible."

These difficulties seem to be practically insurmountable in prognostic studies in child psychopathology. The assumption that adult maladjustment starts in childhood is most probably true, yet it must not be taken in a simplistic manner. Even severely regressed psychotics are not underdeveloped children, and no adult personality resembles a tree turned into a sapling. The psychotic personality structure presents a pitiful picture of adult experiences mixed with early childhood elements, sort of a shambles of a house with base foundations, and the child-adult continuum is subject to qualitative and quantitative changes.

Mental disorder in adults is largely a *regressive* process that may harm or destroy the so-far-achieved level of maturity and integration, but mental disorders in childhood are not miniatures of adult neuroses and psychoses, and there is no straight, simple line leading from an infantile neurosis into an adult neurosis, and every mentally disturbed child is, first of all, a child, that is, a *changing* and *growing* person. Mental disorders in childhood may thwart, distort and block the process of emotional and intellectual maturation, and the personality of a disturbed child represents a most complex combination of progressive and regressive elements. It is perhaps a task of Sisyphus to try to comprehend, predict and prevent mental disorders in children. Certain symptoms are typical for early years, and their role in forming substitution symptoms in adulthood is by no means a matter of common knowledge. Consider enuresis: if a child is a bed-wetter, will he remain a bed-wetter in adulthood?

The entire field of mental health in childhood is still very much in the darkness. The second edition of the *Diagnostic and Statistic Manual of Mental Disorders* published by the American Psychiatric Association (1968) offers rather loose and poorly-defined diagnostic categories (Ross, 1960; Silverman and Ross in this volume). Etiologic studies are still in the beginning, and there is little agreement among research workers and practitioners in the field of child psychopathology (Wolman, 1971). The current trend of shallowness and the superficial, behavioristic approach to personality disorders does not augur to a bright future for prognostic studies.

Unfortunately, psychoanalytic studies have also not been excessively successful and have not produced spectacular results (see

Dr. Sullivan's chapter in this volume). Several psychoanalytic groups have embarked on longitudinal studies of childhood disorders, the research area is vast and the job ahead, enormous. Thus, one must take a rather modest view on predictability, and at the present time one must limit one's prevention proposals to tentative, hypothetical statements, accepting Anna Freud's cautious restatement of Ernst Kris's idea. According to Anna Freud, Ernst Kris regretted that our assessments and diagnostic judgments are not too precise and usually come too late, when the disturbance has already become ingrained. Kris maintained that current diagnostic categories have become inadequate especially since the concept of an "infantile neurosis" had ceased to serve us as a vantage point. Ego psychology has introduced a great number of variations and the concepts of atypical and autistic developments. Current research of the earliest mother-child relationship has discovered that much of what had been considered as innate is actually acquired in early childhood. Small wonder that child psychiatrists and psychoanalysts face great difficulty in understanding "of disturbances of vital functions (sleeping, eating, learning); retardation of ego activities (motility, speech); failures of management (toilet training); fixations and regressions (especially affecting smooth transition in phase development)—all this in addition to the more familiar anxieties, inhibitions, defenses, neurotic, psychotic and borderline appearances" (A. Freud, 1958, p. 96).

Ideally, prediction implies the knowledge of all underlying causes and the ability to infer the effects. Freudian theory represents such a strictly deterministic system in which there are no causes without effects and no effects without causes. Assuming that this is possible, whoever knew *all* the causes could predict *all* the effects. Such an all-knowing mind fits into Spinoza's definition of the causal principle:

> We ought to regard the present state of the universe as the effect of its antecedent state and as the cause of the state that is to follow. An intelligence knowing all the forces acting in nature at a given instant, as well as the momentary positions of all things in the universe, would be able to comprehend in one single formula the motions of the largest bodies as well as of the lightest atoms in the world, provided that its intellect were sufficiently powerful to subject all data to analysis; to it nothing would be uncertain, the future as well as the past would be present to its eyes. The perfection that the human mind has been able to give to astronomy affords a feeble outline of such an intelligence. Discoveries in mechanics and geometry coupled with those in universal gravitation, have

brought the mind within reach of comprehending in the same analytical formula the past and the future state of the system of the world. All the mind's efforts in the search for truth tend to approximate to the intelligence we have just imagined, although it will forever remain infinitely remote from such an intelligence. (Laplace, 1820, preface)

Obviously such a perfect knowledge of all present factors is unattainable, and, therefore, all predictions fall short of perfection. As mentioned above, the dynamic and changing nature of childhood makes prediction even less feasible.

Let us assume that a first rate diagnostic study was performed on a group of children with due consideration to relevant etiologic variables and a proper control group was chosen. Would a correct diagnosis offer an adequate guarantee for a successful prognosis?

Freud shifted the emphasis from the traditional medical nosology toward an etiologic-developmental system. He assumed that (1) the noxious experiences in early childhood are the most important cause of nonorganic mental disorders in later life and (2) mental disorders which start in early childhood continue into adult life. Freud introduced a developmental continuum instead of the discrete and not necessarily related nosological system of Kraepelin.

One must, however, draw a line between continuity and predictability. Freud wrote: "If we start from the premises inferred from the analysis . . . we no longer get the impression of an inevitable sequence of events which could not have been otherwise determined. We notice at once that there might have been another result. . . . Hence the chain of causation can always be recognized with certainty if we follow the line of analysis (i.e. reconstruction), whereas to predict it . . . is impossible" (Freud, 1920, pp. 167–168).

This is apparently a limitation but not an exclusion of predictability. Freud's psychological theory is, fundamentally, a theory of *developmental stages*, and in the famous Freud-Abraham etiologic time table (Abraham, 1924) the origin of mental disorders was linked with fixation in and regression to a particular developmental phase of early childhood.

CONTINUITY AND PREDICTABILITY

Can infantile neurosis serve as a basis for prediction of adult neurosis? In a panel discussion on Problems of Infantile Neurosis chaired by E. Kris (1954), Hartmann analyzed this question: "every behavior of the child that is not according to plan is considered as 'neurotic'. . . . Apart from this, however, many of the very early neuroses are really different from what we are used to calling neurosis in the adult. Many problems in children which we call neurotic are actually limited to a single functional disturbance. . . ."

Adult neurosis is often modeled after infantile neurosis, but "this is not always the case." The fact that "conflicts and fixations of the child resulted also in the formation of a neurosis during childhood is not of necessity an additional pathogenic factor for later life" (Hartmann, 1954, pp. 34–35).

The maturational process creates new "potential conflict situations" but also "new ways of dealing with these conflicts," such as the child's capacity to "neutralize instinctual energy, libidinal and aggressive." There is apparently no unequivocal answer to the question of to what extent infantile neurosis determines future neurosis, psychosis, or normal development.

Obviously, preventive action in mental health must be based on assurance of predictability, but current research indicates that the demand for predictability cannot be met. "At the present time . . . we cannot reliably select out the small group of children with adjustment disturbances who will end in jails and mental hospitals unless treated from the larger group of children with disturbances or from obviously 'bad' environments who will not." This, "positive status on a developmental adaptational trait is more predictive of later absence of maladjustment than is negative status on the trait predictive of later maladjustment on it" (Kohlberg, LaCrosse and Ricks, 1971).

Quantitative and qualitative changes do not exclude predictability. There is a fairly high level of correlation between one's I.Q. at various stages of life from infancy well into adulthood which enables the prediction of one's future mental functioning (Bloom, 1964; Bühler, Keith-Spiegel and Thomas, in press). Piaget's theory of developmental stages is a theory of qualitative changes, yet, analogous to Freud's theory, each consecutive stage follows the preceding one in a predictable manner (Galifret-Granjon, 1971). This predictability applies both to intellectual and moral development so well described in Piaget's numerous works (Piaget, 1948; 1952).

According to Kohlberg (1969) children's moral judgment goes through an invariant sequence of six stages. Despite these distinct changes, the child's moral attitude relative to other children remains fairly constant, and the correlation between the scores of moral maturity at thirteen and twenty-five years of age is r .78 to .92, which indicates quite a high degree of stability of the scores. Kohlberg ascribes these relative stabilities to a parallelism of affective and cognitive factors. Such a parallelism, he believes, helps in prediction of future development in children (Kohlberg, 1969; Kohlberg and Zigler, 1967; Kohlberg, LaCrosse and Ricks, 1971).

Allowing for individual differences and peculiarities in the life histories of various individuals, one tends to accept the idea of continuity in physical and mental growth. Still the question as to whether such a continuity applies to child psychopathology is largely unresolved. For instance, Kagen and Moss (1962) found that one may attain a not too high level of predictability of adult personality traits based on childhood research, but it is rather impossible to derive valid prediction of adult conflict and anxiety from childhood research.

Observational and Follow-Up Studies

Escalona and Heider (1959) wrote as follows:

> Our best predictive successes have occurred in regard to the formal aspects of behavior. With few exceptions, we have been better able to forecast how a child goes about moving, speaking, playing than what he is likely to do, think, speak or play. (Escalona and Heider, 1959).

Certain personality traits are socially accepted and therefore reinforced at a certain age and rejected and inhibited at another age. Consider physical aggression in boys at the age of five and in high school. Five-year-old middle class boys may be quite aggressive and renounce aggressiveness in high school (MacFarlene, Allen, and Honzik, 1962). Thus the continuity of development does not necessarily exclude profound and perhaps unpredictable changes.

Robin's (1966) follow-up study included 524 white, low socioeconomic status children who attended a child guidance clinic. The reason for referrals of seventy-three percent of the children was anti-social behavior; twenty-seven percent were referred for emotional problems and learning difficulties. Only thirty percent of those referred for emotional and learning problems have become well-adjusted as compared to fifty-two percent of controls.

Glueck and Glueck (1959) studied 500 delinquent boys. From

ages nine to seventeen, eighty-six percent were arrested on charges of larceny, burglary or robbery. At the ages of seventeen to twenty-five years, eighty percent were arrested at least once, and at the ages twenty-five to thirty-one, sixty percent were arrested at least once. In contrast to the delinquent group, only ten percent of the control group were ever arrested, and in most cases for minor transgressions. Thus, Glueck and Glueck concluded that antisocial behavior in childhood is a valid indicator of criminal behavior in adulthood.

Psychoanalytic Longitudinal Studies

An essay by Marianne Kris (1957) on prediction in longitudinal studies may shed additional light. The longitudinal studies in the Yale Child Study Center initiated by Ernst Kris and Milton Senn in 1949 were undertaken to search for predictive clues. According to Ernst Kris:

> One way in which we have viewed our data is in terms of their use for prediction. We not only try generally to anticipate 'what will happen next' but we try to focus on specific problems: what kind of predictions are being suggested by any given material; at what point are these predictions expanded; when do new areas of prediction suggest themselves; when are general predictions replaced by more specific ones; what predictions could have been made in the past had we properly evaluated clues. What can be predicted at any given time, that is, the *range* of predictable events is to us more significant than the correctness or incorrectness of any specific prediction. . . .
>
> Past predictions become part of the material for retrospective evaluation. In rediscussing a case we turn to the past material in search of clues which would have suggested a different or more specific prediction. Thus prediction and retrospective evaluation interact. (Quoted after Marianne Kris, 1957, p. 177)

The predictions were made on the basis of psychological examination of the mother during pregnancy. The data obtained on Rorschach and interviews indicate that the mother's "reaction formations toward dirt and messiness would result in attempts at *early* toilet training and in her adopting an over strict attitude" (ibid. p. 178). However, the child was not yet toilet trained at the age of four!

Kris related the error in prediction to some physiological difficulties of the little girl. "We were predicting mother-child relationships with no knowledge of the reality of the child himself" (ibid.). But this factor, no matter how relevant, was only a part of the story. According to Marianne Kris's report, Mrs. C., the mother, "described the first three months as the worst months of her life. During this period Mrs. C. lost all confidence in herself, was incapable of making decisions, and was repeatedly confused by suggestions from neighbors and relatives" (ibid., p. 181).

Some of her co-workers at the Center predicted the possibility of psychotic development. This hypothesis was based on an observation of "unusual sensitivities" in infants who later become schizophrenic (Bergman and Escalona, 1949). One must, however not take at face value these allegedly "unusual sensitivities" reported by worried and probably guilt-ridden mothers (Wolman, 1970).

Marianne Kris gave a detailed description of a variety of observational data. Her report bears witness both to the thoroughness of the observers as well as the complexity of the problem. Yet, one may question the validity of her data. First, there was little said about the neighbors and relatives who "confused" Mrs. C. Were her husband or her mother or her mother-in-law among the confusing relatives? And, if so, perhaps they undermined Mrs. C.'s self-confidence to a much greater extent than the infant's sensitivities. Certainly the infant's physiologic difficulties may bring about modification in maternal attitudes, but the reverse is also true, and the mother's emotional problems may cause difficulties in the infant's behavior. In my studies of schizophrenia (Wolman, 1957; 1965; 1966b; 1970), I failed to discover any "early sensitivities" except those caused by maternal attitudes.

The conclusion is that *every individual case is and must remain unpredictable.* Human behavior and personality development are *over-determined* by hosts of causal factors. There is never a single event produced by a single cause, and in most instances mental symptoms are caused by a cluster of numerous and sometimes nonrelated factors.

According to Ernst Kris, one must ask the question posed by investigators in academic child psychology concerning the usefulness of observational data. Kris wrote (1950, p. 37): "However rich these data, their bearing is limited; they are more useful where mere maturation is concerned, or the development of motility and intelligence is at stake; in other words, they are more useful for certain ego functions than for others."

According to Kris, the psychoanalytical study of child development should integrate the various approaches and deal with the questions of prevention. "How soon can we, from observational data, predict that pathology exists in a given child; how soon can we spot it from the child's behavior, from that of the family unit, or from the history of mother and child? Which therapeutic steps are appropriate to each age level and its disturbance, or to each typical group of disturbances? . . . How much can latency, pre-puberty, or adolescence do to mitigate earlier deviation or to make the predisposition to such disturbances manifest?" (Kris, 1950, p. 38)

In the same volume of the *Psychoanalytic Study of the Child*, Hartmann strongly recommended the combination of direct longitudinal observation of early childhood with reconstructive data supplied by psychoanalytic treatment. Yet both methods cannot yield clear-cut, universally valid data.

According to Hartmann, characteristics of a certain phase may sometimes appear before the main elements of the phase to which they are usually related. Sometimes developmental phenomena make a precocious appearance, especially phase-specific conflicts. When certain aspects of the ego have precociously developed, such precocious development is often related to the autonomous sphere, to early and intense identifications, to an atypical development of the body-ego, or to a number of other reasons. "For instance, reaction formations, like orderliness or cleanliness, displacements, generalized attitudes, which we are accustomed to find correlated with the anal phase, may then appear before problems of anality have come to dominate the child's life. Empirical evidence in this field is unfortunately scarce so far, but some observations seem to suggest this interpretation" (Hartmann, 1950, p. 14).

Certainly there are specific optimal phases for every aspect of adjustment and integration. Thus, the timing and the dosage of child-rearing and preventive mental hygiene rules must be oriented to phase specificity and its genetic determinants. "This orientation can profit greatly from utilizing data of direct observation. Here we meet again the question of the sign function of behavioral data. It points to the necessity of actual or potential conflict—and, which is not the same, of actual or potential pathology. The greatest practical importance of what we are discussing today lies, no doubt, in the field of prevention." (Hartmann, 1950, pp. 14–16)

STRESS AND TRAUMA

It is an overstatement that stress situations necessarily produce mental disorder. Were this true, all discriminated-against and persecuted minority groups would inevitably be afflicted by some sort of mental disorder. Mental disorder should have spread widely amongst Christians persecuted by Romans, Jews persecuted by Christians, Armenians persecuted by Turks, blacks persecuted by whites, and so on. However, this is not the case, and contrary to expectations the ratio of mental disorders *went down* during wars, revolutions, and economic depressions. In many instances a real threat coming from without helped mentally disturbed people to make realistic decisions necessary for survival, and the general mental health has probably improved in days of trial.

Children are undoubtedly more vulnerable than adults. The amount of stress children can take without harm depends on a variety of factors, such as heredity, prenatal, natal, and postnatal experiences.

The smaller the child, the less it is capable of coping with stress situations. Studies by Escalona and Leitch (1953), Glover (1956), Jacobsen (1954), MacFarlane (1954), Murphy (1956; 1961), Pulver (1959), Ribble (1943), Senn (1952), Wolman (1970; 1971a; 1971b) and others have accumulated a wealth of evidence supportive of Freud's ideas concerning the etiological role of stress situations in early childhood.

According to Greenacre neurotic disturbances are related to the Oedipus complex. The specific neurotic manifestations are a product of regression to earlier fixations, rearoused or resorted to in stress situations. The pre-Oedipal areas of disturbances have been unusually dealt with in and through their relation to the Oedipal problems.

In some cases the mental disturbances are particularly severe and numerous, and start in manifest form in the first years. Sometimes they persist later on and appear again accompanying symptoms of a classical neurosis. Quite often these patients develop brief psychotic episodes; thus clinicians regard them as either latently psychotic or severely neurotic.

Patients of this borderline type have generally had early exigencies in the form of internal or external traumata, i.e., unusually untoward conditions (special organic weaknesses, systemic or prolonged local illnesses, nutritional and handling deprivations, as in situations of illness of the mother). These conditions tend in themselves to excite special attitudes of indulgence, anxiety, or rejection in the people around, which sometimes are the result rather than the cause of disturbances in the child and will tend to correct or augment such disturbances as the case may be. Disturbances in the infant produce disturbances in the environment, and vice versa. . . .

In many instances there was a constellation of disturbances from the earlier years, resulting among other things in a gross impairment of the sense of identity, naturally associated with some degree of inadequate separation from the external world, but even more strikingly focused by the first stage of the castration complex, viz., that determined so largely by the discovery of the anatomical differences. (Greenacre, 1954, pp. 18–24)

Yet there is little evidence that a single traumatic experience causes irreversible damage. It seems that patterns or continuous adverse conditions are more harmful to personality development than single traumata. It is, however, an open question which factors are the most harmful. Studies of childhood schizophrenia may illustrate the issue under consideration.

Studies in Childhood Schizophrenia

At the present time, the choice of noxious variables is hypothetical and controversial. Consider the current literature concerning infantile autism. Bender (1959), Bettelheim (1950; 1967), Eveloff (1960), Kanner (1949), Mahler (1958), Rimland (1964), Wolman (1970) and others introduced hypothetical theories concerning the etiology of infantile autism and tested them the best they could. None of them, however, could pursue rigorously controlled experimental research.

Several research workers related childhood schizophrenia to morbid family life and especially mother-child relationships (Bateson et al., 1956; Lidz et al., 1968; Wolman, 1966b; 1970).

Although a disturbed mother-child relationship undoubtedly is a noxious factor that influences the development of pathology in many individual children whom we have studied, is it not true that similar disturbed relationships occur in other children who do not develop mental disorder? We explain this by saying that other factors were operating that counterbalanced the noxious element. . . . When we focus upon an individual child who is mentally ill we presumably have selected from the population someone in whom not only the noxious factor but also the other elements of the multifactorial pathogenic pattern were also present. (Caplan, 1961, pp. 5–6)

In my studies of childhood schizophrenia, (Wolman, 1970) all etiologic findings have been almost uniform. Adult schizophrenia is a process of regression, going in order of severity from paranoid to catatonic, hebephrenic, simple deterioration stages and ending in dementia. Childhood schizophrenia is not regression in personality structure but lack of personality growth. Schizophrenic children are children without childhood, children whose development was squashed before it started.

Childhood schizophrenia represents a reverse order of decreasing severity. Some children were destroyed at the preverbal level even before they had the chance for any ego development; these children seem to suffer from severe mental retardation and are called *pseudo-amentive*. This stage corresponds to the *dementive* stage in adults. Next come the *autistic* children who are afraid of people and afraid to grow up; autism corresponds to *hebephrenic* and *simple* syndrome in adults. Next come the *symbiotic* children who develop a peculiar attachment and dependence on their mothers; this stage corresponds to *catatonia* in adults. The mildest form is the *aretic* stage which corresponds to *paranoid* schizophrenia in adults.

In many cases, the schizo-type of development started in the oral stage. The child apparently sensed the mother's demanding attitude and the father's selfishness. Refusal to suck, vomiting, and sleep disturbances have been among the earliest symptoms, permitting one to hypothesize that these children were too frightened to grow. Fear of eating, inability to chew food, avoidance of new foods, fear of biting, lack of assertiveness, and lack of initiative have been observed by Bettelheim (1950).

In the pseudo-amentive cases of infantile schizophrenia practically everything is affected: motor coordination, homeostasis and metabolism, sleep and waking, food intake, speech, and mental development. In all the cases I have studied since 1937, the child was born normal, but the family pattern was *schizogenic*. In all the patients I have seen, whenever the mothers of any of these children received guidance or therapy, the child has improved.

The nature of symptoms depends primarily on the nature of the offense. Some children are exposed to a schizogenic family pattern from the day they are born. They sense or somehow feel that their mothers did not want them because *the mother herself wanted to be taken care of.*

One mother of a schizophrenic five-year-old child reported that when her husband visited her in the maternity ward, she said, "Now you have to take care of two children. Don't forget me. I am your first child. You must love both of us."

The woman felt resentful toward the infant when it disturbed her husband's sleep. The neonate, so she said, was breaking up the family, disturbing the marital relations, and demanding too much attention. She wondered why her girl friend's infant slept quietly while her child was restless. From the first day she had feeding difficulties. She did not realize that her own impatient attitude caused gastrointestinal and homeostatic troubles in the infant. "As far back as I can recall, the child was peculiar, sensitive, touchy, crying, restless, and demanding all the attention. I had to sacrifice everything for him. He would not let me go out. He would refuse to eat and would vomit frequently. He refused to sleep and screamed for hours. I had to neglect my husband and we began to quarrel. This child brought discord and unhappiness to our home. We had little squabbles before he was born, but since that time life has become torture. I took it in a stoic manner. I realized how selfish my husband was. I became mother and father. I knew I had to take care of everything. In my misery, I resented the child. I wished he were not born, yet I had to take care of him—take care of that little idiot."

This child did not talk, did not feed himself, refused solid food, and was not toilet trained at the age of five. He was frequently whining, whimpering, rocking, banging his head, scratching his face, and pulling and swallowing his hair.

The schizophrenic child is not the "rejected" child, for the schizogenic mother does take care of her child. But she cares in an extremely hostile and pseudovectorial manner: yelling, crying, screaming, beating, and forcing food down the child's throat "for his well-being." Often she goes into a tirade to the infant in the crib: "Why can't you sleep? See how tired I am. You are the worst child ever born!"

The severity of the initial offense and of subsequent ones is an important, if not the most important factor. Most ambulatory or hospitalized adult patients had some years of close to normal or neurotic life, but infantile schizophrenics were never normal or neurotic for there were never any chances for developing ego-protective, neurotic symptoms. Infantile schizophrenia or *vectoriasis praecocissima* usually starts in the first year of the infant's life. Sometimes it is so severe that it affects practically everything: emotions, motility, over-all personality structure, intellectual functions, metabolism, physical growth. The main symptoms of these pseudo-amentive infants resemble severe mental deficiencies. These pseudo-retarded children are frequently institutionalizd as mentally defective. Richards (1951) found twenty-two cases of schizophrenic children in an institution for mental defectives. One of my first patients was diagnosed as a severe imbecile while in reality he was a pseudo-amentive schizophrenic who partially responded to treatment.

My studies indicate that the obsessive-compulsive and phobic neurosis is one of the early phases in the process of maladjustment that *may lead* to a full-blow schizophrenia. Gardner found obsessive-compulsive behavior in thirty percent of boys who became schizophrenic as compared to four percent of boys who later displayed anti-social behavior. Fleming and Ricks (1969) found typical pre-schizophrenic symptoms such as isolation, withdrawal, hypersensitivity and vulnerability in children who later became schizophrenic.

This seems to be the crux of the matter. It is impossible to predict whether a particular case of obsessive-compulsive neurosis will end in schizophrenia, but it is possible to predict that, should an obsessive-compulsive neurotic severely deteriorate and develop psychosis, this psychosis will be schizophrenia. However, it is not easy to predict whether a given case will deteriorate and, if so, how far this deterioration will lead. For instance, some obsessive-compulsive neurotics do not deteriorate, some may develop character-neurotic schizoid personality, while others may end in a latent schizophrenia. Those who will become manifest schizophrenics may develop a variety of symptoms leading to the formation of a catatonic or paranoid syndrome or any other syndrome or combination of syndromes.

The distinction between the so-called "process" and "reactive" schizophrenia (Garmezy and Rodnick, 1959; Kantor et al., 1953; Phillips, 1953; and others) is a case in point. The *process* onset of "process" schizophrenia is gradual and insidious; the patient is called "poor premorbid," his symptoms appear gradually. The "reactive" schizophrenia has a sudden onset and is usually acute. Some authors believe that the prognosis is much better for the reactive type (Chapman et al, 1961; Ullmann and Eck, 1965).

The distinction is at best, inaccurate. How insidious is insidious, and how sudden is sudden? Are personality changes "sudden" if they have gone on unnoticed by friends and relatives? Is schizophrenia "reactive" if it comes after a long period of inner struggle and unnoticeable changes in overt behavior?

One could quote scores of statistical studies based on this ill-conceived distinction; some of the above-mentioned studies strongly support the idea that the prognosis is better for the reactive type. However, often the basis of the distinction is the prognostic estimate, thus the whole thing leads to a vicious cycle.

Moreover, pre-schizophrenic symptoms in childhood are neither a necessary nor a sufficient condition for prediction of adult schizophrenia, for some future schizophrenics develop mild, ego-protective defense mechanisms that hide the schizophrenic conflict. On the other hand, manifest pre-schizophrenic behavior may be mollified by later experiences. The typical schizogenic family dynamics (Wolman, 1965) seem to be an *indispensable* condition for any future full-blown schizophrenia or milder schizo-type disorder, but the *sufficient* conditions for schizophrenia remain largely unknown (Wolman, 1966b).

SOCIO-PSYCHOLOGICAL FIELD

It is impossible to predict the future of an infant even if one knows all the relevant data pertaining to the parent-child relationship simply because such a relationship is not the sole determinant of personality development. It might be possible, however, to compare two groups of infants, one growing up in an unfavorable home environment and the other in a favorable one. Were it possible to match the two groups of infants on all other factors leaving intra-familial relationships as the sole variable that distinguishes between the experimental and the control group, such a study would be invaluable. But such an experimental matching may not be possible. Moreover, a rigorously conducted study in which unfavorable home situations are artificially designed is neither feasible nor morally justified. At best, loosely controlled follow-up and ex post facto studies are certainly indicative of existing problems, but the distinct lack of clear cut evidence undermines their value as guideposts for preventive action.

A study of delinquency conducted by Glueck and Glueck (1959) is a case in point. None of the Gluecks' control group has ever become delinquent, but only twenty-nine percent of the juvenile delinquents have remained delinquents in their early adult years. In Gluecks' study gravitation toward delinquent behavior rapidly decreased in the years seventeen to twenty-nine.

Human beings do not live in a vacuum, and their interaction may carry harmful as well as compensatory influences. Only in a case of totally isolated behavior could a diagnosis have had a considerable prognostic value, but a realistic prognostic estimate must also take environmental factors into consideration. An individual interacting with his environment forms *a psychosocial field*. Even the clinician who observes the child becomes a part of this field.

Contemporary physicists are aware of the bias inherent in assuming that observation of physical phenomena can be objective without taking into consideration the field relationship between the observer and observed. "Every observation," Jeans wrote, "involves a passage of a complete quantum from the observed object to the observing subject, and a complete quantum constitutes a not negligible coupling between the observer and the observed. We can no longer make a sharp division between the two. . . . Complete objectivity can only be regained by treating observer and observed as parts of a single system" (Jeans, 1958, p. 143).

Even intentionally nonparticipant observation of mental patients cannot be conducted without having at least some effect on the patients. Caudill (1958), Stanton and Schwartz (1954), Wolman (1964c), and others conducted extensive nonparticipant observations in mental hospitals. The observers did not treat the patients they observed, nor did they directly participate in making decisions in regard to the observed patients. Yet their very presence influenced, to some extent, the patients' actions.

This influence grows when the interaction is direct and intense. Several research workers have noticed that mental patients, especially schizophrenics, are highly sensitive to who administers a test and how. Shakow (1946), Garmezy (1952), Winder (1960), Rabin and King (1958), Wolman (1959), and scores of others have noticed that the performance of schizophrenics largely depends on who tests them and how it is done and on who interviews or interacts with them. In other words, schizophrenic performance has its ups and downs, depending on rapport. This should not be surprising. Pavlov's dogs became conditioned not only to the metronome but also to the footsteps and to the presence of Pavlov's co-workers. It should be expected that human reactions depend on whom the person interacts with and on the emotional tone of such an interaction.

Interaction includes the totality of social experiences of an individual in his lifetime. Whether one stresses or minimizes the importance of hereditary factors, the fact remains that humans interact with others all their lives. Daily life causes a variety of psychosocial fields. Every child interacts with his parents, siblings, relatives, neighbors, teachers, classmates, and a host of strangers.

Consider prognostic problems of a not-yet-schizophrenic-child. A correct diagnosis of "latent schizophrenia" agrees with Fenichel's definition of latent psychosis. Whether the child will deteriorate and become a manifest schizophrenic or not depends upon a variety of factors. One of them is related to his classroom experience.

> Eleven-year-old Terry developed a profound attachment to the most popular girl in the class. Terry helped her girl friend and served her in many ways in school work, bringing snacks and candies, etc. Terry was not buying her friend's friendship; she was genuinely attached and loyally faithful. When her girl friend was ungrateful or disloyal, Terry sobbed through sleepless nights.

The latent schizophrenic child has little if any chance to be popular with the crowd. Children in the latency period are often clannish, form cliques, and become hostile to those who "do not belong." Manifest schizophrenics, with their bizarre behavior, invite persecution; latent schizophrenics, with their bashful, awkward behavior, invite ostracism or at least a flat rejection.

Most latent schizophrenic children blame themselves. Their superego exercises dictatorial power, and they are prone to blame themselves for whatever injustice is done to them. A twelve-year-old girl felt that her mother was right to force her to take care of her younger sister; her teacher was right in not paying attention to her.

This hostility, turned inward, may sometimes return to the outer world; the latent schizophrenic child may provoke aggression from his schoolmates by teasing, calling names, taking things away, and even pushing and hitting. He may attack bigger children and invite defeat and humiliation as if to prove that he deserves the punishment he receives. At the same time, his provocation to fight enables him to discharge part of the accumulated destrudo energy.

Thomas, Chess, and Birch (1968) reported a ten year longitudinal follow-up study from early infancy through the first years of elementary school. The authors found that "deviant as well as normal development was the result of the interaction between the child with given characteristics of temperament and significant features of the familial and extra familial environment." The child's innate personality traits as such did not cause any noticeable behavior disorder; it was the social interaction at home and in school that caused transient or lasting disorganized behavior. Moreover, according to Thomas, Chess and Birch, anxiety in little children "has not been evident as an initial factor preceding and determining symptom development. Where anxiety has arisen, it has been more a consequence than a cause, though then it affects the symptoms and the expression" (ibid.).

PREVENTIVE POLICY

Epidemiologists and public health workers distinguish three levels of preventive action. *Primary prevention* aims at the reduction of the *ratio of incidence* in a given population. It is tantamount to the lowering of the overall risk of a certain disease, handicap, or disorder. Primary prevention is directed toward the etiologic factors. For instance, if mercury in fish causes poisoning, primary prevention intends to prevent water pollution by mercury.

Secondary prevention copes with an existing disease and aims at preventing disability. Treatment of a disease belongs therefore to the realm of secondary prevention. Tertiary prevention refers to preventing permanent damage and invalidism that may come as an after-effect of a disease.

Anna Freud described the following case which illustrates the difficulty of planning a preventive action.

> [In the Hampstead Child Therapy Clinic, the clinic pediatrician sees an infant] . . . whose mother shows indications of an unsatisfactory attitude toward the child. There is an apparent lack of genuine warmth, no visible pride in the baby's appearance or clothing, a reluctance to fondle or to play with the child's body and a marked clumsiness in distinguishing between the child's needs (whether for nourishment, body comfort, company or entertainment). At the same time the baby is adequately and conscientiously cared for in bodily matters, and there is no question of neglect in its official sense. The mother's attitude to life is revealed, on inquiry, as a depressed and withdrawn one, although not to the degree on which psychiatric diagnoses are based. The baby's responses are predominantly normal, so far, although his social reactions (smiling responses, etc.) were at times somewhat below the age level.
>
> This is where our quandary begins. Our feeling, based on knowledge of typical developments, indicates that subtle harm is being inflicted on this child, and that the consequences of it will become manifest at some future date. But is this foresight backed by sufficient evidence to justify intervention? Further: what are the criteria for choosing between different ways of intervening, such as treatment of the mother (which may be unwelcome to her), introduction

of a second mother figure (which may prove impracticable), or, if it comes to an extreme, separation of mother and child (which may harm the mother)? (A. Freud, 1950, p. 106)

The value of early treatment in preventing or even reducing the danger of mental disorder is highly controversial. According to Levitt (1957; 1963) sixty-six to seventy-five percent of children who have received early psychotherapy improve, but the same percentage improves without therapy.

The success of a preventive action depends primarily upon proper prognostic knowledge, and, in turn, prognosis depends upon diagnosis. In a recent review of the literature Kohlberg, LaCrosse and Ricks (1971) expressed doubts as to whether the diagnosis of emotional disturbances offers sufficient grounds for a prognosis. They were, moreover, critical of provision of mental health services for children diagnosed as those who are most likely to have mental health problems. Thus Kohlberg et al. concluded, "While the provision of mental health services to children does not assume that we can predict which children will have mental health problems as adults, a heavy concentration of these services on a few children through procedures of diagnosis and treatment does rest on this unjustified assumption."

The fact is that even the best primary preventive methods cannot eradicate mental disorder. Even the most rational approach to family planning and psychoanalytic oriented upbringing of children suggested by Bowlby (1951) and Ribble (1943) cannot prevent hereditary, prenatal, natal, and postnatal noxious factors. One can, probably, *reduce* the incidence and severity of mental disorders, but no social system and no preventive policy can totally prevent conflict, frustration and rejection and protect human beings from ever being hurt.

The conclusion of the present study cannot be overly optimistic. The growing numbers and improving quality of etiologic studies is indeed encouraging, but our present knowledge does not permit clear-cut conclusions nor does it enable us to embark upon precise preventive programs. Whatever will be said below is merely an *approximation*, for there is no conclusive evidence concerning etiology.

Guidelines

Contrary to a popular notion, the task of prevention is not to save the child from stress, frustration, and conflict. A child who is never exposed to stress and frustration will never develop proper ability for reality-testing. He may continue to "hallucinate omnipotence" and never accept realistic limitations of his power. A child who is never involved in a conflict situation may not develop the ability for making decisions in a conflict situation.

The question is how to prevent a certain "developmental stage from being so overladen by disagreeable or painful experiences that the child's developmental process is endangered" (Brody, 1961, pp. 168–169). Various answers have been given to this question, but none of them is conclusive.

Brody (1956; 1958; 1961) distinguished what she believed to be signs of mental disturbance in the first year of life and recommended guidance programs for parents based upon intensive observation of infant behavior.

> We should like to minimize, if not to block out, those conditions or experiences which we know are likely to interfere in a lasting way with the ability of the child to struggle continuously and with a moderate degree of energy with those universal and recurring conflicts that may threaten his capacity to function in ways appropriate to his biological maturity and to the demands of reality. We should like to insure that his gratifying and frustrating experiences are so balanced, from day to day, that his motivation to love well and to work well may be held high and fairly constant.
>
> The achievement of any of these aims will bring no dramatic rescues from emotional disorder, and no mass or dramatic cures. The general public will not clamor for the prevention of problems that it hardly knows to exist. Work in prevention rests upon both educational and clinical approaches to problems of psychopathology in childhood. (Brody, 1961, p. 191)

According to Anna Freud, "we have ample evidence that the date at which we take therapeutic action is of extreme importance" (1958, p. 99). Certainly it is advisable to begin therapy "immediately after appearance of trouble," especially in regard to disturbance of sleep, eating, and speech, and phobias and inhibitions.

Bloom (1964) analyzed several longitudinal studies of childhood development. He found that the adult I.Q. is not predictable from the I.Q. in preschool years, but it is predictable at the age of six. According to Bloom, emotional disorders in adulthood are not predictable from early childhood experience, as Freud maintained, but they are predictable from the experiences of later childhood, namely, the years nine to twelve.

The Role of Family

The psychoanalytic emphasis on the role of early childhood experiences in personality development has inspired a multivariant research in family dynamics. The Oedipal conflict is a dramatic entanglement with both parents, and its resolution depends on the intrafamilial interactional patterns. The developmental stages are not rigid patterns but rather general tendencies. All children are inclined to go through these stages, but *how* they go through them depends on a variety of factors, and the most important ones are the parent-child interaction patterns. Certainly the early features of mother-child relations is the area in which observational techniques have contributed most (Kris, 1950).

There is a substantial body of evidence related to the impact of intrafamilial relationships on mental health. Freud's retrospective analysis of early childhood experience has received powerful and almost unanimous supportive evidence from friends and foes. Despite the differences in approach, Abraham and Hartmann, Melanie Klein and Erikson, Jung and Adler, Horney and Sullivan found the roots of mental disorder in intrafamilial dynamics. Socio-cultural studies of Kardiner, Linton, Mead, Childs, Opler, Leighton, Lidz, Wolman and others have pointed to the role of child-rearing practices in personality development.

Moreover, studies in family structure and interactional patterns have contributed an unprecedented wealth of empirical material concerning the impact of family life on mental health (Ackerman, 1961; Bateson, 1956; Brody, 1956; 1961; Caplan, 1961; Flick, 1971; Glueck and Glueck, 1959; Lidz et al., 1968; Mishler and Waxler, 1968; Robins, 1966; Senn, 1947; Wolman, 1965; 1966b; 1970; 1971; and many others).

In brief, there is no proof that family relations are the sufficient and complete condition for mental disorder in the offspring, but there is an impressive body of evidence that, except for clearly organic cases, *family relations* are a *necessary* condition for mental disorders.

Anna Freud stressed the importance of therapeutic work with parents. "A young child . . . may build a complex pathological structure of his own on the basis of the mother's secret or manifest disturbance." In her work at the Hampstead Clinic in London, Anna Freud and her associates have tried to assess the therapeutic chances when only the child is taken into treatment, and they have concluded "that nothing except simultaneous treatment will alter the position where these mental influences are reinforced by actions of the mother which tie the child to her." The mother's incapacity to fulfill the task of mothering may be a result of several factors, and only therapy can change the mother's attitude. However, "since the therapeutic results are slow to come, we have seen repeatedly that the change in the mother comes too late for the child" (A. Freud, 1960, pp. 33–34).

It is however my contention that family structure and parent-child relationships are *not* primary social institutions that determine personality development, but that the famliy itself is a product of more fundamental factors, rooted in the totality of cultural values, in human relations, socio-economic systems and moral standards. Perhaps the best description of a desirable preventive program was given by Ackerman, whom I shall quote in concluding this essay:

> Were we able to build a program of prevention, what would it be? A maximum effort would entail a huge job in social engineering; it would produce nothing less than a social revolution, a fundamental transformation of the values and forms of family and community. A maximum program toward prevention would require family-life education, social therapy, and psychotherapy of parents and the family group. (Ackerman, 1961, p. 143)

REFERENCES

Abraham, K.   A short study of the development of the libido viewed in the light of mental disorders (1924). In *Selected papers*. New York: Basic Books, 1953. 418–501.

Ackerman, N. W.   Preventive implications of family research. In G. Caplan (Ed.), *Prevention of mental disorders in children*. New York: Basic Books, 1961. 142–167.

American Psychiatric Association. *Diagnostic and statistical manual of mental disorders*. (2nd ed.) Washington, D.C.: Author, 1968.

Bateson, G.; Jackson, D. D.; Haley, J.; and Weakland, J.   Toward a theory of schizophrenia. *Behavioral Science*, 1956, 1, 251–264.

Bender, L.   Autism in children with mental deficiency. *American Journal of Mental Deficiency*, 1959, 64, 61–86.

Bergman, J. and Escalona, S. K.   Unusual sensitivities in very young children. *The Psychoanalytic Study of the Child*, 1949, 3–4, 333–352.

Bettelheim, B.   *Love is not enough*. New York: Free Press-Macmillan, 1950.

Bettelheim, B. *The empty fortress.* New York: Macmillan - Free Press, 1967.

Bloom, B. S. *Stability and change in human characteristics.* New York: Wiley, 1964.

Bowlby, J. *Maternal care and mental health.* Geneva: World Health Organization, 1951

Brody, S. *Patterns of mothering.* New York: International Universities Press, 1956.

Brody, S. Signs of disturbance in the first year of life. *American Journal of Orthopsychiatry,* 1958, **28**, 362–368.

Brody, S. Preventive intervention in current problems of early childhood. In G. Caplan (Ed.), *Prevention of mental disorders in children.* New York: Basic Books, 1961.

Bühler, C.; Keith-Spiegel, P.; and Thomas, K. Developmental psychology. In B. B. Wolman (Ed.), *Handbook of general psychology.* Englewood Cliffs, N.J.: Prentice Hall, 1972.

Caplan, G. (Ed.), *Prevention of mental disorders in children.* New York: Basic Books, 1961.

Chapman, L. J.; Day, D.; and Burstein, A. The process reactive distinction and prognosis in schizophrenia. *Journal of Nervous and Mental Diseases,* 1961, **133**, 383–391.

Escalona, S. and Heider, G. *Prediction and outcome: A study of child development.* New York: Basic Books, 1959.

Escalona, S. and Leitch, M. *Early phases of personality development: A non-normatic study of infant behavior.* Evanston, Ill.: Child Development Publications, 1953.

Eveloff, H. H. The autistic child. *Archives of General Psychiatry,* 1960, **3**, 66–81.

Fenichel, O. *The psychoanalytic theory of neurosis.* New York: Norton, 1945.

Flech, S. Some basic aspects of family pathology. In B. B. Wolman (Ed.), *Manual of child psychopathology.* New York: McGraw-Hill, 1971.

Fleming, P. and Ricks, D. F. Emotions of children before schizophrenia and character disorders. In M. Roff and D. F. Ricks (Eds.), *Life history studies in psychopathology.* Minneapolis: University of Minnesota Press, 1969.

Freud, A. Child observation and prediction of development. *The Psychoanalytic Study of the Child,* 1958, **13**, 92–116.

Freud, A. The child guidance clinic as a center of prophylaxis and enlightenment. In J. Weinreb (Ed.), *Recent developments in psychoanalytic child therapy.* New York: International Universities Press, 1960. 25–38.

Freud, A. The symptomatology of childhood: A preliminary attempt at classification. *The Psychoanalytic Study of the Child,* 1970, **25**, 19–44.

Freud, S. The psychogenesis of a case of homosexuality in a woman (1920). In *The standard edition of the complete psychological works of Sigmund Freud.* London: Hogarth Press and the Institute of Psycho-Analysis, 1962. Vol. 18. 145–172.

Galifret-Granjon, N The contribution of Piaget's cognitive theory. In B. B. Wolman (Ed.), *Manual of child psychopathology.* New York: McGraw-Hill, 1971.

Gardner, G. G. The relationship between childhood neurotic symptomatology and later schizophrenia in males and females. *Journal of Nervous and Mental Diseases,* 1967, **144**, 97–100.

Garmezy, N. and Rodnick, E. H. Premorbid adjustment and performance in schizophrenia. *Journal of Nervous and Mental Diseases.* 1959, **129**, 450–466.

Glover, E. *On the early development of mind.* New York: International Universities Press, 1956.

Glueck, S. and Glueck, E. *Predicting delinquency and crime.* Cambridge: Harvard University Press, 1959.

Greenacre, P. Problems of infantile neurosis. In E. Kris, Chairman: Problems of infantile neurosis: A discussion. *The Psychoanalytic Study of the Child,* 1954, **9**, 16–71.

Halpern, F. Diagnostic methods in childhood disorders. In B. B. Wolman (Ed.), *Handbook of Clinical psychology.* New York: McGraw-Hill, 1965. 621–638.

Hartmann, H. Psychoanalysis and developmental psychology. *The Psychoanalytic Study of the Child,* 1950, **5**, 7–17.

Hartmann, H. Problems of infantile neurosis. In E. Kris, Chairman: Problems of infantile neurosis: A discussion. *The Psychoanalytic Study of the Child,* 1954, **9**, 16–71.

Jacobson, E. The self and the object world: Vicissitudes of the infantile cathexes and their influence on ideational and affective development. *The Psychoanalytic Study of the Child,* 1954, **9**, 75–127.

Jeans, J. *Physics and philosophy.* Ann Arbor, Mich.: University of Michigan Press, 1958.

Kagan, J. and Moss, H. Personality and social development: Family and peer influence. *Review of Educational Research,* 1961, **31**, 463–474.

Kanner, L. Problems of nosology and psychodynamics of early infantile autism. *American Journal of Orthopsychiatry,* 1949, **19**, 416–426.

Kantor, R., Wallner, J., and Winder, C. Process and reactive schizophrenia. *Journal of Consulting Psychology,* 1953, **17**, 157–162.

Kohlberg, L. Stage and sequence: The cognitive-developmental approach to socialization. In D. Goslin (Ed.), *Handbook of socialization theory and research.* Chicago: Rand McNally, 1969.

Kohlberg, L., LaCrosse, J., and Ricks, D. The predictability of adult mental health from childhood behavior. In B. B. Wolman (Ed.), *Manual of child psychopathology.* New York: McGraw-Hill, 1971.

Kohlberg. L. and Zigler, E. The impact of cognitive maturity on the development of sex-role attitudes in the years four to eight. *Genetic Psychology Monographs*, 1967, 75, 89–165.

Kris, E. Notes on the development and on some current problems of psychoanalytic child psychology. *The Psychoanalytic Study of the Child*, 1950, 5, 24–46.

Kris, M. The use of prediction in longitudinal study. *The Psychoanalytic Study of the Child*, 1957, 12, 175–189.

Laplace, P. S. *Theorie analytique des probabilités*. Paris: 1820.

Levitt, E. E. The results of psychotherapy with children: An evaluation. *Journal of Consulting Psychology*, 1957, 21, 189–196.

Levitt, E. E. Psychotherapy with children: A further evaluation. *Behavior Research and Therapy Quarterly*, 1963, 1, 45–51.

Lidz, T.; Fleck, S.; and Cornelison, A. R. *Schizophrenia and the family*. New York: International Universities Press, 1968.

Livson, N. and Peskin, H. The prediction of adult psychological health in a longitudinal study. *Journal of Abnormal and Social Psychology*, 1967, 72, 509–518.

MacFarlane, J. *Developmental study of the behavior problems of normal children between 21 months and 14 years*. Berkeley: University of California Press, 1954.

Mahler, M. Autism and symbiosis: Two extreme disturbances in identity. *International Journal of Psycho-Analysis*, 1958, 39, 1–7.

Mednick, S. A. and Schulsinger, F. Factors related to breakdown in children at high risk for schizophrenia. In M. Roff, and D. F. Ricks (Eds.), *Life history studies in psychopathology*. Minneapolis: University of Minnesota Press, 1969.

Mishler, E. C. and Waxler, N. E. *Interaction in families*. New York: Wiley, 1968.

Murphy, L. B. *Personality in young children*. New York: Basic Books, 1956.

Murphy, L. B. Development in the preschool years. In G. Caplan (Ed.), *Prevention of mental disorders in children*. New York: Basic Books, 1961. 218–248.

Phillips, L. Case history data and prognosis in schizophrenia. *Journal of Nervous and Mental Diseases*, 1953, 117, 515–525.

Piaget, J. *The moral judgment of the child*. New York: Free Press—Macmillan, 1948.

Piaget, J. *The origins of intelligence in children*. New York: International Universities Press, 1952.

Pulver, U. *Spannungen und Störungen im Verhalten des Sänglings*. Bern: Hans Huber, 1959.

Ribble, M. *The rights of infants*. New York: Columbia University Press, 1943.

Richards, B. W. Childhood schizophrenia and mental deficiency. *Journal of Mental Science*, 1951, 97, 290–372.

Rimland, B. *Infantile autism.* New York: Appleton-Century-Crofts, 1964.

Robins, L. N. *Deviant children grow up: A sociological and psychiatric study of sociopathic personality.* Baltimore: Williams and Wilkins, 1966.

Ross, N. Panel: An examination of nosology according to psychoanalytic concepts. *Journal of the American Psychoanalytic Association,* 1960, 8, 535–551.

Senn, M. J. E. (Ed.) *Problems of early infancy.* New York: Josiah Macy Jr. Foundation, 1947.

Thomas, A., Chess, S., and Birch, H. *Temperament and behavior disorders in children.* New York: New York University Press, 1968.

Ullmann, L. P. and Eck, R. A. Inkblot perception and process-reactive distinction. *Journal of Clinical Psychology,* 1965, 21, 311–313.

Wolman, B. B. Explorations in latent schizophrenia. *American Journal of Psychotherapy,* 1957, 11, 560–588.

Wolman, B. B. Evidence in psychoanalytic research. *Journal of the American Psychoanalytic Association,* 1964, 12, 717–733.

Wolman, B. B. Family dynamics in schizophrenia. *Journal of Health and Human Behavior,* 1965, 6, 147–155.

Wolman, B. B. Classification of mental disorders. *Psychotherapy and Psychosomatics,* 1966a, 14, 50–65. (a)

Wolman, B. B. *Vectoriasis Praecox or the group of schizophrenias.* Springfield, Ill.: Thomas, 1966 (b).

Wolman, B. B. *Children without childhood: A study in childhood schizophrenia.* New York: Grune and Stratton, 1970.

Wolman, B. B. (Ed.) *Handbook of child psychopathology.* New York: McGraw-Hill, 1971 (a).

Wolman, B. B. *Call no man normal.* New York: International Universities Press, 1971 (b).

16

JOHN J. SULLIVAN

Remarks on Psychoanalytic Research on the Child

It will remain an astonishing document in the history of science that from material so far removed from direct observation of the child as adult neurotics, phenomena of high regularity as biological development could have been so accurately reconstructed. (Hartmann and Kris, 1945, p. 11)

E bbinghaus' (1908) quip about psychology, slightly modified, may be used to describe the psychoanalytic study of the child: The psychoanalytic study of the child has had a long past but a short history. This is due to the nature of psychoanalysis as a psychology.

Beginning as a practitioner's art without the basic science having been fully worked out, psychoanalysis was, as the name implies, uniquely characterized by a method. A distinctive feature of the psychoanalytic method as a psychological discipline was that, because of its aim of curing or alleviating neurotic symptoms, the unit of observation was the functioning person. The strengths and weaknesses of psychoanalysis reside in this global approach to persons. The weakness is due to the fact that the amount of data to be assimilated by the analyst is great and the quality of the data varied. Rather than attempting a detailed theoretical reconstruction of a person, there is a natural tendency by analysts to concentrate on the symptom-related processes and the persisting themes presented by patients. The richness and variety of the data presented to the analyst are also strengths of the system. Not only does the richness of data make possible a close fit of descriptions to individual persons, but analysis of such data requires category systems, theoretical constructs, relational laws, in fact, requires a metapsychology. To bend another quotation (apologies to Kant) to the present topic: Psychoanalytic method without a metapsychology is blind; metapsychology without method is empty.

As a general psychology, however, psychoanalysis is distinguished from other clinical approaches to persons by the stress placed on the specific sub-systems of id, ego, and superego and their interactions. If we are interested in a comparison of the contemporary general psychologies, the question might be asked: How do the fields of perception, learning, memory, emotions, attitudes, values, intelligence, etc., map onto the general psychoanalytic system? This important question will be dismissed with the comment that Hartmann's (See Note A) attempt to expand the notion of ego functions indicated an awareness of scientific developments paralleling those of psychoanalysis and opened the possibility of their selective incorporation into psychoanalytic general psychology.

Within the psychoanalytic movement those analysts engaged in research on children have the same primary task as the general psychoanalyst, namely, the elaboration of the sub-systems and their interactions within an individual in a particular reality setting. A special task of the child analyst is to specify the developmental sequences of the sub-systems and their interactions.

With these prefatory comments in mind, an attempt will be made in this paper to provide ground for the following seven theses:

1. Freud provided the basic paradigm for the psychoanalytic movement.
2. The elaboration of the paradigm and the extensions of its applications constitute the "normal science" of psychoanalysis.
3. The general tasks of elaboration involve further specification of two coordinations: (a) coordination of category systems within one general framework and (b) coordination of the categories with clinical observations of patients' behaviors and assessments of patients' inner states.
4. The establishment of "developmental lines" for the category system is a specific task of psychoanalytic research on children.
5. With singular perspicacity the main tasks have been undertaken by Anna Freud and her close collaborators by the construction of a *Developmental Profile*.
6. The general developmental task was facilitated by the theoretical clarifications of Hartmann and Kris about the nature of genetic "propositions" and their relations to general psychoanalytic doctrines.
7. By analogy with other historical movements in psychology and philosophy, there is some doubt about the future career of psychoanalytic thought.

That Freud's formulations provided the paradigm for the psychoanalytic movement is obviously true. How strong his influence has been and the specific sources most frequently referred to in *The Psychoanaltic Study of the Child* (PSC) will be discussed. The other theses are not particularly controversial, with the possible exception of the last, but an attempt will be made to establish that they *may*, in a nontrivial sense, be true. Since conclusive evidence for these theses is probably unobtainable, to establish that they may be true is to call them to the attention of anyone seriously interested in the nature of psychoanalytic theory and its history.

Just as Jones' biography of Freud (1953, 1955, 1957) and the publication of *The Standard Edition of the Complete Psychological Works of Sigmund Freud* (1953–   ) facilitated the assessment of general psychoanalysis, the publication of *The Writings of Anna Freud* (1965) permits an evaluation of her work and the development of psychoanalytic research on children. From her articles during the period 1945–1956, published in *The Writings of Anna*

Freud, the following comments are extracted. They give added meaning to the phrase "long past but short history" of the psychoanalytic study of the child.

Anna Freud remarks (Vol. IV, pp. 4–5) that the earliest psychoanalytic work was concerned with basic clinical descriptions and the development of technique. During this period the sequence of libidinal development was conceptualized, the Oedipal and castration complexes were described, etc. However, she notes, these findings were not based on the clinical study of children, but were "reconstructed from the analyses of adult neurotics."

The success of this procedure, it is to be remembered, comes from knowing the outcome of childhood experiences and thus tracing back lines of development which actually occurred. By contrast, predicting the development of a child is making an estimate of events in the life of the child which have not yet occurred.

Not until after a couple of decades of basic clinical description and development of techniques were the applications made to the problems of bringing up children. These applications were made without the present understandings of ego psychology. Anna Freud remarks that "The body of psychoanalytic knowledge grew gradually, one small finding being added to the next" (Vol. VI, p. 5).

As a result of the protracted and "piecemeal elaboration," the applications of psychoanalysis to education were unsystematic. In general, the first applications stressed freedom for drive activity, then the conditions of ego strength; more recently emphasis has been on the "intactness of libidinal relations." Due to the method of development of psychoanalytic doctrines, roughly equivalent, as has been said of other sciences, to reconstructing a ship while it is underway, its research has been called "action research."

Anna Freud states that the beginnings of psychoanalytic child psychology are somewhere between Freud's publications: *Studies on Hysteria* (1893–1895) and *The Interpretation of Dreams* (1900). Earlier, Freud worked with propositions which, in the later metapsychological sense, were *dynamic* as well as *logical.* His basic concept was that the conflicting internal forces cannot be brought into harmony with each other because they belong to different strata of the mind: the conscious part, and the unconscious part. *Genetic* propositions were later added, whereby the cause of inner conflict was traced back to the individual past of the patient (Vol. IV, p. 318).

Anna Freud notes (Vol. IV, pp. 128–129) that genetic investigations proceeded from the study of libidinal development to the study of the inhibiting forces of this development. Thus the individual was seen advancing along at least two parallel lines of simultaneous growth. One was from the unconscious and manifested itself in free associations, dreams, and transference phenomena. The other was from the defensive and regulating structures of the ego and superego.

The analysis of the history of psychoanalysis given so succinctly by A. Freud reveals that its development, although piecemeal and unsystematic in structural terms, was largely in a direction, as far as the participants in the history were concerned, that was unconscious. Actually, this development, in retrospect, seems quite reasonable. Of course, the fact that the history took the course it did is some indication that there were adequate causes for the outcomes which were actually obtained. But while the real may be rational, the converse does not hold. The basic imprecision of the field kept its development close to empirical sources as these were progressively discriminated by psychoanalytic practitioners. By contrast, it is a failing of the romantic movement in German philosophy that starting with loose empirical assumptions, the logic of development, unhampered by constant testing in practice, has resulted in philosophical and social monstrosities. By and large, perhaps with the exception of Freud's speculations on death, psychoanalysis avoided such excesses of theoretical imagination.

The judgment to characterize the psychoanalytic research on children through the work of Anna Freud is not arbitrary. After Sigmund Freud, she is the most frequently cited author by the productive contributors to the field. This conclusion was arrived at by a citation analysis of *The Psychoanalytic Study of the Child* (hereafter referred to as PSC).

In Volume XX of PSC (1965) a cumulative author index was published. An inspection of the twenty-one page index indicated that certain contributors, based upon the number of articles published in PSC during the twenty-year span, could be considered "productive." Those called productive by this measure are indicated in Table 16–1. Although he did not strictly qualify as "productive" by the criterion of number of publications in PSC, E. Erikson was added to this list because of interest in his work. This set of writers constituted two and a half percent of the contributors to PSC during the years 1945–1965.

TABLE 16-1 Number of Articles Published by Selected Writers between 1945–1965 in *The Psychoanalytic Study of the Child*

Contributor	Number of Articles
A. Freud	16
Greenacre	13
Hartmann	12
Burlingham	10
Spitz	10
E. Kris	8
K. R. Eissler	8
Fraiberg	8
Mahler	6
Jacobson	6

Following the selection of these productive contributors, each of their articles in PSC was examined. A tabulation was made of the references used in each article.[1] The problem was to ascertain which were the seminal sources of psychoanalytic thought as indicated by the citations of the most productive contributors. Table 16–2 indicates the frequency of citations.

TABLE 16-2 Frequency of Citations by the Highest Contributors in Volumes I-XX of *The Psychoanalytic Study of the Child* for the Years 1945–1965*

Contributor	Number of Citations
S. Freud	246
A. Freud	56
Hartmann	44
Spitz	38
Greenacre	31
Fenichel	24

* After Fenichel there is a gap in the frequency of citation; the order then is Hoffer, Winnicot, Nunberg, Glover, Mahler.

The large number of citations of the works of S. Freud gave an opportunity to sort out those contributions which have been most

[1] This task was performed by Barbara Gerson.

frequently referred to in PSC by the productive contributors. These results appear in Table 16–3.

TABLE 16-3 The Most Frequently Cited References of S. Freud's Work. Citation in order of Frequency by "Productive Contributors" to *The Psychoanalytic Study of the Child**

> *New Introductory Lectures* (1933)
> *Analysis Terminable and Interminable* (1937)
> *The Ego and the Id* (1923)
> *Beyond the Pleasure Principle* (1920)
> *Civilization and its Discontents* (1930)
> *The Problem of Anxiety* (1936)
> *Inhibition, Symptoms, and Anxiety* (1926)
> *Group Psychology and the Analysis of the Ego* (1921)
> *Interpretation of Dreams* (1900)

* The most frequently cited works of A. Freud were: *The Ego and the Mechanisms of Defense* (1936) and *Indications for Child Analysis* (1945). The most frequently cited references to Hartmann were: *Comments on the Formation of Psychic Structure* (1946), *Comments on the Psychoanalytic Theory of the Ego* (1950), *The Genetic Approach to Psychoanalysis* (1945), and *Notes on a Theory of Aggression* (1949).

Two comments may be made about Table 16–3. First, increase in citation frequency is associated with general theoretical articles rather than case studies. Second, the works referred to on the list seem to be the theoretical bases for ego psychology. This list of Freud's works undoubtedly implicitly contains the Freudian paradigm that was developed in PSC. See Note B for an explication of "scientific paradigms" and Note C for the basic references in the works of Hartmann, E. Kris, and A. Freud, which assess the critical elements of the ego psychology paradigm in Freud's works.

To conclude this report of the citation analyses, an attempt was made to see if, over the twenty-year period, there was a discernible shift in the pattern of citations. *All* the references in Volumes I, V, X, XV, and XX were examined for the citations of Sigmund and Anna Freud. No definite trends were observable. The basic works of Freud's late career, as indicated in Table 16–2, continued to have a high rate of citation. One addition was noted, however. Due to the number of case studies in PSC published by the general contributors, there was an increase in the frequency of citation of "The Analysis of a Phobia in a Five-Year-Old Boy" (Freud, 1909).

Anna Freud's *The Ego and the Mechanisms of Defense* continued to have a high frequency of citation up to and through

Volume XV, but in Volume XX it was displaced by "The Concept of Developmental Lines" (1963). Volume V of PSC was the most frequently cited of the PSC volumes. Approximately one-third of all the references were to journal articles and of these, two-thirds were to PSC. Thus, it can be seen that the field of the psychoanalytic study of the child is proceeding on its own literature. The journal most cited other than PSC was *The International Journal of Psycho-Analysis.*

It is clear from the citations that psychoanalytic research is not research in the ordinary sense of the term in the social sciences. It is not a collection of objective measurements followed by an attempt to make a generalization. Nor is it the formulation of hypotheses followed by an attempt to find some measurements that will support the hypotheses on more than a chance basis. Much of the psychoanalytic research on children mirrors the style of Freud in his works cited in Table 16–2. The procedure is one of conjecture and providing evidence or attempting refutations. This procedure is a legitimate scientific procedure, particularly when the variables are difficult to measure exactly. The procedure is one, however, that is easily learned and easily repeated. Under conditions of this sort, the stability of a theory is easily threatened by counter proposals for which some data can be provided. The fractionation of the psychoanalytic movement into sub-groups of Jungians, Adlerians, Reichians, Kleinians, Horneyians, and who knows what will pop up tomorrow, is evidence of the lability of the theoretical procedure. This flexibility undoubtedly helped Freud in his early work, and also made it easy for him to develop and modify his theories. Today it also makes the theory vulnerable to counter proposals. It is not surprising that strong controls are exercised on young psychoanalysts to show that any developments or modifications of doctrine are congruent with what Freud proposed. Hence the style of extensive citation of Freud's works. The review of the literature indicates that the works of A. Freud and Hartmann, in a lesser way, have a similar controlling function.

The need for close control of theoretical proposals was once illustrated by the gestalt psychologists in the following way: In a railroad yard two tracks which, in the beginning, diverge almost imperceptably may end up going in opposite directions.

Quotations out of context are sometimes misleading. Interpretations of the meanings of statements are also quite fallible. There is a tendency in the dialogue of psychoanalysts with psychologists for the analysts to charge that their theories are misunderstood and mis-stated. It is not difficult to detect two attitudes in A. Freud's works, one when she is commenting on psychoanalysts to nonanalysts and another for internal consumption. In talking to psychologists, a sharply polemical and defensive stance is taken and psychoanalysis is defended as if the doctrines were clear and not contradictory. The misunderstandings and mis-statements seem to be attributed to poor scholarship or defects in attitudes. In internal discussions, the differences of doctrine are discussed with a cool detachment remarkably free of polemical style. Rather than summarizing her position, it will be illustrated by a set of quotations from her work. To the charge that the assemblage is out of context and fundamentally misleading, it is hoped that the statements here will provoke more adequate formulation of the psychoanalytic conception of the child and that more than one analyst will agree with the reformulation.

> In the beginning of life, at least, the infant seems to concentrate on the development along those lines which call forth most ostensibly the mother's love and approval, i.e., her spontaneous pleasure in the child's achievement and, in comparison, to neglect others where such approval is not given. This implies that activities which are acclaimed by the mother are repeated more frequently, become libidinized, and thereby stimulated into further growth. (PSC, Vol. VI, p. 86)

> The ego of the young child has the developmental task to master on the one hand orientation in the external world and on the other hand the chaotic emotional states which exist within himself. It gains its victories and advances whenever such impressions are grasped, put into thoughts or words, and submitted to the secondary process. (PSC, Vol. VI, p. 32)

> But in spite of accumulated evidence that adverse environmental circumstances have pathological results, nothing should convince the child analyst that alterations in external reality can work cures, except perhaps in earliest infancy. Such a belief would imply that external factors alone can be pathogenic agents and that their interaction with internal ones can be taken lightly. Such an assumption runs counter to the experience of the analyst. (PSC, Vol. VI, p. 51)

The first of these quotations gives two solutions to the description of the child's behavior: (1) the "infant seems to concentrate on the development . . ." and (2) "activities . . . acclaimed by the mother are repeated more frequently, [and] become libidinalized. . . ." The first description stresses the purposive nature of the infant's acts and the self-directive quality of the behavior; the second stresses the effect of the environment as eliciting behavior from the child and as modifying the child's internal structure (activities become libidinalized).

The second quotation stresses that the modification of the internal states is achieved when the tasks are understood, put into thoughts or words, and put into a context which results in coordination of activities.

The third quotation is a denial that environmental modification works cures. Recall that behavior modifiers like to quote B. F. Skinner to the effect that psychotherapists don't modify the internal structure of individuals, but they modify the patient's environment. If psychoanalysis as a psychotherapy works, the psychoanalyst somewhere in the environment of the patient is important. What is at issue is not that something in the environment affects the patient, but what particular environmental events are most effective. Anna Freud's position seems to be that for the infant, early environmental relations are important. With maturation and the growth of internal structures, the attempt to modify these directly by therapeutic intervention of some sort is more critical. (See Note D.)

The arguments continue about the best ways to manipulate the environment of the child versus the best ways to inject developmental tasks into secondary process thinking, or the best ways to strengthen the ego in its relations to reality, drive regulation, object relations, thought processes, defensive functions, autonomous functions, and synthetic functions. The arguments continue due to the vagueness of the issues, the ambiguity of the referents, missing criteria of therapeutic progress, and poorly controlled evidence. Most lacking is a clear specification of ego strengths, secondary process functions, and what particular environmental, developmental, or therapeutic maneuvers directly influence these functions in a way that is scientifically verifiable. Presumably, therapy or experiences of living strengthen ego functions. Those who believe this should specify (1) ego functions and (2) how specific experiences in and out of therapy sessions influence specific ego functions. In this state of the field, close observation of children and careful categorization of observations seem to have been the major tasks. Anna Freud and her collaborators have attempted to solve this problem by the proposal of a Developmental Profile.

A major research effort in the psychoanalytic study of the child was sponsored by the United States National Institute of Mental Health. The Hampstead Child-Therapy Clinic of London received a grant for a project entitled "Assessment of Pathology in Childhood." The groundwork for this project had been developed by Anna Freud in four lectures given in New York in 1960. The Developmental Profile has undergone a number of modifications from the early proposals (A. Freud, 1962, 1963). It is to be noted that developmental lines had been proposed by Erikson in Volume I of PSC, and as early as 1950 he had proposed a double entry table, age by functions, in *Childhood and Society* (1950). All this is to say that the idea of developmental lines had been previously mentioned but the difficult work of specifying the details and the testing of the Profile was the work of the Hampstead group. Nagera (1963) has published a case study using the Profile on which I shall comment.

In the case reported by Nagera, a child named Arthur was interviewed by a social worker and a psychiatrist and given intelligence tests, presumably by a psychologist. The Profile has the following sections:

I. Reasons for referral
II. Description of the child
III. Family background and personal history
IV. Possibly significant environmental influences
V. Assessment of development
    A. Drive development
        1. Libido
           (a) with regard to phase development
        2. Aggression
    B. Ego and superego development
        1. Ego apparatuses
        2. Ego functions
        3. Defenses
        4. Secondary interferences of defenses with ego functions
    C. Development of the total personality (lines of development and mastery of tasks) or age-adequate responses
VI. Regression and fixation points
    A. Oral level
    B. Anal level
    C. Phallic level

VII.   Dynamic and structural assessment (conflicts)
    A.   External
    B.   Internalized
    C.   Internal conflicts
VIII.   Assessment of some general characteristics
    A.   Frustration tolerance
    B.   Sublimation potential
    C.   Overall attitude to anxiety
    D.   Progressive forces versus regressive tendencies
IX.   Diagnosis

In this brief outline of the major headings of the Profile, because they are of special interest, some of the categories under Section V, Assessment of Development, are included. The Profile, even in its present state, obviously requires a great deal of information and skill to fill out the categories. The outline itself, however, can obviously be expanded at any one of a number of points. The literature on ego functions alone could provide Profile categories at least equivalent to the present scheme. Guilford (1967), for instance, has a structure of intellect model of 120 categories, eighty of which have been isolated in factor analyses; the other forty are now being intensively analyzed. This system does not take into account a drive organization and drive-ego interactions.

The actual use of the Profile, however, indicates that some of the information required, or actually used in the Profile, comes from psychological testing and social worker reports. On the section on Drive development—Libido, with regard to phase developing, Nagera (1963), in filling out the case of Arthur, reports (p. 518):

> Arthur has reached the phallic-oedipal phase. (He giggles and says "ooh" whenever he sees his mother not fully dressed; he makes jokes about girls and laughs about nude pictures with his mother; used to like to write "love letters" to mother when away from her at nine years, etc.) There is evidence that he has very strong fixation points at the oral and anal levels to which large amounts of libido are now regressed.

If the use of the Profile will increase the clinician's awareness of the type of data he actually uses for inferences and the need for precise statements of the grounds for a particular inference, then the Profile can only help the field. One would predict, however, that since it is so easy to construct a case history without this systematic information that the use of the Profile for other than research purposes will be limited. The distinction being made here is the one common in discussions of the relative merits of essay versus objective test items in an examination. The reliability and validity of the essay examination are not high; the person writing it can avoid the mention of aspects with which he is not familiar and can gloss over shady inferences with good style. The objective type examination, however, when well constructed, samples the domain of knowledge and thus has high reliability. The Profile proposed by Anna Freud has the feature that it systematically samples the metatheory of psychoanalysis and ties it down to observations of and judgments about the child. The estimate of this writer is that this procedure is fundamental in any systematic psychoanalytic study of the child. One might press the point even further and suggest that studies that are not done with such systematic sampling will have only incidental value and will not advance the field in the solution of its fundamental problems.

Under the influence of A. Freud, a strong focus of the work of the Hampstead Group is the specification of the observational correlates of the metapsychology. By contrast, the work of the Yale Group has a marked clinical quality. The distinction concerns the location of the work on levels of the psychoanalytic system. The system has levels of explanation and correlated levels of linguistic generality (Sullivan, 1959). This principle of levels is based on the idea of "entailed by," or in perceptual or cognitive terms as "object of." Clinically the "objects of" observations are the behaviors of the patient. The forming of inferences about the "meanings," "inner states," or "processes" of the patient has as its object (and uses the material of) the observations. These observations are put into an explanatory context or sequence and then implied laws are used to explain the occurrence of the events observed. The metapsychology is really an abstraction from the "psychology" and is used to explain it. In this sense "psychology" refers to the relating of the behaviors and the clinical insights about the mechanisms. The direct objects of the metapsychology (what the metapsychology explains) are the mechanisms of thought, feeling, and behavior. Only through these are the clinical observations themselves explained. Strictly speaking, a defense mechanism is not observed. What are observed are instances of behaviors and an inference is made about their relationship. Since the inference is so automatic, the clinician may have the impression of observing the mechanism directly. He may feel sure of it until he meets someone who will make the same observations without sharing the same rules of relating the observations.

The titles of the Yale Group's articles indicate the location of their interest within the psychoanalytic system: The Influence of Early Mother-Child Interaction on Identification Process (Ritvo and Solnit, 1953), Neutralization and Sublimation (E. Kris, 1955), etc. At this level in the psychoanalytic system, the richness of observation may be combined with subtle clinical insights. To push beyond this level of clinical insights is to go to the metapsychology and into abstract theory. The use of observations in the "middle theory" allows for great flexibility of combination in clinically insightful relations.

By contrast, the classification of observations directly by metaphysical categories, thereby short-circuiting through the mechanisms, tends to minimize clinical intuitions at the level most useful to the working psychoanalyst. A creative use of basic observations at the level of formulating the development and interaction of the mechanisms is best exemplified by the work of E. Kris and his collaborators. For E. Kris this activity seemed to give a release from the analysis of the formal problems of psychoanalysis, which he and Hartmann had so ably clarified, and to give free play to the sensitivities peculiarly associated with the functions of an art critic and an historian. By this is meant the intense analysis of what is presented (and its mental representations, *die Vorstellungen*) and their developmental tendencies. Kris's work during this late period seems to be an exemplification of the creative process, as distinguished from talking about it.

The work of both the Hampstead Group and the Yale Group intimately involved the notion of prediction. When the system for which the prediction is made is a relatively open one, the problems of prediction are intrinsically difficult. Assuming the structuralization of the system and the constancy of the environment, prediction is not difficult in principle. Astronomy is replete with such predictions. Postdiction is easier than prediction in that the vicissitudes of the environment may be traced or known, thus eliminating large errors or ambiguity. The solution of the problem of internal structuralization seems to be the conceptualization of developmental lines and the use of this material as baseline reference points. A problem which faces psychoanalysts in studying the child is how precisely the developmental lines can be specified. Without a doubt the simple growth norms of the physician or the development of conflict-free areas of the ego, such as performance on intelligence tests, will not be an adequate model. What the final model will be, however, can be determined only by the work of the type being done by the Hampstead and Yale groups. Undoubtedly the strain on classical psychoanalytic thought will result in decisive modifications and developments.

In "An Appreciation of Herman Nunberg," A. Freud (*Writings,* Vol. V.) notes, "To Nunberg's age group belongs (in alphabetical order) Helene Deutsch, Paul Federn, Edward Hitschmann, Ludvik Jekels; to mine, the Bibrings, Hartmann, Kris, Wilhelm Reich, Waelder" (p. 195). Disregarding Nunberg's group, it is interesting to see how creative were A. Freud's "group." To take at random seven young acolytes in any movement and to have such a distinguished set as A. Freud, Hartmann, E. Kris, and Waelder is nothing short of astonishing. This is not to minimize the contributions of the Bibrings or the early creative work on character structure by Reich. Rather, the suggestion is that the outstanding creativity of this group and the distinctive character of their contributions to ego psychology, in spite of widely differing intellectual styles, is related in some way to the events of that time. The three most generally significant events were the rise of Naziism and the subsequent displacement of these persons, the stage of development of psychoanalytic thought, and the death of S. Freud. Close analysis of the interaction of these events with the details of the careers of this group will be necessary to construct any generalizations at a useful level. As guiding curiosities, it is noted that they successfully weathered the cultural transplantation (became fluent in English, established professionally, etc.); ego psychology had been mentioned and outlined by Freud but not developed in any detail; and, significantly, these persons were reaching the maturity of their professional powers at the death of Freud, thus inheriting the task of the development of psychoanalysis.

The issues that these speculations raise about the future of the psychoanalytic study of the child are serious. We cannot bank on a fertilization of thought by another wave of Viennese psychoanalysts. Anna Freud's generation, whatever their remaining contributions, cannot be expected to do more than consolidate the developments that they started. Who will constitute the next wave? Are they the young psychoanalysts who have recently reached their professional maturity?

Few American-trained psychoanalysts give clear indications of the requisite perceptions, talents, enthusiasms, energies, and control of the social institutions to develop the psychoanalytic system. The United States is not known as the "melting pot" only for the socio-economic assimilation of immigrants. Ideas are as often diluted as melted. In the history of ideas and movements the reputations of the European intellectuals hardly survives until their deaths. The early central European Socialists, the theatrical groups and labor organizations, the anti-Nazi scholars, the Gestalt psychologists, the Logical Positivist philosophers—all were welcomed and given a temporary public platform. But their movements were assimilated as were other immigrant groups. They were welcomed with more or less curious tolerance which turned out to be, in Marcuse's paradoxical phrase, with repressive tolerance. All these intellectual movements got a hearing, some popularity, and a temporary power base. However, they trained no competent followers and rarely survived the deaths of their leading spokesmen.

A. N. Whitehead once remarked something to the effect that the surest sign of the failure of an intellectual movement is the failure to make progress in the solution of its fundamental problems and a turning to the solution of secondary problems. By this criteria, it is estimated that the psychoanalytic study of the child was advanced in a fundamental way by A. Freud's Developmental Profile. The persistent advance in the direction of a greater specification of the theory and attempts to fit the conceptualizations closer and closer in a systematic way to the child under study is clearly the fundamental problem. In measurement terms, the problem is the specification of conditions for assessment and modification of ego strengths by specific analytic procedures. A failure of intellectual impulse here and a concentration on peripheral issues will be fatal.

NOTE A

The interaction of psychoanalytic careers and the academic environment is clear in the case of E. Kris, Hartmann, and to some extent, Waelder. Erikson, who is a contemporary of these analysts but whose career seems to have diverged, seems also to have been the one who had strongest academic affiliations. Erikson has had several appointments in universities, usually with research units; among them were University of California, Berkeley, and Harvard. E. Kris was for many years at the New School for Social Research and City College of New York, and then at Yale. Hartmann, although he had an orthodox medical education, had aspirations as a theorist which made him open to intellectual movements outside of psychoanalysis. Harvard's physicist-philosopher, Philipp Frank, has noted that:

> Rarely were the psychoanalytic doctrines called "meaningless" or "tautological," as representatives of Logical Positivism have often and gladly branded the doctrines of "school philosophy" like Platonism, Thomism or even Kantianism. Otto Neurath, who was one of the leading members of the Vienna Circle and one of the strictest judges on "unscientific" and "meaningless" statements, said repeatedly about psychoanalytical theories that they revealed connections between a great range of new and surprising observed facts; hence one should not discourage this kind of research, although it is far from being logically and semantically satisfactory. This has also been the opinion of Rudolf Carnap and other positivists.
>
> It is certainly a fact that the roots of psychoanalysis and of Logical Positivism grew up in one and the same soil, the intellectual and social climate of Vienna before and after the first World War. It is also a fact that among the workers in psychoanalysis there was a considerable group who attempted to keep contact with the Vienna Circle. We have only to mention Heinz Hartmann, who has been instrumental in keeping psychoanalysis close to scientific methods. (Frank, 1959, pp. 308–309)

NOTE B

Conceptions of the nature of science and the activities of the scientific community have recently undergone a change due to the work of the historians of science. In the broad view science is seen as making progress through the successive accretion of facts as objective methods of research are successfully applied to one field and then another. A closer look, however, indicates not only that the development of science has strong dialectical aspects but that many irrational beliefs become incorporated into a science. Conversely, not all rational beliefs are accepted.

The peculiarities of the belief systems of the scientific communities and the conditions of the incorporation of new beliefs is a topic in either social psychology or sociology that I am not prepared to discuss. When the history of science is approached from the study of both the controversies among scientists and the conditions of acceptance or rejection of a scientific doctrine in a community of scientists, the practice of science can be seen in a new light. Thomas Kuhn (1962) of Princeton has made such a socio-historical approach in *The Structure of Scientific Revolutions.*

I will discuss a few points from Kuhn's works to indicate his definitions of his basic constructs. Kuhn points out that in the early development of a new field, Merton proposes that social needs and values represent a major determinant of the problems to which its practitioners devote their attention. Moreover, the concepts they use in solving problems are conditioned, to a great extent, by contemporary common sense, by the prevailing philosophical tradition, or by contemporary sciences which are most prestigious at that time. The new fields which emerged during the seventeenth century and several of the modern social sciences provide examples of these phenomena. Kuhn argues, however, that the later evolution of a technical specialty is significantly different in ways which were at least suggested by the development of the classical sciences during the Scientific Revolution. The practitioners of a mature science are trained both in a sophisticated body of traditional theory and in instrumental, mathematical, and verbal technique. Therefore, they represent a special subculture, whose members are the exclusive audience for, and judges of, each other's work. The problems on which they work are not presented by the external society but by a personal or internal challenge to increase the scope and precision of the fit between the existing theory and nature. Moreover, the concepts used to resolve these problems are usually closely related to those supplied by prior training for the specialty. "In short, compared with other professional and creative pursuits, the practitioners of a mature science are effectively insulated from the cultural milieu in which they live their extra-professional lives." Kuhn goes on to say:

> That quite special, though still incomplete, insulation is the presumptive reason why the internal approach to the history of science, conceived as autonomous and self-contained, has seemed so nearly successful. To an extent, unparalleled in other fields, the development of an individual technical specialty can be understood without going beyond the literature of that specialty and a few of its near neighbors. Only occasionally need the historian take note of a particular concept, problem, or technique which entered the field from outside. Nevertheless, the apparent autonomy of the internal approach is misleading in essentials, and the passion sometimes expended in its defense has obscured important problems. The insulation of a mature scientific community suggested by Kuhn's analysis is an insulation primarily with respect to concepts and secondarily

with respect to problem structure. There are, however, other aspects of scientific advance, such as its timing. These do depend critically on the factors emphasized by the external approach to scientific development. Particularly when the sciences are viewed as an interacting group rather than as a collection of specialties, the cumulative effects of external factors can be decisive. (Kuhn, 1968, pp. 80–81)

These [paradigms] I take to be universally recognized scientific achievements that for a time provide model problems and solutions to a community of practitioners. Once that piece of my puzzle fell into place, a draft of this essay emerged rapidly. (Kuhn, 1962, p. x)

Normal science, the activity in which most scientists inevitably spend almost all their time, is predicated on the assumption that the scientific community knows what the world is like. Much of the success of the enterprise derives from the community's willingness to defend that assumption, if necessary at considerable cost. Normal science, for example, often suppresses fundamental novelties because they are necessarily subversive of its basic commitments. Nevertheless, so long as those commitments retain an element of the arbitrary, the very nature of normal research ensures that novelty shall not be suppressed for very long. (Kuhn, 1962, p. 5)

NOTE C

Hartmann, E. Kris, and A. Freud suggest the direction of the enlargement of psychoanalytic thought in the concern with "ego psychology." They feel that analytic concepts, as opposed to those of most other branches of psychology, are principally genetic in nature. They encompass mental phenomena having a common origin instead of being merely descriptive. For example, typologies such as oral character, anal character, etc., while defined by the genetic predominance of certain factors also contain elements that are contradictory in a descriptive sense—greediness and wastefulness, sadism and pity, etc. Such an approach is superior because it allows evaluation of the dynamic potentialities of such characteristics, and thus makes predictions more reliable.

This genetic nature of analytic thinking is handicapped by the limitations set by the analytic method, challenging proponents to extend their insight beyond these borders. This extension should proceed along the lines of extrapolation from analytic findings to the preverbal stage, which can be described in terms of basic concepts derived from the study of later stages of development, or, it can be done by direct but analytically informed observation. Both ways must be explored because the study of the preverbal stage is the key to many of the most general analytic assumptions, and is also a prerequisite for theoretical advances. Thus within the framework of discussions on theories of analysis, its interrelations with developmental psychology must be considered.

> Analysis is also, and has always been in Freud's work, general psychology. . . . Actually, the new level of ego psychology has proved decisive for the analysts' renewed interest in problems of developmental psychology and for the possibility to correlate more systematically reconstructive data with data of direct observation—and, vis-à-vis questions of a practical nature, like prevention or education, it proved able to overcome certain limitations inherent in the earlier approach.
>
> Ego development, like libidinous development, is partly based on processes of maturation. And of the ego aspect, too, some of us are agreed that we have to consider it as a partly primary, independent variable, not entirely traceable to the interaction of drives and environment; also that it partly can become independent from the drives in a secondary way. That is what I mean by the terms primary and secondary autonomy in ego development. The secondary autonomy of functions of the ego has a bearing on the stability of its developmental acquisitions. . . . (Hartmann, 1950, pp. 10, 11–12)

E. Kris points out that during the first period of psychoanalytic child psychology there was an interest in the typical reactions of the child, on their sequence, and their genetic, economic and dynamic interrelations. On the other hand, environmental conditions, though recorded in detail, were mainly thought of as the source of such "required" experiences.

Kris proposes that the change in outlook was largely related to the development of ego psychology:

> The way in which this change was effected can best be illustrated if we turn to one of the most crucial applications of ego psychology, to the problem of anxiety. The older toxicological theory, which had assumed that undischarged libidinous tension was transformed into anxiety, was abandoned in favor of one which considered the danger situation as its center. Anxiety as a signal mobilizes defense against danger; anxiety as a symptom may then, in turn, be experienced as danger against which defenses are being mobilized. The theoretical setup is no longer a physiological one but rather a biological one; organism and environment are seen in their interaction. At

the same time, historical factors gain an even greater relevance: the ontogenesis of the reaction to danger, the history of danger experiences and the history of defenses against them are recognized as decisive. The gain for the elaboration of psychoanalytic views on child development was very great indeed. . . . Psychoanalytic child psychology has undoubtedly made a shift towards the environmentalist position. I shall not attempt to give in detail the evidence which brought this shift about. It was inherent in the developments initiating the second phase of psychoanalytic child psychology. Psychoanalytic ego psychology had, as we said, re-emphasized the character of psychoanalysis as a psychology of adaptation, of learning and clinical data have implemented these general assumptions as far as the child's earliest experiences are concerned. (E. Kris, 1950, pp. 27, 30)

In fact, for the accurate assessment of any child's developmental status, no point can be of greater assistance than this particular one which complements what has always happened in analytic diagnosis with regard to the sequence of libidinal, later also of aggressive, stages. So far as I am concerned, I have tried to take care of this by establishing the concept of *developmental lines,* contributed to both from the side of id and of ego development; these developmental lines lead from the child's state of immaturity to the gradual setting up of a mature personality and are, in fact, the result of interaction between maturation, adaptation, and structuralization. (A. Freud, 1969, p. 212)

NOTE D

While Freud's Id-Ego-Superego system is close to Plato's theory of psyche in Book IV of the *Republic,* the psychoanalytic conception of man has classical features that are distinctly Aristotelian. To make a strong distinction between the classical conceptions and those of say, the seventeenth century, the issue can be discussed in terms of the properties given to natural objects, such as stones.

For Aristotle natural objects could be classed into two categories, inanimate and animate. Physics is the study of inanimate and psychology is the study of animate objects. Animate objects have the same properties as the inanimate, but in addition have a principle of life called psyche. Since life forms are quite different, there were three grades of complexity of psyche, that shared by plants, that shared by animals, and that shared by humans. The study of physics (*phusis* in Greek is *nature*) is the study of motion, change or generation, tendencies which are immanent in objects. The fact that motion and change and generation were explained in terms of immanent properties of objects instead of external relations is what distinguishes the classical Aristotelian view from the physics of the seventeenth century. For example, if a stone is dropped it falls to earth due to an immanent tendency to reach its natural place on the ground. The stone when lifted from the ground suffered an unnatural displacement and it is an accident and not part of the essence of the stone that it has been lifted to a position in which it falls to earth. For the seventeenth century physicists, the stone falls because it is in the earth's gravitational field. The external relations of the stone are decisive in its behavior just as the billiard ball's behavior will depend upon how it is hit by other balls rather than its internal structure or natural tendencies.

Aristotle was charged with anthropomorphizing nature. The major problem of the seventeenth century physicists was to eliminate his teleological and to substitute mechanical explanations of natural processes. The success of Newtonian physics led some natural philosophers to construct theories of mind based upon Newtonian models. The first models, by Locke and his contemporaries, followed Aristotle's basic division between animate and inanimate objects, for mind was given mental act (nonphysical) properties. The attempt to construct a theory of mind consonant with physical speculation was developed in England by Hartley, Hume, the Mills, and in France by Condillac and the French Materialists. This movement got a great boost from the Darwinian revolution in biology. The boost was due to the Darwinian stress on adaptation to the environment. The organism's external relations became very important. A study of the external relations of an organism and the behaviors that followed from environmental manipulations led to the psychology of behaviorism. The ultimate application to humans of this behavioristic approach is in the procedures of behavior modification.

It is rather astonishing that the world view of the classical physicists became the model for psychological theorizing in view of the tremendous advances in chemistry in which the structure of the element was decisive in determining its properties. The success of the physicists in analyzing and isolating their problems into elementary particles obscured the point that as the elementary particles combined in various structural relations, the properties of the object became different, and its reaction to environmental events differed. That psychologists and philosophers would tend to model their theories on classical physics and nineteenth century biology can probably be explained on the basis of a wish for low cognitive dissonance with Newtonianism and Darwinism.

For Aristotle, cognitive coherence came from. conceptualizing physics in terms of properties of living organisms. If man can be conceived as having a complex structure whose behavior seems to be striving and purposive and follows a developmental course which ends in the realization of his essential form, then the rest of nature, if nature can be thought of as coherent, can be conceived of in the same terms. Aristotle's physics may have been defective as seen by the seventeenth century, but his psychology should not suffer from the criticism of the physicists. While it may be a mistake to anthropomorphize physics, it is not a mistake to anthropomorphize man.

Undoubtedly one of the sources of the enduring appeals of Greek literature and philosophy is that its humanism is based upon a complex conception of man and stresses the internal responsibility of man for himself and a striving for self-fulfillment. These are qualities at the root of psychoanalytic conceptions of man. The weakness of the classical conception of man can be seen in the fundamental character of Greek tragedy: the hero, true to his inner convictions, runs into either the limitations of the external world or its neutrality or hostility to his strivings. Rather than adapt to the external demands, he affirms himself and his values in heroic death. The weakness of classical psychoanalysis is that its stress on internal structure weakened the stress on relations to the external environment. The weakness of ego psychology is that clinical procedures inherited from the early period have become calcified rationalizations despite the change in the ego psychology stress on maturation, adaptation, and structuralization.

REFERENCES

Cornford, F. M. The Athenian philosophical schools. In *The Cambridge ancient history*. Cambridge, England: Cambridge University Press, 1927. Vol. 6. Pp. 302–351.

Ebbinghaus, H. *Abriss der psychologie*. Leipzig: Veit, 1908.

Erikson, E. H. Childhood and tradition in two American Indian tribes: a comparative abstract, with conclusions. *The Psychoanalytic study of the child*, 1945, 1, 319–350.

Erikson, E. H.   Ego development and historical change: clinical notes. *The Psychoanalytic study of the child*, 1946, **2**, 359–396.

Frank, P.   Psychoanalysis and logical positivism. In S. Hook (Ed.). *Psychoanalysis, Scientific method and philosophy*. New York: New York University Press, 1959, 308–313.

Freud, A.   Indications for child analysis. *The Psychoanalytic study of the child*, 1945, **1**, 127–149.

Freud, A.   Aggression in relation to emotional development: normal and pathological. *The Psychoanalytic study of the child*, 1949, **3/4**, 37–48.

Freud, A.   Some remarks on infant observation. *The Psychoanalytic study of the child*, 1953, **8**, 9–19.

Freud, A.   Psychoanalysis and education. *The Psychoanalytic study of the child*, 1954, **9**, 9–15.

Freud, A.   Child observations and prediction of development: a memorial lecture in honor of Ernst Kris. *The Psychoanalytic study of the child*, 1958, **13**, 92–124.

Freud, A.   Adolescence. *The Psychoanalytic study of the child*, 1958, **13**, 255–278.

Freud, A.   Clinical studies in psychoanalysis: research project of the Hampstead Child Therapy Clinic. *The Psychoanalytic study of the Child*, 1959, **14**, 122–131.

Freud, A.   The concept of developmental lines. *The Psychoanalytic study of the child*, 1963, **18**, 245–265.

Freud, A.   *The writings of Anna Freud*. New York: International Universities Press (six volumes published up to 1969).

Freud, A., Nagera, H.; and Freud, W. E.   Metapsychological assessment of the adult personality: the adult profile. *The Psychoanalytic study of the child*, 1965, **20**, 9–41.

Freud, S.   *The standard edition of the complete psychological works of Sigmund Freud*. London: Hogarth Press, 1953–1958.

Guilford, J. P.   *The nature of human intelligence*. New York: McGraw-Hill, 1967.

Hartmann, H.   Psychoanalysis and developmental psychology. *The Psychoanalytic study of the child*, 1950, **5**, 7–17.

Hartmann, H.   Comments on the psychoanalytic theory of the ego. *The Psychoanalytic study of the child*, 1950, **5**, 74–96.

Hartmann, H.   The mutual influences in the development of the ego and the id. *The Psychoanalytic study of the child*, 1952, **7**, 9–30.

Hartmann, H.   Notes on the reality principle. *The Psychoanalytic study of the child*, 1956, **11**, 31–53.

Hartmann, H.   Comments on the scientific aspects of psychanalysis. *The Psychoanalytic Study of the Child*, 1958, **13**, 127–146.

Hartmann, H.   Concept formation in psychoanalysis. *The Psychoanalytic study of the child*, 1964, **19**, 11–47.

Hartmann, H. and Kris, E. The genetic approach in psychoanalysis. *The Psychoanalytic study of the child*, 1945, 1, 11–30.

Hartmann, H.; Kris, E. and Lowenstein, R. M. Comments on the formation of psychic structures. *The Psychoanalytic study of the child*, 1946, 2, 11–38.

Jones, E. *The life and work of Sigmund Freud.* New York: Basic Books, 3 vol., 1953, 1955, 1957.

Kris, E. Notes on the development and on some current problems of psychoanalytic child psychology. *The Psychoanalytic study of the child*, 1950, 5, 24–46.

Kris, E. Opening remarks on psychoanalytic child psychology. *The Psychoanalytic study of the child*, 1951, 6, 9–17.

Kris, E. Neutralization and sublimation: observations on younger children. *The Psychoanalytic study of the child*, 1955, 10, 30–46.

Kris, E. Decline and recovery in the life of a three-year-old. *The Psychoanalytic study of the child*, 1962, 17, 175–215.

Kris, M. The use of prediction in a longitudinal study. *The Psychoanalytic study of the child*, 1957, 12, 175–189.

Kuhn, T. S. *The structure of scientific revolutions.* Chicago: University of Chicago Press, 1962.

Kuhn, T. S. The history of science. In *International Encyclopaedia of the Social Sciences.* New York: Macmillan Co. and the Free Press, 1968, 74–83.

Nagera, H. The developmental profile: notes on some practical considerations regarding its use. *The Psychoanalytic study of the child*, 1963, 18, 511–540.

Nagera, H. On arrest in development, fixation, and regression. *The Psychoanalytic study of the child*, 1964, 19, 222–239.

Popper, K. R. *Conjectures and refutations.* New York: Basic Books, 1962.

Provence, S. and Ritvo, S. Effects of deprivation on institutionalized infants. *The Psychoanalytic study of the child*, 1961, 16, 189–205.

Ritvo, S., and Solnit, A. J. Influences of early mother-child interaction on identification processes. *The Psychoanalytic study of the child*, 1958, 13, 64–85.

Sandler, J. and Nagera, H. Aspects of the metapsychology of fantasy. The *Psychoanalytic study of the child*, 1963, 18, 159–194.

Spitz, R. A. Hospitalism: an inquiry into the genesis of psychiatric conditions in early childhood. *The Psychoanalytic study of the child*, 1945, 1, 53–74.

Spitz, R. A. Relevancy of direct infant observations. *The Psychoanalytic study of the child*, 1950, 5, 66–73.

Spitz, R. A. Hospitalism: a follow-up report. *The Psychoanalytic study of the child*, 1946, 2, 113–117.

Spitz, R. A. and Wolf, K. M. Anaclitic depression: an inquiry into the genesis of psychotic conditions in early childhood. *The Psychoanalytic study of the child,* 1946, 2, 313–342.

Sullivan, J. J.   From Breuer to Freud. *Psychoanalysis and Psychoanalytic Review,* 1959, 46, 69–90.

Sullivan, J. J.   The development of Plato's theory of psyché. In *Proceedings of 76th Annual Convention of the American Psychological Association.* Washington D.C.: American Psychological Association, 1968.

Author Index

Subject Index

Intimacy, 534, 535, 536, 546, 551, 552, 553, 556, 561
Intrapsychic drive conflicts, 313
Intrapsychic structure, 531
Intra-uterine adaptation, 488
Intra-uterine life, 464
Intra-uterine motility, 39
Introjection, 17, 18, 403, 452, 467, 468, 470
Isakower phenomena, 73
Isolation, 90

Jealousy, 437–440, 475, 482, 549, 551
Jokes, 81
Judgment, 504
Juvenile period, 522–523, 528, 550, 561

Language, 322, 520
  in adolescent analysis, 42
  autistic, 18
  of child, 226–227, 520
  in latency, 85
  modification of, 342
Latency period, 20, 33, 36, 55, 60, 62–98
  achievements in, 103
  adoption during, 37
  aggression in, 67
  defenses, 76
  development in, 71
  drive defense in, 64
  drive dimunition in, 63
  drives in, 72–73, 365
  ego development of, 365
  group life in, 77
  group therapy for, 365–375
  individuation in, 79
  intellectual decline in, 81
  intellectual development in, 64
  lull in, 64
  object choice in, 285, 286
  pregenitality in, 106
  psychoanalytic concept of, 72
  psychohormonal concept of, 71
  psychomotor aspect of, 80
  psychosexual development in, 65
  repression in, 63
  society of child in, 77
  sublimation in, 120
  subphases of, 69
  superego formation in, 65, 90, 91–98
  transition from, 283
Learning, 370, 471, 520, 539
  difficulties, 88
  in latency, 82, 83
  multidisciplinary approach to, 519
Libidinal-aggressive organization, 238
Libidinal
  conflicts, 341
  development, 238, 256, 598, 599, 614
  drive, 313, 483
  energy, 15, 80
  impulses, 365
  phases, 35, 67, 254, 269

relations, 598
types, 54
Libido, 7, 11, 64, 261, 280, 284, 479, 480, 606
  defects, 293
  development of, 35, 133, 154, 294
  maturation of, 53
  narcisstic, 267
  object of, 267
  regression in development of, 271–272
  theory of, 12, 502
  transfer, 36, 37, 72, 270
Logical consequences, 443–444
Logical thought, 82
Loneliness, 524
Longitudinal observation, 577
Longitudinal studies, 571, 575–577, 588
Love, 92, 308, 524, 525, 536, 552, 556
  object, 21, 36, 37, 106, 286
  oral, 21
  self, 68
Lustprinzip, 15
Lying, 118, 274, 275

Manic defense, 470
Manual-exploratory function, 520
Marasmus, 555
Marriage, 478, 483, 484
Masculinity, 127
  feminine, 125, 130
  male, 125
Masculine-active expulsion, 24
Masochism, 12, 14, 41, 56, 89, 91, 107, 113, 290, 563
Mass media, 89
Masturbation, 27, 71, 75, 85, 97, 105, 113, 121, 124, 292, 475
  clitoral, 28, 66
  conflicts, 58, 290, 339
  degree of, 73
  ego in, 73
  fantasies, 70, 73, 75, 81, 257, 314
  group, 313
  guilt, 313
  indirect, 113, 124
  involuntary, 72
  mutual, 117
  passive feminine tendencies in, 73
  phallic, 35, 72, 75, 272
  preadolescent, 107
  pubic, 122
  substitutes, 34, 75, 113
  superego in, 73
  voluntary, 72
Maternal neglect, 543
Maturation, 76, 464–477, 516, 517, 519, 614
  adolescent, 485–492
  changes, 108
  cognitive, 82
  disorders during, 492
  family influence, 477
  father role in, 482
  infant, 541